Reflexing Interfaces:
The Complex Coevolution of Information Technology Ecosystems

Franco Orsucci
University College London, UK &
Institute for Complexity Studies, Italy

Nicoletta Sala
Università della Svizzera Italiana, Switzerland &
Università dell'Insubria, Italy

T0325001

Information Science
REFERENCE

INFORMATION SCIENCE REFERENCE

Hershey · New York

Acquisitions Editor:	Kristin Klinger
Development Editor:	Kristin Roth
Senior Managing Editor:	Jennifer Neidig
Managing Editor:	Jamie Snavely
Assistant Managing Editor:	Carole Coulson
Copy Editor:	Shanelle Ramelb
Typesetter:	Amanda Appicello
Cover Design:	Lisa Tosheff
Printed at:	Yurchak Printing Inc.

Published in the United States of America by
Information Science Reference (an imprint of IGI Global)
701 E. Chocolate Avenue, Suite 200
Hershey PA 17033
Tel: 717-533-8845
Fax: 717-533-8661
E-mail: cust@igi-global.com
Web site: http://www.igi-global.com

and in the United Kingdom by
Information Science Reference (an imprint of IGI Global)
3 Henrietta Street
Covent Garden
London WC2E 8LU
Tel: 44 20 7240 0856
Fax: 44 20 7379 0609
Web site: http://www.eurospanbookstore.com

Library of Congress Cataloging-in-Publication Data

Reflexing interfaces : the complex coevolution of information technology ecosystems / Franco F. Orsucci and Nicoletta Sala, editor.

   p. cm.

  Summary: "This book discusses the application of complex theories in information and communication technology, with a focus on the interaction between living systems and information technologies, providing researchers, scholars, and IT professionals with a fundamental resource on such topics as virtual reality; fuzzy logic systems; and complexity science in artificial intelligence, evolutionary computation, neural networks, and 3-D modeling"--Provided by publisher.

  Includes bibliographical references and index.

  ISBN 978-1-59904-627-3 (hardcover) -- ISBN 978-1-59904-629-7 (ebook)

  1. Information technology. 2. Artificial intelligence. I. Orsucci, Franco. II. Sala, Nicoletta.

  T58.5.R4365 2008

  004--dc22

2007032052

British Cataloguing in Publication Data
A Cataloguing in Publication record for this book is available from the British Library.

All work contributed to this book set is original material. The views expressed in this book are those of the authors, but not necessarily of the publisher.

Table of Contents

Section I
Living Systems and Information Technology

Section II
Application Fields: From Networks to Fractal Geometry

Detailed Table of Contents

Section I
Living Systems and Information Technology

The author identifies the reflexing interfaces that can redefine different approaches in different disciplines in the new millennium. The chapter sets the scene for discussions presented by various subsequent authors.

The author presents the Oedipus myth in the light of interpersonal neurobiology and second-order cybernetics, where observers are self-referentially implicated within the observed. The riddle of the Sphinx is understood as a paradox of self-reference in apparent contradiction with all known laws of science. The chapter describes Oedipus' capacity for full self-reference as equated with the operation of the most powerful universal Turing machine with both implicit and explicit memory of its past.

The authors propose a simple replicator theory of the coevolution of genes and memes. The presented coevolutionary theory assumes that units of information acquired from parents by imitation (memes) are not independent of genes, but are bounded with genes as composites, which are subjects of Darwinian evolution.

Chapter IV
Franco Scalzone, Italian Psychoanalytical Society, Italy
Gemma Zontini, Italian Psychoanalytical Society, Italy

The authors describe some interesting similarities between computer science and psychoanalysis. They formulate some hypotheses by bringing closer the statute of connectionism to the energetic model of the psychic apparatus, as well as OOP (object-oriented programming) to the object relations theory. They explore the man-machine theme, the way in which men relate to machines, especially thinking machines, describing the fantasies they arouse.

Chapter V
John G. Taylor, King's College, UK

The author describes the attention that is analyzed as the superior control system in the brain from an engineering point of view, with support for this from the way attention is presently being understood by brain science. The author remarks that an engineering control framework allows an understanding of how the complex networks observed in the brain during various cognitive tasks can begin to be functionally decomposed.

Chapter VI
Rita M. R. Pizzi, University of Milan, Italy

The author presents the advances of artificial intelligence that have renewed the interest in the mind-body problem, the ancient philosophical debate on the nature of mind and its relationship with the brain. The author remarks that the new version of the mind-body problem concerns the relationship between computational complexity and self-aware thought.

Chapter VII
David Vernon, Canterbury Christ Church University, UK

The author introduces neurofeedback as a mechanism for altering human brain functioning and in turn influencing behavior. He argues that neurofeedback provides a plausible mechanism by which the individual can learn to alter and control aspects of his electrocortical activity.

Chapter VIII
Eleonora Bilotta, Università della Calabria, Italy
Pietro Pantano, Università della Calabria, Italy

The authors present an artificial taxonomy of 2-D, self-replicating cellular automata (CA) that can be considered as proto-organisms for structure replication. The authors highlight the idea that the process of self-reproduction is an important mechanism, and they discuss almost 10 methods of self-replication.

Chapter IX

Marco Tomassini, University of Lausanne, Switzerland
Leonardo Vanneschi, University of Milan-Bicocca, Italy

The authors describe the evolutionary algorithms, focusing their attention on two specific applications. The first is about an important financial problem: the portfolio allocation problem. The second one deals with a biochemical problem related to drug design and efficacy.

Chapter X

Hector Sabelli, Chicago Center for Creative Development, USA
Gerald H. Thomas, Milwaukee School of Engineering, USA

The authors present the notion of quantum computing and how it forces a reexamination of logics. They examine its historical roots in logos, the logic of nature, and the laws of physics, describing the logical design of computers according to the logic of quantum physics that will allow the full use of quantum processes for computation, providing explicit realizations of these ideas.

Section II
Application Fields: From Networks to Fractal Geometry

Chapter XI

Alessandro Giuliani, Istituto Superiore di Sanità, Italy

The author presents the notion of network, which is more and more widespread in all the fields of human investigation, from physics to sociology. He describes some applications of network-based modeling to both introduce the basic terminology of the emergent network paradigm and highlight strengths and limitations of the method.

Chapter XII

Gianni A. Di Caro, Istituto Dalle Molle di Studi sull'Intelligenza Artificiale (IDSIA),
Switzerland
Frederick Ducatelle, Istituto Dalle Molle di Studi sull'Intelligenza Artificiale (IDSIA),
Switzerland
Luca M. Gambardella, Istituto Dalle Molle di Studi sull'Intelligenza Artificiale (IDSIA),
Switzerland

The authors introduce ant colony optimization (ACO), an optimization metaheuristic inspired by the foraging behavior of ant colonies. They describe the characteristics of ACO and they derive from it ant colony routing (ACR), a novel framework for the development of adaptive algorithms for network routing.

Chapter XIII

    Santo Banerjee, JIS College of Engineering, India
    Asesh Roy Chowdhury, Jadavpur University, India

The authors describe a new method for the transmitting and receiving of signals using delayed dynamical systems. The change of the delay parameter at the intermediate state gives extra security to the system. They also propose a method of communication using the synchronization between two coupled, delayed chaotic systems by adaptive coupling-enhancement algorithms.

Chapter XIV

    Lean Yu, Chinese Academy of Sciences, China & City University of Hong Kong, Hong Kong
    Shouyang Wang, Chinese Academy of Sciences, China
    Kin Keung Lai, City University of Hong Kong, Hong Kong

The authors present a double-stage evolutionary algorithm for portfolio optimization. In the first stage, a genetic algorithm is used to identify good-quality assets in terms of asset ranking. In the second stage, investment allocation in the selected good-quality assets is optimized using another genetic algorithm based on Markowitz's theory.

Chapter XV

    Francesco Bertoluzzo, University of Padua, Italy
    Marco Corazza, University Ca'Foscari of Venice, Italy & School for Advanced Studies in
        Venice Foundation, Italy

The authors propose a financial trading system whose trading strategy is developed by means of an artificial neural network approach based on a learning algorithm of recurrent reinforcement type. This approach consists of two parts: first, directly specifying a trading policy based on some predetermined investor's measure of profitability, and second, directly setting the financial trading system while using it. They propose a simple procedure for the management of drawdown-like phenomena, and they apply their financial trading approach to some of the most prominent assets of the Italian stock market.

Chapter XVI

Leonardo Castellano, Matec Modelli Matematici, Italy
Walter Ambrosetti, CNR – Istituto per lo Studio degli Ecosistemi, Italy
Nicoletta Sala, Università della Svizzera Italiana, Switzerland & Università dell'Insubria,
Italy

The authors describe a mathematical model able to simulate the limnological physics of a complex natural body of water: computational fluid dynamics (CFD). They present an experience in progress at CNR-ISE (Italian National Research Council, Italian Institute of Ecosystems Study) of Pallanza in the field of application of mathematical modeling techniques applied to Lake Maggiore (Northern Italy and Switzerland).

Chapter XVII

Renato Saleri Lunazzi, Laboratoire MAP aria UMR 694 CNRS: Ministère de la Culture et
de la Communication, France

The author presents a research task that consists of applying automatic generative methods in design processes. The initial approach briefly explores early theoretical conjectures, starting with form and function balance within former conceptual investigations. He describes original techniques introducing integrated 2-D and 3-D generators for the enhancement of recent 3-D Earth browsers (Virtual Terrain©, MSN Virtual Earth©, or Google Earth©), and cellular automata processes for architectural programmatic optimization.

Chapter XVIII

Ljubiša M. Kocić, University of Niš, Serbia
Liljana R. Stefanovska, Ss Cyril and Methodius University, R. of Macedonia

The authors consider a relationship between spirals as protocomplex shapes and human intelligence organized in an information system, distinguishing between old (precomputer age) and new (computer age) IS. They proposed some methods for extracting spiral forms from pieces of visual arts using modern technologies of IS. The results support the thesis that there is a constant need for systematic recording of this important shape through history.

Chapter XIX

Nicoletta Sala, Università della Svizzera Italiana, Switzerland & Università dell'Insubria,
Italy

The author presents fractal geometry, which can help us describe shapes in nature. It is applied in various fields now, from biology to economy, using two different points of view: spatial fractals and temporal fractals. The author describes some applications of fractal geometry and its properties (e.g., self-similarity) in computer science, particularly for image compression and landscape modeling. Fractional Brownian motion has been observed for controlling traffic in computer networks (local area networks, metropolitan area networks, wireless area networks, and the Internet).

Foreword

Intelligent behavior is characterized by the flexible and creative pursuit of endogenously defined goals. It has emerged in humans through the stages of evolution that are manifested in the brains and behaviors of other animals. Intentionality is a key concept by which to link brain dynamics to goal-directed behavior. The archetypal form of intentional behavior is an act of observation through time and space, by which information is sought for the guidance of future action. Sequences of such acts constitute the key desired property of free-roving, semiautonomous devices capable of exploring remote environments that are inhospitable for humans. Intentionality consists of (a) the neurodynamics by which images are created of future states as goals, (b) command sequences by which to act in pursuit of goals, (c) the prediction of changes in sensory input resulting from intended actions (reafference), (d) the evaluation of performance, and (e) modification of the device by itself in learning from the consequences of its intended actions. These principles are well known among psychologists, philosophers, and engineers (e.g., Ashby, 1952; Clark, 1996; Hendriks-Jansen, 1996; Merleau-Ponty, 1945/1962).

What is new is the development of nonlinear mesoscopic brain dynamics (Freeman, 2000) by which to apply complexity theory in order to understand and emulate the construction of meaningful patterns of endogenous activity that implement the action-perception cycle (Merleau-Ponty, 1942/1963) as exemplified by the perceptual process of observation.

The prototypic hardware realization of intelligent behavior is already apparent in certain classes of robots. The chaotic neurodynamics of sensory cortices in pattern recognition is ready for hardware embodiments, which are needed to provide the eyes, noses, and ears of devices for survival and intentional operation—as distinct from autonomous operation in connoting cooperation with the controller—in complex and/or unpredictable environments.

The three salient characteristics of intentionality are (a) intent or directedness toward some future state or goal, (b) wholeness, and (c) unity. These three aspects correspond to the current use of the term in psychology (with the meaning of purpose), in medicine (with the meaning of the mode of healing and integration of the body), and in analytic philosophy (with the meaning of the way in which beliefs and thoughts are connected with or about objects and events in the world, also known as the symbol-grounding problem).

Intent comprises the endogenous initiation, construction, and direction of behavior into the world. It emerges from brains. Humans, animals, and autonomous robots select their own goals, plan their own tactics, and choose when to begin, modify, and stop sequences of action. Humans at least are subjectively aware of themselves acting, but consciousness is not a necessary property of intention. Unity appears in the combining of input from all sensory modalities into gestalts, in the coordination of all parts of the body, both musculoskeletal and autonomic, into adaptive, flexible, yet focused movements. Subjectively, unity appears in the awareness of self and emotion, but again this is not intrinsic to or a requisite for intention. Wholeness is revealed by the orderly changes in the self and its behavior that constitute the development, maturation, and adaptation of the self, within the constraints of its genes or design principles, and its material, social, and industrial environments. Subjectively, wholeness is revealed in the remembrance of self through a lifetime of change, although the influences of accumulated and integrated experience on current behavior are not dependent on recollection and recognition. In brief, simulation of intentionality should be directed toward replicating the mechanisms by which goal states are constructed, approached, and evaluated, and not toward emulating processes of consciousness, awareness, emotion, and so forth in machines.

Chaotic dynamics has proved to be extremely difficult to harness in the service of intelligent machines. Most studies that purport to control chaos either find ways to suppress it and replace it with periodic or quasiperiodic fluctuations, or to lock two or more oscillators into synchrony, sharing a common aperiodic wave form often as an optimal means for encryption and secure transmission. Our aim is to employ chaotic dynamics as the means for creating novel and endogenous space-time patterns, which must be the means to achieve any significant degree of autonomy in devices that must operate far from human guidance, where in order to function they must make up their courses of action as they go along. We know of no other way to approach a solution to the problem of how to introduce creative processes into machines other than to simulate the dynamics we have found in animal brains. To be sure, there are major unsolved problems in this approach, with the chief among them being that we know too little about the dynamics of the limbic system. Hence, we find it necessary to restrict the development of hardware models to the stage of brain-world interaction that we know best, which is the field of perception. In brief, what are the problems in giving eyes, ears, and a nose to a robot so that it might learn about its environment in something like the way that even the simpler animals do by creating hypotheses and testing them through their own actions?

The formation of a worldview by which the device can guide its explorations for the means to reach its goals depends on the integration of the outputs of the several sensory systems in order to form a multisensory percept known as a gestalt. The sequential frames deriving from sampling the environment must then be integrated over time and oriented in space.

It is also clear that such devices were first built by the pioneer of intentional robotics, W. Grey Walter (1953), and are now in advanced development to meet the challenges of extraterrestrial exploration with intentional robots (Huntsberger, 2001; Huntsberger, Tunstel, & Kozma, 2006; Kozma, in press). The proper path of future management will not be by techniques of passive memory installation or of training and aversive conditioning, but by education with the inculcation of desired values determined by the manufacturers that will govern the choices that must by definition be made by the newly intentional and quasi-autonomous mechanical devices.

This book provides both a toolbox and mapping for the exploration of new landscapes of the human technocultural environment.

Walter J. Freeman
Berkeley, June 2007

REFERENCES

Ashby, W. R. (1952). *Design for a brain.* London: Chapman & Hall.

Clark, A. (1996). *Being there: Putting brain, body, and world together again.* Cambridge, MA: MIT Press.

Freeman, W. J. (2000). *Neurodynamics: An exploration of mesoscopic brain dynamics.* London: Sprinter.

Hendriks-Jansen, H. (1996). *Catching ourselves in the act: Situated activity, interactive emergence, evolution, and human thought.* Cambridge, MA: MIT Press.

Huntsberger, T. (2001). Biologically inspired autonomous rover control. *Autonomous Robots, 11*, 341-346.

Huntsberger, T., Tunstel, E., & Kozma, R. (2006). Onboard learning strategies for planetary surface rovers. In A. Howard & E. Tunstel (Eds.), *Intelligence for space robotics* (chap. 20, pp. 403-422). San Antonio, TX: TCI Press.

Kozma, R. (in press). Neurodynamics of intentional behavior generation. In L. Perlovsky & R. Kozma (Eds.), *Neurodynamics of cognition and consciousness* (Springer Series on Understanding Complex Systems). Heidelberg, Germany: Springer Verlag.

Merleau-Ponty, M. (1963). *The structure of behavior* (A. L. Fischer, Trans.). Boston: Beacon Press. (Original work published 1942)

Merleau-Ponty, M. (1962). *Phenomenology of perception* (C. Smith, Trans.). New York: Humanities Press. (Original work published 1945)

Walter, W. G. (1953). *The living brain.* New York: W. W. Norton.

Preface

...it's a Looking-glass book, of course!
Lewis Carroll

Since the first production of tools at the beginning of human presence on Earth, human evolution is linked to the invention of new tools, usually combined with new environmental adaptations.

The symbiosis of man with tools and environments represents one of the main factors in human evolutionary processes. It is evident how this coupling is based on the biophysics of our bodies and the development of the social memory system called *culture*.

In recent times, computing devices, molecular biology, and new media (all members in different ways of the information communication technology set) are redesigning the human embodiment and its ecological niche.

The studies on interfaces, forming a common boundary between adjacent regions, bodies, substances, or phases, seem located at the core of these new developments (Jonassen & Land, 2000). It is there at the junction, sometimes originating a projection or an incorporation, that humans' new embodied identity evolves. New interfaces are actively reflexive and extend in more and more subtle ways the reflexivity naturally embedded in our bodies.

The cognitive neuroscience of the reflexive function can be one of the main keys to understand how the emergence of new interfaces yields new ways of extending and changing the human presence and consciousness in the world.

The embodied mind emerges and grows (bottom-up) on the basic reflexive function as an order parameter in biological processes. Some authors use these terms synonymously but we prefer to use the different terminology to stress the conceptual and factual difference. Reflexivity will be direct and nonconceptual: It implies an immediate capacity of awareness without effort or intellectualization. Reflectivity is a metacognitive process of higher order, implying secondary self-observation, denotation, and conceptualization (Gladwell, 2005; Siegel, 2007).

In reflexivity, the interface is "under your skin" as we are reminded that the embryological origin of skin, brain, and mind is the same. The ectoderm, our primary interface, is the outermost of the three primary germ layers of an embryo and the source of the epidermis, the nervous system, the eyes, and the ears, that is, interfaces. Reflexions happen at a very precognitive stage, before any higher order metacognition might be established. Primary reflexivity is based on massive nonlinear dynamics and it is probably the basic property of living matter, whose ultimate extension is consciousness. Modern advancements in complexity theory from Henry Poincare to Walter J. Freeman and Stuart Kauffman point in this direction and beyond. Fractal mathematics has extended the isomorphism capabilities in space and time for our technocultural niche (Orsucci, 1998, 2006; Orsucci & Sala, 2005; Sala, 2006; Thelen & Smith, 1994).

The current debate on cyborg identity is, by this perspective, relocated to a more familiar (though maybe not less disconcerting) perspective (Gray, 2001; Hayles, 1999; Marcuse, 1962). Our thesis is that man is a cyborg by default as human intelligence and embodied technology are just as in a Möbius strip: You can change the perspective and it might look different, but the surface is the same. Ancient Greek and Hindi tales describing strange half-flesh, half-metal creatures; golems; talking heads; homunculi; and modern cyborgs are just expressions of the same effort by our intellectual egos to understand and adapt to this natural evolutionary line.

ORGANIZATION OF THE BOOK

The book is divided in two sections. The first section, comprising 10 chapters, explores theoretical perspectives. The second section, including the last 9 chapters, presents a series of examples of applications in different fields.

Chapter I: "Reflexing Interfaces." Franco Orsucci identifies the reflexing interfaces that can redefine different approaches in different disciplines in the new millennium. The chapter sets the scene for discussions presented by various subsequent authors. In particular, it identifies how the cognitive neuroscience of the reflexive function can be a key to understand how the emergence of new interfaces links new ways of projecting human presence and consciousness in the world. In substance, information science and technology are accumulating ground for new possible evolutionary jumps. Computing devices, molecular biology, and new media are redesigning the human embodiment and its environment. An integrated approach, which should include the latest advancements in neuroscience, can draw the map of new possible human evolutions.

Chapter II: "Riddle of the Sphinx: Paradox Revealed and Reveiled." Terry Marks-Tarlow presents the Oedipus myth in the light of interpersonal neurobiology and second-order cybernetics, where observers are self-referentially implicated within the observed. The riddle of the Sphinx is understood as a paradox of self-reference in apparent contradiction with all known laws of science. The author of this chapter describes Oedipus' capacity for full self-reference as equated with the operation of the most powerful universal Turing machine with both implicit and explicit memory of its past.

Chapter III: "Theory of Cooperative Coevolution of Genes and Memes." Vladimir Kvasnicka and Jiri Pospichal propose a simple replicator theory of the coevolution of genes and memes. The presented coevolutionary theory assumes that units of information acquired from parents by imitation (memes) are not independent of genes, but are bounded with genes as composites, which are a subject of Darwinian evolution. A population composed of couples of genes and memes, the so-called m-genes, is postulated as a subject of Darwinian evolution. Three different types of operations over m-genes are introduced: replication (an m-gene is replicated with mutations onto an offspring m-gene), interaction (a memetic transfer from a donor to an acceptor), and extinction (an m-gene is eliminated). Computer simulations of the present model allow us to identify different mechanisms of gene and meme coevolutions.

Chapter IV: "Thinking Animals and Thinking Machines: What Relation? (With Particular Reference to the Psychoanalytical Point of View)." Franco Scalzone and Gemma Zontini describe some interesting similarities between computer science and psychoanalysis. The authors formulate some hypotheses by bringing closer the statute of connectionism to the energetic model of the psychic apparatus, as well as OOP (object-oriented programming) to the object relations theory. They explore the man-machine theme, the way in which men relate to machines, especially thinking machines, describing the fantasies they arouse. In order to do this we will use Tausk's classic *On the Origin of the Influencing Machine in*

Schizophrenia (1919), as well as some of Freud's writings. They also review some ethical issues in the security of electronic commerce.

Chapter V: "Machines Paying Attention." John G. Taylor describes the attention that is analyzed as the superior control system in the brain from an engineering point of view, with support for this from the way attention is presently being understood by brain science. The author remarks that an engineering control framework allows an understanding of how the complex networks observed in the brain during various cognitive tasks can begin to be functionally decomposed. He also presents a machine version of such an attention control system, and he extends it to allow for goals and their reward values also to be encoded in the attention machine. The author briefly discusses the manner in which emotion may then begin to be imbued in the machine and how even some glimpse of consciousness may then arise.

Chapter VI: "Artificial Mind." Rita Pizzi presents the advances of artificial intelligence that have renewed the interest in the mind-body problem, the ancient philosophical debate on the nature of the mind and its relationship with the brain. The author says the new version of the mind-body problem concerns the relationship between computational complexity and self-aware thought. She also introduces the progresses of micro-, nano-, and biotechnologies that allow creating the first bionic creatures, composed by biological cells connected to electronic devices. Creating an artificial brain with a biological structure could allow verifying if it possesses peculiar properties with respect to an electronic one, comparing them at the same level of complexity.

Chapter VII: "Neurofeedback." David Vernon introduces neurofeedback as a mechanism for altering human brain functioning and in turn influencing behavior. The author argues that neurofeedback provides a plausible mechanism by which the individual can learn to alter and control aspects of his electrocortical activity. He highlights some of the findings from both clinical and optimal performance research, showing the benefits of neurofeedback training, and outlines some of the important issues that remain to be addressed.

Chapter VIII: "Biological Traits in Artificial Self-Reproducing Systems." Eleonora Bilotta and Pietro Pantano present an artificial taxonomy of 2-D, self-replicating cellular automata (CA) that can be considered as proto-organisms for structure replication. The authors highlight that the process of self-reproduction is an important mechanism, and they discuss almost 10 methods of self-replication. These systems produce structures that are very similar to those found in biological systems. After examining self-replicating structures and the way they reproduce, the authors consider this behavior in relation to the patterns they realize and to the function they manifest in realizing an artificial organism.

Chapter IX: "Evolutionary Algorithms in Problem Solving and Machine Learning." Marco Tomassini and Leonardo Vanneschi describe the evolutionary algorithms, a family of powerful optimization heuristics based on the metaphor of biological evolution, especially genetic algorithms and genetic programming. The authors focus their attention on two specific applications. The first is about an important financial problem: the portfolio allocation problem. The second one deals with a biochemical problem related to drug design and efficacy.

Chapter X: "The Future Quantum Computer: Biotic Complexity." Hector Sabelli and Gerald H. Thomas present the notion of quantum computing and how it forces a reexamination of logics. The authors examine its historical roots in logos, the logic of nature, and the laws of physics. They also describe the logical design of computers according to the logic of quantum physics that will allow the full use of quantum processes for computation, providing explicit realizations of these ideas.

The second section is composed of nine chapters.

Chapter XI: "Networks: Uses and Misuses of an Emergent Paradigm." Alessandro Giuliani presents the notion of network, which is more and more widespread in all the fields of human investigation, from physics to sociology. It evokes a systemic approach to problems able to overcome the limitations of reductionist approaches as evidenced for some decades. The author describes some applications of network-based modeling to both introduce the basic terminology of the emergent network paradigm and highlight strengths and limitations of the method.

Chapter XII: "Theory and Practice of Ant-Based Routing in Dynamic Telecommunication Networks." Gianni A. Di Caro, Frederick Ducatelle, and Luca M. Gambardella introduce ant colony optimization (ACO), an optimization metaheuristic inspired by the foraging behavior of ant colonies. The authors describe the characteristics of ACO and they derive from it ant colony routing (ACR), a novel framework for the development of adaptive algorithms for network routing. They also state, through the concrete application of ACR's ideas to the design of an algorithm for mobile ad hoc networks, that the ACR framework allows the construction of new routing algorithms.

Chapter XIII: "Cryptography, Delayed Dynamical Systems, and Secure Communication." Santo Banerjee and Asesh Roy Chowdhury present nonlinear systems with time-delayed feedback, whose dynamics are governed by delay-differential equations. The authors describe a new method for the transmitting and receiving of signals using those delayed dynamical systems. The change of the delay parameter at the intermediate state gives extra security to the system. They also propose a method of communication using the synchronization between two coupled, delayed chaotic systems by adaptive coupling-enhancement algorithms.

Chapter XIV: "Portfolio Organization Using Evolutionary Algorithms." Lean Yu, Shouyang Wang, and Kin Keung Lai present a double-stage evolutionary algorithm for portfolio optimization. In the first stage, a genetic algorithm is used to identify good-quality assets in terms of asset ranking. In the second stage, investment allocation in the selected good-quality assets is optimized using another genetic algorithm based on Markowitz's theory. The authors discuss the experimental results that highlight that their double-stage evolutionary algorithm for portfolio optimization provides a useful tool to assist investors in planning their investment strategy and constructing their portfolio.

Chapter XV: "Automatic Financial Trading Systems: Is Recurrent Reinforcement Learning the Way?" Francesco Bertoluzzo and Marco Corazza propose a financial trading system whose trading strategy is developed by means of an artificial neural network approach based on a learning algorithm of recurrent reinforcement type. This approach consists of two parts: first, directly specifying a trading policy based on some predetermined investor's measure of profitability, and second, directly setting the financial trading system while using it. The authors take into account as a measure of profitability the reciprocal of the returns weighted direction symmetry index instead of the widespread Sharpe ratio. They propose a simple procedure for the management of drawdown-like phenomena and apply their financial trading approach to some of the most prominent assets of the Italian stock market.

Chapter XVI: "About the Use of the Computational Fluid Dynamics (CFD) in the Framework of Physical Limnological Studies on a Great Lake." Leonardo Castellano, Walter Ambrosetti, and Nicoletta Sala describe a mathematical model able to simulate the limnological physics of a complex natural body of water: computational fluid dynamics (CFD). The authors present an experience in progress at the CNR-ISE (Italian National Research Council, Italian Institute of Ecosystems Study) of Pallanza, Italy. The main features of the current state of the art in this field of application of mathematical modeling techniques are summarized and the characteristics of the computer code now in use for their studies on Lake Maggiore (Northern Italy and Switzerland) are described in detail.

Chapter XVII: "Urban and Architectural 3-D Fast Processing." Renato Saleri Lunazzi presents a research task that consists of applying automatic generative methods in design processes. The initial approach briefly explores early theoretical conjectures, starting with form and function balance within former conceptual investigations. The author, following experiments, describes original techniques introducing integrated 2-D and 3-D generators for the enhancement of recent 3-D Earth browsers (Virtual

Terrain©, MSN Virtual Earth©, or Google Earth©), and cellular automata processes for architectural programmatic optimization.

Chapter XVIII: "Reflections of Spiral Complexity on Art." Ljubiša M. Kocić and Liljana R. Stefanovska consider a relationship between spirals as protocomplex shapes and human intelligence organized in an information system. The authors distinguish between old (precomputer age) and new (computer age) IS. It seems that actual intelligent machines, connected in an efficient network, inherit a much older structure: a collective consciousness being formed by an international group of artists that exchange their ideas of beauty with amazing speed and persistence. The authors proposed some methods for extracting spiral forms from pieces of visual arts using modern technologies of IS. Sometimes, these forms are a consequence of a conscious and sometimes of an unconscious action of the artist. The results support the thesis that there is a constant need of systematic recording of this important shape through history.

Chapter XIX: "Fractal Geometry and Computer Science." Nicoletta Sala presents fractal geometry that can help us describe shapes in nature (e.g., ferns, trees, seashells, rivers, mountains). It is applied in various fields now, from biology to economy, using two different points of view: spatial fractals and temporal fractals. Spatial fractals refer to the presence of self-similarity observed in various enlargements. Temporal fractals are present in some dynamic processes that evidence a wide range of time scales with scale-invariant power-law characteristics. The author describes some applications of fractal geometry and its properties (e.g., self-similarity) in computer science, particularly for image compression and landscape modeling. Fractional Brownian motion has been observed for controlling traffic in computer networks (local area networks, metropolitan area networks, wireless area networks, and the Internet). The chapter highlights that self-similarity, which characterizes some fractal objects, is a unifying concept. In fact, it is an attribute of many laws of nature and is present in different fields of computer science.

CONCLUSION

In the Kubrick and Clarke's movie *2001: A Space Odyssey* (1968), a savannah-dwelling ape has a eureka-like flash of inspiration in realizing the awesome power of the bone tool in his hands. He tosses it skyward, where it morphs into a space station at the dawn of this millennium (Ambrose, 2001).

This book is a multifaceted mirror on how human evolution has had a constant psychobiological link with the development of new tools and environmental changes. Discoveries and technological innovations in information and communication science and technology (ICST) are paving the ground for new evolutionary steps. Computer devices could play a central role in this evolution as Giovanni Degli Antoni (1988) affirms: "Computers become mirrors in which the real lives his new reality beyond space and the time."

In the book *Through the Looking-Glass* (1872), the sequel to *Alice's Adventures in Wonderland* (1871), Lewis Carroll described many mirror experiences lived by Alice. Alice's adventures beyond the mirror could be considered a metaphor for ICST realities. If Alice were a modern child, certainly her mirror could be a computer screen. She would be used to experiencing how actions in a real world are transformed in other actions in the virtual world, and vice versa. These transformations follow interesting mathematical and physical processes that Lewis Carroll would certainly be interested in; Degli Antoni named these new processes *bi-causality* (Pizzi, 1989).

The isomorphism between biocognitive structures and the ICST niche we inhabit is progressively blurring boundaries between *res cogitans* and *res extensa*. Our new insights in neurocognition and the multiple reflexions implied in our sensory-perceptive processes are leading to new interfaces and new media. Reflexing interfaces are extensions of human embodiment just as the bone tool tossed skyward by a savannah-dwelling ape. Time flows, always different yet similar.

As Varela, Thompson, and Rosch stated aphoristically, "Readiness-for-action is a micro-identity and its corresponding level a micro-world: we embody streams of recurrent micro-world transitions" (1991).

We are the flow of micro and macro worlds, nested and intermingled. The stream of time flows here and there, generating multiple cascades, reflexing in billions of infinitesimal mirrors, and radiating in what we used to call consciousness.

REFERENCES

Ambrose, S. H. (2001). Paleolithic technology and human evolution. *Science, 291*, 1748-1753.

Degli Antoni, G. (1988). Il computer, il reale, l'artificiale. *Note di Software*, 41.

Gladwell, M. (2005). *Blink: The power of thinking without thinking.* Little, Brown.

Gray, C. H. (2002). *Cyborg citizen: Politics in the posthuman age.* London: Routledge.

Hayles, N. K. (1999). *How we became posthuman: Virtual bodies in cybernetics, literature, and informatics.* Chicago: University of Chicago Press.

Jonassen, D. H, & Land, S. M. (2000). *Theoretical foundations of learning environments.* Mahwah, NJ: Lawrence Erlbaum Associates Inc.

Kubrick, S. (Producer/Writer/Director), & Clarke, A. C. (Writer). (1968). *2001: A space odyssey* [Motion picture]. Borehamwood, United Kingdom: MGM.

Marcuse, H. (1962). *Eros and civilization: A philosophical inquiry into Freud.* New York: Vintage Books.

Orsucci, F. (Ed.). (1998). *The complex matters of the mind.* Singapore: World Scientific.

Orsucci, F. (2006). The paradigm of complexity in clinical neuro-cognitive science. *The Neuroscientist, 12*(4), 1-10.

Orsucci, F., & Sala, N. (2005). Virtual reality, telemedicine and beyond. In D. Carbonara (Ed.), *Technology literacy applications in learning environments* (pp. 349-357). Hershey, PA: Idea Group.

Pizzi, R. (1989). Through the looking glass: Una metafora della realtà artificiale. In *Verso la comunicazione elettronica* (pp. 7-16). Milan, Italy: Sole 24 HTE (High Tech and Education).

Sala, N. (2006). Complexity, fractals, nature and industrial design: Some connections. In M. M. Novak (Ed.), *Complexus mundi: Emergent pattern in nature* (pp. 171-180). Singapore: World Scientific.

Siegel, D. J. (2007). *The mindful brain: Reflection and attunement in the cultivation of well-being.* New York: Norton.

Tausk, V. (1919). Uber die entstehung des beeinflussungsapparates. In der Schizophrenie, *Inter.Zeitsch. Psychoan.* 5

Thelen, E., & Smith, L. B. (1994). *A dynamic systems approach to the development of cognition and action.* Cambridge, MA: MIT Press.

Varela, F. J., Thompson, E., & Rosch, E. (1991). *The embodied mind, cognitive science and human experience.* Cambridge, MA: MIT Press.

Acknowledgment

The editors would like to acknowledge the contributions of all people involved in the project's collation and review processes, without whose support the book could not have been satisfactorily completed.

Our gratitude goes to all the authors, whose creativity added multiple reflexing perspectives to this looking-glass book. We wish to thank all of the authors for their insight and excellent contributions. We also want to thank all of the people who assisted us in the reviewing process.

Special thanks also go to all the staff at IGI Global, whose contributions throughout the whole process from inception of the initial idea to final publication have been invaluable. In particular, thanks go to Kristin Roth (development editor), Deborah Yahnke and Ross Miller (editorial assistants), Jan Travers (managing director), and Mehdi Khosrow-Pour (executive editor) whose enthusiasm motivated us to initially accept his invitation for taking on this project.

Finally, we want to thank our families for their love and support throughout this project.

Franco Orsucci, MD, and Nicoletta Sala, PhD
Editors
London (UK) and Mendrisio (CH)
June 2007

Section I
Living Systems and Information Technology

Chapter I
Reflexing Interfaces

Franco Orsucci

University College London, UK & Institute for Complexity Studies, Italy

ABSTRACT

Since the first production of tools at the beginning of human presence on Earth, evolutionary jumps mark human development. Sometimes these punctuations were triggered by inventions of new tools, combined with new environmental adaptations. Affordances, as specialized forms of symbiotic embodiment with tools and environments, represent one of the main factors for human evolutionary processes. The cognitive neuroscience of the reflexive function can be one of the main keys to understand how the emergence of new interfaces yields new ways of projecting the human presence and consciousness in the world.

INTRODUCTION

In the movie 2001: A Space Odyssey (Ambrose, 2001), a savannah-dwelling ape has a eureka-like flash of inspiration in realizing the awesome power of the bone tool in his hands. He tosses it skyward, where it morphs into a space station at the dawn of this millennium.

Since the first production of tools at the beginning of human presence on Earth, evolutionary jumps mark human development. Sometimes these punctuations were triggered by inventions of new tools, combined with new environmental adaptations.

Affordances, as specialized forms of symbiotic embodiment with tools and environments, represent one of the main factors for human evolutionary processes.

The cognitive neuroscience of the reflexive function can be one of the main keys to understand how the emergence of new interfaces yields new ways of projecting the human presence and consciousness in the world. In recent times, information science and technology are accumulating ground for new possible evolutionary jumps. Computing devices, molecular biology, and new media (all members in different ways of the ICT set) are redesigning the human embodiment and its environment. An integrated approach of ICT and neuroscience can design a map for new possible human evolutions.

SETTING

Stone-tool technology, robust australopithecines, and the genus Homo appeared almost simultaneously 2.5 million years ago. Once this adaptive threshold was crossed, technological evolution continued to be associated with increased brain size, population size, and geographical range. Traits of behavior, economy, mental capacities, neurological functions, the origin of grammatical language, and sociosymbolic systems have been inferred from the archaeological record of Paleolithic technology (Ambrose, 2001).

Homo habilis is, obviously, considered the first toolmaker. The contiguity in the brain of Broca's area, involved in oro-facial fine motor control and language, to the area for precise hand motor control might be more than casual. The hand of Homo habilis resembles that of modern humans. Its brain was significantly larger (600 to 800 cm³) than that of earlier and contemporary australopithecines and extant African apes (450 to 500 cm³), and its teeth were relatively small for its body size, suggesting a relation between tool use, quality of diet, and intelligence.

The production of tools and artifacts is linked to the development of language, culture, and cognitive functions. This happened as tools and artifacts were, just as other sociolinguistic processes, mediating and reflexing interfaces in environmental and social interactions.

We need to know more about the ways in which speaking, tool using, and sociality are interwoven into the texture of everyday life in contemporary human groups. The birth of technique was incubated in the complex system of material resources, tools, operational sequences and skills, verbal and nonverbal knowledge, and specific modes of work coordination that come into play in the fabrication of material artifacts. It is a process—a complex interplay of reflexivity between sensory-motor skills, symbolic cognition, tools, artifacts, and environment.

James J. Gibson (1979), in this context, originally proposed the concept of affordance to refer to "all action possibilities" latent in a specific environment, objectively measurable,

Figure 1. Neurocognitive dynamics in affordance, for example, grasping a mug (Arbib, 2002)

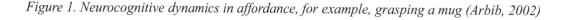

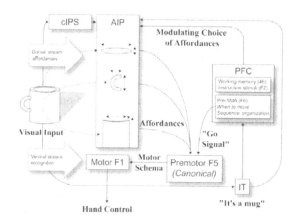

and independent of the individual's ability to recognize those possibilities. Furthermore, these action possibilities are dependent on the physical capabilities of the agent. For instance, a set of steps with risers 4 feet high does not afford the act of climbing if the actor is a crawling infant. Therefore, we should measure affordances along with the relevant actors.

Donald Norman (1988) introduced the term affordance in human-machine interaction, which made it a very popular term in the interaction design field. Later, he clarified he was actually referring to a perceived affordance as opposed to an objective affordance (Norman, 1999). This new definition clarified that affordances are determined not only by the physical capabilities of the agent, but also by the individual and social knowledge embedded in objects and interactions of everyday life.

For example, if an agent steps into a room with a chair and a book, Gibson's definition of affordance allows a possibility that the agent may look at the chair and sit on the book as this is objectively possible. Norman's definition of perceived affordance captures the likelihood that the actor will sit on the chair and look at the book because of the embodiment and social knowledge embedded as affordance in these objects.

As Figure 1 clearly presents, affordances are rooted in motor schemes and neurocognitive dynamics.

FOCUS

The significance of evolutionary theory to the human sciences cannot be fully appreciated without a better understanding of how phenotypes in general, and human beings in particular, modify significant sources of selection in their environments, thereby codirecting subsequent biological evolution. Empirical data and theoretical arguments suggest that human technocultural activities have influenced human genetic evolution by modifying sources of natural selection and altering genotype frequencies in some human populations (Bodmer & Cavalli-Sforza, 1976). Technocultural traits, such as the use of tools, weapons, fire, cooking, symbols, language, and trade, may have also played important roles in driving hominid evolution in general and the evolution of the human brain in particular (Aiello & Wheeler, 1995). It is more than likely that some cultural and scientific practices in contemporary human societies are still affecting human genetic evolution. Modern molecular biologists do interfere with genes directly on the basis of their acquired scientific experiences, though this practice might be too recent to have already had an enduring impact on human genetic evolution. In any case, it already brings a new reflexive loop in our development.

Other evolutionary biologists maintain that culture frequently does affect the evolutionary process, and some have begun to develop mathematical and conceptual models of gene-culture coevolution that involve descriptions not only of how human genetic evolution influences culture, but also of how human culture can drive, or codirect, some genetic changes in human populations (Feldman & Laland, 1996). These models include culturally biased, nonrandom mating systems; the treatment of human sociocultural or linguistic environments as sources of natural selection (Aoki & Feldman, 1987); and the impact of different cultural activities on the transmission of certain diseases (Durham, 1991). The common element among these cases is that cultural processes change the human selective environment and thereby affect which genotypes survive and reproduce.

Culture works on the basis of various kinds of transmission systems (Boyd & Richerson, 1985), which collectively provide humans with a second, nongenetic knowledge-carrying inheritance system.

Niche construction from all ontogenetic processes modifies human selective environments,

Figure 2. Evolutionary dynamics involving genes and technoculture (Laland et al., 2000)

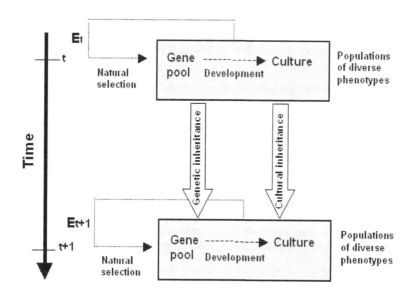

generating a legacy of modified natural selection pressures that are bequeathed by human ancestors to their descendants. Figure 2 best captures the causal logic underlying the relationship between biological evolution and cultural change (Laland, Odling-Smee, & Feldman, 2000).

If the technocultural inheritance of an environment-modifying human activity persists for enough generations to produce a stable selective pressure, it will be able to codirect human genetic evolution. For example, the culturally inherited traditions of pastoralism provide a case in point. Apparently, the persistent domestication of cattle, sheep, and so forth and the associated dairying activities did alter the selective environments of some human populations for sufficient generations to select for genes that today confer greater adult lactose tolerance (Durham, 1991). Although other species of animals have their "proto-cultures" (Galef, 1988), it has generally been assumed that Homo sapiens is the only extant species with a

technocultural transmission stable enough to codirect genetic evolution (Boyd & Richerson, 1985). We may conclude that our technoculture is part of our ecological niche.

Building on ideas initially developed by Lewontin (1983), Laland previously proposed that biological evolution depends not only on natural selection and genetic inheritance, but also on niche construction (Laland et al., 1996a). Niche construction refers to the activities, choices, and metabolic processes of organisms through which they define, choose, modify, and partly create their own niches. It consists of the same processes that Jones et al. (1997) call "ecosystem engineering."

For example, to varying degrees, organisms choose their own habitats, mates, and resources, and construct important components of their local environments such as nests, holes, burrows, paths, webs, dams, and chemical environments. Many organisms also partly destroy their habitats

Table 1. Techno-cultural niche construction (Laland et al., 2000)

Source of niche construction	Feedback to biological evolution	Feedback to cultural change
Population genetic processes	Web spiders marking web or building dummy spiders (Edmunds 1974)	Sex differences in human mating behaviour (Barkow et al. 1992; Daly & Wilson 1983)
Information acquiring ontogenetic processes	Woodpecker finch, by learning to grub with a tool, alleviates selection for a woodpecker's bill (Alcock 1972; Grant 1986)	Learning and experience influence the adoption of cultural traits (Durham 1991)
Cultural processes	Dairy farming selects for lactose tolerance (Feldman & Cavalli-Sforza 1989)	Invention of writing leads to other innovations such as printing, libraries, e-mail

through stripping them of valuable resources or building up detritus, processes we refer to as negative niche construction.

Organisms may niche construct in ways that counteract natural selection, for example, by digging a burrow or migrating to avoid the cold, or they may niche construct in ways that introduce novel selection pressures, for example, by exploiting a new food resource, which might subsequently select for a new digestive enzyme. In every case, however, niche construction modifies one or more sources of natural selection in a population's environment.

One theoretical construct that captures some, but not all, of the consequences of niche construction is Dawkins' (1982) "extended phenotype." Dawkins argues that genes can express themselves outside the bodies of the organisms that carry them. For example, the beaver's dam is an extended phenotypic effect of beaver genes. Like any other aspect of the phenotype, extended phenotypes play an evolutionary role by influencing the chances that the genes responsible for the extended phenotypic trait will be passed on to the next generation. Dawkins emphasizes this single aspect of the evolutionary feedback from niche construction.

However, the beaver's dam sets up a host of selection pressures, which feed back to act not only on the genes responsible for the extended phenotype, but also on other genes that may influence the expression of other traits in beavers, such as the teeth, tail, feeding behavior, susceptibility to predation or disease, social system, and many other aspects of their phenotypes. It may also affect many future generations of beavers that may inherit the dam, its lodge, and the altered river or stream, as well as many other species of organisms that now have to live in a world with a lake in it.

An example of contemporary environmental niches in information technology can be obviously found in the computer mouse and its related iconic desktop-like interface. An evolution of the creation of virtual spaces that can change the way we perceive and interact with other dimensions of our realities is presented in new commercial and experimental interfaces. It is clear that every human interface tends to use biomechanical and physiological properties of the human body in order to reach a possible perfect symbiosis between man and machine.

The result is the possibility of a real-time interaction with a real or a conceptual object within a learning environment based on augmented reality, adding new dimensions to our usual everyday reality and, at the same time, giving a new reality to scientific "mind objects." For instance, the Wii Remote for Nintendo video games is a sophisticated controller, fusing the familiarity of a remote control with motion or neurophysiologic sensing technology.

Figure 3. Interacting with a physico-mathematical structure in augmented reality, the Roessler attractor (courtesy of Studierstübe)

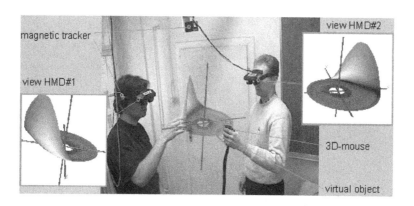

Other experimental devices or prototypes might be interesting examples: Eye movements, brain waves, and other biosignals are captured and amplified to translate them into useful logic commands and neural-signal interpretation (such as emotions).

MIRRORS

In "Language within our Grasp," Rizzolatti and Arbib (1998) showed that the mirror system in monkeys is the homologue of Broca's area, a crucial speech area in humans, and they argued that this observation provides a neurobiological missing link for the long-argued hypothesis that primitive forms of communication based on manual gesture preceded speech in the evolution of language. "Language readiness evolved as a multimodal manual/facial/vocal system with proto-sign (manual-based protolanguage) providing the scaffolding for proto-speech (vocal-based protolanguage). There was the "neural critical mass" to trigger the emergence of language (Arbib, 2002, 2005) via the mirroring between neurons

at the dendrite and axon level. The neurodynamic result of this critical mass was the possibility to reach the threshold, which in terms of dynamical systems is the number of degrees of freedom necessary for effective psychodynamics (Freeman, 1975; Orsucci, 1998).

The mirror-system hypothesis states that the matching of neural code for execution and observation of hand movements in the monkey is present in the common ancestor of monkey and human. It is the precursor of the crucial language property of parity, namely that an utterance usually carries similar meaning for speaker and hearer. Imitation plays a crucial role in human language acquisition and performance: Brain mechanisms supporting imitation were crucial to the emergence of Homo sapiens.

Rizzolatti & Arbib (1998) hypothesize several stages of this evolution.

a. Grasping
b. A mirror system for grasping (i.e., a system that matches observation and execution)
c. A simple imitation system for grasping
d. A complex imitation system for grasping

Figure 4. Neurodynamics of mirror systems during an observed action (Rizzolatti & Arbib, 1998)

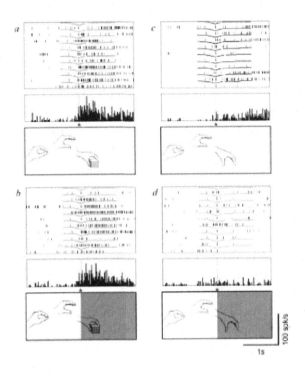

e. A manual-based communication system
f. Speech, characterized as being the open-ended production and perception of sequences of vocal gestures, without implying that these sequences constitute a language
g. Verbal language

A mirror system for grasping in the monkey has been found in area F5 of the premotor cortex, while data have been found consistent with the notion of a mirror system for grasping in humans in Broca's area, which is homologous to monkeys' F5 but in humans is most often thought of as a speech area. Following their findings and hypothesis, language evolved from a basic mechanism not originally related to communication: the mirror system with its capacity to generate and recognize a set of actions.

There are some difficult questions posed by the interaction between new media and the mirror system. The different kinds of reality experience produced by new media might activate, via direct perception, presentations or action-like brain effects, or enduring plasticity effects. We are not referring just to the banal imitation induction we might experience after an immersive movie, but also to the longer lasting molding of the brain by the mirroring induced by all the most various contents provided by new media. It is a problem older generations never encountered, and the spreading of diagnoses such as attention deficit/hyperactivity disorder can be related to this (as we will see later on).

The linguist Noam Chomsky (e.g., 1975) has argued that since children acquire language rapidly despite the "poverty of the stimulus," the basic structures of language are encoded in the brain, forming a universal grammar encoded in the human genome. For example, it is claimed that the universal grammar encodes the knowledge that a sentence in a human language could be ordered as subject-verb-object, subject-object-verb, and so forth, so that the child simply needs to hear a few sentences of his first language to "set the parameter" for the preferred order of that language. Against this, others have argued that in fact the child does have a rich set of language stimuli, and that there are now far more powerful models of learning than those that Chomsky took into account, allowing us to explain how a child might learn from its social interactions aspects of syntax that Chomsky would see as genetically prespecified. The reader may consult Lieberman (1991) for a number of arguments that counter Chomsky's view. Here we simply observe, for example, that many youngsters today easily acquire the skills of Web surfing and video-game playing despite a complete poverty of the stimulus, namely the inability of their parents to master these skills. We trust that no one would claim that the human genome contains a Web-surfing gene. Instead, we know the history of computers, and know that technology has advanced over the last 55 years to take us from an interface based on binary coding to a mouse-and-graphics interface so well adapted to human sensory motor capabilities that a child can master it.

We reject Chomsky's view that many of the basic alternatives of grammatical structure of the world's current languages are already encoded in the human genome so that the child's experience merely sets parameters to choose among prepackaged alternative grammatical structures. The experimental evidence of this hypothesis, years after it was proposed, is still weak. The different view, which I support, holds that the brain of the first Homo sapiens was language-ready, but it required many millennia of invention and technocultural evolution for human societies to form human languages in the modern sense.

The structure of a language-ready brain had reached a critical neural mass action (Freeman, 1975) of connections and feedback redundancies capable to provide reflexivity and the emergence of consciousness. The mirror neurons finding is based on the massive increment of feedback and regulations embedded in the human brain architecture. In this sense, mirroring and reflexivity are embedded in the usual functioning of all neurons and structured in some more specialized ones. Chomsky and his followers instead, in some way, present a Platonist approach claiming that the so-called deep structures—symbols and genes—are primary and antecedent to bio-psycho-physical experiences. We prefer a more realistic complexity approach that recognizes different biological and nonbiological factors in language development (Orsucci, 2002; Tomasello, 2003).

In this framework, it is quite interesting to consider how Rizzolatti and Arbib (1998) propose that at Stage 5, the manual-based communication system broke through the fixed repertoire of primate vocalizations to yield a combinatorial open repertoire, so that Stage 6, speech, did not build upon the ancient primate vocalization system, but rather rested on the invasion of the vocal apparatus by collaterals from the communication system based on F5 or Broca's area. In discussing the transition to Homo sapiens, they stress that our predecessors must have had a relatively flexible, open repertoire of vocalizations, but this does not mean that they, or the first humans, had language. They hold that human language (as well as some dyadic forms of primate communication) evolved from a basic mechanism that was not originally related to communication: the capacity to recognize actions.

Psychoanalytical studies highlight the important perspective of mirroring in emotional development. The reflexive function is central also in the definition of identity and relations. Freud (1920/n.d.) had focused on a child's game, becoming famous as *Fort/Da*, in which a mirror can be used by the child to represent the disappearance of the caregiver. Lacan (1937/2005) proposed a specific stage in child development, called *le stade du miroir*, in which the child reaches recognition of his or her image in a mirror. This stage, linked to a crucial step in the integration of the central nervous system, is evident also in some primates and was considered crucial in the establishment of a self-conscious identity. Gaddini (1969) explored imitation as a primary form of identification. Winnicott (1987) extended this notion to reflexive responsiveness a child can receive from the caregiver, the family, and the extended social environment. Fonagy and Target (1997) state that reflective function is the developmental acquisition that permits the child to respond not only to other people's behavior, but to his or her conception of their beliefs, feelings, hopes, pretense, plans, and so on: "Reflective function or mentalization enables children to 'read' people's minds." Paulina Kernberg (2006) recalls how the mirror function of the mother is expanded to the idea of attunement between mother and child (Stern, 1983), resonating affectively, visually, vocally, and by movement and touch.

EVOLUTION

Judging from the anatomical and cultural remains left by hominids and early humans, the most important evolutionary steps were concentrated into a few transition periods when the process of change was greatly accelerated, and these major transitions introduced fundamentally new capacities. Merlin Donald (1997), within the same research line, proposes some evolutionary punctuation in the development of the human embodied mind.

The first transition is mimetic skill and autocueing. The rationale for the first transition is based on several premises: (a) The first truly human cognitive breakthrough was a revolution in motor skill—mimetic skill—which enabled hominids to use the whole body as a representa-

tional device, (b) this mimetic adaptation had two critical features—it was a multimodal modeling system, and it had a self-triggered rehearsal loop (that is, it could voluntarily access and retrieve its own outputs), (c) the sociocultural implications of mimetic skill are considerable and could explain the documented achievements of Homo erectus, (d) in modern humans, mimetic skill in its broadest definition is dissociable from language-based skills, and retains its own realm of cultural usefulness, and (e) the mimetic motor adaptation set the stage for the later evolution of language.

Mimesis can be just an emergent property of the mass action in the nervous system as the mirror function is a specialization of the arousal and feedback neural processes. The embodiment of mind processes becomes, in this way, a neurobiological necessity. As the whole body becomes a potential tool for expression, a variety of new possibilities enter the social arena: complex games, extended competition, pedagogy through directed imitation (with a concomitant differentiation of social roles), a subtler and more complex array of facial and vocal expressions, and public action-metaphor, such as intentional group displays of aggression, solidarity, joy, fear, and sorrow. The emergence of religious practice could also be considered, in its animistic beginnings, as an inclusive extension of mimetic functions to the living and nonliving environment.

The second transition is the lexical invention. The rationale for the second transition is briefly as follows: (a) Since no linguistic environment yet existed, a move toward language would have depended primarily on developing a capacity for lexical invention, (b) phonological evolution was accelerated by the emergence of this general capacity for lexical invention, and included a whole complex of special neuronal and anatomical modifications for speech, (c) the language system evolved as an extension of lexical skill, and gradually extended to the labeling of relationships between words, and also to the imposition of more and more complex metalinguistic skills that govern the uses of words, (d) the natural collective product of language was narrative thought (essentially, storytelling), which evolved for specific social purposes and serves essentially similar purposes in modern society, and (e) further advanced products are technical jargons and mathematical notations. These new representational acts—speech and mimesis—both are performed covertly as well as overtly.

Covert speech has been called inner speech or inner dialogue to stress how it is equivalent to the activation of the central aspects of articulation, without actual motor execution. The mental operation we call imagination can similarly be seen as mimesis without motor execution of imagined acts and situations. The control of mimetic imagination (probably even of visual generative imagery, which is facilitated by imagined self-movement) presumably lies in a special form of kinematical imagery. Autoretrievability is just as crucial for covert imaginative or linguistic thought as it is for the overt or acted-out equivalent. Thus, given a lexicon, the human mind became able to self-trigger recall from memory in two ways: by means of mimetic imagination, and by the use of word-symbols, either of which could be overt or covert.

The third transition is grammar and other metalinguistic skills. According to the competition model proposed by Bates and MacWhinney (1987), the whole perisylvian region of the left hemisphere of the brain is diffusely dedicated to language, with function words and grammatical rules being stored in the same tissue as other kinds and aspects of lexical entries. However, we readily admit that this issue, like many others in this field, is still not conclusively resolved; there is electrophysiological evidence that function words—those most relevant to grammar—might have a different cerebral representation from open-class words (Neville, 1992).

SYNCHRONIZATIONS

In the classical sense, the word synchronization (literally, from ancient Greek, *sharing time*) means: "adjustment or entrainment of frequencies of periodic oscillators due to a weak interaction." Synchronization is a basic nonlinear phenomenon in physics, discovered in interactions between pendulums at the beginning of the modern age of science. More recently, Maturana and Varela (1980) had suggested that sync is a form of structural coupling, a process that occurs when two structurally plastic systems repeatedly perturb one another's structure in a nondestructive way over a period of time. This leads to the development of structural fit between systems. There is an intimate relationship between this process and the emergence of appropriate behavior from the interplay between interacting systems because the structure of a system determines its responses to perturbing environmental events. Maturana (2002) stressed this dynamical approach in semiotic terms within a coevolutionary perspective: "Language is a manner of living together in a flow of coordination of coordinations of consensual behaviours or doings that arises in a history of living in the collaboration of doing things together." This dynamical systems' approach leads to control and synchronization in chaotic or complex systems. Pecora and Carroll (1990) and Ott, Grebogi, and Yorke (1990) opened a new and reliable way to contemporary research on control and synchronization of complex systems.

We have been investigating sync during natural conversations, finding that it is a quite complex phenomenon happening at the same time as the nonverbal, phonetic, syntactic, and semantic levels (Orsucci, 2006; Orsucci, Giuliani, & Zbilut, 2004; Orsucci, Walters, Giuliani, Webber, & Zbilut, 1999). The statistical tool we consider most suitable for this kind of study is recurrence quantification analysis (Eckmann, Kamphorst, & Ruelle, 1987; Marwan, 2003; Webber & Zbilut, 1994). Coordination between conversation partners occurs at multiple levels, including the choice of syntactic structure (Branigan, Pickering, & Cleland, 2000). A number of outstanding questions concerning the origin of this coordination require novel analytic techniques. Our research can be considered complementary to a study by Shockley, Santana, and Fowler (2003), in which interpersonal coordination during conversation was based on recurrence strategies to evaluate the shared activity between two postural time series in a reconstructed phase space.

In a study on speech and rhythmic behavior, Port et al. (1999) found that animals and humans exhibit many kinds of behavior where frequencies of gestures are related by small integer ratios (like 1:1, 2:1, or 3:1). Many properties like these are found in speech as an embodied activity considered as an oscillator prone to possible synchronizations. Our findings in the synchronization of conversation dynamics can be relevant for the general issue of the structural coupling of psychobiological organizations. Implications are related with psycho-chrono-biology research and

the clinical field. Data on synchronization suggest that this dynamic behavior can be evident also in semiotic and cognitive dynamics, besides the well-established research on biological oscillators. For example, Dale and Spivey (2006) used this method to explore lexical and syntactic coordination between children and caregivers in conversation. Results indicate that children and caregivers coordinate sequences of syntactic classes, and that this coordination diminishes over development. Similar studies highlight synchronization of eye movements in conversations (Richardson & Dale, 2005).

Synchronization is a crucial area to study in order to bridge biophysics, neuroscience, and information technologies. Sharing time, in different time frames, is critical for neurodynamics, consciousness, and cooperation with humans and nonhumans (machines included). We might cite, for example, applications from several research groups as some key areas of the current research in information science and technology in which synchronization is so important, though it might not be fully recognized.

Figure 5. Synchronization during a natural conversation (Orsucci et al., 2004)

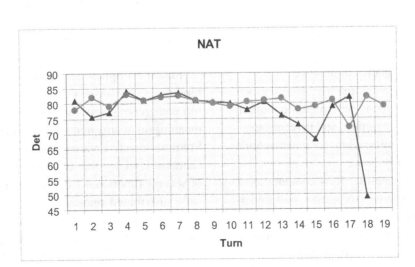

a. Robotic Life: How to build cooperative. machines that work and learn in partnership with people

b. Object-Based Media: How to create communication systems gaining an understanding of the content they carry and use it to make richer connections among users

c. Sociable Media: How to create better online environments and interfaces for human communication

d. Biomechatronics: How technology can be used to enhance human physical capability

e. Tangible Media: How to design seamless interfaces among humans, digital information, and the physical environment

f. Software Agents: How software can act as an assistant to the user rather than as a tool by learning from interaction and by proactively anticipating the user's needs

g. Ambient Intelligence: How ubiquitous, personalized interfaces can be responsive to our interests and expand our minds

h. Society of Mind: How various phenomena of mind emerge from the interactions among many kinds of highly evolved brain mechanisms

i. Smart Cities: How buildings and cities can become more intelligently responsive to the needs and desires of their inhabitants

j. Future of Learning: How to redefine and expand the conceptual framework and language of learning by creating new technologies and spheres of practice

k. Responsive Environments: How sensor networks augment and mediate human experience, interaction, and perception

l. Mobile Dynamics: How to make mobile devices socially aware

m. Affective Computing: How computational systems can sense, recognize, and understand human emotions and respond

n. Learning Environments: How to engage people in creative learning experiences

o. Wearable Computing: How to embed computing devices in clothes and accessories

REFLEXIONS

Time, as we have seen, is a crucial factor in synchronization. Mirroring needs some coincidences in space and time, though its definition can be quite complex: Depending on the context, the framing of sync can change. Subjective and neurocognitive time in experience is quite different from time as measured by a clock. Time in experience presents itself not only as linear, but also as having a complex texture (evidence that we are not dealing with a "knife-edge" present), a texture that dominates our existence to an important degree (Varela as cited in Petitot, 1999).

This overall approach to cognition is based on situated embodied agents. Varela, Thompson, and Rosch (1991) and Thompson (2001) have proposed the adjective *enactive* to designate this approach more precisely. It comprises two complementary aspects.

1. Ongoing coupling of the cognitive agent, a permanent coping that is fundamentally mediated by sensory-motor activities

2. Autonomous activities of the agent whose identity is based on emerging, endogenous configurations (or self-organizing patterns) of neuronal activity

Enaction implies that sensory-motor coupling modulates, but does not determine, an ongoing endogenous activity that it configures into meaningful world items in an unceasing flow. From an enactive viewpoint, any mental act is characterized by the concurrent participation of several functionally distinct and topographically distributed regions of the brain and their sensory-motor embodiment. From the point of view of the neuroscientist, it is the complex task of relating and integrating these different components that is at the root of temporality. These various components require a frame or window of simultaneity that corresponds to the duration of lived subjective present. These kinds of present are not necessarily conscious; often they are not, though they might not be unconscious in the folk Freudian way (Orsucci, Giuliani, Webber, Zbilut, Fonagy, & Mazza, 2006). There are three possible scales of duration to understand the temporal horizon just introduced (though other scales of extended present, considered in chronobiology, might considered).

- basic or elementary events (the 1/10 scale)
- relaxation time for large-scale integration (the 1 scale)
- descriptive-narrative assessments (the 10 scale)

The first level is already evident in the so-called fusion interval of various sensory systems: the minimum distance needed for two stimuli to be perceived as nonsimultaneous, a threshold that varies with each sensory modality. These thresholds can be grounded in the intrinsic cellular rhythms of neuronal discharges, and in the temporal summation capacities of synaptic integration. These events fall within a range of 10 ms (e.g., the rhythms of bursting interneurons) to 100 ms (e.g., the duration of an EPSP/IPSP sequence in a cortical pyramidal neuron). These values are the basis for the 1/10 scale. Behaviorally, these elementary events give rise to microcognitive phenomena variously studied as perceptual moments, central oscillations, iconic memory, excitability cycles, and subjective time quanta. For instance, under minimum stationary conditions, reaction time

Figure 6. Windows of time (Varela et al., 1991)

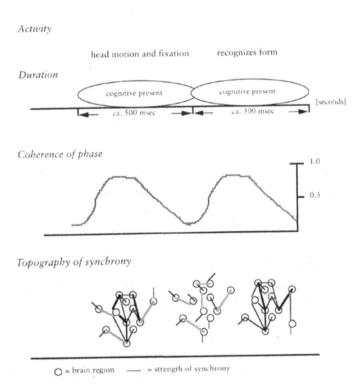

or oculomotor behavior displays a multimodal distribution with a 30- to 40-millisecond distance between peaks; in average daylight, apparent motion (or "psi-phenomenon") requires 100 ms.

This leads naturally to the second scale, that of long-range integration. Component processes already have a short duration, about 30 to 100 ms; how can we understand such experimental psychological and neurobiological results at the level of a fully constituted, normal cognitive operation? A long-standing tradition in neuroscience looks at the neuronal bases of cognitive acts (perception-action, memory, motivation, and the like) in terms of cell assemblies (CAs) or, synonymously, neuronal ensembles. A CA is a distributed subset of neurons with strong reciprocal connections.

The diagram depicts the three main time frames considered here. A cognitive activity (such as head turning) takes place within a relatively incompressible duration: a cognitive present. The basis for this emergent behavior is the recruitment of widely distributed neuronal ensembles through increasingly frequent coherence in the gamma (30-80 Hz) band. Thus, we might depict the corresponding neural correlates of a cognitive act as a synchronous neural hypergraph of brain regions undergoing bifurcations of phase transitions from a cognitive present content to another.

Recently, this view has been supported by widespread findings of oscillations and synchronies in the gamma range (30-80 Hz) in neuronal groups during perceptual tasks. Thus, we have neuronal-level constitutive events that have a duration on the 1/10 scale, forming aggregates that manifest as incompressible but complete cognitive acts on the 1 scale. This completion time is dynamically dependent on a number of dispersed assemblies and not on a fixed integration period; in other words, it is the basis of the origin of duration without an external or internally ticking clock.

"Nowness," in this perspective, is therefore presemantic in that it does not require a remembering in order to emerge. The evidence for this important conclusion comes, again, from many sources. For instance, participants can estimate durations of up to 2 to 3 seconds quite precisely, but their performance decreases considerably for longer times. Spontaneous speech in many languages is organized such that utterances last 2 to 3 seconds and short, intentional movements (such as self-initiated arm motions) are embedded within windows of this same duration.

This brings to the fore the third duration, the 10 scale, proper to descriptive-narrative assessments. In fact, it is quite evident that these endogenous, dynamic horizons can be, in turn, linked together to form a broader temporal horizon. This temporal scale is inseparable from our descriptive-narrative assessments and linked to our linguistic capacities. It constitutes the "narrative centre of gravity" in Dennett's (1991) metaphor: the flow of time related to personal identity. It is the continuity of the self that breaks down under intoxication or in pathologies such as schizophrenia or Korsakoff's syndrome. As Husserl (1980) points out, commenting on similar reasoning in Brentano, "We could not speak of a temporal succession of tones if…what is earlier would have vanished without a trace and only what is momentarily sensed would be given to our apprehension." To the appearance of the just-now, one correlates two modes of understanding and examination (in other words, valid forms of donation in the phenomenological sense): (a) remembrance or evocative memory, and (b) mental imagery and fantasy.

The "Urimpression" is the proper mode of nowness, or in other words, it is where the new appears; impression intends the new. Briefly, impression is always presentational, while memory or evocation is representational.

These neurophysiologic events are correlated to microcognitive phenomena and behavioral elements variously studied as perceptual moments, central oscillations, iconic memory, excitability cycles, and subjective time quanta: the elementary particles of reflexions we can share with humans and media. Coupling and sharing between humans and machines are happening at this level, when metacognitive and mental skills are certainly unusual. It is the "a-conscious" level and modality, preliminary to any unconscious or preconscious modes. The kind of reflexivity implied in these processes concerns the embodied mind. It is a kind of cognitive capacity fully incorporated in bodily actions and reactions. These kinds of processes involve a presentational intentionality, not a representational intellect. It is a form of direct cognition, not a self-conscious metacognition.

The embodied mind emerges and grows (bottom-up) on the basic reflexive function as a direct parameter in biological processes. Reflection is a metacognitive function (top-down): "the overall reflective process can embed more conceptual and linguistic functions in the brain than the reflexive component alone" (Siegel, 2007). Some authors use the terms synonymously, but we prefer to use a different terminology to stress a conceptual and factual difference. Reflexivity will be direct and nonconceptual: It implies an immediate capacity of awareness without effort or intellectualization. In reflexivity, the interface is just like your own skin, and it is useful remember that the

embryological origin of skin, brain, and mind is the same. The ectoderm, our primary interface, is the outermost of the three primary germ layers of an embryo and the source of the epidermis, the nervous system, the eyes, and the ears, that is, the interfaces.

Reflexions happen at a very precognitive stage, before any higher order metacognition might be established. We have been exploring some important implications of mirror neuron research. New findings by Libet (1993) and Libet, Freeman, and Sutherland (1999) on the so-called readiness potential extend our perspectives on this matter.

Kornhuber and Deecke (1965) had found that all actions are preceded by a slow potential easily detected in an EEG. They gave this potential a German name, *bereitschaft-potential*, but nowadays it is more frequently called in English readiness potential (RP). A question was quite immediate: As the RP was happening at about 550 ms before action, in which timing (and maybe causal) sequence was it placed with representations and decisions concerning that same action? It was found that every conscious representation and

Figure 7. Libet et al. (1999)

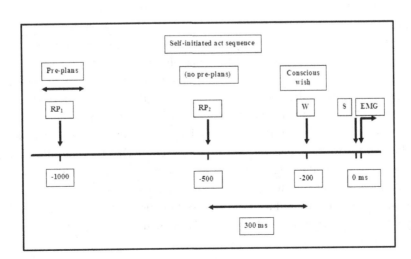

decision of acting (or not) were placed at just 200 ms before action, so they were following the RP at about 300 ms. Benjamin Libet, an American neurophysiologist, has been expanding research in this area both in the sensory and the motor fields, including some possible psychological and philosophical implications (Libet, 1993; Libet et al., 1999). His vantage point might be summarized in this way: We do not have free will, but we do have free denial. We have the possibility to facilitate or stop an action after it has been started in an a-conscious way. Recent advancements in the complex neurodynamics of time could provide seminal contributions in advancing our understanding of ethical issues on the personal responsibility of actions (Gazzaniga, 2005).

It is not surprising then that some recent research is showing evidence on how new media have a direct neurocognitive impact, including probable long-term evolutionary results (Chan & Rabinowitz, 2006). New media are exploiting our physiological capacity of direct sensation and reaction through a-conscious interactions. New media constitute a technocultural niche, an enriched or enhanced environment, based on forms of direct knowledge—a knowledge not mediated by intellectual representations.

Every generation has raised concerns regarding the negative impact of media on social skills and personal relationships. The Internet and other new media types are reported to have important social and mental health effects on everyone, especially on adolescents, probably because they are heavy users and their brains and psychology are still very moldable.

Video-game playing, for example, enhances the capacity of visual attention and its spatial distribution. Video-game training enhances task-switching abilities as well as decreasing the attention blink. Thus, both the visual and amodal bottlenecks identified during temporal processing of visual information are reduced in video-game players. Clearly, these individuals have an increased ability to process information over time; however, whether this is due to faster target processing, such as faster selection and stabilization of information in memory, or to an increased ability to maintain several attention windows in parallel, cannot be determined from our current data.

By forcing players to simultaneously juggle a number of varied tasks (detect new enemies, track existing enemies, and avoid getting hurt, among others), action-video-game playing pushes the limits of three rather different aspects of visual attention. It leads to detectable effects on new tasks at untrained locations after only 10 days of training. Therefore, although video-game playing may seem to be rather mindless, it is capable of radically altering visual attention processing. There are several ways by which video-game training could lead to such enhancements. Changes in known attention bottlenecks is certainly a possibility; however, speeded perceptual processes and/or better management of several tasks at the central executive level are also likely to contribute. It will be for future studies of the effect of video-game practice to determine the relative contribution of these different factors to skill learning (Green & Bavelier, 2003)

For example, there has been reported a statistical association between television viewing and obesity, attention disorders, school performance, and violence (Mathiak & Weber, 2006). A significant relationship between Internet use and attention deficit/hyperactivity disorder (ADHD) has also been shown in elementary school children (Yoo et al., 2004). The relationship between video games and ADHD is unknown. The incidence of ADHD continues to rise and it is a significant challenge on medical, financial, and educational resources. ADHD is a complex disorder that often requires input from the affected child or adolescent, teachers, parents, and physicians in order to be diagnosed correctly and treated successfully. Adolescents who play more than 1 hour of console or Internet video games a day may have more or more intense symptoms of ADHD or inattention than those who do not (Straker, Pollock, Zubrick, & Kurinczuk, 2006).

New media and new reflexions are already part of the technocultural niche of our age: This is part of a new evolutionary step we can better understand considering studies on learning and enriched environments. At Harvard, David Hubel and Torsten Wiesel studied cats raised blind in one eye, and by 1962 they had demonstrated that such deprivation caused profound structural changes in the cats' visual cortex. Hubel and Wiesel's work made it clear that severe deprivation during critical developmental periods could have catastrophic effects on a growing brain, but the question of whether the opposite was true remained suspended for a while. By 1964, the Berkeley team led by Mark Rosenzweig completed a series of experiments that began to answer those questions. They found that rats raised in an enriched environment, with toys and nice social activities, were not only smarter than rats raised in impoverished environments, but that the improvement in performance correlated with an increase in the weight of the rats' cerebral cortex. The idea that the brain, like a muscle, might respond to cerebral exercise with physical growth was surprising to many, and gave strength to an increasingly powerful theory suggesting that all aspects of the mind—from memory, to dreams, to emotions—have physical correlates. The classical statement by William James (as cited in McDermott, 1967) has found an experimental validation: "Experience is remoulding us at every moment: Whilst we think, our brain changes." Studies on enriched environments are still growing, but they have already established evidence that the brain modifies its structure (not necessarily its size) depending on the kind of niche that Rosenzweig called environmental complexity and training. These studies are now extended to human learning environments (Carbonara, 2005; Orsucci & Sala, 2005).

CONCLUSION

This book is a multifaceted mirror on how human evolution has had a constant psychobiological link with the development of new tools and environmental changes. Discoveries and technological innovations in information and communication science and technology are paving the ground for new evolutionary steps.

Our new insights in neurocognition and the multiple reflexions implied in our sensory-perceptive processes are leading to new interfaces and new media. The isomorphism between biocognitive structures and the ICT niche we inhabit is progressively blurring boundaries between *res cogitans* and *res extensa*. Reflexing interfaces are extensions of human embodiment just as the bone tool tossed skyward by a savannah-dwelling ape. Time flows, always different yet similar. As Varela et al. (1991) stated aphoristically, "Readiness-for-action is a micro-identity and its corresponding level a micro-world: we embody streams of recurrent micro-world transitions."

We are the flow of micro and macro worlds, nested and intermingled. The stream of time flows here and there, generating multiple cascades, reflexing in billions of infinitesimal mirrors, and radiating in what we use to call consciousness.

REFERENCES

Aiello, L. C., & Wheeler, P. (1995). The expensive-tissue hypothesis. *Current Anthropology, 36*, 199-221.

Ambrose, S. H. (2001). Paleolithic technology and human evolution. *Science, 291*, 1748-1753.

Aoki, K., & Feldman, M. V. (1987). Toward a theory for the evolution of cultural. *Proceedings of the National Academy of Sciences, 84*, 7164-7168.

Arbib, M. A. (2002). The mirror system, imitation, and the evolution of language. In C. Nehaniv & K. Dautenhahn (Eds.), *Imitation in animals and artifacts*. The MIT Press.

Arbib, M. A. (2005). From monkey-like action recognition to human language: An evolutionary framework for neurolinguistics. *Behavioral and Brain Sciences, 28*, 105-167.

Bates, E., & MacWhinney, B. (1987). Competition, variation and language learning. In B. MacWhinney (Ed.), *Mechanisms of language acquisition* (pp. 157-193). Hillsdale, NJ: Erlbaum.

Bodmer, W. F., & Cavalli-Sforza, L. L. (1976). *Genetics, evolution and man*. San Francisco: Freeman.

Boyd, R., & Richerson, P. J. (1985). *Culture and the evolutionary process*. Chicago: University of Chicago Press.

Branigan, H. P., Pickering, M. J., & Cleland, A. A. (2000). Syntactic co-ordination in dialogue. *Cognition, 75*, B13-B25.

Carbonara, D. (Ed.). (2005). *Technology literacy applications in learning environments*. Hershey, PA: Idea Group.

Chan, P. A., & Rabinowitz, T. (2006). A cross-sectional analysis of video games and attention deficit hyperactivity disorder symptoms in adolescents. *Ann Gen Psychiatry, 5*, 16.

Chomsky, N. (1975). *Reflections on language*. New York: Pantheon.

Dale, R., & Spivey, M. J. (2006). Unravelling the dyad: Using recurrence analysis to explore patterns of syntactic coordination between children and caregivers in conversation. *Language Learning, 56*, 391-430.

Dawkins, R. (1982). *The extended phenotype*. San Francisco: Freeman.

Dennett, D. C. (1991). *Consciousness explained*. Boston: Little, Brown & Co.

Donald, M. (1997). Origins of the modern mind: Three stages in the evolution of culture and cognition. *Behavioral and Brain Sciences, 16*(4), 737-791.

Eckmann, J.-P., Kamphorst, S. O., & Ruelle, D. (1987). Recurrence plots of dynamical systems. *Europhysics Letters, 5*, 973-977.

Feldman, M. W., & Laland, K. N. (1996). Gene-culture coevolutionary theory. *Trends in Ecology and Evolution, 11*, 453-457.

Fonagy, P., & Target, M. (1997). Attachment and reflective function: Their role in self-organization. *Development and Psychopathology, 9*, 679-700.

Freeman, W. J. (1975). *Mass action in the nervous system*. New York: Academic Press.

Freud, S. (n.d.). Beyond the pleasure principle. In J. Strachey (Ed. & Trans.), *The standard edition of the complete psychological works of Sigmund Freud* (Vol. 18, pp. 1-64). London: Hogarth Press. (Original work published 1920)

Gaddini, E. (1969). On imitation. *International Journal of Psycho-Analysis, 50*, 475-484.

Gazzaniga, M. S. (2005). *The ethical brain*. New York: The Dana Press.

Gibson, J. J. (1979). *The ecological approach to visual perception*. NJ: Lawrence Erlbaum Associates.

Green, C. S., & Bavelier, D. (2003). Action video game modifies visual selective attention. *Nature, 423*, 534-537.

Griffiths, M. (2000). Does Internet and computer "addiction" exist? Some case study evidence. *CyberPsychology & Behavior, 3*(2), 211-218.

Husserl, E. (1980). *Collected works*. Boston: The Hague.

Kernberg, P. F. (2007). *Beyond the reflection: The role of the mirror paradigm in clinical practice.* New York: Other Press.

Kornhuber, H. H., & Deecke, L. (1965). Hirnpotentialänderungen bei willkürbewegungen und passiven bewegungen des menschen: Bereitschaftspotential und reafferente potentiale. *Pflügers Arch. Ges. Physiol., 284*, 1-17.

Lacan, J. (2005). The mirror stage. In *Ecrits.* W. W. Norton. (Original work published 1937)

Laland, K. N., Odling-Smee, J., & Feldman, M. W. (2000). Niche construction, biological evolution, and cultural change. *Behavioral and brain sciences, 23*, 131-175.

Lewontin, R. C. (1983). Gene, organism, and environment. In D. S. Bendall (Ed.), *Evolution from molecules to men.* Cambridge University Press.

Libet, B. (1993). *Neurophysiology of consciousness: Selected papers and new essays.* Boston: Birkhauser.

Libet, B., Freeman, A., & Sutherland, K. (1999). *The volitional brain, towards a neuroscience of free will.* Thorverton, United Kingdom: Imprint Academic.

Lieberman, P. (1991). *Uniquely human: The evolution of speech, thought, and selfless behavior.* Cambridge, MA: Harvard University Press.

Marwan, N. (2003). *Encounters with neighbours.* Unpublished doctoral dissertation, University of Potsdam.

Mathiak, K., & Weber, R. (2006). Toward brain correlates of natural behavior: fMRI during violent video games. *Human Brain Mapping, 27*(12), 948-956.

Maturana, H. (2002). Autopoiesis, structural coupling and cognition: A history of these and other notions in the biology of cognition. *Cybernetics & Human Knowing, 9*(3-4), 5-34.

Maturana, H. R., & Varela, F. J. (1980). *Autopoiesis and cognition: The realization of the living.* Dordrecht, the Netherlands: D. Reidel Publishing Co.

McDermott, J. J. (Ed.). (1967). *The writings of William James.* New York: Random House.

Norman, D. A. (1988). *The design of everyday things.* New York: Doubleday.

Norman, D. A. (1999). Affordances, conventions, and design. *Interactions, 6*(3), 38-41.

Orsucci, F. (Ed.). (1998). *The complex matters of the mind.* Singapore: World Scientific.

Orsucci, F. (2006). The paradigm of complexity in clinical neuro-cognitive science. *The Neuroscientist, 12*(4), 1-10.

Orsucci, F., Giuliani, A., Webber, C., Zbilut, J., Fonagy, P., & Mazza, M. (2006). Combinatorics & synchronization in natural semiotics. *Physica A: Statistical Mechanics and its Applications, 361*, 665-676.

Orsucci, F., Giuliani, A., & Zbilut, J. (2004). Structure & coupling of semiotic sets. *Experimental Chaos: AIP Proceedings, 742*, 83-93.

Orsucci, F., & Sala, N. (2005). Virtual reality, telemedicine and beyond. In D. Carbonara (Ed.), *Technology literacy applications in learning environments* (pp. 349-357). Hershey, PA: Idea Group.

Orsucci, F., Walters, K., Giuliani, A., Webber, C., Jr., & Zbilut, J. (1999). Orthographic structuring of human speech and texts. *International Journal of Chaos Theory and Applications, 4*(2), 80-88.

Ott, E., Grebogi, C., & Yorke, J. A. (1990). *Phys. Rev. Lett., 64*(11), 1196.

Pecora, L. M., & Carroll, T. L. (1990). *Phys. Rev. Lett., 64*, 821.

Petitot, J. (1999). *Naturalizing phenomenology: Issues in contemporary phenomenology and cognitive science.* Stanford, CA: Stanford University Press.

Richardson, D. C., & Dale, R. (2005). Looking to understand: The coupling between speakers' and listeners' eye movements and its relationship to discourse comprehension. *Cognitive Science, 29*, 39-54.

Rizzolatti, G., & Arbib, M. A. (1998). Language within our grasp. *Trends in Neuroscience, 21*, 188-194.

Shockley, K., Santana, M.-V., & Fowler, C. A. (2003). Mutual interpersonal postural constraints are involved in cooperative conversation. *Journal of Experimental Psychology: Human Perception and Performance, 29*, 326-332.

Siegel, D. J. (2007). *The mindful brain.* New York: Norton.

Stern, D. (1985). *The interpersonal world of the infant.* New York: Basic Books.

Straker, L. M., Pollock, C. M., Zubrick, S. R., & Kurinczuk, J. J. (2006). The association between information and communication technology exposure and physical activity, musculoskeletal and visual symptoms and socio-economic status in 5-year-olds. *Child Care Health Development, 32*(3), 343-351.

Thompson, W. I. (1996). *Coming into being: Artefacts and texts in the evolution of consciousness.* New York: St. Martin's Press.

Tomasello, M. (2003). *A usage-based theory of language.* Cambridge, MA: Harvard University Press.

van der Maas & van Geert (Eds.). (1999). *Non-linear analysis of developmental processes.* Amsterdam: Elsevier.

Varela, F. J., Thompson, E., & Rosch, E. (1991). *The embodied mind, cognitive science and human experience.* Cambridge, MA: MIT Press.

Webber, C. L., Jr., & Zbilut, J. P. (1994). Dynamical assessment of physiological systems and states using recurrence plot strategies. *Journal of Applied Physiology, 76*, 965-973.

Winnicott, D. W. (1987). *The child, the family, and the outside world.* Reading, MA: Addison-Wesley Publishing Co.

Yoo, H. J., Cho, S. C., Ha, J., Yune, S. K., Kim, S. J., Hwang, J., et al. (2004). Attention deficit hyperactivity symptoms and Internet addiction. *Psychiatry Clinical Neuroscience, 58*(5), 487-494.

Chapter II
Riddle of the Sphinx:
Paradox Revealed and Reveiled

Terry Marks-Tarlow
Institute for Fractal Research, Kassel, Germany & Private Practice, Santa Monica, California, USA

ABSTRACT

This chapter interprets the myth of Oedipus in light of interpersonal neurobiology and second-order cybernetics, where observers are self-referentially implicated within the observed. The riddle of the Sphinx, "What walks on four legs in the morning, two legs at noon, and three legs in the evening?" is understood as a paradox of self-reference in apparent contradiction with all known laws of science. From a developmental perspective, traumatic residues from King Laius' attempted infanticide uniquely prepare Oedipus to solve the Sphinx's riddle. Oedipus' capacity for full self-reference is equated with the operation of the most powerful universal Turing machine with both implicit and explicit memory of its past. That Oedipus could move beyond literal thought to interpret morning, noon, and evening as stages of human life proves pivotal. Oedipus' use of metaphor and abstraction to solve a paradox of self-reference signals humankind's transition to greater levels of internal complexity, including more fully self-reflective consciousness.

INTRODUCTION

Mythology the world over helps to organize cultural categories and mores by providing roles, rules, models, and narratives about life in the past in preparation for life in the future. Ancient and traditional peoples often treat myths literally as stories about real people and concrete events (e.g.,

Jaynes, 1976). Especially heralded by the work of Carl Jung (e.g., 1961), contemporary psychology brings a more symbolic, self-referential focus to the ways that myths can illuminate the inner world and culture of the mythmakers themselves.

If one myth rises above all others to signal entry into modern consciousness, it is that of Oedipus. This tale has been analyzed throughout the millennia by well-known thinkers such as Aristotle, Socrates, Nietzsche, Lévi-Strauss, Lacan, and Ricoeur. Some (e.g., Lévi-Strauss, 1977; Ricoeur, 1970) have understood the Oedipus myth as the individual quest for personal origins or identity; others (e.g., Aristotle, 1982, Nietzsche, 1871/1999) have used sociopolitical and cultural lenses to focus on the tale's prohibitions against the very taboos it illustrates. Prohibitions against infanticide, patricide, and incest help to establish the modern day state by erecting boundaries to protect society's youngest and most vulnerable members while serving as social glue to bind individuals into larger collective units. From an evolutionary vantage point, these prohibitions prevent inbreeding and maximize chances for survival and healthy propagation within the collective gene pool.

Perhaps the most noted analyst of the Oedipus myth is Sigmund Freud. At the inception of psychoanalysis, Freud's discovery of this myth fused his theory of psychosexual developmental with his topographical metaphor of the psyche. That this tragic hero killed his father and then married and seduced his mother staked out the psychological lay of the land, so to speak, which became immortalized as the Oedipus complex. Whereas Freud (1900/1966) viewed this myth quite literally in terms of unconscious impulses and fantasies toward real people, his successor Jung (1956) interpreted the Oedipus story symbolically as an intrapsychic reflection of healthy individuation.

This chapter revisits early origins of psychoanalysis that pivot around the Oedipus myth in order to introduce a second-order cybernetic point of view. Whereas cybernetics establishes the study of information, second-order cybernetics views information science self-referentially by implicating the observer within the observed (see Heims, 1991). From the vantage point of self-reference, the Oedipus story yields important clues about how the modern psyche became more complex through recursive loops in consciousness whereby implicit memory processes become explicit and lead to an increased capacity for self-reflection.

In the section to follow, I refresh the reader's memory by briefly recounting the Oedipus myth. Then I apply the approach of Lévi-Strauss to treat the myth structurally by introducing a new level of abstraction. I regard the Sphinx's riddle as a paradox of self-reference, arguing that both the riddle of the Sphinx and the life course of Oedipus bear structural similarities that signify the self-reflective search for origins. This interpretation establishes a foundation to regard the shift within the early history of psychoanalysis from a literal, Freudian interpretation to a more symbolic Jungian one. I demonstrate how this shift itself emerges in part self-referentially through the concrete enactment of the Oedipus myth within the real relationship between Freud as father and king, and Jung as prince and heir apparent.

Next, I follow Feder (1974/1988) to examine the clinical profile of Oedipus, whose restless, relentless search for his own origins plus infantile, primitive attempts to blot out what he ultimately sees are driven by psychobiological symptoms of separation and adoption trauma combined with the physical abuse of attempted murder by his biological father. Then I link Feder with contemporary research on the psychoneurobiology of implicit vs. explicit memory plus a cybernetic perspective that implicates the power of universal Turing machines to fully harness implicit and explicit memory. I conclude with claims that affective, imagistic, and cognitive skills necessary to advance from concrete to metaphorical thinking relate to implicit processes within Lakoff and Johnson's (1999) embodied philosophy and mature, abstract cognition within Jean Piaget's (e.g., Flavell, 1963) developmental psychology. Recursive loops in consciousness by which the observer can be detected within the observed signal enhanced internal complexity and the power of self-reflection to break intergenerational chains of abusers unwittingly begetting abusers.

Although I refer to Sigmund Freud amply throughout this chapter, my purpose is primarily historical and contextual. I do not intend to appeal to Freud as the ultimate authority so much as the originator of psychoanalysis and precursor to contemporary thought and practice. Especially since Jeffrey Masson (1984) documented Freud's projection of his own neuroses onto his historical and mythological analyses, including the invention of patients to justify his theories, Freud largely has been decentered, if not dethroned, within many contemporary psychoanalytic communities. Yet, just as contemporary neuropsychoanalysis reinstates some of Freud's early claims about the nature of the human unconscious (Solms, 2004; Solms & Turnbull, 2002), I hope that this cybernetic reading of Oedipus can reestablish the majesty of this myth to the human plight without sacrificing any gains and insights gleaned by psychoanalysts and other psychotherapists since Freud's time.

THE MYTH OF OEDIPUS

In the myth of Oedipus, which dates back to Greek antiquity, King Laius of Thebes was married to Queen Jocasta, but the marriage was barren. Desperate to conceive an heir, King Laius consulted the oracle of Apollo at Delphi, only to receive a shocking prophecy. The couple must remain childless, for any offspring of this union would grow up to murder his father and marry his mother. Out of fear of conceiving an heir, Laius ordered Jocasta confined within a small palace room and placed under strict prohibitions against sleeping with him.

But Jocasta was not to be stopped. She arrived at a plot to intoxicate and fornicate with her husband. The plot worked, and a son was born. Once again desperate to prevent fulfillment of the oracle, Laius ordered the boy's ankles be pinned together and proclaimed that he be left upon a mountain slope to die. However, the shepherd earmarked to carry out this order took pity on the boy, and took him instead to another shepherd who delivered him to King Polybus in the neighboring realm of Corinth. Likewise, suffering from a barren marriage, Polybus promptly adopted the boy as his own. Due to his pierced ankles, the child was called Oedipus. This name, which translates either to mean *swollen foot* or *know where*, is most telling given Oedipus' lifelong limp plus his relentless search to know where he came from.

As Oedipus matured, he overheard rumors that King Polybus was not his real father. Eager to investigate his true heritage, Oedipus followed in the footsteps of his biological father to visit the oracle at Delphi. The oracle grimly prophesized that Oedipus would murder his father and marry his mother. Horrified, Oedipus also attempted to avoid this fate. Still believing Polybus his real father, Oedipus decided not to return home, but instead took the road from Delphi toward Thebes rather than back to Corinth.

Unaware of the underlying truth, Oedipus met his biological father at the narrow crossroads of three paths that separated and connected the cities of Delphi, Corinth, and Thebes. King Laius ordered the boy out of the way to let royalty pass. Oedipus responded that he himself was a royal prince of superior status. Laius ordered his charioteer to advance so that he might strike Oedipus with his goad. Enraged, Oedipus grabbed the goad to strike and kill Laius plus four of his five retainers, leaving only one to tell the tale.

Upon Laius' death appeared the Sphinx, a lithe monster perched high on the mountain top. This creature possessed the body of a dog, the claws of a lion, the tail of a dragon, the wings of a bird, and the breasts and head of a woman. The Sphinx began to ravage Thebes, stopping all mountain travelers who attempted to enter the city, presenting them with a riddle: "What goes on four feet in the morning, two at midday, and three in the evening?"

Whereas the priestess of the oracle at Delphi revealed a glimpse of the future to her visitors, often concealed in the form of a riddle, the Sphinx, in contrast, killed anyone unable to answer her riddle correctly. The Sphinx either ate or hurled her victims to their death on the rocks below. Until the arrival of Oedipus, the riddle remained unsolved. With no visitors able to enter the city, trade in Thebes had become strangled while the treasury was depleted.

Confronted with the Sphinx's riddle, Oedipus responded correctly without hesitation, indicating that it is mankind who crawls on four legs in the morning, stands on two in midday, and leans on a cane as a third in the twilight of life. Horrified at being outwitted, the Sphinx suffered her own punishment by casting herself to death on rocks far below. Thebes was freed, and as reward for saving the city, Oedipus was offered its throne plus the hand of the widow Jocasta. Still unaware of his true origins, Oedipus accepted both honors. He ruled Thebes and married his mother, with whom he multiplied fruitfully. In this manner, Oedipus fulfilled the second part of the oracle.

But the city of Thebes was not finished suffering. Soon it became stricken with a horrible plague and famine that rendered all production barren. Eager to end the affliction, Oedipus once again consulted the oracle. He was told that in order to release Thebes from its current plight, the murderer of Laius must be found. Wanting only what was best for the city, Oedipus relentlessly pursued his quest for truth. He declared that whenever Laius' murderer was found, the offender would be banished forever from Thebes.

Oedipus called in the blind prophet Tiresias for help, but Tiresias refused to reveal what he knew. Intuiting the truth and dreading the horror of her sins exposed, Jocasta committed suicide by hanging herself. Soon Oedipus discovered that the one he sought was none other than himself. After learning that he had murdered his father and married his mother as predicted, Oedipus was unable to bear what he saw. He tore a brooch off Jocasta's hanging body to blind himself. Oedipus then faced consequences he himself had determined

for Laius' murderer and was subsequently led into exile by his sister-daughter Antigone.

Here ended the first of Sophocles' tragedies, *King Oedipus*. The second and third of this ancient Greek trilogy, *Antigone* and *Oedipus at Colonus*, detail Oedipus' and his sister-daughter's extensive wanderings. Tragic insight into unwittingly having committed these crimes of passion brought Oedipus to wisdom. Eventually he reached a mysterious end in Colonus, near Athens, amidst the utmost respect from his countrymen. Despite his sins, Oedipus' life ended with the blessings of the gods. To complete one more self-referential loop, his personal insight informed the very land itself, and Colonus became an oracular center and source of wisdom for others.

NEW TWISTS TO AN OLD MYTH

To Freud, the tale of Oedipus was initially conceived in terms of real sexual and aggressive impulses toward real parents until his seduction theory later was revised and downplayed to the level of fantasy and imaginary impulses. Within Freud's three-part, structural model of the psyche, the id was the container for unbridled, unconscious, sexual and aggressive impulses; the superego was a repository for social and societal norms, and the ego was assigned the difficult task of straddling these two warring, inner factions while mediating the demands and restrictions of outside reality.

According to Freud, symptoms formed out of the tension between conscious and unconscious factors, including conflicting needs both to repress and express. Among many different kinds of anxiety Freud highlighted, an important symptom was castration anxiety. Castration anxiety consisted of the fear that one's incestuous desire for one's mother would be discovered by the father, and punished by the father by cutting off his penis. Both desire for the mother and fear of castration were sources of murderous impulses toward the father. Working through these feelings and symptoms in psychoanalysis involved lifting the repression barrier and gaining insight into the unconscious origins of the conflict.

Note that Freud's developmental model of the psyche was primarily intrapsychic. Because he emphasized the Oedipus complex as a universal struggle within the internal landscape of all (the adaptation for girls became known as the Electra complex in honor of another famous Greek tragedy), it mattered little how good or bad a child's parenting was. Most contemporary psychoanalytic theories, such as object relations (e.g., Klein, 1932), self-psychology (e.g., Kohut, 1971), or intersubjectivity theory (e.g., Stolorow, Brandchaft, & Atwood, 1987), have abandoned the importance of the Oedipus myth partly by adopting a more interpersonal focus. Within each of these newer therapies, psychopathology is believed to develop out of real emotional exchanges (or their absence) between infants and their caregivers. Symptoms are maintained and altered within the relational context of the analyst-patient dyad.

Prior to these relational theories, near the origins of psychoanalysis, the myth of Oedipus took on an ironic, self-referential twist by becoming embodied in real life. Carl Jung, a brilliant follower of Freud, had been earmarked as the "royal son" and "crown prince" slated to inherit Freud's psychoanalytic empire (see Jung, 1961; Kerr, 1995; Monte & Sollod, 2003). The early intimacy and intellectual passion between these two men gave way to great bitterness and struggle surrounding Jung's creative and spiritual ideas. In his autobiography, Jung (1961, p. 150) describes Freud as imploring, "My dear Jung, promise me never to abandon the sexual theory. This is the most essential thing of all. You see, we must make a dogma of it, an unshakable bulwark...against the black tide of mud...of occultism."

For Jung, Freud's topography of the psyche maps only the most superficial level of the personal unconscious, which contains personal memories and impulses toward specific people. Partly on the basis of a dream, Jung excavated another even deeper stratum he called the "collective unconscious." This level has a transpersonal flavor by containing archetypal patterns common in peoples of all cultures and ages.

By acting as if there was room only for what Jung called the personal unconscious within the psyche's subterranean zone, Freud appeared compelled to reenact the Oedipus struggle in real life. He responded to Jung as if to a son attempting to murder his symbolic father. This dynamic was complicated by yet another even more concrete level of enactment: Both men reputedly were competing for the loyalties of the same woman, initially Jung's patient and lover, and later Freud's confidant, Sabina Speilrein (see Kerr, 1995).

Freud and Jung acted out the classic Oedipal myth at multiple levels, with Jung displacing Freud both professionally (vanquishing the king) and sexually (stealing the queen). An explosion ensued when the conflict could no longer be contained or resolved. As a result, the relationship between Freud and Jung became permanently severed. Jung suffered what some believe was a psychotic break (Hayman, 1999) and others termed a creative illness (Ellenberger, 1981), and then recovered to the symbolic wealth of his own unconscious.

Jung overcame his symbolic father partly by rejecting the Oedipus myth in favor of Faust's tale: "Jung meant to make a descent into the depths of the soul, there to find the roots of man's being in the symbols of the libido which had been handed down from ancient times, and so to find redemption despite his own genial psychoanalytic pact with the devil" (Kerr, 1995, p. 326). After his break with Freud, Jung self-referentially embodied his own theories about individuation, which took the form of the hero's journey. Whereas Jung underscored the sun hero's motif and role of mythical symbols, mythologist Joseph Campbell (1949/1973) differentiated three phases of the hero's journey: separation (from ordinary consciousness), initiation (into the night journey of the soul), and return (integration back into consciousness and community). This description certainly fits Jung's departure from ordinary sanity, his nightmarish descent into haunting symbols if not hallucinations, and his professional return to create depth psychology.

Jung and his followers have regarded the Oedipus myth less literally than Freud. In hero mythology, as explicated by one of Jung's most celebrated followers, Eric Neumann (1954/1993), to murder the father generally and the king in particular was seen as symbolic separation from an external source of authority in order to discover and be initiated into one's own internal source of guidance and wisdom.

Whereas Freud viewed the unconscious primarily in terms of its negative, conflict-ridden potential, Jung recognized the underlying universal and positive potential of the fertile feminine. However, in order to uncover this positive side, one first had to differentiate and confront the destructive shadow of the feminine. At the archetypal level, some aspects of the feminine can feel life threatening. To defeat the Sphinx was seen as conquering the terrible mother. In her worst incarnation, the terrible mother reflected the potential for deprivation and destructive narcissism within the real mother. In some cultures, for example, as portrayed in the Germanic fairytale of Hansel and Gretel, the terrible mother appeared as the Vagina Dentate, or toothed vagina, a cannibalistic allusion not to the Freudian fear of castration by the father, but rather to the Jungian anxiety about emasculation by the mother.

Symbolically, once the dark side of the terrible mother was vanquished, her positive potential could be harvested. To have incest and fertilize the mother represented overcoming fear of the feminine, of her dark chaotic womb, in order to tap into riches of the unconscious and bring new life to the psyche. Psychologically we can see how the Sphinx and incest fit together for Neumann (1954/1993): The hero killed the mother's terrible female side so as to liberate her fruitful and

bountiful aspect. For Jung, to truly individuate was to rule the kingdom of one's own psyche by overthrowing the father's masculine influence of power, the ultimate authority of consciousness, while fertilizing and pillaging the mother's feminine territory, that of the unconscious. By breaking with Freud and finding his way through his psychosis, Jung killed the king and overcame the terrible mother to harvest her symbolism for his own creative development, both in theory and in self.

Judging from the drama of real life, Freud and Jung each arrived at their ideas partly self-referentially by experientially living them out. Along with affirming Ellenberger's (1981) notion of "creative illness," this coincides with Atwood and Stolorow's (1979/1993) thesis that all significant psychological theory derives from the personal experience and worldview of its originators.

RIDDLE AS PARADOX

In the last several decades, the Freudian interpretation of the Oedipus story has largely been laid aside. With the early advent of feminism, the significance of the tale to a woman's psyche was challenged. With the recognition that sexual abuse was often real and not just fantasy, later feminist thought challenged Freud's early abandonment of his seduction theory. As knowledge about the psychophysiology of the posttraumatic stress condition increases (e.g., Rothschild, 2000; Schore, 2007), so has clinical interest in vertical, dissociative splits within the psyche vs. the horizontal splits that maintain Freud's repression barrier (see Kohut, 1977). Greater relational emphasis among contemporary psychoanalysts shifts interest toward early mother-infant attachment dynamics, as well as here-and-now intersubjective relations between psychotherapist and patient. Finally, the current climate of multiculturalism disfavors any single theory, especially one universalizing development.

In the spirit of Lévi-Strauss, I propose a different way of looking at the Oedipus myth. I aim to harvest meaning primarily by sidestepping narrative content to derive an alternative interpretation that is both structural and cybernetic in nature. When understood literally, both the improbable form the Sphinx embodies plus her impossible-seeming riddle present paradoxes that appear to contradict all known laws of science. Surely no creature on earth can literally walk on four, two, and then three limbs during the very same day. With the possible exception of the slime mold, no animal changes its form of locomotion this radically, and not even the slime mold undergoes such complete metamorphosis in the course of a single day.

The Sphinx's riddle presents the type of ordinary paradox that science faces all the time. Here, a paradox is loosely conceptualized as a set of facts that contradicts current scientific theory. Just as Darwin's embodied evolution proceeds in fits and starts (e.g., Gould & Eldredge, 1977), so too does the abstract progression of scientific theory. Kuhn (1962) described the erratic evolution of scientific theory, when the resolution of ordinary contradiction leads to abrupt paradigm shifts that offer wider, more inclusive contexts in which to incorporate previously discrepant facts.

However, the Sphinx's riddle went beyond this type of ordinary scientific paradox to present itself more formally as a paradox of self-reference. Its solution, humanity, required deep understanding of the nature of being human, including knowledge of self. In order to know what crawls on four legs in the morning, walks on two in midday, and hobbles on three in the evening, Oedipus had to understand the entire human life cycle. He needed to possess intimate familiarity with physical changes in his own body, ranging from the dependency of infancy, through the glory of maturity, to the waning powers of old age.

To approach the riddle without self-reference was to look outward, use a literal understanding, and miss the potential for a metaphorical interpretation. To approach the riddle with self-reference was to seek knowledge inward through introspection. Oedipus was uniquely positioned to apply the riddle to himself: Almost killed at birth and still physically handicapped, he harbored virtual, vestigial memories of death in life. His limp and cane were whispers of a helpless past and harbingers of a shattered future.

Self-referentially, Oedipus' own life trajectory showed the same three parts as the Sphinx's riddle. Through the kindness of others Oedipus survived the traumatized helplessness of infancy. In his prime, he proved more than able to stand on his own two feet: strong enough to kill a king, clever enough to slay the proverbial monster, and potent enough to marry a queen and spawn a covey of offspring. Ironically, in the case of our tragic hero, it was Oedipus' very insight into his own origins that led to the loss of his kingdom and wife-mother, leaving him to hobble around blindly in old age, leaning on his cane, and dependent upon the goodness of others, primarily his daughter-sister Antigone.

The namesake and body memories of Oedipus connected him with chance and destiny, past and future, infancy and old age. Recall that the name Oedipus means both *swollen foot* and *know where*. Feder (1974/1988) analyzed the Oedipus myth in terms of the clinical reality of adoption trauma. Like many adopted children, Oedipus was relentlessly driven to seek his own origins in order to know where he came from both genetically and socially.

Taking this approach a step further, we can see the impact of early physical abuse—attempted infanticide—on the neurobiology of different memory systems. Oedipus knows where he came from implicitly in his body due to his swollen foot, even while ignorant of the traumatic origins explicitly in his mind. This kind of implicit memory has gained much attention in recent clinical lore (e.g., Rothschild, 2000; Siegel, 2001). In early infant development, implicit memory is the first kind to develop. It helps tune ongoing perception and emotional self-regulation in the nonverbal context of relationships with others. In this way, contingent vs. noncontingent responses of caretakers become hardwired into the brain and body via particular neural pathways. While alluded to by others, for example, Ornstein (1973), Allan Schore (2001) specifically proposes that implicit memory exists within the right, nonverbal hemisphere of the human cerebral cortex to constitute the biological substrate for Freud's unconscious instincts and memories. Although hotly contested, neurobiological evidence mounts for Freud's repression barrier as hardwired into the brain (e.g., Solms, 2004).

Schore (2001) proposed a vertical model of the psyche, where the conscious, verbal mind is localized in the left hemisphere of the brain, while the unconscious and body memory is mediated by the nonverbal right hemisphere (for most right-handed people). The hemispheres of the brain and these different modes of processing are conjoined as well as separated by the corpus callosum. Early trauma plus his secret origins caused a haunting and widening of the gap between what Oedipus' body knew vs. what his mind knew. Oedipus' implicit memory of his early abandonment and abuse became the invisible thread that provided deep continuity despite abrupt life changes. His implicit memory offered a clue to the commonality beneath the apparent disparity in the Sphinx's three-part riddle.

Structurally, to solve the riddle became equivalent to Oedipus' self-referential quest for explicit memory of his own origins. This interpretation meshes with anthropologist Lévi-Strauss' (1977) emphasis on structural similarities within and between myths, plus the near universal concern with human origins. It also dovetails with Bion's (1983, p. 46) self-referential understanding of the Sphinx's riddle as "man's curiosity turned upon himself." In the form of self-conscious examination of the personality by the personality, Bion uses the Oedipus myth to illuminate ancient origins of psychoanalytic investigation.

METAPHORICAL THINKING AND COGNITIVE DEVELOPMENT

In order to solve both the riddle of the Sphinx as well as that of his own origins, Oedipus had to delve beneath the concrete level of surface appearances. Here he would have lived happily, but in ignorance, as children and innocents are reputed to do. Ignorance may be bliss, but it does not necessarily lead to maturity. Prior to Oedipus solving the riddle, humankind lived in an immature state, an idea supported by the work of Julian Jaynes (1976). Writing about the "bicameral mind," Jaynes speculated that ancient humanity hallucinated gods as living in their midst. Here myths were concretely embodied, serving as external sources of authority before such executive functions became internalized within the cerebral cortex of the modern psyche, including our increased capacities for self-reflection, inner guidance, and self-control.

The Sphinx's riddle was a self-referential mirror reflecting and later enabling explicit memory and knowledge of Oedipus' traumatic origins. Upon successfully answering the riddle, Oedipus bridged the earlier developmental territory of the right mind with the evolutionarily and developmentally later left brain (Schore, 2001). In the process, Oedipus healed and matured on many levels. Not only did he address his castration fears by conquering the terrible mother in the form of the Sphinx after killing the terrible father, but also and perhaps more significantly, Oedipus made the leap from concrete to metaphorical thinking. By understanding morning, midday, and evening as stages of life, he demonstrated creativity and mental flexibility characteristic of internal complexity. Cognitive psychologists Lakoff and Johnson (1980) have suggested that metaphor serves as the basis for all abstract thinking. More recently, Lakoff and Johnson (1999) argued that metaphor forms part of the implicit memory of the cognitive unconscious, where its immediate conceptual mapping is hardwired into the brain.

The leap from concrete to metaphorical thinking not only was an important developmental step in the history of consciousness, but it also can be understood within the historical trajectory of the individual. Here Jean Piaget's developmental epistemology (e.g., Flavell, 1963) becomes relevant. Though details are still disputed, overall, Piaget's theory has remained one of the most important and universal accounts of intellectual development to date (Sternberg, 1990). Using careful observation and empirical studies, Piaget mapped the shift from a sensorimotor period of infancy, through the preconcrete and concrete operations of early childhood, into a formal operations stage of later childhood characterizing the adult, mature mind. Piaget's hallmark of maturity involved freedom from the particulars of concrete situations, granting cognitive flexibility necessary for both abstract and metaphorical thinking.

SELF-REFERENCE AND UNIVERSAL TURING MACHINES

So far, I have suggested that self-reference is central to a metaphorical solution of the Sphinx's riddle. However, self-reference also proves to be an essential part of cybernetics, the sciences of information. A computational model views the human psyche as a recursive system, where present behavior depends upon how it has processed its past behavior. Within abstract machines, different computational powers depend deterministically upon a system's retrospective access to memory.

In computational science, power is ranked according to Chomsky's hierarchy. At the bottom of the hierarchy lies the finite-state automaton. This machine possesses only implicit memory for its current state. In the middle lies the pushdown automaton. This machine possesses explicit memory, but with only temporary access to the past. At the top of Chomsky's hierarchy lies the universal Turing machine. This abstract machine possesses unrestricted, permanent, and explicit memory for all past states.

Cyberneticist Ron Eglash (1999) provides a text analogy to contrast these differences: The least powerful machine is like a person who accomplishes all tasks instinctively, without the use of any books; in the middle is a person limited by books removed once they have been read; at the top is a person who collects and recollects all books read, in any order. The power of the universal Turing machine at the top is its capacity to recognize all computable functions.

The point at which complete memory of past actions is achieved marks a critical shift in computational power. It is the point when full self-reference is achieved, which brings about the second-order cybernetic capacity of a system to analyze its own programs. My reading of the Oedipus myth illustrates this very same point in time—that powerful instant when full access to memory dovetails with self-reference to signal another step in the "complexification" of human consciousness.

THE RIDDLE AS MIRROR

Just as the Sphinx presented a paradigm of self-reference to hold a mirror up to Oedipus, the myth of Oedipus also holds up a mirror to us as witnesses. The story of Oedipus reflects our own stories in yet another self-referential loop. Like Oedipus, each one of us is a riddle to him- or herself. The story rocks generation after generation so powerfully partly because of this self-referential quality, which forces each one of us to reflect upon our own lives mythically.

Throughout the tale, there is dynamic tension between knowing and not knowing, in Oedipus and in us. Oedipus starts out naïvely not knowing who he is or where he came from. We start out knowing who Oedipus really is, but blissfully unaware of the truth in ourselves. By the end of the tale, the situation reverses: Oedipus solves all three riddles, that of the oracle of Delphi, that of the Sphinx, and that of his origins, while ironically, we participants and observers are left not knowing. We harbor a gnawing feeling of uncertainty, almost as if another riddle has invisibly materialized—as if we face the very Sphinx herself, whose enigma must be answered upon threat of our own psychological death.

Eglash (1999) notes that the power of the universal Turing machine lies in its ability to not know how many transformations or applications of an algorithm a system would need ahead of time, before the program can be terminated. Paradoxically, to achieve full uncertainty about the future and its relationship to the past is symptomatic of increasing computational power. This kind of fundamental uncertainty is evident collectively within the modern sciences and mathematics of chaos theory, stochastic analyses, and various forms of indeterminacy. For example, Heisenberg's uncertainty principle states the impossibility of precisely determining both a quantum particle's speed as well as its location at the same time. Meanwhile, chaos theory warns of the impossibility of precisely predicting the long-term future of highly complex systems, no matter how precise our formulas or capacity to model their past behavior.

Experientially, we must deal with fundamental uncertainty with respect to the riddle of our own lives, a task that leaves us ultimately responsible to glean meaning from this self-reflective search. The Oedipus myth presents a self-referential mirror through which each one of us individually enters the modern stage of self-reflective consciousness. Capabilities for full memory, to consider the past and future, to contemplate death, to confront paradox, to self-reflect, and to consider self-reference all represent critical levels of inner complexity that separate human from animal intelligence, the infant from the mature individual, plus the weakest from the most powerful computing machines.

CONCLUSION

Every myth remains alive in the collective psyche so long as people continue to milk meaning from its narrative. With this purpose in mind, I revisit the myth of Oedipus through lenses of contemporary neuroscience and computational studies. Whereas Freud found a story about psychosexual development and Jung told a tale about individuation, this chapter highlights the centrality of paradoxes of self-reference for affective, cognitive, and behavioral integration. However, here is the irony: To see deeply into our own origins is as impossible as to know our own DNA through self-reflection or to glimpse the back of our eyeballs through their rotation. Yet the very act of facing an impossible quest is what develops inner complexity. Within the human psyche, full self-reference serves as a springboard, if not a prerequisite, to a fully self-actualized human being. To possess thorough access to memory of the past plus the cognitive flexibility to not have to know the future represents integration—between left and right brain hemispheres, between body and mind, and between implicit, procedural memory vs. explicit memory for events and facts. The negotiation and continual renegotiation of this integration maximizes our potential to be spontaneous, original, and creative, all hallmarks of successful maturation and individuation.

In conclusion, I argue that a complex state of "good-enough" self-reflective awareness is central to conscious self-fulfillment and is necessary to break the tragic intergenerational chain of fate and trauma symbolized by Greek tragedy in general and the Oedipus myth in particular. Echoed by a Greek chorus, the observation that those born into abuse unwittingly grow up to become abusers lies at the heart of the Oedipus myth. Laius' unsuccessful attempt to kill his son all but sealed Oedipus' fate to escalate this loop of violence by successfully killing his father. From a neurobiological standpoint, abusers beget abusers by means of posttraumatic residues of the original abuse when emotional unregulation plus amygdala-driven fight, flight, and freeze reactions are carried by implicit processes that are disconnected from higher cortical levels and controls. The only way out of this fatalistic tragedy is enough conscious insight to unearth violent instincts before the deed is done, followed by the exertion of sufficient self-control to resist and transcend such instincts. The telltale sign of these capacities is the ability to tell a cohesive, self-referential narrative. Multigenerational, prospective research within the field of attachment (e.g., Siegel, 1999) suggests that the best predictor of trauma prevention plus secure attachment in children is their parents' success relaying a cohesive narrative about their own early childhoods. It matters little whether the quality of this narrative is idyllic or horrific. What counts is that parents possess enough self-reflective insight to maintain memories concerning their origins that can be cohesively woven into the fabric of current life without affective disruption during recall. I believe this kind of self-referential reflection carries the full computational power of a universal Turing machine, the only platform strong enough to break intergenerational chains of emotional and physical abuse. Only by having full access to the past can we be freed from the necessity of its repetition.

REFERENCES

Aristotle. (1982). *Poetics* (Vol. 23, Loeb Classical Library). Cambridge, MA: Harvard University Press.

Atwood, G., & Stolorow, R. (1993). *Faces in a cloud: Intersubjectivity in personality theory.* Northvale, NJ: Jason Aronson. (Original work published 1979)

Bion, W. (1983). *Elements of psycho-analysis.* Northvale, NJ: Jason Aronson.

Campbell, J. (1973). *The hero with a thousand faces.* Princeton, NJ: Bollingen Series, Princeton University. (Original work published 1949)

Eglash, R. (1999). *African fractals: Modern computing and indigenous design.* NJ: Rutgers University Press.

Ellenberger, H. (1981). *The discovery of the unconscious.* New York: Basic Books.

Feder, L. (1988). Adoption trauma: Oedipus myth/clinical reality. In G. Pollock & J. Ross (Eds.), *The Oedipus papers.* Madison, CT: International Universities Press. (Original work published 1974)

Flavell, J. H. (1963). *The developmental psychology of Jean Piaget.* New York: Van Nostrand.

Freud, S. (1966). *The interpretation of dreams* (J. Strachey, Trans.). New York: Basic Books. (Original work published 1900)

Gould, S. J., & Eldredge, N. (1977). Punctuated equilibria: The tempo and mode of evolution reconsidered. *Paleobiology, 3*, 115-151.

Hayman, D. (1999). *The life of Jung.* New York: W. W. Norton.

Heims, S. (1991). *The cybernetics group.* Cambridge, MA: The MIT Press.

Jaynes, J. (1976). *The origin of consciousness in the breakdown of the bicameral mind.* Boston: Houghton Mifflin.

Jung, C. (1956). Symbols of transformation. In *Collected works.* London: Routledge & Kegan Paul.

Jung, C. (1961). *Memories, dreams, reflections.* New York: Random House.

Kerr, J. (1995). *A most dangerous method.* New York: Vintage Books/Random House.

Klein, M. (1932). *The psycho-analysis of children.* London: Hogarth.

Kohut, H. (1971). *The analysis of the self.* New York: International Universities Press.

Kohut, H. (1977). *The restoration of the self.* New York: International Universities Press.

Kuhn, T. (1962). *The structure of scientific revolutions.* Chicago: University of Chicago Press.

Lakoff, G., & Johnson, M. (1980). *Metaphors we live by.* Chicago: University of Chicago Press.

Lakoff, G., & Johnson, M. (1999). *Philosophy in the flesh: The embodied mind and its challenge to Western thought.* New York: Basic Books.

Lévi-Strauss, C. (1977). *Structural anthropology 1* (C. Jacobson & B. G. Schoepf, Trans.). Harmondsworth, United Kingdom: Penguin.

Masson, J. (1984). *The assault on truth: Freud's suppression of the seduction theory.* Horizon Book Promotions.

Monte, C., & Sollod, R. (2003). *Beneath the mask: An introduction to theories of personality.* New York: John Wiley & Sons.

Neumann, E. (1993). *The origins and history of consciousness.* Princeton, NJ: Princeton. (Original work published 1954)

Nietzsche, F. (1999). *The birth of tragedy and other writings* (Cambridge texts in the history of philosophy). Cambridge, United Kingdom: Cambridge University Press. (Original work published 1871)

Ornstein, R. (Ed.). (1973). *The nature of human consciousness.* San Francisco: W. H. Freeman.

Pollock, G., & Ross, J. (1988). *The Oedipus papers.* Madison, CT: International Universities Press.

Ricoeur, P. (1970). *Freud and philosophy.* Cambridge, MA: Yale University Press.

Rothschild, B. (2000). *The body remembers: The psychophysiology of trauma and trauma treatment.* New York: W. W. Norton.

Schore, A. (2001). Minds in the making: Attachment, the self-organizing brain, and developmentally-oriented psychoanalytic psychotherapy. *British Journal of Psychotherapy, 17*(3), 299-328.

Schore, A. (2007). Dissociation chapter Schore on implicit memory

Siegel, D. (2001). Memory: An overview, with emphasis on developmental, interpersonal, and neurobiological aspects. *Journal of the Academy of Child & Adolescent Psychiatry, 40*(9), 997-1011.

Solms, M. (2004). Freud returns. *Scientific American*, pp. 83-89.

Solms, M., & Turnbull, O. (2002). *The brain and the inner world: An introduction to the neuroscience of subjective experience.* New York: Other Press/Karnac Books.

Sternberg, R. (1990). *Metaphors of mind: Conceptions of the nature of intelligence.* New York: Cambridge University Press.

Stolorow, R., Brandchaft, B., & Atwood, G. (1987). *Psychoanalytic treatment: An intersubjective approach.* Hillsdale, NJ: The Analytic Press.

Chapter III
Theory of Cooperative Coevolution of Genes and Memes[1]

Vladimir Kvasnicka
Slovak University of Technology in Bratislava, Slovakia

Jiri Pospichal
Slovak University of Technology in Bratislava, Slovakia

ABSTRACT

This chapter proposes a simple replicator theory of the coevolution of genes and memes. The presented coevolutionary theory assumes that units of information acquired from parents by imitation (memes) are not independent of genes, but are obligatorily bounded with genes as composites, which are subjects of Darwinian evolution. A population composed of couples of genes and memes, the so-called m-genes, is postulated as a subject of Darwinian evolution. Three different types of operations over m-genes are introduced: replication (an m-gene is replicated with mutations onto an offspring m-gene), interaction (a memetic transfer from a donor to an acceptor), and extinction (an m-gene is eliminated). Computer simulations of the present model allow us to identify different mechanisms of gene and meme coevolutions.

INTRODUCTION

Memes belong to very controversial concepts of theory of human culture (Aunger, 2001; Blackmore, 1999; Dawkins, 1976; Dennett, 1995).

This meme concept was initially introduced by evolutionary biologist Richard Dawkins in his seminal book *The Selfish Gene* (1976) as an information unit copied from a human brain to another human brain by an imitation. Moreover, he postulated that memes have properties of replicators and therefore their population may be a subject of evolution (see also Blackmore; Dennett). Memetics (a science about memes) offers conceptually simple explanations about the nature and evolution of human culture: A paradigm of memes as replicators looks very attractive for an audience mostly outside social sciences. On the other hand, memetics is strongly rejected by many social scientists as a theoretical approach based on dubious postulates and superficial analogies. Hot disputes continue in the following three directions: (a) whether culture is properly seen as composed of independently transmitted information units, (b) whether memes have the necessary qualification to serve as replicators, and (c) whether evolutionary approaches such as memetics offer the most natural framework for a theory of culture. Recently, Aunger's *Darwinizing Culture* (2001) was the first book to attempt a thorough critical and conservative appraisal of the potential of memetics. This text summarizes the points of agreement and/or disagreement on memetics and concludes with some suggestions for the progressive directions, particularly with respect to the means by which empirical research in this area may be undertaken. Many biologists or social scientists (Aunger; Laland, Odling-Smee, & Feldman, 1999) doubt whether memes may directly affect the fitness of genes. They suggest overcoming this serious problem of memetics such that an environmental niche is introduced; it is postulated that memes may affect only this niche and gene fitness is specified by its structure plus an interaction between gene and environmental niche.

The purpose of this communication is to suggest a replicator model (Eigen, 1971; Eigen & Schuster, 1977; Kvasnicka & Pospichal, 2003) of the coevolution of genes and memes (Boyd & Richerson, 1985; Cavalli-Sforza & Feldman, 1981; Durham, 1991; Feldman & Laland, 1996; Laland et al.; Kvasnicka, & Pospichal, 1999b), where it is postulated that a memetic environment may

change the selection of genes; in other words, gene fitness is affected by memes. In our approach, memes are not independent from genes. They form couples composed of a gene and a meme (these couples are called m-genes). A subject of Darwinian evolution is a population composed of these couples instead of two relatively independent populations, one composed of genes and one composed of memes. In the proposed coevolutionary approach, the fitness of m-genes is composed of two parts: the fitness of the respective gene itself and the interaction fitness between the respective gene and the respective meme. This second term reflects an influence of memes onto genes and may be characterized as a (direct or indirect) cultural influence onto genes through a (cultural) modification of the environment (niche) in which genes exist. The memes coevolve simultaneously with genes; a Darwinian selection exists only for gene-meme composites. Three different types of m-gene transformations are postulated.

1. **Replication:** A randomly selected m-gene is copied with mutations onto another m-gene. There exist two possibilities as to how to create a meme of emerging offspring: The first one is a simple copy with the mutations of the parental meme, whereas the second possibility consists of a local optimization of the new meme in the nearest neighborhood of the parental meme. This second possibility may be interpreted as a kind of social learning, where an offspring adapts the parental meme to a form more appropriate for its gene. The replication causes the so-called vertical transfer of memes from parents onto offspring.

2. **Interaction:** Two randomly selected m-genes (that are classified as a donor and an acceptor) are transformed in such that a way that an acceptor meme is substituted with a modified donor meme. In a similar way as replication, the creation of a new donor meme may be done through two possibilities.

The first one consists of a simple mutation of the donor meme, whereas the second one consists of a local optimization of the donor meme. In other words, the approach to create a donor meme may be considered genuine social learning, where the acceptor adapts the donor meme to an optimal form with respect to its gene. The interaction process performs the so-called horizontal transfer of memes from a donor to an acceptor. Since at another time the role of donor and acceptor may be swapped, the whole process results in knowledge exchange.

3. **Extinction:** A randomly selected m-gene is eliminated from the population. This simple process is immediately applied when a replication process is used, which increases the number of m-genes in the population by one. It means that the extinction process ensures a constant number of m-genes in the population.

We have specified two types of social learning processes that may appear when either vertical or horizontal meme transfers are applied; both learning processes are connected with a local optimization of memes (for a fixed respective gene). There exists also another quite different possibility consisting of a local optimization of the gene with respect to a fixed respective meme (when genes code the architecture of cognitive organs, e.g., brains). This interesting alternative approach to the learning of gene parts of m-genes is applicable for the calculation of fitness, in particular when the gene part of fitness is locally optimized. We get the so-called effective fitness that reflects an evolvability of m-genes on the fitness landscape (this approach to calculation of fitness is often called in literature the Baldwin effect; Baldwin, 1896; Belew & Mitchel, 1996; Kvasnicka, & Pospichal, 1999b).

The fitness of m-genes is evaluated by making use a generalized version of Kauffman *KN* functions (Altenberg, 1998; Kauffman, 1993), which recently became very popular for constructions of realistic rugged fitness landscapes. The same type of fitness landscape was recently used by Bull, Holland, and Blackmore (2000) in their simulation of the coevolution of genes and memes. They studied coevolution, where two independent populations are considered, one for genes and another for memes. The present approach to coevolution of genes and memes is quite different from Bull et al.'s approach. We will study only one population composed of couples, each made of a gene and a meme (m-genes), and this population is a subject of Darwinian evolution.

Figure 1. A population P is comprised of m-genes that are represented by compositions (determined by a cross product) of genes and memes. Darwinian evolution runs over the population P and not separately over genes and memes. This approach is a manifestation of our postulation that memes may exist only in coexistence with genes.

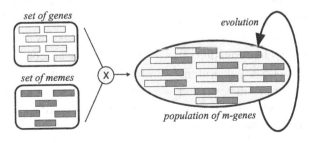

35

A COOPERATIVE COEVOLUTION OF GENES AND MEMES

Let us consider two different sets that are composed of all possible genes and memes, $\mathcal{G} = \{g, g', ...\}$ and $\mathcal{M} = \{m, m', ...\}$, respectively. A composition, called the m-gene, is defined by $(g, m) \in \mathcal{G} \times \mathcal{M}$, and a population is a finite multiset composed of A m-genes (see Figure 1).

$$\mathcal{P} = \{(g_1, m_1), (g_2, m_2), ..., (g_A, m_A)\} \qquad (1)$$

Each m-gene (g, m) is evaluated by a *fitness function f*:

$$f[(g, m)] = (1 - \omega)F(g) + \omega H(g, m) \qquad (2)$$

where the function F evaluates a gene g by a nonnegative real number from the closed interval [0,1], specifying an evolutionary quality of a gene g, $F: \mathcal{G} \rightarrow [0,1]$, and the function H evaluates an m-gene by a real number from [0,1] that corresponds to a cultural interaction between a gene g and a meme m, $H: \mathcal{G} \times \mathcal{M} \rightarrow [0,1]$. The parameter $0 \leq \omega \leq 1$ is a measure of mutual interaction between genes and memes (it will be called the cultural parameter); a maximal value of fitness is specified by $f(g, m) \leq f_{max} = 1$. The fitness may be formally specified by $f: \mathcal{G} \times \mathcal{M} \rightarrow [0,1]$. Darwinian evolution (Wright, 1931) over the population $\mathcal{P}$ may be considered as an optimization algorithm that looks for a global maximum on a composed $\mathcal{G} \times \mathcal{M}$ fitness landscape.

$$(g_{opt}, m_{opt}) = \arg \max_{(g, m) \in \mathcal{G} \times \mathcal{M}} f[(g, m)] \qquad (3)$$

This discrete and very complex optimization problem belongs to a class of hard numerical NP-complete problems. This is the main reason why the optimization problems like equation (3) are solved by the so-called evolutionary algorithms (Holland, 1975). We will use a very simple version of evolutionary algorithms tightly related to the idea of "chemostat" (Dittrich, 1999; Gillespie,

1977), which is very popular in artificial chemistry (Dittrich; Kvasnicka et al., 2002).

Let us postulate three elementary reactions that are fundamental for the proposed chemostat evolutionary algorithm over a population of m-genes.

1.   Replication: An m-gene (g, m) is replicated to another m-gene (g', m') (see Figure 2).

$$\underbrace{(g, m)}_{parent} \rightarrow \underbrace{(g, m)}_{parent} + \underbrace{(g', m')}_{offspring} \qquad (4)$$

Components of the offspring m-gene (g', m') from the right-hand side of equation (4) are closely related to the respective parent components (usually with a small distance) and are specified as follows:

$$g' = O_{mut}^{(gene)}(g) \qquad (5a)$$

and

$$m' = \arg \max_{\tilde{m} \in U(m)} H(g', \tilde{m}), \qquad (5b)$$

where $O_{mut}^{(gene)}$ is a gene mutation operator (Holland, 1975; mutability is specified by a probability $P_{mut}^{(gene)}$). The second formula means that an offspring meme m' is created as a solution of a local maximization problem in the neighborhood $U(m) = \{\tilde{m} = O_{mut}^{(meme)}(m)\}$ with fixed cardinality U_{card} (considered as a parameter of the method), and $O_{mut}^{(meme)}$ is a meme mutation operator (mutability is specified by a probability $P_{mut}^{(meme)}$). It means that an offspring meme m' is not a simple mutation of the parent meme m, but it results from a local hill-climbing memetic learning process with respect to a fixed offspring gene g'. In other words, we may say that the offspring does not automatically accept a parent meme, but is trying to locally optimize (a kind of social learning process) the parent meme m with respect to its gene g' transferred genetically from its parent. If

Figure 2. Diagrammatic interpretation of the replication process in equation (4). (a) A randomly selected parent m-gene is replicated; both components of an offspring m-gene are specified as slightly mutated versions of their parent counterparts (manifested by an appearance of thin vertical columns in the offspring). (b) Schematic outline of the replication process in a population; the randomly selected parent m-gene is replicated (with mutations) to an offspring m-gene, and the randomly selected m-gene is eliminated from the population.

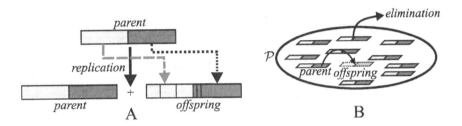

we state U_{card} = 1, then equation (5b) is reduced to the simple formula $m' = O_{mut}^{(meme)}(m)$.

Formally, the replication process may be expressed by a stochastic operator:

$$(g',m') = O_{repli}(g,m). \qquad (6)$$

In a limiting case, a resulting m-gene (g',m') may be simply equal to the argument (g,m). We have to emphasize that for replication processes, we distinguish two types of mutation operators: The first one is a gene mutation and the second one is a meme mutation, where both are characterized by different mutation probabilities $P_{mut}^{(gene)}$ and $P_{mut}^{(meme)}$, respectively. This distinguishing feature allows us to separate processes of gene and meme mutations; it implies that we may introduce different evolutionary rates of genes and memes. A probability of an application of the replication operator (an analog to the kinetic rate constant k) is specified by

$$prob_{(g,m)(g',m')} = exp\left[\alpha\left(f(g,m) - f_{max}\right)\right], (7)$$

where f_{max} =1+ω is an estimated maximal value of the fitness and α>0 is the so-called slope pa-

rameter (its greater values, $\alpha \to \infty$, cause negligible value of probability, $prob_{(g,m)(g',m')} \to 0$, for $f(g,m) < f_{max}$). It means that a replication process is more probable for those m-genes that have fitness closely related to its maximal value f_{max}. The preferable selection of m-genes with higher fitness for replication is of great importance for accomplishing a global solution (or its tightly related approximation) of the optimization problem in equation (3) by the proposed evolutionary algorithm based on the metaphor of chemostat (Dittrich, 1999; Gillespie, 1977).

2. Interaction: Two m-genes (g,m) (called the donor) and (g',m') (called the acceptor) mutually interact in such a way that there exists an oriented memetic transfer of a meme from the donor to the acceptor (see Figure 3).

$$\underbrace{(g,m)}_{donor} + \underbrace{(g',m')}_{acceptor} \to \underbrace{(g,m)}_{donor} + \underbrace{(g',m'')}_{\substack{modified \\ acceptor}} \qquad (8)$$

The memetic part of the acceptor is created from the transferred donor meme by its local optimization with respect to its fixed gene part g' (cf. equation (5b)).

*Figure 3. Diagrammatic interpretation of the interaction process in equation (8). (a) A randomly selected donor transfers its meme **m** to a randomly selected acceptor, and then this meme is locally optimized with respect to the original acceptor gene **g**'. (b) Schematic outline of the interaction process in a population; two randomly selected m-genes interact such that a meme from the donor is transferred (represented by an oriented arrow) to the acceptor and is locally optimized with respect to the acceptor gene.*

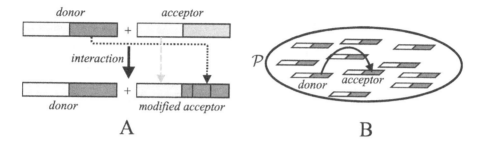

$$m'' = arg \max_{\tilde{m} \in U(m)} H\left(g', \tilde{m}\right) \qquad (9)$$

Equation (9) is similar to equation (5b), it means that an acceptor meme m'' is created as a solution of a local maximization problem in the neighborhood $U\left(m\right) = \left\{ \tilde{m} = O_{mut}^{(meme)}\left(m\right) \right\}$ with fixed cardinality (considered as a parameter of the method) U_{card}. The modified acceptor is composed of a meme, which is originated from the donor and modified by a local optimization with respect to the original acceptor gene g'. This interaction process corresponds to one of the fundamental properties of memetic systems [5]; in particular, memes are spreading throughout the population not only vertically by replication, but also horizontally when a donor offers its meme to other acceptors by the interaction process. The interaction process may be expressed by a stochastic operator

$$\left(g', m''\right) = O_{int\,eract}\left(\left(g, m\right), \left(g', m'\right)\right). \qquad (10)$$

In a limiting case, if this operator could not be applied to arguments, then the resulting m-gene (g', m'') is simply equal to the second argument (acceptor) (g', m'). In order to get a complete specification of the interaction operator, we have to introduce a probability of its application to the arguments:

$$prob_{(g,m)(g',m')} = max\left\{0, 1 - exp\left[\alpha\left(f\left(g', m'\right) - f\left(g, m\right)\right)\right]\right\}. \qquad (11)$$

$\alpha > 0$ is the so-called slope parameter (its greater values cause a dichotomy-like behavior, either zero or the unit) of the probability. The probability is positive if the fitness of the donor is greater than the fitness of the acceptor, $f\left(g, m\right) > f\left(g', m'\right)$, and it is proportional to a difference $f\left(g, m\right) - f\left(g', m'\right)$. This means that there exists a one-way memetic transfer from a donor, which must have greater fitness than the acceptor.

3. Extinction: An m-gene (g, m) is removed from the population $\mathcal{P}$:

$$\underbrace{\left(g, m\right)}_{parent} \to \varnothing . \qquad (12)$$

Each replication process is automatically accompanied by extinction. Since replication increases the number of m-genes in the population by one (cf. equation (4)), an application of extinction (a randomly selected m-gene is eliminated from the population) ensures a constant number of m-genes in chemostat (i.e., the size of chemostat population is invariant in the course of evolution).

In the proposed evolutionary algorithm based on the metaphor of chemostat (Dittrich, 1999; Gillespie, 1977), a selection pressure in the population of m-genes is created by replication and interaction processes based on fitness. M-genes with greater fitness have a greater chance to take part in a replication or interaction process (a measure of quality of m-genes); on the other hand, m-genes with little effective fitness are rarely used in the replication process or as a donor in the interaction. This simple manifestation of Darwin's natural selection ensures a gradual evolution of the whole population. In the present approach, the mentioned principle of the fitness selection of m-genes is preserved, but it is now combined with an additional selection pressure due to a constancy of the number of m-genes in the chemostat. An m-gene outgoing from the replication reaction eliminates a randomly selected m-gene. Moreover, we have to distinguish between a performance of replication and a performance of interaction; the replication process should be applied with substantially higher frequency than the interaction process. That is, simple replications of parents onto offspring are more frequent than transfers of a meme from donors to acceptors (see Algorithm 1).

Algorithm 1.

```
1  chemostat P is randomly generated;
2  for t:=1 to tmax do
3  begin (g,m):=Oselect(P);
4     if random<prob(g,m) then
5     begin (g',m'):=Orepli(g,m);
6        (g'',m''):=Oselect(P);
7        (g'',m'')←(g',m');
8     end;
9     while random<Pinteract then
10    begin (g,m):=Oselect(P);(g',m'):=Oselect(P);
11       if random<prob((g,m),(g',m')) then
12       begin (g',m''):=Ointeract((g,m),(g',m'));
13          (g',m')←(g',m'');
14       end;
15    end;
16 end;
```

The algorithm is initialized by a population composed of randomly generated m-genes that are all evaluated by fitness (see Row 1). The algorithm is composed of two blocks that are activated with different probabilities: the first one (with a probability P_{repli}) for a replication (Rows 5-8) and the second one (with a probability $P_{interact}$) for an interaction (Rows 9-15). The replication block is initiated by a random selection (realized by an operator O_{select}) of an m-gene (g,m); this m-gene is further replicated (with a probability specified by prob(g,m)) by an operator O_{repli}. The resulting product (g',m') is evaluated by fitness and then is returned to the population such that it eliminates a randomly selected m-gene (g'',m''). The interaction block is repeated with a probability $P_{interact}$, two m-genes are randomly selected, and then both undergo an interaction.

FURTHER GENERALIZATION OF THE PRESENT THEORY

One of the most serious restrictions of the present theory is a postulate that a particular gene interacts only with one meme. In many cases of theoretical interest (in theoretical memetics), this severe restriction seriously limits the applicability of the present theory; therefore, we suggest its generalized version, which to some extent overcomes the mentioned restriction. Moreover, this simple generalization nicely demonstrates the flexibility and efficiency of the present theoretical approach, which allows not only simple computational simulations, but also its power to be simply modified and generalized.

As a simple application of this generalized coevolutionary theory of genes, we present its

Figure 4. Diagram A shows a type of used interaction in a cooperative model with an environmental niche that mediates an interaction between memes and genes. Diagram B is a special situation where composite genes are created from three different parts: gene, environment, and meme.

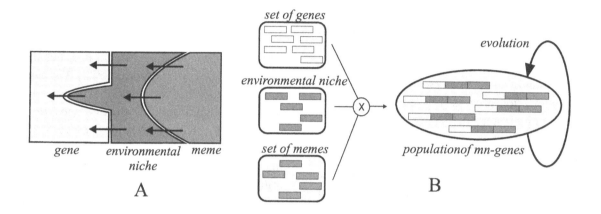

specification when an environmental niche is explicitly considered. In particular, many biologists or social scientists (Aunger, 2001; Laland et al., 1999) doubt whether memes may directly affect the fitness of genes. They suggest overcoming this serious problem of memetics such that an environmental niche is introduced; it is postulated that the memes may affect only this niche, and gene fitness is specified by its structure plus an interaction between gene and environmental niche (see Diagram A in Figure 4). It means that within this model, a vicarious interaction does not exist between genes and memes, but this is mediated by an environmental niche. Subjects of Darwinian evolutions are composites called mn-genes that are created by a gene, environmental niche, and meme (see Diagram B in Figure 4). Their fitness is calculated as follows:

$$f\left[(g,n,m)\right] = (1-\omega)F(g) + \frac{\omega}{2}\left(H_{GN}(g,n) + H_{NM}(n,m)\right),$$
(13)

where H_{GN} (H_{NM}) represents an interaction term between gene and environmental niche (environ-

mental niche and meme). We see that a memetic part of an mn-gene does not interact directly with a particular gene, but interacts vicariously through an environmental niche.

CHEMOSTAT SIMULATION OF COEVOLUTION OF GENES AND MEMES

The chemostat approach outlined previously will be used as an algorithmic framework for a simulation of Darwinian coevolution between genes and memes. An initial composition of chemostat is done by identical binary strings. Numerical values of single parameters are specified in Table 1.

We specify functions F and H that are needed for the fitness evaluation of m-genes (see equation (2)) by Kauffman's rugged functions (Altenberg, 1998; Kauffman, 1993). Their general properties are summarized by Altenberg. In particular, the function F is specified as a standard NK function, where $N=40$ and $K=3$ (number of pleotropisms).

Table 1. Numerical values of parameters used in numerical simulations

No.	Parameter	Numerical Value
1	N, length of genes and memes	40
2	$P_{mut}^{(gene)}$, probability of one-point gene mutation	0.0001
	$P_{mut}^{(meme)}$, probability of one-point meme mutation	0.001
3	$P_{interact}$, probability of an interaction event (see Algorithm 1)	0.5
4	α, slope parameter for calculation of probabilities in equations (7) and (11)	4
5	ω, cultural parameter in equation (2)	0.1
6	A, size of population	500
7	t_{max}, maximal number of elementary evolutionary epochs	2×10^6
8	U_{card}, size of neighborhood in equations (5b) and (9)	1 (10)
9	$U_{card}^{(eff)}$, size of neighborhood in equation (13), Baldwin effect	1 (10)

Figure 5. Typical plots of mean values of functions F and H obtained for parameters specified in Table 1. We see that a plot for F (corresponding to the fitness of an isolated gene) forms a typical nondecreasing staircase graph, whereas a plot of H (corresponding to an interaction between genes and memes) is not monotonous and mostly random.

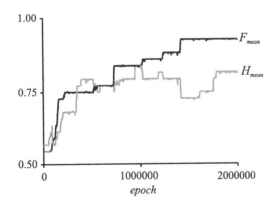

Slightly more complicated is a specification of the function H that expresses an interaction between genes and memes; we used the so-called generalized function *NKCS* (we put $C=S=1$), which Kauffman introduced as a proper model to allow the systematic study of various aspects of natural evolution between interacting species. A plot of typical results is displayed in Figure 5 (for parameters specified in Table 1). This figure nicely demonstrates the basic property of all our simulations, in particular that the plot of the mean value of function F (it corresponds to the fitness of an isolated gene) is nondecreasing and is of a staircase form. On the other hand, the plot of the mean value of H (it corresponds, loosely speaking, to the fitness of the meme with respect to its partner gene) is not monotonous and mostly random. This very important conclusion may be formulated as a first observation obtained from our simulations.

First Observation. *A gene part F of fitness always forms a nondecreasing staircase function, whereas a memetic part H of fitness is not monotonous and may contain both decreasing as well as increasing stages.*

This first observation has a very interesting, almost philosophical interpretation. A biological evolution is always of a cumulative and nondecreasing character, but its memetic counterpart, though partially of an increasing character, contains also a considerable random part (i.e., it is not of a cumulative and nondecreasing character). This interesting feature of our simulations is caused by the fact that memes form only an environment (we may say a cultural niche) for the evolution of genes, while memes are evolutionary pulled only indirectly through their interaction with genes.

The fitness (2) contains a positive parameter ω, with the help of which an interaction (cultural) term H may be gradually incorporated into fitness.

We have done a series of simulations with the parameters specified in Table 1, where the parameter ω was gradually changed from the initial value 0.1 to its final value 2.0. The obtained results may be summarized by the following observation.

Second Observation. *There exists a critical value ω_{crit} of the cultural parameter (for a fixed value of interaction probability $P_{interact}$); for $\omega < \omega_{crit}$ a gene part F of fitness is not very affected, but for $\omega > \omega_{crit}$, part F is substantially decelerated (see Figure 6).*

A similar phenomenon was also observed by Bull et al., 2000. They interpreted the observation such that there exists a phase transition depending on the parameter ω. There exist two different types of plots such as were displayed in Figure 7. If parameter ω exceeds its critical value, then the type of plot is dramatically changed to the other type.

Figure 6. Two different plots of mean values of function F, which corresponds to a gene part of the fitness. Diagram A contains a plot for those values of parameter ω that are smaller than a critical value ω_{crit}. This plot shows that gene fitness is gradually increased to almost its maximal unit value. Diagram B contains a similar plot, but for such values of ω that are greater than the critical value ω_{crit}. In this case, a gradual increase of function F is substantially decelerated.

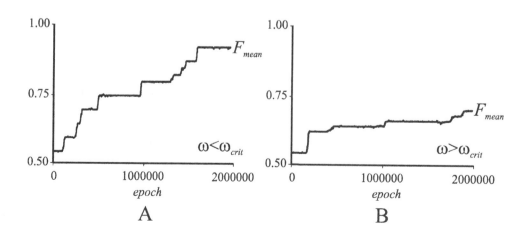

The chemostat algorithm (see Algorithm 1) contains an important parameter corresponding to a probability $P_{interact}$ that controls stochastically an inclusion of interaction between two randomly selected m-genes. We have done two independent simulations: the first one for smaller values of probability $P_{interact}$ and the second one for its increased value $P'_{interaction}$; the obtained results are summarized by the following observation.

Third Observation. *An interaction probability $P_{interact}$ does not affect substantially the gene part F of fitness while a cultural part H is accelerated by increasing the probability (see Figure 7).*

As was already mentioned, the probability $P_{interact}$ controls a horizontal transfer of memes. Its intensification by increasing the probability caused an increasing of the selection pressure

Figure 7. Plots of mean values of functional parts F and H of the fitness for two different values of probabilities $P_{interact}$ and $P'_{interact} > P_{interact}$. Diagrams A and C correspond to $P_{interact} = 0.5$, whereas Diagrams B and D correspond to $P'_{interact} = 0.95$. We see that an increase of the probability (Diagrams A and B) does not affect the plots of the gene fitness part F; on the other hand, an increased value of probability substantially changes (Diagrams C and D) the plots of interaction fitness part H, which is considerably accelerated to higher functional values.

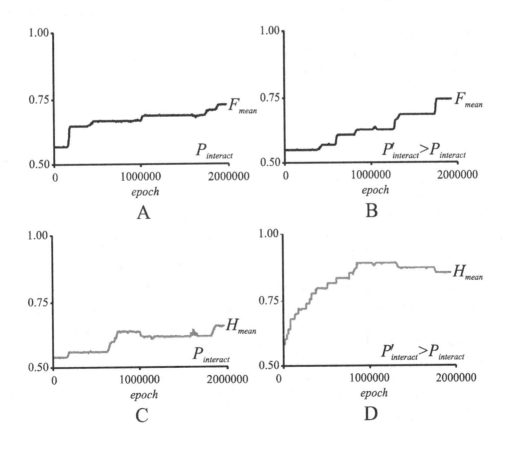

between memes, which is manifested by an acceleration of memetic evolution. In other words, it means that a frequency of horizontal memetic transfer belongs to important parameters of the present coevolutionary theory; it may partially control the relative evolutionary rate of memes with respect to genes.

CONCLUSION

Although the scientific value of memetics remains a matter of opinion in social sciences (Aunger, 2001), in computer sciences (Conte, Hegselmann, & Terna, 1997; Kvasnicka & Pospichal, 1999a, 1999b, 1999c, 2000), particularly in artificial societies and social simulations, it belongs to very popular approaches on how to overcome the information limits of Darwinian evolution. Since it is impossible to realize genetically a transfer of acquired information from parents onto offspring, and some of this information is vitally important for the successful survival of the offspring, there must exist something other than the genetic transfer of information. It seems that most natural solutions to these problems are meme approaches (Aunger, 2001; Blackmore, 1999; Dawkins, 1976; Dennett, 1995) based on a postulation that genes and memes form composites, called in this chapter m-genes. The present coevolutionary theory is fully based on a postulation that memes are not independently and freely appearing with respect to genes, but are obligatorily bounded with genes as composites, which are subjects of Darwinian evolution. It represents a formal attempt to suggest a coevolution of genes and memes by introducing a population of m-memes with specified types of elementary interactions. Loosely speaking, this approach may be alternatively understood as a performance of a multiagent system, where each agent is specified not only by a gene (e.g., it specifies an architecture of its cognitive organ), but also by a meme (a knowledge database that facilitates an agent surviving in its environment).

REFERENCES

Altenberg, L. (1998). B2.7.2. NK fitness landscapes. In T. Baeck, D. F. Fogel, & Z. Michalewicz (Eds.), *Handbook of evolutionary computation.* New York: Oxford University Press.

Aunger, R. (Ed.). (2001). *Darwinizing culture: The status of memetics as a science.* New York: Oxford University Press.

Baldwin, J. M. (1896). A new factor in evolution. *American Naturalist, 30,* 441-451.

Belew, R. K., & Mitchel, M. (Eds.). (1996). *Adaptive individuals in evolving populations: Models and algorithms.* Reading, MA: Addison-Wesley.

Blackmore, S. (1999). *The meme machine.* New York: Oxford University Press.

Boyd, R., & Richerson, P. J. (1985). *Culture and the evolutionary process.* Chicago: University of Chicago Press.

Bull, L., Holland, O., & Blackmore, S. (2000). On meme-gene coevolution. *Artificial Life, 6,* 227-235.

Cavalli-Sforza, L. L., & Feldman, M. W. (1981). *Cultural transmission and evolution: A quantitative approach.* Princeton: Princeton University Press.

Conte, R., Hegselmann, R., & Terna, P. (Eds.). (1997). *Simulating social phenomena.* Berlin, Germany: Springer Verlag.

Dawkins, R. (1976). *The selfish gene.* Oxford: Oxford University Press.

Dennett, D. (1995). *Darwin's dangerous idea.* Hammondsworth, United Kingdom: The Penguin Press.

Dittrich, P., Ziegler, J., & Banzhaf, W. (2001). Artificial chemistries: A review. *Artificial Life, 7, 225-275.*

Durham, W. H. (1991). *Coevolution: Genes, culture and human diversity.* Stanford, CA: Stanford University Press.

Eigen, M. (1971). Self organization of matter and the evolution of biological macro molecules. *Naturwissenschaften, 58,* 465-523.

Eigen, M., & Schuster, P. (1977). The hypercycles: A principle of natural evolution. *Naturwissenschaften, 64,* 541; *65,* 7; *65,* 341.

Feldman, M. W., & Laland, K. N. (1996). Gene-culture coevolutionary theory. *Trends in Ecology and Evolution, 11,* 453-457.

Gillespie, D. T. (1977). Exact stochastic simulation of coupled chemical reactions. *Journal of Phys. Chem., 81,* 2340- 2361.

Hofbauer, J., & Sigmund, K. (1988). *The theory of evolution and dynamical systems.* Cambridge: Cambridge University Press.

Holland, J. H. (1975). *Adaptation in natural and artificial systems.* Ann Arbor, MI: University of Michigan Press.

Jones, B. L., Enns, R. H., & Rangnekar, S. S. (1976). On the theory of selection of coupled macromolecular systems. *Bulletin of Mathematical Biology, 38,* 15-23.

Kauffman, S. (1993). *The origins of order: Self-organization and selection in evolution.* Oxford, United Kingdom: Oxford University Press.

Kvasnicka, V., & Pospichal, J. (1999a). Evolutionary study of interethnic cooperation. *Advances in Complex Systems, 2,* 395-421.

Kvasnicka, V., & Pospichal, J. (1999b). Simulation of Baldwin effect and Dawkins memes by genetic algorithm. In R. Roy, T. Furuhashi, & P. K. Chawdhry (Eds.), *Advances in soft computing* (pp. 481-496). London: Springer-Verlag.

Kvasnicka, V., & Pospichal, J. (1999c). Simulation of evolution of Dawkins memes. *Evolution and cognition, 5,* 75-86.

Kvasnicka, V., & Pospichal, J. (2000). An emergence of coordinated communication in populations of agents. *Artificial Life, 5,* 319-342.

Kvasnicka, V., & Pospichal, J. (2003). Artificial chemistry and molecular Darwinian evolution in silico. *Collection of Czechoslovak Chemical Communications, 68*(1), 139-177.

Laland, K. N., Odling-Smee, J., & Feldman, M. W. (1999). Niche construction, biological evolution and cultural change. *Behavioral and Brain Sciences, 23,* 131-175.

Wright, S. (1932). The roles of mutation, inbreeding, crossbreeding, and selection in evolution. *Proceedings of the Sixth International Congress of Genetics, 1,* 356-366. Retrieved from http://www.blackwellpublishing.com/ridley/classictexts/wright.pdf

ENDNOTE

[1] This work was supported in part by grants from the Slovak Scientific Grant Agency (No. 1/4053/07) and the Slovak Research and Development Agency (No. APVV 20-002504).

Correspondence concerning this article should be addressed to Vladimir Kvasnicka or Jiri Pospichal, Institute of Applied Informatics, Faculty of Informatics and Information Technologies, Slovak Technical University, 842 16 Bratislava, Slovakia. E-mail: kvasnicka@fiit.stuba.sk or pospichal@fiit.stuba.sk

Chapter IV
Thinking Animals and Thinking Machines:
What Relations?
(with Particular Reference to the Psychoanalytical Point of View)

Franco Scalzone
Italian Psychoanalytical Society, Italy

Gemma Zontini
Italian Psychoanalytical Society, Italy

ABSTRACT

In this chapter we will examine some similarities between computer science and psychoanalysis, and we will formulate some hypotheses by bringing closer the statute of connectionism to the energetic model of the psychic apparatus, as well as OOP (object-oriented programming) to the object relations theory. We will make some remarks on the machine and people theme, the way in which people relate to machines, especially "thinking machines," describing the fantasies they arouse. In order to do this, we will use Tausk's classic (1919/1933) "On the Origin of the 'Influencing Machine' in Schizophrenia," as well as some of Freud's writings.

PSYCHOANALYSIS AND ARTIFICIAL INTELLIGENCE: A NEW ALLIANCE?

In this chapter we will examine, with a panoramic view, some similarities between computer science and psychoanalysis, and we will formulate some hypotheses by bringing closer the statute of connectionism to the energetic model of the psychic apparatus, as well as OOP (object-oriented programming) to the object relations theory. Finally, we will make some remarks on the machine and people theme, the way in which people relate to machines, especially "thinking machines," describing the fantasies they arouse. We will then propose a psychoanalytical interpretation. In order to do this, we will use Tausk's classic (1919/1933) "On the Origin of the 'Influencing Machine' in Schizophrenia,"[1] as well as some of Freud's writings.

CONNECTIONISM

"Computers are not appropriate models of brain, but they are the most powerful heuristic tool we have with which to try to understand the matter of the mind." (Edelman, 1992, p. 194)

As Turkle (1988) points out, what we may call classic artificial intelligence (AI) is too often viewed only as computation or as procedures for information processing; it is therefore mainly connected to cognitivism. Such conceptual collocation has driven away from AI the interests of many psychoanalysts, notwithstanding many attempts, such as Erdelyi's (1985), Bucci's (1997), and others', to build a bridge between psychoanalysis and cognitive psychology.

AI studies intelligence in an indirect way, trying to build machines capable of intelligent behavior but without paying too much attention to the peculiar features of human intelligence. Its method is the programming of calculators so that they may show some intelligent capabilities. We may say that there are essentially two ways to try and simulate intelligent human processes through computer modeling: Either we start from the symbolic functions of a higher level then try to break them down into lower level subfunctions (top-down method), or we start from the attempt to reproduce low-level functions, or even the hardware, to then make our way up to high-level symbolic functions.

Edelman (1992), with his neural Darwinism theory, shows us just how our brain is able to operate in a bottom-up mode through the theory of neural group segregation (TNGS)—that is to say, able to self-learn and self-organize when faced with an unlabelled world. We can say that the first method to simulate cognitive processes is the one carried out by classic AI, which some would like to merely call cognitive simulation, and the second one is the one carried out by emergent AI.

If we consider the reductionistic position that homologizes mind and calculator, we see that, for the time being, the only mental activities that can be simulated on a calculator are the perceptive cognitive and logical ones. As it is known, the latter are the simplest ones to simulate through ad hoc algorithms while much harder, for instance, is the simulation of perceptive processes.

We witness the apparent paradox of how the processes that appear as mental activities difficult for people to carry out, such as complex mathematical calculations, are rapidly performed by computers. On the contrary, psychological functions, which we deem as simple (common sense) and are all capable of performing without even realizing it, pertain to subjectivity and cannot be so easily expressed in as formalized a way through an algorithm; they also entail extreme processing complexity and a difficult theoretical explanation, making them impossible, at least for now, to be simulated on a computer.

AI has found remarkable difficulties every time it has been faced with the solution of aleatory problems, as in the simulation of vision in order to recognize forms with irregular contours, or in analogical reasoning, for instance. Also, emotions are indirect and secondary products of the functioning of the structure and of the way in which it is organized, and they cannot be reproduced through an effective procedure or through a program. What a machine would be lacking is the qualitative character of the conscious experience (qualia). They, the emotions, can be found in no place and in no particular level; they too are distributed functions and emerge from the complexity of the structural organization.

Another difficulty is the fact that human mathematical skills also possess the nonalgorithmic capacity to recognize mathematical truths, which would spring from some sort of intuition that would not use physical symbols manipulated by following algorithmic procedures.

Nowadays, calculators are able to simulate mainly logical thinking—the type of system that, according to Basch-Kahre (1985), is innate to the brain; in fact, she assumes that a primitive form of logic has existed since the gestation period of the fetus. We are saying this to underline how the forms of thinking that at times seem to be the most fully developed, that is, logical thinking, can probably be also very ancient and perhaps seem to be more connected to the physical structure of the brain (hardwired) than other types of mental functioning. A Boolean network, for instance, that is, a nonintentional system, is already able to solve self-learning problems by using logical functions. However, one must also say that our brain, when performing logical thinking and using logical language, neither reveals nor operates on the low level of the neural network but on the high levels of a sophisticated symbolic functioning with a symbolic language.

Already, von Neumann (1958) wrote that the external forms of our mathematical language are absolutely irrelevant in the evaluation of the logical or mathematical language actually used in the central nervous system. Furthermore, the brain, unlike calculators and Boolean networks, is a system capable of intentional self-organization.

Taking into account what we have said and pushing inferences a little forward, we can say that the computational aspects of the mind (considering their higher accessibility to being simulated on a calculator, though considered as superior functions) show a higher feasibility both by using,

for instance, a machine with a von Neumann-like architecture, or Turing machine,[2] and by using a neural-network architecture working with parallel processing. The functioning of the second type is certainly more similar to the functioning of the brain-machine, especially as regards the part that we would call the unconscious.

The term simulation is employed in computer science with many different shades of meaning, ranging from the possibility to build perfect sequences of symbolic thinking, like the one about the logic processes of thought, to the possibility of deceit, through which the naive spectator is fooled when showed that the machine has intelligence and a relational skill similar to the human being's but that, at least for the time being, it does not possess. By simulation here, we do not mean simulation of the mind expressed through computer programs, for example, as shown by programs such as PARRY by Colby or ELIZA[3] by Weizenbaum, which look more like artifacts to us if not funny and sophisticated bluffs. Programs like ELIZA, which in its section called DOCTOR simulates a Rogersian psychotherapist, only simulate the initial and final parts of human behavior and therefore, like the Turing test, deal with the mind just as if it were a black box. By studying merely the initial conditions (the inputs) and the final ones (the outputs), they reduce the whole test to the utilization of verbal behavior. Such a method is unacceptable because one cannot reduce intelligence and emotionality to being expressed only verbally. In fact, Weizenbaum underlined, when rightly criticizing his disciple Colby's program PARRY, which simulates a paranoid mind, that when the program was having some trouble, it would shut down, thus refusing to answer and confirming to the interlocutor a kind of behavior that showed anxiety of the persecutory type. Therefore, a program that is completely passive, causing the interlocutor to find himself facing a blank screen, would have perfectly represented the simulation of an autistic patient.

Simulations are not simply and only supposed to reproduce phenomena, but they must try to reproduce the mechanisms and processes that lie behind phenomena; they are another way of expressing theories without turning to symbols. Furthermore, they are useful also to formulate some empirical previsions and then verify them: They realize an experimental laboratory in which virtual phenomena occur within an artificial reality. The simulations that we are referring to are made possible by the presence of the computer. The advantages in using simulations are manifold; for instance, they allow us to study phenomena that, due to physical and temporal reasons, cannot be studied any other way or phenomena impossible to reproduce for ethical reasons, and so forth. Moreover, they are extremely useful in order to study complex systems that present strong unpredictability and unrepeatability, that are difficult to face, and whose theories are complex.

By simulation we here mean, according to the connectivism paradigm, simulating the functioning of the brain and therefore of the mind, including its internal structural organization, just the way they operate perhaps in real people. It is true that there is the risk of excessive reductionism, but this simulation is highly sophisticated and therefore very different from the reductionism of classic AI. However, simulation techniques are only in their early stages, and we shall have to wait for future development to fully appreciate their real possibilities.

For a long time now, a different field of AI has been raising interest: connectionism. It employs the calculator not by using programs that work in a sequential way according to instructions and rules provided by the program to manipulate data, but by using software that simulates neural networks, which perform parallel processing; that, in a way, is much more similar to the operational mode of the brain. A neural network is a set of neurons linked by connections that carries out feedback when the cells are stimulated. When Hebb in 1949 put forward such a model, scientists had little knowl-

edge of the real connections present in the brain. One may also utilize proper parallel-architecture machines in which there are a high number of processors operating in parallel: Such architecture speeds up processing in a remarkable way. Within connectionism, information processing is carried out by the interaction of a great number of simple units appropriately connected. The architecture of most digital calculators, instead, is the classic one by von Neumann (1958) in which the memory and the central processing unit (CPU) are separated. In order to perform a program, data are called back by memory, processed within the central unit, and then reallocated into memory: This is a sequential architecture because operations are carried out one at a time and the process then can hardly be speeded up over certain limits because of the existence of bottlenecks that slow down the performing of programs.

We must particularly underline one characteristic that differentiates traditional programming from neural-network programming. In classic AI, the machine must be explicitly programmed by man who provides the instructions for the performing of a certain procedure; this is obtained through one or more algorithms that will be written in a chosen programming language and that will form the program. Instead, in connectionism a person provides, randomly, a series of weights entered into the input units of the network, and then the network is able to modify itself by performing self-learning based on experience. All of this will determine the behavior of the network; in other words, the network is able to find by itself those weights on the connections that will allow it to realize the performance required, and therefore it is able to self-organize.

It is interesting to report here a passage by Freud (1892-1895/n.d.-a, p. 291) that exemplifies the functioning of conscience:

For there is some justification for speaking of the "defile" of consciousness. The term gains meaning and liveliness for a physician who carries out an analysis like this. Only a single memory at a time can enter ego-consciousness. A patient who is occupied in working through such a memory sees nothing of what is pushing after it and forgets what has already pushed its way through. If there are difficulties in the way of mastering this single pathogenic memory—as, for instance, if the patient does not relax his resistance against it, if he tries to repress or mutilate it—then the defile is, so to speak, blocked. The work is at a standstill, nothing more can appear, and the single memory which is in process of breaking through remains in front of the patient until he has taken it up into the breadth of his ego. The whole spatially-extended mass of psychogenic material is in this way drawn through a narrow cleft and thus arrives in consciousness cut up, as it were, into pieces or strips. It is the psychotherapist's business to put these together once more into the organization which he presumes to have existed. Anyone who has a craving for further similes may think at this point of a Chinese puzzle.

Conscious processes then, also according to Freud, are carried out in a sequential way and therefore conscience would work along the lines of an architecture similar to von Neumann's. Unconscious, instead, would work in parallel, a mode that is much more similar to neural-network processing. Here, the parallelism is meant as the spatial development of a complex performing algorithm and not as several independent processes in a simultaneous performance. Therefore, parallel time has a limit because it is bound to sequential space and thus the series of intermediate data, which must be periodically memorized, represents the space needed to solve the problem.

In the final part of the above-mentioned quotation by Freud, we can see how the mass of psychic materials, in order to be used by conscience, must first be translated into words and then processed and conveyed, as it occurs, for instance, in the conscious work of an analysis, and must then be "drawn through a narrow cleft and thus arrives

in consciousness cut up, as it were, into pieces or strips." It is evident here the evocation of the paper tape of the sequential functioning in a Turing machine. Freud had attributed the difference between *Ucs* and *Prec* to the fact that preconscious representation is linked to language, that is, to word representation. He therefore believed that for unconscious contents (thing representations) to become conscious, they needed linking to word representations, and therefore such linkage to language, as a matter of fact, made consciousness a typically sequential process (AI).

Returning to our subject, other machines, instead, have a parallel architecture; that is, they are made up of many microprocessors functioning simultaneously, which are each provided with their own memory. The processing is thus remarkably speeded up compared to von Neumann-designed machines.

Nowadays, neural networks can be realized on a calculator, a network of simple elements that simulate a network of neurons and that can be implemented both on parallel processing machines and on normal personal computers: They simulate the nervous system of an organism or artificial life, which uses genetic algorithms. The networks are made up of three components: input units connected to internal units that are in turn connected to output units. These simulations or parallel machines, when simulating the mind, have a functioning that is more similar to the functioning of the Ucs system in which several processes operate in parallel simultaneously. In the case of artificial life, we also have the simulation of the environment in which the organism lives. A neural network is a simulated system that transforms patterns of activation of neurons into other patterns of activation of neurons; therefore, there are no symbols.

We have here spoken about feed-forward neural networks, whose characteristics are limited because, for example, there is no representation of time. In order to realize this, we need recurrent networks, that is, networks in which there are paths of ascending and descending or recurring information, as in the brain, enabling them to have some sort of short-term memory. A network of this type can generate complex successions of activation vectors even without any input. However, the true innovation is when not only the software but also the hardware is structured through platforms specialized for the processing of particular algorithms (neuronal chip). This allows one to not be limited to using simple simulations programmed on a serial machine, which is slow, but to use real hardware networks able to carry out the parallel distributed calculation at high speed.

For the paradigm of strong AI, then, the properly programmed calculator is a mind because it possesses cognitive states. Conversely, weak AI considers the calculator only as a powerful work tool to study the mind.

Classic AI studied mental functioning trying to reproduce procedures that might provide the same results of mental operations, neglecting the architecture of the physical device: functionalism. The important element was the software, the set of algorithmic procedures implemented in the biological hardware, without any interest either in the machine or in the processes occurring inside of it, therefore not even inside of the person.

Emergent AI, on the contrary, strives to reproduce also the neural organization in which the brain is structured and therefore it can investigate the birth of the microstructure of the cognitive processes of the system to then get to the macrostructure as the set of emerging properties. Cognitivism tried to reproduce only the external results of mental workings; connectivism, instead, tries to reproduce the mechanisms and the internal functioning mode. That is, it tries to reproduce not only the functioning of the mental machine, but also its physical correlate and its organizational architecture. Finally, classic AI operates by simulating a type of top-down knowledge, which means starting from highly symbolic levels, while neural networks proceed in the opposite way, bottom-up, starting from the level of sub or

presymbolic configuration; Freud would say, in the "Project for a Scientific Psychology" (1895/n.d.-b), it starts from quantity to get to quality, that is, to the conscious being.

The connectionistic idea that the quantity of the weight can be viewed as a measure of the conductivity of the relative connection makes us think of the Freudian idea, once again expressed in the "Project" and regarding the description of the functioning of the neuronic apparatus, about the facilitations that the nervous impulse may encounter in passing through the contact barriers of the neurons of ψ system, which is connected to memory. As we know, when the passing of excitation from one neuron to the other through the contact barriers causes a permanent diminishing of resistances, there will be a facilitation so that excitation will in the future choose the path that has been facilitated. We would like to remind our readers that for Freud, the mnestic trace is nothing but a particular configuration of facilitations. Both processes, the connectionistic one and the psychoanalytical one, are then referred to the construction of memory by means of the organization of neuronic configurations in which certain circuits and certain neuronal groups, more stable because they are facilitated, are favored compared to others when meeting, in the future, signals of a similar type. Long-term changes of the forces of synapses then supply the basis to learning and memory.

Freud, also in the case of memory, does not always present to us the same ideas; sometimes he seems to be talking of a localized, static, addressed memory based on set memory traces that once activated, produce memories, and at other times he presents to us a much more developed picture of a dynamic memory, arranged in a distributed structure and capable of constant recategorizations, which he described in a letter to Fliess (Masson, 1985) as a "rearrangement" in accordance with fresh circumstances—a retranscription. The categorization indicates the possibility to generalize: to enter perceived objects into preconstituted empty forms. Recategorization means that the recalling of a particular categorical response does not occur in the form in which it occurred the first time (even though such possibility cannot be excluded). The response, that is, memory, in general is modified and enriched by the ongoing changes. This type of memory is both associative and inaccurate, unlike the replicative memory of computers, but it is dynamic and capable of generalizations because it is founded upon probabilistic perceptive categorizations based upon values and continuous recategorizations.

We are here going to sum up some of the fundamental characteristics of the functioning of networks. First, we would like to highlight the subformal, subsymbolic approach of the system that brings it closer to the functioning of the unconscious: It is capable of producing an internal representation of the quantitative-type concept. The organization of knowledge (perception, memory) is distributed and not localized; this means that it is represented by a set of network units, while with classic AI knowledge is conceived in terms of symbolic representation and information processing in accordance with sequential programs founded upon rules that manipulate data, just like in cognitivism, which utilizes a computational model of the mind. Memory is neither localized nor simply addressed, but it is a procedural and distributed memory thus able to be continually recategorized; it is a property of the system. It is then a nonreplicative memory that depends for its form on the dynamics of degenerative and associative networks. Such a characteristic about distributed functions allows the system to react to lesions without replying with a breakdown of the system itself but only with a slow decaying of the net due to its tolerance to defaults, as it occurs with the brain. Finally, we would like to underline the capacity to learn through experience, not by resorting to the transmission either of data in the form of information or of programs, which reveal how to process them, but by using procedures that assess any aleatory perturbations

from the outside and then process them according to its own purposes.

Learning can be carried out, for instance, according to the backpropagation[4] learning method or by means of simulated annealing.[5] The system has therefore the possibility to self-organize and evolve in an adaptive way.

Connectionism does not limit itself to studying the mind with models inspired by the brain, but it studies both the mind and the brain as particular cases of a larger class of systems characterized by a large number of simple elements that are in intersection among themselves according to nonlinear and complex dimensions. This means that the dualism between mind and brain is overcome not by simply reducing the former to the latter, but by including the study of both into the more general study on a particular class of phenomena of nature, or if you wish, of reality.

This initial approach to AI, the one of the connectionistic type, can be compared to the energetic drive model of psychoanalysis because we can compare, for instance, the quantitative concept of weight or value to the one of charge. During the training of neural networks, as we said, patterns of activation are assigned to the input units and then the correctness of the output patterns will be verified.

OBJECTS

Another point of convergence between AI and psychoanalysis is found by Turkle (1988), on the one hand in OOP and on the other in the object relations theory.

Both postulate particular entities or agents inside the system: Objects, though obviously not superimposable, can be viewed as analogous and can be, besides plain homophony, a different and common way to approach the organization and the functioning of inner reality. We will briefly try and touch upon the aspects the two concepts may share.

We know that in psychoanalysis the objects theory is becoming increasingly articulated and that there are by now several theories of objects because scholars at times put forward very different concepts of what is meant by an object. Here we will accept the extensive definition given by Greenberg and Mitchell (1983) who talk about the object relations theory as concerning the study of relations between external real people and internal images and residues of relations with them, and the significance these residues have for psychic functioning. As for object relations instead, they speak of interactions of individuals with other internal and external people (real and imaginary) and of the relation between their inner and outer object worlds.

The object is a module with an interface. Object-based programming is then a modular programming of the bottom-up type with predisposed basic modules operating on the data. Modules (objects) are built from the bottom toward the top and thus the stage regarding the choosing of low-level modules is very important. The object is an abstract type of datum. Modules are predisposed through a clearly defined interface in which the data structure is concealed within the module, which appears as a black box, therefore the user (or the subject, the person) knows the interface but not the data structure. Similarly, the internal objects of psychoanalytical theory and their dynamics inform us of their state and their interactions with the individual's internal world, that is, the other objects, and with the external one represented by interpersonal relationships. Psychoanalytical objects can also be nested inside each other, as we can see in some versions of the Kleinian theory (see Wisdom, 1961).

In OOP, as a programming technique, it is important to take some concepts into consideration: the class to which objects belong, the hereditariness of the characteristics (data and functions), polymorphism, modularization, and information hiding. These classes of objects can,

for instance, define the state in which objects are at a particular moment. Due to their modularity, objects cannot be manipulated directly but only through the functions that constitute the interfacing with the rest of the system and with the external environment.

Already, many attempts have been made in psychoanalysis to theorize mixed models of the mind to try to harmonize the drive model and the object model, but for the time being, no satisfactory results have been achieved.

In psychoanalysis, however, object theory still risks being a theory that slides into a homunculus conception of psyche and therefore it may lead to an endless regression because the subject constantly escapes individuation and thus only the relations with other objects are left to investigate: On the whole, it will be about an interpersonal relations theory both in its external and in its interiorized dimension.

Also, the self can be seen as an object among many and therefore the subject is either defined as an emergence from the complex organization of the interaction between objects, a mere representation, or as a deus ex machina coming down from above when we find ourselves faced with theoretical difficulties. Are internal objects in psychoanalysis homunculi with their own personality, their own memory, their own feelings and thoughts? Or are they assimilable with simplified models of a part of the total individual and of some functions of the internalized exterior ones, and therefore are necessitated not only to interact with the other objects of the internal world but also, for instance, to draw upon central memory and upon a single thinking apparatus? Conversely, can they think or even think of themselves: That is, can they be a thought of thought? Is the self a simple internal representation or is it an autonomous agent? The questions that need answering could multiply immeasurably.

The object theory in psychoanalysis, however, while placing the drive theory in the back seat though without necessarily refusing it, lends itself to a dialogue with emergent AI and perhaps to a simulation on the calculator.

Finally, internal objects are assimilable to modules, which cannot be attacked in a direct way but, as for the whole mental set, allow only for an indirect access through particular routes and functions. Therefore, we may consider objects as modules, and the mind as a modular mind (see Fodor, 1983; Minsky, 1985).

For example, we may consider internal objects as encapsulated modular agents forming a matrix in which the self is immersed: agents, that is, able to operate a preprocessing of emotions before being totally recognized as an integral part of the self.

They too, the objects, like units of sense, would in their turn be encapsulated modules, probably made up of smaller modules more or less integrated among themselves: partial objects.

Such an organization would be used to avoid that the true and proper self, as a narcissistically organized central system, may excessively affect the inner world with its emotional setup, which already existed when the internal objects appeared. If we then consider internal objects as a sort of doubles of the external ones, we may assume that there existed a preobject state of the psyche and that, following the maturation process, a sort of internal virtual reality was organized in which objects are utilized to relate oneself to the external world and to experience through an informational redundancy new configurations and emotional (ideative) responses without altering by a short circuit the individual's emotional setup. It is as if the individual could mentally experiment with more solutions before taking on the responsibility of the definitive decision about situations he or she is faced with in relational life, and not as if there were the need to function just to react to stimuli. Yet, we must always take into account the reference to the existence of the real machine, which is placed under the virtual machine and al-

lows the latter to exist; obviously, in our case it is constituted by the neuronal network of the brain. We may then either side with those who consider virtual reality as reality tout court, therefore able to provide real sensations, or with those who see the real machine (hardware) as the only reality (reductionism) and virtual reality as a plain phenomenal reality or simulation: Therefore, it is always a question of levels of reality. However, in both cases the effects of virtual reality will be real effects when considering both the "magical" link between the psyche and external world and the one between the psyche and soma.

Freud in his "Project for a Scientific Psychology" (1895/n.d.-b) actually tried to start from the neuronal level characterized by movements of quantity (energy) to then reach the conscience capable of recognizing the quality of the mental set, but he himself was not as presumptuous as to think he had solved the problem and claimed:

No attempt, of course, can be made to explain how it is that excitatory processes in the ω neurones bring consciousness along with them. It is only a question of establishing a coincidence between the characteristics of consciousness that are known to us and processes in the ω neurones which vary in parallel with them. And this is quite possible in some detail. (p. 311)

However, we would like to point out that, especially at the beginning of his studies, Freud prevented the hardware—the brain—from becoming absorbed, therefore invisible in respect to the software or psyche. Only later on, as it is well known, did he opt for psychological inquiry, but he never wanted to unhook psychoanalysis from the somatic bedrock for fear of wandering too far away from other sciences.

We must finally underline, so that there may not be any misunderstanding, that obviously the modular model of the mind and the distributed one are almost irreconcilable, as are the drive model and the object one in psychoanalysis. Yet, we have dealt with them here in order to show the availability of more than one model of mental functioning that might be used, for instance, for different cerebral hemispheres (right or left), different functional areas, or for different periods of mental maturation. We must also say that the modular organization of objects in AI could be arranged in its internal part as a neural network and the objects could be connected among themselves with a network-like distributed organization. Then, the distributed model could be likened to a type of primary functioning of the mind preceding the operational closure of the modules when there is still a strong transmodularity, while the object-oriented modular model could be likened to the more mature functioning of the individual when both sensory modules and the object ones are closed to the conditioning of central systems—to the self. Also, in the mature individual, objects could live in a drive atmosphere and seek pleasure through object relations; but maybe this chapter is still to be written. However, we know that the two functioning modes may still keep on coexisting all through one's life without maturation suppressing any of the two, even though the former mode is probably concealed by the latter.

REGARDING "BEEINFLUSSUNGAPPARATES" (INFLUENCING MACHINE) AND THINKING MACHINES: AN EXAMPLE DRAWN FROM PSYCHOANALYTICAL LITERATURE

Over the last few years, the issue concerning the relation between human and machine has been present more than ever. We will now make some remarks on how people view machines, describe the fantasies they arouse, and then put forward an interpretation. In order to achieve such purposes we will use the classic work by Tausk

(1919/1933) "On the Origin of the 'Influencing Machine' in Schizophrenia" as well as some of Freud's works.

Tausk (1919/1933) talks of delusions of influence that sometimes present themselves in psychoses, in particular schizophrenia, which are enacted through an influencing machine that would have characteristics drawn from the technical and scientific knowledge of the time; it would be structured in an articulate and complex way and would influence individuals through levers, beams, and various devices. It would also be responsible for visions, stimulations, and various bodily sensations.

Tausk claims that the influencing machine represents the projection of the genital organs of the human body. The stimuli coming from such organs are perceived as something threatening and unfamiliar—erection, for instance—that are out of the ego's control. The excitement deriving from them is felt as being outlandish and therefore menacing and is then projected into the machine, which thus takes on a threatening and alien aspect. However, the influencing machine can also represent a projection of the whole body, meant as a pregenital body or even as a nongenital body. The entire body and the sensations deriving from it are perceived as something the ego cannot control and are therefore projected outside the individual and attributed to the machine.

From an evolutionary moment onward, a swift technological development will start that, through exteriorization processes of a series of functions and operational programs, will lead to the ever-increasing liberation of time, which will then become spare time. The possibility to exteriorize the motor brain into tools will pave the way to a lengthy process toward the realization of machines and, later on, to the exteriorization of memory and of logic-mathematical thought (symbolic thought). However, while tools are the material prolongation of an organ, the effectiveness of which is thus increased, the machine is a more or less complex system built by people in order to carry out various operations through the use of some form of energy. Scientific discoveries themselves always need an instrument to be realized and made applicable. Later on, we will dwell particularly on the computer, which allows humans extraordinary calculation skills. Also, these machines belong to those phenomena of the externalization of human mental faculties, which developed through a long and complex evolutionary process that began with the invention of the abacus as an externalization of calculation faculties and constitutes the base for the realization of new writing techniques, immense electronic memories, audio-visual systems, communicational cyberspaces,[6] and so forth. Every time people provide themselves with new artificial organs, whether they act as sensory detectors or as performing machines, they integrate into their system another part of the world and must deal, also emotionally, with the consequent change. Regarding this topic, we would like to underline that the more powerful the machine is, the more outlandish and alien it appears, and all the more so it lends itself to being the target of projections: The more powerful it is, the more frightening.

From such an evolutionary process, feelings seem to be left out if we do not consider that they too are exteriorized all the same through the mechanism of the projection onto people and objects.

We will now examine how such projections manifest themselves, for instance, not only in our patients, but also in the life of clinically sane individuals in their fantastic relation with machines.

FANTASIES OF OMNIPOTENCE, COMPUTERPHILIA, AND COMPUTERPHOBIA

The calculator-machine, as we know, is almost always seen as a mechanism capable of logical operations but, in any case, uncannily devoid of emotions and restraint. This particular characteristic easily turns it into a persecutory or protective object, as the expression of the other face of the same fantasy, and is therefore highly threatening because it arouses the fear that it might escape rational control, as if having feelings were in itself a warranty for goodness. In order to refute this assumption, we must draw the reader's attention to three robotics rules invented by Asimov in his sci-fi novel *I, Robot* (1950), which strictly forbid automata to commit acts that might be harmful to people: Robots are therefore subjected to a sort of cybernetics taboo. Its features make the machine alien on the one hand, but disquietingly similar to us on the other—a replica. In fact, both the idea that suddenly the robot could come alive like a golem[7] and the fear that people might lose their feelings and be regulated by a plain mechanism, that is, turn out to be cold machines or automata, is uncanny.

In our view, however, it is not just the lack of emotions that represents the difference between calculator-machine (artificial machine) and human (natural machine), but also the radically different way of treating symbols and therefore the possession or nonpossession of symbolic thought. Furthermore, machines have no or very little tolerance for contradictions, uncertainties, or ambiguity; they have no initiative, common sense, or opinions. Finally, they do not have any intentionality or self-organizational skills. Our brain, unlike other machines, uses processes that modify the brain itself: The mind is a complex system.

Machines, as we said, are unable to understand the meaning of the symbols they manipulate while people, conversely, by understanding their meaning, can operate with the instrument of thought; they possess, therefore, a "sixth-sense organ": conscience. Conscience is a nonspecialized sense, a sort of universal processing and perceptive faculty. Moreover, people are able to free themselves of the testimony of senses through developing representations and logical thinking and can operate some sort of mental experiments (*gedankenexperimente*) as a test for the subsequent getting into action. Riedl (1988) rightly notices that the advantage consists of the fact that instead of jeopardizing one's life, people can put at risk only a mental experiment; the assumption may die instead of who formulated it.

But now let us get back to the texts. In the article by Freud "The Uncanny" (1919/n.d.-c), we come across Olimpia Spallanzani's daughter, "a mysteriously laconic and still doll"; unmistakably a sign of a narcissistic vocation, she is nothing but an automaton. The fact that Nathaniel, the main character in Hoffman's short story, falls for her shows us the charm that a machine may exercise, all the more so when it has feminine features.

It is our opinion that one of the attractions some programs simulating human beings have, at least at the start and for little experienced people, is the one about being able to pretend to posses the capacity to manipulate verbal symbols, to have some sort of linguistic behavior from which the presence of a mental activity may be inferred though only testified by the capacity to communicate by writing on a screen. Actually, thought is a peculiar capacity of the human being, which, as a matter of fact, the machine does not yet possess; it does not possess an apparatus to think thoughts because it is unable to understand the meaning of words it uses, though it is able to manipulate them in a syntactically correct way (see Searle, 1981). Already, Turing in 1948 wrote that possessing a human (so to say) cortex would be virtually useless if no attempt were made to organize it.

Simulation in machines, even of the plain human exterior aspect, increases the interlocutor's disorientation. That is the reason why a human being's exact copy, though artificial, capable of imitating all types of behavior and not just the linguistic ones, would seriously embarrass us in case we had to decide, for instance, whether or not to assign it the capacity to think and to suffer

or experience any other kind of feeling, that is, to be a person. The fact is that we must consider ourselves content with indirect signs, the same ones we use when dealing with other people, as we do not yet have at our disposal any direct and error-proof heuristic that might reveal to us the existence or the nonexistence of consciousness, or rather intentionality as one would say nowadays, provided we were able to define it in an exact way.

CONCLUSION: MACHINE AND PEOPLE

At this point we are faced with the troubling issue of thinking machines; upon it we would like to dwell, though very briefly. We are about to approach the subject in a rather vague fashion in order to talk of the problems facing analysts when the possibility arises of comparing, if not even defining, the human or its mind as a machine—a mechanism—though of a very particular kind.

However, saying that the brain is a calculator is not like saying that a person can be likened to a machine because it all depends on what we mean by machine. We would like to point out how Varela speaks of a person as an "ontologic machine," Dawkins as (genetic) "machines of survival," Maturana and Varela as living beings and therefore humans as being self-poietic machines, and so forth. Thus, they are convinced that such definition does not belittle humans' dignity but, on the contrary, opens up new studying opportunities, not only regarding the body as an ontological machine, but also the mind and brain: the body-mind unity.

We must not then prejudicially be scared off by such an eventuality if first we do not provide a definition of the word *machine* that can be acceptable also to psychoanalysts.

Even Freud in a letter to Fliess in 1895 wrote (Masson, 1985)

Now listen to this. During an industrious night last week, when I was suffering from that degree of pain which brings about the optimal condition for my mental activities, the barriers suddenly lifted, the veils dropped, and everything became transparent—from the details of the neuroses to the determinants of consciousness. Everything seemed to fall into place, the cogs meshed, I had the impression that the thing now really was a machine that shortly would function on its own. (p. 146)

Here, by "machine" Freud meant a system made up of well-identifiable parts and with a precise and predictable functioning, still within the limits of what is possible, which could be studied through concepts drawn from natural sciences.

Surely we can date back to Descartes the idea of describing the body as a machine (*res extensa*), at least in its more modern conceptualization. Later on, early AI scholars wondered about the possibility of finding intelligent behavior, or even a mind, in machines or calculators. Today we may explore the idea that mind is a machine, though of a very particular type. Although we do not believe that the brain is a calculator, we may not only utilize the calculator to simulate parts of the brain, but we may assume, at least in principle, the possibility of building an artifact endowed with conscience, as Edelman (1992) claims. Then, whether or not we are able to carry out such a project with the technologies currently available is quite another matter.

Machines make us think of predictable and precise systems provided with mechanisms and operating processes that are easily individuated and, moreover, studied through natural laws, especially physics. Now, human beings are not mechanical because they are not simple systems, but complex ones that present unpredictable behaviors and are capable of learning and adapting and so forth.

A remarkable significance along this scientific route has been taken on by the Turing test, which, invented by an outstanding English mathematician, is a procedure to test any given machine capable of manipulating fully developed symbols in order to decide whether or not it has an intelligent kind of behavior, if not a mind. In brief, the inventor would set into communication a man and a calculator, ruling out any possibility of using eyesight, through a keyboard and a printing machine with which questions could be sent and answers received. One has to be able to find out whether the interlocutor is a man or a machine. An endless number of articles have been written both in favor and against this original way of testing machines, which its inventor oddly called The Imitation Game; we would like to add in a Gaddini sort of way that it is imitation *in order to be*.

We would like to specify here that the test would need a significantly long time of execution because it is easy to deceit the interlocutor in a short amount of time and yet so far no simulation program on computers has ever overcome the Turing test.

At this point, we have to say something regarding the issue of consciousness and the possibility of its implementation onto the machine, referring our readers to other texts for an in-depth study on the subject.

For instance, if we take into account what Edelman (1992) claims, we see that he distinguishes between two types of conscience: primary conscience and higher order consciousness, that is, the conscience of being conscious. It is important to remember that also Edelman claims that conscience is a function emerging from the bottom-up self-organization of the neural network. He likens primary conscience to a sort of remembered present resulting from processes of self-categorization of the brain obtained by matching past perceptive categorizations that originate in the thalamus-cortical system with systems of value coming from the brain stem and limbic system connected by means of reentrant rings. Instead, the higher order consciousness is possible thanks to symbolic memory and is closely connected to language in its phonological, semantical, and syntactical aspects. We would like to remind the reader that Freud, who defines conscience as an "organ of sense for the perception of psychic qualities," closely connected mental contents becoming conscious to the possibility of being verbally expressed, that is, to language. Therefore, conscious representation consists, according to Freud, of the representation of an (unconscious) thing plus word representation.

If we now move on to the possibility of implementing conscience into machines, as part of the system's awareness, we may use, for instance, Trautteur's (1987) proposal, which, also by drawing upon Jaynes' ideas (1976, 1995), hypothesizes an algorithm that might realize, at least theoretically, a functional, but not analogical, simulation of the nervous system.

First of all, Trautteur views algorithms as physical systems, as effective procedures located where their symbols are, and therefore deemed as material processes as well as mental processes whenever they are performing; they, as widespread and active entities, belong then both to *res cogitans* and to *res extensa* (Trautteur, 1997). He takes into consideration the realization of a system that includes three identical systems that are distinguishable according to their differentiated activities. There would then be a speaker, a listener, and a bystander injected at a later moment into the speaker, able to witness and record what is happening and to recursively and dynamically recall itself. In this sense, there would be a bystander, internalized by now, whose behavior would be the same, or better isomorphic, as the description from the outside. Thus, there would take place some sort of doubling of identity that reiterates itself in the following calls of the system, which will later be recorded in some stack.[8] The first call would have the character of an analyzer and the second would constitute the internal bystander: interiority. The realization of

this "one and trine" algorithm would be able to carry out in the machine something very similar to awareness because it is able, for example, to answer questions of a personal type.

However, there would still be left to specify whether the machine is able to understand the meanings of the symbols it manipulates, as Searle (1981) and others highlight, or it is limited to the display of linguistic behavior, which is only externally meaningful. Searle's criticism, expressed in the experiment of the Chinese chamber,[9] consists of underlining that the kind of syntax calculator programs have is not sufficient to determine semantics, which is what characterizes human minds. The human mind is not a plain computational mind, as cognitivism would state, which manipulates symbols only in an algorithmic fashion, but it does it also in a semantic way. In any case, this kind of criticism is, in its turn, criticized because of the doubt about the existence of an intrinsic meaning.

A completely different possibility would be to train a neural network by means of self-learning and at a certain point be able to verify, once reaching the critical mass in the complex system, the possibility that this machine is able to talk to us about itself and therefore testify to the emerging of intentionality. Regarding this alternative, hypotheses might be helpful and perhaps even more interesting for analysts, as the ones by Edelman (1976) who, starting from TNGS, indicates to us how it is possible from neurons, ascending through the production of reentrant maps, categorizations, recategorizations, and so forth, to get to the birth of a primary conscience and then, through semantic self-elevation with the advent of language, to the appearance of a higher order consciousness. These models, at least in principle, can be implemented on an evolved parallelism computer: Then a simulation can be realized. However, there still remains the fact that neural-network learning always needs a human operator who establishes at least the initial instructions in order to carry out the learning rules; that is, it is not based, as in brain development, on selection or on an autonomous neural Darwinism.

For the time being, we may say that a thinking machine does not yet exist and perhaps it never will, if by mental activity and its product, thought, we mean what a man's mind is able to elaborate. The fact is, however, that there can be a series of activities that can be processed by a machine or attributed to it by our activity, for instance, by our fantasy. The human mind is able to avail itself of the calculator and of machines in general, as a prolongation, prothesis, or simple tool for an exteriorized function of itself. Such possibility may allow us to build worlds that mirror the mind's fantasies to then make them independent realities to be shared with others, as before was done only with films and books. However, while cinema is only passively enjoyed, virtual reality and cyberspace are modifiable by the operator, can be shared with others, and are navigable. Furthermore, one experiences, through virtual realities, real sensations, though here there is the risk that sensory experiences of assimilation and extension of the self may turn into sensual experiences mediated by an erotization of the process. Part of the human mental activity can be implemented onto the machine and one can make it run: That means that one can follow its functioning and modify it. One of the dangers might be to utilize all this in a magically and omnipotently defensive way in order to reduce the surrounding environment, that is, external reality, to being a plain extension of the self at the magical service of the self with the intention of avoiding persecutory anxieties that would entail recognizing the other from the self.

However, for analysts, maybe, it is not so interesting to establish whether machines have a mind as to establish whether the mind is a machine. The problem, then, is not just the technical realization of building a conscious and intelligent machine, but succeeding in defining, in a way that can be

shared, what intelligence is, what consciousness is, and, we would add, the strategies to diagnose the entities that possess them through definite heuristics; it is essentially this that keeps us away from building an intelligent artificial system: the lack of an explicative theory about intelligent entities, and not the unrealizability of an artificial intentionality or the limits of silicon compared to carbon. After having done this, one should similarly move on to the definition of emotions and to the possibility of diagnosing them and simulating them on models of mental machines. The main problem is exactly having a good theory of consciousness, or at least an acceptable one.

Through consciousness we become aware of the phenomenal present. We can state, as we have already said, that mental processes take place in parallel, or rather we can say that conscious processes are serial and the unconscious ones, instead, are parallel. Concerning this aspect, Johnson-Laird (1988) lists three types of machines: Cartesian machines that are incapable of using symbols and being self-aware, Craikian automata that are capable of building symbolic models of the world and basic awareness, and finally machines that possess the recursive capacity of including models within models, of having a model of their own operating system, and of applying the one to the other; these systems would also be self-reflective and intentional. However, all this would still be insufficient to make sure that such a machine is provided with consciousness, like the human one. For the time being, a machine supplied with conscience does not exist, but this does not mean that it will be possible when our technology will be more refined.

The decisive fact that still blocks us is that we do not possess a sure heuristics that can help us claim whether or not a system has any consciousness, and therefore even if there were a machine with consciousness we would not be able to easily demonstrate it. For this reason, perhaps we may say, parodying Dennett (1978), that in the meantime it is better to avoid kicking calculators—they might kick us back.

Therefore, the thinking machine, that is, the calculator, can be experienced also in a persecutory way, like a Tauskian influencing machine that can take our powers away from us and take them on itself, thus making us totally helpless and subjected to it. We then move from a tolerant disparagement of the calculator to a really delusional "computerphobia," whereas "computerphilia" is the other side of the coin. We cannot forget that also in this case we must consider the role played by sexuality and sexual organs in order to retrace an interpretative route. Tausk (1919/1933) also writes, *"Indeed, the machines produced by man's ingenuity and created in the image of man are unconscious projections of man's bodily structure. Man's ingenuity seems to be unable to free itself from its relation to the unconscious"* (p. 555).

Furthermore, he writes,

The evolution by distortion of the human apparatus into a machine is a projection that corresponds to the development of the pathological process which converts the ego into a diffuse sexual being, or—expressed in the language of the genital period—into a genital, a machine independent of the aims of the ego and subordinated to a foreign will. It is no longer subordinated to the will of the ego, but dominates it. Here, too, we are reminded of the astonishment of boys when they become aware for the first time of erection. And the fact that the erection is shortly conceived as an exceptional and mysterious feat, supports the assumption that erection is felt to be a thing independent of the ego, a part of the outer world not completely mastered. (p. 556)

Thus, as erection can be perceived by the child as an autonomous and uncontrollable process, but powerful and magic, also the machine, onto which the genital projection has been made, may escape, as mind itself, the control of the mind: The endogenous excitation is then perceived as being aroused from the outside, some sort of real seductive suggestion which, being no longer controllable, becomes persecutory.

After all, Freud reminds us how the gods inherited just from the genitalia their divine functions of omnipotence and omniscience.

We may here try to hypothesize the following process: Initially humans, through technology, externalized cortical functions by building different kinds of tools, among which, the calculator. This technical process is accompanied by a fantastical psychical activity through which they project, onto the structure of the machine, genitals and the relative functions that still enjoy divine worship as the legacy of animism and the fantasy of realizing the omnipotence of thought, which is conveyed to all the new activities learned by the same humans, including the capacity of processing by means of calculators. It seems to us that thinking machines exercise great seductive power and that one of the reasons for this fascination consists of an idealization of their capacity of processing, which gives the illusion, by manipulating and controlling them, of being able to magically realize, even though only through their help, the ancient dream of omniscience through the omnicomprehensiveness of information archives, of mastering multiplicity, and of the computational and logic omnipotence of thought. We have to highlight, here, the distinction that must be taken into account between the magical use of magic thought and the magical use of logic thought: They are very similar but still there is a difference. The latter is more treacherous, and therefore more dangerous, because it can more easily be mistaken for real scientific thinking while, instead, it does nothing but convey a very primitive animistic thought with defensive purposes.

With the passing of time, when the idealization of machines began to fade away because people realized it couldn't keep the promise about an impossible omnipotence, people repossessed the divine part, which is now summed up by pure mental activity, and the rest, that is, the technical instrument calculator or genital organ, falls prey to contempt, thus paving the way to persecutory delusions. Only a few "madmen" remain slave of the machine, which, as the Tauskian one, is the menacing heir of the power of genitalia by now perceived as being prey only to the instinctual component no longer restrained by reason. This means that problems arise when there is a splitting of the rational parts from the instinctual ones and a drive de-fusion with the consequent freeing of a destructive element that rebels against the individual along the lines of the dynamics of the persecutory type. It is the despised rest, split and projected, that unleashes persecutory anxieties, only at times denied and concealed with a rationalized and reassuring depreciation of the machine-persecutor. The fact is that the invention and the use of the machine gives the illusion of a greater control over one's emotional life: that is, avoiding the recognition of the other and the encounter with separation anxieties by actively generating confusion between the inside and outside and between subject and object through the narcissistic relation with a mechanized object. Delusion, as well as extreme technological competence, obeys the same need about controlling the huge, and therefore feared, power of the primary object. This is the reason why the delusion of the paranoid person represents the extreme defensive attempt to prevent the intrusion of the object into one's mind. Moreover, we have to notice that the calculator can become, in somebody's fantasy, either a fetish, a symbolic substitute for the maternal penis that might help to deny castration anxieties or, worse, an autistic object that helps protect against unthinkable anxieties of fragmentation and separation and their tragic consequences. In actual fact, even the calculator is not a real thinking machine, but at most is a machine devoid of any initiative and creativity and that can only be programmed by people, as already Lady Lovelace in the 19th century had understood. Therefore, though presently things are already changing and some neural networks are able to show some sort

of unpredictable behavior (very limited, actually), the calculator is able to process or think only the thought the programmer projects into it, just the way it happens with delusion of influence. The fact that many fear the calculator makes people demential (as well as an excessive masturbation), because it carries out operations that should be accomplished by man who in his turn is impoverished every time he uses such proxy, is an idea that finds its reasons only within persecutory fantasies about psychophysical harm. In actual fact, the calculator takes on the task of performing mainly those long, repetitive, and monotonous calculations that would waste our time and, by freeing ourselves of this burden, it allows us to deal with more creative things: obviously only as long and as far as we are capable of it.

Threats coming from machines (computers) therefore do not derive from their inhumanity; on the contrary, they are the product of the far too human tendency, which we have inserted into machines, mostly in those built by fantasy, and which these machines, when they are capable of it, provide on their part to develop and potentiate. The fact is that the clash is not between human and machine, but between human and human or between humans and their inner world.

REFERENCES

Asimov, I. (1950). *I, robot.* Boston: Gnome Press.

Basch-Kahre, E. (1985). Patterns of thinking. *International Journal of Psychoanalysis, 66*(4), 455-470.

Bruer, J., & Freud, S. (1895). *Studies on hysteria.* SE 2.

Bucci, W. (1997). *Psychoanalysis and cognitive science.* New York: Guilford Press.

Dennett, D. C. (1978). *Brainstorms.* Cambridge, MA: MIT Press/Bradford Books.

Edelman, G. M. (1992). *Bright air, brilliant fire: On the matter of the mind.* London: Penguin Group.

Erdelyi, M. H. (1985). *Psychoanalysis: Freud's cognitive psychology.* New York: W. H. Freeman & Company.

Fodor, J. A. (1983). *The modularity of mind.* Cambridge, MA: *MIT Press.*

Freud, S. (n.d.-a). Studies on hysteria. In J. Strachey (Ed. & Trans.), *The standard edition of the complete psychological works of Sigmund Freud* (Vol. 2). London: Hogarth Press. (Original work published 1893-1895)

Freud, S. (n.d.-b). Project for a scientific psychology. In J. Strachey (Ed. & Trans.), *The standard edition of the complete psychological works of Sigmund Freud* (Vol. 1, pp. 295-391). London: Hogarth Press. (Original work published 1895)

Freud, S. (n.d.-c). The "uncanny." In J. Strachey (Ed. & Trans.), *The standard edition of the complete psychological works of Sigmund Freud* (Vol. 17, pp. 217-256). London: Hogarth Press. (Original work published 1919)

Gaddini, E. (1992). On imitation. In Limentani (Ed.), *A psychoanalytic theory of infantile experience.* London: Routledge. (Original work published 1969)

Gaddini, E. (1989). Fenomeni PSI e processo creativo. In *Scritti.* Milan: Cortina. (Original work published 1969)

Galatzer-Levy, R. (1988). On working through: A model from artificial intelligence. *Journal of the American Psychoanalytic Association, 38*(1), 125-151.

Greenberg, J. R., & Mitchell, S. A. (1983). *Object relations in psychoanalytic theory.* Cambridge, MA: Harvard University Press.

Jaynes, J. (1976). *The origin of consciousness in the breakdown of bicameral mind.* New York: Houghton Mifflin.

Jaynes, J. (1995). The diachronicity of consciousness. In G. Trautteur (Ed.), *Consciousness: Distinction and reflection.* Napoli, Italy: Bibliopolis.

Masson, J. M. (Ed.). (1985). *The complete letters of Sigmund Freud to Wilhelm Fliess 1887-1904.* Cambridge, MA: Belknap.

Minsky, M. (1985). *The society of mind.* New York: Simon & Schuster.

Searle, J. R. (1980). Minds, brains, and programs. *Behavioural and Brain Sciences, 3,* 417-424.

Tausk, V. (1933). On the origin of the "influencing machine" in schizophrenia. *Psychoanalytic Quarterly, 2,* 519-556. (Original work published 1919)

Trautteur, G. (1987, February). *Intelligenza umana e intelligenza artificiale.* Paper presented at Centro Culturale San Carlo of Milan.

Trautteur, G. (1997-1998). Distinzione e riflessione. *ATQUE, 16,* 127-141.

Turing, A. M. (1964). *Minds and machines.* Englewood Cliffs, NJ: Prentice Hall. (Original work published 1950)

Turkle, S. (1988). Artificial intelligence and psychoanalysis: A new alliance. *Daedalus, 117*(1), 241-268.

von Neumann, J. (1958). *The computer and the brain.* London: Yale University Press.

Wisdom, J. O. (1961). A methodological approach to the problem of hysteria. *International Journal of Psychoanalysis, 42,* 224-237.

ENDNOTES

[1] Tausk's paper was published, oddly enough, in the same year, 1919, in which Freud published "The Uncanny," about which we will later talk.

[2] By the name Turing machine, it is usually meant the conception of a machine that is abstract but that can actually be realized.

[3] Programs like Weizenbaum's ELIZA, which in its DOCTOR section simulates a Rogersian psychotherapist, simulate only the initial and final parts of human behavior and therefore, on par with the Turing test, treat the mind as if it were a black box.

[4] Backpropagation is a technique of learning by or training of neural networks obtained through correcting weights on the connections along an antidromic route.

[5] Simulated annealing is a technique for the training of neural networks consisting of simulating the process through which, in metallurgy, metals are tempered by means of heating and cooling, or rather freezing, in order to free them of any impurities.

[6] Cyberspace is a word coined by the sci-fi author William Gibson. It indicates a new parallel universe created by global networks of communication via computers.

[7] The Golem is a legendary figure created by Rabbi Löw from Prague.

[8] A stack is a type of data structure ordered according to the L.I.F.O. (last in first out) arrangement (set of rules); that is, the last element enters the structure and the first one exits it.

[9] The Chinese chamber experiment allows us to swiftly manipulate formal symbols, Chinese characters, and to answer incoming questions in Chinese by using only the instructions and rules written in our language, but without us ever understanding the meaning of what we are being asked or of what we are answering, still in Chinese; the entire operation is carried out correctly from a grammatical and syntactical point of view.

Chapter V
Machines Paying Attention

John G. Taylor
King's College, UK

ABSTRACT

Attention is analyzed as the superior control system in the brain from an engineering point of view, with support for this from the way attention is presently being understood by brain science. Such an engineering-control framework allows an understanding of how the complex networks observed in the brain during various cognitive tasks can begin to be functionally decomposed. A machine version of such an attention control system is then discussed and extended to allow for goals and their reward values also to be encoded in the attention machine. The manner in which emotion may then begin to be imbued in the machine is briefly discussed and how even some glimpse of consciousness may then arise.

INTRODUCTION

The brain, itself a complex system, is able to be very effective in processing complex environments in a manner unmatched yet by the powers of any so-called intelligent machine. Attention is now being increasingly recognized as a crucial feature of the powerful abilities shown in such human information processing. Without attention being paid, serious errors may occur, accidents will more often happen, and effective decisions are impossible to achieve. It is therefore natural to probe this faculty of attention possessed by the brain further in order to understand how these complexities, especially of the human brain and how it is so efficiently processing complex environments, are handled. In this way it might be possible to create a new breed of machines, those possessing attention in such a way as to even enable a level of real intelligence to be included.

It is unclear how to develop intelligence along human lines. Present machine intelligence is increasingly effective in pattern processing and recognition, in classification, and in prediction, across a range of task domains. However, the neural or other architectures needed to create a machine possessing true cognitive powers, those of reasoning, thinking, and even creativity, are still unknown. Our human ability to reason, possessed also at some level, as it is now being recognized, by an increasing number of animals, has not yet been understood, nor has the basis of that most subtle cognitive feat of all, that of being conscious. However, all of these faculties are accompanied by the power of focused attention and our ability to move it at will. Moreover, it is now being realized that more specifically attention plays an important role in emphasizing some internal stimulus representations while inhibiting others. Even further, attention is being recognized as at the basis of our ability to change things in our minds, to transform them into new activities, or delete them altogether. Such processes appear as the basic ones in thinking. Thus, attention should be regarded as an important faculty to include in machines if we wish them to begin to be truly intelligent in a human-like manner, and also to begin to handle the complexity of the external (and internal) world.

To this end, the chapter begins an investigation of attention in order to uncover its secrets, especially how it can handle complexity but at the same time how it could support higher order cognitive processing. We start with a description of attention as it is now being increasingly better understood through various investigations in brain science. We then turn to a high-level description of attention in engineering-control terms. In this way, the complex networks observed in the brain during the carrying out of various cognitive tasks under attention control can begin to be understood in terms of their various functional decompositions. How attention processing can be created in a machine is then discussed and extended to allow for goals and their reward values also to be encoded in such a machine. The manner in which emotion may then begin to be imbued in the machine is briefly discussed and how even some glimpse of consciousness may then arise.

BACKGROUND ON ATTENTION

The Control Nature of Attention

It is now accepted that attention involves a process of selection of part of a scene for analysis, thereby acting as a filter on the input. This is especially important for complex scenes with many distracters. This is now recognized as being achieved in the brain by attention through the process of amplification to the attended input and inhibition of distracting inputs. These processes occur in various sensory and motor cortical regions in the brain; they can also be observed in higher regions (such as the temporal lobe face and object maps in the fusiform gyrus, or goal representations in the prefrontal cortex). The temporal dynamics of such amplification signals have been observed in action (Mehta, Ulbert, & Schroeder, 2000). Furthermore, there are regions of the brain that have now been accepted as generating the control signals that create these amplificatory or inhibitory signals that are to be sent to the regions mentioned earlier. These control regions are sited in the parietal and prefrontal cortices. A parietal or prefrontal network for shifting attention has been detected by a PET study in an attention movement paradigm (Corbetta & Shulman, 2002). The modulation of cells in area V4 by attention to their receptive fields has been observed (McAdams & Maunsell, 1999).

Thus overall, attention movement involves brain sites with two different functions.

1.   Amplification or decrease of sensory input or motor output (in sensory and motor cortical regions)
2.   Creation of control signals to achieve the relevant control signal. This creation is now recognized as occurring in the parietal and prefrontal cortex.

As concluded by Kastner and Ungerleider (2001, p. 1263; see also Kastner & Ungerleider,

2000), "Attention-related activity in frontal and parietal areas does not reflect attentional modulation of visually evoked responses, but rather the attentional operations themselves."

Given this clear control function that attention performs, it is to be expected that sites with more specific functions will be expected to be observed in the brain (goals, monitors or error assessors, feedback signals, control signal generators). In order to bring some order to the increasing number of brain sites being observed as relevant in attention control, it was proposed in 2000 to use the engineering-control approach for attention (J. G. Taylor, 2000), which has been developed more fully since then (J. G. Taylor, 2002a, 2002b, 2003a, 2003b, 2003c).

Models of Attention

There are already various models of attention that have been studied in the recent past, ranging from those of a descriptive form, such as the influential "biased competition" model of attention (Desimone & Duncan, 1995) to the more detailed neural-network-based models involving large-scale simulations, such as those of Deco and Rolls (2005) or of Mozer and Sitton (1998). These approaches to attention, developed by an increasing number of research groups (Deco & Rolls; Mozer & Sitton; Hamker, Grossberg, & Raizada; for reviews and earlier references see J. G. Taylor, Nobre, & Shapiro, 2006), have been effective in showing how experimental data from various types of paradigms can be fitted together, especially those involving changes in the receptive field size of posterior cortical neurons or behavioral responses in search tasks. In spite of this level of success, none of these models have been developed explicitly to explore the manner in which attention can function so as to support higher order cognitive processes as involved in rehearsal or maintenance, the substitution of one image by another, the retrieval of past memories, the transformation of images on working memory

(WM) into new images achieving certain goals, and even to help understand models of thinking and reasoning involving internal motor models under the control of attention. It is these aspects of attention that are crucial to understand and model in order to create an attention framework for intelligence machines.

More generally it is to be noted that the neural models of attention referred to above have not had a clear overarching functional model guiding their construction. If we consider the recent results on attention of brain imaging experiments mentioned above (Corbetta & Shulman, 2002; Corbetta, Tansy, Stanley, Astafiev, Snyder, & Shulman, 2005; Kanwisher & Wojciulik, 2000) then we find that the language of engineering-control theory applies very effectively and flexibly to help understand the complex-looking network of modules observed through brain imaging as involved in attention effects.

In more detail, the experiments cited in the earlier subsection show without doubt that there are regions in the parietal lobe and prefrontal cortex that send out a signal independent of the stimulus input itself, but only depending on the nature of the attention task. Thus, there is evidence for this prefrontal and parietal brain component as generating the necessary attention control signal that is observed to be sent to posterior sensory sites, or to motor control sites in the case of motor control (Binkofski et al., 2002; Mehta et al., 2000; Rushworth, Ellison, & Walsh, 2001). Moreover, this control system can be fractionated into an inverse model controller (IMC) and a goal-holding site. The latter is well supported by many experiments, both using brain imaging as well as from clear behavioral deficits, in which it is noted that the relevant prefrontal sites (in the lateral prefrontal cortex) are functioning as goal sites, holding desired goal states; prefrontal deficits from damage to such sites is well known in terms of loss of power in decision making and increased perseverance in light of contrary information. The attention control signal, guided by the goal signal, thus acts so as to filter out activity of the attended stimulus, which is then to be employed in these higher level cognitive and intelligent processes occurring in higher level cortices.

The presence of a goals module, an attention movement control generator (an IMC module in the language of control theory), and a "plant" being controlled (as are posterior cortical regions) already indicates the relevance of ballistic control ideas to attention. However, engineering-control approaches to complex tasks, as well as observations and modeling in motor control, support the extension of this simplest ballistic control system approach to attention to a more sophisticated one, in which there is also involvement of a corollary discharge, or efference copy, of the signal of attention movement from the IMC. There is considerable support for the existence of a forward model, using a copy of the motor control signal, for motor control in the brain (Desmurget, Epstein, Turner, Prablanc, Alexander, & Grafton, 1999; Desmurget & Grafton, 2000; Miall & Wolpert, 1996; Wolpert & Ghahramani, 2000). An internal model and associated attention copy signal was proposed in J. G. Taylor (2000) and associated support obtained for it more recently as will be discussed shortly. This attention copy enables the speedup of error correction as well as other features, as the references cited indicate clearly. This is the basis of the CODAM model (corollary discharge of attention movement) of J. G. Taylor (2000, 2002a, 2002b, 2003a, 2003b, 2003c, 2004, 2005, 2006). The extension by addition of an attention copy signal leads to the expectation of further components able to use this rapid attention copy signal to make attention movement faster and with reduced error, as well as providing a way to support attention learning by means of the associated forward model and errors thereby produced in prediction. This extended control model for attention implies the existence of an overall executive control system for attention that is complex, involving both the parietal lobes as well as various components of the prefrontal cortex. It also avoids the problems of earlier suggestions of Feinberg (1978) and Frith (1992) that schizophrenia and other disturbances of thought were purely based on deficits in the brain's internal motor control models; this has been extended to suggested deficits mainly in the attention control circuitry of the brain (J. G. Taylor, 2002a, 2002b, 2003, 2006). This and related questions are presently being investigated by brain imaging methods.

MACHINES WITH ATTENTION

In order to build an effective attention machine, it is necessary to consider the tools to be used to achieve this. This can be done by developing more fully the CODAM model mentioned earlier and discussing how it can best be implemented for machine use in which executive or cognitive functions are made more explicit.

As already emphasized, the engineering-control approach to attention employed here was already developed in the CODAM model in J. G. Taylor (2000; see also J. G. Taylor, 2002a, 2002b; J. G. Taylor & Fragopanagos, 2005) and used in J. G. Taylor and Rogers (2002) to simulate the Posner benefit effect in vision (where attention focused on a target stimulus leads to faster response, the Posner benefit, as compared to if the focus of attention were elsewhere). The CODAM model was applied to the hard task of the attentional blink (AB; in which a subject tries to detect a target letter in a fast stream, say at 10 Hz, of such letters almost immediately after detecting a previously chosen letter, for example, with greatest difficulty for the second target 270 ms after the first) in Fragopanagos, Kockelkoren, and Taylor (2005), and more recently in numerous applications of CODAM to working-memory tasks (J. G. Taylor, Fragopanagos, & Korsten, 2006) as well as to help understand results observed by brain imaging of paradigms involving emotion and cognition in interaction (J. G. Taylor & Fragopanagos, 2005).

CODAM uses the notion that the purpose of attention is to select out from the complexity of posterior cortical activities the stimulus activity for an attended stimulus so as to make this activity of use for higher level activities, such as thinking, reasoning, and remembering for later recall. Such a process requires short-term storage of this attended activity in order that it is accessible without having also to carry the activity associated with distracters in any later neural computations. Thus, we must consider the manner in which working memory enters into attention and in particular into a CODAM-type model.

Working Memory

There has been a considerable advance in understanding WM through the distributed concept of Baddeley (1986) now widely accepted after considerable justification through brain imaging experiments. Baddeley proposed that there are several lower level "slave" or buffer working-memory modules in various modalities that hold activity over several seconds for later use. Thus, there is a phonological store in audition for holding phonemes, a visuospatial sketch pad in vision for holding object shapes, and so on. At a higher level is an executive system, able to perform operations on the neural activity at lower levels in one or more of the various buffers. There has been considerable support from brain imaging and deficits studies for such a neural architecture in the brain.

Although working memory has traditionally been viewed as a distinct functionality mainly focused in the prefrontal cortex, recent evidence points to a more enlarged circuitry. The posterior and parietal cortices are found to be involved in WM tasks (D'Esposito, Postle, & Rypma, 2000; Fuster & Alexander, 1971; Passingham & Sakai, 2004; Petrides, 2000). Strikingly, these areas are

Figure 1. The architecture of the CODAM model of attention

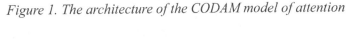
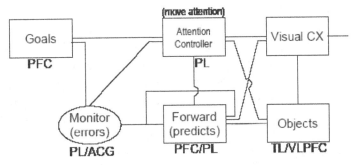

This model was mentioned in the text. It consists of input arriving at the visual cortex being sent to an object coding module (objects). Attention feedback from the IMC (attention controller) thereby amplifies the input and helps it attain the buffer working memory (forward model), which then allows the resulting buffered activity to be used in higher level processing. The attention controller is guided by the goals module. The forward model can send a signal to the error monitor so as to be compared with the desired state from the goals site. Any error causes increased attention feedback. This allows an explanation of specific timing features of the attentional blink.

very similar to those often found to be active in attentional tasks as described above. This suggests, as noted by Awh and Jonides (2001) and Awh, Jonides, and Reuter-Lorenz (1998), an overlap in functionality as well as localization of WM and attention. In addition, the attention boosting of off-line stimuli in working memory, rather than online stimuli present in the visual field, has been found to take place (Griffin & Nobre, 2003).

The original form of CODAM already possessed a buffer working-memory site to hold activity (for 1-2 seconds) that had been able to access it through attention amplification. The architecture of CODAM is shown in Figure 1, and a possible mathematical implementation of it is outlined in the appendix.

The CODAM model of Figure 1 contains a buffer working-memory site functioning exactly as expected: to hold activity only of that attended to and amplified sufficiently to access the buffer site. An aspect of this accession, and of allowing only the attended activity to access the WM site, was suggested (J. G. Taylor, 2000) as arising from the use of the attention copy signal to amplify only the attended stimulus representation and inhibiting activity of distracters; this was used as a crucial component in the more recent simulation of the attentional blink (Fragopanagos et al., 2005). Recent experimental data (Sergent, Baillet, & Dehaene, 2005) has supported this notion of the inhibition of the attention copy signal and distracter-based inputs to the WM buffer. Thus, we consider this aspect of attention, the existence of an attention copy signal, as an important component of attention.

A Formal Approach to Attention

The neural-based mathematical implementation of goal-biased attention feedback in the appendix may be too specialized for general application of the notion of attention. Not only is the formulation implemented in graded neurons, but it is also based on neurons themselves. Here a brief development

will be given of a more general definition of attention in a control framework.

Consider an information-processing machine M. The state of the external world W is represented in M by a state vector X. This vector will consist of a set of subvectors if M has a modular structure so that each subvector component of X will correspond to a representation of W as achieved in its module. In the brain, the modules form several hierarchies in the different modalities, leading to highest level representations as of objects (in vision or touch) and of tonal sequences (in audition). More generally, then, we can expect

$$X = U_n X(n), \qquad (1)$$

where X(n) is the component of X associated with the module labeled by n.

The action of attention as a filter is to be expressed as an operator A(g) acting on X:

$$X \rightarrow A(g)X, \qquad (2)$$

where g denotes a goal state biasing the projection of attention toward the components of X that are g-like. Thus, A(g) has a form like a projector along the space G in M of goals, represented by a set of individuals g. It is expected that G has state representations similar to those of X, although this is not essential. In the case of attention caused by the appearance of a salient stimulus in the external world (exogenous attention), it is expected that the related goal state would be directly related to the external stimulus. However, in the case of an internal (endogenous) goal, such identification may be incorrect, but even in the exogenous case, such as if a fire alarm sounds when you are in a building, the goal to get outside is created by the stimulus but is not at all related to it.

The nature of the operator A has not been defined above except for its general projection properties toward the goal states. However, these goals may be very complex in higher cognition and not directly related to object representations of the external world as contained in X. The filtered states as presented in equation (2) will be expected to depend on X in a roughly reductive manner, as given by A(g) having a support (in terms of what it focuses on) determined by g so that when g is a stimulus representation, then the action of A(g) on states with no g-like object present would be zero. Beyond that one can consider a generalization of the way that feedback to neurons in X are amplified or inhibited, as described in more detail in the appendix; that will not be considered further here.

The goal states g are expected to be related to the states of the world W. However, they also crucially involve internal structures of M, such as drives and rewards, which allow M to continue existing and become more efficient at obtaining its rewards from W. It is through the interaction with the world W that M can achieve this, so M must also have a set of responses {Act} that enable M to change the world state it is in so as to obtain a reward r(Act) from the world for an action Act made on it. Through this assumed structure of the world, we can introduce a utility function U and assume that M chooses actions so as to maximize U. This requires that M has set up (say, by genetic inheritance) an apparatus to estimate U and to maximize it.

Having set up a general framework for the system [M, {Act}, U, {r(Act)}, {X}; W], let us now return to the attention powers we wish to insert into the machine M, as introduced under equations (1) and (2). We regard the states X of M as sensory states, and the states Act as action states. The former provide a representation of W as obtained from all sensors that M is equipped with. The latter, the actions Act, provide representations of all actions that can be taken by M on the external states of the world. Then we can use attention to filter out extraneous representation components in either the sensory or action spaces (or both at once). Thus, there are two operators: A(g) acting on the sensory states of M, as in equation (2), and B(g) acting on the action states of M, as in

$$Act \rightarrow B(g)Act. \qquad (3)$$

We also note that it may be necessary to modify A(g) and B(g) to contain specifications of what actions are to be taken to achieve the assumed sensory goals g, or even replace them altogether by action goals. Thus, one can specify a goal as a cup of coffee, or as getting a cup of coffee in a specific way, or even, as in athletics, just making a movement of specific form such as a perfect golf swing. However, this extension can be prevented, as seems to occur in the brain, by use of sensory feedback from actions (especially by proprioception as used by the brain) so that only sensory specifications are needed for goals (with additional chunking to make automatic sequences of actions, so reducing the capacity needed to solve sequential goals).

Numerous extensions of the formal structure given by equations (1), (2), and (3) are needed to provide some sort of inner executive structure in M. These are the following.

a.   Which goals are used presently will depend on the associated rewards they are predicted to bring (by their associated utility U); those expecting to produce the greatest reward will be more likely to have attention focused on them. This bias by U can be written in terms of a competition as in

$$g(X) = argminU(X, g'), \qquad (4)$$

where $U(X, g')$ is the predicted reward form the environment X for the goal g'.

b.   Attention to actions is needed in order to avoid activation of a range of actions that might be inappropriate. This is obtained by use of the attention projector of equation (3) so as to reduce the level of action possibilities, where the error

$$|B(g)Act - Act(des)| \qquad (5)$$

can be used to refocus motor attention on the desired action Act(des) so as to ensure it is achieved.

c. So far, time has not been explicitly introduced. However, it is needed to enable a machine to run in real time. Time dependence enters by the introduction of a buffer site WM that is accessed by the attended state activity Act(g)X provided it is large enough. So, we can define a working-memory operator WMOper(g, X) as corresponding to the activation on the buffer site (being held over a longer period of time than would be the activity of X):

$$WM = WMOper(g, X)[Act(g)X]. \quad (6)$$

It is this further projected state that is used on cognitive activity.

d. A crucial component of executive function is a monitor or error assessor, which uses an attention copy of A(g) to assess the expected error between the goal state and the predicted goal state. This error is obtained by use of the attention copy and a suitable forward model FM(A(g)):

$$|g - FM(A(g))|. \quad (7)$$

The error level of equation (7) is to be used to increase the attention level output A(g); a simple constant increase of A(g) proportional to equation (7) would be suitable in case the mechanisms in M have a degree of linearity.

We have outlined above a general framework for machine attention beyond that based on coupled neural modules (as occurs in the brain). However, in order to move the attention forward in detail, especially for its executive functionality, we will need to return to the brain for guidance.

Executive Functionality

We now need to turn to further aspects of executive function in order to consider more clearly what components of intelligence we will concentrate on in attention machines.

There are numerous executive functions of interest, all involving the faculty of attention in one way or another, and arising in reasoning, thinking, and planning. These include the following.

1. Encoding, storage, and retrieval of memories in the hippocampus (HC) and related areas
2. Rehearsal of desired inputs in working memory
3. Comparison of goals with new posterior activity
4. Transformation of buffered material into a new, goal-directed form (such as spatial rotation of an image held in the mind)
5. Inhibition of prepotent responses (Houde & Tzourio-Mazayer, 2003)
6. The development of forward maps of attention in both sensory and motor modalities so that possible consequences of attended actions on the world can be imagined and used in reasoning and planning
7. Determination of the value of elements of sequences of sensory-motor states as they are being activated in forward model recurrence
8. Learning of automatic sequences (chunks) so as to speed up the cognitive process

The rehearsal, transformation, inhibition, and retrieval processes are those that can be carried out already by a CODAM model (Fragopanagos et al., 2005; Korsten et al., 2006; J. G. Taylor, 1999; with an additional hippocampus for encoding and retrieval). CODAM can be used to set up a goal, such as the transformed state of the buffered image or its preserved level of activity on the buffer, and transform what is presently on the buffer by the inverse attention controller into the desired goal state. Such transformations arise by use of the monitor in CODAM to enable the original image to be transformed or preserved under an attention feedback signal, generated by an error signal from the monitor and returning to the inverse model generating the attention movement control signal so as to modify (or preserve) attention and hence what is changed (or held) in the buffer for later report or even use as a goal. Longer term storage of material for much later use would proceed in the hippocampus under attention control. The comparison process involves yet again the monitor of CODAM.

The use of forward models mentioned in equation (6) allows for careful planning of actions and the realization and possible valuation of the consequences. This can be done with no actions on the external world, but purely by virtual processes, so corresponding to reasoning. Multiple recurrences through forward models and associated inverse model controllers allow prediction of the consequences of several further action steps.

Automatic processing is created by sequence learning in the frontal cortex, using FCX $\rightarrow$ basal ganglia $\rightarrow$ thalamus $\rightarrow$ FCX, as well as with cerebellum involvement, so as to obtain the recurrent architecture needed for learning chunks (although shorter chunks can also be learned in the hippocampus).

Attention agents have been constructed (Kasderidis & Taylor, 2004) and most recently combined with reward learning (Kasderidis & Taylor, 2005). Also, reward learning, using TD methods, can be allied with an attention-based processing model such as CODAM to enable the learning of values of goals and the strength of values to be attached to their representation in the prefrontal sites in the brain. In this manner, emotions are included at a minimal level, although far more complex processes (rules, appraisal processes, etc.) need to be incorporated before the full-blown emotions of humans are expected to be included in such a model.

Finally, it has been suggested in the CODAM series of publications (J. G. Taylor, 2000; 2002a, 2002b, 2003a, 2003b, 2003c, 2004, 2005, 2006) that CODAM provides a control model of consciousness, extending that, for example, of Gallagher (2000) to allow for the presence of the prereflective self (Zahavi, 1999). This occurs by the use of the N2 signal, the first one in the brain to be regarded as part of the attention control system, but being 100 to 200 ms before the P3, regarded as the access of content to consciousness. It has been proposed in the CODAM model that the N2 is a signal of a content-free kind detected in various higher level cortical sites. It has been observed, for example, by Hopf et al. (2000) and Ioannides and Taylor (2003). However, this is still very conjectural but could provide a brain basis for support for the notion of immunity to error through misidentification of the first-person pronoun, as discussed, for example, in Shoemaker (1968).

Toward an Attention Machine

We have now presented our picture of attention in engineering-control terms with its extensions in a variety of ways toward various aspects of executive control, including value maps and emotions. Various simulations of these processes have been referred to in which connected modules of neurons have been used to show how the related architectures can begin to explain some of the recent brain imaging data. We have also presented a more general framework for machines with attention, although the details of the executive processes would have to be developed further in a general manner in order to have a nonneural basis if that were thought important.

A basic problem with this approach is that it is somewhat academic. Thus, it does not tackle the main problems being presently realized as important in developing a truly cognitive and flexible attention machine system.

1. It is not necessarily embodied, so has no connection to the external work and only exists, for example, as a passive spectator of the play of patterns and lights that can be observed by the system. We introduced actions and action-based attention in the previous subsection, but this was only at a very general level: The approach needs more teeth.

2. It is not able to be flexible in that the system cannot develop its cognitive powers and be able to go into a new environment and explore it in any cognitive manner so as to be able to survive and especially to flourish. This is partly due to the lack of embodiment noted above, but also due to no inclusion of any object learning system, so it cannot develop new object stimulus representations or actions on the new objects (even beyond the lack of embodiment of the system).

3. There is no clear developmental pattern of learning, so that the complexity of external stimuli (both singly and combined with many others in real environments) cannot be handled so as to be able to incorporate these new objects into the attention filter process and into higher executive processes to enable cognition to be used to solve any tasks that arise. Thus, there is no specification, for example, of any of the numerical values of any of the connection weights defined in the equations for the CODAM model in the appendix.

We will first turn to discuss how to resolve these problems and then turn to how we need to proceed to develop machines able to employ the architecture suggested at the end of the previous section.

Embodiment can be resolved in several ways: by use of a virtual robot environment, such as webbots, or to take an embodiment in terms of a simple moveable robot, with a gripper or grippers so as to be able to manipulate various objects. For example, in the GNOSYS project (see http://ics.forth.gr/gnosys), a four-wheeled self-steering platform has been developed that also has a gripper on its platform as well as two cameras that can be used for object recognition (as well as other sensors). Besides low-level control software employing standard algorithms for route planning and obstacle avoidance, a software G-brain has been created. This possesses adaptive powers of perception and concept formation so as to possess some flexibility of a suitable form. The object concepts are also able to be used as goals, to attend to, if so required (internally or by external command), the order of attention across a set of stimuli being determined by a TD-learning-based value map for the various possible object representations created by learning. Thus, the GNOSYS robot can respond to a stimulus if commanded to go to it and touch it.

Learning is crucial here. This is where a neural instantiation enables learning to proceed incrementally (or in one shot, as seems to occur in the hippocampus). In the GNOSYS robot, we have used space-time-dependent potentiation, where a synapse is increased if the presynaptic neuron causes the postsynaptic neuron to fire, with synapse reduction if there is anticausality, both being in a certain time window of each other.

Very soon, one meets a severe problem of computational complexity. If a realistic visual scene is being viewed by the robot cameras, it will need up to several thousands of neurons and over a million connection weights to obtain useful representations of several objects that can be able to be distinguished from each other. This takes time and a large-enough computer system.

There are also limitations if the resulting software brain is wanted to be of use in real time for robot control and exploration. So, it may be necessary to reduce the size of the weight files by suitable tricks in order to enable the system to run, for example, on a 3GHz dual processor.

FUTURE TRENDS

There are numerous problems facing the program of creating machines with attention so as to begin the climb toward truly intelligent machines with reasoning powers.

a. There is computational complexity in creating the initial perception-based framework so that it is flexible. This was discussed in the previous section, where neural-network simulations with adaptive synapses were proposed as a solution. However, here, in order to enable the creation of truly lightweight systems, the complexity issue may be seen as being solvable by the creation of suitable hardware. A hierarchy of neural chips is suggested, created so as to possess the gross topology of various early cortical modules (V1, V2, V3, V4). Given a rough Gaussian connectivity from one to another, the training (and associated pruning of excess connections) may be feasible with the latest VLSI technology.

Such a hardware basis does not, however, address the question of the creation of attention feedback. In the GNOSYS project, that was done by learning from the feedback from neurons most active for a given object to the inputs onto these neurons when the objects were being attended to. How that can be created in hardware is uncertain.

b. Learning or prewiring is a further problem. There is considerable prewiring in the brain, but then further learning and associated pruning allow for appropriate sculpting of

the neural connectivity patterns. A strongly developmental approach can be used here, in which learning onto V1 is first achieved on exposure to bars in the visual scene. Then, intersecting bars are used to train from V1 to V2, then further partial boundaries of various shapes are used, and so on. Such a hierarchical learning scheme for the hierarchical set of visual modules appears to be somewhat close to that of the infant.

c. The difficulty of proceeding with learning to higher sites, and especially the learning of the attention feedback control structures, may ultimately be solved by a more general approach that uses a rough topography of connections in the higher sites but allows for extensive training, especially using inhibitory connection strengths, of these higher sites to develop like the various control modules described earlier in the chapter. The mechanism to achieve this is most likely in the order of the processing allowed, together with the degrees and spreads of inhibitory modules associated with the excitatory cortical ones.

d. The pressure is great to produce more intelligent machines. Indeed, the present view of machines as unintelligent is correct. Yet, the progress to real human-like intelligence is clearly hard, as seen by the problems raised so far. An important component to help this along could be language, allied with the perception and concept representations being created by learning in a variety of environments. Here again there are daunting tasks ahead due to the complex nature of environments and their needed internal representations, as described above. Thus, robots with a primitive range of internal object representations and limited vocabulary are very likely the first embodied devices to aim for with some modicum of real human-like intelligence.

e. Finally, we should consider the viability of

what would be the most complex machine of all: that is, one with consciousness. This is of increasing interest amongst those concerned with the creation of cognitive machines. The CODAM model gives one (conjectured in J. G. Taylor 2000, 2002a, 2002b) way to approach this construction. However, besides the need for a CODAM-like attention control structure, there are also subtle problems associated with the actual implementation of such a faculty. Would it require, for whatever model of consciousness it was instantiating, a real-time dynamics associated with active neurons? If so, and there is support for this (Whoever heard of a weather simulation raining on its simulators?), then a suitably complex physical embodiment would be necessary to achieve consciousness. That fits onto the comments made earlier about the need for hardware implementations of lower level processing. If this present view were followed, the whole machine would be needed to be implemented in hardware to acquire any conscious experience—but then that is for some time in the future.

CONCLUSION

In this chapter, a general account has been given of a new branch of control: attention machines. These are control systems that perform a filtering process on the plant being controlled so as to enable further higher level processing on the low-level plant activity. Thus, if the plant is an image of the noisy, chaotic world, the filtered image may only be a small part of that totality and thus be much more amenable and effective for further processing by other higher level modules. The processes involved in attention were described, the higher level executive functions performed on the filtered lower level activity were listed, and some possible models of some of them were

described. A neural instantiation of this attention processing was given in an appendix; a more general approach to attention machines, outside solely a neural instantiation, was sketched in the text. Finally, brief remarks were made about the possibility of creating a conscious machine.

ACKNOWLEDGMENT

The author would like to thank the EC under the GNOSYS Cognitive Systems Unit for financial support while this work was being completed, as well as his colleagues N. Fragopanagos, N. Korsten, M. Hartley, and N. Taylor for stimulating discussions over numerous aspects of attention.

REFERENCES

Awh, E. & Jonides, J. (2001). Overlapping mechanisms of attention and spatial working memory. *Trends in Cognitive Sciences, 5*, 119-126.

Awh, E., Jonides, J., & Reuter-Lorenz, P. A. (1998). Rehearsal in spatial working memory. *Journal of Exp. Psychol. Hum. Percept. Perform., 24*, 780-790.

Baddeley, A. D. (1986). *Working memory.* Oxford, United Kingdom: Oxford University Press.

Binkofski, F., Fink, G. R., Geyer, S., Buccino, O., Grfuber, O., Shah, N. J., et al. (2002). Neural activity in human motor cortex areas 4a and 4p is modulated differentially by attention to action. *Journal of Neurophysiology.*

Burgess, N., & Hitch, G. (2005). Computational models of working memory: Putting long-term memory into context. *Trends in Cognitive Sciences, 9*(11), 535-541.

Corbetta, M., & Shulman, G. L. (2002). Control of goal-directed and stimulus-driven attention in the brain. *Nature Reviews, Neuroscience, 3,* 201-215.

Corbetta, M., Tansy, A. P., Stanley, C. M., Astafiev, S. V., Snyder, A. Z., & Shulman, G. L. (2005). A functional MRI study of preparatory signals for spatial location and objects. *Neuropsychologia, 43,* 2041-2056.

Deco, G., & Rolls, E. T. (2005). Attention, short-term memory, and action selection: A unifying theory. *Prog. Neurobiol., 76,* 236-256.

Desimone, R., & Duncan, J. (1995). Neural mechanics of selective visual attention. *Annual Reviews of Neuroscience, 18,* 193-222.

Desmurget, M., Epstein, C. M., Turner, R. S., Prablanc, C., Alexander, G. E., & Grafton, S. T. (1999). Role of the posterior parietal cortex in updating reaching movements to a visual target. *Nature Neuroscience, 2,* 563-567.

Desmurget, M., & Grafton, S. (2000). Forward modeling allows feedback control for fast reaching movements. *Trends in Cognitive Neurosciences, 4,* 423-431.

D'Esposito, M., Postle, B. R., & Rypma, B. (2000). Prefrontal cortical contributions to working memory: Evidence from event-related fMRI studies. *Exp. Brain Res., 133,* 3-11.

Feinberg, I. (1978). Efference copy and corollary discharge: Implications for thinking and its disorders. *Schizophrenia Bulletin, 4,* 636-640.

Fragopanagos, N., Kockelkoren, S., & Taylor, J. G. (2003). A neurodynamic model of the attentional blink. *Cognitive Brain Research, 24,* 568-586.

Frith, C. (1992). *The cognitive neuropsychology of schizophrenia.* Hillsdale, NJ: Erlbaum.

Fuster, J. M., & Alexander, G. E. (1971). Neuron activity related to short-term memory. *Science, 173,* 652-654.

Gallagher, S. (2000). Philosophical conceptions of the self. *Trends in Cognitive Sciences, 4*(1), 14-21.

GNOSYS. (2006). Retrieved from http://www.ics.forth.gr/gnosys

Griffin, I. C., & Nobre, A. C. (2003). Orienting attention to locations in internal representations. *Journal of Cognitive Neuroscience, 15,* 1176-1194.

Hopf, J.-M., et al. (2000). Neural sources of focused attention in visual search. *Cerebral Cortex, 10,* 1231-1241.

Houde, O., & Tzourio-Mazayer, N. (2003). Neural foundations of logical and mathematical cognition. *Nature Review, Neuroscience, 4,* 507-514.

Ioannides, A. A., & Taylor, J. G. (2003). Testing models of attention with MEG. *Proceedings of IJCNN'03.*

Kanwisher, N., & Wojciulik, E. (2000). Visual attention: Insights from brain imaging. *Nature Review, Neuroscience, 1,* 91-100.

Kasderidis, S., & Taylor, J. G. (2004). Attentional agents and robot control. *International Journal of Knowledge-Based & Intelligent Systems 8,* 69-89.

Kasderidis, S., & Taylor, J. G. (2005). *Rewarded attentional agents.* Proceedings of ICANN2005, Warsaw, Poland.

Kastner, S., & Ungerleider, L. G. (2000). Mechanisms of visual attention. *Annual Reviews of Neuroscience, 23,* 315-341.

Kastner, S., & Ungerleider, L. G. (2001). The neural basis of biased competition in human visual cortex. *39,* 1263-1276.

McAdams, C. J., & Maunsell, J. H. R. (1999). Effects of attention on orientation tuning functions of single neurons in macaque cortical area V4. *Journal of Neuroscience, 19*(1), 431-441.

Mehta, A. D., Ulbert, I., & Schroeder, C. E. (2000). Intermodal selective attention in monkeys II: Physiological mechanisms of modulation cerebral cortex. *10*, 359-370.

Miall, R. C., & Wolpert, D. M. (1996). Forward models for physiological motor control. *Neural Networks, 9*(8), 1265-1279.

Mozer, M. C., & Sitton, M. (1998). Computational modeling of spatial attention. In H. Pashler (Ed.), *Attention* (pp. 341-393). New York: Taylor & Francis.

Nobre, A. C. (2001). The attentive homunculus: Now you see it, now you don't. *Neuroscience and Biobehavioral Reviews, 25*, 477-496.

Passingham, D., & Sakai, K. (2004). The prefrontal cortex and working memory: Physiology and brain imaging. *Current Opinion in Neurobiology, 14*, 163-168.

Petrides, M. (2000). Dissociable roles of mid-dorsolateral prefrontal and anterior inferotemporal cortex in visual working memory. *Journal of Neuroscience, 20*, 7496-7503.

Phillips, C., & Harbour, R. (2000). *Feedback control systems*. NJ: Prentice Hall.

Pisella, L., Grea, H., Tillikete, C., Vighetto, A., Desmurget, M., Rode, G., et al. (2000). An "automatic pilot" for the hand in human posterior parietal cortex: Toward reinterpreting optic ataxia. *Nature Neuroscience, 3*, 729-736.

Praamstra, P., & Oostenveld, R. (2003). Attention and movement-related motor cortex activation: A high density EEG study of spatial stimulus-response compatibility. *Cognitive Brain Research, 16*, 309-323.

Ramachandran, V. S., & Hirstein, W. (1998). The perception of phantom limbs. The DO Hebb lecture. *Brain, 121*, 1603-1630.

Rushworth, M. F. S., Ellison, A., & Walsh, V. (2001). Complementary localization and lateralization of orienting and motor attention. *Nature Neuroscience, 4*(6), 656-661.

Rushworth, M. F. S., Krams, M., & Passingham, R. E. (2001). *Journal of Cognitive Neuroscience, 13*, 698-710.

Rushworth, M. F. S., Nixon, P. D., Renowden, S., Wade, D. T., & Passingham, R. E. (1997). The left parietal cortex and motor attention. *Neuropsychologia, 35*(9), 1261-1273.

Sabes, M. (2000). The planning and control of reaching movements. *Current Opinion in Neurobiology, 10*, 740-746.

Schluter, N. D., Krams, M., Rushworth, M. F. S., & Passingham, R. E. (2001). Cerebral dominance for action in the human brain: The selection of actions. *Neuropsychologia, 39*, 105-113.

Schwoebel, J., Boronat, C. B., & Coslett, H. B. (2002). The man who executed "imagined" movements: Evidence for dissociable components of the body schema. *Brain and Cognition, 50*, 1-16.

Sergent, C., Baillet, S., & Dehaene, S. (2005). Timing of the brain events underlying access to consciousness during the attentional blink. *Nature Neuroscience, 8*, 1391-1400.

Sergent, C., & Dehaene, S. (in press). Is consciousness a gradual phenomenon? Evidence for an all-or-none bifurcation during the attentional blink. *Nature Neuroscience.*

Shapiro, K. L., Arnell, K. M,. & Raymond, J. E. (1997). The attentional blink. *Trends in Cognitive Science, 1*, 291-295.

Shapiro, K. L., Hillstrom, A. P., & Husain, M. (2002). Control of visuotemporal attention by inferior parietal and superior temporal cortex. *Current Biology, 12*, 1320-1325.

Shinba, T. (1999). Neuronal firing activity in the dorsal hippocampus during the auditory discrimination oddball task in awake rats. *Cognitive Brain Research, 8*, 241-350.

Shoemaker, S. (1968). Self-reference and self-awareness. *Journal of Philosophy, 65*, 556-570.

Taylor, J. G. (1996). Breakthrough to awareness. *Biological Cybernetics.*

Taylor, J. G. (2000). Attentional movement: The control basis for consciousness. *Society for Neuroscience Abstracts, 26*, 2231.

Taylor, J. G. (2002a). From matter to mind. *Journal of Consciousness Studies, 6*, 3-22.

Taylor, J .G. (2002b). Paying attention to consciousness. *Trends in Cognitive Sciences, 6*(5), 206-210.

Taylor, J.G. (2003a). *The CODAM model and deficits of consciousness.* Proceedings of the Conference of Knowledge-Based Expert Systems, Oxford, United Kingdom.

Taylor, J.G. (2003b). Neural models of Consciousness. In M. A. Arbib (Ed.), *The handbook of brain theory and neural networks* (pp. 263-267). Cambridge, MA: MIT Press.

Taylor, J. G. (2003c). Paying attention to consciousness. *Progress in Neurobiology 71*, 305-335.

Taylor, J. G. (2004). A review of brain-based cognitive models. *Cognitive Processing, 5*(4), 190-217.

Taylor, J. G. (2005). From matter to consciousness: Towards a final solution? *Physics of Life Reviews, 2*, 1-44.

Taylor, J. G. (2006). *The mind: A user's manual.* Wiley & Son.

Taylor, J. G., & Fragopanagos, N. (2003). Simulation of attention control models of sensory and motor paradigms. *Proceedings of IJCNN'03.*

Taylor, J. G., & Fragopanagos, N. (2005). The interaction of attention and emotion. *Neural Networks, 18*(4), 353-369.

Taylor, J. G., Fragopanagos, N., & Korsten, N. (2006). *Modelling working memory through attentional mechanisms.* Proceedings of the International Conference on Artificial Neural Networks (ICANN06), Athens, Greece.

Taylor, J. G., Nobre, C. A., & Shapiro, K. (Eds.). (2006). Special issue on brain and attention. *Neural Networks, 19*(7).

Taylor, J. G., & Rogers, M. (2002). A control model of the movement of attention. *Neural Networks, 15*, 309-326.

Taylor, N., Hartley, M., & Taylor, J. G. (2006). *Value learning for goal decisions* (KCL preprint).

Wolpert, D. M., & Ghahramani, Z. (2000). Computational principles of movement neuroscience. *Nature Neuroscience, 3*, 1212-1217.

Zahavi, D. (1999). *Self-awareness and alterity.* Evanston, IL: North-Western University Press.

APPENDIX 1: A SIMPLE NEURAL INSTANTIATION

In this appendix, we present a mathematical form of the CODAM model using the simplest of possible neurons as having a graded (continuous) response, and the modules of the figure being modeled as two-dimensional neural fields. We will start with ballistic control (in which there is a control signal set p at the beginning of the control process, and no feedback is used to correct for any errors that may have occurred in either setting up the initial control signal or in implementing it in a control signal generator module, an IMC, as denoted earlier).

In discussing attention earlier, we applied the language of engineering-control theory and so assumed the existence in higher cortical sites of an inverse model for attention movement, as an IMC, the signal being created by use of a bias signal from prefrontal goal sites. The resulting IMC signal amplifies (in contrast gain, singling out the synapses from lower order attended stimulus representations) posterior activity in semantic memory sites (early occipital, temporal, and parietal cortices). This leads to the following ballistic model of attention control.

Goal bias (PFC) → Inverse model controller IMC (Parietal lobe) → Amplified lower level representation of attended stimulus (in various modalities in posterior CX) (A1)

We denote the state of the lower level representation as $\mathbf{x}(\ ,t)$, where the unwritten internal variable denotes a set of coordinate positions of the component neurons in a set of lower level modules in the posterior cortex. Also, we take the states of the goal and IMC modules to be $x(\ ,t;\ goal)$, $x(\ ,t;\ IMC)$. The set of equations representing the processes in equation (1) are

$$\tau dx(goal)/dt = -x(goal) + bias \qquad (A2a)$$

$$\tau dx(IMC)/dt = -x(IMC) + x(goal) \qquad (A2b)$$

$$\tau dx(,t)/dt = -x(,t) + w*x((IMC) + w'**x(IMC)I(t) \qquad (A2c)$$

In equation (A2c), the single-starred quantity $w*x$ denotes the standard convolution product $\int w(r, r')IMC(r')dr'$ and $w**x(IMC)I(t)$ denotes the double convolution product $\int w(r, r', r'')$ $x(r';$ $IMC)I(r'')$, where I® is the external input at r. These two terms involving the weights w and w' and single and double convolution products correspond to the additive feedback and contrast gain suggested by various researchers.

Equation (A2a) indicates a bias signal (from the lower level cortex) as in exogenous attention, an already present continued bias as in endogenous attention, or in both a form of value bias as is known to arise from the orbito-frontal cortex and amygdala. The goal signal is then used in equation (A2b) to guide the direction of the IMC signal (which may be a spatial direction or in object feature space). Finally, this IMC signal is sent back to lower level cortices in either a contrast gain manner (modulating the weights arising from a particular stimulus, as determined by the goal bias, to amplify relevant inputs) or in an additive manner. Which of these two is relevant is presently controversial, so we delay that choice by taking both possibilities. That may indeed be the case.

The amplified target activity in the lower sites is then able to access a buffer working memory sited in posterior cortices (temporal and parietal), which acts as an attended state estimator. The access to this buffer has been modeled in the more extended CODAM model (J. G. Taylor, 2000, 2003, 2005) as a threshold process, arising possibly from two-state neurons being sent from the down to the up state (more specifically, by two reciprocally coupled neurons almost in bifurcation, so possessing long lifetime against decay of activity). Such a process of threshold access to a buffer site corresponds to the equation

$$x(WM)=xY[x-threshold], \qquad (A3)$$

where Y is the step function or hard threshold function. Such a threshold process has been shown to occur by means of the modeling of experiments on priming (J. G. Taylor, 1996) as well as in detailed analysis of the temporal flow of activity in the AB (Sergent & Deheane, in press); the activity in the buffer only arises from input activity above the threshold. Several mechanisms for this threshold process have been suggested but will not occupy us further here, in spite of their importance.

The resulting threshold model of attended-state access to the buffer working-memory site is different from that usual in control theory. State estimation usually involves a form of corollary discharge of the control signal so as to allow for rapid updating of the control signal if any error occurs. However, the state being estimated is usually that of the whole plant being controlled. In attention it is only the attended stimulus whose internal activity representation is being estimated by its being allowed to access the relevant working-memory buffer. This is a big difference from standard control theory and embodying the filtration process being carried out by attention. Indeed, in modern control theory partial measurement on a state leads to the requirement of state reconstruction for the remainder of the state. This is so-called reduced-order estimation (Phillips & Harbour, 2000). In attention control it is not the missing component that is important, but that which is present, as the attended component, that is important.

Access to the sensory buffer, as noted above, is aided by an efference copy of the attention movement control signal generated by the inverse attention model. The existence of an efference copy of attention was predicted as being observable by its effect on the sensory buffer signal (as represented by its P3); this has just been observed in an experiment on the AB, where the N2 of the second target is observed to inhibit the P3 of the first when T2 is detected (Sergent et al., 2005).

The corollary discharge activity is thus to be represented most simply as

$$x(CD)=x(IMC) \qquad (A4)$$

The presence of this copy signal modifies the manner in which updates are made to the IMC and to the monitor:

$$\tau dx(IMC)/dt=-x(IMC)+x(goal)+w''*x(CD), \qquad (A5a)$$

$$\tau dx(,t)/dt=-x(,t)+w*x((IMC)+w'**x(IMC)I(t)+x(MON), \qquad (A5b)$$

$$x(MON)=|x(goal)-x(CD)|+|x(goal)-x(WM)|, \qquad (A5c)$$

where the monitor is set up so as to take whichever is first of the error signals form the corollary discharge and the buffer activations, but then discard the first for the latter when it arrives (the first having very likely died away in the meantime).

It is also the corollary discharge aspect of the attention control model that is beyond that of earlier models, such as biased competition. It is important to appreciate this as acting in two different ways (as emphasized in J. G. Taylor, 2002b).

1. As a contributor to the threshold battle ongoing in the posterior buffer in order to gain access by the attended lower level stimulus. It was conjectured in J. G. Taylor (2000) that this amplification occurred by a direct feedback of a corollary discharge copy of the IMC signal to the buffer (at the same time with inhibition of any distracter activity arriving there).

2. Used as a temporally early proxy for the attention-amplified stimulus activity, being used in a monitor module to determine how close the resulting attended stimulus achieves the prefrontally held goal.

Both of these processes were shown to be important in a simulation of the attentional blink (Fragopanagos et al., 2005); the spatially separated and temporally detailed EEG (electroencephalograph) data of Claire and Sergent required especially the first of these as the interaction of the N2 of the second target T2 and the P3 of the first target T1. The resulting CODAM model (J. G. Taylor, 2000) takes the form of Figure 1 shown earlier.

Numerous other features have been added to the CODAM model.

a.   More detailed perception and concept processing system (GNOSYS)

b.   Addition of emotional evaluation modules, especially modeled on the amygdala (Korsten et al., 2006)

c.   Addition of a value-learning system similar to the OFC (N. Taylor, Hartley, & Taylor, 2006)

The relation of the attention copy approach contained in the above equations to those of standard engineering-control theory is summarized in Table 1.

We note in Table 1 that the main difference between the two columns is in the entries in the lowest row, where the buffer working memory in attention control contains an estimate of the state of the attended activity in the lower level cortex; this is clearly distinguished from that for standard engineering-control theory, where the estimated state in the equivalent site is that of the total plant and not just a component of it.

Table 1. Comparison of variables in engineering-control theory and attention

Variable	In Engineering Control	In Attention
x(t)	State of plant	State of lower level cortical activity
x(IMC)	Control signal to control plant in some manner	Control signal to move attention to a spatial position or object
x(goal)	Desired state of plant	Desired goal causing attention to move
x(CD)	Corollary discharge signal to be used for control speedup	Corollary discharge to speed up attention movement
x(WM)	Estimated state of plant (as at present time or as predictor for future use) often termed an observer	Estimated state of attended lower level activity (at present time or as predictor for future use)

Chapter VI
Artificial Mind

Rita M. R. Pizzi
University of Milan, Italy

ABSTRACT

The advances of artificial intelligence (AI) have renewed the interest in the mind-body problem, the ancient philosophical debate on the nature of mind and its relationship with the brain. The new version of the mind-body problem concerns the relationship between computational complexity and self-aware thought. The traditional controversy between strong and weak AI will not be settled until we are able in the future to build a robot so evolved to give us the possibility to verify its perceptions, its qualitative sensations, and its introspective thoughts. However, an alternative way can be followed: The progresses of micro-, nano-, and biotechnologies allow us to create the first bionic creatures, composed of biological cells connected to electronic devices. Creating an artificial brain with a biological structure could allow verifying if it possesses peculiar properties with respect to an electronic one, comparing them at the same level of complexity.

INTRODUCTION

The attempt to understand the nature of mind goes back to the time of the Greek philosophers. In modern times, the behavioral movement concentrated on the external behavior, excluding the importance of the internal mental processes. Only in the last decades the cognitive sciences and the artificial intelligence (AI) research attracted attention on mental processes, reviving the interest in the nature of intelligence and reflexive thought.

The development of computer technology opened a new research method by means of computer simulations of functions typical of the human brain.

After the enthusiasm of the first times, when many prototypes were developed, the successes of AI research faded in the '80s due to the difficulty to move the AI algorithms in the complexity of the real world.

However, although the wide, excessively expensive and ambitious AI systems that concentrated on specific problems were once renounced, in the last decade, swift developments have produced many applications in robotics and several useful algorithms applied to all kinds of fields, where the complexity of the problems is greater and traditional algorithms cannot reach significant results.

Nonetheless, the solutions proposed for the problem of the nature of mind remain debatable.

The development of AI created a diatribe between the supporters of the so-called strong and weak AI. Following weak AI, the computer is just a powerful tool that allows us to verify hypotheses and to implement useful functionalities, but it will never have the features of a human mind.

Following strong AI, the computer can be considered a real mind that in the future, endowed with evolved programs, will possess all the features of the mind and cognitive states.

This unsolved diatribe changed over time into a dispute between materialists and nonmaterialists. The purpose is not anymore to decide if the technology will succeed in developing robots with an intelligence similar to the human one (we understood that this is a very far goal but that we will reach it for all practical purposes), but to understand the very nature of mind and its relationship with the brain.

This problem is seen today not only as a philosophical but also as a scientific goal, whose application to AI development will be an important consequence.

BACKGROUND

Weak AI vs. Strong AI

One of the most famous and sharp criticisms of strong AI is John Searle's work (1980) and its "Chinese room" thought experiment. An English man is closed in a room. He does not understand Chinese. He receives a sheet containing a story and some questions on the story written in Chinese, and a set of rules to draw Chinese symbols in reply to the questions. The man follows the rules and answers the questions.

The rules correspond to a computer program. The man corresponds to a computer that processes the program specified by means of formal rules. The man can become so clever that his answers are indistinguishable from those of a Chinese man.

Strong AI maintains that the computer understands the story, but the man in the room does not understand the story at all. He does not know the meaning of the Chinese symbols. Many objections have been raised by Searle's conclusion about this thought experiment, and Searle always rejected them with extremely smart considerations.

However, it is clear that the English man accomplishes in the room only a careful but stupid copying task from a lookup table and does not perform a learning algorithm such as those AI (and all the more reason for the human mind) is able to accomplish.

The man in the room could try to understand the connection between the lookup table items and the story, and finally he could learn Chinese. The same could be accomplished by a machine using, for example, an artificial neural network or other symbolic knowledge representation techniques. Thus, it seems that the progresses of AI succeed without difficulties in giving a computer the ability to understand the connections between information, and to memorize and learn them.

Douglas Hofstadter (1979; see also Hofstadter & Dennett, 1981), one of the most convincing and famous strong-AI supporters, maintains that a growing complexity of the computer processes, including the interaction between different cognitive levels, could lead a machine not only to the ability of understanding and learning, but also to the emergence of the ability of self-reflection that is the basis of consciousness.

Hofstadter hypothesizes that consciousness rises from the closure of a tangled loop between the high (symbolic) level and low (neurophysiological) level, bounded to each other by a chain of causalities. The most central and complex symbol of the high level is the one we call *I*. This closed loop allows the representational system to perceive its own state inside a set of concepts.

Currently, many AI programs already possess the ability to know their own structures and react to variations of these structures, exhibiting a rudimental kind of control of the self. In conclusion, Hofstadter affirms that the mind can be reproduced inside a computer because it can be simulated by a program, thus it does not reside in the biological structure of the brain.

The "Hard Problem"

The above considerations seem to lead to the assertion that a computer could in the future present all the features of a human mind, including consciousness. However, the problem is not so easily solved.

Following David Chalmers (Chalmers, 1995, 1997), to be able to develop an intelligent machine that is aware, understands, learns, and possesses a control of its own self as a human being does is not equivalent to state that this machine possesses a mind in the subjective and qualitative sense that we experience.

He coined the term "hard problem" to indicate the problem to understand the origin of the subjective and qualitative component of the mind experience differently from "easy problems," that is, the problems that concern the integration between internal mental states and sensorial perceptions, selective attention, emotional behavior, and so forth. These problems should in principle be solved in the future by means of the neurophysiological research and the computer science approach.

In the future, a computer could also be able to reproduce faithfully the human thought in a third-person fashion, but nothing indicates that the computer would have a first-person experience of what it is elaborating.

As an example, Minsky's emotion machine (Minsky, 2006) could soon reproduce many typically human functionalities, like emotions and the idea of self, but there is no reason to think that the computer would experience emotions and the sense of self in the same subjective way as we do.

The hard problem is not a problem about how functions are performed, but the problem to understand why the performance of the functions is associated with conscious experience.

We are not able to explain why, for instance, when the brain processes a specific wavelength of light, we have the experience of a specific color (the "blueness" of blue).

Consciousness and Laws of Nature

Chalmers does not deny that the biological structure of the brain is heavily implied in the onset of the phenomenon of consciousness, but he affirms that the connection between conscious processes and their neural correlates are not obvious. However, both Chalmers and Searle (1980) believe that the difference between man and machine could be connected with the specific properties of the brain physiology. The exact reproduction of the neural physiology, even with a different chemistry, could lead to reproduce also the experiential properties of consciousness.

Another way to face the problem, as Chalmers suggests, is to admit that consciousness is an irreducible phenomenon, that is, an a priori property of nature. In this way, consciousness would obey laws similar to the other fundamental physical laws like gravity or electromagnetism.

The key observation is that not all the entities in science are explained in terms of more primitive physical entities. For instance, space-time, mass, and charge are considered fundamental entities of the universe because they are not reducible to something easier.

In the case of consciousness, the goal would be to affirm that the brain state B produces the conscious state C due to the fundamental law X. We could come to a theory of everything that includes the laws of consciousness inside the set of the laws of nature.

A possibility to include consciousness in the laws of nature has been opened by quantum mechanics, in whose fundamentals the role of the observer is extremely critical. Several idealistic or interactionist theories are still competing with the traditional Copenhagen interpretation: Erwin Schrödinger (1956) first approached the Oriental monism in the frame of quantum mechanics, putting the accent of the indissolubility between the physical event and observer's mind. After him, J. Archibald Wheeler (1983), Eugene Wigner (1961, 1972), and in more recent times Josephson and Pallikari-Viras (1991) and Henry Stapp (1993) maintained quantum theories where consciousness is crucial in the objectivity of physical reality.

In particular, Stapp (1993) proposes an interpretation where consciousness, intended as an a priori phenomenon, is the cause of the wave function collapse. On the other hand, Chalmers' hypothesis is that a way to include consciousness in the frame of the laws of nature is to develop a theory of everything based on the concept of information, hypothesizing that information has two aspects: a physical one and an experiential one. Systems with equal structural organization include equal information. This idea is compatible with Wheeler's (1983) theory that information is a fundamental concept of physics. The laws of physics could be re-coined in informational terms, satisfying the congruence between physical and psychophysical structures.

Although the role of the observer in quantum mechanics remains an extremely controversial issue, in the last few years several quantum mind theories have been developed (Hagan, Hameroff, & Tuszynski, 2002; Matsuno, 1999; Tuszynski, Trpisova, Sept, & Sataric, 1997) that intend to connect the biophysical properties of the brain to quantum physics. The most authoritative is the Penrose-Hameroff theory (Hameroff & Penrose, 1996; Penrose, 1994), which hypothesizes that in microtubules, cellular structures inside the neuron, quantum reductions take place associated with simple consciousness events. Microtubules possess the physical properties suitable to obey quantum laws, thus they could play a fundamental role in the phenomenon of consciousness.

THE MIND-BODY PROBLEM IN THE 21ST CENTURY

Both the hypothesis that intelligence and self-awareness could spring from the complexity of the brain, or an artificial structure perfectly homologous to the brain, and the parallel hypothesis that consciousness is an a priori entity of nature and could be connected to the fundamentals of quantum physics are at the moment indemonstrable. However, thanks to the progresses of electronics and of computer technology, we can start to build the bases of an empirical proof of these theories.

During the past decade, several laboratories in the world carried out experiments on direct interfacing between electronics and biological neurons in order to support neurophysiological research, but also to pioneer future hybrid human-electronic devices, bionic robotics, biological computation, and bioelectronic prostheses (Akin, Najafi, Smoke, & Bradley, 1994; Canepari, Bove, Mueda, Cappello, & Kawana, 1997; Egert et al., 2002; Maher, Pine, Wright, & Tai, 1999; Potter, 2001). Progress in this research field is quick and continuous.

During the early '90s, Fromherz's group (Max Planck Institute of Biochemistry) first pioneered the silicon-neuron interface. The group keeps developing sophisticated techniques to optimize this kind of junction (Fromherz, 2002; Fromherz, Muller, & Weis, 1993; Fromherz, Offenhäusser, Vetter, & Weis, 1991; Fromherz & Schaden, 1994).

Many other experiments have been carried out with different aims: Garcia, Calabrese, DeWeerth, and Ditto (2003) and Lindner and Ditto (1996) at Georgia Tech tried to obtain simple computations from a hybrid electronic leech creature. As the neurons do not behave as "on-off" elements, it has been necessary to send them signals and interpret the neural output using the chaos theory.

In 2000, a team of the Northwestern University of Chicago, University of Illinois, and University of Genoa (Reger, Fleming, Sanguineti, Alford, & Mussa-Ivaldi, 2000) developed a hybrid creature consisting of lamprey neurons connected to a robot. In front of light stimuli, the creature behaves in different ways: follows light, avoids it, and moves in circle.

In 2002, De Marse, Wagenaar, and Potter at Georgia Tech created a hybrid creature made of a few thousand living neurons from a rat cortex placed on a special glass Petri dish instrumented with an array of 60 microelectrodes, also able to learn from its environment.

In 2003, Duke University's group (Carmena et al., 2003) succeeded in connecting 320 microelectrodes to monkey cells in the brain, allowing them to directly translate the electrical signals into computer instructions and to move a robotic arm.

In 2005, the SISSA group (Ruaro, Bonifazi, & Torre, 2005) experimented with the possibility to use neurons on MEAs (microelectrode arrays) as "neurocomputers" able to filter digital images.

Despite these astonishing results, neurophysiological research is far from understanding in detail the learning mechanism of the brain and fails to interpret the cognitive meaning of the signals coming from the neurons.

Our group, the Living Networks Lab, since 2002 has carried out experiments on networks of biological human neurons directly connected to MEAs (Figure 1).

A Bionic Brain

The neurons, adhering directly to an MEA support, are stimulated by means of simulated perceptions in the form of digital patterns, and the output signals are analyzed. In previous experiments, we verified that the neurons reply selectively to different patterns and show similar reactions in front of the presentation of identical or similar patterns (Pizzi, Fantasia, Gelain, Rossetti, & Vescovi, 2004a; Pizzi, 2007).

On the basis of these results, we developed a bionic creature able to decode the signals coming

Figure 1. MEA support and magnification of neural stem cells adhering on the MEA

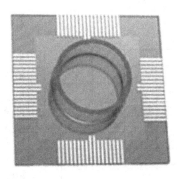
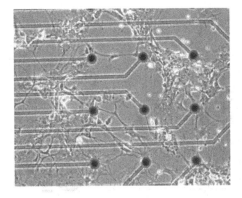

Figure 2. Block diagram of the hardware

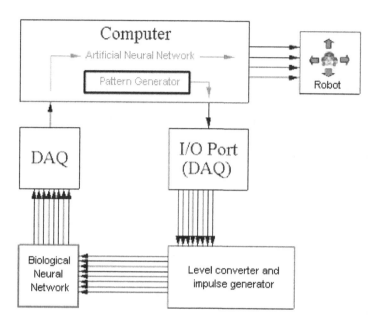

from a network of neurons stimulated by digital patterns. The whole hybrid system is shown in Figure 2 (Pizzi, 2008).

We arranged on the MEA eight input channels picked from eight electrodes, on which living cells were attached. The cells were cultured on the connection sites of the MEA and were con-

nected to each other as in the case of a Hopfield (1980) artificial neural network.

The first phase of the experiment consisted of stimulating the neurons with a set of simulated perceptions in the form of four digital patterns (Figure 3).

Figure 3. The four patterns: forward, backward, left, right

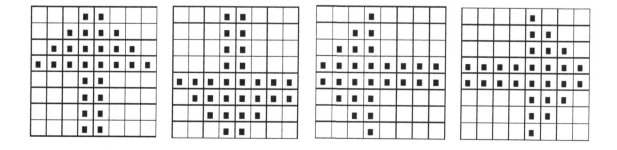

The stimulation occurs with a 100 mV positive voltage followed by a brief -100 mV depolarization pulse. The stimulation frequency is 433 Hz, and the sampling rate is 10 kHz.

Each pattern is constituted by a matrix of 8x8 bits. Every bit lasts 300 ms. The cells are stimulated 2.4 seconds for each pattern. Each stimulation is followed by a 1-second pause and is repeated 10 times for each pattern in order to allow the neurons to learn.

Once the training phase was finished, a testing phase was carried out. During this phase, we sent to the neurons several stimulations corresponding to one of the four patterns in a random order.

The reactions of the neurons have been sent to an artificial neural network that classified the answers on the basis of the neural reactions recorded after the training phase. The model of the artificial neural network, a novel architecture called ITSOM (Inductive Tracing Self Organizing Map; Pizzi, de Curtis, & Dickson, 2002), was developed considering that a self-organizing architecture was necessary as we had no set of known outputs to train with.

In the described experiment, we tested the hybrid system with 25 random patterns. The evaluation of the proposed model presents an accuracy of 80.11% and a precision of 90.50%. These results (Table 1) allow us to consider the effectiveness of our hybrid classifier quite satisfactorily.

This research shows a way to deeply analyze the behavior of networks of neurons and to decode their signals in reply to simulated perceptions.

After an adequate increase of the number of electrode connections, the system should be able to receive real perceptions from suitable sensors and to react to them.

Our challenge consists of studying in detail the behavior of networks of neurons and of verifying if this bionic system, after a suitable increase of complexity, will allow the emergence of behaviors typical of a human mind in an artificial structure with features homologous to the brain structure.

Possible Quantum Processes in Cultured Neurons

Another research line of our group concerns the search for possible quantum processes inside the neurons. Our system is constituted by networks of human neural stem cells cultured on a set of MEAs. We verified that weak electromagnetic stimulations are able to produce action potentials in networks of neurons under extremely strict conditions of optical and electrical shielding.

The first results showed very high values of cross-correlation and frequency coherence during electromagnetic pulses (Pizzi, Fantasia, Gelain, Rossetti, & Vescovi, 2004b); these results encouraged us to continue the experimentations.

During the last 3 years, we prepared and carried out several other experiments, improving both the hardware detection and controlling system and the shielding techniques. We also took the maximum care in preparing the experimental

Table 1. Performance of the hybrid classifier

	Pattern F	Pattern B	Pattern L	Pattern R	Total
Sensitivity	100%	45.45%	75%	100%	80.11%
Specificity	94.44%	100%	83.33%	84.21%	90.50%

protocols devoted to exclude possible biases and alternative hypotheses.

All the experiments confirm the presence of spikes in neurons under tested conditions of optical and electrical shielding. On the basis of the experimental findings and the bench tests, it is possible to state that the spikes appearing in the neural signals simultaneously with the electromagnetic pulses are not due to interference.

The reactivity of neurons to the electromagnetic pulses could be due to the presence of microtubules in their cellular structure. The microtubules, formed by wrapped tubulin molecules, are structurally similar to carbon nanotubes. Actually, the structures are empty cylinders; the diameter of a microtubule is around 20 nm and its length is around some micron, whereas a carbon nanotube's dimensions can be similar to or less than those of the microtubule. Interesting optical, electrical, and quantum properties of carbon nanotubes are known (Andrews & Bradshaw, 2005; Gao, Cagin, & Goddard, 1998; Katura, 1999; Lovett, Reina, Nazir, Kothari, & Briggs, 2003; Wang et al., 2005). It is also known that both microtubules and nanotubes behave as oscillators (Marx & Mandelkow, 1994; Sept, Limbach, Bolterauer, & Tuszynski, 1999), and this could make them superreactive receivers able to amplify the signal.

The reported experimental findings need further exploration and confirmation. Nevertheless, they constitute an attempt to investigate on possible quantum processes in the brain: Experimental proofs are necessary to yield a validation of the quantum mind theories and to try to find an empirical solution of the mind-body problem.

FUTURE TRENDS

These preliminary results encourage us to continue our research with more and more complex experiments. As regards the research on possible quantum processes in neurons, many other ex-periments will be needed that must be confirmed by analogous experiments carried out by other groups. On the other hand, several theoretical physicists and cognitive scientists are developing new theories on the ontological implications of quantum physics and in particular on the theme of the quantum mind.

As regards our experiments on learning in the bionic brain, better performance can be reached in the future with a better tuning of the artificial neural network that decodes the neural signals. During an off-line experiment, we already tested a new procedure able to reach better performance. In the future, it will be possible to test the system with a higher number of electrodes and endow it with sensors that allow real perceptions instead of the simulated ones. Our goal is to create a bionic creature that reacts autonomously to environmental stimulations, and to improve the complexity of its neural networks.

Only the growth in complexity of the system could give rise to nonstereotyped behaviors, and make possible new answers to the problem of the relationship between mind, brain, and machines. On the other side, several scientists are implementing complex software systems able to emulate functionalities of the human brain. Also in this case, only a sharp increase of complexity of these intelligent systems can yield some indications on the real possibility to simulate the most evolved features of the human mind. Currently, several intelligent systems are able to exhibit performance similar or better than human ones, but this performance does not concern the sphere of emotions and self-awareness, and they are only partially able to perceive and learn autonomously from the environment and to improve their abilities over time.

Although the way toward the development of an artificial mind is still quite long, certainly AI is taking many important technological contributions in all the fields of our lives, by means of software embedded in instrumentations and computers, and of more and more evolved robots that facilitate many tasks in the past only pertinent to humans: from health to industry to domestic life.

In the particular case of our Living Networks Lab, we hope that the by-products of our research activity could be useful to deepen neurophysiological knowledge, test the possibility of biological computation, and develop bionic prostheses useful to people who suffer from neurological damage.

CONCLUSION

The success of the cognitive sciences, of AI, and of the neurosciences removed the problem of the nature of the mind and consciousness from the category of the philosophical problems and put it at the center of the attention of science.

The lack of ultimate answers on this issue is in part due to the poor complexity of the current artificial systems in comparison with the complexity of the brain, making it impossible to compare artificial and human performance and features. Therefore, a huge amount of work is still to be done, but some important courses have been drawn out, both in the field of the development of the software simulation of intelligent behavior, and in the field of the development of bionic systems that reproduce the neurophysiological structure of the brain.

Also, theoretical physics has still to yield an ultimate answer on its fundamentals in order to clarify the role of the person in the objective reality in such a way as to shed light on the nature of consciousness.

Despite the difficulty of the problems that neurosciences, informatics, and physics have to solve in this frame, the quantity of scientific material related to the issue of consciousness and to the implementation of AI hardware and software systems has grown exponentially during the last

few years. This trend will certainly contribute to consider the birth of a real artificial mind and the solution of the mystery of consciousness as not so far and not so impossible events.

ACKNOWLEDGMENT

I feel deeply indebted to all the members of the Living Networks Lab (D. Rossetti, G. Cino, D. Marino, and many others), and to Professor A. L. Vescovi (SCRI DIBIT S. Raffaele, Milan) and Professor G. Degli Antoni (University of Milan) for their valuable support.

REFERENCES

Akin, T., Najafi, K., Smoke, R. H., & Bradley, R. M. (1994). A micromachined silicon electrode for nerve regeneration applications. *IEEE Transactions of Biomedical Engineering, 41*, 305-313.

Andrews, D. L., & Bradshaw, D. S. (2005). Laser-induced forces between carbon nanotubes. *Optics Letters, 30*(7), 783-785.

Canepari, M., Bove, M., Mueda, E., Cappello, M., & Kawana, A. (1997). Experimental analysis of neural dynamics in cultured cortical networks and transitions between different patterns of activity. *Biological Cybernetics, 7*, 153-162.

Carmena, J. M., Lebedev, M. A., Crist, R. E., O'Doherty, J. E., Santucci, D. M., Dimitrov, D. F., et al. (2003). Learning to control a brain-machine interface for reaching and grasping by primates. *M.A.L. PLoS Biology, 1*, 193-208.

Chalmers, D. (1995). Facing up the problem of consciousness. *Journal of Consciousness Studies, 2*(3), 200-219.

Chalmers, D. (1997). *The conscious mind: In search of a fundamental theory.* Oxford University Press.

De Marse, T. B., Wagenaar, D. A., & Potter, S. M. (2002). *The neurally controlled artificial animal: A neural computer interface between cultured neural networks and a robotic body.* Proceedings of SFN 2002, Orlando, FL.

Egert, U., Schlosshauer, B., Fennrich, S., Nisch, W., Fejtl, M., Knott, T., et al. (2002). A novel organotypic long-term culture of the rat hippocampus on substrate-integrated microelectrode arrays. *Brain Resource Protocol, 2,* 229-242.

Fromherz, P. (2002). Electrical interfacing of nerve cells and semiconductor chips. *Chemphyschem, 3,* 276-284.

Fromherz, P., Muller, C. O., & Weis, R. (1993). Neuron-transistor: Electrical transfer function measured by the patch-clamp technique. *Physical Review Letters, 71.*

Fromherz, P., Offenhäusser, A., Vetter, T., & Weis, J. (1991). A neuron-silicon-junction: A Retzius-cell of the leech on an insulated-gate field-effect transistor. *Science, 252, 1290-1293.*

Fromherz, P., & Schaden, H. (1994). Defined neuronal arborisations by guided outgrowth of leech neurons in culture. *European Journal of Neuroscience, 6.*

Gao, G., Cagin, T., & Goddard, W. A., III. (1998). Energetics, structure, mechanical and vibrational properties of single walled carbon nanotubes (SWNT). *Nanotechnology, 9,* 184-191.

Garcia, P. S., Calabrese, R. L., DeWeerth, S. P., & Ditto, W. (2003). Simple arithmetic with firing rate encoding in leech neurons: Simulation and experiment. *Proceedings of the XXVI Australasian Computer Science Conference, 16,* 55-60.

Hagan, S., Hameroff, S., & Tuszynski, J. (2002). Quantum computation in brain microtubules? Decoherence and biological feasibility. *Physical Reviews E, 65.*

Hameroff, S. R., & Penrose, R. (1996). Orchestrated reduction of quantum coherence in brain microtubules: A model for consciousness? In S. R. Hameroff, A. W. Kaszniak, & A. C. Scott (Eds.), *Toward a science of consciousness: The first Tucson discussions and debates* (pp. 507-540). Cambridge, MA: MIT Press.

Hofstadter, D. R. (1979). *Gödel, Escher, Bach: An eternal golden braid.* New York: Basic Books.

Hofstadter, D. R., & Dennett, D. C. (1981). *The mind's I: Fantasies and reflections on self and soul.* New York: Basic Books.

Hopfield, J. J. (1984). Neural networks and physical systems with emergent collective computational abilities. *Proceedings National Academy of Sciences US, 81.*

John, A., Wheeler, J. A., & Zurek, W. H. (1983). *Quantum theory and measurement.* Princeton University Press.

Josephson, B. D., & Pallikari-Viras, F. (1991). Biological utilisation of quantum nonlocality. *Foundations of Physics, 21,* 197-207.

Katura, H. (1999). Optical properties of single-wall carbon nanotubes. *Synthetic Metals, 103,* 2555-2558.

Lindner, J. F., & Ditto, W. (1996). Exploring the nonlinear dynamics of a physiologically viable model neuron. *AIP Conference Proceedings, 1,* 375-385.

Lovett, B. W., Reina, J. H., Nazir, A., Kothari, B., & Briggs, G. A. D. (2003). Resonant transfer of excitons and quantum computation. *Physics Letters A, 315,* 136-142.

Maher, M. P., Pine, J., Wright, J., & Tai, Y. C. (1999). The neurochip: A new multielectrode device for stimulating and recording from cultured neurons. *Neuroscience Methods, 87,* 45-56.

Marx, A., & Mandelkow, E. M. (1994). A model of microtubule oscillations. *European Biophysics Journal, 22*(6), 405-421.

Matsuno, K. (1999). Cell motility as an entangled quantum coherence. *BioSystems, 51*, 15-19.

Minsky, M. (2006). *The emotion machine: Commonsense thinking, artificial intelligence, and the future of the human mind.* Simon & Schuster.

Penrose, R. (1994). *Shadows of the mind.* Oxford University Press.

Pizzi, R., de Curtis, M., & Dickson, C. (2002). Evidence of chaotic attractors in cortical fast oscillations tested by an artificial neural network. In J. Kacprzyk (Ed.), *Advances in soft computing.* Physica Verlag.

Pizzi, R., Fantasia, A., Gelain, F., Rossetti, D., & Vescovi, A. (2004a). *Behavior of living human neural networks on microelectrode array support.* Proceedings of the Nanotechnology Conference and Trade Show 2004, Boston.

Pizzi, R., Fantasia, A., Gelain, F., Rossetti, D., & Vescovi, A. (2004b). *Non-local correlations between separated neural networks.* Proceedings of the SPIE Conference on Quantum Information and Computation, Orlando, FL.

Pizzi, R., Rossetti, D., Cino, G., Gelain, F., & Vescovi, A. (2007). Learning in human neural networks on microelectrode arrays. *BioSystems*, 88, 1-15.

Potter, S. M. (2001). Distributed processing in cultured neuronal networks. In M. A. L. Nicolelis (Ed.), *Progress in brain research.* Elsevier Science B.V.

Reger, B., Fleming, K. M., Sanguineti, V., Alford, S., & Mussa-Ivaldi, F. A. (2000) Connecting brains to robots: An artificial body for studying the computational properties of neural tissues. *Artificial Life, 6*, 307-324.

Ruaro, M. E., Bonifazi, P., & Torre, V. (2005). Toward the neurocomputer: Image processing and pattern recognition with neuronal cultures. *IEEE Transactions on Biomedical Engineering, 3.*

Schrödinger, E. (1956). *Science and humanism.* Cambridge University Press.

Searle, J. R. (1980). Minds, brains, and programs. In *The behavioral and brain sciences* (3). Cambridge University Press.

Sept, D., Limbach, H.-J., Bolterauer, H., & Tuszynski, J. A. (1999). A chemical kinetics model for microtubule oscillations. *Journal of Theoretical Biology, 197*, 77-88.

Stapp, H. (1993). *Mind, matter, and quantum mechanics.* Springer-Verlag.

Tuszynski, J. A., Trpisova, B., Sept, D., & Sataric, M. V. (1997). The enigma of microtubules and their self-organizing behavior in the cytoskeleton. *BioSystems, 42*, 153-175.

Wang, Y., Kempa, K., Kimball, B., Carlson, J. B., Benham, G., Li, W. Z., et al. (2004). Receiving and transmitting light-like radio waves: Antenna effect in arrays of aligned carbon nanotubes. *Applied Physics Letters, 85*, 2607-2609.

Wigner, E. (1961). Remarks on the mind-body question. In I. J. Good (Ed.), *The scientist speculates.* London: W. Heinemann.

Wigner, E. (1972). The place of consciousness in modern physics. In C. Muses & A. M. Young (Eds.), *Consciousness and reality.* New York: Outerbridge & Lazard.

Chapter VII
Neurofeedback:
Using Computer Technology to Alter Brain Functioning

David Vernon
Canterbury Christ Church University, UK

ABSTRACT

This chapter introduces neurofeedback as a mechanism for altering human brain functioning and in turn influencing behavior. It argues that neurofeedback provides a plausible mechanism by which the individual can learn to alter and control aspects of his electrocortical activity. The chapter highlights some of the findings from both clinical and optimal performance research, showing the benefits of neurofeedback training, and outlines some of the important issues that remain to be addressed. It is hoped that outlining some of the issues that have yet to be resolved will serve a dual purpose. Initially it will assist in the understanding of some of the theoretical and methodological limitations that may be holding the field back. In addition, it is hoped that such information will stimulate researchers to work toward designing more efficient and effective research protocols and paradigms.

INTRODUCTION

This chapter provides an introduction to some of the uses of neurofeedback and highlights some of the issues from the field that are as yet unresolved. The first section describes how the electrocortical activity of your brain can be recorded and separated into a range of preset frequency components. This is followed by an overview of neurofeedback as an operant-conditioning paradigm that can enable you to learn how to use computer technol-ogy to alter specific aspects of your brain wave activity. The next section provides some evidence for the use of neurofeedback in practice, both in clinical and optimal performance settings. The chapter then focuses on some of the key issues relating to the use of neurofeedback in the field. These are the modality of the feedback given, the specific number and configuration of sensors used to record electrocortical activity, the use of standard preset training frequency ranges, the specific effect of neurofeedback training on cortical activity, issues relating to the duration and frequency of the training, and the transferable effects of neurofeedback training and whether the effects of such training are long lived or not. By highlighting some of the issues that currently limit our understanding of the effectiveness of neurofeedback training, I hope to stimulate future researchers to empirically address them. The final section of the chapter identifies the possible future trend of using full scalp recording and the feedback of multiple frequency components to provide a more comprehensive training package.

THE ELECTROENCEPHALOGRAM

Whether you are awake or asleep your brain remains active, with millions of tiny brain cells called pyramidal cells firing in synchrony representing your thoughts and dreams. However, it was not until Hans Berger discovered that by placing a number of sensors on the human scalp that such electrical activity could be recorded. What Berger originally recorded is now commonly referred to as the electroencephalogram or EEG. The EEG signal itself represents the difference in electrical potential between two sensors, where one is placed over an active region, such as your brain, and the other is placed over what

is assumed to be in inactive reference site, such as your earlobe.

The main aspects of the EEG are its frequency, amplitude, and coherence. Frequency refers to the number of oscillations of EEG activity per second while amplitude is measured as half the distance between the high and low points of an oscillation. Coherence refers to how much the EEG signals recorded from two separate active sites are synchronized such that the crests and troughs of the waves occur simultaneously (see Figure 1).

The EEG recorded from a single active sensor produces a raw trace, which if then converted and replayed on a computer screen looks like a long squiggly line. However, this single trace can then be broken down into a range of predefined frequency components. Much in the same way as white light can be split by a prism into its spectral components of red, orange, yellow, and so forth, the raw trace of the EEG can be divided into a range of frequency components using a fast Fourier transform (FFT; see Figure 2).

Traditionally, the raw EEG trace has been divided into five main frequency bands. These are delta (1-4 Hz), theta (4-7 Hz), alpha (8-12 Hz), beta (13-30 Hz), and gamma (35+ Hz; see, e.g., Andreassi, 2000). As such, the EEG represents a noninvasive technique to record specific

Figure 1. Showing amplitude, frequency, and coherence of the EEG

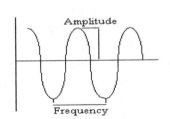

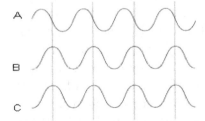

Waveforms A and B are not synchronised but waveforms B and C are

Figure 2. Showing the conversion of the raw EEG trace into four of the classic frequencies (i.e., delta, theta, alpha, and beta)

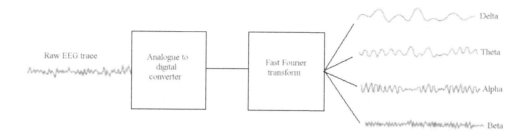

frequency components of your electrocortical activity.

NEUROFEEDBACK

Neurofeedback represents a sophisticated form of EEG biofeedback based on specific aspects of cortical activity. The aim of neurofeedback is to encourage you to learn how to modify some aspect of your cortical activity. This may include learning to change the amplitude, frequency, and/or coherence of distinct electrophysiological components of your brain. The goal of neurofeedback training is to teach you what specific states of cortical arousal feel like and how to reactivate such states voluntarily. For example, during neurofeedback training, your EEG is recorded and the relevant components are extracted and fed back to you using an online feedback loop in the form of audio, visual, or combined audiovisual information. For example, it may be that your aim is to enhance the amplitude of your alpha activity and simultaneously inhibit the surrounding theta and beta frequencies. As such, each of these frequency components may be represented on a computer screen as colored bars, with the amplitude of the relevant frequency component represented by the size of the bar, such that the higher the bar the greater the amplitude. Given this, your task would then be to increase the size of the training frequency bar (alpha) and simultaneously decrease the size of the bars representing the inhibitory frequencies (theta and beta). You attempt to do this by trying to remember and re-creating the thoughts and feelings you had when the bar was high. On meeting this goal, a tone may sound and a symbol may appear to indicate a point scored, with the aim to score as many points as possible. Such training can provide you with the opportunity to learn to alter a range of brain wave activity.

Neurofeedback as a technique to enable humans to control their brain activity was developed back in the 1960s when Joe Kamiya was examining how different states of consciousness were associated with distinct patterns of electrical activity in the brain. In particular, he was interested in the activity of the alpha frequency as this was associated with a calm resting state. He conducted a two-part study examining whether an individual could influence his or her brain activity when such information was fed back (Kamiya, 1968). In the first part of his study, participants were seated with eyes closed and when a tone sounded were asked to say whether they thought they were producing alpha waves or not. He found that some individuals could learn to identify when their brain was producing alpha waves and as a consequence were able to increase their production. In the second part of the study, participants were asked to go into alpha when a bell rang once and not go into the state when the bell rang twice. Once again, some of the participants were able to enter the state on command. Others, however, could not control it at all. Nevertheless, the results were significant and very attractive, showing for the first time that it was possible for someone to voluntarily control the production of a particular aspect of cortical activity.

NEUROFEEDBACK IN PRACTICE

Neurofeedback as a technique for change has been used in a wide range of clinical settings as well as in the optimal performance field more recently. For example, two prominent areas of clinical research utilizing neurofeedback are epilepsy and attention deficit/hyperactivity disorder (ADHD).

The research on epilepsy is based on some serendipitous findings from early work by Barry Sterman and colleagues. While tracking the EEG of cats, Sterman and colleagues found that they exhibited an increase in brain wave frequencies between 12 to 16 Hz when they were given reinforcement to suppress a motor activity. This 12 to 16 Hz activity was termed the sensorimotor rhythm (SMR) because it occurred predominantly over the sensorimotor cortex. This may have led to nothing if Sterman had not then received a request from the U.S. Air Force to examine the effects of exposure to a rocket fuel that was known to produce seizures. He tested this by injecting the chemical into cats, some of which had been involved in his previous EEG study. He found that most of the cats suffered a seizure, but the onset of the seizure was considerably later for a subset of the cats. Trying to understand why this might have occurred, he examined his protocol again

and realized that the resilient cats were the ones that had been involved in his previous conditioning tests. This led him to surmise that enhancing the SMR had reduced seizure onset for the cats, which in turn spurred a study to examine whether training epileptic patients to enhance their SMR would have similar beneficial effects (Sterman & Friar, 1972). A number of studies have since shown that the motor seizure incidence of epileptic patients may be lowered significantly by training them to enhance their SMR using neurofeedback (Sterman, 1973, 2000; Sterman & Macdonald, 1978; Sterman, Macdonald, & Stone, 1974).

These early findings led others like Joel Lubar to wonder whether neurofeedback training to enhance SMR, which required the individual to remain mentally alert but motorically quiet, would aid in the reduction of some of the hyperactive and impulsive behaviors exhibited by children with ADHD (Lubar & Shouse, 1976). This research produced some initially positive findings showing improvements in both the behavior and academic performance of such children (Linden, Habib, & Radojevic, 1996; Lubar, Swartwood, Swartwood, & O'Donnell, 1995; for a review see Vernon, Frick, & Gruzelier, 2004). More recently, this intervention has gained support from quantitative EEG studies showing that up to 80% of children with ADHD exhibit distinct differences in their cortical profile when compared to a nonclinical group (Chabot, di Michele, Prichep, & John, 2001). For instance, when compared to nonclinical controls, children with ADHD exhibit an excess of slow theta activity, predominantly in the frontal regions, and lower levels of the faster beta activity (Clarke, Barry, McCarthy, & Selikowitz, 1998; Clarke, Barry, McCarthy, Selikowitz, & Brown, 2002; Mann, Lubar, Zimmerman, Miller, & Muenchen, 1992). These findings have led to a new range of neurofeedback training protocols aimed at training children with ADHD to inhibit the excessive slow wave theta activity and simultaneously attempt to enhance the faster beta activity (Monastra, Monastra, & George, 2002; Thompson &

Thompson, 1998). However, because of the lack of large-scale randomized controlled studies, the evidence suggesting that neurofeedback has a beneficial effect is equivocal at present.

These studies provide suggestive evidence that neurofeedback may enhance the attentional abilities of clinical groups. This, along with findings showing specific patterns of cortical activity associated with particular patterns of behavior, has led to an increasing use of neurofeedback in the optimal performance field. Here the aim is to enhance the performance of healthy participants beyond and above its current status. To date, neurofeedback has been utilized in enhancing sporting performance, a range of cognitive abilities, and artistic performance (see Vernon, 2005).

For instance, one group of researchers examined whether neurofeedback training to enhance low-frequency activity prior to the execution of a physical skill would benefit performance (Landers et al., 1991). Landers et al. examined the performance of two groups of pre-elite archers receiving neurofeedback training. The neurofeedback training required one of the groups to increase the low frequency activity in their left temporal region. This was based on the assumption that an increase in low-frequency activity represented a reduced level of cognitive activation, which would result in a reduced level of covert verbalizations of the left brain allowing the visual-spatial processing of the right hemisphere to become more dominant. The second neurofeedback group was included to control for motivational or expectancy effects associated with the use of the neurofeedback equipment and as such received the same type of training over their right temporal region. Both groups completed 27 shots at a target positioned 45 m away, with the level of performance measured as the distance between the arrow and the center of the target. This was followed by a number of neurofeedback training sessions, which continued until each participant reached a preset criterion with regard to changes in the amplitude of their

EEG. Then both groups completed a further 27 target shots. They found that those trained to enhance low-frequency activity in their left temporal region showed a significant improvement in their performance. In contrast, those trained to enhance low-frequency activity in their right temporal region performed significantly worse following the neurofeedback training. These findings led Landers et al. to conclude that neurofeedback training may be used as a method of enhancing the performance of pre-elite archers.

Research has also examined whether neurofeedback training to alter the faster beta frequencies can influence the cognitive abilities of healthy participants (Egner & Gruzelier, 2001; Rasey, Lubar, McIntyre, Zoffuto, & Abbott, 1996; Vernon et al., 2003; Vernon, Egner, et al., 2004). For instance, Egner and Gruzelier (2001) trained a group of 22 participants to enhance their low beta activity in the 12 to 15 Hz range over the right central region of the brain and 15 to 18 Hz range over the left central region while simultaneously inhibiting the surrounding lower theta (4-7 Hz) and higher beta (22-30 Hz) frequencies. The participants completed a total of 10 neurofeedback training sessions while pre- and postmeasures of cognition were examined using a computerized continuous performance task (CPT; Greenberg, 1987) and an event-related potential (ERP) measure of attention. The continuous performance task involved presenting a range of stimuli on screen, some of which were targets that required the participant to respond as quickly and as accurately as possible, and some of which were lures or nontargets. In this instance, the participant was required to refrain from responding. The ERP task involved presenting a range of tones to the participant that changed in pitch; the participant was required to actively monitor and detect such changes while EEG was recorded. The researchers found that, following the neurofeedback training, participants showed a significant improvement on the CPT task and an increase in the amplitude of a generalized

P3b ERP component that is thought to represent an updating of information in working memory (Donchin & Coles, 1988). They also found some correlations between changes in participants' EEG as a function of neurofeedback training and improvements in cognitive processing. This led them to conclude that the results represented a "successful enhancement of attentional performance in healthy volunteers through EEG operant conditioning techniques" (p. 9).

More recently, my colleagues and I found that neurofeedback training to enhance the low beta (12-15 Hz) frequency can influence semantic working memory performance (Vernon et al., 2003; Vernon, Egner, et al., 2004). We trained two groups of participants to enhance a range of different EEG frequencies and then examined the effect of such training on a range of cognitive tasks. The first group trained to enhance slow theta (4-8 Hz) activity while simultaneously inhibiting the surrounding delta (1-4 Hz) and alpha (8-12 Hz) frequencies. The second group underwent neurofeedback training to enhance the amplitude of their low beta (12-15 Hz) frequencies while simultaneously inhibiting the theta (4-8 Hz) and high beta (18-22 Hz) frequencies. All participants completed a range of cognitive tasks designed to measure attention and semantic working memory, followed by eight sessions of neurofeedback training with the sensor placed on the central position of the scalp; they then repeated the measures of cognitive performance. Contrary to our expectations, we found that those training to enhance their theta activity actually showed a marginal reduction of theta and exhibited no change in their cognitive performance. In contrast, those training to enhance their low beta showed significant changes in their EEG in line with the neurofeedback training protocol. In addition to this, the low-beta training group also showed a significant improvement in semantic working memory. We attempted to account for this by suggesting that enhancing the 12 to 15

Hz range aids the maintenance of the working memory representation utilized in semantic working memory.

With regard to artistic performance, recent research has reported on two successive experiments aimed at utilizing neurofeedback to enhance music performance (Egner & Gruzelier, 2003). In the first experiment, Egner and Gruzelier report on a group of music students who underwent neurofeedback training to enhance a combination of frequency ranges, including low beta (12-15 Hz and 15-18 Hz) and theta (5-8 Hz) at different scalp locations. Before and after the neurofeedback training, all participants were required to play a piece of music for 15 minutes, which was recorded. Their performance was assessed internally by a panel of judges from the Royal College of Music and externally by a set of experts examining the video recordings of each performance. Researchers found that the neurofeedback training resulted in marginal improvements in musical performance. These findings led them to conduct a second experiment that utilized a similar design but had a separate group of participants undergo neurofeedback training to enhance the level of their theta activity over that of their alpha activity (commonly referred to as alpha-theta training). Here they found that when participants' post-training musical performances were examined, they showed significant improvements in overall quality, musical understanding, stylistic accuracy, and interpretative imagination. This led Egner and Gruzelier (2003) to conclude that neurofeedback training can benefit the musical performance of healthy individuals.

Given the findings outlined above from the clinical and optimal performance literature, it would seem that neurofeedback represents a useful mechanism for providing you with the ability to alter your brain activity and in doing so change your behavior. However, while this evidence is suggestive, there are many issues relating to the use of neurofeedback that remain unresolved, limiting our understanding of its use and its acceptance in the wider field. These include which type of feedback is most effective, the specific recording and monitoring setup of the EEG, the use of standard training frequencies, and the assumption that training to enhance a single frequency range will only influence that component. In addition, there are questions concerning the neurofeedback training sessions themselves that need to be answered, for instance, how many neurofeedback training sessions are required, how long should a session last, and how often should they take place. An important question relating to the use of neurofeedback is whether the effect of neurofeedback training is transferable to situations outside of the training setting. Furthermore, are the effects of such training long lived or not? Each of these issues will be examined below.

ISSUES

Modality of Feedback

Information recorded from the EEG can be fed back to the individual in a number of different formats, such as auditory, visual, or a combination of auditory and visual feedback. The type of feedback is important as it needs to be considered as capable of providing sufficient information for the feedback loop to operate effectively.

Traditional biofeedback research suggests that the attentional demands placed upon the participant during training by the feedback signal may influence performance. For instance, presenting two simultaneous signals (e.g., visual and auditory) may enhance attention to the task (Qualls & Sheehan, 1981). As attention to one of the signals wanders, the remaining signal may be capable of redirecting attention back to the task. To some extent this idea is supported by research showing enhanced attention, as indexed by quicker response times, to multimodal information (Giray & Ulrich, 1993).

For neurofeedback, there are no clear empirical data either way. However, while comparisons across studies may be limited by possible differences in method and focus, they can also provide some useful insights. For instance, research examining the effect of alpha neurofeedback training has produced some interesting results in terms of the modality of feedback used (Bauer, 1976; Vernon & Withycombe, 2006). Bauer trained a group of participants to enhance their level of alpha activity across four 1-hour sessions. During the training, the participants sat in a dimly lit room and were given feedback in the form of a 400 Hz tone to signify the presence of alpha. Following this, the participants were given a range of memory tasks while simultaneously attempting to produce alpha. Bauer found that the neurofeedback training helped participants to produce approximately 25% more alpha activity. However, more recently a colleague and I trained a group of participants to enhance the level of their alpha activity by having them focus on a computer screen and providing them with both auditory and visual feedback signifying the presence or absence of alpha. The neurofeedback training took place over ten 10-minute sessions. Unlike Bauer, we found no evidence that the participants were able to enhance the level of their alpha activity.

Although caution is needed when making comparisons between studies that are not methodologically matched, the above findings are suggestive. It may be that, for alpha at least, auditory feedback is more effective than either visual or a visual-auditory combination. Such a possibility is consistent with early research showing that participants can learn to increase the level of their alpha activity when given auditory feedback with their eyes closed (Kamiya, 1968). Nevertheless, a rigorous examination of the effectiveness of the different modalities of feedback on all EEG frequencies is needed to fully elucidate this issue.

Montage

The electrical potentials recorded from sensors placed on the scalp are all referential in the sense that the potentials from one location are measured with respect to those at another location. The precise number and configuration of sensors used to record this information is commonly referred to as the montage and follows a preset pattern on the scalp according to an international EEG nomenclature called the 10-20 system; it is based on the relationship between the location of an electrode and the underlying area of the cerebral cortex (Jasper, 1958). It is called the 10-20 system because the sensors are placed at distances of either 10% or 20% apart from each other or set points on the head. In addition to this, each site is identified by a letter, which corresponds to the underlying cortical lobe, and another letter or number to denote the location. For example, the letters F, T, C, P, and O stand for the frontal, temporal, central, parietal, and occipital lobes, respectively. In addition to this, any accompanying even numbers (2, 4, 6, 8) refer to the right hemisphere and odd numbers (1, 3, 5, 7) refer to the left hemisphere, with the letter z denoting a sensor placed on the midline. Thus, the position Cz refers to the central region of the scalp along the midline, and C3 refers to the central position of the scalp on the left. See Figure 3 for an illustration of some the commonly used scalp locations.

Traditionally, neurofeedback training has been conducted with single-channel recordings using either a referential (monopolar) or sequential (bipolar) montage. It is important to note that an assumed difference between the referential and sequential montages is the degree to which each is thought to measure cortical activity at a given location. However, this is not necessarily the case as any recorded potential reflects the integration

Figure 3. Showing EEG sensor placement according to the 10-20 system

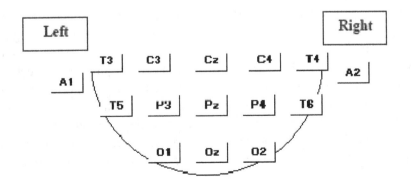

of the electric field along any path between two points. As such, any potential measured at a point on the scalp is not necessarily a characteristic of that point alone, but also represents the path to that point (Katznelson, 1981). Hence, the potentials recorded can only be interpreted as activity just below the active sensor if you assume a single stable generator located beneath the skull and no other additional dipoles at other locations or orientations. Such a scenario has been suggested to be unlikely (for more information on this point see Nunez, 1981).

If these assumptions are accepted, then referential training is thought to provide a measure of the amplitude at a single active site (e.g., Cz) compared to a neutral reference location. As such, neurofeedback training using this type of montage relies on the participant's ability to alter the relevant EEG component at or near the site of the active sensor. Hence, one advantage of this type of montage is that it allows you to identify activity at a particular location.

In contrast, identifying precisely what is being trained using a sequential montage is more ambiguous. For example, a sequential montage provides a picture of the relationship between two active sites (e.g., Cz and Fz) but cannot provide clear information concerning what is happening at each individual site. As is the case for the referential montage, what is observed in sequential neurofeedback training is what remains in the EEG following rejection of the common mode. Thus, the potentials that are recorded and fed back to the trainee represent a measure of how the activity at the two different sites differs. This means that an increase in amplitude of a set frequency may be the result of either (a) increasing the synchronous synaptic potentials at site A and decreasing them at site B, or vice versa, or (b) altering the phase relationship between the two points (for a discussion of these issues see Putman, 2001). Thus, in contrast to the referential montage that is assumed to provide information on cortical activity at a set location, the sequential montage results in feedback that reflects the relationship between different regions of the cortex.

No research has yet been conducted that directly compares the two montages to ascertain which may be the more effective in facilitating changes in EEG. However, some illumination and guidance may be provided from the research literature. For instance, Beatty et al. (1974) used a bipolar montage set between O1 and P3 to train a group of participants to suppress theta activity and were successful in achieving this goal. My colleagues and I, however, failed to elicit any changes in the participants' EEG when we trained them to enhance theta using a referential montage at Cz (Vernon et al., 2003). Of course, caution is needed to not overinterpret this comparison given the range of other differences between the two studies. Nevertheless, it may be that neurofeedback training to alter theta activity is more responsive when a sequential montage is used. In contrast, we found that neurofeedback training utilizing a referential montage was efficacious in facilitating significant changes in the EEG for the low beta frequency range. It may be the case that different montages differentially suit the training of different EEG frequency components. As such, future research could help to elucidate this by conducting clear comparisons between the two montages for each of the main frequency ranges.

Training Standard Frequency Ranges

Most if not all of the neurofeedback training to date has focused on encouraging the participant to alter one or more of the traditional set EEG frequency components (i.e., delta, theta, alpha, beta, and gamma). This sort of training assumes that a traditional set frequency, alpha (8-12 Hz), for example, is the same for everyone. However, such an assumption is questionable given the research showing that the peak alpha frequency can vary to a considerable extent in normal-age-matched participants (Klimesch, Schimke, Ladurner, & Pfurtscheller, 1990; Klimesch, Schimke, & Pfurtscheller, 1993). As such, the future of neurofeedback training may be better served by initially identifying each participant's individual alpha frequency using their mean peak frequency as an anchor point and allocating a 2 Hz window below the peak as lower alpha and a 2 Hz window above the peak as upper alpha (see Klimesch et al., 1990, for a description of this method). Identifying the EEG frequency ranges individually for each participant may enable them to alter their cortical activity more effectively.

Effect of Neurofeedback Training on the EEG

The underlying rationale of using neurofeedback training to enhance performance is one based upon associations. By identifying associations between particular patterns of cortical activity and specific states or aspects of behavior that are classified as optimal, one can attempt to train an individual to enhance performance by mirroring the pattern of cortical activity seen during such optimal states. An implicit assumption that permeates the neurofeedback literature and underpins current practice is that the training process will lead to changes in the EEG, which in turn produces changes in behavior. However, it should be noted that the link between these components is not well established in either performance enhancement (see, e.g., Egner, Zech, & Gruzelier, 2004) or the clinical literature (see, e.g., Vernon, Frick, et al., 2004), especially with respect to predictable changes and correlations between changes and outcome variables. For instance, research has shown that healthy participants learning to enhance low beta (11.7 to 14.6 Hz) at Cz exhibited a posttraining decrease in low beta in the prefrontal region and a decrease in alpha (7.8-11.7 Hz) at left frontal regions (Egner et al., 2004), while learning to

raise theta (3.9-7.8 Hz) over alpha (7.8-11.7 Hz) at Pz was associated with a posttraining reduction of beta (14.6-17.5 Hz) at prefrontal scalp sites. Furthermore, additional examination of these effects only managed to partially replicate these findings, showing that raising theta over alpha was associated with a reduction in prefrontal beta. This shows that learning to temporarily enhance the amplitude of a specific frequency component of the EEG during neurofeedback training does not necessarily translate to increased activity in that component while at rest. The reason for this pattern of effects is, as yet, unclear. It is possible that the difficulty in producing a clear and consistent effect on baseline EEG levels is due to the underlying complexity of the neural dynamics of the EEG. Nevertheless, further systematic investigation is imperative to examine and produce empirical validation of predictable neurophysiological outcomes as a result of neurofeedback training.

Neurofeedback Training Sessions

Neurofeedback training is both labor and time intensive. As such, it would be beneficial to know, for both clinical and optimal performance paradigms, what the ideal duration and frequency of training sessions should be in order to elicit a positive change in the EEG profile as well as producing sustainable changes in behavior and cognitive performance.

Although there is a great deal of research examining the efficacy of neurofeedback, both as a clinical intervention and to enhance the performance of healthy participants, there is as yet no research comparing the duration, frequency, and total number of neurofeedback sessions required to elicit a positive outcome. Furthermore, there is not always a great deal of consistency in how the different researchers approach the neurofeedback training sessions. Looking at the research literature, it may be the case that attempting to train different frequency components of the EEG may require distinct training regimes. For instance, Beatty et al. (1974) found changes in the theta frequency range of their participants following two 1-hour sessions. In contrast, my colleagues and I found no changes in our participants' theta levels following eight 10-minute sessions (Vernon et al., 2003). This would suggest that neurofeedback training to alter the theta frequency component may be more effective if the training sessions are longer and more intensive. Again, there are other differences between the two studies that make such a comparison less than ideal. For instance, the participants in the study conducted by Beatty et al. were undergoing neurofeedback training to suppress their theta activity, while the participants in our study were attempting to enhance their theta activity, and it may be that learning to suppress a particular EEG frequency component is somehow easier than enhancing it (yet another empirical question that awaits to be resolved).

Furthermore, attempts to alter the low beta frequency range of the EEG in an effort to influence cognition have also produced some inconsistent effects, which may be due to the frequency of the training sessions (Egner & Gruzelier, 2004; Vernon et al., 2003). For instance, Egner and Gruzelier trained a group of participants to enhance their low beta activity across ten 15-minute sessions completed once a week. Although there were some changes in attentional performance, there was no clear change in the participants' EEG. In contrast, we trained a group of participants to enhance their low beta across eight 10-minute sessions carried out twice per week. Not only did we find a clear improvement in semantic working memory, but we also found that the participants exhibited a significant enhancement of their low beta activity. This would suggest that neurofeedback training to enhance the low beta frequency range may be more effective if the training is carried out in multiple weekly sessions.

Such interpretations, while tenuous, highlight the need for a systematic investigation of these issues to make the training process more efficient.

Transferable Effects of Neurofeedback

One issue that has received little attention is whether the effects of neurofeedback training can easily transfer to situations outside of the training session. That is, do you have to complete neurofeedback training at the same time as completing the task in order for the training to have a positive effect, or can what you have learned during the training be transferred, allowing you to utilize this skill at a later date? Needless to say that if what is learned during the neurofeedback training is capable of being transferred to situations beyond the training session, this makes neurofeedback a potentially powerful mechanism for change.

Unfortunately, there is no evidence relating directly to this issue and the findings from the literature are ambiguous. For instance, Beatty et al. (1974) found that having a group of participants simultaneously undergo both neurofeedback training to suppress theta activity and a radar monitoring task resulted in improved attentional monitoring of the radar task. This would suggest that the neurofeedback training needs to be conducted at the same time as any test performance. However, Bauer (1976) had a group of participants simultaneously attempt to produce alpha while completing recall and digit span tasks and found no evidence of an effect on cognition. More recently, we have shown that neurofeedback training to enhance the low beta rhythm not only led to enhanced activity in the target frequency range, but was also associated with better performance on a posttraining semantic working memory task (Vernon et al., 2003). This would suggest that what is learned during the neurofeedback training is transferable to a posttesting situation. However, it may be the case that what is learned during the neurofeedback training is also influenced by the targeted range of EEG frequencies, the particular dynamics of the training session, and the behavior under examination. Nevertheless, the transferability of what is learned during neurofeedback training is an important issue that needs to be addressed and as such remains the domain of future research.

Long-Term Effects of Neurofeedback Training

A final issue relates to how long the effects of neurofeedback training last. Given the labor- and time-intensive nature of the training, it would be useful to know whether any changes resulting from neurofeedback training are merely a temporary adaptation or of lasting benefit. In terms of optimal performance training for healthy participants, the research does not allow any inferences to be drawn as none of the researchers conducted any long-term follow-up analyses. However, there is some limited evidence from the clinical literature that the effects of neurofeedback may be long lived (Monastra et al., 2002; Tansey, 1993; Tansey & Bruner, 1983).

Tansey and Bruner (1983) reported on a 10-year-old boy they treated with neurofeedback. Directly following the treatment, the boy was able to produce more activity in the target frequency range of 14 Hz and showed improvements in behavior. Ten years after the termination of his treatment, Tansey (1993) once again examined the boy and found him to exhibit a normalized EEG profile as well as showing evidence of academic success. Such a case, while interesting, needs to be treated with caution as it relies on the data from a single participant. However, more recently Monastra et al. (2002) conducted a 1-week follow up analysis of children with ADHD that had received neurofeedback as part of their treatment package. They found that the children that had received neurofeedback training as part of their treatment showed a consistent decrease in their theta-beta ratios compared to a group that did not receive neurofeedback, as well as attentional performance that was judged to be within normative limits.

The clinical data suggest that neurofeedback may provide long-term benefits. Such a view is consistent with the suggestion that the gains made during neurofeedback training are likely to be long lived and are a result of a learning process that involves the acquisition of self-regulatory skills through operant conditioning (Lubar, 1995). Nevertheless, it is essential then that future research, particularly in the optimal performance arena, ensure that long-term follow up analyses are conducted to ascertain precisely what the long-term benefits of neurofeedback training are.

FUTURE TRENDS

Although neurofeedback has been around since the 1960s, its popularity in recent years has grown, not only in clinical practice but also in optimal performance training. At present, all neurofeedback training is conducted using single or dual sensors placed in either a referential or sequential montage. Such an approach, while useful, has its limitations in terms of what can be trained and where. As our understanding of the nature and complexity of the brain improves and our ability to build computers that are capable of processing more information at faster speeds evolves, the neurofeedback training of the future may be very different from the type of training undertaken today. Instead of attempting to enhance a sct frequency range recorded from a single sensor placed at a fixed location, we may be able to train a whole range of frequency components, recorded from across the whole scalp. Full-cap neurofeedback training with multiple frequencies being fed back to the participant in real time may open up a whole new range of possibilities concerning what can be trained.

CONCLUSION

Neurofeedback represents an interesting example of human-computer interaction that has evolved over time to be used in a range of different settings. The use of a computer to provide you with information concerning your electrocortical activity, of which you were consciously unaware, provides a mechanism enabling you to take some degree of conscious control over the activation of various EEG frequencies and in doing so alter some aspect of your behaviour. The possible benefits of such training are only beginning to become known.

Recent years have seen a dramatic increase in the availability and use of neurofeedback in both clinical and optimal performance settings, with research suggesting that such training has a great deal of potential, only some of which is currently realized. However, while the present research findings are encouraging, there are a number of issues that remain to be resolved in order to help us optimize the nature of the training and in doing so provide a neurofeedback training regime that is both more efficient and more effective. It is not clear from the present research what the limits of neurofeedback training may be, and this may change as new methods are developed and adopted. However, it is clear that such findings speak of interesting possibilities in terms of what may be achieved, although at present these possibilities remain the domain of future researchers to explore.

REFERENCES

Andreassi, J. L. (2000). *Psychophysiology: Human behaviour and physiological response* (4th ed.). Mahwah, NJ: LEA.

Bauer, R. H. (1976). Short-term memory: EEG alpha correlates and the effect of increased alpha. *Behavioural Biology, 17*, 425-433.

Chabot, R. J., di Michele, F., Prichep, L., & John, E. R. (2001). The clinical role of computerized EEG in the evaluation and treatment of learning and attention disorders in children and adolescents. *Journal of Neuropsychiatry and Clinical Neuroscience, 13*(2), 171-186.

Clarke, A. R., Barry, R. J., McCarthy, R., & Selikowitz, M. (1998). EEG analysis in attention-deficit/hyperactivity disorder: A comparative study of two subtypes. *Psychiatry Research, 81*(1), 19-29.

Clarke, A. R., Barry, R. J., McCarthy, R., Selikowitz, M., & Brown, C. R. (2002). EEG evidence for a new conceptualisation of attention deficit hyperactivity disorder. *Clinical Neurophysiology, 113*(7), 1036-1044.

Donchin, E., & Coles, M. G. H. (1988). Is the P300 component a manifestation of context updating. *The Behavioral and Brain Sciences, 11*, 406-425.

Egner, T., & Gruzelier, J. (2003). Ecological validity of neurofeedback: Modulation of slow wave EEG enhances musical performance. *NeuroReport, 14*(9), 1221-1224.

Egner, T., & Gruzelier, J. (2004). EEG biofeedback of low beta band components: Frequency-specific effects on variables of attention and event-related brain potentials. *Clinical Neurophysiology, 115*, 131-139.

Egner, T., & Gruzelier, J. H. (2001). Learned self-regulation of EEG frequency components affects attention and event-related brain potentials in humans. *NeuroReport, 12*(18), 4155-4159.

Giray, M., & Ulrich, R. (1993). Motor coactivation revealed by response force in divided and focused attention. *Journal of Experimental Psychology, Human Perception and Performance, 19*(6), 1278-1291.

Greenberg, L. (1987). An objective measure of methylphenidate response: Clinical use of the

MCA. *Psychopharmacology Bulletin, 23*(2), 279-282.

Jasper, H. H. (1958). Report of the committee on methods of clinical examination in electro-encephalography. *Electroencephalography and Clinical Neurophysiology, 10,* 370-375.

Kamiya, J. (1968). Conscious control of brain waves. *Psychology Today, 1,* 57-60.

Katznelson, R. D. (1981). Normal modes of the brain: Neuroanatomical basis and a physiological theoretical model. In P. L. Nunez (Ed.), *Electric fields of the brain: The neurophysics of EEG* (pp. 401-442). New York: Oxford University Press.

Klimesch, W., Schimke, H., Ladurner, G., & Pfurtscheller, G. (1990). Alpha frequency and memory performance. *Psychophysiology, 4,* 381-390.

Klimesch, W., Schimke, H., & Pfurtscheller, G. (1993). Alpha frequency, cognitive load and memory performance. *Brain Topography, 5*(3), 241-251.

Landers, D. M., Petruzzello, S. J., Salazar, W., Crews, D. J., Kubitz, K. A., Gannon, T. L., et al. (1991). The influence of electrocortical biofeedback on performance in pre-elite archers. *Medicine and Science in Sports and Exercise, 23*(1), 123-129.

Linden, M., Habib, T., & Radojevic, V. (1996). A controlled study of the effects of EEG biofeedback on cognition and behaviour of children with ADD and LD. *Biofeedback and Self Regulation, 21*(1), 35-49.

Lubar, J. F. (1995). Neurofeedback for the management of attention-deficit/hyperactivity disorders. In M. S. Schwartz (Ed.), *Biofeedback: A practitioner's guide* (2nd ed., pp. 493-522). New York: Guildford Press.

Lubar, J. F., & Shouse, M. N. (1976). EEG and behavioral changes in a hyperkinetic child con-current with training of the sensorimotor rhythm (SMR): A preliminary report. *Biofeedback and Self Regulation, 1*(3), 293-306.

Lubar, J. F., Swartwood, M. O., Swartwood, J. N., & O'Donnell, P. H. (1995). Evaluation of the effectiveness of EEG neurofeedback training for ADHD in a clinical setting as measured by changes in T.O.V.A. scores, behavioural ratings, and WISC-R performance. *Biofeedback and Self Regulation, 20*(1), 83-99.

Mann, C. A., Lubar, J. F., Zimmerman, A. W., Miller, C. A., & Muenchen, R. A. (1992). Quantitative analysis of EEG in boys with attention-deficit-hyperactivity disorder: Controlled study with clinical implications. *Pediatric Neurology, 8*(1), 30-36.

Monastra, V. J., Monastra, D. M., & George, S. (2002). The effects of stimulant therapy, EEG biofeedback and parenting style on the primary symptoms of attention deficit/hyperactivity disorder. *Applied Psychophysiology and Biofeedback, 27*(4), 231-249.

Nunez, P. L. (1981). *Electric fields of the brain: The neurophysics of EEG.* New York: Oxford University Press.

Putman, J. A. (2001). Technical issues involving bipolar EEG training protocols. *Journal of Neurotherapy, 5*(3), 51-58.

Qualls, P. J., & Sheehan, P. W. (1981). Role of the feedback signal in electromyograph biofeedback: The relevance of attention. *Journal of Experimental Psychology, General, 110*(2), 204-216.

Rasey, H. W., Lubar, J. F., McIntyre, A., Zoffuto, A. C., & Abbott, P. L. (1996). EEG biofeedback for the enhancement of attentional processing in normal college students. *Journal of Neurotherapy, 1*(3), 15-21.

Sterman, M. B. (1973). Neurophysiologic and clinical studies of sensorimotor EEG biofeedback training: Some effects on epilepsy. *Seminal Psychiatry, 5*(4), 507-525.

Sterman, M. B. (2000). Basic concepts and clinical findings in the treatment of seizure disorders with EEG operant conditioning. *Clinical Electroencephalography, 31*(1), 45-55.

Sterman, M. B., & Friar, L. (1972). Suppression of seizures in an epileptic following sensorimotor EEG feedback training. *Electroencephalography and Clinical Neurophysiology, 33*(1), 89-95.

Sterman, M. B., & Macdonald, L. R. (1978). Effects of central cortical EEG feedback training on incidence of poorly controlled seizures. *Epilepsia, 19*(3), 207-222.

Sterman, M. B., Macdonald, L. R., & Stone, R. K. (1974). Biofeedback training of the sensorimotor electroencephalogram rhythm in man: Effects on epilepsy. *Epilepsia, 15*(3), 395-416.

Tansey, M. A. (1993). Ten-year stability of EEG biofeedback results for hyperactive boy who failed fourth grade perceptually impaired class. *Biofeedback and Self Regulation, 18*(1), 33-44.

Tansey, M. A., & Bruner, R. L. (1983). EMG and EEG biofeedback training in the treatment of a 10-year-old hyperactive boy with a developmental reading disorder. *Biofeedback and Self Regulation, 8*(1), 25-37.

Thompson, L., & Thompson, M. (1998). Neurofeedback combined with training in metacognitive strategies: Effectiveness in students with ADD. *Applied Psychophysiology and Biofeedback, 23*(4), 243-263.

Vernon, D. (2005). Can neurofeedback training enhance performance? An evaluation of the evidence with implications for future research. *Applied Psychophysiology and Biofeedback, 30*(4), 347-364.

Vernon, D., Egner, T., Cooper, N., Compton, T., Neilands, C., Sheri, A., et al. (2003). The effect of training distinct neurofeedback protocols on aspects of cognitive performance. *International Journal of Psychophysiology, 47*(1), 75-85.

Vernon, D., Egner, T., Cooper, N., Compton, T., Neilands, C., Sheri, A., et al. (2004). The effect of distinct neurofeedback training protocols on working memory, mental rotation and attention performance. *Journal of Neurotherapy, 8*(1), 100-101.

Vernon, D., Frick, A., & Gruzelier, J. (2004). Neurofeedback as a treatment for ADHD: A methodological review with implications for future research. *Journal of Neurotherapy, 8*(2), 53-82.

Vernon, D., & Withycombe, E. (2006). *The use of alpha neurofeedback training to enhance mental rotation performance.* Paper presented to the Society of Applied Neuroscience, Swansea, United Kingdom.

Chapter VIII
Biological Traits in Artificial Self–Reproducing Systems

Eleonora Bilotta
Università della Calabria, Italy

Pietro Pantano
Università della Calabria, Italy

ABSTRACT

This chapter presents an artificial taxonomy of 2-D, self-replicating cellular automata (CA) that can be considered as proto-organisms for structure replication. We found that the process of self-reproduction is a widespread mechanism. In fact, self-reproducers in 2-D CA are very common and we discovered almost 10 methods of self-replication. The structures these systems produce, from ordered to complex ones, are very similar to those found in biological endeavor. After examining self-replicating structures and the way they reproduce, we consider their behavior in relation to the patterns they realize and to the function they manifest in realizing artificial organisms. According to us, many methods produced by CA are based on universal models of biological cell development. The relevance of such work consists in the goal of modeling the evolution of living systems that can lead us to a better understanding of the essential properties of life.

INTRODUCTION

What is the evolutionary process that has brought about the generation of self-reproducing systems and how do such configurations form and unite, giving life to more complicated organisms through a process of self-reproduction? What are the fundamental mechanisms that bring about the creation of self-reproducers? And what are the internal mechanisms that make self-reproducers create some forms rather than others? How have the tails of tigers been formed, or the wings of a butterfly, or even the cellular structures that cover our bodies, the epithelium (*Groves, Wilson, &*

Reeder, 2005)? What are the functional motives in evolution that have created self-reproducers, or rather structures capable of replicating themselves with a purpose or even without one, to follow other specific objectives of the system or environment in which such organisms are found? In other words, what is the function of self-reproduction and how can such a function be reproduced in the digital machines now in our possession?

Almost all the applications that deal with the simulation and synthesis of living systems are related to the influential work of John von Neumann (1966), who proposed a machine capable of reproducing itself: the universal constructor. In fact, the automatic treatment of the self-reproducing process has become a mathematical problem—the "logic of life" or rather how to extract mathematical algorithmic structures from biological phenomena, structures that can be useful to the understanding of the biology of the phenomena and their possible reinvention in digital worlds.

The study of self-reproducing structures has continued to search for a minimum system capable of nontrivial reproduction (Langton, 1984; Morita & Imai, 1996), other computing capabilities of the self-reproducers (Perrier, Sipper, & Zahnd, 1996; Tempesti, 1995), and the self-reproducers' emergence and evolution (Chou & Reggia, 1997; Lohn & Reggia, 1995; Sayama, 1998, 2000). Here we propose an alternative approach, through which, using genetic algorithms on two-dimensional cellular automata (CA), we obtain the emergent phenomena of self-replication. We have found and classified different kinds of self-reproducer systems that have genetic maps, as if they were biological agents in a real environmental situation (Bilotta, Lafusa, & Pantano, 2003). We argue that the study of these self-reproducing systems may be deeply significant for both natural and artificial evolutionary systems.

In this chapter, we present a taxonomy of self-reproducers that are particularly interesting and

present behavior analogous to that of biological nature, and we analyze how these construct colonies. The nature of these colonies, apart from the complexity of the structure of the self-reproducer, is regulated by precise rules of fractal nature, which throw light on the growth of the form.

The chapter is organized as follows. The second section discusses CA and GA formal aspects. The third section reports on self-reproducers' taxonomy. Finally, conclusions are presented.

FORMAL ASPECTS

The considered environment is a two-dimensional CA, which can be thought of as the following tuple.

$$A = (d, S, N, f), \tag{1}$$

where d is a positive integer that indicates the CA dimension (one-, two-, three-dimensional or more), S a set of finite states, $N = (x_1,....., x_n)$ is a neighborhood vector of n different elements of Z^d, and f is a local rule defined as

$$f : S^n \rightarrow S. \tag{2}$$

In our case d=2, and the neighborhood identifies the cells with a local interaction ray r, so equation (2) to the $(2r + 1)^2$ elements of S associates with another element of S, that is,

$$\begin{pmatrix} \cdots & \cdots & \cdots \\ \cdots & s_{ij} & \cdots \\ \cdots & \cdots & \cdots \end{pmatrix} \mapsto s_{ij} \tag{3}$$

with $s_{ij} \in S$ for $\forall i, j$.

A rule that discriminates all possible cases is expressed in exhaustive form and considers all $k^{(2r+1)}$ possible cases. With the increase of k=|S| and of r, the exhaustive rule becomes not very manageable. Here we define a particular form of rule (called hereafter k-totalistic rule), considering rules that do not distinguish the position of neighbors in the surrounding area, but just consider how many cells are in a given stage (Bilotta, Lafusa, & Pantano, 2002, 2003).

Let $h_s(t)$ be the number of cells in the neighborhood that is in stage s at time t. We denote as V the set of all possible configurations of the neighborhood whose elements can be represented by a numerical string $(h_0h_1....h_{k-1})$; h_i values are not arbitrary, but they must satisfy the following constraints:

$$h_0 + h_1 + ... + h_{k-1} = (2r + 1)^2 \text{ and } h_i \geq 0,$$
$$\text{for } i = 0,1,..., k - 1. \tag{4}$$

By definition, a totalistic rule T is an application that associates with any configuration $v \in V$ an S element:

$$T : V \rightarrow S. \tag{5}$$

The explicit formula of this application can be considered the CA rule table, where

$$(h_0h_1....h_{k-1}) \in V \mapsto T(h_0h_1....h_{k-1}) \in S.$$

In particular, equation (5) can be represented explicitly as a table that associates with the first k-1 totals (for the constraints in equation (4), the last of which depends on the others) a number included between 0 and k-1. For example, according to the constraints in equation (4), the string (240) for a CA $k=4$ and $r=1$ indicates that two elements of the neighborhood, composed of nine cells, are in Stage 0, four elements are in Stage 1, zero are in Stage 2, and three are in Stage 3. To the string (240) will correspond one element $q \in S$. In this case, 220 local rules of this kind will exist.

The presence of the constraints in equation (4) allows a substantial lowering of the number of possible configurations. To estimate this value,

we consider the problem as being the same as that of placing $2r + 1$ undistinguishable objects in k containers. From elements of combinatorial analysis, such a number is given by

$$N_T = \binom{k + (2r+1)^2 - 1}{(2r+1)^2} = \frac{(k + (2r+1)^2 - 1)}{(2r+1)^2!(k-1)}. \tag{6}$$

The table of rules that allows the association of an element of S with any configuration of the neighborhood can be represented as a numeric sequence of N_T length:

$$l = (s_1, s_2, ..., s_{(k)^{N_T}}) \tag{7}$$

with $s_i \in S$. To make a configuration $(h_0h_1....h_{k-1}) \in V$ correspond to an s_i value of the string in equation (7) and vice versa, we establish the convention that $s_i \in S$ corresponds to the ith configuration in lexicographical order. A configuration $(h_0h_1....h_{k-1}) \in V$ represents a path along an oriented tree, whose leaf is s_i. For $k=2$, the k-totalistic rules become the well-known totalistic rules for binary CA. In this way, the dimension of the k-totalistic rule, given by equation (5), becomes treatable for values higher than k (number of stages) and r (radius of the neighborhood).

GENETIC ALGORITHMS

We used the string in equation (7) as a genotype of the genetic algorithm (Bilotta et al., 2002, 2003) and defined an index of complexity as a fitness function. The input entropy is an index of the degree of order-chaos that we applied to the k-totalistic rules, following the same method as Wuensche (1999) for exhaustive rules. In Bilotta et al. (2002, 2003), we used a standard method for implementing a genetic algorithm (Holland, 1975; Mitchell, 1996) that searches for self-reproducing systems and employs as fitness functions the characteristics of entropy. The evolutionary runs produced a rich number of complex rules, many of which contain self-reproducer systems.

TAXONOMY OF SELF-REPRODUCERS

In a recent study (Bilotta & Pantano, 2006), we demonstrated that self-reproduction in the CA, far from being an isolated and improbable phenomenon, in fact interferes in many complex rules. These self-reproducers emerge spontaneously from the primordial soup, are quite stable with regard to genetic variations, and manifest highly characteristic forms and functions.

We have attempted to categorize the huge quantity of muted self-reproducing systems. A preliminary taxonomy is displayed in Figure 1.

Now we shall consider in detail the characteristics of this taxonomy, with some examples of self-reproducers.

Linear Self-Reproducers

The first category deals with systems, which reproduce themselves developing in different directions in the grid. The self-reproducer presents two poles of growth in opposite directions. Along these directions, the structure grows until it divides itself in two or three distinct configurations, which in turn become two or three self-reproducers.

For example, the first reproducer (Figure 1) is composed of three elements that are yellow

Figure 1. Taxonomy of the self-reproducing systems

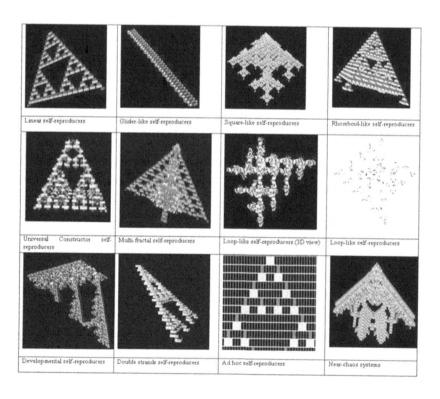

Figure 2. Behaviour of Reproducer 1 during the course of 16 temporal steps

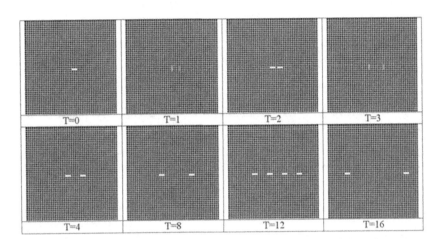

in color, the behavior of which in the course of reproduction is identified in Figure 2.

The figure shows that the reproducer develops in a linear manner. After one temporal step, it produces two structures that are red in color and orthogonal in direction. At the next step, the two red structures transform into yellow, completing the first process of reproduction. The two resulting structures have the same direction as the starting reproducer. The subsequent growth of the colony is regulated by a double law: birth by reproduction and death by overpopulation. The final result is that the structures produced, before beginning a new cycle of reproduction, have to distance themselves sufficiently one from the other.

Another reproducer with a linear development is shown in Figure 3. In this case the initial datum is more complex than in the preceding case. It is formed by a ring that is red and yellow in color: Specifically, it can be represented by a 3x4 matrix.

In this case, the process of reproduction, again of a linear kind, comes about in eight evolutionary steps. The process recalls that which is typical

of a cellular division: The reproducer presents two poles of growth in opposite directions; as the two poles separate, the structure grows until it divides into two different structures, which subsequently will complete themselves in the starting reproducer. The spatial-temporal pattern will now emerge as much more complex than in the preceding case, yet there are, however, many similarities.

The third self-reproducer that we present also manifests linear reproduction. Though similar to Reproducer 1, it manifests some interesting differences. In this case, the linear structure composed of three white states revolves 90° and transforms into a structure of three red states. With the next step, the structure is reproduced in three structures similar to that at the beginning (there is a new 90° rotation and a tripling of the base structure). Subsequently, the process continues, following the usual logic of distancing of the structures in order to favor the start of a new cycle, constituted of reproduction and death through overpopulation.

Figure 3. The behaviour of Reproducer 2

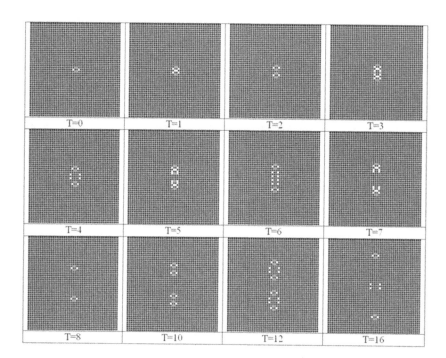

Glider-Like Self-Reproducers

The second category shares some characteristics with the first since these systems reproduce themselves repetitively with each step of the simulation. This kind of behavior is useful for bringing information in different places, choosing some sources as starting points. It can be similar to the diffusion of the same program starting from one or many sides.

Square and Rhomboidal-Like Self-Reproducers

The third and the fourth categories regard systems that develop both into square-like or rhomboidal patterns. The initial self-reproducers realize four or more copies of themselves.

We will now analyze a process of reproduction with a square development (Figure 4). The behavior of these systems, with a simple initial datum such as a cell, is characterized by a very interesting phenomenon. The self-reproducing process goes on by developing first a new square-like structure formed of nine cells, and then four copies of the initial datum. Inside these copies a new different-colored cell appears that in turn reproduces itself with each of the four steps of the simulation. This new cell does not influence the process of self-replication of the former. The latter cell evolves into four new cells, organized in square-like or rhomboidal configurations, which in turn reproduce them. So, the self-replication process contains three nested subprocesses.

The behavior of this self-reproducer is very simple even though it contains within itself dy-

Figure 4. Reproduction behavior of Self-Reproducer 4

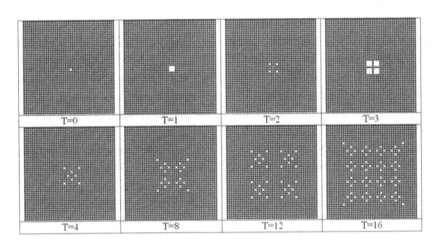

namics that are highly interesting and are worth analyzing in detail. The process of reproduction with square development takes place in two steps: In the first, the simple small white point produces a new square-shaped structure composed of nine white stages, and at the next step, the structure appears to be composed of four white points positioned at the points of a square. The reproductive process produces from the starting structure a quadruple effect, resulting in four new structures in the form of squares. The process continues in time, through multiplication by four and death through overpopulation until a new cycle begins. What makes this self-reproduction particular is that in the second step, a new structure composed of a red point is produced. This structure does not influence the reproductive cycle of the white structure and in its turn it reproduces in a cycle of four steps. The red self-reproducer evolves using the white one (which now functions perhaps as an enzyme). The red one is a structure parasitical of the preceding one, which exploits the reproduction of the white structure in order to reproduce itself. The logic of the red self-reproducer is analogous to that of the white, but now its period is double

that of the white. Yet the phenomenon is not yet complete because the red, in its turn, presents a yellow parasite that exploits the self-reproduction of the red structure in order, in its turn, to reproduce itself. In effect, in the rule examined, the white self-reproducer allows the reproduction of the red, which in its turn allows for the reproduction of the yellow. The yellow produces a rhomboid structure even though the colony develops according to the logic of the white self-reproducer's square development.

Universal-Constructor Self-Reproducers

The universal-constructor category has systems that have some special features. They are able to reproduce any initial data as they have a general constructive capacity (von Neumann, 1966).

Any macrostructure generated in this way and formed by the arbitrary combination of simple structures made by one of these reproducers is in turn a self-reproducing system. This property has been observed for different self-reproducers. In order for any components of whatever structure we want to replicate to interact correctly, it is necessary that each element have the same orientation, or the elements must be turned around to a certain degree with respect to each other, and that each element is at a distance of a determined number of cells in the grid, or at a distance from these cells. The mechanism of reproduction of these components connected together is similar to simple reproducer behavior. The interesting feature is that it is possible to reproduce any image you can draw by means of the simple structure arranged together.

For example, the universal reproducer in Figure 1 also has a square development. Its reproductive behavior takes place in a cycle of eight steps and it shows how structure that is linear in symmetry can manifest a reproductive behavior that has a square symmetry (Figure 5). The reproducer now presents itself in a CA with five stages.

The base structure that will reproduce itself is composed of three stages in a square form represented by the following matrix.

At the first stage of the evolutionary process, the structure will create a new structure composed of three stages that are separate. At the next step, the starting structure will double: The two resultant structures will rotate by 90° and -90° with respect to the base structure and in phases opposite to each other. After two more steps, the structures will have become four, of which two will be equal to the base structure and two will be rotated by 180° with respect to it. The higher structures will be in a phase opposed to that of the lower ones. It is interesting to note that the configuration is the same when the initial datum is reflected with respect to a horizontal axis. The resultant structure is unvaried with respect to a reflection in the initial datum while the reflec-

Figure 5. Reproductive behavior of Self-Reproducer 5

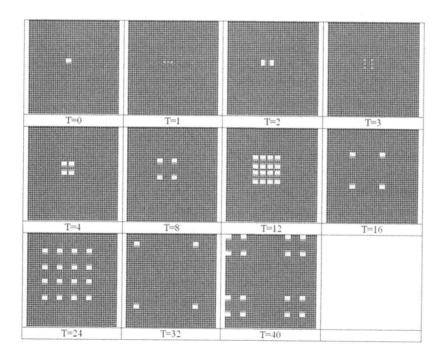

tive symmetry with respect to a vertical axis is maintained in the reproductive process. The behavior of this self-reproducer is analogous to that at eight stages discussed in the study (Bilotta et al., 2002).

The subsequent development process of the colony does not emerge as being different with regard to the preceding cases, manifesting a process of distancing constituted of reproduction and death through overpopulation with the aim of initiating a new process of reproduction.

The population of structures evolves toward macrostructures, which are ever more complex. The macrostructures that form are in their turn self-reproducing structures in which the macroscopic mechanism of self-reproduction is the same as the microscopic.

The most interesting phenomenon with regard to this system is the possibility of reproducing arbitrary structures, due to the fact that every macrostructure formed by the drawing together of simple structures is, in its turn, a self-reproducing structure (see Figure 6). We will call these macrostructures second-level self-reproducers.

Clearly, the structures at the next level (that is, formed by self-reproducers at second level or higher) are self-reproducing.

We have discovered this characteristic by simulating this system for initial stages that are completely casual, and by observing that because of the contemporary emergence of several structures, approaches manifest themselves (or macrostructures) differently from those observed in the evolution of a single structure that led to self-reproduction. This mechanism of self-reproduction, provided certain limitations are respected, can be used to reproduce any figure of any given complexity.

Figure 6. Second level of the self-reproducing mechanism for the universal-constructor category

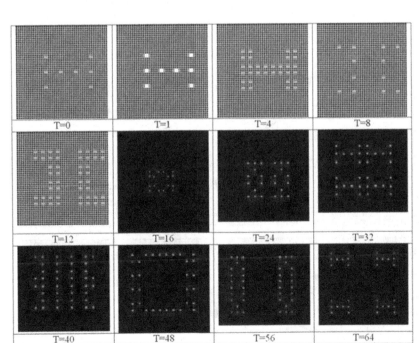

Multifractal Self-Reproducers

These are systems that instead of reproducing a simple structure, in a Sierpinski-like configuration, create a complex patterning phenomenon that foresees the realization of a structure in different-oriented planes of a multidimensional space. Usually, these systems organize their structures around an axis of rotation, from which the other configurations seem to develop.

The Loop Self-Reproducers

This class presents complex phenomena of reproduction like the famous Langton's loop. Usually, we have found different kinds of self-reproducing loops, but generally the self-replicating structures create four different directions of the replication process, each generating many copies and giving life to a population of other entities, which in

turn begin to reproduce. Besides this, during the explosion of the population, many gliders are produced, so these systems, and globally the emerging macrostructures, behave like glider guns.

Developmental Self-Reproducers

The evolution of these systems is very complex as the structures, before reproducing, undergo a nonlinear growth process designed in two distinct phases. In the first, the structures become bigger, and after relevant steps of simulation, reproduce a copy of themselves. In this phase, the self-reproducers grow as biological organisms do and give life to child copies of themselves, which in turn grow and procreate after many steps of simulation. The child copies behave and develop in the opposite direction with respect to their mothers. Yet the growth process of the mothers does not stop: After many steps of simulation and varied

Figure 7. The first process of development and procreation of Self-Reproducer 6

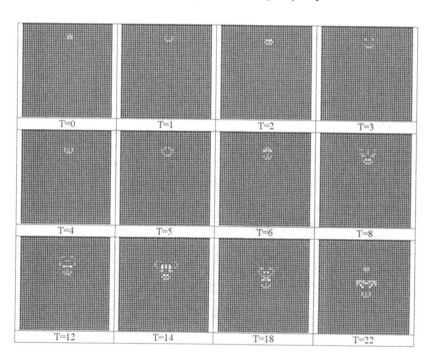

modifications of their morphological configurations, the mother structures begin to create different configurations while the other child structures undergo the same processes at different times in their evolution. These self-reproducers exploit different temporal and nested processes. The main process is produced by the self-reproducers, which produce the coordinated ones; each of the children in turn generates asynchronous processes. These processes are emergent and are not realized by external procedures (Nehaniv, 2002).

The behavior of this self-reproducer with linear development emerges as being highly complex with respect to previous cases (see Figure 7). The CA that allows for the presence of this reproducer is in five stages.

A structure that is quite simple composed of a matrix of type

$$\begin{pmatrix} 0 & 2 & 0 \\ 4 & 2 & 4 \\ 4 & 2 & 4 \end{pmatrix}$$

in 21 steps manages to reproduce itself. This process of reproduction, however, is highly complex because the structure, before reproduction, has to undergo a process of growth. This process is entirely nonlinear; on the one hand there is growth in the structure, while on the other there is growth of an appendage, which, passing through various phases, eventually expels a new structure of the same kind as the starting one. After 22 steps, the staring structure will have become mature and will give life to a new structure in an infantile state, which, in its turn, will grow and procreate after 22 steps. The daughter structure will move and procreate in a direction opposite to that of the mother one. In effect, the process of growth and development of the mother structure does not stop, but, in its turn, it produces significant changes before giving birth to other processes of procreation (see Figure 8).

The second process of development and procreation of the mother structure is even more complex than the preceding one. After various growth phases and changes in form, the mother structure, after 53 steps, acquires a form that is large and stable. After 12 steps this form presents

Figure 8. The second process of development and procreation of the mother structure

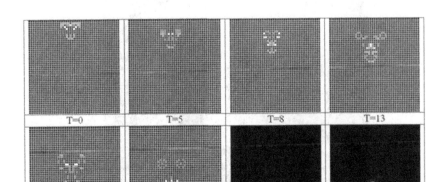

itself as before, now with a daughter structure that travels in a direction opposite that of the mother. The daughter structure now has the form that the initial structure had after four evolutionary steps (see Figure 9). In Figure 10, the spatial-temporal pattern of the developmental self-reproducing mechanism is presented. In particular, this figure shows the mother's reproduction.

Double-Strand Self-Reproducers

This class of self-reproducers develops in a linear way, but at the same time these systems undergo a translation in a specific spatial direction. The resulting spatial-temporal patterns lie on the face of a pyramid. On a two-dimensional view, it is possible to note the two strands of the self-repro-

Figure 9. The reproduction process of the mother figure. Every 12 steps a daughter structure is reproduced.

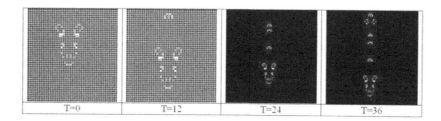

Figure 10. The reproduction process of the mature figure. The mother figure moves to the left and produces three daughter structures. The first, which moves toward the right, has reached its first maturity and produces, in its turn, a daughter structure that moves toward the right and is about to encounter the second daughter structure, causing annihilation.

duction process. The first is made up of a structure whose stage corresponds to a yellow configuration. The second is made up of a structure whose stage corresponds to a cyan configuration. The two strands are synchronized and both realize a Sierpinski configuration.

Ad Hoc Mixed Systems

We have realized a computational system (Bilotta & Pantano, 2005) which, by identifying a module in the generated pattern of a self-reproducer (the basic self-reproducer or a subset of it), allows the simulation of the two-dimensional CA by means of an ECA rule (Wolfram, 2002). A module is a mathematical entity governed by Boolean cellular automata. The module can overlap the self-reproducing initial data or more modules can be put together in order to obtain the self-reproducer initial data.

The mathematical formula that realizes this process is the following:

$$P_T = P_M + P_1 + P_2 + P_3,$$

where P_T is the final pattern, P_M is the pattern generated by the basic module, and P_1, P_2, and P_3 are the remaining differences. We can say that the final pattern can be obtained by combining a subset of the same pattern. Each of these substructures is governed by an ECA rule that sets its development at different levels of scale.

Near-Chaos Systems

In this class, the systems, which are not self-reproducers, use the disorder of chaotic configurations to evolve. In the apparently random patterns, however, it is possible to reveal ordered configurations that seem to degrade step by step toward more disordered ones. This means that it could be possible to model the parameters within which systems will stay stable or change.

The genetic code (Bilotta et al., 2003; Bilotta & Pantano, 2005) is economic in the first four classes of this taxonomy and it varies, going from networks composed from 5 to 11 characters. These systems are very common in the evolutionary runs for different k and r values. The networks grow exponentially in the other classes of the taxonomy.

CONCLUSION

Each of these self-reproducing systems can generally give rise to infinite sets of other self-reproducing automata. The automata within such sets are characterized as sharing a particular constructing automaton. The process is allowed by a set of hidden rules that impose constraints on how structures are put together, and the final pattern is repeated many times at different levels, with the same substructure that it is possible to see in the whole structure. This is the concept of self-similarity expressed by the triangle of Sierpinski. This means that all the automata within such a set share the same formal genetic language and give rise to open-ended evolution. We have realized an artificial context in which a life-like self-reproducer undergoes mutations (Bilotta & Pantano, 2005, 2006). This artificial organism has been identified by a set of genetic rules, which is maintained constantly in order to preserve its form and function in 2-D cellular automata. Form is intended as the self-reproducer's geometrical shape and color (conventionally chosen in relationship with its k and r values); the function is its behaviour in the self-reproduction cycle. The set of genetic rules, or the self-reproducer's template, has been detected by realizing a computational model, through which it has been possible to see how many times the self-reproducer consults the rule table (the genotype) in order to realize its own form (phenotype) and function (self-replication process). In turn, we found that a network of potential mutations connects them.

As von Neumann (1966) argued, if the description of the self-reproducing automata is changed (mutated) in such a way as to not affect the basic functioning of (A+B+C), then the new automaton (A + B + C)' will be slightly different from its parent. Furthermore, he proposed that nontrivial self-reproduction should include this "ability to undergo inheritable mutations as well as the ability to make another organism like the original" to distinguish it from naive self-reproduction, like growing crystals.

On the basis of von Neumann's (1966) suggestions, we realized a computational model that allowed us to identify exactly the characters each self-reproducer consults in the rule table during its evolution. These rules can be considered the genetic code of the self-reproducing systems. In this way, self-reproducers can be regarded as biological agents since they inherit a genetic code from their parents to evolve and change, thus realizing the spontaneous formation of well-organized structures. Like biological systems and as in life, self-reproducing systems realize forms of computation, such as the transmission, storage, and modification of information, creating beautiful patterns.

REFERENCES

Bilotta, E., Lafusa, A., & Pantano, P. (2002). Is self replication an embedded characteristic of artificial/living matter? In R. K. Standish, M. A. Bedau, & H. A. Abbass (Eds.), *Artificial life VIII* (pp. 38-48). Cambridge, MA: The MIT Press.

Bilotta, E., Lafusa, A., & Pantano, P. (2003). Life-like self-reproducers. *Complexity, 9*(1), 38-55.

Bilotta, E., & Pantano, P. (2005). Emergent patterning phenomena in 2D cellular automata. *Artificial life, 11*(3), 339-362.

Bilotta, E., & Pantano, P. (2006). Structural and functional growth in self-reproducing cellular automata. *Complexity, 11*(6), 12-29.

Chou, H. H., & Reggia, J. A. (1997). Emergence of self-replicating structures in a cellular automata space. *Physica D, 110*(3-4), 252-276.

Groves, C., Wilson, D. E., & Reeder, D. M. (Eds.). (2005). Mammal species of the world (3ʳᵈ ed.). Johns Hopkins University Press.

Holland, J. (1975). *Adaptation in natural and artificial systems.* Ann Arbor, MI: The University of Michigan Press.

Langton, C. G. (1984). Self-reproduction in cellular automata. *Physica D, 10*, 135-144.

Lohn, J. D., & Reggia, J. A. (1995). Discovery of self-replicating structures using a genetic algorithm. In *Proceedings of 1995 IEEE International Conference on Evolutionary Computation* (ICEC'95, pp. 678-683).

Mitchell, M. (1996). *An introduction to genetic algorithms.* Cambridge, MA: The MIT Press.

Morita, K., & Imai, K. (1996). Self-reproduction in a reversible cellular space. *Theoretical Computer Science, 168*, 337-366.

Nehaniv, C. L. (2002). Evolution in asynchronous cellular automata. In R. K. Standish, M. A. Bedau, & H. A. Abbass (Eds.), *Artificial life VIII* (pp 65-73). Cambridge, MA: The MIT Press.

Perrier, J. Y., Sipper, M., & Zahnd, J. (1996). Toward a viable, self-reproducing universal computer. *Physica D, 97*, 335-352.

Sayama, H. (1998). Introduction of structural dissolution into Langton's self-reproducing loop. In C. Adami, R. K. Belew, H. Kitano, & C. E. Taylor (Eds.), *Artificial life VI* (pp.114-122). Los Angeles: MIT Press.

Sayama, H. (2000). Self-replicating worms that increase structural complexity through gene transmission. In M. A. Bedau, J. S. McCaskill, N. H. Packard, & S. Rasmussen (Eds.), *Artificial life VII* (pp. 467-476). MIT Press.

Tempesti, G. (1995). A new self-reproducing cellular automaton capable of construction and computation. In F. Morán, A. Moreno, J. J. Merelo, & P. Chacón (Eds.), *Lecture notes in computer science: Vol. 929. ECAL'95: Third European Conference on Artificial Life* (pp. 555-563). Heidelberg, Germany: Springer-Verlag.

von Neumann, J. (1966). *Theory of self-reproducing automata* (Edited and completed by A. W. Burks). IL: University of Illinois Press.

Wolfram, S. (2002). *A new kind of science*. Champaign, IL: Wolfram Media.

Wuensche, A. (1999). Classifying cellular automata automatically: Finding gliders, filtering and relating space-time patterns, attractors basins and the Z parameter. *Complexity, 4*(3), 47-66.

Chapter IX
Evolutionary Algorithms in Problem Solving and Machine Learning

Marco Tomassini
University of Lausanne, Switzerland

Leonardo Vanneschi
University of Milano-Bicocca, Italy

ABSTRACT

In the first part of the chapter, evolutionary algorithms are briefly described, especially genetic algorithms and genetic programming, with sufficient detail so as to prepare the ground for the second part. The latter presents in more detail two specific applications. The first is about an important financial problem: the portfolio allocation problem. The second one deals with a biochemical problem related to drug design and efficacy.

INTRODUCTION

Evolutionary algorithms (EAs) are a broad class of stochastic optimization algorithms, inspired by biology and in particular by those biological processes that allow populations of organisms to adapt to their surrounding environment: genetic inheritance and survival of the fittest. These concepts were introduced in the 19th century by Charles Darwin and are still today widely acknowledged as valid, even though they are complemented with further details.

The first proposals in that direction date back to the mid '60s, when John Holland (1975), of the University of Michigan, introduced genetic algorithms (GAs). Fogel, Owens, and Walsh (1966), of the University of California in San Diego, started their experiments on evolutionary programming, and Ingo Rechenberg (1973), of the Technical University of Berlin, independently began to work on evolution strategies. Their pioneering work eventually gave rise to a broad class of optimization methods particularly well suited for solving hard problems where little is known about the underlying search space in a reasonable amount of computational time. What makes EAs interesting in real-life application is the fact that, in the eventuality they are not able to generate a perfect solution to a given problem, they always return an approximated one. For this reason, EAs are usually included in the research field known as soft computing (Tettamanzi & Tomassini, 2001), which traditionally also includes artificial neural networks, fuzzy systems, and so forth. One of the last developments in the EA research area is so-called genetic programming (GP), introduced by John Koza (1992) of Stanford University at the beginning of the '90s. Recent texts of reference and synthesis in the field of EAs are Michalewicz (1996) and Eiben and Smith (2003).

An evolutionary algorithm maintains a population of candidate solutions for the problem at hand, and makes it evolve by iteratively applying a (usually quite small) set of stochastic operators, known as mutation, recombination, and selection. Mutation randomly perturbs a candidate solution, recombination decomposes two distinct solutions and then randomly mixes their parts to form novel solutions, and selection replicates the most successful solutions found in a population at a rate proportional to their relative quality. The initial population may be either a random sample of the solution space or may be seeded with solutions found by simple local search procedures, if these are available. The resulting process tends to find locally or globally optimal solutions to the problem much in the same way as how natural populations of organisms tend to adapt to their surrounding environment.

GENETIC ALGORITHMS

Essentially, EAs make use of a metaphor whereby an optimization problem takes the place of the surrounding environment for biological populations; feasible solutions are viewed as individuals living in that environment. Finally, an individual's degree of adaptation to its surrounding environment is the counterpart of the objective function (often called the fitness function) evaluated on a feasible solution. In the same way, a set of feasible solutions take the place of a population of organisms. In EAs, selection operates on data structures stored in computer memory and, in time, their functionalities evolve in a way substantially analogous to how populations of living organisms evolve in a natural setting. Although the computer model introduces sharp simplifications with respect to the real biological mechanisms, EAs have proved capable of making surprisingly complex and interesting structures emerge. Each structure, or individual, may be viewed as a representation, according to an appropriate encoding, of a particular solution to a problem, for example, a strategy to play a game, a picture, or even a simple computer program.

Representation

In GAs, individuals are just strings of digits (typically binary digits). As computer memory is made up of an array of bits, anything that can be stored in a computer can also be encoded for by a bit string of sufficient length. In a sense, representing solutions to a problem as bit strings is the most general encoding that can be thought of.

The Evolutionary Cycle

An evolutionary algorithm starts with a population of randomly generated potential solutions to the problem (individuals from now on), though it is also possible to use a previously saved population or a population of individuals encoding for solutions provided by a human expert or by another heuristic algorithm. In the case of genetic algorithms, the initial population will be made up of random bit strings. Once an initial population has been created, an evolutionary algorithm enters a loop. At the end of each iteration, a new population will have been created by applying a certain number of stochastic operators to the previous population. One such iteration is referred to as a generation.

The first operator to be applied is selection. Its aim is to simulate the Darwinian law of survival of the fittest. In GAs, this law is enforced by so-called fitness-proportionate selection in order to create a new intermediate population of n parents: n independent extractions of an individual from the old population are performed, where the probability for each individual of being extracted is linearly proportional to its fitness. Therefore, above-average individuals will expectedly have more copies in the new population, while below-average individuals will risk extinction. There are several other selection methods (see, for example, Eiben & Smith, 2003; Michalewicz, 1996), but although there are technical differences among them, the general idea is the same.

Once the population of parents, that is, the individuals that have been selected for reproduction, has been extracted, the individuals for the next generation are produced through the application of a number of reproduction operators, which can involve just one parent, thus simulating asexual reproduction (in which case we speak of mutation), or more parents, thus simulating sexual reproduction (in which case we speak of recombination). In GAs, two reproduction operators are used: crossover and mutation. To apply crossover, couples are formed with all parent individuals; then, with a certain probability, called the crossover rate, each couple actually undergoes crossover: The two bit strings are cut at the same random position and their second halves are swapped between the two

individuals, thus yielding two novel individuals, each containing characters from both parents. After crossover, all individuals undergo mutation. The purpose of mutation is to simulate the effect of transcription errors that can happen with a very low probability when a chromosome is duplicated. This is accomplished by flipping each bit in every individual with a very small probability, called the mutation rate. In other words, each 0 has a small probability of being turned into a 1 and vice versa. In principle, the above-described loop is infinite, but it can be stopped when a given termination condition specified by the user is met. Examples of termination conditions are the following.

- A predetermined number of generations or time has elapsed.
- A satisfactory solution has been found.
- No improvement in solution quality has been taking place for a predetermined number of generations.

All of the above termination conditions are acceptable under some assumptions relevant to the context the EA is used in. The evolutionary cycle can be summarized by the following pseudocode.

```
generation = 0
seed population
while not termination condition do
    generation = generation + 1
    calculate fitness
    selection
    crossover
    mutation
end while
```

GENETIC PROGRAMMING

GP is a new evolutionary approach that extends the genetic model of learning to the space of programs. It is a major variation of GAs in which the evolving individuals are themselves computer programs instead of fixed-length strings from a limited alphabet of symbols. GP is a form of program induction that allows one to automatically discover programs that solve or approximately solve a given task. The present form of GP is principally due to Koza (1992). Individual programs in GP might be expressed in principle in any current programming language. However, the syntax of most languages is such that GP operators would create a large percentage of syntactically incorrect programs. For this reason, Koza chose a syntax in prefix form analogous to LISP and a restricted language with an appropriate number of variables, constants, and operators defined to fit the problem to be solved. In this way, syntax constraints are respected and the program search space is limited. The restricted language is formed by a user-defined function set F and terminal set T. The functions chosen are those that are a priori believed to be useful for the problem at hand, and the terminals are usually either variables or constants. In addition, each function in the function set F must be able to accept as arguments any other function return value and any data type in the terminal set T, a property that is called syntactic closure. Thus, the space of possible programs is constituted by the set of all possible compositions of functions that can be recursively formed from the elements of F and T.

As an example, suppose that we are dealing with simple arithmetic expressions in three variables. In this case, suitable function and terminal sets might be defined as

$$F = \{ +,-,*,/ \} \quad \text{and} \quad T = \{ A, B, C \}.$$

The following are simple examples of legal programs:

$$(+ \ (* \ A \ B) \ (/ \ C \ D)) \quad \text{and} \quad (* \ (- \ (+ \ A \ C) \ B) \ A).$$

It is important to note that GP does not need to be implemented in the LISP language. Any language that can represent programs internally as parse trees is adequate. Thus, most GP packages today are written in C, C++, or Java rather than LISP. Programs are thus represented as trees with ordered branches in which the internal nodes are functions and the leaves are the terminals of the problem. Thus, the examples given above would give rise to the trees in Figure 1.

Evolution in GP is analogous to GAs, except that different individual representations and genetic operators are used. Once suitable functions and terminals have been determined for the

Figure 1. The graphical representation of two legal GP individuals that can be built with the sets $F = \{ +,-,*,/ \}$ and $T = \{ A, B, C \}$

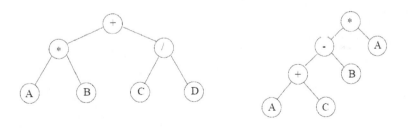

problem at hand, an initial random population of trees (programs) is constructed. From there on, the population evolves as with a GA, where fitness is assigned after actual execution of the program (individual) and genetic operators are adapted to the tree representation. Fitness calculation is a bit different for programs. In GP we usually would like to discover a program that satisfies a given number N of predefined input-output relations: These are called the fitness cases. For a given program p_i, its fitness f_i on the ith fitness case represents the difference between the output g_i produced by the program and the correct answer G_i for that case. The total fitness $F(p_i)$ is the sum over all N fitness cases of some norm of the cumulated difference:

$$F(p_i) = \sum_{k=1}^{N} \| g_k - G_k \|.$$

Obviously, a better program will have a lower fitness under this definition, and a perfect one will score zero fitness.

The crossover operation starts by selecting a random crossover point in each parent tree and then exchanging the subtrees, giving rise to two offspring trees, as shown in Figure 2. The crossover site is usually chosen with nonuniform probability in order to favor internal nodes with respect to leaves.

Mutation is usually implemented by randomly removing a subtree at a selected point and replacing it with a randomly generated subtree.

One problematic step in GP is the choice of the appropriate language for a given problem. In general, the problem itself suggests a reasonable set of functions and terminals, but this is not always the case. Although experimental evidence has shown that good results can be obtained with slightly different choices of F and T, it is clear that the choice of language has an influence on how hard the problem will be to solve with GP. For the time being, choosing suitable language sets requires problem knowledge and is more an art than a rigorous scientific process.

A controversial issue has to do with the size of the GP trees. The depth of the trees can in principle increase without limits under the influence of crossover, a phenomenon that goes under the name of bloat. The increase in size is often accompanied by stagnant population fitness. Most GP systems have a parameter that prevents trees from becoming too deep, thus filling all the available memory and requiring longer evaluation times. To further avoid bloat, a common approach is to introduce a size-penalty term into the fitness expression, possibly in a self-adapting way. There

Figure 2. Example of crossover of two genetic programs

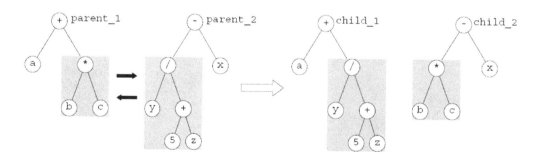

is still some debate among practitioners in the field as to whether one should let the trees breed and grow until the maximum depth or whether to edit and simplify them along the way in order to obtain shorter programs. The argument for larger trees is that the often redundant genetic material has a richer set of breeding possibilities and may lead to increased diversity in successive populations. On the other hand, the use of parsimony or size penalties may give rise to compact and efficient solutions in some cases. The issue is difficult to settle due to our currently limited knowledge about the dynamics of the evolution of program populations.

GP is particularly useful for program discovery, that is, the induction of programs that correctly solve a given problem with the assumption that the form of the program is unknown and that only the desired behavior is given, for example, by specifying input-output relations. GP has been successfully applied to a wide variety of problems from many fields, described in Koza (1992) and Banzhaf, Nordin, Keller, and Francone (1998).

A GA APPLICATION: PORTFOLIO OPTIMIZATION

To provide a practical feel of the issues involved with applying EAs to real-world problems, this section examines a financial application, namely, asset allocation using nontrivial indices of risk. A more detailed analysis appears in Tettamanzi and Tomassini (2001).

The central problem of portfolio theory concerns selecting the weights of assets in a portfolio that minimize a certain measure of risk for any given level of expected return. According to mainstream portfolio theory (Markowitz, 1959), a meaningful measure of risk is the variance of the distribution of portfolio returns. However, while leading to elegant analytical results and easy practical implementation, this approach fails to

capture what an investor perceives as the essence of risk, that is, the chance of incurring a loss. In this respect, the economic literature has recently proposed alternative measures of risk; an interesting family of measures, defined as lower partial moments (Harlow, 1991), refers to the downside part of the distribution of returns and has therefore become known under the name of downside. A number of difficulties are encountered when trying to apply this new approach even to simple problem instances. First of all, the nature of these risk measures prevents general analytical solutions from being devised, and quadratic optimization techniques cannot be applied because the shape of the objective surface is in general nonconvex. Moreover, the typical size of real-world portfolio selection problems is in the order of several tens or even hundreds of assets. Expected return and risk may be calculated by using historical series made up of hundreds of historical returns, or may be suggested by rather sophisticated financial forecasting techniques. Even the software packages that apply the conventional mean-variance approach through quadratic optimization suffer limitations as the size of the problem grows beyond a certain threshold. Things become more involved as it is usual practice among fund managers to impose various constraints on their optimal portfolios.

Downside Risk

In summary, let θ be a threshold beyond which the investor judges the result of his investment a failure. Adapting the formula for semivariance to this subjective threshold gives the formula of target semivariance,

$$TS(\theta) = \sum_{i:W_i < \theta} Pr(i)(\theta - W_i)^2,$$

where *Pr(i)* is the probability of scenario *i* and *Wi* is the wealth in that scenario. This measure can be usefully generalized into downside risk, having as a parameter a risk aversion coefficient $q > 0$:

$$\mathrm{DSR}(\theta; q) = \sum_{i:W_i < \theta} \mathrm{Pr}(i)(\theta - W_i)^q.$$

A higher aversion to risk corresponds to a larger value of q.

Problem Formulation

Portfolio optimization can be viewed as a convex combination parametric programming problem in that an investor wants to minimize risk while maximizing expected return. This can be expressed as a two-objective optimization problem:

$$
\begin{aligned}
&\underset{\mathbf{w}}{\text{minimize}} && \mathrm{Risk}(\mathbf{w}) \\
&\underset{\mathbf{w}}{\text{maximize}} && \mathrm{ER}(\mathbf{w}) \\
&\text{subject to} \\
& && \sum_i w_i = 1, \\
& && w_i \geq 0.
\end{aligned}
\tag{1}
$$

The set of Pareto-optimal, that is, nondominated, solutions to this two-objective optimization problem is called the efficient frontier. On the efficient frontier, a larger expected return always corresponds to a greater risk. The two objectives in equation (1) can be parametrized to yield a convex combination parametric programming problem with objective

$$\underset{\mathbf{w}}{\text{minimize}} \; \lambda \mathrm{Risk}(\mathbf{w}) - (1 - \lambda)\mathrm{ER}(\mathbf{w}), \tag{2}$$

where λ is a trade-off coefficient ranging between 0 and 1. When $\lambda = 0$, the investor disregards risk and only seeks to maximize expected return. When $\lambda = 1$, risk alone is being minimized, whatever the expected return. Since there is no general way to tell which particular trade-off between risk and

return is to be considered the best, optimizing a portfolio means finding a whole range of optimal portfolios for all the possible values of the trade-off coefficient; the investors will thus be able to choose the one they believe appropriate for their requirements.

The Evolutionary Approach

A natural way to achieve the stated objective within an evolutionary setting is to have several distinct populations evolve for a number of trade-off coefficient values. The greater this number, the finer the resolution with which the investor will be able to explore the efficient frontier. Because it is likely that slight variations in the trade-off coefficient do not significantly worsen a good solution, a natural way to sustain the evolutionary process is to allow migration or crossbreeding between individuals belonging to populations corresponding to values of the trade-off coefficient that are close together. Encoding portfolio selection is a typical example of what is called a pie problem, so we can use the straight encoding suggested for this kind of problem (Tettamanzi & Tomassini, 2001): Each asset *i* is encoded as an integer g_i between 0 and 255. The actual weight *u>i* of asset *i* is computed as

$$w_i = \frac{g_i}{\sum_j g_j}.$$

Objective Function and Fitness. The objective function is defined, according to equation (2), as

$$z(\mathbf{w}; \lambda) = (1 - \lambda)\mathrm{ER}(\mathbf{w}) - \lambda \mathrm{DSR}(\mathbf{w}), \tag{3}$$

where both return and downside risk are appropriately scaled. By adopting the convention that lower fitness is better, we scale fitness in such a way that the best possible individual for each subpopulation always has zero fitness. The fitness of individual **g**, corresponding to portfolio **w**, of a subpopulation associated with trade-off coefficient **A** is calculated as

$$f(\mathbf{g}) = \frac{z^{\max}(\lambda) - z(\mathbf{w};\lambda)}{z^{\max}(\lambda) - z^{\min}(\lambda) + 1}, \qquad (4)$$

where $\mathbf{z}^{\max}(\mathbf{A})$ and $z^{min}(X)$ stand for the greatest and smallest value of the objective function in the subpopulation.

Genetic Operators. A variation of uniform crossover, which we may call uniform balanced crossover, was adopted. Let γ and κ be two parent chromosomes. For each gene *i* in the offspring, it is decided with equal probability whether it should inherit from one parent or the other. Suppose that the ith gene in γ, γ_i, has been chosen to be passed on to a child genotype substring ζ. Then, the value of the ith gene in ζ is

$$\zeta_i = \min\left(255, \gamma_i \frac{\sum_{j=1}^{N} \gamma_j + \sum_{j=1}^{N} \kappa_j}{2\sum_{j=1}^{N} \gamma_j}\right).$$

The main motivation behind this operation is to preserve the relative meaning of genes, which depends on their context. Indeed, genes have a meaning with respect to the other genes of the same portfolio since the corresponding weight is obtained by normalization. Therefore, crossing the two substrings (1, 0, 0) and (0, 0, 10) to obtain (1, 0, 10) would not correctly interpret the fact that the 1 in the first substring means to put everything on the first asset. A mutation operator that worked quite well on this problem alters a gene either by an increment or decrement of one. This ensures that a chromosome undergoing mutation will not experience abrupt changes.

Selection and Algorithm. The evolutionary algorithm for one-period portfolio selection is steady state with elitist selection, with multiple populations connected according to a linear (or stepping-stone) topology, in such a way that

adjacent subpopulations have the closest values of λ.

Experiments and Results. The evolutionary algorithm described above was packaged in a decision support system, called DRAGO, on behalf of the mutual fund management branch of a prominent Italian bank. Since its implementation, DRAGO has undergone a comprehensive testing in the field, with portfolios ranging from a few dozens to hundreds of assets, proving quite successful in approximating the efficient frontier for a wide variety of problems.

A GP APPLICATION: ASSESSMENT OF HUMAN ORAL BIOAVAILABILITY OF DRUGS

In recent years, the introduction of high-throughput screening (HTS) and combinatorial chemistry techniques has deeply changed the process of drug discovery. Libraries of millions of chemical compounds could now be tested in order to evaluate their affinity to a particular pathology-associated protein. Results of tests could then be used to design modifications to be done on the molecules for optimizing their properties. Nevertheless, this is not enough; in fact, compounds with putative pharmacological value have not only to show a good target binding, but also have to reach the target in vivo. In other words, it is necessary that compounds follow the appropriate way into the human body without altering the health of the patient. About half of the failures in pharmacological development were made at this stage (Kennedy, 1997), with an unacceptable burden on the research and development budget of pharmaceutical companies. For this reason, the behavior of the molecules must be evaluated through the so-called ADMET processes (adsorption, distribution, metabolism, excretion, and toxicity). One important parameter directly correlated with ADMET processes is the human oral bioavailability, which is the parameter that measures the percentage of initial drug dose that effectively reaches the systemic blood circulation. This parameter is particularly relevant for pharmaceutical industries because oral consumption is usually the preferred way for supplying drugs to patients and because it is a representative measure of the quantity of active principle that effectively can actuate its biological effect. Various medium- and high-throughput in vitro screens are therefore now in use to predict ADMET parameters, and there is an increasing need for good tools for predicting them. This serves two aims: first to reduce the risk of late-stage attrition at the design stage of new compounds and compound libraries, and second, to optimize screening and testing by looking at only the most promising compounds (Smola & Scholkopf, 1998). Here, we show that GP is a promising and valuable tool for quantitative predictions of the human oral bioavailability of drug candidates. A first attempt in this direction can be found in Langdon and Barrett (2004). A more detailed description of the application presented here can be found in Archetti, Lanzeni, Messina, and Vanneschi (2006).

In particular, we present some experiments that we have performed using a canonic version of GP, three variants of GP in which the fitness function and/or the set of terminal symbols have been modified and a set of well-known non-evolutionary machine learning methods were used, such as linear and least square regression, feed-forward artificial neural networks, and two different versions of support vector machines (SVMs). Before describing GP variants used here and the way in which they have been used in our experiments, and before presenting the experimental results, in the following sections we describe data collecting and preparation, the computation of molecular descriptors, and the strategy used for data-set partitioning. The non-evolutionary machine learning methods are not described here to save space. Nevertheless, they are standard, and documentation can be found in

Akaike (1973), Hall (1998), Haykin (1999), Jolliffe (1986), Rousseeuw and Leroy (1987), Smola and Scholkopf (1998), Van de Waterbeemd et al. (2003), and Weka (2006).

Data-Set Collecting and Preparation

We collect from Yoshida and Topliss (2000) and from the Drug Bank public database (*Drug Bank*, 2006) the chemical structure, expressed as SMILES (simplified molecular input line entry specification) string, and the human oral bioavailability experimental measurements for 360 FDA- (Food and Drug Administration) approved drugs and drug-like compounds. SMILES is a string codifying the 2-D molecular structure of a compound in an extremely concise form, introduced by Chemical Information Systems Inc. (2006). Chemical strings are transformed into bi-dimensional formulas and used as input for ADMET Predictor (software produced by Simulation Plus Inc., 2006) for calculating 241 bi-dimensional molecular descriptors. Now we dispose of a matrix H of m rows and n columns, where m represents the number of molecules for which we have the experimental bioavailability measurements, and n represents the number of molecular descriptors. The known values of human oral bioavailability are placed in the m-dimensional vector %F. A random splitting of the data set is performed before model construction by partitioning it into a training and a test set: 70% of the molecules are randomly selected with uniform probability and inserted into the training set, while the remaining 30% forms the test set. In other words, H is spitted into $H^{(TRAIN)}$ and $H^{(TEST)}$. The first of these two matrixes has m^+ rows (where m^+ is the number of molecules selected for constructing the training set) and n columns, whereas $H^{(TEST)}$ has $m-m^+$ rows and n columns. Analogously, also the vector %F is partitioned in %F$^{(TRAIN)}$ and %F$^{(TEST)}$, where %F$^{(TRAIN)}$ of course contains the same indexes of %F as the ones in $H^{(TRAIN)}$.

We have not used feature selection for any of the GP versions presented below in our experiments, while we have used the well-known correlation-based feature selection (Jolliffe, 1986) for all the other machine learning techniques. The choice of this feature selection strategy is motivated by an experimental study not shown here (Archetti et al., 2006).

Genetic Programming Settings

Four (slightly) different versions of GP have been used to obtain the results presented here. They have been called the following.

- Canonic (or standard) GP (stdGP)
- Linear scaling with two criteria (LS2-GP)
- Linear scaling with two criteria and random constants (LS2-C-GP)
- Dynamic fitness GP (DF-GP)

They are described below.

Canonic or Standard GP

The first GP setting that we have used was a deliberately simple version of standard tree-based GP (Koza, 1992). In particular, we have chosen to use a parameter setting and the sets of functions and terminal symbols as similar to the ones that have originally been used in Koza as possible for symbolic regression problems. Each molecular feature H_{ij} has been represented as a floating point number. Potential solutions (GP individuals) have been built by means of the set of functions F={+, *, -,÷} (where ÷ is the protected division, i.e., it returns 1 if the denominator is 0) and the set of terminals T composed by n floating point variables (where n is the number of columns in the training set, i.e., the number of molecular features of the compounds). The fitness of each individual has been defined as the root mean squared error (RMSE) measured on the data used to construct the bioavailability model; that is, only the data

contained in the training set have been used as fitness cases. In other words, given an individual k producing the bioavailability predictions %F$^{(PRE)}$ on the training set, we define the fitness of k ($RMSE_k$) as

$$RMSE_k = f(k) = \sqrt{\frac{\sum_{i=1}^{m^+} (\% F_i - \% F_i^{(PRE)})^2}{m^+}}.$$

For each individual k, we also evaluate the RMSE measured on the test set H$^{(TEST)}$, whose data, of course, are not used at all during the evolution. The RMSE on the test set will be used for comparing GP results with the ones of the other machine learning methods.

Linear Scaling with Two Criteria

The second version of GP that we present uses the same parameter setting as stdGP, but a different fitness function. In particular, the fitness of a GP individual is obtained by executing two steps. The first step consists of applying linear scaling to $RMSE_k$ as it has been defined in equation (1). Linear scaling (Keijzer, 2003) is a technique that transforms the $RMSE$ in such a way that formulas that have the same form as the target function are assigned a good fitness. The second step consists of calculating a weighted average between the value of the $RMSE$ with linear scaling and the statistical correlation between the real bioavailability values of the molecules belonging to the training set and the bioavailability predictions calculated by GP individuals on the same molecules.

Linear Scaling with Two Criteria and Random Constants

The third GP version presented here is similar to LS2-GP with the only difference that a set of ephemeral random constants (ERCs) is added to the set of terminal symbols to code GP expressions. These ERCs are generated uniformly at random from the range [*m*, *M*], where *m* and *M* are the minimum and the maximum values of bioavailability of the molecules in the training set respectively. In the experiments presented here, a number of ERCs equal to the number of variables (i.e., equal to 241) have been used. This choice has been empirically confirmed to be suitable by a set of GP runs in which different numbers of ERCs extracted from different ranges have been used.

Dynamic Fitness

The fourth version of GP presented here differs from the previously presented ones since this time the fitness function used by GP dynamically changes during the evolution. In particular, the evolution starts with the correlation coefficient used as the only optimization criterion. When at least 10% of the individuals in the population reach a value of the correlation coefficient that is larger or equal to 0.6, the fitness function changes, and it becomes the following one.

$$f(k) = \begin{cases} bad\_fitness \quad f \quad CORR_k < 0.6 \\ RMSE_k \qquad\quad otherwise \end{cases}$$

In this way, the selection pressure operates as a pruning algorithm, giving a chance to sur-vive for mating only to those individuals whose correlation is largest or equal than 0.6. The idea behind this method is that the search space is too large for GP to perform efficiently; furthermore, we hypothesize that individuals with a good, although not optimal, correlation coefficient between outputs and goals will have the largest generalization ability and thus should take part in the evolutionary process. Some experiments (whose results are not shown here for lack of space) have empirically confirmed that the threshold value 0.6 for the correlation coefficient is large enough to avoid underfitting and small enough to reduce overfitting.

EXPERIMENTAL RESULTS

Table 1 shows the RMSE and correlation coefficient for all the presented nonevolutionary machine learning techniques with correlation-based feature selection. The best results, both for RMSE and correlation coefficients, are returned by linear regression.

In Table 2, RMSE and the correlation coefficient for all the considered GP versions are shown. In particular, we report the performance of the individual with the best RMSE value contained in the population at termination over 20 independent runs.

Table 1. Experimental comparison between different machine learning techniques for bioavailability predictions using correlation-based feature selection

Method	RMSE on Test Set	Correlation Coefficient
Linear Regression	27.5212	0.3141
Least Square Regression	31.7826	0.1296
Multilayer Perception	32.5782	0.2308
SVM Regression (first degree polynomial kernel)	28.8875	0.2855
SVM Regression (second degree polynomial kernel)	29.7152	0.2787

Table 2. Experimental results of the different GP versions. These results concern the individuals with the best RMSE value in all the populations over 20 independent runs.

Method	RMSE on Test Set	Correlation Coefficient
stdGP	30.1276	0.1661
LS2-GP	26.5909	0.3735
LS2-C-GP	26.0126	0.4245
DF-GP	27.3591	0.3304

Comparing the results shown in this table with the previously presented ones, we remark that all the GP versions outperform the other machine learning methods both for RMSE and the correlation coefficient, except for stdGP, which is outperformed by SVM and linear regression. The technique that has returned the best solution is LS2-C-GP. Comparing the results returned by LS2-C-GP with the ones of the nonevolutionary methods, we can remark that LS2-C-GP has found a better RMSE and a remarkably higher correlation coefficient value. We hypothesize that this is due to two main reasons. First of all, using two criteria to evolve solutions on the training set allows us to generate solutions that are good on both the criteria and that are optimal on none of them. In this way, we prevent the evolutionary process from generating too good solutions on the training set for one single criterion, which could lead to overfitting. In doing that, we also use the correlation coefficient as an optimization criterion, which is an important measure for results accuracy. Secondly, the use of ERCs may help to asses the relevance of the features in the proposed solutions.

Finally, we remark that the genotype of the best GP individual obtained using LS2-C-GP uses only 17 2-D molecular descriptors over the 241 that we have used. In other words, GP has automatically performed a strong feature selection. This normally very expansive phase (if performed explicitly) can be done implicitly by none of the other machine learning techniques that we have studied. In this application, feature selection plays a very important role (bioavailability can be expressed as a function of some molecular descriptors, not necessarily all), and we claim that this is one of the reasons why GP may be a suitable technique to solve this kind of problems.

CONCLUSION

In this chapter we have described evolutionary algorithms, a family of powerful optimization heuristics based on the metaphor of biological evolution. These heuristics have nowadays a quite rigorous theoretical basis and have been proven useful in approaching many hard problems. Among the many successful real-life applications that could be described, we have presented two case studies, one in the economic domain (for which genetic algorithms have been used), and the other in the biotechnology area (which has been solved by means of genetic programming). Both case studies clearly show that evolutionary algorithms are a particularly flexible and powerful heuristic approach that may outperform many other machine learning techniques on a significant and continuously increasing set of applications.

ACKNOWLEDGMENT

We acknowledge Professor Francesco Archetti, Professor Enza Messina, and Dr. Stefano Lanzeni for their collaboration on the application of the automatic assessment of human oral bioavailability of drugs.

REFERENCES

Akaike, H. (1973). Information theory and an extension of maximum likelihood principle. *2ⁿᵈ International Symposium on Information Theory* (pp. 267-281).

Archetti, F., Lanzeni, S., Messina, E., & Vanneschi, L. (2006). Genetic programming for human oral bioavailability of drugs. *Proceedings of the Genetic and Evolutionary Computation Conference* (GECCO'06, pp. 255-262).

Banzhaf, W., Nordin, P., Keller, R. E., & Francone, F. D. (1998). *Genetic programming: An introduction.* San Francisco: Morgan Kaufmann.

Chemical Information Systems Inc. (2006). *The company that introduced SMILES molecule representation.* Retrieved January 10, 2007, from http://www.daylight.com/dayhtml/smiles

Drug Bank, a recently developed database of FDA approved and experimental drugs. (2006). Retrieved January 10, 2007, from http://redpoll.pharmacy.ualberta.ca/drugbank/

Eiben, A. E., & Smith, J. E. (2003). *Introduction to evolutionary computing.* Berlin, Germany: Springer.

Fogel, L. J., Owens, A. J., & Walsh, M. J. (1966). *Artificial intelligence through simulated evolution.* New York: John Wiley.

Harlow, H. V. (1991). Asset allocation in a downside-risk framework. *Financial Analysts Journal,* pp. 30-40.

Haykin, S. (1999). *Neural networks: A comprehensive foundation.* London: Prentice Hall.

Holland, J. H. (1975). *Adaptation in natural and artificial systems.* Ann Arbor, MI: The University of Michigan Press.

Jolliffe, I. T. (1986). *Principal component analysis* (2ⁿᵈ ed.). Berlin, Germany: Springer

Keijzer, M. (2003). Improving symbolic regression with interval arithmetic and linear scaling. In C. Ryan et al. (Eds.), *Lecture notes in computer science: Vol. 2610. Genetic Programming: Proceedings of the 6ᵗʰ European Conference* (pp. 71-83). Berlin, Germany: Springer.

Kennedy, T. (1997). Managing the drug discovery development interface. *Drug Discovery Today, 2,* 436–444.

Koza, J. R. (1992). *Genetic programming.* Cambridge, MA: MIT Press.

Langdon, W. B., & Barrett, S. J. (2004). Genetic programming in data mining for drug discovery. In *Evolutionary computing in data mining* (pp. 211-235). Berlin, Germany: Springer.

Markowitz, H. M. (1959). *Portfolio selection.* New York: John Wiley.

Michalewicz, Z. (1996). *Genetic algorithms + data structures = evolution programs* (3ʳᵈ ed.). Berlin, Germany: Springer.

Rechenberg, I. (1973). *Evolutionsstrategie: Optimierung technischer systeme nach prinzipien der biologischen evolution.* Stuttgart, Germany: Fromman-Holzboog Verlag.

Rousseeuw, P. J., & Leroy, A. M. (1987). *Robust regression and outlier detection.* New York: Wiley.

Smola, A. J., & Scholkopf, B. (1998). A tutorial on support vector regression (Tech. Rep. No. NC2-TR-1998-030). NeuroCOLT2.

Tettamanzi, A., & Tomassini, M. (2001). *Soft computing: Integrating evolutionary, neural, and fuzzy systems.* Berlin, Germany: Springer.

Yoshida, F., & Topliss, J. G. (2000). QSAR model for drug human oral bioavailability. *Journal of Medicinal Chemistry, 43,* 2575-2585.

Chapter X
The Future Quantum Computer:
Biotic Complexity

Hector Sabelli
Chicago Center for Creative Development, USA

Gerald H. Thomas
Milwaukee School of Engineering, USA

ABSTRACT

Quantum computing forces a reexamination of logic. We examine its historical roots in logos, the logic of nature, and it is manifested by the laws of physics. A new logic comes out of this inquiry and it is applied to quantum computing. The logical design of computers according to the logic of quantum physics will allow the full use of quantum processes for computation and also adapt our humanly conceived computer logic to the actual logic of nature. The basic principles of quantum physics are homologically repeated in fundamental processes at all levels of organization. Thus, the principles of action, opposition such as charge and spin, chromatic structure, and the creation of novelty, diversity, and complexity can guide logic. Explicit realizations of these ideas are provided.

INTRODUCTION

Here we explore a logical design for computers that matches the logic of quantum physics. This will allow the full use of quantum processes for computation. As an added and larger advantage, it will also adapt our humanly conceived computer logic to the actual logic of nature.

Quantum processes involve actions (rather than static states) and the universal superposition of opposite states (e.g., spins). We envision quantum decision gates that use the superposition of quantum opposites to generate complex logical functions beyond those of Boolean logic. Such devices serve for generic computation because opposites actually coexist in natural and human processes at every level of organization. Thus, we hope to model social and mathematical processes more directly with a biotic logic, which will be a new approach from the current approach based on traditional static logic.

The general-purpose digital computer is constructed from electrical circuits connecting logical gates that represent Boolean logic functions. This corresponds to a mechanical, static, nonevolutionary worldview in which opposites exclude each other, as they do in the case of abstract mathematical objects (principle of no contradiction). Such general-purpose computers in fact are not able to solve all problems equally well: For example, complex problems such as weather prediction demand an impractical amount of time, and quantum systems can be simulated on classical computers only at an exponential cost.

The development of the proposed new computers corresponds to a worldview focused on processes, evolution, and the creation of complexity via the interaction of opposites such as electrical charges and biological sexes.

The logical theory that connects this view and the quantum decision gates is bios theory (Sabelli, 2005) and its realization via physical models of decision making (Thomas, 2006). Decision theory is a newly proposed extension to the theory of games that is based on the same logic as are causal processes in nature. Bios is a newly discovered causal process in nature that follows chaos in the evolution from simple to complex (Sabelli), and is illustrated in mathematical recursions (Figure 3) in which trigonometric functions model bipolar feedback (Kauffman & Sabelli, 1998). Here the opposites are bipolar and bi-dimensional, as they are in quantum processes. The Schrödinger equation produces a biotic pattern (Sabelli & Kovacevic, 2006; Thomas, Sabelli, Kauffman, & Kovacevic, 2006), that is to say, a sequence of morphologically organic-like forms (complexes; Figure 4), diversification (increased variance with time), novelty (more changes than its randomized copy), and nonrandom complexity as observed in biological processes (hence the term bios, meaning life).

Figure 1

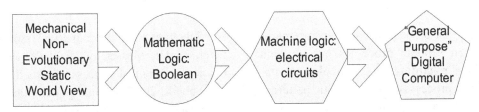

Figure 2

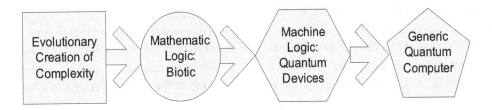

Figure 3. A simple model $A(t+1) = A(t) + g*sin(A(t))$ of bipolar feedback that generates steady state, bifurcation, unifurcation, bifurcation tree, chaos, bios, and leaps as the parameter g increases. Leaps are not presented in the picture. Both unifurcations and leaps are catastrophes.

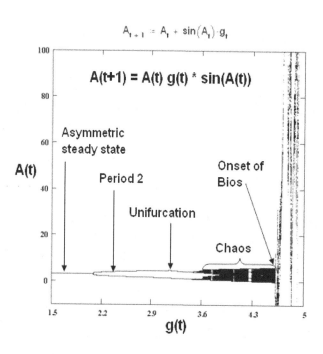

The fact that biotic processes generate more novelty than random processes has obvious implications regarding quantum phenomena. As quantum processes generate biotic patterns, we propose to develop quantum biotic devices as logical gates. Quantum computations should not be restricted to static molds. Quantum biotic processes can be useful for generic computation because biotic patterns exist everywhere at all levels of organization: in the temporal distribution of galaxies and of quasars (Sabelli & Kovacevic, 2003, 2006; Thomas et al., 2006), geographical structures, meteorological processes, DNA base sequences (Sabelli, 2005), heartbeat series (Carl-son-Sabelli et al., 1994; Sabelli, Carson-Sabelli, Patel, Zbilut, Messer, & Walthall, 1995), and other physiological processes (Sabelli & Carl-son-Sabelli, 2005), animal populations (Sabelli & Kovacevic, 2006), economic processes (Levy-Carciente, Sabelli, & Jaffe, 2004; Patel & Sabelli, 2003; Sabelli & Carlson-Sabelli, 2005; Sugerman & Sabelli, 2003), and some musical compositions (Levy, Alden, & Levy, 2006) and literary texts (Sabelli, 2005).

The objective of this chapter is to sketch the general principles of a logic that incorporates the biotic complexity of quantum processes as a foundation for quantum computation.

LOGIC AND RATIONALITY

Rationality consists of thinking according to the mathematical structure of nature at all levels of organization (Galileo's hypothesis). The term logic has at least four distinct uses: the logic of nature, the science of reasoning, mathematical logic, and computer logic, in decreasing order of extension. The term logic derives from logos, the term used by Heraclitus to indicate that the organization of nature corresponds to that of human reason. Nature is rational, not random or chaotic.

It is desirable to examine the logic of quantum physics as a foundation for computational logic. If one really understands the physical process, one should be able to deduce its logic without waiting for philosophers to provide an interpretation or for the symbolic logicians to complete their formalization. However, interpretations do not emerge from nature: They are processed by humans immersed in a given culture. Many presentations of

quantum physics imply that it demonstrates that nature is illogical, entities are in no specific state unless observed, the coexistence of contradictory properties must be accepted without question, and changes occur without cause. Feynman's famous remark "nobody understands quantum mechanics" reflects its current formulation, which Einstein, Schrödinger, Bohm, and Bell, among others, find objectionable. Thus, the task of developing a logic for quantum computation also involves the formulation of a realistic and rational interpretation of quantum phenomena.

The universe is creative and life-like (biotic), proposed the Greek founders of science. Processes are created by the interaction of opposites (Heraclitus, Empedocles). The coexistence of opposites in nature demands a method of reasoning in which opposition plays a central role, that is, Socrates' dialectics, which is the foundation and context of Aristotle's logic. Logic was developed in ancient Greece along with arithmetic and geometry. These

Figure 4. Time series and recurrence plot of biotic pattern generated by the Schrödinger equation. We show an example of a bound particle in a one-dimensional box, which is a useful idealization of an electron bound inside an atom. Bound particles have many quantum states, which can be represented as an infinite number of simple trigonometric functions. Each state evolves over time. An initial packet formed from a superposition of states will, over time, spread out. This behavior is biotic, as shown with both discrete (Sabelli & Kovacevic, 2006) and continuous (Thomas et al., 2006) models.

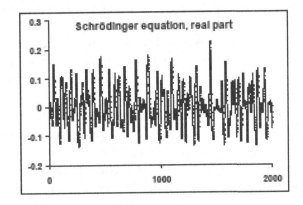
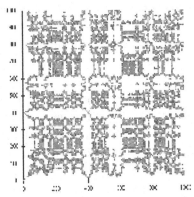

are historically the three roots of mathematics. However, logic is not a purely mathematical discipline. Logic was conceived as the study of reason, a study that they viewed as both descriptive and normative. So it was seen by Aristotle and again by Boole, who clearly called his book *The Laws of Thought*. In our times, logic has gone beyond a descriptive and normative science of thinking to become an engineering of computing, calculating, ordering, organizing, and other forms of thinking. Historically, the first computational devices were analog: The differential gear of a car first appeared in early computational devices.[a] Later on, Shannon (1938) discovered the possibility of mapping Boolean logical functions onto simple electronic gates. Boolean logical functions allow the mathematization and thereby mechanization of logic, that is, computation.

Three essential tenets of Aristotelian logic have been consistently ignored by his medieval followers and later thinkers: first, the existence of a third open value (neither true nor false) for what has not yet come to pass, thus allowing for creativity; second, the superiority of states of coexisting opposites (the "golden middle"); and third, the local character of the principle of no contradiction. Opposites do not coexist at the same time, at the same place, and in the same context. Opposites can otherwise coexist. Thus, true Aristotelian logic is compatible with process concepts; in fact, Aristotle pioneered the notion of causal development. Computational logic may be expanded by including these essential tenets of Aristotelian logic. In contrast, standard contemporary logic has adopted the static perspective of medieval logic, excluding third values and rendering noncontradiction an absolute, universal principle.

The science of reason, logic, need not be based on the simplest branch of mathematics, as Russell attempted to do. The notion that one can formulate logical norms without attending to the physics of nature and the psychobiology of thinking seems at best overconfident. In any case, such logic fails to describe reality—an obvious example is its inability to describe quantum phenomena as well as natural reasoning—and even to provide sufficient bases for arithmetic (Gödel's theorem). Static two-value logic based on set theory fails as a science of reason by the following.

1. Advancing a static concept of identity A=A that does not describe either physical actions or personal identity, both of which continually change
2. Postulating the separation and mutual exclusion of opposites[b]
3. Portraying processes and properties as spatial and separate atomic-like entities rather than as actions and interactions

Physicists have also considered the coexistence of opposites from the perspective of oriental philosophy. The Taoist concept of the complementarity of opposites was adopted by N. Bohr as central to quantum physics (Capra, 1975), and it was explored as a logic of systems (Sabelli, 1989, 1998; Xu & Li; 1989), but computer scientists so far have not made use of this concept.

Following the rediscovery of Heraclitus' texts, the notion of creative opposition was named dialectics by Hegel, reshaped by Marx, and made famous by his followers. Dialectic logic has been proposed as an alternative to standard logic (Joja, 1969; Lefebvre, 1947; Planty-Bonjour, 1965), but it has not been possible to use it in computation because it has not been formulated mathematically, although some attempts have been made (Gauthier, 1984; Kosok, 1984; Sabelli, 1971, 1984). Because it is a vague verbal formulation, dialectics allows for all kinds of abuse in reasoning (as illustrated by the rejection of quantum mechanics by Soviet Marxists).

Mathematical dynamics provides tools to expand Boolean logic. Based on mathematics, natural science, and psychobiology, bios theory focuses on fundamental opposites, such as quantum conjugates, electric charge, and biological sexes, that generate bifurcations, triads, chaos, bios, atoms, and organisms, rather than neutralizing each other in equilibrium or dialectic synthesis.

PHYSICAL BASES FOR COMPUTATIONAL LOGIC AND FOR BIOS THEORY

The physical bases for rationality are (a) quantum of action, (b) electrodynamics, (c) chromodynamics, and (d) relativistic cosmological nucleation and expansion. Here we reformulate bios theory on these physical foundations.

The Quantum of Action

Action is the change of energy in time.[c] Planck's constant involves energy and time. While for Planck h was a mathematical constant, Einstein explained the photoelectric effect by assuming that light quanta were actual particles, which he called photons. Quanta are the units of action in nature. Action is the one and sole constituent of the universe (Sabelli, 2005). Just as inertia, not rest, is intrinsic to mechanical movement, energy continually transforms itself; action, not stasis (resting equilibrium), is the simplest spontaneous condition. Action requires time: There are no instantaneous interactions at a distance. Action involves conservation and change as inseparable aspects. Energy is transformed and conserved (first law of thermodynamics[d]), so actions cause change, and conversely there cannot be events without cause (chance).[e] Correspondingly, time is unidirectional, asymmetric, unipolar, and irreversible.[f] Ordered in space-time, actions form lattices, one of the three mother structures of mathematics according to Bourbaki (1948/1962; see also Piaget, 1950).[g]

The principle of least action describes action as an integral quantity used to determine the evolution of a physical system between two defined states, that is, a change of energy in time; imbued of the economic spirit, the principle requires the action to be least.[h] Students, who conserve their critical faculties, question how natural processes know how to evolve in such economic fashion. Actually, at the quantum level, an entity does not follow a single path, but its behavior depends on all imaginable paths and the value of the actions of each path (Feynman, 1974).[i] Regardless of their diversity, these various definitions of action show time and energy as inseparable; they do not change independently from each other. We can extend this definition of action to all levels of organization. For instance, cardiac action involves the force and time (timing, duration,

Figure 5. Conjugate opposites

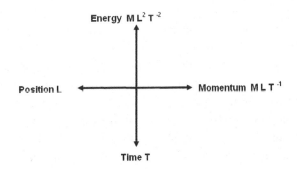

and frequency) of contractions; in psychological processes, mania is characterized by high-energy fast processing while depression is characterized by low energy and motor retardation (Sabelli, 2005). In the context of classical mechanics, the Lagrangian is the kinetic energy of a mechanical system minus its potential energy. In quantum physics, time and energy are conjugates and hence noncommutative—Boolean logic is commutative. Action is the integral of differences. This is a noteworthy union of opposites.[j] Differences are directional, not commutative; going from A to B is the opposite, not the same, as going from B to A. Action actually involves two orthogonal pairs of conjugated opposites: energy and time, position and momentum. Position and time are locations in four-dimensional space-time, while energy and momentum represent self-causing, self-changing substance.

Electrodynamics

Electrical charge is a coexistence of opposites (bipolarity) that constructs complex arrangements from atoms to organisms, and generates electromagnetic radiation that carries information among distant galaxies as well as in brains and computers. (Nuclear forces and gravitation act in smaller or larger realms; they do not currently play a direct role in the function of the computer.) Information, so fundamental in genetics and computer science, does not need to appear as a separate dimension in physics: Electrical charge is information. More generally, information is encoded in opposition and other gauge symmetries[k]. Physical symmetries are abstracted by groups, another basic structure of mathematics according to Bourbaki (1948/1962).

Opposition embodies information: Two values are necessary and sufficient to encode information. Thus, complexity results from successive bifurcations. This new conception of information (Sabelli, 2005) renders it causal and gives equal significance to repetition and to difference as its

carriers; this is in contrast to a focus on uncertainty (Heisenberg) and probability (Shannon, 1948), and the definition of information as entropy, difference, or distinction. Shannon's entropy refers to the communication of information along wires, explicitly excludes meaning, and presupposes the distinction among two or more values as the embodiment of information. Distinction requires asymmetry (Sabelli); partition alone is not sufficient. In fact, distinction does not require a partition into separate classes, as in Aristotelian and Boolean logic, set theory, or the theory of form (Spencer-Brown, 1969/1979). Two-ness is a simple and familiar form of opposition and it is widely used to encode information. However, opposites can be contained in an asymmetry within a unity, such as the direction of an action, the polarity of a magnet, or the spin of a quantum. The Möbius ribbon, the Klein bottle, and fractals further illustrate that opposites are not determined by boundaries. Distinction involves either change or repetition. Difference or change carries information (Bateson, 1979), but only in a static system; in changing processes, it is repetition that conveys pattern (Sabelli). For instance, messengers such as light are always described by periodic repetition characterized by a frequency.

Besides charge, there are other fundamental oppositions, such as spin, which has only two values: ½ and −½ for electrons. Pauli's exclusion principle states that two identical fermions (electrons, protons, neutrons, quarks) cannot simultaneously occupy the same quantum state. If two fermions 1 and 2 are in states a and b respectively, the corresponding wave function ψ is

$$\psi = \psi_1(a)\,\psi_2(b) - \psi_1(b)\,\psi_2(a).$$

This antisymmetric wave function requires two such entities located in the same place (e.g., two electrons in the same orbital) to have opposite spin. In a way, Pauli's principle updates Aristotle's principle of local noncontradiction, and thereby imposes a dialectic.

The information carried by electrical charge also creates structure. Matter, often described as neutral, actually is bipolar; atoms are made by positive nuclei and negative electrons. Their separation forms structure.

Nuclear Structure

Structures, starting with matter itself, are formed as nucleations around centers, not as bounded systems; this fact alone indicates the limitation of sets, classes, and systems as fundamental logical entities. The fundamental centers are the tridimensional baryons (protons and neutrons) formed by quarks of three colors (quantum chromodynamics) and their further nucleation as atomic nuclei. There is a not understood but significant relation between triadicity, stability, and transformation. Protons are extremely stable; their decay has not been observed. Neutrons outside the nucleus, however, are extremely unstable, and it is the conversion between protons and neutrons via the weak force that creates higher forms of matter. Structures are not static. They are engines, like enzymes, even creative engines, as accelerators that create new particles and elements.

Material Organization

Macroscopically, matter is further organized in heterogeneous forms generated by gravitation in four-dimensional space-time. At this level, organization involves both nucleation and its opposite expansion, as well as stability and its opposite transformation. The organization of matter in N-dimensional space is abstracted by topology, the third basic structure of mathematics according to Bourbaki (1948/1962), with its ancestor, geometry, stressing the tri-dimensionality of actual physical space.

PSYCHOBIOLOGICAL AND MATHEMATICAL BASES FOR BIOTIC LOGIC

Bios theory generalizes these four physical processes as generic dynamics present at all levels of organization (Sabelli, 2005). Generalizing the notion of action quanta, we propose unipolar discrete action at all levels of organization (e.g., action potentials, cardiac contractions, individual persons). Generalizing quantum electrodynamics, we derive the notion that information is bipolar and that fundamental opposites exist at each level of organization, as illustrated by sex, cooperation and conflict, abundance and scarcity, and true and false. Generalizing from the weak nuclear force and the strong nuclear force (quantum chromodynamics), we seek and find connectedness and tri-dimensionality at all levels of organization. At all levels there will be the three dimensions of physical space because all is material, as well as specific dimensions such as primary colors.

We have here encountered the small integers (1, 2, 3, 4) as fundamental features of quantum processes. This is not surprising as actions are quantic and ordered in time; numbers are unit quantities (cardinal numbers) and ordered (ordinal numbers). Numbers are also forms. Numbers such as the small integers and π are generic forms present at multiple levels of organization (Pythagoras, Galileo, Pierce, Jung; Robertson, 1995). We propose to seek these numerical forms at each level and in each process (Sabelli & Carlson-Sabelli, 1996). At all levels there are units, pairs, and triads. At all levels there is unidirectionality, symmetry, and spatial organization. At all levels there is a linear flow in time, two-way transformations, and hierarchical feedbacks. At all levels there is oneness of substance, a partition into two classes, and hierarchy of three levels. Triadicity is a fundamental form that repeats in many processes at multiple levels of organization, as illustrated by macroscopic physical space, π atomic orbitals, DNA codons, family triads, conceptual triads, and symbolic triads including Trinitarian concepts of God. Triads are fundamental not only because of Aristotelian logic and examples from quantum physics (three colors for quarks), but also because of Sarkovskii's theorem (Peitgen, Jūrgens, & Saupe, 1992) that shows Period 3 as the end of an ordered series of periodicities, including infinity. This theorem is central to modern nonlinear dynamics. The infinite periodicities implied by Period 3 have been interpreted as chaos, and in fact gave the name to this field. While logic and dialectics focus on two-ness, and others propose instead a three-valued logic, we consider it necessary to consider both two-ness and triadicity. We further speculate that the four-dimensional space-time of relativity theory may help us some day to understand the fundamental role of quaternity at many levels of organization.[1]

The same basic natural forms (action, opposition, and spatial organization) appear in abstract form as arithmetic, logic, and geometry, which are the historical foundations of mathematics. They reappear in an even more abstract manner in lattice, group, and topology, the "mother structures" of mathematics. Lattices are sets of discrete units ordered by an asymmetric and transitive order relation < that abstracts actions, which are quantic and ordered in unidirectional time rather than hierarchies and always involve bidirectional interactions. The other basic quantum concepts are symmetries modeled by gauge groups: electrical charge by U(1), the weak force by SU(2), and the strong force by SU(3);[m] gravity also is a gauge symmetry, but as yet not integrated into the standard model. These gauge symmetries are actions, not static symmetries as one may find in a crystal. Symmetry vs. asymmetry is the basic opposition underlying information. Paraphrasing Heraclitus, asymmetry is the father and symmetry is the mother of all things.

The tridimensional organization of matter and concepts determines hierarchical interactions that are bidirectional (like cycles) and asymmetric (like actions) insofar as the simpler echelons have temporal priority, have greater energy and duration, and generate more complex organizations that acquire supremacy. The human central nervous system displays the asymmetry of action from back to front, the bilateral symmetry of opposition, and a hierarchy from simple and older levels to complex and newer ones (cortical supremacy) in the vertical dimension (Sabelli, 1989).

These basic forms—unidirectional action, bipolar opposition, and spatial organization—are also reflected in cognitive processes. Cognition begins in the infant with actions that construct the bifurcation between self and world. At the other extreme of complexity, human mathematics, a product of the mind, truthfully reflects the mathematical organization of the universe, a wonder that marveled Einstein and should not cease to marvel us. The brain naturally represents reality correctly because it is constructed by natural evolution out of natural components, and shaped by millions of years of activity and selection through cooperation, competition, and sexual matching (Sabelli, 1989; Vandervert, 1988). The biological bases of informatics are the innate ability to count, communicate (e.g., innate language grammar; Chomsky, 1976), and navigate (e.g., cognitive maps of spatial location), which developed into arithmetic, logic, and geometry, and later on into lattice, group, and topology. The mother structures of mathematics also are the basic cognitive structures in child development (Piaget, 1950). We propose that these structures constitute the universal logic of nature and thought (Sabelli, 2001, 2005). At all levels we have unidirectional action, bipolar opposition, tridimensional space, and other fundamental forms. The existence of homologous forms at multiple levels of organization allows the development of general-purpose computers.

Mathematics as a totality offers tools to mechanize logic. Lattice order (discrete sets ordered by a transitive and asymmetric relation) provides a dynamic concept of identity applicable to discrete and causal actions in unidirectional time. Groups (closed sets with inverses modeling natural cycles and two-way communication) provide a scheme for the separation (self-other), contradiction (true-false), and mutual transformation and implication of opposites. Topology (abstracting connectedness in space-time, i.e., continuity in both conservation and change) offers multiple designs for logical operations. Dynamic systems that incorporate recursive action, bipolar opposition, and topological connectedness generate processes with creative, life-like (biotic) features. Taking mathematics as totality a science of reason, we explore how to develop a new computational logic that is homological with quantum physical processes.

BIOTIC LOGIC: ACTION AS DYNAMIC IDENTITY

Physical action may serve as a principle of dynamic identity, that is, becoming, which is required to understand the continuity of identity through time (e.g., the evolution of a tree from acorn to oak) and the multiple expressions of identity in different contexts (e.g., the behavior of a person at work and at home). Action is self-referential: Action produces interactions and hence change. Static identity A=A is valid only for abstract entities, for short periods of time, and for macroscopic entities and is never true for actions. Reflexivity A=A means idempotency; self-interaction does not produce change: A and A= A or A = A. In the case of dynamic identity, reflexivity means self-transformation, so $A(t)$ implies $A(t+1)$. Dynamic identity implies transformation (not equality) and temporal asymmetry (not symmetry). Beyond the copula *to be* and the *if-then* implication, we may include in logic also other actions, that is, active verbs such as *to do*.

The various properties of action have significant implications regarding computation. First, macroscopic energy flow produces heat and interactions produce an incoherence of quantum superposition. Second, interactions are not instantaneous; they are communications via messengers, and therefore they involve time. Thus, interactions are processes of mutual feedback. Feedback is an important component of creative biotic processes. Third, as an action, a message or communication is the end result of a multiplicity of an infinity of imaginable paths. Information is contained in the message, the sequence of terms, and the sentence, not the letters.

BIOTIC LOGIC: OPPOSITION AS INFORMATION

Opposites are primarily forces[n] rather than different classes. The term opposite means both partner and antagonist; this ambiguity of meaning reflects the inseparability of these opposites. The opposition of the thumb shows that opposition is essential for synergy. Procreation reminds us that opposition is fundamentally creative.

Opposition is Universal, Diverse, and Tautological

All fundamental processes contain pairs of matching and contrasting complementary opposites (Heraclitus, Lao-tzu, Hegel) such as quantum conjugates (energy and time), electrical charge, spin, and biological sexes. Obviously, these are very diverse forms of opposition. Opposites are inseparable, just as left and right, which persist no matter how we divide the object: right if and if only left. There is an A if and only if there is a no-A. Real opposition is tautological.

Fundamental opposites are connected, complementary, connate (same origin), similar, and cocreative. Their pairing is necessary and fundamental. They are not simply mutually exclusive as in standard logic, nor simply polar, complementary, or antithetic as in dialectics.º Opposition is self-referential: Opposites are similar and different, synergic and antagonistic, connected and separate. Opposites carry information and produce or arrest change, thereby creating pattern and structure.

Quantum electrodynamics provides a physical embodiment of information for computation. As charge, information is bipolar (1 and –1). At the quantum level, there are many properties that can also encode information, such as spin, nuclear spin, color, and so forth, all of which can in principle be measured simultaneously. A spin state can be thought of as representing a direction in one dimension in physical space. The spin is continually and rapidly changing in the three dimensions of space. Thus, even when the initial state is specified (such as up), over time it will change. When we measure the spin of an electron in one dimension, we necessarily affect its spin in every other dimension of space. A property such as spin must be expressed by two complex Schrodinger-Dirac equations, thus four real numbers at every point in space. A measurement process for spin in one dimension (e.g., Stern and Gerlach experiment) filters the system into two distinguishable states: up (+½ spin) and down (–½ spin) in physical space. Although the terms up and down mean linear opposition, in quantum mechanics they are used to refer to orthogonal states that we can combine in various proportions. The quantum state

$$|\psi> = \alpha \ |0> + \beta \ |1>$$

is usually described as a superposition of opposite orthogonal basis states. Actually, there is no difference between basis and intermediate states other than what we choose as a basis in which to measure. Superposition means nothing other than taking the linear combination of orthogonal states. Although a given measurement selects a basis and we can determine only the fraction in each basis

state $|0>$ or $|1>$, the intermediate states have real, verifiable consequences, which are significant for computation. We learn partial information about the complex numbers α and β.

The qubit is thus described by four real numbers constrained by the absolute square of the wave function being constant. The qubit resides on the surface of a three-sphere and is locally described by a three-dimensional subspace, involving three orthogonal diameters and three pairs of opposites. Spin continually changes direction. Groups thus offer a fruitful model for negation: Rotation separates and connects opposites. While logic and dialectics focus on twos, it seems necessary to develop a 2^N valued logic, starting with the quaternity: the cross or square of opposites that emerges from the repetition of bifurcation.

Mutual Implication of Opposites Imply Each Other

No A necessarily implies A; destruction implies previous existence and creation. The implication of complementary classes in extensional logic is asymmetric. That there is an x implies that there is a no-x. However, that there is a no-x does not imply (or exclude) that there is an x. If there is a unicorn, there are some things that are not unicorns; otherwise, we could not distinguish the unicorn from the rest of the universe. But the fact that there are things that are not unicorns does not imply that there are unicorns.

The mutual implication of opposites is most evident in their alternation, which is ubiquitous in nature. Period 2 is widely observed in natural and human processes, for example, day and night, walking, conjugated carbons in aromatic molecules, the rise and fall of waves. Period 2 captures some important aspects of the seminal but vague dialectic concept of negation as being similar to, and reinforcing, the original assertion. The dialectic concept of negation (sublate, conserve, negate, and supersede) also includes a notion of hierarchy. ᴾ

To model sublation, one can use lattice-like sets. Opposites also alternate in nonperiodic fashion, such as chaotic and biotic patterns. By alternating in space and/or time, opposites coexist globally while remaining separated locally.

Bios Principle of Quantum Superposition, Local Partition, and Global Complementarity

At the quantum level, there are fundamental conjugates such as energy and time, and there are fundamental properties such as spin that come in pairs. Furthermore, these opposites superpose. A quantum entity exists in a continuum of different states (superposition) and continuously changes. This enormous amount of information, however, is not directly observable. Whenever we interact with a quantum property, let us say, spin, to measure it, we obtain either one result or its opposite (the collapse of the wave function), demonstrating a fundamental two-ness in nature.[q] Central to quantum physics is that opposites add linearly (meaning adding states with complex coefficients, each coefficient being two real parameters). Opposites such as opposite spins are diametric opposites in tridimensional physical space and orthogonal in the four-dimensional parameter space. The law of opposition is that there always is such two-ness, not that there are pure mutually exclusive opposites like the true and false of standard logic. Logic and dialectics focus on two-ness. Quantum physics demonstrates that two-ness is both fundamental and incomplete. Moreover, at the quantum level, two particles that have interacted continue determining each other even after they are separated (entanglement), no matter how distant they are from each other (quantum nonlocality).

At macroscopic levels, opposites are locally and partially separated in time, space, or context (local principle of no contradiction), not in all three. Positive and negative charges necessarily coexist in every atom, albeit in different particles. Male and female necessarily coexist in the same species but usually in different individuals. Life and death coexist but separate in time or place. Every living organism eventually dies, and while alive it is continually replacing its cells, literally living and dying at once. Rarely if ever are there entities that, showing one property P, are entirely free of its opposite −P. Opposite classes represent asymmetric distribution of opposite properties: There is a class of entities in which $+P > -P$, and a class of entities in which $-P > +P$.

Globally, opposites coexist and codetermine each other (dialectics); they form systems and cocreate new entities.

In summary, opposites superpose at the quantum level, and split at macroscopic levels into distinct components that together make up every process. Biotic logic integrates physics, logic, and dialectics by proposing that opposite processes display three different forms of interaction according to the size and complexity of the level of organization: quantum superposition, local macroscopic separation (logical noncontradiction), and global complementarity (dialectic contradiction; Sabelli, 2001).

An opposition thus involves the commonality between the opposing actions (let us say, the absolute value of P), the actual opposition +P and −P, the structures that embody the opposition (such as the class of entities in which $+P > -P$ and the class of entities in which $-P > +P$), and the system formed by the coexistence and interaction of these opposite forces and of the members of opposite classes. Sexuality involves the commonalities between all members of a species (far greater than their differences), the distinction between femaleness and maleness, separate classes of females and males, the coexistence and interaction of feminine and masculine traits in each person, and the coexistence and intercourse of males and females. Protons and electrons are particles with mass and charge; their mass is very different, their charge is opposite, and their coexistence generates atoms.

The existence of multiple levels of opposition corresponds to the multiple levels in which we can consider physical processes. A light ray as conceived in geometric optics is actually a wave, manifested in diffraction phenomena, that at a more elementary level is constituted by the multiple paths of action described by Feynman. We may regard these paths as multiple "biotic opposites." The periodic oscillation of radiation corresponds to the helical models of opposition commonly advanced in dialectics, while the linear geometric models correspond to linear logic. The concept of multiple, elementary biotic opposites is being explored as an alternative to philosophical notions of complementarity.

We thus conceive three levels of opposition: (a) the macroscopic logical or mechanical, in which paths are linear in the sense of geometric optics, (b) the dialectic or periodic in the sense of waves, as in periodic oscillations that include among its most important cases Period 2 alternation, Period 3, and the infinite periodicities it implies, and (c) the biotic or creative, which involves multiple components that generate new ones.

Opposition: Quantity, Quality, and Polarity

Oppositions can be unipolar (a set and its complement in two-valued logic, as in matter and void, construction and destruction, proton and neutron with regard to electrical charge), bipolar and asymmetric (proton and electron), or bipolar and symmetric (positron and electron). Fundamental opposites (such as electrical charge and male and female) are similar in substance and opposite in information. To represent this relation, one needs to consider opposite sign or bipolarity (like 1 and -1). Polarity is bipolarity; antimatter is not a deficit in matter, and evil is not a deficit of goodness. Opposition implies at least three values—positive, negative, and zero—in contrast to the widely used 0 to 1 scales. However, opposites are not simply poles in a linear continuum. Opposites also are synergistic in some respects and antagonistic in others.

Insofar as opposites are linear, opposition is bipolar in sign and unipolar in quantity. One aspect of opposition is a difference in some quantity (e.g., temperature, regarding hot and cold sensations); in this sense, opposites are poles of a continuum in which as one waxes, its opposite wanes. This concept underlies mechanics as well as probabilistic and fuzzy logics. But even at the extremes, each opposite contains the other in a diminished form, as represented symbolically by the yin-yang of Taoism, and as clearly observed in fractals.

Differences in quantity imply differences in quality (Galileo) and changes in quantity generate changes in quality (Hegel, Engels). There are nonlinear, sudden jumps in quality (dialectic leaps), as illustrated by biological thresholds and leaps in the process equation. Opposites are different from their less extreme forms (as highlighted by Taoism) and in some ways similar to each other and opposite to moderation (as avowed by popular wisdom). In this respect, Freud's a potiori argument (learn about a phenomenon by examining its extreme form) can be misleading.

Standard logic makes opposites mutually exclusive. If A is true (1) then no-A is false (0). Polar models (including versions of Taoism and dialectics) likewise postulate that increases in one extreme result in decreases of its opposite; other versions postulate conjoint increase (polarization) or decrease. The fact is that opposites can wax and wane together or autonomously rather than reciprocally; for instance, anger and fear often coexist and enhance each other. This relative independence of opposites requires that we plot them in separate axes. Two dimensional plots also allow one to consider the nonlinear aspects of opposition, that is, the simultaneous existence of similarity and difference, and of synergy and antagonism. Note that these three dimensions—amount or intensity of each opposite, similarity or difference, and synergy or antagonism—do not coincide; for example, similar entities are allies in some contexts and compete in others.

Opposites are orthogonal (like 1 and i, the square root of -1) as is the case for the basis states of a qubit. A qubit includes orthogonal diameters of polar opposites: 1 and – 1 or i and –i. Bipolarity and orthogonality are two separate forms of opposition that coexist in the qubit. Orthogonal variables often represent necessarily coexisting (i.e., complementary) dimensions.[r] We coin the term "conjugate opposites" to describe fundamental opposites that imply each other.[s] The expression "complementary opposite" has been used in the context of so many different theories[t] that it no longer conveys a specific meaning.[u] The meaning of Bohr's concept of complementarity is still open to question and should not be interpreted to mean the dismissal of the logical principle of no contradiction.[v]

Negation and Bifurcation

Oppositions are actions. Opposites are bifurcations from a common origin, alternate with each other periodically or aperiodically, and interact, influencing each other and creating new entities. Bifurcations do not create dichotomies that separate opposites; they create cycles that contain and connect opposites. These cycles may be periodic, chaotic, or biotic. In static logic, opposition is simple negation, leading to paradoxes of self-reference such as "I am lying" (or its equivalent, Russell's paradox), which is nothing more than Period 2, an alternation of opposites. Dialectics also highlights Period 2, but adds a hierarchical character to it as well as a constructive role, so negation is more powerful than assertion, and the negation of the negation is the synthesis of opposites. Bifurcation involves an increase in diversity from periodic to chaotic to biotic patterns.[w] Thus, bifurcation creates multiple qualities and structures.

BIOTIC LOGIC: STRUCTURES, CLASSES, AND DIMENSIONS

Processes create structures. Actions, oppositions, and nucleation precede and create structures, objects, and sets of objects. Actions and structures carry multiple types of information (qualities). They manifest as properties from the viewpoint of isolated entities, and as relations when regarded in context. Although processes, properties (information, dimension), and classes (matter, extension) are correlated, there is no exact overlap between them. Opposites exist as qualities and as classes, but the two do not exactly overlap: There are women and men, and there is masculinity and femininity, but both sexes partake, in different proportions, of both sets of qualities. The usually made assumption that properties such as being red can be defined by the set of red things is of limited value. Opposite properties are statistically but not absolutely divided in separate classes at the macroscopic level.

The logic of classes is itself a complex matter. Kauffman (2002, 2004) is developing a bio-logic where he explores the boundary between biology and the study of formal systems (logic). He arrives at a summary formalism, a chapter in boundary mathematics where there are not only containers <> but also "extainers" ><, entities open to interaction and distinguishing the space that they are not. The boundary algebra of containers and extainers is to bio-logic what Boolean algebra is to classical logic. He shows how this formalism encompasses significant parts of the logic of DNA replication, the Dirac formalism for quantum mechanics, formalisms for protein folding, and the basic structure of Temperley-Lieb algebra at the foundations of topological invariants of knots and links.

We conceptualize qualities, that is, information, as dimensions (Sabelli, 1989; Thomas, 2006) rather than as classes. The traditional focus on classes has been extremely useful regarding the classification of elementary particles, chemical elements, and biological species. Classes are used by philosophers to encode qualities by the extension of the entities that manifest a given property, at least since Aristotle, but dimensions are preferable because they can also provide quantitative information (e.g., not only that X is red but also how red it is) and also encode the coexistence of qualities (e.g., X is so much red and so much green). Using dimensions also solves some simple conundrums, such as "Does the American flag belong to the class of red objects or to the class of nonred objects?"

Dimensions encode qualities. In physics, which for good reasons is the model reference science, properties are represented as dimensions. [x] The concept of dimension involves quantity and quality, and thus formalizes their essential unity (Galileo, Hegel, Engels), which is the foundation of modern science insofar as it hinges on measurement. Current stress on qualitative science and scale-free phenomena, while valuable in themselves, should not obscure the dialectic unity of quantity and quality. Besides involving both quantity (measurement) and quality (properties and relations), dimensional analysis in physics involves a theoretical system. All fundamental physical processes can be expressed in terms of combinations of three basic dimensions: mass (M), length (L), and time (T), which allows us to define other physical dimensions. (Although one may use other concepts as the basic dimensions, each choice of a possible fundamental dimension implies what others can be chosen.)

Dimensions belong to reality; they are not human arbitrary decisions. Attending to dimensions reveals the fundamental aspects of a concept. The essence of action in physics is its dimensionality $M L^2 T^{-1}$, indicating self-causation (energy) and asymmetry (time). Dimensions are conserved in a unidirectional manner: The dimensions of the simpler components are by necessity present in their composites. Causality stems from the conservation of dimension. The dimensions of cause and effect must by necessity be the same. This implies that causation must be natural and deterministic; never can it be supernatural or aleatory. Also, the dimensions of the simple must be considered in every complex process.

Furthermore, attending to these most fundamental properties of action serve to see the relation between physical action and more complex forms (chemical, biological, social, psychological). To understand biological, social, and even psychological processes it is necessary to consider their physical dimensions: How would we practice medicine without measuring fever or pulse rate? How will the economy fare if the global temperature continues increasing?

Biology, sociology,[y] and psychology of course also involve more complex qualities, such as form,[z] which is desirable to conceptualize as dimensions new forms, not different forces or substance than physical ones. We do not possess as yet a system of dimensions to organize and measure these processes, but this does not mean that biological and psychological dimensions do not exist.[aa]

Dimensional analysis is the conceptual tool we apply to understand physical situations involving a mix of different kinds of physical quantities. We may generalize its use to all sciences to replace extensional logic based on set theory. To define a system of fundamental dimensions for human processes, as it has been done in physics, it is cogent to start with social dimensions as these are fewer and older than psychological ones. We thus first consider age (a continuous variable) and generation (child, parent, grandparent), sexuality (femininity and masculinity,), socioeconomic role, and cultural, national, and religious roots.

There are no barriers to the practical use of dimensions. The number of dimensions necessary to describe, for instance, a person's race is no larger, only more accurate, than the number of classes offered to describe it. Dimensions are routinely used in psychiatric diagnosis. Multiple dimensions enter in mathematics without any difficulty, and quantum processes are described in Hilbert space, a Euclidean-like space of infinite dimensions.

Obviously, there are many dimensions that we have not defined, but the existence of which is made evident by time series analyses (e.g., correlation dimension, embedding dimension, etc.); instead of considering them as convenient mathematical conventions, we regard them as abstract representations of real dimensions, and more specifically as dimensions of form. Taking dimensionality as complexity, we construe creativity as dimensiogenesis (Sabelli, 2005).

To construct a general logic of quality, we propose as a general principle that for each level of organization, there must be dimensions homologous to unidirectional action, bi-dimensional and bipolar information, a tridimensional space with different quality in each direction (like color), and the more complex forms generated by them. Starting with the concept of action, entities are represented in phase space, and the portrait of opposites requires a plane rather than a one-dimensional scale.

THE PHASE SPACE OF OPPOSITES

The multidimensional space of quantum physics offers a natural realization for a dimensional logic. Let us illustrate the ideas with the much simpler case of the two-dimensional representation of a process. Any process involves the interaction of forces that can be represented by vectors, and that are in part synergistic and in part antagonistic. These forces share dimensions of energy and time, and often many other properties since they participate in the same process. They are additive in some dimensions and subtractive in others. We thus represent the process in terms of opposite forces. Opposites are similar; what distinguishes them is sign (information). Electron and positron annihilate each other but their mass is converted to energy. Each of the two opposite vectors should then be decomposed into two orthogonal components: one corresponding to the properties they share and the other portraying their differences and antagonism. To represent opposition requires at least two orthogonal dimensions. This is the phase plane of opposites, a method that was devised to collect and analyze empirical data (Carlson-Sabelli, Sabelli, Patel, & Holm, 1992; Carlson-Sabelli & Sabelli, 1992; Sabelli, 1995).

Opposites such as supply and demand, cooperation and competition, and attraction and repulsion are plotted using orthogonal axes, thus creating a phase plane where we can plot trajectories in time. The plane allows the representation of linear as well as nonlinear, complementary and partial opposites, and shows similarities and differences between them. The concept also provides an interpretation for phase portraits and return maps, both in terms of opposition and of energy and information. For instance, these two-dimensional plots reveal and measure how opposite motivations and interpersonal feelings coexist and may be positively correlated or uncorrelated, not inversely proportional or mutually exclusive as implicit in the linear scales standard in psychology and sociology. The diamond of opposites allows quantity, change, and the coexistence of opposites to be considered in all classes.

A preliminary understanding of the diamond of opposites is to regard its four quadrants as a 2x2 table (iterated negation). But a 2x2 table classifies entities into four mutually exclusive classes, while the diamond offers a two-dimensional field within which processes flow, often gradually, from one point to another. Moreover, the opposites coexist in all cases, including those in the two quadrants in which one opposite predominates and the neutral cases in which neither appears to dominate over the other.

Figure 6. Phase plane of opposites (right); a bi-dimensional representation of opposites, contrasted with categorical and linear scales (left). The phase plane allows one to represent the trajectory of processes as observed empirically as well as to relate these observations to underlying opposite forces and to physical theory.

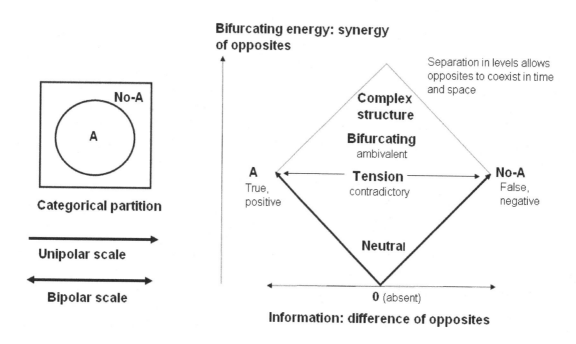

The phase plane allows one to examine how the interaction of opposites produces different outcomes or choices (Carlson-Sabelli et al., 1992). Given simultaneous attraction and repulsion, their difference is the information that determines the choice (selection or rejection), and the sum of the attraction and repulsion gives the energy of the choice. For simple fold catastrophes, the energy (the sum of opposites) is the bifurcating factor while the information (provided by the difference of opposites) is the asymmetric factor. These observations lead us to regard Thom's catastrophes as logical operations.

Catastrophes as mathematical structures represent the simplest of the complex structures generated by interacting opposites. This relation between energy, information, and opposites may also apply to more complex situations, such as the formation of structures in nature.

BIOTIC LOGIC

In brief, a biotic logic involves the following concepts: (a) action as dynamic identity, (b) opposition as a fundamental two-ness that is self-referential (opposites overlap and separate, cooperate and conflict, persist and bifurcate), (c) tridimensional conceptual space, (d) the generation of higher levels of complexity (information) that are homologous (new forms of action, opposition, space, and generation), and (e) mutual feedback between simpler actions that have priority and complex levels that have the supremacy of a higher density of information.

Though we cannot develop here a complete quantum biotic logic, Table 1 sketches some similarities and differences with Boolean and dialectic logics.

The implementation of a complex logic is not a matter of choice. From set theory (Boolean logic) we cannot generate real numbers, from real numbers we cannot generate topological groups, and even more complex mathematics is needed to portray nature.

Lattice theory describes important aspects of logic processes. Implication displays the properties of the partial order relation <. Negation involves not only the symmetry implicit in A = no-no-A, but also an asymmetry: 1f A is true, then no-A implies A. Dialectic negation (sublation) explicitly includes hierarchy. The notion of hierarchical negation may be modeled by lattice-like sets (Sabelli, 1971, 2005).

Helicoids are sets ordered by a relation sublation ↓ that is asymmetric (if A ↓ B then not B ↓ A) and indirectly transitive (if A ↓ B, B ↓ C, and C ↓ D then A ↓ D); A is not sublated by C. There are two classes of elements (Figure 7). From these postulates we can infer A < C. Thus, C is similar (in color) and stronger than A. In his modern

classic *Proofs and Refutations*, Lakatos (Worrall & Zahar, 1976) offers a heuristic in which a counterexample is used to improve the original conjecture, thus unifying proofs and refutations in a single dialectic process of creation. The refutation (falsification) of the refutation of a hypothesis serves as its confirmation as an alternative to the inductive definition of confirmation that leads to Hempel's paradox[ab] (Sabelli, 1989). Helicoids have also been used to model neural pathways through the study of drug antagonisms (Sabelli, 1972).

MULTIPLE TYPES OF QUANTUM GATES

To approach the complexity of nature, computers may need to use multiple types of gates, including complex gates. There will necessarily be Boolean-like gates channeling action as they form lattices ordered in space-time; also, by necessity, every quantum computer must include macroscopic connections.

The notion of iterated negation (Sabelli, 1979, 1984, 1989) expands the use of Boolean logic. Opposition is universal; it repeats in time and space. Thus, opposition does not imply dichotomy. On the contrary, each single bifurcation expands to multiple bifurcations. Cascades of bifurcations

Figure 7. Helicoids

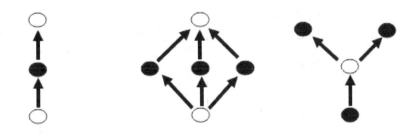

Table 1. Biotic, Boolean, and dialectic logic

	Logic		
	Biotic	**Boolean**	**Dialectic**
Formulation	Physical (classic and quantum) and mathematical (lattice, group, and topology)	Mathematical (set theory)	Verbal
Identity	Physical action, the integral of temporal change in energy	Static A = A valid for mathematical entities	Dynamic, as evident in sociology and psychology
Negation	Multiple forms: Lattice dual, group inverse, topological bifurcations	Set theory complementation	Sublation: To end and simultaneously conserve
Opposites	Similar, synergic, and/or antagonistic, 2^2 bifurcations, elementary biotic opposites	Differences stressed, black or white thinking	Similarities or differences stressed in different contexts
Implication and Exclusion of Opposites	Mutual implication of opposites, exclusion of identical fermions (Pauli)	Mutual implication of complementary sets, mutual exclusion of opposites in logic	Contradiction (Hegel) and conflict (Marx) are universal
Contradiction	Aristotle's local principle of no contradiction (exclusion for same place, time, and context)	Absolute principle of no contradiction	Contradiction must lead to conflict resolved by either synthesis or destruction of one or both
Verbs Modeled	Catastrophes, chaos, bios, and leaps as models for active verbs	To be, to imply	No formal models
Logical Values	Opposite signs and varying quantities: N and – N for bifurcations, and similar to N^2 for decision gates	0 and 1	Not formalized but implicit opposites of varying quantities
Third Value	Triads, quantum chromodynamics, categories, Aristotelian third value open to future, Sarkovskii's theorem	Exclusion	Polarization excludes intermediate classes
Information	Information = opposition as in repetition or difference	Probabilistic information theory uses logical values 0 and 1	Probabilistic information theory, developed along the same lines
Graphic Representation	Phase space of opposites and decision theory	Venn diagram	None
Negation of the Negation	$A_t < A_{t+2}$, A < no-no-A, ubiquitous Period 2 in time, space, context, helicoid model	Identical: A = no-no-A.	Third term (synthesis) similar but superior to thesis, ubiquitous Period 2 in time, space, context

continued on following page

Table 1. continued

	Logic		
	Biotic	**Boolean**	**Dialectic**
Logical Operations	Iterated negation, catastrophes, quantum gates, decision gates	And, or	Dialectic synthesis, no formal model
Quality	Dimensions	Classes	Classes (e.g. socioeconomic)
Quantity and Quality	Quantitative parameters of catastrophes, chaos, bios, and leaps	Regarded as separate categories	Necessary and nonlinear relation between them, dialectic leaps
Simplicity and Complexity	Bipolar and asymmetric feedback (priority of the simple and supremacy of the complex)	Focus on simplicity, complex analyzed into simple components	Focus on single composition, material (Marx) or ideal (Hegel)
Logical Properties Included	Asymmetry and symmetry, noncommutativity, direct and indirect transitivity	Reflexive identity, asymmetric negation, directly transitive implication	Not formalized but implicit asymmetry and direct and indirect transitivity
Heuristic	Homology across levels, refutation of refutation as confirmation	Proof by refutation of the opposite, confirmation by induction	dialectic of proof and refutation (Lakatos)
Computation	Planning quantum computer with biotic logic	Developing quantum computer with Boolean logic	No computer application
Innovation Processes	Causal and creative development by synergy and conflict (bipolar feedback)	Mechanical determinism, innovation only by chance	Innovation by synthesis, frequent use of deterministic models
Human Processes	"Sociatry" (collective psychotherapy), bio-socio-psychological medicine	Unchanging human nature, competition leading to conflict (Malthus, standard economics, social Darwinism, racism)	Conflictual models (Darwinian evolution, Marxian class war, Freudian Oedipus conflict)

(Feigenbaum, 1983) generate 2^N complexity in mathematical recursions. In biology, cell division and differentiation represents the most elementary step in growth, development, and evolution. In physics, cosmological evolution consists of a sequence of symmetry breakings. In mathematics, a fork bifurcation splits one process into complementary opposites. In a process, there are 2^N, not just two, opposites. The first bifurcation gives you two opposites, 1 and 0 or 1 and -1, which is negation in logic. Iterating negation in two-valued logic generates 2^N values; the bifurcation of a bifurcation thus allows one to accommodate dialectic contradiction within the context of mathematical logic.

We start by constructing a 2x2 table in which one side of the table is one action (present or absent) and the other is its opposite (present or absent). In other words, we generate a four-valued logic by iterating the standard two-valued negation. Iterated negation thus generates four values: A, its opposite A^{-1}, both, and neither. While in two-valued logic A = 1 implies no-A = 0 and conversely A = 0 implies no-A = 1, we admit the relative independence of opposites, so in a given situation both may exist A = 1 and no-A = 1 (contradiction, ambivalence, or complexity) or neither may be present (neither A nor no-A). Iterated negation represents the second step in a cascade of bifurcations. Just as the combination of two entities provides 16 logical functions in Boolean logic, the iteration of negation generates 16 combinations of opposites.

Some forms of opposition, including negation, may be modeled by catastrophes. Thom's catastrophes provide a good starting point to go beyond the standard *and* and *or* gates. First, according to Thom's theorem, we need to consider only a few control forms.[ac] The limited number of archetypal morphologies that Thom identified is assumed to be universal. Certainly, forms are created and constrained by physical factors that also extend across the chemical, biological, social, and psychological domains. We may apply this concept to logical statements. Second, it is a good starting point because catastrophe forms appear in the study of choice (Carlson-Sabelli et al., 1992). Third, Thom (1983) and others have already explored how catastrophes can be used to model active verbs representing actions, as contrasted to Boolean logic that only models the inactive copula *to be*. Thom gives a constructive and a destructive interpretation to each catastrophe. For instance, the fold represents to begin and to end, the cusp represents to engender or unite and to capture

and to break, and the butterfly represents to give and to receive, as well as to exfoliate.

In our view, a fold catastrophe abstracts the *or* exclusive (A or B but not both) while A and no-A may be modeled by bifurcation. Butterfly catastrophes generate three possible outcomes and may thus relate to creative processes. Catastrophes may serve to implement some forms of dialectic reasoning: Given A, find no-A by increasing or decreasing a catastrophe parameter.

According to Thom (1980), the universe can be understood in terms of structures that are momentarily stable and that are not of an infinite variety, but are drastically constrained by factors of space and time. However, processes that generate catastrophes do so only within limits, beyond which they generate more complex patterns (Sabelli, 2005). Biotic processes (quantum, biological, economic, etc.) involve continual change. They do not jump from one attractor to another, but they evolve within and between complexes (which some interpret as attractors). We thus need to go beyond catastrophes to model higher order logical operations. Trigonometric functions modeling bipolar opposition generate bifurcation trees, chaos, and bios. Quantum physical processes may also generate bios as illustrated by the Schrödinger equation. Quantum gates (Nielsen & Chuang, 2000) offer even richer models for opposition. While in standard logic opposition leads to one operation—negation, mechanized by the *not* gate in standard computers—quantum computation already involves several types of one-qubit gates, providing for modeling implication of opposites.

Quantum computing may also allow us to implement more complex forms of processing. In this manner we can examine the following.

- Codetermination: How A and no-A coexist and determine each other through processes of mutual feedback
- Cocreation paradigm: How A and no-A cocreate, for example, by their synthesis

- Conegation: Negate both terms of a dichotomy to create a new third possibility as the negation of both opposites, a practical notion when confronted with an undesirable alternative

DECISION THEORY

We may use physical dynamics as a basis for a theory of decision making (Thomas, 2006) that allows one to develop different types of complex gates; complex gates are advantageous in the processing of complex problems and may become the core of a computational machine. Let us introduce the idea with a relatively simple bi-triadic gate. Consider two armies: the Red and the Green. Both armies have a symmetric set of choices: Fight from the high ground, fight from the low ground, or fight as archers. The one that chooses high ground defeats the one that chooses low ground, but will be vulnerable to attack by archers some of the time. The one that picks low ground defeats the archers by hand-to-hand combat, but will be defeated if the enemy chooses high ground. The one that chooses archers will defeat the enemy on high ground some of the time, but will be defeated some of the time by the enemy on low ground. The following matrix portrays the output reflecting these choices at each play.

These outputs are logical values or, from the perspective of game theory, utilities. No pure strategy is optimal; for instance, if Green chooses high ground every time, Red is capable of choosing archers every time. There is a clear advantage in not letting the other side know what choice you are going to make. A mixed set of strategies, chosen so as to not let the other know which choice will actually be made yet made in certain proportions, is optimal (i.e., gives the best outcome for each player independent of what the other player chooses), and is of course the same for each player: $\frac{2}{7}$ high, $\frac{1}{7}$ low, and $\frac{4}{7}$ archers. The decision a player makes is not random, though random elements may exist to hide the choice from the other player. The decision is based on imperfect information; it is based on not knowing what decision the other player will make. Moreover, decision making is a repetitive activity, and the decision made at each time depends on what has happened in the past. Thus, over time a player can determine even the mix of strategies of their opponent and adjust their own mix accordingly; the optimal strategy is one that reflects a steady state and is a particular view of reality, a reality that leads to no dynamic changes. We know that there are dynamic changes, and these are not accounted for in the standard game theory. In decision theory, the output of the gate influences its input for the next step, as well as the parameters of the gate that determine the decision. This includes the standard game theory as a special case, but allows for dynamic changes.

Decision theory allows history to be represented. This is bipolar feedback, the same as those that generate biotic processes. Decision

Table 2. Example of output matrix in a decision gate

Output matrix for bi-triadic gate (two three-valued inputs, seven distinct outputs)		Red		
		High	Low	Archers
Green	High	0	100	-25
	Low	-100	0	50
	Archer	25	-50	0

theory achieves this feedback by considering the physical process involved. The standard approach invokes an optimal strategy to mean that there is presumed and idealized feedback from the output to the next input such that only a steady state occurs; the gate is at equilibrium. This means the decision values of the gate and the mixed strategies are all constant. Decision theory allows both to change in time. It in fact meets the criteria described earlier for a biotic logic, and provides an existence proof that such logic can be constructed at other levels of complexity from the physical or chemical world. On the flip side, biotic logic provides a philosophical foundation for theories such as decision theory, a reason why such theories should and must be considered as relevant for processes at their level.

Consistent with the notion that processes are homologous at different levels of organization, decision theory is based on action, charge, and space. The conceptual space is formed from time T and the input strategies S that indirectly reflect that all decisions occur in the physical time and space. Over time, the state of a gate moves in this conceptual space. The conceptual space is a gauge symmetric differential geometry homologous to physical space-time (i.e., Minkowski space-time) where distances between points in space-time are specified by a metric g_{ab}. In Minkowski spaces, there is a limiting velocity for message transfer that relates units of time to units of input. This along with the fundamental unit of action specifies two of the three units in the theory.

Charge is an attribute of the state of the gate. Related to charge, we expect electric and magnetic fields to be generated from the motion of charge, and from Einstein we expect such fields to combine to form an antisymmetric matrix. Note that the output matrix of the bi-triadic gate we are using as an example is antisymmetric (intuitively, look at the distribution of numbers relative to the diagonal, and you see that they change signs). For any decision gate, we can always form an appropriate antisymmetric output.

We associate this field with the motion of the charge. In the theory of differential geometry of gauge theories, such fields are associated with messenger fields (in physical theory, the photon) that carry the group structure information. In decision theory, the output matrix is associated with this messenger field, and the interaction of the charge of the gate with this messenger field determines the motion of the gate. This proves the coexistence of opposites in decision theory, and it is due to the charge of the gate.

Generalizing to all types of gates (involving two players), we write the output matrix as

$$F_{ab} = \begin{pmatrix} & n & m & \text{time} = "0" \\ \hline n & 0 & -G^T & m_0^{-1}G^T X \\ m & G & 0 & -m_0^{-1}GY \\ "0" & -m_0^{-1}X^T G & m_0^{-1}Y^T G^T & 0 \end{pmatrix},$$

where F_{ab} is the output matrix of the gate G for an $m \times n$ gate. The X and the Y represent the equilibrium mixed strategy inputs for the two players. The subscripts represent any of the dimensions in the conceptual space of inputs and time. Similar structures hold when there are more than two players. In Minkowski space, the messenger field defined by the output matrix determines the motion of the gate and the motion of the gate generates the field. An electric current (moving charges) generates a magnetic field. There is feedback from the motion to the field. Thus, the output matrix values are not static entities of game theory, but dynamic entities that adjust. It makes sense that such adjustments take place because, over time with feedback, there is some information that becomes available to the decision gate based on history. The gate is in fact a learning gate.

Actualization

Action, not static states, determines the logic. Figure 8 illustrates the biotic nature of actions in a decision gate. To actualize a functioning

Figure 8. Recurrence plot of the biotic pattern generated by a decision gate (see Thomas, 2006, p. 124). At Dimension 10, N = 2000. The demonstration that decision gates can generate biotic patterns indicates that a biotic logic is possible.

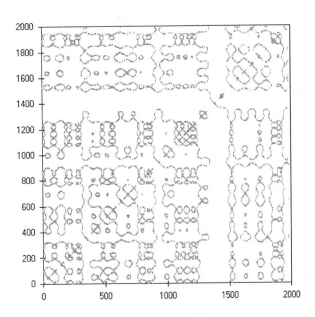

computer, one needs equations that allow for measurement. The next paragraphs sketch the nature of the equations (see Thomas, 2006, for the mathematical details).

The starting point is that the behavior of decision gates is determined by an action principle applied to a gauge theory in a Minkowski-conceptual space-time. The mathematics for this conceptual space is homologous to the theory of relativity by Einstein. The significant point is that the equations provide all the quantitative behaviors of this biotic logic. When the action is large compared to the quantum of action, the motion follows the path of least action. This results in equations of motion that generalize that the Newtonian force equals mass times acceleration: The equations consist of two parts—a part that depends only on the metric and a part that depends on the sources[ad] and the metric.

The source part is determined by the energy-momentum tensor T_{ab}, which is the relativistic generalization of the notions of energy and momentum stresses for an elastic medium. In an elastic medium, energy and momentum do not instantly appear or disappear, but flow in a continuous fashion from one region of the media to another. We say that the flow of energy and momentum density is conserved.

The second part of the equation is determined by the curvature tensor and the metric $R_{ab} - \frac{1}{2}Rg_{ab}$, where the curvature components R_{ab} and R determine the curvature properties of the conceptual space and are known functions of the metric and its derivatives up to the second order with respect to space and time. The principle of least action equates these two parts into the famous and well-publicized equation of Einstein:

$$R_{ab} - \tfrac{1}{2} R g_{ab} = -k\, T_{ab}\,.$$

These equations are significant because they determine all the quantitative behavior of the decision gates: Starting with known values of the output matrix and metric, and known positions of the gates, all values at subsequent points in time are determined. In this theory there are only three dimensional qualities: time, the common dimension of each direction in the conceptual space, and the dimension of mass that characterizes the inertia.

The theory provides a number of interesting feedbacks. First, the messenger fields (that include all the gauge fields including gravity and the output matrix fields) are determined by the motion of the sources, which have charge and mass (inertia). A subset of these relations is homologous to Maxwell's equations, which united a number of natural laws: Coulomb's law governing the static attraction or repulsion of charges, Faraday's law that changing magnetic fields generate electric currents and fields, and Ampère's law that moving charges generate a magnetic field. The theory goes much further, however, by providing feedback of the source fields on the metric field: The metric field is determined by the motion of the sources. The metric and output matrix fields play a similar role as both exist because of gauge symmetry.

There is inverse feedback as well. The metric and output matrix fields determine the motion of the sources. The motion is determined by the forces, including forces associated with the magnetic and electric components of the output matrix, as well as new forces associated with the metric. Einstein identified these metric forces with the Newtonian gravitational field, though with a profound difference. The multiple components of the metric field propagate with a finite velocity (the velocity of light), whereas Newtonian gravity has a single component that propagates instantly from one point of space to the next. Decision theory is characterized by a metric with a homologous

property. Since it is generated by sources, by all forms of energy, it will be an attribute that one particularly associates with mass. It is matter that determines the qualities of this force and determines the metric, and it is the metric that determines the motion of the gate in the force.

Decision theory has a concept of matter that is homologous to ordinary matter: It is a continuous medium characterized by an energy density, a pressure, charges (associated with each player), and a flow. A detailed analysis of these forces allows a decomposition of the forces acting on a fluid that is homologous to those of Euler and Bernoulli. There will be a contribution due to the charge of the gate and the flow of charged matter, a contribution due to the mass of the gate in the metric field (gravitational), and a contribution that is determined by the pressure gradient of the fluid. These three types of forces have different characteristics. The magnetic force generates circular motion proportional to the matter's charge. The electric force generates attraction or repulsion depending on opposite or like charges, whereas the gravitational force generates attraction toward other matter or energy. The pressure gradient generates repulsion away from areas of high pressure: The change in pressure over distance produces a force well known in weather as wind moves from high pressure to low pressure, accounting for lift in airplanes and the ability to sail close to the wind in sailboats. We expect there to be a rich variety of phenomena based on these forces that have conflicting properties, of which Figure 7 is a simple example. Steady-state phenomena will be the exceptions.

In decision theory, the phase planes of opposites are equivalent to the phase plane of the conjugate variables of directions in the space and their conjugate momenta. Phase plane plots are standard in physics, chemistry, and thermodynamics and have vast usefulness. They support the claim of the general ideas of biotic logic.

We connect with the ideas of game theory in the rather special case that decisions are static. In this case, there is no acceleration, so that flows are constant. We ignore the effects of gravitation and of pressure change so that the only forces are those of the messenger field and the output matrix. In this case, the force is zero for strategies that are at equilibrium.

The output of decision gates in time displays a pattern that carries information, lowest for steady state and increasing for more complex patterns: periodic, chaotic (local sensitivity to initial conditions results in unpredictable terms but predictable range), and biotic (global sensitivity to initial conditions results in unpredictable terms and range).

ENGINEERING

Quantum computation faces enormous technical difficulties, starting with working at single-atom and single-photon scales, and then putting quantum gates together into circuits and preventing incoherence. All over the world, many scientists are developing many different physical implementations for quantum computers, including photons (Zeilinger, Weihs, Jennewein, & Aspelmeyer, 2005). Quantum dots allow one to employ single electrons. Recent experiments show that it is feasible to operate single-electron spins in quantum dots as quantum bits (Koppens et al., 2006).

The engineering of quantum computers depends on how quantum physics is conceived and developed. Probabilistic models of quantum processes are taught as fact, but the fundamental equations of quantum physics are entirely deterministic; this is compatible with a causal interpretation of physics à la Einstein and Schrödinger rather than with stochasticity.[ae] An important implication is that quantum processes are always in specific states. Being actions, quantum entities are in continual, spontaneous change until an interaction (such as a measurement) determines, that is, fixes, one parameter. Many physicists question whether or not a quantum entity is in a particular state if nobody observes it (Wheeler, 1957). A qubit is said by some to exist in more than one state until measuring causes that superposition to collapse into one state or the other. Also, Schrödinger's cat is said to exist in more than one state until we open the cage. With apologies to many authors who misquote Schrödinger, we must let the cat out of the bag: He intended, and in our opinion succeeded, to refute the notion that the state of a physical system is undefined until observed by the fact that the cat is alive or dead regardless of our knowing it. Claiming that quantum particles are in no particular state unless observed pushes us into metaphysical idealism akin to that of Bishop Berkeley, who doubted whether or not a falling tree makes a sound when nobody hears it.

Another practically important issue is energy consumption. Quantum processes do not generate heat and entropy; electrons moving in atomic orbitals do not heat up and radiate. Could then reversible gates work like Maxwell's demons, generating information without increasing entropy? Even if this could be possible, computation involves macroscopic processes such as measurement. Although information can be expressed in different ways (e.g., as voice, written words, or action potentials in brain neurons) without changing it, they all involve macroscopic processes in irreversible time that increase entropy. Macroscopic physical processes are not reversible. Computers cannot work like Maxwell's demons. Feynman (Hey & Allen, 1996) has calculated the minimum energy required for computation.

In order to minimize energy consumption, one needs to perform computations using quantum processes and reduce as much as possible the number of macroscopic interactions such as measurement and communication with the human operator. In physical processes, there is immense information involved in quantum superposition that is not communicated; communication reduces it to two complementary opposites. This is relevant to quantum computation: We can process much at the quantum level without producing heat (entropy) until we measure it. At the psycho-biological level, there is an immense amount of information at the biological level that remains largely unconscious, and only the small tip of the iceberg becomes conscious. The existence of two levels of information in both natural and mental processes indicates an interesting parallel between them. The existence of two levels of information seems a very general phenomenon. For instance, the chemical properties of an atom are given by the valence electrons, not by the core electrons and the nucleus.

A current focus in quantum computing is the design of logically reversible gates that could minimize energy cost (Landauer's principle). Note, however, that irreversibility emerges from creation, not only from destruction. We cannot "postdict" the past, and we cannot predict the future. A dynamic logic by necessity must include logically irreversible gates. Irreversibility is a sine qua non of creativity, and also appears in simpler processes. Although equilibrium is often highlighted as emblematic of reversibility, equilibration is an irreversible process as once trajectories reach the attractor, we cannot know their point of origin. The Schrödinger equation generates bios, and biotic processes are not mathematically reversible (Sabelli, 2005).

CONCLUSION: BIOTIC LOGIC IN CLASSIC AND QUANTUM COMPUTATION

The real power of quantum computation has been the development of new algorithms that allow the exploitation of quantum superposition. As a result, we can now solve problems such as factorization, and come up with new methods to deal with encryption. We propose here to make further use of quantum superposition to develop a logic that is dialectic rather than classificatory. Philosophical dialectics provides a threat of Ariadne that guides us beyond static views. Quantum

processes provide in principle a way to move from a static to a dynamic biotic logic that incorporates mathematical structures, physical principles, and psychological insights far beyond philosophy. Biotic logic (Sabelli, 1984, 1995, 2005) has been substantially expanded here.

In summary, we outline a new approach that adapts the logic of the computer to the logic of nature as embodied by both quantum computing devices and by natural and human processes. Regarding quantum physics as the fundamental logic of nature demands us to consider its theory as logical principles. To find a logical interpretation to quantum principles may thus not be regarded as a proposal, or a matter of choice, but is a task to be accomplished. While we are far from attaining it, such a goal can be reached. The continuity of evolution requires that the same fundamental forms must be expressed at all levels of organization, so the principles of quantum physics and the principles of rational thinking must be homologous.

Logic (mathematical, computational, and philosophical) develops in a tension between the logic of nature—quantum and classic physics—and the logic of human behavior—socioeconomics and psychology. Note that both the physical and the human logic each involves at least two levels. Thus, even from the perspective of physics, computation involves quantum processes that have priority and macroscopic interactions that have supremacy. Material realities, physical and economic, have priority, while ideological and psychological interpretations have supremacy. Thus, electrons are in particular states, albeit continuously changing, regardless of whether we observe them or not, and quantum computers are designed according to ideological presuppositions, not simply as determined by quantum physics. Strict adherence to the different meanings of terms in common language and in the various disciplines is required for interdisciplinary communication and for clear thinking. Attending to both physical and human processes, both of which are at least biotic and often much more complex,

Figure 9. Two types of logic and two types of computer

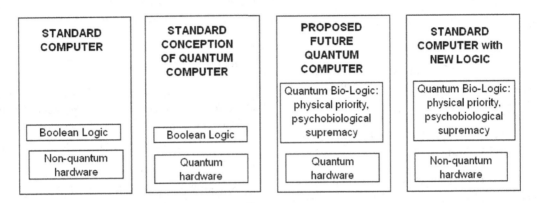

we propose a quantum bio-logic. Our attempts in this direction include Sabelli's biotic logic that stresses the priority of physics and the supremacy of ideological and psychological factors, Thomas' physical models of economic decision making, and Kauffman's bio-logic.

A biotic quantum logic may help construct functioning quantum computers, but even before the enormous engineering problems involved in this enterprise are solved, it can guide the logic of current computers (Figure 9). Conversely, models for biotic logic in digital computers may help one to develop quantum computation.

ACKNOWLEDGMENT

We are thankful to the Society for the Advancement for Clinical Philosophy (SACP) for its support, and to Mrs. Maria McCormick for her gifts to SACP. This chapter benefited from discussion with our colleagues at the Chicago Center for Creative Development: Louis Kauffman, Craig Brozefsky, Warren Grimsley, Lisa Maroski, Lazar Kovacevic, Valerie Busch-Zurlent, Keelan Kane, and Linnea Carlson-Sabelli.

REFERENCES

Bateson, G. (1979). *Mind and nature: A necessary unity.* Toronto, Canada: Bantam.

Bourbaki, N. (1962). L'architecture des mathématiques. In F. Le Lionnais (Ed.), *Les grands courants de la pensée mathématique.* Blanchard. (Reprinted from *Cahiers du Sud,* 1948)

Capra, F. (1975). *The Tao of physics.* Boulder, CO: Shambala.

Carlson-Sabelli, L., Sabelli, H., Patel, M., & Holm, K. (1992). The union of opposites in sociometry: An empirical application of process theory. *The Journal of Group Psychotherapy, Psychodrama and Sociometry, 44,* 147-171.

Carlson-Sabelli, L., & Sabelli, H. C. (1992). Phase plane of opposites: A method to study change in complex processes, and its application to sociodynamics and psychotherapy. *The Social Dynamicist, 3,* 1-6.

Carlson-Sabelli, L., Sabelli, H. C., Zbilut, J., Patel, M., Messer, J., Walthall, K., et al. (1994). How the heart informs about the brain: A process analysis of the electrocardiogram. *Cybernetics and Systems, 94*(2), 1031-1038.

Chomsky, N. (1975). *Reflections on language.* New York: Pantheon Books.

Feynman, R. P. (1974). Statistical mechanics: A set of lectures. *American Journal of Physics.*

Feynman, R. P., Leighton, R. B., & Sands, M. (1963). *The Feynman lectures on physics, v1-3.* Reading, MA: Addison-Wesley.

Gauthier, Y. (1984). Hegel's logic from a logical point of view. In R. S. Cohen & M. W. Wartofsky (Eds.), *Hegel and the sciences* (pp. 303-310). New York: D. Reidel Publishing Co.

Hey, A. J. G., & Allen, R. W. (Eds.). (1996). *Feynman lectures on computation.* Reading, MA: Addison-Wesley Publishing Company.

Joja, A. (1969). *La lógica dialéctica y las ciencias* [M. Serrano Pérez, Trans.]. Buenos Aires, Argentina: Juárez.

Kauffman, L., & Sabelli, H. (1998). The process equation. *Cybernetics and Systems, 29*, 345-362.

Kauffman, L. H. (2002). Biologic II. In N. Tongring & R. C. Penner (Eds.), *Woods hole mathematics: World Scientific series on knots and everything 34* (pp. 94-132). Singapore: World Scientific.

Kauffman, L. H. (2004). Biologic. *AMS Contemporary Mathematics Series, 304*, 313 - 340.

Koppens, F. H. L., Buizert, C., Tielrooij, K. J., Vink, L. T., Nowack, K. C., Meunier, T., et al. (2006). Driven coherent oscillations of a single electron spin in a quantum dot. *Nature, 442*, 766-771.

Kosok, M. (1984). The dynamics of Hegelian dialectics, and nonlinearity in the sciences. In R. S. Cohen & M. W. Wartofsky (Eds.), *Hegel and the Sciences* (pp. 311-348). New York: D. Reidel Publishing Co.

Landauer, R. (1961). Irreversibility and heat generation in the computing process. *IBM Journal of Research and Development*, 183-191.

Lefebvre, H. (1947). *Logique formelle, logique dialectique.* Paris: Editions Sociales.

Levy, A., Alden, D., & Levy, C. (2006, August). *Biotic patterns in music.* Paper presented at the Society for Chaos Theory in Psychology & Life Sciences 16th Annual International Conference, Baltimore.

Levy-Carciente, S., Sabelli, H., & Jaffe, K. (2004). Complex patterns in the oil market. *Interciencia, 29*, 320-323.

Nielsen, M. A., & Chuang, I. L. (2000). *Quantum computation and quantum information.* Cambridge, United Kingdom: Cambridge University Press.

Ogden, C. K. (1967). *Opposition.* London: Indiana State University. (Original work published 1932)

Patel, M., & Sabelli, H. (2003). Autocorrelation and frequency analysis differentiate cardiac and economic bios from 1/F noise. *Kybernetes, 32*, 692-702.

Peitgen, H., Jürgens, H., & Saupe, D. (1992). *Chaos and fractals.* New York: Springer.

Piaget, J. (1950). *Introduction à l'épistémologie génétique* (3 Vols.). Paris: Presses Universitaires de France.

Planty-Bonjour, G. (1965). *Le catégories du matérialisme dialectique.* Paris: Presses Universitaires de France.

Robertson, R. (1995). *Jungian archetypes.* York Beach, ME: Nicholas-Hay.

Sabelli, H. (1971). An attempt to formalize some aspects of dialectic logic. In W. R. Beyer (Ed.), *Hegel-Jahrbuch 1970* (pp. 211-213). Meisenheim am Glan, Germany: Verlag Anton Hain.

Sabelli, H. (1989). *Union of opposites: A comprehensive theory of natural and human processes.* Lawrenceville, VA: Brunswick.

Sabelli, H. (1995). Non-linear dynamics as a dialectic logic. *Proceedings of International Systems Society* (pp. 101-112).

Sabelli, H. (1998). The union of opposites: From Taoism to process theory. *Systems Research, 15,* 429-441.

Sabelli, H. (2001). The co-creation hypothesis. In G. Ragsdell & J. Wilby (Eds.), *Understanding complexity.* London: Kluwer Academics/Plenum Publishers.

Sabelli, H. (2005). *Bios: A study of creation.* Singapore: World Scientific.

Sabelli, H., & Carlson-Sabelli, L. (1989). Biological priority and psychological supremacy: A new integrative paradigm derived from process theory. *American Journal of Psychiatry, 146,* 1541-1551.

Sabelli, H., & Carlson-Sabelli, L. (1996). As simple as one, two, three. Arithmetic: A simple, powerful, natural and dynamic logic. *Proceedings of International Systems Society* (pp. 543-554).

Sabelli, H., & Carlson-Sabelli, L. (2005). Bios: A process approach to living system theory. In honor to James and Jessie Miller. *Systems Research and Behavioral Science, 23,* 323-336.

Sabelli, H., Carlson-Sabelli, L., Patel, M., Zbilut, J., Messer, J., & Walthall, K. (1995). Psychocardiological portraits: A clinical application of process theory. In F. D. Abraham & A. R. Gilgen (Eds.), *Chaos theory in psychology* (pp. 107-125). Westport, CT: Greenwood Publishing.

Sabelli, H., & Kovacevic, L. (2006a). Biotic population dynamics and the theory of evolution. *International Journal* 2006. Retrieved from http://www.interjournal.org/manuscript_abstract. php?82762892

Sabelli, H., & Kovacevic, L. (2006b). Quantum bios and biotic complexity in the distribution of galaxies. *Complexity, 11,* 14-25.

Sabelli, H. C. (1972). A pharmacological approach for modeling neuronal nets. In H. Drischeland & P. Dattmar (Eds.), *Biocybernetics* (Vol. 4, pp. 1-9). Jena, Germany: Veb Gustav Fischer Verlag.

Sabelli, H. C. (1984). Mathematical dialectics, scientific logic and the psychoanalysis of thinking. In R. S. Cohen & M. W. Wartofsky (Eds.), *Hegel and the sciences* (pp. 349-359). New York: D. Reidel Publishing Co.

Saunders, P. T. (1980). *An introduction to catastrophe theory.* Cambridge, United Kingdom: Cambridge University Press.

Shannon, C. E. (1938). A symbolic analysis of relay and switching circuits. *Trans. Am. Inst. Elec. Eng., 57,* 713-723.

Shannon, C. E. (1948). *A mathematical theory of communication. Bell System Technical Journal, 27,* 379-423, 623-656.

Spencer-Brown, G. (1979). *Laws of form.* New York: E. P. Dutton. (Original work published 1969)

Sugerman, A., & Sabelli, H. (2003). Novelty, diversification and nonrandom complexity define creative processes. *Kybernetes, 32,* 829-836.

Thom, R. (1983). *Mathematical models of morphogenesis.* Chichester, United Kingdom: Ellis Horwood.

Thomas, G. H. (2006). *Geometry, language and strategy.* Singapore: World Scientific.

Thomas, G. H., Sabelli, H., Kauffman, L. H., & Kovacevic, L. (2006). Biotic patterns in Schrödinger's equation and the evolution of the universe. *International Journal.* Retrieved from http://www.interjournal.org/manuscript_abstract. php?1161328888

Vandervert, L. R. (1988). Systems thinking and a proposal for a neurological positivism. *Systems Research, 5,* 313-321.

Wheeler, J. A. (1957). Assessment of Everett's "relative state" formulation of quantum theory. *Reviews of Modern Physics.*

Worrall, J., & Zahar, E. (Eds.). (1976). *Proofs and refutations.* Cambridge, United Kingdom: Cambridge University Press.

Xu, L. D., & Li, L. X. (1989). Complementary opposition as a systems concept. *Systems Research, 6,* 91-101.

Zeilinger, A., Weihs, G., Jennewein, T., & Aspelmeyer, M. (2005). Happy centenary, photon. *Nature, 433,* 230-238.

ENDNOTES

[a]   Much older calculation devices include the abacus for arithmetic, and the octant and the sextant for navigation.

[b]   Moreover, representing negation by set theory complementation generates meaningless aggregates unless the complement is defined within a narrow universe of discourse (e.g., nonred includes hippopotamus, hippocampus, triangles, and blue objects). A negation must always be a concrete negation (Hegel) that includes the other (e.g., the negation of man is woman; the negation of going to the movies implies a possibility of going).

[c]   The concept of action transforms process philosophy into physics-based science.

[d]   Energy is conserved in all physical processes, and is in fact more basic than thermodynamics.

[e]   In this chapter, we challenge the usual statistical interpretation of quantum mechanics that takes quantum probability theory as a genuine doctrine of chances.

[f]   Time is irreversible not only from the perspective of biology, but also in physics. Charge, parity, and time together are conserved (CPT invariance), but the observed violation of CP invariance implies that time is not reversible, although time reversibility is claimed as fact in many descriptions of classic, relativistic, and quantum mechanics, and in theoretical discussions of quantum computation.

[g]   The partial rather than total order of lattices corresponds to the limitations in the definition of simultaneity implicit in relativity theory.

[h]   Actually, action must be at a minimum, a maximum, or a saddle point for small perturbations about the true evolution. The derivative of the function equals zero; this is described as extreme or stationary, although in other contexts stationary means that the mean, variance, and autocorrelation do not change over time.

[i]   Hamilton's view provides useful insight into the relationship between classical and quantum physical processes. Hamilton's view identifies the variables that are conjugate, and in fact demonstrated that they fundamentally do not commute. His view of action also provides a connection to the view that classical physics provides a geometric optics approximation to the real world of quantum phenomena. In general, the kinetic energy is a quadratic function of the velocities: $T = \sum m_{jk}(q_j)\dot{q}_j\dot{q}_k$. The system will be composed of many components, each with its own position in space, so the totality of unconstrained coordinates will be large. The coefficients may depend on these coordinates. The generalized space determined by the unconstrained coordinates can be given a metric suggested by this form of the kinetic energy: $ds = \sum m_{jk}(q_j)dq_jdq_k$. Hamilton studied the behavior of physical systems by studying their motion in this space, and

wrote his principle of least action using this measure for distance: $\Delta \int \sqrt{T} \, ds = 0$. The principle of least action is homologous to the principle applied to light traveling through a material with an index of refraction $\sqrt{T}$. Though light is a wave, when the wave length of light is sufficiently small compared to the size of the optical medium in which it travels, light takes the path of least time subject to the proviso that its speed in a medium is determined by the index of refraction. The modern formulation (Feynman's quantum electrodynamics) of the behavior of light is in terms of the Lagrangian (as opposed to the Hamiltonian). It incorporates the view that light consists of quanta, and that the behavior of physical processes is described by the integration of the complex number $e^{iS/\hbar}$ over all possible paths, where the rate of change of the phase S with time is the Lagrangian function $dS/dt = L$. The phase is Lagrange's action. In this view, the principle of least action arises when the actions are sufficiently larger than the unit of action, Planck's constant $\hbar$. This is the limit of geometrical optics, which we now apply to all phenomena, not just light.

[j] Newton's use of the term action, currently dismissed as obsolete, calls attention to the inseparability of action and counteraction at the simplest level.

[k] Gauge symmetry is a symmetry transformation that can be performed not only globally but also locally—a transformation in a particular region of space-time does not affect what happens in another region. This requirement is a generalized version of the equivalence principle of general relativity. A gauge process involves a messenger (no instantaneous action at a distance), such as the photon for electromagnetic interactions that is sensitive to the force it carries. Gauge theories provide a unified framework (the standard model) to describe electro-magnetism, the weak force, and the strong force with the gauge group U(1) × SU(2) × SU(3).

[l] Thus, quaternity is noted regarding the two conjugated oppositions in action, in the fundamental structure of the qubit, in the four vales generated by the bifurcation of a bifurcation that allows for iterated negation and the incorporation of dialectic contradiction in Boolean logic, and in the need for four or more factors for the generation of biotic expansion, diversification, and novelty (Sabelli & Carlson-Sabelli, 2005). Psychologically, quaternity corresponds to concepts of justice (Jung; see Robertson, 1995).

[m] Electric charge has a fundamental oneness (one in the complex plane is the phase, hence it is a one that is topologically the circle, not the line). The two-ness of the weak force is a sphere in a two-dimensional complex plane, hence it is really more complicated and shares the same structure as rotations in three dimensions. Going along in the same fashion, the three-ness of quarks is really an eightfold way because the three are in a space with three complex dimensions, and a sphere in that space is eight dimensional.

[n] "Opposition is not to be defined as maximum degree of difference, but as a very special kind of repetition, namely of two similar things that are mutually destructive in virtue if their similarity. They are always a couple or duality, opposed as tendencies or forces, not as beings nor yet as states." (Ogden, 1932/1967)

[o] A dialectic antithesis is not inevitably necessary and fundamental: For instance, a cognitive-emotional dissonance (e.g., being Christian and homosexual) may be the pair of thesis and antithesis that moves the psychological process of a person, but it is not a fundamental, generic opposition because

its terms are not necessarily coexisting and inseparable.

p From the German *aufheben*, literally *out* or *up*, or *lifting*

q As a measurement it is nothing more than an interaction, a similar determination of a single state rather than a continuum of incessantly changing states, that must occur whenever processes interact; this may be the basis for the transition from the quantum superposition of opposites to the macroscopic exclusion of opposites (local no contradiction). In a similar manner, particle properties may emerge from waves when they interact with other entities.

r Orthogonal does not mean independent. Conjugates are orthogonal and inseparable. Space dimensions are orthogonal and inseparable. Opposites are paired (inseparable) in phase space just as material dimensions are triadic (inseparable) in physical space. In both cases they are orthogonal. Our use of the term orthogonal departs from current usage in statistics and in the social sciences, where variables that affect a particular result are said to be orthogonal if they are independent, and independence is understood to mean that by varying each separately, one can predict the combined effect of varying them jointly because there are no synergistic or antagonistic effects.

s The term conjugate means *joined together*, especially coupled in a pair. Thus, conjugate means time and energy, or position and momentum in quantum physics, an acid and a base differing in one proton in chemistry, words derived from a common source in linguistics, and inversely or oppositely related with respect to one of a group of otherwise identical properties in mathematics, for instance, the complex conjugate of a complex number $z = a + ib$ is $z^* = a - ib$.

t Complementarity has been discussed in the context of Greek physiology, Chinese Taoism, medieval scholasticism, German dialectics, the Copenhagen interpretation of quantum mechanics, and systems theory, among others. Linear opposites vary inversely: as one waxes, the other wanes; complementary angles vary in such a way. This is not the way in which complementarity is understood in quantum mechanics or in philosophy, where it refers to the coexistence of opposites.

u Unipolar opposites (like 0 and 1) are regarded by some authors as paradigmatic of complementary opposites, showing that the concept of complementarity is only vaguely defined.

v The fact that at the present state of our knowledge we need to describe entities as having both particle-like and wave-like properties (de Broglie's duality) does not mean that we must give up rationality. Perhaps quantum entities are neither waves nor particles. Some physicists model quantum entities as particles. Schrödinger proposed a precise mathematical description of quantum processes as waves. Feynman described such action wave as the adding together of the actions of all the histories that include a given event, and that together correspond to the least action of macroscopic physics. While these models are often interpreted in terms of probability, one may also regard them as portraits of the real form of the quantum entities. In this interpretation, an observation is an interaction. A quantum process appears as a particle in exactly one place when the wave interacts with another wave or with a structure, but a photon interferes with itself because it is a wave made up of multiple smaller particles each of which follows one of Feynman's paths that together constitute the action wave. This is of course a very simplistic version of elaborate theories being developed by string theorists.

w Bifurcation cascades generate increasingly diverse periodic series, then chaos and bios.

Chaotic series show local sensitivity to initial conditions (change in trajectory) and diversification (increase in variance with embedding) only at low embedding dimensions. Biotic series show global sensitivity to initial conditions (change in the range of trajectories) and diversification (increase in variance with embedding) at low and high embedding dimensions.

x   A dimension (Latin, *measured out*) is a parameter required to describe the relevant characteristics of an object or process as its position within a physical or conceptual space—where the dimensions of a space are the total number of different parameters used for all possible entities and objects that must be considered. A Cartesian coordinate system is used to uniquely determine each point in the plane through two numbers, in space using three coordinates, and in higher dimensions with as many parameters as necessary. In this manner, we can plot changes in quantity and quality. A Euclidean space (also called Cartesian space) is a generalization that applies Euclid's concept of distance, and the related concepts of length and angle, to a coordinate system in any number of dimensions. A Hilbert space is a generalization of a Euclidean space that is not restricted to finite dimensions. Hilbert spaces are of crucial importance in the mathematical formulation of quantum mechanics. Differential geometry provides a different type of generalization to spaces that are locally Euclidean, but whose large scale properties are not flat. A sphere is a good example of this since at very small distances it appears flat, but at a large scale the curvature is evident. Differential geometry allows coordinates that are not Cartesian. A general coordinate system specifies the distance ds between neighboring points x^a and $x^a + dx^a$ in terms of a metric g_{ab}, which is a matrix of numbers, and a prescription for calculating such small distances in terms of the product of the coordinate distances and the matrix:

$$ds = \sqrt{\sum_{a,b} g_{ab} dx^a dx^b}.$$

The prescription is to multiply the product of the shown distances by the indicated metric element and sum over all the possible directions of the space. The resultant distance is the square root of this quadratic form. By considering new coordinates that are linear combinations of the original, a new quadratic form can be formed; it is always possible to make a choice so that the resultant form is either Euclidean or more generally a diagonal form in which some squares are added and some subtracted. Spaces that are not Euclidean are called Minkowski spaces. Newtonian physics is formulated for a Euclidean space whereas Einstein's physics is formulated for a Minkowski space with time being treated differently from the space dimensions.

y   Regarding qualities as dimensions instead of classes has evident implications for sociology where age, sex, and socioeconomic and national classes play an important role. Dividing people as belonging to one race increases discrimination and conflict, and is false. (Most "Blacks" are largely "White"; "Hispanics" are of any color; Italian or Jewish brothers can become one "Hispanic" and the other "White" if born in different places.) The reality is that a person is female to some degree and male to some other, shares several races and cultures, continuously changes age, and relates in three ways regarding socioeconomic class: over some, under others, and at the same level as many others.

z   Physics focuses on generic processes rather than on the specific form of physical mountains or galaxies.

aa   The fact that we still have not agreed upon units to measure biological or psychological dimensions is an incentive to define them clearly, not an objection against conceptualizing them as dimensions. Dimensions are not the same as units. Dimensionless quantities may have units, for example, angles. Dimensions are objective facts of nature.

ab   Defining confirmation as the empirical demonstration of a case, the hypothesis "All ravens are black" is supported by finding a red shoe, as "All A are B" is equivalent, in standard logic, to "No no-B is A."

ac   "[T]he number of qualitatively different configurations of discontinuities that can occur depends not on the number of state variables, which is generally very large, but on the control variables, which is generally very small. In particular, if the number of control variables is not greater than four, then there are only seven types of catastrophes, and in none of these more than two state variables are involved." (Saunders, 1980)

ad   When the action is small compared to some action scale, it is possible to envision a quantum version of the decision theory. This has not yet been done, though if possible it would be a more complete instantiation of biotic theory complete at all levels of comparison with known physical theories. The known difficulties are that the known physical theories have not yet integrated gravitation successfully, though string theories are working hard to accomplish that. It may be many generations, however, before this comes to fruition.

ae   Even if we need statistical methods involving multiple observations to measure a quantum process (as it may be necessary for computation), this does not imply that quantum processes are inherently probabilistic. We use statistical methods in biology for many reasons while never implying that the processes are in themselves probabilistic.

Section II
Application Fields:
From Networks to Fractal Geometry

Chapter XI
Networks:
Uses and Misuses of an Emergent Paradigm

Alessandro Giuliani
Istituto Superiore di Sanità, Italy

ABSTRACT

The term network is more and more widespread in all the fields of human investigation from physics to sociology. It evokes a systemic approach to problems able to overcome the limitations reductionist approaches have evidenced for some decades. Network-based approaches gave very brilliant results in fields like biochemistry, where the consideration of the whole set of metabolic reactions of an organism allowed us to understand some very important properties of the organisms that cannot be appreciated by the simple enumeration of single biochemical reactions. Nevertheless, the lack of consciousness that networks are modeling tools and not real entities could be detrimental to the exploitation of the full potential of this paradigm. Some applications of network-based modeling will be presented to both introduce the basic terminology of the emergent network paradigm and highlight strengths and limitations of the method.

INTRODUCTION

The network paradigm is the prevailing metaphor in today's natural sciences. We can read about gene networks (De Jong, 2002; Gardner & Faith, 2005), protein networks (Bork, Jensen, Von Mering, Ramani, Lee, & Marcotte, 2004), metabolic networks (Nielsen, 1998; Palumbo, Colosimo, Giuliani, & Farina, 2005), ecological networks (Lassig, Bastolla, Manrubia, & Valleriani, 2001), and so forth. This metaphor went well outside the realm of natural science to invade more humanistic and less formalized fields like sociology and psychology (McMahon, Miller, & Drake, 2001).

The network paradigm is a horizontal construct (Palumbo, Farina, Colosimo, Tun, Dhar, & Giuliani, 2006), basically different from the classical top-down paradigms of modern science, dominant until not so many years ago when there was a privileged flux of information (and a consequent hierarchy of explanation power) from more basic atomisms (fundamental forces in physics, DNA in biology) down to the less fundamental phenomenology (condensed matter organization, physiology).

The general concept of a network as a collection of elements (nodes) and the relationships among these (arcs) cannot be separated by the definition of a system in dynamical systems theory, where the basic elements (nodes) are time-varying functions and relationships are differential or difference equations. In this respect, the two definitions are very similar. While the emphasis of the term network is on topology (i.e., the static wiring diagram of the modeled reality), the term dynamical system refers to the dynamics emerging from the interaction of components, that is, the actual behavior of the network when observed in time. This analogy is at the root of the recently renewed interest in systems biology (Klipp, Herwig, Kowald, Wierling, & Lehrach, 2005).

Psychology, as well as other soft sciences, is not new to the systems approach; the names of Von Bertalanffy, Wiener, and so forth are not new to sociology and psychology students. The cultural scene from the '40s to '70s was dominated by concepts borrowed from systems science, like feedback, stability, and trajectory. This systemic approach came to an eclipse when apparently more fascinating metaphors came from hard sciences or, better, from what appeared to be the most innovative technology around. When the charisma of the most powerful technology shifted from servomechanisms to digital computers, the "dynamical system" became the "sequential machine" whose operational behavior was embodied in a suitable memory and a processor able to read along the correct steps. Nowadays, the fascination comes

from the World Wide Web that is unanimously considered the most powerful and innovative object around, thus it is not strange anything must be equated to a network. In the subsequent part of this work, we will try and go beyond this idolatrous way of thinking and to understand how and when the network-based metaphors and modeling can be useful in day-to-day research work.

DISCUSSION

What a Network Is

As we said before, a network is simply a set of nodes connected by arcs as in Figure 1 that depicts a portion of the metabolic network of a cell.

The nodes can be anything you want: metabolites in the case of a biochemical pathway as the one depicted in the figure, airports in the case of airway transport systems, or people in the case of a social network. Consequently, the arcs can represent any meaningful relation between the nodes, so in the case of biochemical pathways, an arc between node i and node j simply means a metabolite i can be transformed into metabolite j; in the case of airway transportation, the arc points to the fact there is a direct flight between airport i and airport j, while in the case of the social network, the arc implies a friendship relation between the two connected nodes. The important thing for a network model to be useful (instead of being a pure rhetorical exercise) is that we can derive some relevant information on the general behavior of the modeled system by the sole knowledge of a network wiring diagram (who is connected with whom).

It is important to stop and think about the previous statement: In the case of dynamical system theory, we do not only need information about the topology of the system but, more important, we need information about the nature and strength of the arcs (the relations between the elements of the system). In other words, in order to build

Figure 1.

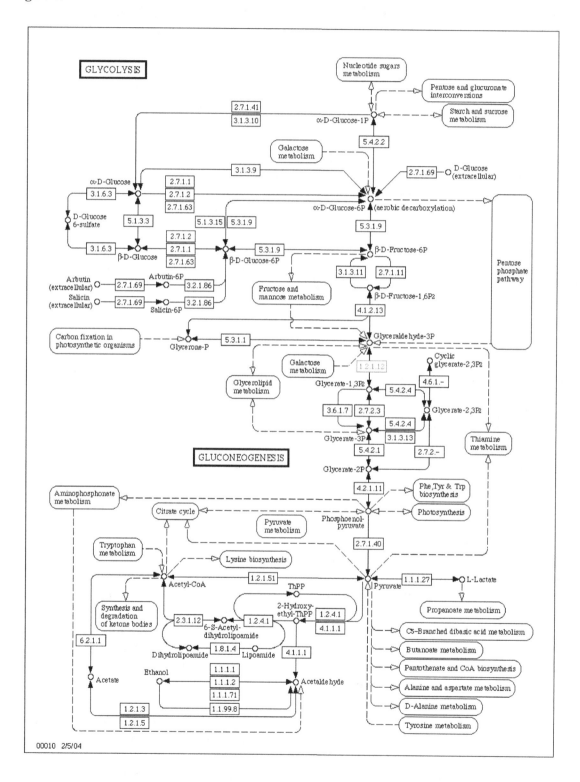

a differential-equation-based model, it is not sufficient to say molecule i is transformed into molecule j, or airport i is connected to airport j by a direct flight. We need to know in advance the rate of formation of j starting from i (and vice versa) and the time needed to fly from i to j. This requirement is at the basis of the substantial failure of dynamical system analysis of complex systems. Simply, we cannot give all the needed information because they are outside the reach of empirical investigation or because they cannot be assumed to be invariant during the system's actual functioning. The shift from the dynamical system approach to networks is then an admission of our limits of going in deep into complex systems' fine structure.

The basic mathematical model to approach the topological study of networks is the graph. The graph is defined as a tuple (V,E), with V as a set of vertices (or nodes) and E as a set of edges (or arrows, arcs). The degree of a node is the number of arcs connected to it (Palumbo et al., 2006).

In the case of a directed graph, or digraph, the set of edges is composed of directed arcs and is defined as a tuple (i,j) of vertices where i denotes the head and j the tail of the edge. Arrows on the arcs are used to encode the directional information.

In a directed graph, vertices have both in-degree and out-degree. The in-degree is the number of distinct arcs leading to that vertex, and the out-degree is the number of arcs leading away from that vertex. A walk through a directed graph is a sequence of nodes connected by arcs corresponding to the order of nodes in the sequence; a path is a walk with no repeated nodes. The distance between two vertices corresponds to the number of arcs in the minimum path.

All the applications of the network paradigm are based on the possibility to operate some sort of classification of the elements of the network relying on features based on their connectivity pattern alone, with no use of specific properties of the nodes external to the network wiring.

The most basic of these network features is the possibility to reach a given node i starting from another node j by a path along a graph: This possibility defines an equivalence relation "to be connected to" that partitions a given graph G in equivalence classes called components made by all the nodes that are connected among them. The set of nodes mutually reachable inside a given graph is called a connected component. A graph G is called connected if it is made by only one component. The number of distinct paths connecting two nodes can be considered an index of connectivity on the graph nodes: The greater the number of paths connecting the two nodes, the greater the two nodes are correlated, and the higher their connectivity index.

This allows for a straightforward application of clustering algorithms able to individuate supernodes, that is, groups of nodes highly connected among each other and forming functional modules. This metric property of topological graph representation was exploited in many different fields extending from organic chemistry, where the graphs are the molecules with atoms as nodes and chemical bonds as edges (Lukovits, 2000), to protein domains where the nodes are amino-acid residuals and the edges are the structural contiguity relation (Rao & Caflisch, 2004). It is worth noting that the generation of classifications (families of nodes) derives directly from the pattern of mutual relations between the nodes without any explicit involvement of features of the nodes other than their connectivity pattern in the network. This implies a complete inversion of the classic reductionist approach. In the case of the network paradigm, the properties of the elements of the system are derived from the properties of the entire system (the connectivity pattern of the graph) and not vice versa. In other words, each node is completely identical to any other as for its nature: Its specific determination stems from its peculiar pattern of relations with all the other elements of the network; that is to say that, when adopting the network modeling style, we opt for an intrinsic, context-dependent geometry of the studied system in which the single elements are not measurable independently of the topology of the whole system.

How Networks are Described

The study of complex graphs for which detailed topological information was lacking started in 1950. In this realm, the pioneering work of two Hungarian mathematicians, Erdos and Renyi, can be considered of much importance (Erdos & Renyi, 1960; Palumbo et al., 2006). They introduced the concept of random graphs, in which the number of connections linking the different nodes is defined by stochastic variables. Each node of the graph can be defined by the number of nodes connected to it (degree). This gives rise to the degree distribution P(k) describing the general wiring pattern of the network having as the abscissa the number k of connections and as the y axis the number of nodes having k connections. In analogy with statistical mechanics, these distributions are defined as scaling laws (Barabasi & Albert, 1999).

Humanities scientists are acquainted with Zipf's law linking the length of words and their frequency of occurrence. This is another scaling law, whose specific shape allows us to make some inference on the system at hand (Perline, 1996). Statisticians simply refer to these laws as distributions, wisely attenuating the arrogance of the term *law* frankly exaggerated for what is simply an empirical observation. In the case of networks, what happens is that if there are too many nodes, it is impossible to enumerate the degree of connectivity of each single node, and we need to perform some statistics, that is, to use some meaningful summary of what is going on.

These statistical distributions can give us some useful information on the general shape of the analyzed networks. Figure 2 shows two typical kinds of distributions. The panel on the left shows a Poisson distribution in which there is a privileged scale of the number of connections and a decreasing number of nodes having less than average or more than average links. The panel on the right depicts a so-called scale-free network (Palumbo et al., 2006) in which there is a huge majority of nodes with a low number of connections and a very small number of nodes having a large number of links. These highly connected nodes are called hubs. This kind of architecture often leads to a "small-world" property (Watts & Strogatz, 1998); that is, each node is, on average, near any other in terms of the number of arcs connecting them.

Albert, Jeong, and Barabasi (2000) investigated the tolerance of both random and scale-free networks after the removal of several nodes. The deletion of a node causes an augmentation of the distance between the nodes in the network. The authors distinguish between two kinds of deletion: failure and attack. The former consists of

Figure 2.

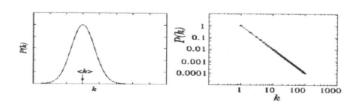

the removal of a randomly selected set of nodes, while the latter consists of the deletion of the most connected nodes of the network. The robustness of a scale-free network is due to its particular connection distribution. As a few nodes are highly connected, an informed attack will provoke the deletion of a hub and, as a consequence, the isolation of many nodes. On the other hand, a random failure has only a small probability to significantly alter the structure of the scale-fee network because the majority of the nodes have a few connections and the probability to damage a highly connected node (with consequently limited effects on the entire network) is quite high.

There is a vast debate about the different distributions present in biological networks (Palumbo et al., 2006); this debate stems from the lack of reliable experimental data and from the controversial definition of what a connection is. A particular enlightening example are protein networks for which there is a big debate on how to measure a protein-protein interaction. Thus, I think it is better to concentrate on the simple possibility to describe real networks by means of statistical indexes derived from $P(k)$ distribution without paying attention to the classification of a network as small-world or Poissonian: The relevant thing is that these indexes can give us some good prediction about the behavior of the modeled system.

The tendency of having subsets of nodes that are strongly connected can be measured by the so-called aggregation coefficient. Let us consider a generic i node f the network having $k(i)$ edges connecting it to other $k(i)$ nodes. In order for these nodes to possess the maximal connectivity (each node connected to each other), we should have a total number of edges equal to

$$k(i)*(k(i)-1)/2. \qquad (1)$$

Expression (1) corresponds to the maximal number of connections among $k(i)$ nodes when self-connections are avoided. Thus, it is perfectly

natural to define the aggregation coefficient in terms of the ratio between the number of actually observed Ei and the maximal number of connections expressed by Expression 1. Thus, the aggregation coefficient relative to node i, Ci, is expressed as

$$Ci = 2*(Ei/k(i)*(ki-1)). \qquad (2)$$

The aggregation coefficient for the entire network corresponds to the average of Ci over all the nodes. The operative counterpart of the clustering tendency is the concept of modularity, that is, the possibility to isolate portions of a more general network that can be considered as partially independent subnetworks, that is, modules, that can be studied as such without necessarily referring to the whole network, given the by-far greater relevance of inside-module links with respect to the between-module ones. This is nothing different from the concept of stable classification in classical multidimensional statistics, in which well-behaved clusters are defined collections of statistical units very near each other (in the network language, having a lot of mutual connections) and distant from the elements of the other cluster (in the network language, having only few arcs connecting to elements of different modules).

A Case Study

Let us shift now to an example in which network-based modeling allowed us to rationalize a relevant biochemical phenomenon: the essential character of a metabolic reaction (Palumbo et al., 2005). The metabolism of an organism (in this case the yeast Saccharomyces Cerevisiae) can be thought of as a network in which the metabolites are the nodes and the arcs correspond to enzymes converting a metabolite i into a metabolite j. The elimination of an enzyme by a specific mutation corresponds to the elimination of the arc directly connecting the two metabolites at its ends. Adopting a purely network-based approach to the study of this system implied the task of inferring the lethal character of each mutation (i.e., the arcs whose elimination ends in the death of the microorganism) on the pure basis of its position into the wiring diagram, without any reference to the nature of the catalyzed reaction.

The metabolic network of microorganisms, at odds with other biological networks like protein-protein interaction networks or genetic regulation networks, is very well understood and characterized. It corresponds to Boeheringer's charts of metabolism pinned on the walls of almost every biochemistry laboratory in the world, having enzymatic reactions as edges and metabolites as nodes.

A metabolic network can be imagined (Figure 3) as composed of four distinct classes of nodes. The first one is the strong connected components (SCC), made of nodes linked to each other by direct paths. Reactant subsets consist of metabolites entering the system as reactants called sources because they can reach SCC from the external environment. Another class is constituted by the product subset: Such metabolites are positioned

at the end of a given pathway and thus exit the system as products (they are called sinks in opposition to the sources). The metabolites in the last class, called the isolated subset, are inserted in autonomous pathways with respect to SCCs. This architecture can be found in many scale-free networks such as the World Wide Web, the electric power transmission grid, and airplane connections (Crucitti, Latora, Marchiori, & Rapisarda, 2004).

Since an enzymatic reaction is catalyzed by one or more enzymes, an arc represents the enzymes involved in the reaction. This opens the way to a straightforward analysis of the possibility to derive biologically meaningful features from the network topology. Relying on the existing database of the experimentally verified effects of yeast mutations (http://www-sequence.stanford.edu/group/yeast_deletion_project/deletions3.html), we checked the possibility to pick up a connectivity descriptor able to unequivocally define essential enzymes (those enzymes whose lack provokes yeast death). If this can be done, this is proof of the possibility to consider the

Figure 3.

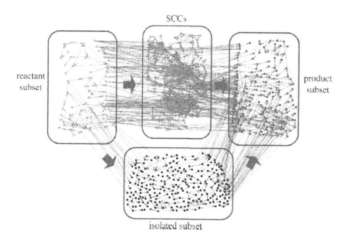

whole metabolism as a biological entity per se, from whose structure the biological relevance of the single elements of the system (the specific enzymes) derives. In other words, the biological role of a given enzyme is not fully definable in isolation from the whole set of interactions it is embedded into, so falsifying the basic tenet of a great part of scientific and technological applications of molecular biology.

Figure 4 is a graphic representation of the Saccharomyces Cerevisiae metabolic network. The labels of the nodes correspond to the codes of the different metabolites according to the KEGG database (Ma & Zeng, 2003). Yellow bars show where essential enzymes are positioned in the network. Nodes colored in blue, light blue, violet, and green belong to the strong connected components of the network. These components constitute the cores of the network and all of the

nodes belonging to one of them can reach one another because they are fully connected.

Our conjecture was that the lethal mutations can unequivocally be defined by those isolating one or more nodes from the entire network; that is, lethal mutations are those that do not allow for an alternative pathway to reach one or more nodes. This was actually the case, thus pointing to a much more crucial role played by peripheral portions of the network with respect to hubs. As a matter of fact, nodes in SCCs are protected by the redundancy of paths (high connectivity), thus it is extremely difficult that a single arc deletion can isolate a node in an SCC; on the contrary, a lateral node, due to its low connectivity, can be easily isolated by an arc deletion.

The demonstration of the possibility to exactly predict a biological phenomenon (essential character of an enzyme) from the pure analysis of

Figure 4.

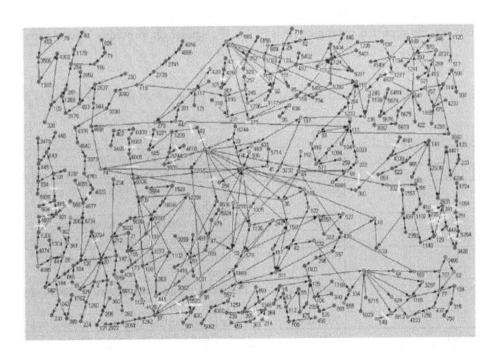

the connectivity pattern of the metabolic network without referring to any biochemical notion of a single enzyme's physiology is strong proof of the possible usefulness of the network approach and of the feasibility of a holistic approach in biology.

Obviously, even if the results give the impression that something we can call a metabolic network does in fact exist, we must pay the maximal attention to the fact that all the things we speak about in science are not real entities but (at their best) are useful toy models of what does effectively exist. This is a basic point to keep in mind in order to not ingenerate the dangerous mistake of applying a successful model to anything in the world. The basic question is then "When is it convenient to model something like a network?"

Are networks everywhere? Yes and no; clearly the basic definition of a network is sufficiently vague to be applied to anything by means of a minimal formalization effort. This is a relatively easy (and basically trivial) exercise developed in Table 1.

Table 1 reports a possible network formalization (in terms of nodes and arcs) for eight different systems. The interested reader could both enlarge the reported list or invent more smart network formalizations for the reported examples (it is

worth noting I can choose different nodes and arcs for the same object, depending on which of the multiple relations present in a given object I decide to assume as the privileged view, as in the case of Internet where a software view of the system instead of the hardware one was privileged). For each of these formalizations I can easily derive all the topological descriptors we discussed above and thus identify hubs and nonhub connectors (the essential enzymes of the case study), measuring different connectivity indexes and so forth.

The basic question to decide if my network formalization is worth it is thus simply, "Can I derive some useful information from the topology of the network?" Let us try and play the game of useful-trivial for the above-sketched examples.

Building: This is useful, but only if the building is very big (has a lot of rooms) and you are the architect who must connect node families (modules) with different functions (let us think of a building hosting different work activities). The corresponding network of modules and different activities is probably a useful optimization principle.

Railway: This model is trivial if you are a passenger. It provides information you can

Table 1.

System	Nodes	Arcs (An arc does exist when)
Building	rooms	It is possible to go from room i to room j directly
Railway	stations	Station *j* can be reached from station *i* with no intermediate stop
Office	clerks	Two clerks collaborate in the same job
Scientific Literature	authors	Author *i* and j have coauthored one or more papers
Lego	bricks	Two bricks are directly connected with no intermediate brick
Computer Network	computers	There is a physical connection between computers *i* and *j*
Internet	Web sites	There is a direct link between two sites *i* and *j*
Gene Expression	genes	Genes *i* and *j* share the same promoter

derive from any railway book; the relevant information is the time needed to go from one place to another to help in choosing the best travel schedule. It is only useful if you must plan the railway because you could optimize the topology in relation to the traffic fluxes.

Office: The network is useful if two clerks pertaining to two different departments collaborate more often than two clerks of the same department, which could cause an error in human resources allocation.

Scientific Literature: This kind of exercise is only useful to increase scientists' pomposity (and equates to selling refrigerators at the North Pole).

Legos: This is trivial because the bricks are basically interchangeable.

Computer Network: This is very important and useful for optimizing the connections in terms of the physical location of computers and of the shared work.

Internet: Knowing that reciprocal links between different sites mirror relative arguments, it could be useful for someone that is interested in developing a study about the ecology of Web users.

Gene Expression: This is debatable, even if the current vision seems to answer trivial because sharing the same promoter does not seem to be as biologically meaningful as it was considered some years ago and, more important, it does not seem that these networks have a stable topology.

The useful-trivial game was played with a semantic attitude, that is, having in mind the use we can make of a network formalization. We could equally play a syntactic version of the game in which the decision of the relevance of the network modeling is based on how straightforward and natural the translation of the specific system is.

Basically, a network is made of nodes and arcs: Nodes are locations where activity (or energy or

matter) is especially concentrated with respect to the rest of environment, and arcs are links between these locations along which something happens (chemical transformations, flux of energy or of information, chemical bonding, etc.). When this partition of the space is clear cut and unambiguous, network formalization is syntactically correct (then obviously we must decide about its semantic justification). Thus, it is perfectly fit to think of a highway system as a network: The cities are the nodes, the highways connecting them are the arcs. The population density, function, landscape, and so forth inside the cities (nodes) are basically different from that of the country along which the highways go. Thus, modeling the system as a network is perfectly natural and unambiguous. This is no more the case when we want to model the streets inside a town as a network: Who plays the role of node? Who plays the role of arc? We can decide for different choices but there is not a most natural one.

In conclusion network-based modeling of complex systems is a potentially very powerful tool; the important thing to keep in mind is that it is a tool and not the real thing. So it is important to avoid unjustified philosophical speculations on its use and maintain an operational attitude on the use of this paradigm.

CONCLUSION

The message I tried to convey in these pages, mainly oriented toward biochemical sciences given my specific research interests, is that network formalization is neither the brilliant new paradigm of the future, opening our minds to a different view of the world, nor an abstruse and mathematically intensive tool to approach complex systems in the definitive way. Simply, they are analysis tools, like the more ordinary but equally effective (and extremely more versatile) multidimensional statistics that, instead of the philosopher's enthusiasm, generally elicits boring expressions. Like any analysis tool, we decide when to use a network algorithm on the basis of the problem at hand, taking into consideration its structural characteristics besides any epistemological or theoretical predisposition.

REFERENCES

Albert, R., Jeong, H., & Barabasi, A. L. (2000). Error and attack tolerance of complex networks. *Nature, 406*, 378-382.

Barabasi, A. L., & Albert, R. (1999). Emergence of scaling in random networks. *Science, 286*, 509-512.

Bork, P., Jensen, L. J., Von Mering, C., Ramani, A. K., Lee, I., & Marcotte, E. M. (2004). Protein interaction networks from yeast to human. *Current Opinion on Structural Biology, 7*, 292-299.

Crucitti, P., Latora, V., Marchiori, M., & Rapisarda, A. (2004). Error and attack tolerance of complex networks. *Physica A, 340*, 388-394.

De Jong, H. (2002). Modeling and simulation of genetic regulatory systems: A literature review. *Journal of Computational Biology, 9*, 67-103.

Erdos, P., & Renyi, A. (1960). On the evolution of random graphs. *Publ. Math. Inst. Hung. Acad. Sci., 2*, 17-61.

Freeman, L. C. (2004). *The development of social networks analysis: A study in the sociology of science.* Vancouver, Canada: Booksurge Publishing.

Gardner, T. S., & Faith, J. J. (2005). Reverse-engineering transcriptional control networks. *Physics of Life Review, 2*, 65-88.

Klipp, E., Herwig, R., Kowald, A., Wierling, C., & Lehrach, H. (2005). *Systems biology in practice.* Weinheim, Germany: Wiley-VCH.

Lassig, M., Bastolla, U., Manrubia, S. C., & Valleriani, A. (2001). Shape of ecological networks. *Physical Review Letters, 86*, 4418-4421.

Lukovits, I. (2000). A compact form of adjacency matrix. *Journal of Chemical Information and Computer Sciences, 40*, 1147-1150.

Ma, H. W., & Zeng, A. P. (2003). The connectivity structure, giant strong component and centrality of metabolic networks. *Bioinformatics, 19*, 1423-1430.

McMahon, S. M., Miller, K. H., & Drake, J. (2001). Networking tips for social scientists and ecologists. *Science, 293*, 1604-1605.

Nielsen, J. (1998). Metabolic engineering: Techniques of analysis of targets for genetic manipulations. *Biotechnology & Bioengineering, 58*, 125-132.

Palumbo, M. C., Colosimo, A., Giuliani, A., & Farina, L. (2005). Functional essentiality from topology features in metabolic networks: A case study in yeast. *FEBS Letters, 579*, 4642-4646.

Palumbo, M. C., Farina, L., Colosimo, A., Tun, K., Dhar, P., & Giuliani, A. (2006). Networks everywhere? Some general implications of an emergent metaphor. *Current Bioinformatics, 1*(2), 219-234.

Perline, R. (1996). Zipf's law, the central limit theorem, and the random division of the unit interval. *Physical Review E, 54*, 220-223.

Rao, F., & Caflisch, A. (2004). The protein folding network. *Journal of Molecular Biology, 342*, 299-306.

Watts, D. J., & Strogatz, S. H. (1998). Collective dynamics of "small world" networks. *Nature, 393*, 440-442.

Chapter XII
Theory and Practice of Ant–Based Routing in Dynamic Telecommunication Networks

Gianni A. Di Caro
Istituto Dalle Molle di Studi sull'Intelligenza Artificiale (IDSIA), Switzerland

Frederick Ducatelle
Istituto Dalle Molle di Studi sull'Intelligenza Artificiale (IDSIA), Switzerland

Luca M. Gambardella
Istituto Dalle Molle di Studi sull'Intelligenza Artificiale (IDSIA), Switzerland

ABSTRACT

Modern telecommunication networks are becoming increasingly complex and dynamic. This is due to their size and heterogeneity, and to the complex interactions among their elements. Classical techniques for network control were not conceived to face such challenges. Therefore, new algorithms are needed that are adaptive and robust, work in a self-organized and decentralized way, and are able to cope with heterogeneous large-scale systems. In this chapter, we argue that the reverse engineering of natural processes can provide a fruitful source of inspiration for the design of such algorithms. In particular, we advocate the use of ant colony optimization (ACO), an optimization metaheuristic inspired by the foraging behavior of ant colonies. We discuss the characteristics of ACO and derive from it ant colony routing (ACR), a novel framework for the development of adaptive algorithms for network routing. We show through the concrete application of ACR's ideas to the design of an algorithm for mobile ad hoc networks that the ACR framework allows the relatively straightforward construction of new routing algorithms that can deal with all of the challenges mentioned above.

INTRODUCTION

Telecommunication networks are becoming increasingly large, dynamic, and heterogeneous. The global Internet is rapidly evolving toward a highly complex system that comprises and integrates a number of wired and wireless networks covering the needs of different communities of users and ranging from small-body area networks to global satellite networks. It is just a matter of time before the *all the time, everywhere access* foreseen in the view of pervasive computing (Saha & Mukherjee, 2003) will be put into practice, allowing continual access to data, users, and services. Core features of current and forthcoming network scenarios are the continual mobility and appearance or disappearance of users; the continual updating, migration, and reorganization of available data and services; and the tight interaction between wireless and wired communication nodes with totally different characteristics in terms of capacity and delivered quality of service. It is apparent that the control and management of network systems with such characteristics is a highly complex task. Existing protocols and algorithms were conceived to deal with rather static and homogeneous network environments, and rely on human intervention in case of major problems and tuning. Therefore, a paradigm shift is necessary to deal with the challenges posed by extremely large, dynamic, and heterogeneous networks. Novel control and management protocols have to be designed that show the following essential properties.

- *Adaptivity* to changes (in traffic, topology, services, etc.)
- *Robustness* to deal with component failures, transmission errors, and small perturbations
- *Self-organizing* and *decentralized* behavior
- Scalability in terms of performance vs. overhead and usage of network resources
- *Ability* to work across (sub)networks that are heterogeneous in terms of transmission technology and/or node and topology characteristics
- *Independent behavior*, that is, being able to self-tune internal parameters, self-manage, self-configure, self-govern, and so forth

The central idea contained in this wish list is that novel algorithms should continually and robustly learn about the current network status and user context, and accordingly adapt their internal characteristics and decision policies. In a broad sense, this is the approach advocated, with different perspectives, in the two recent frameworks of *traffic engineering* (Freeman, 2004) and *autonomic communications* (Kephart & Chess, 2003). For the latter, the term autonomic precisely stresses the need for a design that lets the different network components be fully autonomous to control and manage the whole network through self-organizing social interaction. The central aim is to minimize human intervention while maximizing the overall performance and efficiency.

The design from scratch of novel protocols and algorithms with the listed properties is in general a very challenging task, also considering the rather large number of different network systems with different characteristics that are available nowadays (e.g., wired wide area networks, Wi-Fi networks, wireless mesh networks, sensor networks, etc.). On the other hand, we can draw some basic inspiration from biological systems. In fact, a number of systems that can be observed in nature precisely show the general properties we wish to have in a network control system. As a matter of fact, biological systems have evolved the ability to effectively adapt in terms of both structure and behavior to constantly changing environments. Most of these systems can be seen as composed of a large number of dynamic, autonomous, and distributed units that generate a variety of useful effective behaviors at the system level as a result of local interactions and self-organization. Moreover, biological systems are usually robust to handle internal perturbations or loss of units, and are able to survive and evolve over a wide range of different environments. Nature has already served as a source of inspiration for a number of successful algorithms and frameworks. For instance, neural networks (Bishop, 1995; Hopfield & Tank, 1985) were originally designed after the brain's neurons, evolutionary computation (Fogel, 1995; Holland, 1975) stems from the observation of the processes underlying evolution and natural selection, and swarm intelligence (Bonabeau, Dorigo, & Theraulaz, 1999) finds its roots in both the swarm and social behaviors of groups of animals.

In this chapter, we show that taking basic inspiration from nature's complex adaptive systems to design novel routing algorithms to tackle the intrinsic complexity of modern networks is a general and effective way to proceed. In particular, we discuss *ant colony optimization* (ACO) Di Caro, 2004; Dorigo & Di Caro, 1999; Dorigo, Di Caro, & Gambardella, 1999; Dorigo & Stützle, 2004), a combinatorial optimization framework that reverse engineers and formalizes the basic mechanisms at work in the shortest path behavior observed in *ant colonies* (Deneubourg, Aron, Goss, & Pasteels, 1990; Goss, Aron, Deneubourg, & Pasteels, 1989). It has been observed that ants in a colony are able to converge on the shortest among multiple paths connecting their nest and a food source. The driving force behind this behavior is the use of a volatile chemical substance called pheromone. While moving, ants lay pheromone on the ground, and they also go in the direction of higher pheromone intensities. This mechanism allows ants to implicitly mark paths to guide subsequent ants, and let good paths arise from the overall behavior of the colony. Details about the mechanism are explained further on.

ACO is based on the *iterative construction of multiple solutions* for the optimization problem under consideration. The aim is to learn about the characteristics and the regularities of the search space, and recursively use this knowledge to direct the solution construction processes. These solution construction processes are defined in the terms of *sequential decision processes* and are driven by a parametric *stochastic decision policy*. ACO's strategy consists of the *progressive learning of the parameters used by this decision policy* in order to eventually discover a global policy that can allow the generation of good or optimal solutions to the problem at hand. Solution construction processes are designed after ant behavior and are termed ants, while the parameters that are the object of learning play the role of pheromone, and are termed *pheromone variables* (see Figure 1).

ACO's recipe has been applied with success to a number of combinatorial optimization problems. For many problems of both practical and theoretical interest, ACO implementations represent the state of the art. Its general application to *routing problems* is a relatively straightforward task due to a somehow natural mapping between the characteristics of ACO and those of typical network routing tasks. As a matter of fact, most ACO implementations for routing share a common structure and strategies. Each ant is actually a lightweight mobile agent (usually implemented as an "intelligent" control packet) responsible for discovering a routing path between the generating source node and an assigned destination node. The network routing policy is encoded in pheromone variables, which are stored in a distributed way in the nodes of the network. Ants actively explore the network, collect useful information along the followed path (e.g., about the congestion status), and use this information to learn about the network dynamics and to continually update the parameters of the routing policy in order to track network changes.

Based on the common underlying structure and set of strategies that can be singled out from actual ACO-based routing algorithms, in this chapter we

Figure 1. Circular relationship between repeated solution generation and policy adaptation

Pheromone variables bias solution construction

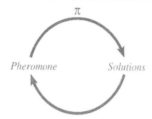

Outcomes of solution construction are used to modify pheromone values

informally define the ant colony routing (ACR) framework. ACR is a high-level distributed control architecture that specializes the core ideas of the ACO approach to the specific case of network routing and, at the same time, provides a generalization of these same ideas to define a fully distributed architecture for autonomic routing. We show by means of a general discussion and a concrete example of an ACR algorithm that, following the ACR guidelines, it is relatively straightforward to design novel routing algorithms that possess most of the characteristics reported in the wish list made up earlier on. Moreover, we show that the same core ideas can be applied with success over a range of dynamic network scenarios obtaining state-of-the-art performance.

The rest of this chapter is organized as follows. We first provide some general background on the class of problems and on the methods discussed throughout the chapter. In particular, we provide a general discussion about the problem of routing in networks, we describe the shortest path behavior in ant colonies in nature and single out all the basic mechanisms at work, and we report the definition of the ACO metaheuristic and a discussion of its properties. Then, we concentrate on the application of ACO to routing in networks. First, we provide the general definition of ACR and discuss its characteristics. Next, we describe

the practical implementation of AntHocNet, an ACO/ACR algorithm for routing in the extremely dynamic *mobile ad hoc networks* (MANETs). AntHocNet's characteristics are described and a number of experimental results over several network scenarios are reported in order to provide a sound validation of the ACR approach. We conclude the chapter with a summary of its contents and a discussion of future developments.

GENERALITIES ON NETWORK ROUTING

In this section we discuss general characteristics of network routing. The reader can find more detailed and insightful discussions on routing in Bertsekas and Gallager (1992), Tanenbaum (2002), Steenstrup (1995), Walrand and Varaiya (1996), Royer and Toh (1999), and Di Caro (2004).

A telecommunication network can be represented as a directed weighted graph $G=(V,E)$, where each node in the set V represents a processing and forwarding unit and each edge in E is a transmission system with certain capacity, bandwidth, and propagation characteristics. Two nodes are adjacent in the graph if they can communicate directly by means of wired or wireless transmission, and are called neighbors. Data traffic originates from a source node $s \in V$ and is directed to a set $d \subseteq V$ of destination nodes. In this chapter we consider only the case where all data have a unique destination node which is called unicast traffic. The routing component of a network control system addresses the basic issue of finding and setting up feasible paths to forward data packets from source to destination nodes. In packet-switched networks (e.g., the Internet), data packets are independently forwarded at each node according to a local routing decision policy parameterized by a local data structure called a routing table, which holds routing information. In the general case, entries in the routing table associate for each destination of interest and for each neighbor a measure of the cost of reaching the destination through the neighbor. In this sense, a network routing system can be seen as a distributed decision system.

A good routing strategy is one that selects the feasible paths optimizing the overall network performance, which is usually expressed in terms of maximizing the number of delivered data packets while minimizing their end-to-end latency and interarrival jitter time. Optimized path selection is a complex task since it involves the concurrent optimization of multiple and often conflicting objectives and requires taking into account the dynamic evolution of the network in terms of input traffic patterns and network characteristics like topology and link transmission delays. When all this knowledge is available, the problem of routing assignments can in principle be solved to optimality following *optimal routing* approaches (Bertsekas & Gallager, 1992; Gallager, 1977), which look at routing as a multicommodity flow problem (Papadimitriou & Steiglitz, 1982). Unfortunately, in most cases of practical interest, perfect and reliable knowledge about the dynamics of input traffic and network structure and characteristics is not available. Therefore, on the one hand, the routing decision policy at the nodes should be dynamically updated to keep track of network changes. On the other hand, updating can only be

based on imperfect knowledge about the current and future status of the network. In dynamic (or adaptive) routing strategies, this knowledge is collected online at the nodes (e.g., by monitoring the congestion level of the connected links) and possibly shared among the nodes, and is used to *automatically adapt* the local routing policies to changing network conditions. In the case of static (or oblivious) routing systems, routing paths are determined without regard to the current network state. Paths are usually chosen as the result of some off-line optimization process based on prior knowledge and are statically assigned and used. Adaptive routing is in principle the most attractive choice. However, it has as a drawback in that it can cause oscillations and inconsistencies in the selected paths, which in turn can cause circular paths, as well as large fluctuations in measured performance. Moreover, the general nonstationary quality of the network environment makes parameter setting in adaptive routing a very challenging task.

As a matter of fact, the great majority of the routing algorithms at work in deployed networks are basically static with respect to traffic variations and are only adaptive with respect to topological variations. For instance, this is the case for popular intradomain protocols like OSPF (Moy, 1998) and RIP (Malkin, 1999), which are at the very core of the wired Internet. Other intradomain protocols like CISCO's EIGRP come with only simple traffic adaptivity schemes. This is justified by the fact that *topological adaptivity* is an essential property to guarantee the basic functioning of any network. On the other side, adaptivity to other aspects of the network environment can be more regarded as performance or resource optimization, and since it is in a sense a harder task than topological adaptivity, it is usually not included in the protocols used in real-world applications. Often, the boosting of performance is obtained not by injecting intelligence into the network, but rather by adding more or redundant resources. However, this way of proceeding by overdimensioning is not always possible (e.g., like in the case of *mobile ad hoc networks* that are generated on the fly; Royer & Toh, 1999), can happen only on a slow time scale, and requires a major economical investment.

The ACO-based approach that is the focus of this chapter shows that it is possible to obtain both traffic and *topological adaptivity* in a very efficient, robust, and scalable way through a totally distributed and self-organizing strategy.

THE ANT COLONY OPTIMIZATION METAHEURISTIC

Biological Inspiration: The Shortest Path Behavior of Ant Colonies

A lot of species of ants have a trail-laying and trail-following behavior when foraging for food (Hölldobler & Wilson, 1990). While moving, individual ants deposit on the ground a volatile chemical substance called pheromone, forming in this way pheromone trails. Ants can sense pheromone and, when choosing their way, they tend to prefer, in probability, the paths marked by stronger pheromone concentrations. In this way, the pheromone distribution modifies the way the environment is perceived by the ants, acting as a sort of attractive field. This evolved characteristic of ant colonies is useful in finding their way back to the nest and food sources, in finding the location of food sources discovered by nest-mates, and in recruiting other ants to carry out cooperative tasks where it is necessary. Between the end of the 1980s and the beginning of the 1990s, a group of researchers of the Université Libre de Bruxelles in Brussels, Belgium (S. Aron, R. Beckers, J.-L. Deneubourg, S. Goss, and J.-M. Pasteels), ran several experiments and obtained original theoretical results concerning the influence of the pheromone fields on the ant decision patterns. Their works seemed to indicate that pheromone acts as a sort of dynamic collective

memory of the colony, a repository of all the most recent foraging experiences of the ants belonging to the same colony. By continually updating and sensing this chemical repository, the ants can indirectly communicate and influence each other through the environment. Indeed, this basic form of indirect communication termed stigmergy (Dorigo et al., 1999; Grassé, 1959; Theraulaz & Bonabeau, 1999), coupled with a form of positive feedback, can be enough to allow the colony as a *whole* to discover the *shortest path* connecting a source of food to the colony's nest.

This fact can be understood considering the following binary bridge experiment described in Goss et al. (1989; see Figure 2). The nest of a colony of Argentine ants *Linepithema humile* and a food source have been separated by a diamond-shaped double bridge with branches of different length. Ants are then left free to move between the nest and the food source. The percentage of ants that choose one or the other of the two branches is observed over time. The experimental observation is that, after a transitory phase that can last a few minutes, most of the ants use the shortest branch. It is also observed that the colony's probability of selecting the shortest path increases with the difference in length between the long and the short branches. The mechanism works as follows. The first ants able to arrive at the food source are those that traveled along the shortest branch. Accordingly, the pheromone that these ants have laid on the shortest branch while moving forward toward the food source makes it so that this branch is marked by more pheromone than the longest one. These higher levels of pheromone stimulate these same ants to probabilistically choose again the shortest branch when moving backward to their nest. This recursive behavior can be described as a self-sustaining positive *feedback effect* because the very fact of choosing a path increases its probability of being chosen again in the near future. During the backward journey, additional pheromone is released on the shortest path. In this way, pheromone is laid on the shortest branch at a higher rate

Figure 2. Effect of laying and following pheromone trails in a colony of Argentine ants, Linepithema humile, crossing an asymmetric bridge (modified from Goss et al., 1989)

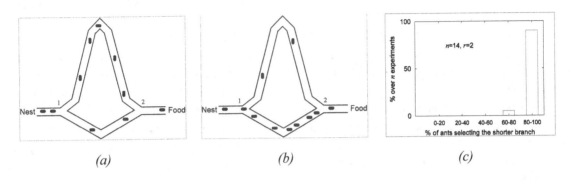

(a)   *(b)*   *(c)*

than on the longest branch. This reinforcement of the pheromone intensity on the shorter path is the result of a form of *implicit path evaluation*: The shorter path is completed earlier than the longer one, and therefore it receives pheromone reinforcement more quickly. Consequently, for the same number of ants choosing either the shortest or the longest branch at the beginning (Figure 2a), since the pheromone on the shortest branch is accumulated at a higher rate than on the longest one, the choice of the shortest branch becomes more and more attractive for the subsequent ants at both the decision points. The result (see Figure 2b and Figure 2c) is that after an initial transitory phase during which some oscillations can appear, ants tend to converge on the shorter path.

According to the described experiment, the ability of ant colonies to select shortest paths can be understood as the result of the synergistic interaction among a number of elements such as:

- A population (colony) of foraging ants
- Fforward-backward path following
- Step-by-step laying and sensing of pheromone
- A sequence of stochastic decisions biased by local pheromone intensity
- Positive feedback

- (implicit) path evaluation
- Iteration over time

In computational terms, the ants in the colony can be seen as *minimalist autonomous agents* that act in a completely *asynchronous, concurrent,* and *distributed fashion* to collectively solve a shortest path problem. Stigmergic communication makes the ant system self-organizing. Multiple paths (solutions) are repeatedly tried out as ants are moving back and forth, and some information related to each followed path is released on the environment, encoded in the pheromone trails, representing a shared distributed memory of the system. In turn, the local content of this memory affects the stochastic decisions of the ants, such that, when there is a significant difference in the lengths of the possible paths, *implicit path evaluation* gets to work and, coupled with positive feedback, results in a distributed and collective path optimization mechanism. Given enough time (depending on the number of ants, length and relative length difference of the paths, and other factors), this can result in the convergence of all the ants in the colony on the shortest among the possible paths. Each ant gives a contribution to the overall behavior. However, although a single ant is capable of building a solution (i.e., finding a path between its nest and a food reservoir), it is only the simultaneous presence and synergistic action of an ensemble of ants that makes the convergence to the shortest path behavior possible. So, the shortest path finding behavior is a property of the colony and of the concurrent presence of all the discussed ingredients, and not a property of the single ant.

All these mechanisms have been abstracted, reverse engineered, and put to work almost as they are in *ant colony optimization*, resulting in a general framework for the design of robust, distributed, and adaptive multiagent systems for the solution of shortest path problems. This class of problems is a very important one and encompasses a vast number of other problems (e.g., see Bertsekas, 1995). Graphs whose nodes represent possible alternatives or states and whose edges represent the distances, losses, rewards, and costs associated with node transitions are graphical models for a huge number of practical and theoretical decision and optimization problems. In general, almost any combinatorial optimization, network flow, or sequential decision problem can be modeled in terms of a shortest path problem. Having in hand an effective procedure to handle this class of problems opens endless opportunities for applications, especially considering the distributed, adaptive, and self-organizing properties of the approach.

ACO: Definition and General Properties

ACO is a metaheuristic for combinatorial optimization problems. An instance of a combinatorial optimization problem is a pair (S,J), where S is a finite set of feasible solutions and J is a function that associates a real cost to each feasible solution, $J : S \rightarrow \Re$. The problem consists of finding the element $\sigma^* \in S$ that minimizes the function J:

$$\sigma^* = \arg\min_{\sigma \in S} j = J(\sigma) \qquad (1)$$

It is common practice to define an instance of a combinatorial problem using a more compact definition of the type (C, Ω, J). In this definition, C is a finite set of components $\{c_0, c_1, ..., c_n\}$, used to define a solution, and Ω is a set of mathematical relations defining constraints on the way C's elements have to be selected in order to produce a feasible solution $\sigma \in S$. For the class of problems we are interested in in this chapter, namely, routing in telecommunications networks, the set S is represented by the set of all possible node paths joining each pair (s,d) of source and destination nodes involved in data exchange. The component set C is the set of all nodes belonging to the network, while Ω defines the consecutive nodes in a solution path that must be able to communicate (i.e., a wired or a wireless physical transmission channel must allow data exchange between the two nodes, and no infinite loops must be present). The cost of a path is the sum of the costs (e.g., time delays) associated with the transmission between two adjacent nodes c_t and c_{t+1} belonging to the path. In the following, we restrict the discussion to the class of combinatorial problems whose costs are additive in this way (e.g., this is true for important problems such as the traveling salesman problem; Garey & Johnson, 1979).

A combinatorial optimization problem can be approached with a variety of different solution methods, each having different properties in terms of the optimality of the produced solution, and in terms of the time required to reach this solution (Garey & Johnson, 1979; Vazirani, 2001). For important classes of problems, like the NP-hard ones, the time required for an exact method to produce an optimal solution might be prohibitive for large instances, and it is therefore often necessary in practice to rely on heuristics. These are solution methods that attempt to provide a near-optimal solution in reasonable time without any formal guarantee on performance. ACO is what is called a metaheuristic. That is a high-level strategy that guides the development of heuristics. A metaheuristic can be seen as a general algorithmic framework that can be applied to a possibly wide range of different optimization problems with relatively few modifications.

ACO's heuristic recipe is the following. Reverse engineering the mechanisms at work in ant colonies, ACO is based on the repeated sampling of multiple solutions to the problem at hand and on the use of the outcomes of these solutions to update the value of variables, playing the role of pheromone in ant colonies that biases in turn the process of solution generation. The aim is to progressively learn an assignment to these pheromone values that is able to capture regularities associated with good solutions and that eventually allows the generation of optimal or near-optimal solutions to the problem under consideration.

The precise characterization of what pheromone variables represent is related to fact that in ACO, the single solutions are incrementally constructed. That is, starting from an empty set $x_0 = \{\}$, a complete feasible solution $x_s \in S$ is built stepwise by adding one new component $c_i \in C$ at a time. This way of proceeding means that each solution is the result of a sequence of decisions about the next component to include in the current partial solution, represented by the sequence $x_s = [c_0, c_1, ..., c_E]$. Therefore, the generation of a solution coincides with the output of a sequential decision process. This process actually mimics ants building a path from the nest to a source of food. Accordingly, we speak of these processes in terms of ant-like agents, or, shortly, artificial ants.

As in the ant colony case, the single decisions are issued according to a stochastic decision policy π parameterized by a set of real-valued variables τ, called pheromone variables. A policy is a rule that associates the state of a process with an action, selected from among those actions that are feasible in that state, that is, according to the constraints Ω in our case. A stochastic policy defines a distribution of probability over the feasible actions, assigning in practice a selection probability to each action. Then an action is actually selected according to a chosen random scheme that takes

into account the different probability values (e.g., a random proportional scheme selects proportionally to the probability values).

In many ACO implementations, the model used to represent the decision process is such that the states of the process are mapped one to one onto the components of the optimization problem. This means that at step t the decision policy selects the next component $c_{t+1} \in C$ conditionally to the fact of being in state c_t, and among the subset of components that are still feasible. After issuing the decision, the current state becomes c_{t+1}. For the case of routing, where the problem components (and thus the states of the decision process) correspond to the network nodes, this means that a next hop is chosen conditionally to the fact of currently being at node c_t and among those nodes that are neighbors of c_t, which is a natural way of proceeding. After selecting the next hop, the new node becomes the current state.

Following this approach, whereby optimized complete solutions result from a sequence of single decisions about movements between states (or problem components), it is important to have a way to estimate the quality of each state transition $c_t \rightarrow c_{t+1}$. This is the role of the pheromone variables τ, which are used in ACO to associate a real-valued quality with each state transition. In practice, τ_{ij} represents a measure of the desirability of having the pair (c_i, c_j) in the solution sequence in the perspective of eventually building a good complete solution. For instance, in the case of routing, τ_{ij} represents the desirability of moving from c_i to c_j in order to reach destination d in the perspective of optimizing the final path from the source node s to d (e.g., obtaining a path with very low time latency for transmitting data packets from s to d). τ values are the parameters of the decision policy. They are used to calculate the relative probability of each feasible decision by normalization: If $N_{x_t}(c_i)$ is the set of components still feasible in state c_i given the current partial solution, then the probability of each $c_j \in N_{x_t}(c_i)$ is calculated as,

$$P_{ij} = \frac{\tau_{ij}}{\sum_{c_j \in (c_i)} \tau_{ij}}. \qquad (2)$$

The stochastic policy π takes as input the probabilities P_{ij} and uses them to select the next component according to some random selection rule.

The ACO fingerprint is that the pheromone quality estimates, which bias solution construction in this way, are built up and continually revised according to the outcomes of the solution generation process itself. The objective is to *adaptively learn*, through a continual sampling of solutions, a value assignment to the parameters of the policy that can eventually allow us to generate good, possibly optimal, solutions to the combinatorial problem under consideration. Basically, the idea is to reward those state transition decisions that belonged to good complete solutions. The underlying assumption of the ACO approach is that good solutions possess common features that can be learned through repeated solution sampling. The single solutions are supposed to be constructed according to a *computationally light scheme* in order to allow the sampling of a relatively large number of different solutions, realizing in this way an effective directed exploration of the search set.

Figure 3 shows in C-like pseudo-code the very general structure of the ACO metaheuristic.

Figure 3. High-level description of the behavior of the ACO metaheuristic

```
procedure ACO_metaheuristic()
  while (¬ stopping_criterion)
    schedule_activities
      construct_solutions_using_pheromone();
      pheromone_updating();
      daemon_actions();        /* OPTIONAL */
    end schedule_activities
  end while
  return best_solution_generated;
```

The algorithm is organized in three main logical blocks. The daemon_actions() block refers to all those optional problem-specific activities that share no relationship with the biological context of inspiration of the metaheuristic and that do not really make use of pheromone information. For instance, it is common practice to interleave ant solution generation with local search procedures (Dorigo & Gambardella, 1997).

Precisely in the spirit of a metaheuristic, ACO does not specify the implementation details of its different components. This is clear from the pseudo-code, which does not specify how the ant agents should construct the solutions, or how pheromone is updated following the evaluation of the generated solutions. Neither the characteristics of the pheromone mapping nor the modalities of the ant generation processes are specified. On the other side, since quite a large number of ACO algorithms have been designed so far, there are quite consolidated and rather standard ways of designing new ACO algorithms. The reader is referred to the mentioned bibliography for examples of ACO implementations, especially concerning classical combinatorial optimization problems (e.g., traveling salesman, quadratic assignment, task scheduling, etc.), which are static and can be solved in a fully centralized way. In the following we show how ACO's recipe can be adopted almost as it is to design new state-of-the-art routing algorithms for modern dynamic networks.

ACO FOR ROUTING IN DYNAMIC NETWORKS

In the introduction we discussed the reasons behind the high complexity associated with the control of modern telecommunications networks. We proposed a wish list of characteristics that algorithms for these modern networks would have to possess, including adaptivity, robustness, scalability, self-organization, etc. The main claim of this chapter is that the nature-inspired ACO

Table 1. ACO algorithms for dynamic routing problems in telecommunication networks. Applications are listed in alphabetical order and grouped in three classes depending on the kind of network they were designed for and the kind of service they deliver. Algorithm names are either those used by the authors, or assigned by us if the authors did not explicitly provide a name.

Problem Name	Authors	Algorithm Name	Year
Wired IP best-effort networks	Di Caro and Dorigo	AntNet, AntNet-FA	1997
	Subramanian, Druschel, and Chen	ABC Uniform Ants	1997
	Heusse, Snyers, Guérin, and Kuntz	CAF	1998
	Rothkrantz and van der Put	ABC-Backward	1998
	Oida and Kataoka	DCY-AntNet, NFB-Ants	1999
	Gallego-Schmid	AntNet NetMngmt	1999
	Doi and Yamamura	BntNetL	2000
	Baran and Sosa	Improved AntNet	2000
	Jain	AntNet Single-Path	2002
	Kassabalidis et al.	Adaptive-SDR	2002
Wired circuit-switched and QoS (quality of service) networks	Schoonderwoerd et al.	ABC	1996
	White, Pagurek, and Oppacher	ASGA	1998
	Di Caro and Dorigo	AntNet-FS	1998
	Bonabeau, Henaux, Guérin, Snyers, Kuntz, and Theraulaz	ABC Smart Ants	1998
	Oida and Sekido	ARS	2000
	Di Caro and Vasilakos	AntNet+SELA	2000
	Michalareas and Sacks	Multi-Swarm	2001
	Sandalidis, Mavromoustakis, and Stavroulakis	Ant-Based Routing	2001
	Subing and Zemin	Ant-QoS	2001
	Tadrus and Bai	QColony	2003
	Sim and Sun	MACO	2003
	Carrillo, Marzo, Fàbrega, Vila, and Guadall	AntNet-QoS	2004
Wireless networks	Câmara and Loureiro	GPS-ANTS	2000
	Matsuo and Mori	AAR	2001
	Sigel, Denby, and Heárat-Mascle	ACO-LEO	2002
	Kassabalidis et al.	Wireless Swarm	2002
	Günes, Sorges, and Bouazizi	ARA	2002
	Marwaha, Tham, and Srinivasan	Ant-AODV	2002
	Baras and Mehta	PERA	2003
	Heissenbüttel and Braun	MABR	2003
	Di Caro, Ducatelle, and Gambardella	AntHocNet	2004
	Tatomir and Rothkrantz	ABC-AdHoc	2004
	Zhang, Kuhn, and Fromherz	SC, FF, and FP Ant Routing	2004
	Zheng, Guo, and Liu	ADRA	2004
	Rajagopalan and Shen	ANSI	2005
	Liu, Kwiatkowska, and Constantinou	EARA	2005
	Liu and Feng	AMQR	2005

framework can provide basic guidelines to design in a rather straightforward way novel state-of-the-art routing algorithms showing exactly those properties.

From the discussions of the previous sections, it results that the fingerprint of the ACO approach consists of repeated solution construction by means of lightweight agents, the use of a stochastic decision policy to build the solutions, and progressive learning of the decision policy parameters from the observation of the outcomes of the solution generation process. All these characteristics are a natural match for the characteristics of routing and other network problems. This can be easily understood by considering the following simple facts. First, given the distributed nature of a network, the most natural way of proceeding to discover a feasible source-destination path consists of hopping from one node to the other until the final destination is reached. This precisely means following a construction approach when creating feasible solutions. Second, pheromone entries, which in ACO are the parameters of the construction policy, play exactly the same role of the entries in the node routing tables. Finally, due to the dynamic and distributed nature of a network environment, it is intrinsically necessary to keep exploring the network and collecting useful information. That is, much like in ant colonies, repeated sampling of full routing paths through the continual generation of ant agents (i.e., "smart" control packets) is expected to be an effective strategy to learn about network status and to consequently adapt the routing policy to it.

The good matching between the characteristics of ACO and those of network routing has in recent years attracted the interest of a relatively large number of researchers, resulting in a number of routing algorithms designed according to ACO guidelines. An overview of existing ACO routing algorithms is given in Table 1. For more extensive references and reviews, see, for example, Di Caro (2004). The great majority of these algorithms are explicitly derived from the first two ACO implementations for *routing problems*: ABC (Schoonderwoerd, Holland, Bruten, & Rothkrantz, 1996) and AntNet (Di Caro, 2004; Di Caro & Dorigo, 1998), which have addressed respectively routing in circuit-switched telephone networks and in packet-switched IP (Internet protocol) data networks. The empirical evidence is that well-designed ACO algorithms for routing perform comparably or much better than other classical state-of-the-art approaches. This is the case for AntNet and AntHocNet (described later in the chapter) developed by the authors of this chapter.

In practice, a common underlying structure and set of strategies can be singled out from all these ACO-based routing algorithms. Here we use this evidence to informally define the ACR framework, a high-level distributed control architecture that specializes the general ideas of the ACO approach to the case of network routing and, at the same time, provides a generalization of the same ideas for the autonomic control of generic distributed systems. In the next two subsections, we first sketch the general underlying scheme common to most ACO implementations for routing, and then we show how we make at the same time a generalization and a specialization of it in order to provide an effective recipe for the design of novel routing algorithms based on ACO's principles. Finally, we describe the AntHocNet routing algorithm as an example of how ACR can be adapted for a specific type of environment (in this case *mobile ad hoc networks*).

Common Characteristics of ACO Implementations for Routing

In the approach that is common to most ACO-based routing algorithms, nodes make use of ant packets to sample paths toward destination nodes of interest (e.g., end-points of frequent communications). Ants are usually generated according to simple periodic schemes. Each ant traveling forward to its destination constructs a solution, that is, a feasible path to its destination, in an incremental way by hopping between adjacent nodes. The task of an ant is to find a good path to the destination on the basis of the selected metrics of interest (e.g., time latency). Each node that can be chosen as a next hop has a vector of pheromone variables associated with it. These variables indicate how good it is to choose the given next hop, with respect to the selected optimization metrics, when traveling to the different possible destinations. Ants select their next hops according to a stochastic policy based on this pheromone information, and possibly also on further local heuristic information such as the length of the packet queues associated with the next hops. Once an ant has reached its destination, it evaluates the relative quality of the followed path and, carrying this information with it, retraces the path back to its source. At each of the visited nodes, the backward traveling ant provides this information to the node to let it update its pheromone information according to the fresh network information gathered by the ant during its journey. This general scheme is independently and concurrently actuated by each node and by each generated ant. It is derived from the general ACO scheme consisting of the repeated pheromone-biased construction of solutions (paths), multiple successive solution evaluations, and recursive updating of the pheromone variables that directed the path construction in the first place, with the general objective of dynamically learning properties of the problem at hand (here, the dynamically changing network environment). Clearly, different ACO instances show specific ways of implementing the different aspects of the general scheme, depending also on the specific characteristics of the network at hand. For instance, in some cases (e.g., cost-symmetric networks) the forward traveling ant can update pheromone information about the path leading back to its source so that it is not necessary to travel backward to the source (this is the design choice made in the mentioned ABC). Furthermore, in some cases using a periodic ant

generation scheme is not appropriate. For example, in those cases in which bandwidth is scarce, like in wireless multihop ad hoc networks, ant generation is usually made according to on-demand schemes that use bandwidth in a much wiser way (e.g., Baras & Mehta, 2003; Di Caro et al., 2004; Günes et al., 2002).

The Ant Colony Routing Framework

The ACR framework inherits all the essential characteristics of the general scheme derived above, but at the same time introduces new basic types of agents, defines their hierarchical relationships, and points out the general characteristics and strategies that are expected to be part of a distributed control architecture based on the ACO approach. In a sense, ACR's definition aims to make clear what an ant-based approach to network problems is and what it is not. ACR provides concrete guidelines for the design of adaptive routing algorithms for dynamic networks.

In the ACR view, the network is under the control of a system that consists of a distributed society of adaptive autonomous agents, with one agent for each node in the network. Each controller is called a node manager. Its internal status is defined by the values of the local pheromone tables and of possibly other additional data structures that are needed in the considered network scenario. Each entry in the pheromone table is associated with a different control action locally available to the node manager, and represents a statistical estimate of the goodness of taking that action. The controller adopts a stochastic decision policy that is parameterized by the pheromone and possibly by other local heuristic variables. The target of each controller is to locally and autonomously learn a decision policy in terms of pheromone variables such that the distributed society of controllers can jointly learn to optimize some global performance. Each controller is expected to learn good pheromone values by continually monitoring the network environment and the effect of its decisions on it, and by making use of the observed data to adaptively change the pheromone values as well as other parameters regulating its monitoring and control behavior. Local monitoring (also called passive monitoring) is realized directly by the node managers (e.g., monitoring of local traffic flows). Nonlocal monitoring, for the gathering of nonlocal network information, is done through the explicit generation of lightweight ant agents (active monitoring) acting as active long-range perceptions of the node managers.

The task of an ant agent is to explore the network with the aim of discovering a good path to an assigned destination, collect useful information about the quality and the status of the network along the path, and communicate this information back to the node managers to let them update their pheromone values accordingly. Typically, an ant samples a full, feasible network path, evaluates its quality, and retraces the path back to allow pheromone updates at the node managers along the path. Ants explore the network adopting a stochastic routing policy based on the node pheromone values. They can show a locally adaptive behavior, for instance, by replicating (or proliferating) when there is more than one single good alternative, or self-destroying in case of excessive local congestion. The term active perception refers both to the fact that a nonlocal information gathering act is explicitly issued and to the fact that each one of these perceptual acts can actually be generated with specific characteristics (e.g., different levels of exploratory attitude) in order to get precisely the information needed.

Node managers act concurrently and without any form of global coordination. Therefore, they must act socially and possibly cooperate (e.g., exchange messages or even their decision policies) in order to get positive synergy (e.g., not injecting too many ants in case of congestion).

The design of an ACR algorithm involves several critical choices, such as strategies for (a) local monitoring, (b) proactive and on-demand scheduling of ant agents, (c) the definition of the internal characteristics for the generated ants, (d) the development of ant policies, and (e) the use of the gathered information in order to learn effective decision policies for routing and to tune other internal node parameters regulating, for instance, the rate of proactive ant generation.

General Properties and Innovative Aspects of ACR

Writing a novel routing algorithm (or, more generally, a network control algorithm) according to ACR guidelines results in an algorithm that is expected to enjoy one or more properties that can be seen as highly desirable for the control of modern dynamic networks. We discuss these expected properties one by one in the following.

Self-Organization and Robustness

The control system is fully distributed and self-organizing. Each controller is an independent learner and exchanges information with other controllers either by local message passing or through the generation of path sampling ants. Decision policies are learned in a strictly local way, which makes the whole self-organizing process of collective learning highly robust in response to network changes. This fact can be understood by considering that at each node manager, the updating of pheromone estimates is based on the direct sampling experiences reported by the ants and is realized independently from estimates calculated in other nodes. This way of proceeding differs substantially from that followed in the most consolidated routing frameworks such as distance-vector and link-state routing (e.g., see Bertsekas & Gallager, 1992; Di Caro, 2004), which popular Internet routing protocols such as the already mentioned RIP and OSPF are derived from. Distance-vector strategies are based on information bootstrapping. Bootstrapping is a technique that characterizes dynamic programming (Sutton & Barto, 1998). Nodes derive an estimate for the cost of a path to a destination by combining the cost estimate provided by the next node on the path with the locally estimated cost of going to this next node. Basing cost estimates on those provided by neighboring nodes is a powerful technique that can save a lot of computation. However, the mutual dependence of the cost estimates used by the nodes also makes the system vulnerable. Especially when the network is highly dynamic, bootstrapping can be harmful. In fact, since each local estimate is propagated step by step throughout the whole network and used in turn to build new estimates, each estimate that becomes incorrect due to local changes will affect the entire network and the new correct estimate has to be repropagated to all the network nodes. An analogous problem can arise in link-state algorithms, where each node holds a complete representation of the entire network in terms of a weighted graph. Each node builds an estimate of the cost of its local links (e.g., in terms of queue length) and periodically floods these estimates into the network. On reception of cost estimates, each node updates the weights of its network representation and recalculates minimum cost paths to define its local routing policy. Again, the approach is very effective in the quasi-stationary case but suffers from the same problems of bootstrapping-based algorithms in case of dynamic situations.

On the other hand, in ACR's approach, which is termed Monte Carlo learning in reinforcement learning jargon (Sutton & Barto, 1998), routing information is at no point derived from estimates provided by other nodes. This approach is expected to be less effective in the (uncommon) quasi-stationary case while it is a lot more robust when the system is highly dynamic since no unnecessary dependencies among node policies are created. ACR is also robust when it comes to losses of control packets (ants). In fact, if an ant gets lost or has to be discarded because of hardware errors

or buffer overflows, the impact on the system is minimal. It will likely just result in a slower update of the pheromone tables for a single specific source-destination pair.

Monitoring and Adaptivity

Passive and *active network monitoring* is the key to obtain adaptive behavior. In ACR algorithms, node managers are able to progressively adapt the used decision policies to network changes precisely through continual monitoring. Clearly, monitoring creates an overhead, especially in terms of the repeated generation of ant agents. The challenge of any ACR implementation consists of finding the right trade-off between the rate and the amount of gathered information and the resulting overhead in order to obtain good and scalable performance.

Active monitoring has rarely been implemented in routing strategies precisely due to its potential negative impact in terms of overhead (e.g., see the use of packet-probing techniques for capacity estimation in Dovrolis, Ramanathan, & Moore, 2004). On the other hand, later in this chapter we show that even in the challenging environment of *mobile ad hoc networks*, we could define in our AntHocNet algorithm an effective way to minimize the overhead due to active monitoring by ant agents while providing at the same time state-of-the-art performance.

Multiple Paths, Stochastic Data Routing, Resource Optimization, and Scalability

Routing tables in ACR algorithms consist of pheromone entries. This means that for each destination of interest d and for each neighbor node n, an estimate of expected quality of the path that goes through n to eventually reach d is available at the nodes. In practice, this means that for each pair of source and destination nodes, a *bundle of paths*, each with an associated estimated quality, is available as the result of the ant path sampling activities. Both the paths and their estimates are continually updated to track network changes. This path bundle can be used to implement multiple path routing of data packets and to provide backup paths in case of sudden changes or failures in the network. Multiple path routing is realized through probabilistic routing schemes, whereby for each data packet a next hop is chosen with a probability that is relative to the hop's pheromone value. This is similar to the way ants are forwarded, with the difference being that for data packets, the preference for the best paths is normally increased so that the lowest quality paths are avoided. Concurrent probabilistic spreading of data packets across the best multiple paths results in automatic load balancing and performance optimization (e.g., throughput increase). When the path bundle is used for backup purposes, the adaptive response of the system to sudden changes is expected to be robust and smooth. Both different uses of the available path bundle result also in good scalability of the system since they allow thorough resource optimization.

Generally speaking, the use of multiple paths is by no means free of problems. Issues such as the number of paths to use, path selection criteria (which is particularly challenging in interfering wireless environments), and data distribution policy are very complex to deal with at design time (e.g., see Nelakuditi & Zhang, 2001). Again, in the next section, we show through experimental results that AntHocNet's design can deal in a rather automatic way with these issues using the adaptive quality estimates associated with each available path by means of pheromone values.

AntHocNet: ACO for Routing in Mobile Ad Hoc Networks

In the remainder of this section, we describe an example of how the ACR framework can be applied to develop an adaptive routing algorithm for a specific network environment. We focus on best-effort routing in MANETs. MANETs form a particularly challenging type of network in which all the properties of modern networks mentioned earlier in our wish list, such as adaptivity, robustness, decentralized working, and so forth, are essential. The ACR algorithm we describe is AntHocNet. This algorithm has been thoroughly discussed and evaluated in a number of recent papers (Babaoglu et al., 2006; Di Caro et al., 2004, 2005a, 2005b, 2006; Ducatelle, Di Caro, & Gambardella, 2005a, 2005b, 2006, 2007). Here we provide a summary description of its behavior. The interested reader can find more detailed descriptions and discussions in the given references.

In MANETs, all nodes are mobile and can enter and leave the network at any time. They communicate with each other via wireless connections. All nodes are equal and there is neither centralized control nor fixed infrastructure (e.g., ground antennas) to rely on. There are no designated routers: All nodes can serve as routers for each other, and data packets are forwarded from node to node in a multihop fashion. The wireless channel is shared among the peer nodes and the access must be arbitrated according to a medium access control (MAC) layer protocol. MANETs represent some of the most dynamic, constrained, and complex examples of real-world networks. MANET control definitely needs algorithms that meet the requirements of the wish list we proposed in the introduction. MANETs can find their application in a variety of scenarios needing the creation of a network on the fly due to the unavailability of a connecting infrastructure. This is a situation typical in battlefields, disaster or remote areas, or in geographically challenging areas where specific communities of users must temporarily interact.

Providing reliable data transport in MANETs is quite difficult, and a lot of research is being devoted to this. The routing problem is especially very hard to deal with due to the constant changes in topology and traffic, and due to the limited bandwidth that is available from the shared wireless channel. In recent years, a number of routing algorithms have been proposed (e.g., see Broch, Maltz, Johnson, Hu, & Jetcheva, 1998; Royer & Toh, 1999; Stojmenovic, 2002), but even current state-of-the-art protocols are quite unreliable in terms of data delivery and delay.

The main challenge when developing ant-based routing schemes for MANETs consists of finding the right balance between the rates of ant generation and the resulting network overhead. In fact, on the one hand, repeated path sampling is at the very core of ACR algorithms: More ant agents means that an increased and more up-to-date amount of routing information is gathered, possibly resulting in a better adaptation of the routing policy at the nodes. On the other hand, an excessive generation of routing packets can cause network congestion, thereby leading to a decrease rather than an increase in performance. This is due to the fact that the radio channel is a shared resource, such that multiple radio collisions can happen in case of high traffic load in dense node areas, with consequent underutilization of the nominal bandwidth. In the final part of this section, we show by reporting experimental results that AntHocNet's design is such that a good balance can actually be achieved while providing at the same time good adaptivity with respect to traffic and topology, as well as good robustness and scalability.

Algorithm Description

In MANET jargon, AntHocNet is termed a hybrid algorithm since it makes use of both reactive and proactive strategies to establish routing paths. It is reactive in the sense that a node manager only starts gathering routing information for a specific destination when a local traffic session needs to communicate with this destination. It is proactive because from the moment that the communication starts, and for as long as it continues, the nodes

proactively try to keep the routing information related to the ongoing flow up to date with network changes. The reactive component of the algorithm deals with the phase of path setup and is focused on the generation of ant agents to find a good initial path for the new data session. The proactive component of the algorithm implements path maintenance and improvement. During the course of a session it proactively adapts the paths of the session to network changes. Path maintenance and improvement is realized by a combination of ant path sampling and slow-rate pheromone diffusion: The routing information obtained via ant path sampling is spread between the node managers and is used to update the pheromone tables according to an information bootstrapping scheme that in turn provides main guidance for the exploration behavior of the ants. *Link failures* are dealt with using a local path repair process or via the generation of ant agents carrying explicit notification information. Stochastic decisions are used both for ant exploration and to spread data packets over multiple paths. In the following we provide a concise description of each of the components of the algorithm.

Pheromone Metrics Used to Define Path Quality

As in any ACR algorithm, paths are implicitly defined by the pheromone variables contained in pheromone tables, which play the role of routing tables. An entry $\tau_{nd}^i \in R$ in the pheromone table of node i contains a value indicating the estimated goodness of going from i over neighbor n to reach destination d.

In principle, in the complex MANET environment several aspects can be used to define how good a path is: the number of hops, end-to-end delay, signal quality, congestion level, battery usage, node speed, and so forth. AntHocNet defines the pheromone variables in terms of a combination of these metrics. In particular, the pheromone variables used in the experiments reported later make use of a combination of a number of hops and signal-to-noise ratio (for a discussion on the use of different combinations of metrics and on their relative evaluation, see Ducatelle et al., 2006). This means that the algorithm tries to find paths characterized by a minimal number of hops and good signal quality between adjacent nodes. The use of such composite pheromone values allows us to optimize multiple objectives simultaneously, which can be very important in complex networks.

Reactive Path Setup

When a source node s starts a communication session with a destination node d, and no pheromone information is available about the path to d, the node manager needs to gather long-range information about possible paths. Therefore, it broadcasts a reactive forward ant. This constitutes a reactive approach to ant generation, aimed at improving the efficiency of the system by focusing on gathering information that is strictly necessary. Broadcasting is equivalent to replicating the ant agent to all neighboring nodes. At each node, the ant is either unicast or further broadcast, according to whether or not the current node has pheromone information for d. If pheromone information is available, the ant makes use of a random proportional rule to select its next hop. Each neighbor n is given a selection probability P_{nd} which depends on the relative goodness of n as a next hop as expressed by the value of the associated pheromone variable $\tau^{i;nd}$:

$$P_{nd} = \frac{(t_{nd}^i)^\beta}{\sum_{j \in N_d^i} (t_{jd}^i)^\beta}, \beta \geq 1, \qquad (3)$$

where N_d^i is the set of neighbors of i over which a path to d is known, and β is a parameter that controls the exploratory behavior of the ants. The expression for P_{nd} is equivalent to the generic one for ACO described in equation (2). If no pheromone is available, the ant is broadcast.

Due to subsequent broadcasts, many duplicate copies of the same ant travel to the destination. A node manager that receives multiple copies of the same ant only accepts the first and discards the other.

Each forward ant keeps a list of the nodes it has visited. Upon arrival at the destination d, it is converted into a backward ant, which travels back to the source retracing the path. At each intermediate node i, coming from neighbor n, the ant information is used to update the entry τ_{nd}^i in i's pheromone table. The way the entry is updated depends on the path quality metrics used to define pheromone variables. For instance, in the simplest case when the pheromone is expressed using only the number of hops as a measure of path goodness, at each hop the backward ant increments an internal hop counter and the inverse of this value is used to locally assign the value τ_d^i which is used to update the pheromone variable τ_{nd}^i as follows:

$$\tau_{nd}^i = \gamma\tau_{nd}^i + (1-\delta)\tau_d^i, \delta \in [0,1] \qquad (4)$$

For different metrics, the calculation of τ_d^i is more complex but follows the same logic. For instance, if delay is used, the ant needs to incrementally calculate at each node a robust estimate of the expected delay to reach the destination (see Di Caro et al., 2005; Ducatelle et al., 2005).

Once the backward ant has returned, a single path is made available between source and destination. During the course of the communication session, more paths are added via the proactive path maintenance and exploration mechanism discussed next.

Proactive Path Maintenance and Exploration

During the course of a communication session, managers at source nodes periodically send out proactive forward ants to update the information about currently used paths and to try to find new and potentially better paths. They follow phero-mone and update pheromone tables in the same way as reactive forward ants do. Such continual sampling of paths corresponds to a proactive approach of ant generation, with the aim to keep monitoring the situation along the used paths. However, in MANETs the ant sending frequency that is needed to faithfully keep track of the constant network changes is in general too high compared to the available bandwidth. Moreover, to find entirely new paths, blind explorations through random walks or broadcasts are required. Therefore, we keep the ant-sending rate low and integrate ant sampling actions with a lightweight information bootstrapping process called phero-mone diffusion. This process provides a second way of updating pheromones on existing paths, while at the same time it can provide useful in-formation to guide exploratory ant behavior.

In the pheromone diffusion process, each node n periodically and asynchronously broadcasts beacon messages. In each beacon message, it includes a list of destinations it has information about, indicating for each of these destinations d its best pheromone value τ_{m*d}^n. A node manager at node i receiving such a message from a node n first of all registers that n is its neighbor. This is a form of local monitoring performed by the node managers. Then, for each destination d listed in the message, it derives an estimate of the goodness of going from i to d over n by combining the cost of hopping from i to n with the reported pheromone value τ_{m*d}^n. We call the obtained estimate β_{nd}^i bootstrapped pheromone, since it is built up by bootstrapping on the value of a path quality estimate received from an adjacent node. The bootstrapped pheromone can in turn be forwarded in the next beacon message sent out by n. The concurrent iteration of this pro-cess by all the nodes gives rise to a bootstrapped pheromone field over the MANET. As has been pointed out earlier, this is the typical way of cal-culating estimates implemented by the routing approaches based on dynamic programming, such

as the class of distributed Bellman-Ford routing algorithms (Bertsekas & Gallager, 1992) and the reinforcement learning routing algorithms derived from Q-learning (Sutton & Barto, 1998). Bootstrapping is an efficient process, but it is not appropriate for highly dynamic environments. Also, in our case, due to the slow multistep forwarding, a bootstrapped pheromone does not provide the most accurate view of the current situation and has difficulties to properly track the distributed changes in the network. We can say that the pheromone diffusion process is efficient and lightweight, but gives potentially unreliable information. The key element in AntHocNet is that pheromone diffusion is not the only source of routing information, but rather serves as a second-ary process to complement the ant-based Monte Carlo path sampling process. It is important to take care when and how to use the bootstrapped pheromone information.

For path maintenance, a bootstrapped phero-mone is used directly. If i already has a pheromone entry τ_{nd}^i in its routing table for destination d going over neighbor n, we know that the path from i to d over n has in the past been sampled by ants. This path can therefore be considered reliable. b_{nd}^i is then just treated as an update of the goodness estimate of this reliable path, and is used directly to replace τ_{nd}^i. This way, the pheromone on current paths is kept up to date.

On the other hand, for path exploration, a boot-strapped pheromone is used indirectly only after an explicit checking. If i does not yet have a value for τ_{nd}^i in its pheromone table, b_{nd}^i could indicate a possible new path from i to d over n. However, this path has never been explicitly tried out by an ant, so that it is unclear whether the path has not disappeared during the information forwarding through the slow multistep pheromone diffusion process, or if it does not contain undetected loops or dangling links. It is therefore not safe to use for data forwarding before being checked. This is the task assigned to proactive forward ants, which make use of both regular and bootstrapped pheromones on their way to the destination. They check out promising pheromone, and if the associated path is there and has the expected good quality, they can turn it into a regular path available for data. This increases the number of paths available for data routing, which grows to a full mesh, and allows the algorithm to exploit new opportunities in the ever changing topology.

The approach followed in this proactive path maintenance and exploration process and the earlier described reactive path setup process illustrates the generality of ACR node managers. Rather than mere ant generators, they are general learning agents, which can use different monitoring and learning strategies to obtain their goals. In the case of AntHocNet, reactive and proactive ant-based Monte Carlo sampling is combined with information bootstrapping to obtain adaptivity, reliability, and efficiency.

Stochastic Data Routing

The path setup phase together with the proactive path improvement actions create a mesh of multiple paths between source and destination nodes, expressed in a distributed way in the pheromone tables of the nodes of the network. Data are forwarded according to a stochastic policy depending on these pheromone values. When a node has multiple hops for the destination d of the data, it randomly selects one of them, with probability P_{nd}, which is calculated in the same way as for reactive forward ants in equation (3), but with a higher exponent β, in order to be greedy with respect to the better paths.

In the experiments, β was set to 20 for data. Setting the routing exponent so high means that if several paths have similar quality, data will be spread over them. However, if one path is clearly better than another, it will almost always be preferred. According to this strategy, we do not have to choose a priori how many paths to use: their number will be automatically selected in function of their quality.

If estimates are kept up to date (which is done using the pheromone diffusion and ant sampling processes), the dynamic availability of multiple paths leads to automatic load balancing, the optimization of resource utilization, and an increase in throughput. This is a common characteristic in ACR implementations.

Link Failures

Nodes can detect link failures (e.g., a neighbor has moved away) through local monitoring. Specifically, link failures are assumed to have taken place when unicast transmissions (of data packets or ants) fail, or when expected pheromone diffusion messages were not received. When a neighbor is assumed to have disappeared, the node manager takes a number of actions. In the first place, it removes the neighbor from its neighbor list and all the associated entries from its routing table.

Further actions depend on the event that was associated with the discovered disappearance. If the event was a failed transmission of a control packet, the node broadcasts a link failure notification message. Such a message contains a list of the destinations to which the node lost its best path, and the new best routing estimates for this destination (if it still has entries for the destination). All its neighbors receive the notification and update their pheromone table using the new estimates. If they in turn lost their best or their only path to a destination due to the failure, they broadcast the notification further, until all concerned nodes are notified of the new situation.

If the event was the failed transmission of a data packet, the node does not include the destination of the data packet in question in the link failure notification. For this destination, the node starts a local route repair process. The node manager broadcasts a route repair ant that travels to the involved destination like a reactive forward ant: It follows available routing information when it can, and is broadcast otherwise. One important difference is that it has a maximum number of broadcasts (which we set to 2 in our experiments), so that its proliferation is limited. The node waits for a certain amount of time (in the experiments it was set to 5 times the estimated end-to-end delay of the lost path), and if no backward repair ant is received by then, it concludes that it was not possible to find an alternative path to the destination. Packets that were in the meantime buffered for this destination are discarded, and the node sends a new link failure notification about the lost destination.

Experimental Results

AntHocNet's performance has been extensively evaluated against state-of-the-art algorithms under a range of different MANET scenarios for both open space and realistic urban conditions. We have studied the behavior of the algorithm under different conditions for network size, connectivity, change rate, data traffic patterns, and node mobility. Performance was measured in terms of data delivery ratio, end-to-end packet delay, and delay jitter as measures of effectiveness, and routing overhead in the number of control packets per successfully delivered data packet as a measure of efficiency. Here we report only a small subset of these results with the aim of supporting the claim that AntHocNet shows superior performance in terms of general efficacy and efficiency, and in terms of adaptivity, robustness, and scalability. The reader is referred to the mentioned AntHocNet references for the full set of results (some of the results presented here, namely, Figure 5 up to Figure 10, have appeared earlier in Babaoglu et al., 2006).

All experiments are carried out in simulation using QualNet (Scalable Network Technologies, Inc., 2006), a commercial state-of-the-art simulator for telecommunications networks. The open-space scenarios used in the tests reported on here were all derived from the same base scenario. In this scenario, 100 nodes are randomly placed in an open-space area of 2400×800 m^2.

Each experiment is run for 900 seconds. Data traffic is generated by 20 constant bit rate (CBR) sources sending four 64-byte packets per second using UDP at the transport layer. Each source starts sending at a random time between 0 and 180 seconds after the start of the simulation, and keeps sending until the end. A two-ray path-loss model is used in the radio propagation model. The radio range of the nodes is 250 meters, and the data rate is 2 Mbit/s. At the MAC layer we use the IEEE 802.11b DCF protocol, as is common practice in MANET research. The MANET nodes move according to the random waypoint (RWP) mobility model (Johnson & Maltz, 1996): They choose a random destination point and a random speed, move to the chosen point with the chosen speed, and rest there for a fixed amount of pause time before they choose a new destination and speed. The speed is chosen between 0 and 10m/s, and the pause time is 30 seconds.

The urban scenario models a realistic urban environment where a MANET could be actually deployed and used. The scenario is derived from the street organization of downtown Lugano, Switzerland. Figure 4 shows the city map we considered as a reference. It corresponds to an area of $1561 \times 997 m^2$, which covers most of downtown Lugano. Streets define the open spaces where nodes are free to move. Buildings are inaccessible to the nodes and basically play the role of obstacles that put constraints on agent movements and shield radio signal propagation. Three classes of nodes live in the scenario: nodes moving at typical urban car speed, nodes simulating walking people, and nonmobile users. Most of the basic settings used in the open-space scenarios have been transferred directly to the urban one. The characteristics and complexity of the urban scenario are quite different from those of the open-space ones. Here we report just a few results for the urban case with the aim of showing that the ACR approach is effective over radically different classes of network scenarios. The interested reader can find more experimental results in Di Caro et al. (2006), and Ducatelle et al. (2007).

To assess the performance of our algorithm relative to the state of the art in the field, we compare each time to *ad hoc on-demand distance vector routing* (AODV) (Perkins & Royer, 1999) and *optimized link state routing* (OLSR) (Clausen, Jacquet, Laouiti, Muhlethaler, Qayyum, & Viennot, 2001), two important reference algorithms in the field. AODV is a reactive algorithm, while OLSR is based on a proactive strategy. All points reported in the data plots are the average over 15 simulation runs with different random placements of the nodes.

Scalability: Varying the Number of Nodes in Open Space

We increase the number of nodes from 100 to 800 nodes. The MANET area was increased accordingly to keep the node density constant. The results are presented in Figure 5 and Figure 6. For

OLSR we report only results up to 500 nodes as simulation run times became prohibitively large beyond that, and performance was very low. We can see that AntHocNet's advantage over both other algorithms grows for all measures of effectiveness for larger networks. This is an indication that it is a scalable algorithm. Also, in terms of efficiency, AntHocNet seems to be scalable: While its overhead is comparable to that of the other algorithms for small networks, it increases less quickly and is much lower for the larger networks.

Adaptivity to Topological Changes: Varying the Pause Time in Open Space

In this set of experiments, we study the effect of increased mobility by changing the RWP pause time. This has a direct effect on the change rate of the network topology. Results are reported in Figure 7 and Figure 8. AntHocNet's average end-to-end delay is about half that of AODV for

Figure 4. The map of the city of Lugano, Switzerland, used for the experiments in the urban scenario

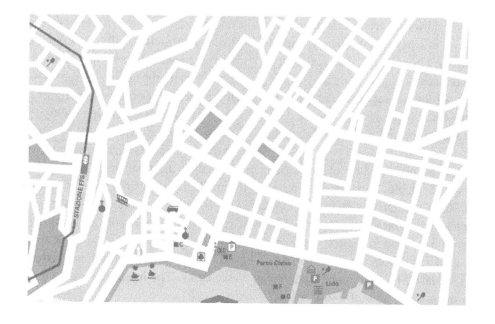

Figure 5. Average delay (left) and delivery ratio (right) for an increasing number of nodes

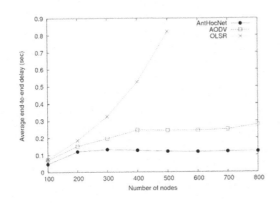 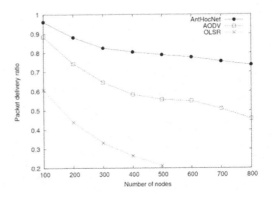

Figure 6. Average jitter (left) and routing overhead (right) for an increasing number of nodes

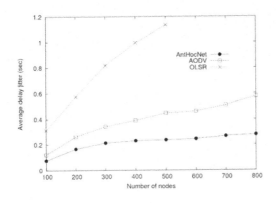 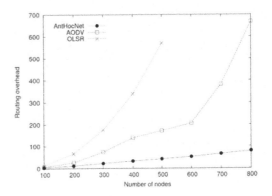

low pause times, and around one third for high pause times. In terms of delivery ratio, the difference is less striking but still significant. OLSR is always performing very badly. Also, in terms of jitter, we can see a large advantage of AntHocNet over the two other algorithms. Again, the better performance of AntHocNet is not paid back in terms of higher routing overhead. These results seem to indicate the effectiveness of AntHocNet to adapt robustly to very different rates of topological changes inside the network.

Scalability and Adaptivity to Traffic Loads: Varying the Number of Data Sessions in Open Space

Here we report the results for varying the total number of active data traffic sessions (Figure 9 and Figure 10). In this way we aim to study the response of the algorithms to an increase in data load. This gives important indications about both the scalability of the algorithms with respect to data traffic, and their ability to cope with a very dynamic situation at the local level caused by the

Figure 7. Average delay (left) and delivery ratio (right) for increasing pause times

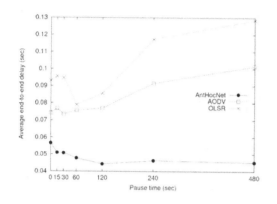 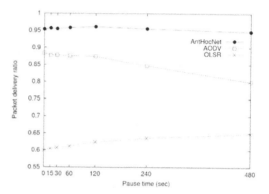

Figure 8. Average jitter (left) and routing overhead (right) for increasing pause times

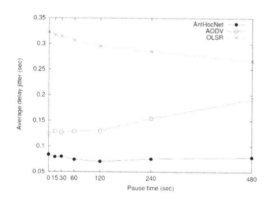 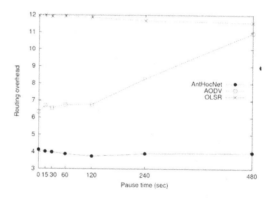

continual transmission of large amounts of data packets. Also, this set of experiments shows a significantly superior performance of AntHocNet with respect to both AODV and OLSR for the considered metrics. These results provide a further validation of the characteristics of adaptivity and scalability of the approach.

Scalability: Varying the Number of Nodes in the Urban Scenario

We increase the number of nodes in the urban scenario from 200 to 500 nodes. The total number of active CBR traffic sessions is kept constant at 30, as well as the number of nodes moving at car speed, which is fixed at 25; 30% of the nodes are

Figure 9. Average delay (left) and delivery ratio (right) for an increasing number of data sessions

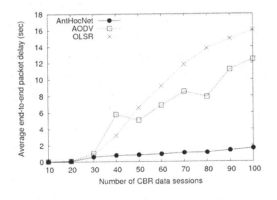 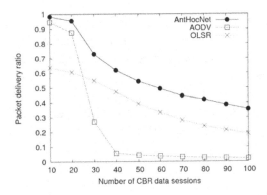

Figure 10. Average jitter (left) and routing overhead (right) for an increasing number of data sessions

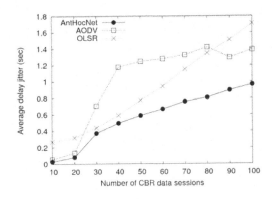 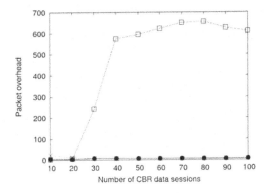

nonmobile. Basically, increasing the number of nodes in the radio-constrained urban scenario makes the task easier since it brings more local connectivity. However, the algorithm has to show the ability to profit from the increase in connectivity, as well as the ability to deal with the radio and movement constraints imposed by the urban structure. Results are shown in Figure 11 and Figure 12. OLSR's performance is not reported since in all the experiments we carried out in

the urban environment, OLSR was performing very poorly. We can see that the difference in performance between AODV and AntHocNet is this time approximately constant but still always clearly in favor of AntHocNet. Again, also this set of experiments, run in a scenario with quite different characteristics from the previous ones, confirms the good scalability and adaptivity of our approach, as well as its overall robustness in providing superior performance over a wide range of different scenarios.

CONCLUSION AND FUTURE TRENDS

In this chapter we have considered the problem of designing novel routing algorithms for complex, dynamic, and heterogeneous modern networks. In the introduction we stated a wish list of desirable properties a network control algorithm should have in order to cope with this high complexity. We need algorithms that are as much as possible

adaptive, *robust*, *scalable*, and *self-organizing*. Our claim is that a biologically inspired framework like ACO can provide the basic guidelines to implement in a relatively straightforward way novel routing algorithms possessing precisely these characteristics. We described the biological process from which ACO was derived, that is, the pheromone-mediated ability of the ants in ant colonies to find in a totally distributed and

Figure 11. Average delay (left) and delivery ratio (right) for an increasing number of nodes in the urban scenario

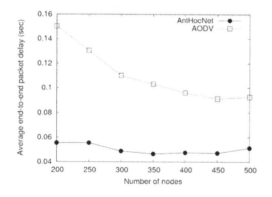
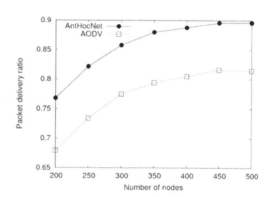

Figure 12. Average jitter (left) and routing overhead (right) for an increasing number of nodes in the urban scenario

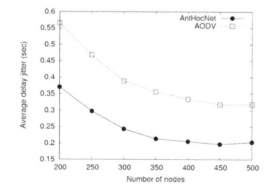
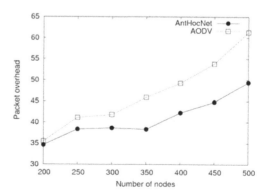

dynamic way shortest paths joining their nest with sources of food. We defined ACO after this *shortest path behavior*. We described it as a general recipe to solve combinatorial optimization problems by repeated construction of multiple solutions according to a step-by-step stochastic decision policy depending on real-valued variables that play the role of pheromone in ant colonies. The outcomes of the solution generation process are used in turn to adaptively modify the values of these pheromone variables. The aim is to *learn a decision policy* that eventually allows the generation of good solutions for the optimization problem at hand. We showed that this way of proceeding is particularly suitable to attack *routing problems* in network environments. Then, starting from the general ACO, we derived ACR, a specialized framework for the design of autonomic routing systems based on adaptive learning components. We discussed the general properties expected from a properly designed ACR algorithm, and we pointed out that it would be relatively easy to obtain the desirable properties stated in the wish list. To show this in practice, we have described and thoroughly evaluated AntHocNet, a routing algorithm for *mobile ad hoc networks*, which form a very complex and dynamic class of networks. AntHocNet's performance was evaluated in both open-space and urban scenarios. The experimental results seem to strongly suggest that the algorithm is able to provide superior performance and to show those characteristics of adaptivity, scalability, robustness, and self-organization that we were looking for.

In this chapter, we have not provided any formal justification or theoretical analysis of our claims. Therefore, we can only speak on the basis of empirical evidence. However, the amount of experiments that we and other researchers in the field have carried out so far over a large number of different network scenarios provides significant statistical evidence of the overall efficacy and effectiveness of the ACR general guidelines for the design of state-of-the-art routing algorithms

showing autonomic properties.

In terms of future work, we can see two important research directions. In the first place, it is important to carry out theoretical work in the direction of understanding under which dynamic conditions an adaptive learning approach like ACR is really useful. In fact, if the system dynamics are too fast or hectic to be tracked and in some sense understood in a distributed way, it is probably better to rely on simple purely reactive schemes instead of trying to collect information that becomes too rapidly out of date. On the other hand, if the system is rather static, nonadaptive approaches might prove to perform better. The second important research direction is of practical nature. Most of the protocols that are currently in use at the diferent layers, like TCP (transmission-control protocol), were not designed to interact with highly adaptive or probabilistic schemes. Therefore, to really bring adaptivity in modern networks, it will likely be necessary to rewrite or radically modify many existing network protocols. This is at the moment a major impediment for the real-world implementation and use of novel autonomic network controllers like AntHocNet.

REFERENCES

Babaoglu, O., Canright, G., Deutsch, A., Di Caro, G. A., Ducatelle, F., Gambardella, L. M., et al. (2006). Design patterns from biology for distributed computing. *ACM Transactions on Autonomous and Adaptive Systems (TAAS), 1*(1).

Baran, B., & Sosa, R. (2000). *A new approach for AntNet routing.* Proceedings of the Ninth International Conference on Computer Communications Networks, Las Vegas, NV.

Baras, J., & Mehta, H. (2003). A probabilistic emergent routing algorithm for mobile ad hoc networks. *WiOpt03: Modeling and Optimization in Mobile, Ad Hoc and Wireless Networks.*

Bertsekas, D. (1995). *Dynamic programming and optimal control* (Vol. 1-2). Athena Scientific.

Bertsekas, D., & Gallager, R. (1992). *Data networks*. Prentice-Hall.

Bishop, C. M. (1995). *Neural networks for pattern recognition*. Oxford University Press.

Bonabeau, E., Dorigo, M., & Theraulaz, G. (1999). *Swarm intelligence: From natural to artificial systems*. Oxford University Press.

Bonabeau, E., Henaux, F., Guérin, S., Snyers, D., Kuntz, P., & Theraulaz, G. (1998). Routing in telecommunication networks with "smart" ant-like agents. *Proceedings of IATA'98, Second International Workshop on Intelligent Agents for Telecommunication Applications*.

Broch, J., Maltz, D. A., Johnson, D. B., Hu, Y.-C., & Jetcheva, J. (1998). A performance comparison of multi-hop wireless ad hoc network routing protocols. *Proceedings of the Fourth Annual ACM/IEEE International Conference on Mobile Computing and Networking (MobiCom98)*.

Câmara, D., & Loureiro, A. (2000). A novel routing algorithm for ad hoc networks. *Proceedings of the 33rd Hawaii International Conference on System Sciences*.

Carrillo, L., Marzo, J., Fàbrega, L., Vila, P., & Guadall, C. (2004). Ant colony behaviour as routing mechanism to provide quality of service. *Ants Algorithms: Proceedings of ANTS 2004, Fourth International Workshop on Ant Algorithms*.

Clausen, T., Jacquet, P., Laouiti, A., Muhlethaler, P., Qayyum, A., & Viennot, L. (2001). Optimized link-state routing protocol. *Proceedings of the IEEE International Multi Topic Conference (INMIC)*.

Deneubourg, J.-L., Aron, S., Goss, S., & Pasteels, J.-M. (1990). The self-organizing exploratory pattern of the Argentine ant. *Journal of Insect Behavior, 3*, 159-168.

Di Caro, G. A. (2004). *Ant colony optimization and its application to adaptive routing in telecommunication networks*. Unpublished doctoral dissertation, Faculté des Sciences Appliquées, Université Libre de Bruxelles, Brussels, Belgium.

Di Caro, G. A., & Dorigo, M. (1997). Adaptive learning of routing tables in communication networks. *Proceedings of the Italian Workshop on Machine Learning*.

Di Caro, G. A., & Dorigo, M. (1998a). AntNet: Distributed stigmergetic control for communications networks. *Journal of Artificial Intelligence Research (JAIR), 9*, 317-365.

Di Caro, G. A., & Dorigo, M. (1998b). Extending AntNet for best-effort quality-of-service routing. *ANTS'98: From Ant Colonies to Artificial Ants. First International Workshop on Ant Colony Optimization*.

Di Caro, G. A., Ducatelle, F., & Gambardella, L. M. (2004). AntHocNet: An ant-based hybrid routing algorithm for mobile ad hoc networks. In *Lecture notes in computer science: Vol. 3242. Proceedings of Parallel Problem Solving from Nature (PPSN) VIII* (pp. 461-470). Springer-Verlag.

Di Caro, G. A., Ducatelle, F., & Gambardella, L. M. (2005a). AntHocNet: An adaptive nature-inspired algorithm for routing in mobile ad hoc networks. *European Transactions on Telecommunications, 16*(5), 443-455.

Di Caro, G. A., Ducatelle, F., & Gambardella, L. M. (2005b). Swarm intelligence for routing in mobile ad hoc networks. *Proceedings of the IEEE Swarm Intelligence Symposium*.

Di Caro, G. A., Ducatelle, F., & Gambardella, L. M. (2006). *Studies of routing performance in a city-like testbed for mobile ad hoc networks* (Tech. Rep. No. 07-06). Lugano, Switzerland: Istituto Dalle Molle di Studi sull'Intelligenza Artificiale.

Di Caro, G. A., & Vasilakos, T. (2000). Ant-SELA: Ant-agents and stochastic automata learn adaptive routing tables for QoS routing in ATM networks. *ANTS2000: From Ant Colonies to Artificial Ants. Second International Workshop on Ant Colony Optimization.*

Doi, S., & Yamamura, M. (2000). BntNetL: Evaluation of its performance under congestion. *Journal of IEICE B.*

Dorigo, M., & Di Caro, G. A. (1999). The ant colony optimization meta-heuristic. In D. Corne, M. Dorigo, & F. Glover (Eds.), *New ideas in optimization* (pp. 11-32). McGraw-Hill.

Dorigo, M., Di Caro, G. A., & Gambardella, L. M. (1999). Ant algorithms for discrete optimization. *Artificial Life, 5*(2), 137-172.

Dorigo, M., & Gambardella, L. M. (1997). Ant colony system: A cooperative learning approach to the traveling salesman problem. *IEEE Transactions on Evolutionary Computation, 1*(1), 53-66.

Dorigo, M., & Stützle, T. (2004). *Ant colony optimization.* Cambridge, MA: MIT Press.

Dovrolis, C., Ramanathan, P., & Moore, D. (2004). Packet-dispersion techniques and a capacity-estimation methodology. *IEEE/ACM Transactions on Networking, 12*(6), 963-977.

Ducatelle, F., Di Caro, G. A., & Gambardella, L. M. (2005a). Ant agents for hybrid multipath routing in mobile ad hoc networks. *Proceedings of the Second Annual Conference on Wireless on Demand Network Systems and Services (WONS).*

Ducatelle, F., Di Caro, G. A., & Gambardella, L. M. (2005b). Using ant agents to combine reactive and proactive strategies for routing in mobile ad hoc networks. *International Journal of Computational Intelligence and Applications, 5*(2), 169-184.

Ducatelle, F., Di Caro, G. A., & Gambardella, L. M. (2006). An analysis of the different components of the AntHocNet routing algorithm. In *Lecture notes in computer science: Vol. 4150. Proceedings of ANTS 2006, Fifth International Workshop on Ant Algorithms and Swarm Intelligence* (pp. 37-48). Springer-Verlag.

Ducatelle, F., Di Caro, G. A., & Gambardella, L. M. (2007). *A study on the use of MANETs in an urban environment* (Tech. Rep. No. 01-07). Lugano, Switzerland: Istituto Dalle Molle di Studi sull'Intelligenza Artificiale.

Fogel, D. B. (1995). *Evolutionary computation.* IEEE Press.

Freeman, R. L. (2004). *Telecommunication system engineering.* Wiley-IEEE Press.

Gallager, R. (1977). A minimum delay routing algorithm using distributed computation. *IEEE Transactions on Communications, 25,* 73-84.

Gallego-Schmid, M. (1999). Modified AntNet: Software application in the evaluation and management of a telecommunication network. *Genetic and Evolutionary Computation Conference (GECCO-99).*

Garey, M. R., & Johnson, D. S. (1979). *Computers and intractability.* W. H. Freeman & Company.

Goss, S., Aron, S., Deneubourg, J.-L., & Pasteels, J. M. (1989). Self-organized shortcuts in the Argentine ant. *Naturwissenschaften, 76,* 579-581.

Grassé, P. P. (1959). La reconstruction du nid et les coordinations interindividuelles chez bellicositermes natalensis et cubitermes sp: La théorie de la stigmergie. Essai d'interprétation du comportement des termites constructeurs. *Insectes Sociaux, 6,* 41-81.

Günes, M., Sorges, U., & Bouazizi, I. (2002). ARA: The ant-colony based routing algorithm for MANETS. *Proceedings of the 2002 ICPP*

International Workshop on Ad Hoc Networks (IWAHN).

Heissenbüttel, M., & Braun, T. (2003). Ants-based routing in large scale mobile ad-hoc networks. *Kommunikation in Verteilten Systemen (KiVS03).*

Heusse, M., Snyers, D., Guérin, S., & Kuntz, P. (1998). Adaptive agent-driven routing and load balancing in communication networks. *Advances in Complex Systems, 1*(2).

Holland, J. (1975). *Adaptation in natural and artificial systems.* University of Michigan Press.

Hölldobler, B., & Wilson, E. O. (1990). *The ants.* Berlin, Germany: Springer-Verlag.

Hopfield, J., & Tank, D. W. (1985). Neural computation of decisions in optimization problems. *Biological Cybernetics, 52.*

Jain, P. (2002). *Validation of AntNet as a superior single path, single constrained routing protocol.* Unpublished master's thesis, Department of Computer Science and Engineering, University of Minnesota, MN.

Johnson, D. B., & Maltz, D. A. (1996). Dynamic source routing in ad hoc wireless networks. In *Mobile computing* (pp. 153-181). Kluwer.

Kassabalidis, I., Das, A., El-Sharkawi, M., Marks, R., II, Arabshahi, P., & Gray, A. (2002). Intelligent routing and bandwidth allocation in wireless networks. *Proceedings of the NASA Earth Science Technology Conference.*

Kassabalidis, I., El-Sharkawi, M., Marks, R., II, Arabshahi, P., & Gray, A. (2002). Swarm intelligence for routing in communication networks. *Proceedings of the IEEE World Congress on Computational Intelligence.*

Kephart, J., & Chess, D. (2003). The vision of autonomic computing. *IEEE Computer, 36*(1), 41-50.

Liu, L., & Feng, G. (2005). A novel ant colony based QoS-aware routing algorithm for MANETs. *Proceedings of the First International Conference on advances in Natural Computation (ICNC).*

Liu, Z., Kwiatkowska, M., & Constantinou, C. (2005). A self-organised emergent routing mechanism for mobile ad hoc networks. *European Transactions on Telecommunications (ETT), 16*(5).

Malkin, G. S. (1999). *RIP: An intra-domain routing protocol.* Addison-Wesley.

Marwaha, S., Tham, C. K., & Srinivasan, D. (2002). Mobile agents based routing protocol for mobile ad hoc networks. *Proceedings of IEEE Globecom.*

Matsuo, H., & Mori, K. (2001). Accelerated ants routing in dynamic networks. *2nd International Conference on Software Engineering, Artificial Intelligence, Networking and Parallel/Distributed Computing.*

Michalareas, T., & Sacks, L. (2001a). Link-state and ant-like algorithm behaviour for single-constrained routing. *IEEE Workshop on High Performance Switching and Routing (HPSR).*

Michalareas, T., & Sacks, L. (2001b). Stigmergic techniques for solving multi-constraint routing for packet networks. *Proceedings of the First International Conference on Networking (ICN), Part II.*

Moy, J. (1998). *OSPF anatomy of an Internet routing protocol.* Addison-Wesley.

Nelakuditi, S., & Zhang, Z.-L. (2001). On selection of paths for multipath routing. In *Lecture notes in computer science: Vol. 2092. Proceedings of the International Workshop on QoS (IWQoS)* (pp. 170-182).

Oida, K., & Kataoka, A. (1999). Lock-free Ant-Net and its evaluation for adaptiveness. *Journal of IEICE B.*

Oida, K., & Sekido, M. (2000). ARS: An efficient agent-based routing system for QoS guarantees. *Computer Communications*, 23(14-15). Papadimitriou, C. H., & Steiglitz, K. (1982). *Combinatorial optimization*. NJ: Prentice-Hall.

Perkins, C. E., & Royer, E. M. (1999). Ad-hoc on-demand distance vector routing. *Proceedings of the Second IEEE Workshop on Mobile Computing Systems and Applications*.

Rajagopalan, S., & Shen, C. (2005). ANSI: A unicast routing protocol for mobile ad hoc networks using swarm intelligence. *Proceedings of the International Conference on Artificial Intelligence*.

Rothkrantz, L., & van der Put, R. (1998). Routing in packet switched networks using agents. *First International Workshop on Ant Colony Optimization (ANTS)*.

Royer, E. M., & Toh, C.-K. (1999). A review of current routing protocols for ad hoc mobile wireless networks. *IEEE Personal Communications, 6*(2), 46-55.

Saha, D., & Mukherjee, A. (2003). Pervasive computing: A paradigm for the 21st century. *IEEE Computer, 36*(3).

Sandalidis, H., Mavromoustakis, K., & Stavroulakis, P. (2001). Performance measures of an ant based decentralized routing scheme for circuit switching communication networks. *Soft Computing, 5*(4).

Scalable Network Technologies, Inc. (2006). *Qualnet simulator, Version 3.9*. Retrieved from http://www.scalable-networks.com

Schoonderwoerd, R., Holland, O., Bruten, J., & Rothkrantz, L. (1996). Ant-based load balancing in telecommunications networks. *Adaptive Behavior, 5*(2), 169-207.

Sigel, E., Denby, B., & Heárat-Mascle, S. L. (2002). Application of ant colony optimization to adaptive routing in a LEO telecommunications satellite network. *Annals of Telecommunications, 57*(5-6).

Sim, K., & Sun, W. (2003). Ant colony optimization for routing and load-balancing: Survey and new directions. *IEEE Transactions on Systems, Man, and Cybernetics: Part A, 33*(5).

Steenstrup, M. E. (Ed.). (1995). *Routing in communications networks*. Prentice-Hall.

Stojmenovic, I. (Ed.). (2002). *Mobile ad-hoc networks*. John Wiley & Sons.

Subing, Z., & Zemin, L. (2001). A QoS routing algorithm based on ant algorithm. *Proceedings of the IEEE International Conference on Communications (ICC)*.

Subramanian, D., Druschel, P., & Chen, J. (1997). Ants and reinforcement learning: A case study in routing in dynamic networks. *Proceedings of IJCAI-97, International Joint Conference on Artificial Intelligence*.

Sutton, R. S., & Barto, A. G. (1998). *Reinforcement learning: An introduction*. Cambridge, MA: MIT Press.

Tadrus, S., & Bai, L. (2003). A QoS network routing algorithm using multiple pheromone tables. *Proceedings of the IEEE/WIC International Conference on Web Intelligence*.

Tanenbaum, A. (2002). *Computer networks*. Prentice-Hall.

Tatomir, B., & Rothkrantz, L. (2004). Dynamic routing in mobile wireless networks using abc-adhoc. *Proceedings of the Fourth International Workshop on Ant Colony Optimization and Swarm Intelligence (ANTS)*.

Theraulaz, G., & Bonabeau, E. (1999). A brief history of stigmergy. *Artificial Life, 5*, 97-116.

Vazirani, V. V. (2001). *Approximation algorithms*. Berlin, Germany: Springer-Verlag.

Walrand, J., & Varaiya, P. (1996). *High-performance communication networks*. Morgan Kaufmann.

White, T., Pagurek, B., & Oppacher, F. (1998). ASGA: Improving the ant system by integration with genetic algorithms. *Proceedings of the Third Genetic Programming Conference.*

Zhang, Y., Kuhn, L. D., & Fromherz, M. P. J. (2004). Improvements on ant routing for sensor networks. *Proceedings of the Fourth International Workshop on Ant Colony Optimization and Swarm Intelligence (ANTS).*

Zheng, X., Guo, W., & Liu, R. (2004). An ant-based distributed routing algorithm for ad-hoc networks. *Proceedings of the International Conference on Communications, Circuits and Systems (ICCCAS).*

Chapter XIII
Cryptography, Delayed Dynamical Systems, and Secure Communication

Santo Banerjee
JIS College of Engineering, India

Asesh Roy Chowdhury
Jadavpur University, India

ABSTRACT

The idea of using synchronized chaotic circuits for sending and receiving signals when they are masked using classical cryptography is extended to the case of delayed dynamical systems. It is observed that due to the existence of the delayed parameter τ, the mode of communication is more secure due to the fact that the delayed parameter is changed at a fixed interval by both the sender and receiver. It is shown how an extended set of secret keys could be constructed to send a message containing both numerical and alphabetical sequences. Again, a secure communication scheme is also discussed based on the synchronization of two coupled delayed dynamical systems with a varying coupling parameter.

INTRODUCTION

The **synchronization** of chaotic systems is one of the most interesting phenomena initially discovered by Pecora and Caroll (1990). They first observed that when two such chaotic dynamical systems are synchronized, it becomes possible to send a **message** from one system to the other. In particular, the use of chaotic synchronization in communication systems has been investigated by several authors like Cuomo and Oppenheim (1993), Kocarev, Halle, Eckert, Chua, and Parlitz (1992), Lozi and Chua (1993), Cuomo, Oppenheim, and Strogatz (1993), Parlitz, Chua, Kocarev, Halle, and Shang (1992), Halle, Wu, Itoh, and Chua (1993), and Wu and Chua (1993). The information signal is transmitted using a chaotic signal as a **broadband carrier**, and synchronization is necessary to recover the information at the receiver. There are many implementations of this basic idea, for example, in the works of Cuomo and Oppenheim, Kocarev et al., Lozi and Chua, and Cuomo et al. The information signal is added to the chaotic signal. Cuomo and Oppenheim, and Parlitz et al. used a **parametric modulation** for the transmission of digital signals. Other approaches to use chaos for the purpose of communication include **controlling techniques** to **encode** binary information as Hayes, Grebogi, and Ott (1993) did and methods that make use of the quick decay of the correlation function for chaotic signals as in the work of Parlitz and Ergezinger (1994). Later it was shown that this can be used to create **keys** for **cryptography** and be very effective in the process of **masking** an actual signal for private communication. This process gives rise to the subject of cryptography using chaos. Traditionally, cryptography was used mainly for military and diplomatic purposes. However, in recent years the need for security has increased manifold due to the extensive use of remote log-in, the Internet, intranets, and so forth. So it was observed that if a signal could be masked with the help of a set of secure keys that are pseudo-random, chaotic synchronization can really be an effective tool. Figure 1 shows a block diagram of a cryptosystem using synchronization process.

Nonlinear **delay differential dynamics** has shown a growing interest in optics in the last 30 years through numerous theoretical, numerical, and experimental investigations like the works of Ikeda (1979), Gibbs, Hopf, Kaplan, and Schoemacker (1981), Arecchi, Gadomski, and Meucci (1986), and Aida and Davis (1992). These dynamics were explored at first mainly for fundamental interests such as in Farmer (1982) and Dorizzi, Grammaticos, Berre, Pomeau, Ressayres, and Tallet (1987).

Such an interest is due to, among other reasons, an amazing feature: These dynamical systems exhibit extremely complex chaotic behavior (with an arbitrary high attractor dimension), although

Figure 1. Block diagram of a chaotic communication system

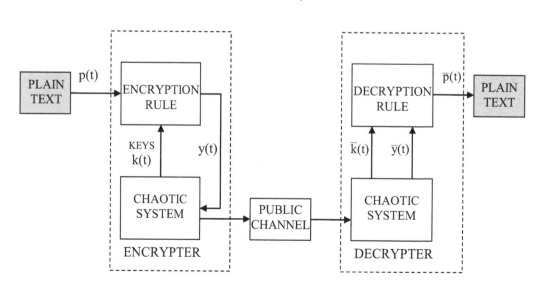

their mathematical description can be as simple as a scalar first-order differential equation. Nonlinear phenomena induced by the **delay** in the feedback loop have many applications in laser systems as Ikeda, Kondo, and Akimoto (1982) have shown; Mackey and Glass (1977), Plant (1981), Mackey and Heiden (1984), and Milton, Heiden, Longtin, and Hlackey (1990) have shown in **physiological** systems; and Marcus and Westervelt (1989) have shown in **artificial neural network** models. **Delay-differential equations** have very interesting properties that make them appealing for information storage purposes like in Ikeda and Matsumoto (1987), Aida and Davis (1992), and Mensour and Longtin (1995). These properties can be summarized as follows.

- They are **infinite-dimensional** dynamical systems because we need to specify a function over one delay interval as the initial condition.
- They are multistable at large delays; that is, different initial functions lead to different attractors.
- In the chaotic regime, their attractors have a finite fractal dimension proportional to the delay.
- The solutions exhibit series of connected plateaus in the singular limit, where the delay is much greater than the response time. In this limit, certain properties of the delay differential equation can be studied using a discrete time map.

On the other hand, it has been observed by many researchers that one may get a hold of the basic parameters used behind a set of keys and the **security** may be broken. This generates a need for a newer method of **chaotic communication**. Here in this chapter we have shown that the usual set of nonlinear dynamical systems used in chaotic synchronization can be replaced by delayed dynamical systems, and the existence of an extra

parameter makes the whole process more secure. Also, it has been observed that it is not very easy to estimate the delay parameter from a given time series without a priori information that it is an output of a delayed system.

Finally, we have shown that the **cryptosystem** becomes more secure if the synchronization between two delayed systems occurs with the synchronization coupling k, which is not a constant but varying with time. The sender and receiver can choose the equation of the coupling parameter k(t) by themselves. The equation of the coupling signal may be an ordinary differential equation or one that contains an additional time delay τ, which can hide the state of the system. In this way, the total cryptosystem becomes more secure and an attacker cannot find the secret keys with unidirectional coupling. Time-delayed coupling has been studied recently and is also observed in systems such as coupled lasers and spiking neurons.

FORMULATION

The System

To start with, we consider the **delayed Rössler systems** coupled with a similar one via a one-way coupling. The corresponding equations are:

$$\dot{x}_1 = -x_2 - x_3 + \alpha_1 x_1 (t - \tau)$$
$$\dot{x}_2 = x_1 + \beta_1 x_2$$
$$\dot{x}_3 = x_3 (x_1 - \gamma) + \beta_2 \qquad (1)$$

$$j \neq i$$
$$\dot{x}_5 = x_4 + \beta_1 x_5 + k(x_2 - x_5)$$
$$\dot{x}_6 = x_6 (x_4 - \gamma) + \beta_2 \qquad (2)$$

where τ is the delay parameter; α_1 is the geometric factor; β_1, β_2, and γ are the usual parameters of a standard Rössler System, and k is the one-way coupling parameter. The fixed points of System 1 are,

$$E_i = (x_{0i}, y_{0i}, z_{0i}),$$

where the following applies.

1. $E_1 = (-\beta_1 X_+, X_+, \frac{\beta_2}{\beta_1 X_+ + \gamma})$

2. $E_2 = (-\beta_1 X_-, X_-, \frac{\beta_2}{\beta_1 X_- + \gamma}),$

where

$$X_\pm = \frac{-\gamma \pm \sqrt{\gamma^2 A^2 - 4A\beta_1\beta_2}}{2A\beta_1}$$

provided $\gamma^2 A^2 \geq 4A\beta_1\beta_2$ where $A = 1 + \alpha_1\beta_1$.

The characteristic equation of System 1 around any fixed point (x_0, y_0, z_0) is

$$P_1(\lambda) + e^{-\lambda\tau} P_2(\lambda) = 0 \qquad (3)$$

where,

$$P_1(\lambda) = \lambda^3 + \lambda^2 (\gamma - x_0 - \beta_1) + \lambda(1 + z_0 - \beta_1 \gamma + \beta_1 x_0)$$
$$\quad + (\gamma - x_0 - \beta_1 z_0)$$
$$P_2(\lambda) = -\alpha_1 \{ \lambda^2 + \lambda (\gamma - x_0 - \beta_1) - \beta_1 (\gamma - x_0) \}.$$

To analyze the stability of the steady state of System 1, we consider the following two lemmas.

Lemma 1

Consider the general delay dynamical system.

$$\dot{x}(t) = A_0 x(t) + \sum_{k=1}^{n} A_k x(t_{\tau k}),$$

where $A_0, A_k \in C^{d \times d}$ are constant complex matrices, and $x(t_{\tau k}) = (x_1(t - \tau_{k1}), x_2(t - \tau_{k2}), \ldots, x_d(t - \tau_{kd})$ stand for constant delays.

For a complex matrix W, let $\mu(W)$ be the logarithmic norm of W and $\mu(W) = \lim_{\Delta \to 0+} \frac{\|I + \Delta W\| - 1}{\Delta}$.

If the condition $\mu(A_0) + \sum_{k=1}^{n} \|A_k\| < 0$ holds, then System 1 is asymptotically stable.

Lemma 2

A steady state with characteristics in equation (3) is stable in the absence of delay, and becomes unstable with increasing delay if and only if A_1, A_2, and A_3 are not all positive and the following conditions hold.

1. $\gamma - x_0 - \beta_1 - \alpha_1 > 0$
2. $\gamma - x_0(1 + \alpha_1 \beta_1) - \beta_1 z_0 + \alpha_1 \beta_1 \gamma > 0$
3. $-(\alpha_1 + \beta_1)\{x_0^2 + \beta_1 + \alpha_1 - 2\gamma)x_0 + \gamma^2 + 1 - \alpha_1\gamma\}$
   $-x_0 z_0 + (z_0 + \beta_1^2 + \alpha_1 \beta_1)(\gamma - \alpha_1) > 0$
4. either $A3 < 0$ or $A_3 > 0$ and $A_1^2 - 3A_2 > 0$ and
   $4(A_2^2 - A_1 A_3)(A_1^2 - 3 A_2) - (9A_3 - A_1 A_2)^2 > 0,$

where A_1, A_2, and A_3 are the coefficients of the characteristic equation of System 1, which has been calculated following the work of Ghosh, Saha, and Chowdhury (in press) given by,

$$A_1 = (x_0 - \gamma)^2 - 2(1 + z_0) + (\beta_1^2 - \alpha_1^2)$$

$$A_2 = (x_0 - \gamma)^2(\beta_1^2 - \alpha_1^2 - 2) + (1 + z_0^2) - \beta_1^2(\alpha_1^2 + 2z_0)$$

$$A_3 = (x_0 - \gamma)^2 (1 - \alpha_1\beta_1^2) + \beta_1^2 z_0^2 + 2\beta_1 z_0 (x_0 - \gamma).$$

We consider the fixed point E_1 with the parameter values $\beta_1 = \beta_2 = 0.2$, and $\gamma = 1.2$, then the range of values for α_1 that satisfies Lemma 2 is $0.9714 < \alpha_1 < 23.6171$. In this range, we consider $\alpha_1 = 1.0$. When the delay lies $2.3 < \tau < 2.6$ we get a limit cycle, which becomes unstable with increasing τ, leading to chaos by an intermittency route. The corresponding situation is depicted in Figure 2 where τ is the bifurcation parameter. From Figure 2, we can see that System 1 becomes chaotic for the above parameter values with $\tau > 2.6$.

Figure 2. Bifurcation diagram with respect to the delay parameter τ

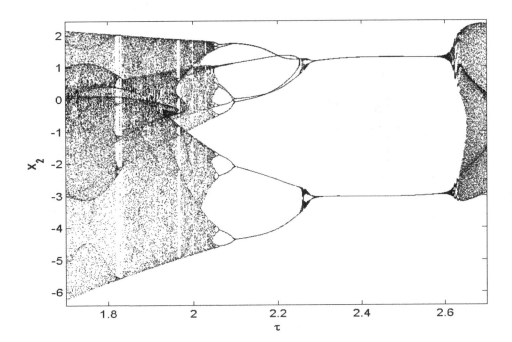

The Cryptosystem

We now consider $\tau = 2.67$. The state of synchronization between Systems 1 and 2 that was achieved can be visualized by plotting the difference $x_1 - x_4$ and $x_3 - x_6$, which tends to be zero as shown in Figures 3 and 4 respectively.

We now wish to utilize these two synchronized chaotic systems for communication using **cryptographic encoding**. The sender uses System 1 and the receiver uses System 2. They choose the values of the variables x_3 and x_6 respectively as the secret keys after some time, say $t = 10.0$. To take the values of the secret keys as integers, they choose $k = [1000z]$ where z represents values either of x_3 or x_6. Since they consider the coupled chaotic systems with time delay to be more secure, they both agree to change the values of τ after every eight messages. The values of τ are increased by

0.1 by both of them at this interval. The data from z_1 picked up by the sender and the corresponding secret keys are shown in Table 1.

Let us first describe how the process is generated. The actual **message** that a **sender** wants to send to the receiver is called **plaintext**. The plaintext and the corresponding **ciphertext** can be divided into message units. **He** and **Vaidya** (1998) showed that each unit of message is a single alphabet and they used 26 letters equivalent to the numbers 0 to 25. The corresponding formula for the **ciphertext** message is,

$$c = p + k \bmod (26), \qquad (4)$$

and the decrypted message can be obtained by

$$p = c - k \bmod (26). \qquad (5)$$

Figure 3. Time variation of $x_1 - x_4$ showing synchronization between Systems 1 and 2

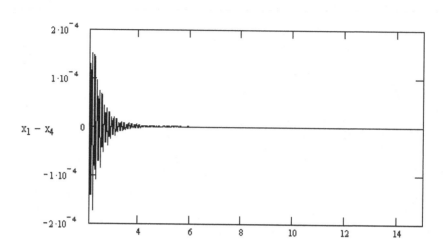

Figure 4. Variation of $x_3 - x_6$ with respect to time t

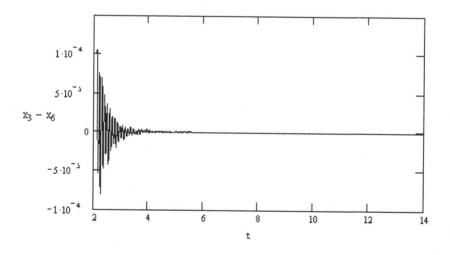

In the present chapter, we have made a generalization of this procedure. Suppose our message contains both letters as well as numbers. In the work of He and Vaidya (1998) the received word or message was "GOODMORNING" instead of "GOOD MORNING." An improved version of this method is one in which the unit of message (it may be a word, line, or paragraph) is not only the alphabet but also numbers, decimals, and spaces between two words or sentences. The

Table 1

Number Assigned	0	1	2	3	4	5	6	7	8	9	10	11	12	13	...	37
Unit Message	0	1	2	3	4	5	6	7	8	9	_	.	A	B	...	Z

corresponding numbers were merely 0 to 25, but there should be more than that. We assign the numeric numbers 0 to 9 to the numbers 0 to 9 respectively. The blank space (gap) between two words is represented by 10. The decimal (or full stop between two sentences or any punctuation marks) is given as 11. The 26 letters from A to Z are assigned the numbers 12 to 37 respectively. Table 1 shows the complete assignment.

The corresponding formula can be written as,

$$c_i = p_i + k_i \mod (38)$$
$$p_i = c_i - k_i \mod (38),$$

where k_i is the secret key to unmask the message. Corresponding to every message unit, we use one and only one message key, which is randomly generated. For a complete message, the secret keys are a series of numbers $k_1, k_2, k_3, \ldots k_n$. Actu-

ally, the key k_j hides and secures the message unit p_j. Let us consider the message in the form of a sentence that contains numbers also.

MORNING STARTS AT 7.30 FOR ME

Table 2 shows the message units and the corresponding keys.

Next in Table 3 and Table 4 we show the value of the corresponding dynamical variable $x_3(t)$ and $x_6(t)$, the keys, plaintext, time, the time lag τ, and **ciphertext** for both the sender and receiver.

In general, synchronous chaotic systems using ODEs are easy to implement. Here we have shown how a delayed ODE can be substituted for it, where we have an extra parameter τ, the **time delay**. The important fact is that after a fixed interval of time, this τ can be changed even maintaining the **synchronization** and hence can

Table 2

Keys	k_1	k_2	k_3	k_4	k_5	k_6	k_7	k_8	k_9	k_{10}	k_{11}	k_{12}	k_{13}	k_{14}	k_{15}
Unit Message	M	O	R	N	I	N	G	_	S	T	A	R	T	S	_

Keys	k_{16}	k_{17}	k_{18}	k_{19}	k_{20}	k_{21}	k_{22}	k_{23}	k_{24}	k_{25}	k_{26}	k_{27}	k_{28}	k_{29}
Unit Message	A	T	_	7	.	3	0	_	F	O	R	_	M	E

Table 3. Ciphertext sent by the sender

Time Lag τ_1	Time T	$x_3(t)$	Keys k	Plaintext p	Ciphertext $c = p + k \bmod (38)$
2.67	10.0	2.2138...	2213	M (24)	33
	11.0	3.0080...	3008	O (26)	29
	12.0	3.7198...	3719	R (29)	62
	13.0	4.2952...	4295	N (25)	26
	14.0	4.6781...	4678	I (20)	22
	15.0	4.8226...	4822	N (25)	59
	16.0	4.2737...	4273	G (18)	35
	17.0	2.5082...	2508	- (10)	10
2.77	18.0	0.9300...	930	S (30)	39
	19.0	2.0703...	2070	T (31)	40
	20.0	2.6764...	2676	A (12)	20
	21.0	3.2704...	3270	R (29)	30
	22.0	4.3766...	4376	T (31)	34
	23.0	4.8609...	4860	S (30)	42
	24.0	5.2752...	5275	- (10)	41
	25.0	5.5942...	5594	A (12)	16
2.87	26.0	5.7825...	5782	T (31)	34
	27.0	5.7899...	5789	- (10)	23
	28.0	5.5464...	5546	7 (7)	43
	29.0	4.9637...	4963	. (11)	34
	30.0	3.9593...	3959	3 (3)	10
	31.0	2.5211...	2521	0 (0)	13
	32.0	0.6906...	690	- (10)	13
	33.0	0.3253...	325	F (17)	38
2.97	34.0	0.2458...	245	O (26)	43
	35.0	0.3584...	358	R (29)	37
	36.0	0.7322...	732	- (10)	15
	37.0	0.8103...	810	M (24)	30
	38.0	0.7244...	724	E (16)	17

make the **communication** more secure. It is to be pointed out that keys should be used only once and are shorter than the message length.

Next, we will show that an analytical signal can also be transmitted with the help of the system so described. For example, suppose we have a plaintext signal in the form of a sine curve:

$$u(t) = \sin(7t). \tag{6}$$

The transmitter and receiver are the coupled Rössler systems with one way coupling:

$$\dot{x}_1 = -x_2 - x_3 + \alpha_1 x_1(t - \tau) + F_T(t)$$
$$\dot{x}_2 = x_1 + \beta_1 x_2$$
$$\dot{x}_3 = x_3(x_1 - \gamma) + \beta_2 \tag{7}$$

and

Table 4. The plaintext deciphered by the receiver

Time Lag τ_1	Time T	$x_6(t)$	Keys k	Ciphertext c	Plaintext $p = c - k \bmod (38)$
2.67	10.0	2.2138...	2213	33	24 (M)
	11.0	3.0080...	3008	29	26 (O)
	12.0	3.7198...	3719	62	29 (R)
	13.0	4.2952...	4295	26	25 (N)
	14.0	4.6781...	4678	22	20 (I)
	15.0	4.8226...	4822	59	25 (N)
	16.0	4.2737...	4273	35	18 (G)
	17.0	2.5082...	2508	10	10 (-)
2.77	18.0	0.9300...	930	39	30 (S)
	19.0	2.0703...	2070	40	31 (T)
	20.0	2.6764...	2676	20	12 (A)
	21.0	3.2704...	3270	30	29 (R)
	22.0	4.3766...	4376	34	31 (T)
	23.0	4.8609...	4860	42	30 (S)
	24.0	5.2752...	5275	41	10 (-)
	25.0	5.5942...	5594	16	12 (A)
2.87	26.0	5.7825...	5782	34	31 (T)
	27.0	5.7899...	5789	23	10 (-)
	28.0	5.5464...	5546	43	7 (7)
	29.0	4.9637...	4963	34	11 (.)
	30.0	3.9593...	3959	10	3 (3)
	31.0	2.5211...	2521	13	0 (0)
	32.0	0.6906...	690	13	10 (-)
	33.0	0.3253...	325	38	17 (F)
2.97	34.0	0.2458...	245	43	26 (O)
	35.0	0.3584...	358	37	29 (R)
	36.0	0.7322...	732	15	10 (-)
	37.0	0.8103...	810	30	24 (M)
	38.0	0.7244...	724	17	16 (E)

$$\dot{x}_4 = -x_5 - x_6 + \alpha_1 x_4(t - \tau) + F_R(t)$$
$$\dot{x}_5 = x_4 + \beta_1 x_5 + k(x_2 - x_5)$$
$$\dot{x}_6 = x_6(x_4 - \gamma) + \beta_2 \qquad (8)$$

where $F_T(t) = x_1 + u(t)$ is the transmitted signal and $F_R(t)$ is the received signal. All other parameters are kept in the chaotic region for the two systems to remain synchronized. The corresponding transmitted and received signals are shown in Figures 5 and 6.

On the other hand, one can also have a chaotic time series as the input signal instead of the $sin(7t)$. In our case, we consider the $x(t)$ variable of the usual chaotic Rössler system. The transmitted signal is $F_T(t) = x_3(t) + x(t)$. The corresponding time series diagrams of the Rössler variable and

$F_R(t)$ are given in Figures 7 and 8 respectively. Figure 9 is the signal recovered.

Cryptography Using Adaptive Synchronization

In this section, we use the synchronization between two coupled **delayed dynamical systems** by an adaptive mechanism. Consider two one-way, coupled, identical chaotic delayed systems described by

$$\dot{x}(t) = F(x, x_\tau) \tag{9}$$

and

$$\dot{y}(t) = F(y, y_\tau) + k(t)[x(t) - y(t)] \tag{10}$$

Figure 5. The transmitted signal $F_T(t)$

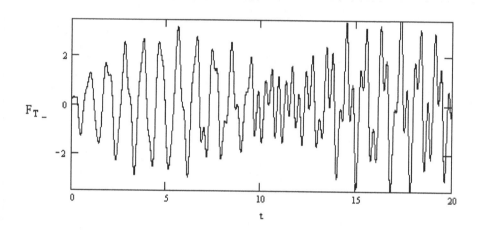

Figure 6. The received signal $F_R(t)$

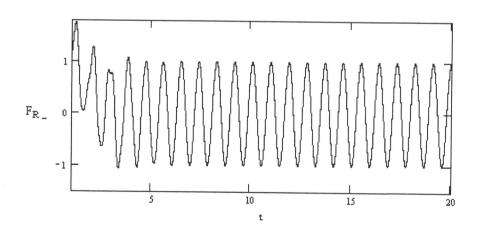

Figure 7. x-variable of the usual Rössler system varying with time

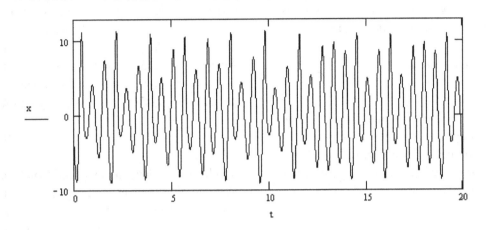

Figure 8. The transmitted signal $F_T(t)$

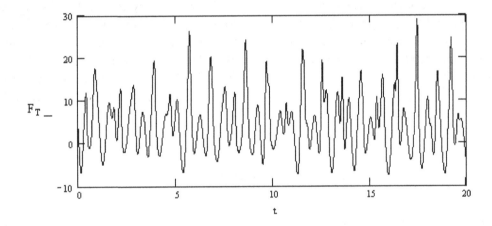

Figure 9. The received signal $F_R(t)$

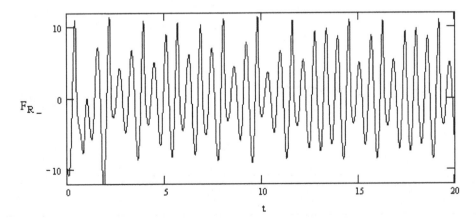

where $x = [x_1, x_2, x_{3,....}, x_n]^T, y = [y_1, y_2, y_{3,....}, y_n]^T \in \Re^n$ is the state of the coupled systems, $x_\tau = x(t-\tau)$. The coupling matrix $k(t) = diag [k_1(t), k_2(t), ... k_n(t)]$ is a diagonal matrix with the following relation:

$k_i(t) \equiv k(t)$ for any i and
$k_j(t) \equiv 0$ for $j \neq i$.

Therefore, Systems 9 and 10 are linearly coupled through their i state variables, and k(t) represents the coupling strength. The adaptive algorithms for the coupling strength is described by Wang (2002) as

$$\dot{k}(t) = g_k [x_i(t) - y_i(t)]^2 [k^* - k(t)],$$
$$k(0) = k_0, \tag{11}$$

where γ_k and k^* are positive adaptive gain and maximum allowed coupling strength respectively.

In our case, we consider Systems 1 and 2 with the coupling parameter $k = k(t)$ with the following adaptive algorithm:

$$\dot{k}(t) = \gamma_k [x_2 - x_5]^2 [k^* - k(t)], \tag{12}$$

For numerical simulation, we have set the parameter values $\beta_1 = \beta_2 = 0.2$, $\gamma = 1.2$, $\gamma_k = 0.1$ and $k^* = 5.0$. Figures 10 and 11 are the time variations of x_1-x_4 and x_3-x_6 respectively, which shows synchronization. So Systems 1 and 2 with the coupling Algorithm 12 can be used as a cryptosystem.

To be more secure we introduce another **delay parameter** τ_1 and the new coupling algorithm

$$k(t) = \gamma_k [x_2 - x_5]^2 [k^* - k(t - \tau_1)] \tag{13}$$

which is also a **delay differential equation**. The Systems 1 and 2 synchronize with same parameter values with $\tau_1 = 1.2$. Figures 12 and 13 are the time variations of x_1-x_3 and x_4-x_6 respectively, showing synchronization.

We now want to send a continuous signal using the above cryptosystem. If there are any hidden patterns and structural changes in data, it is better to analyze the signal graphically using **recurrence plots**. The **recurrence plot** of a dynamical system is a new technique for the qualitative assessment of time series. In visual recurrence analysis (VRA),

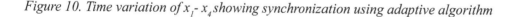

Figure 10. Time variation of x_1-x_4 showing synchronization using adaptive algorithm

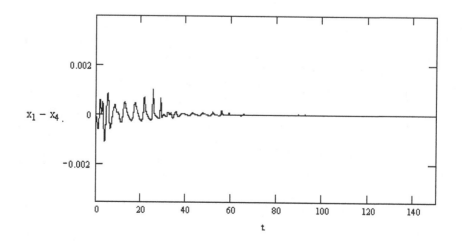

Figure 11. x_3- x_6 varying with time t

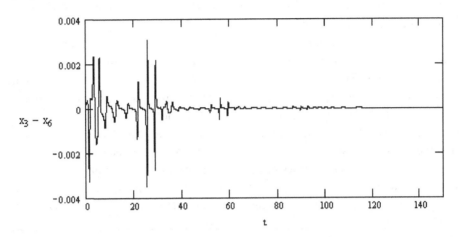

Figure 12. Time variation of x_1- x_4 showing synchronization with τ_1=1.2

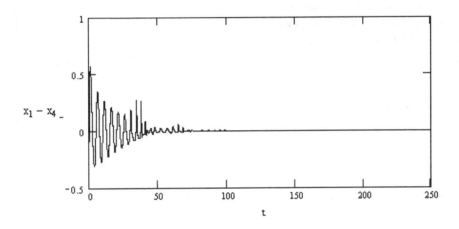

Figure 13. Time variation of x_3- x_6 with τ_1=1.2

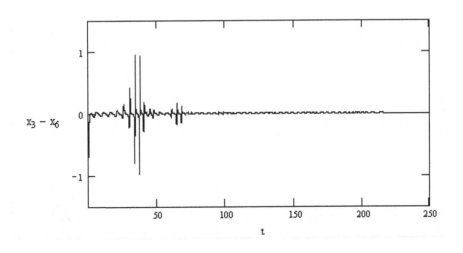

a one-dimensional time series from a data file is expanded to a higher dimensional space, in which the dynamics of the underlying generator takes place by using the delayed coordinate **embedding technique,** which is found in Eckmann, Kampshort, and Ruelle (1987).

Let us first send a chaotic signal, which is, in our case, the x variable of the usual chaotic Lorenz system. Therefore, the original signal is $i(t) = x(t)$, and the transmitted signal is $s(t) = x(t) + x_1(t)$ where $x_1(t)$ is the first variable of System 1. Figures 14 and 15 show the recurrence diagram of the original signal i(t) and the transmitted signal s(t) respectively.

Figure 16 shows the recovered signal.

One can check the minimum embedding dimension of the transmitted and the received signal using the method of **false nearest neighbors** (Abarbanel & Kennel, 1993; Kennel, Brown, & Abarbanel, 1992).

For each vector $X = (x_1, x_2, x_3, \dots x_n)$ in the **time series** of a chaotic signal, find its **nearest neighbor** $Y = (y_1, y_2, y_3, \dots y_n)$ in an n-dimensional space. Let $R = |x_{n+1} - y_{n+1}|$. This distance R is essentially a distance between the images of vectors X and Y. We can also define y_{n+1} as a predictor for x_{n+1}, so R is then the prediction error. The idea is that when the attractor is completely unfolded in n dimensions, the distance R between the $(n+1)^{th}$ components of vectors X and Y will be small. To detect if the nearest neighbor just found is false, we compare the prediction error with the errors that would have been made by a trivial predictor. If the error made by the trivial predictor is less than R, we denote the nearest neighbor as false.

Therefore we can say

If $|x_{n+1} - y_{n+1}| = |x_{n+1} - x_n|$,

the nearest neighbor is labeled as false.

Figure 14. Recurrence diagram of the x variable of the chaotic Lorenz system

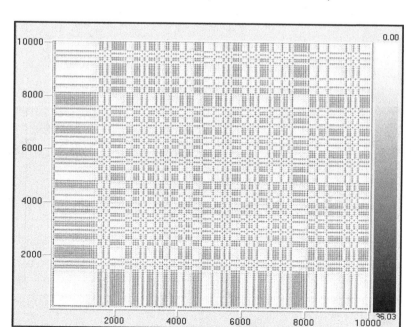

Figure 15. Recurrence diagram of the transmitted signal s(t)

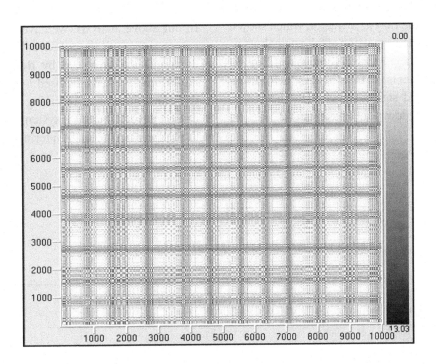

Figure 16. Recurrence diagram of the received signal

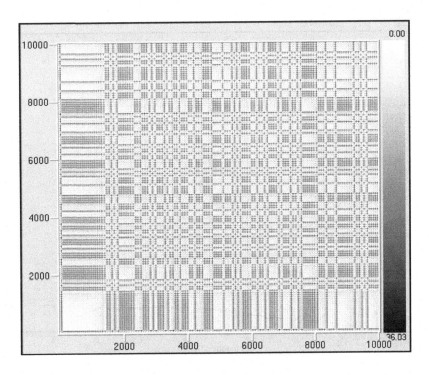

Figure 17 is the percent of false neighbors plotted against the embedding dimension of the time series of the Lorenz attractor, which shows that the minimum proportion of false neighbors is reached somewhere between Dimensions 2 and 3. Figure 18 represents the **false nearest neighbors** of the recovered signal, which also shows the minimum embedding dimension near 2.

CONCLUSION

In our above analysis, we have studied nonlinear systems with time-delayed feedback whose dynamics are governed by **delay-differential equations**. We have devised a new method for the transmitting and receiving of signals using those delayed dynamical systems. The change of the delay parameter at the intermediate state gives

Figure 17. Percent of false neighbors of the Lorenz system

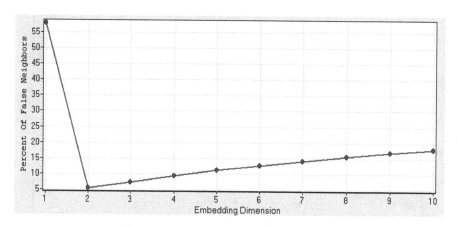

Figure 18. Percent of false neighbors of the recovered signal

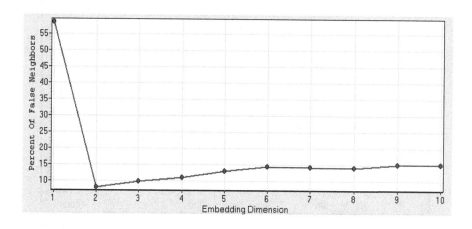

extra security to the system. Any form of analytic signal can be sent, either periodic or chaotic. Our **encryption keys** allow both an alphabetic and numerical form of message to be sent. We also proposed a method of communication using the synchronization between two coupled delayed chaotic systems by adaptive coupling-enhancement algorithms.

REFERENCES

Abarbanel, H. D. I., & Kennel, M. B. (1993). Local false nearest neighbors and dynamical dimensions from observed chaotic data. *Physics Review E, 47*, 3057-3068.

Aida, T., & Davis, P. (1992). Oscillation modes of laser diode pumped hybrid bistable system with large delay and application to dynamical memory. *IEEE Journal of Quantum Electronics, 28*(3), 686-699.

Arecchi, F., Gadomski, W., & Meucci, R. (1986). Generation of chaotic dynamics by feedback on a laser. *Physical Review A, 34*, 1617-1620.

Cuomo, K. M., & Oppenheim, A. V. (1993). Circuit implementation of synchronized chaos with applications to communications. *Physical Review Letters, 71*, 65-68.

Cuomo, K. M., Oppenheim, A. V., & Strogatz, S. H. (1993). Robustness and signal recovery in a synchronized chaotic system. *International Journal of Bifurcation and Chaos in Applied Sciences and Engineering, 3*(6), 1629-1638.

Dorizzi, B., Grammaticos, B., Berre, M. L., Pomeau, Y., Ressayres, E., & Tallet, A. (1987). Statistics and dimension of chaos in differential delay systems. *Physical Review A, 35*, 328-339.

Eckmann, J. P., Kampshort, S. O., & Ruelle, D. (1987). Recurrence plots of dynamical systems. *Europhysics Letters, 4*, 973-977.

Farmer, J. D. (1982). Chaotic attractors of an infinite-dimensional dynamical system. *Physica D, 4*, 366-393.

Ghosh, D., Saha, P., & Chowdhury, A. R. (in press). Multiple delay Rössler system-bifurcation and chaos control. *Chaos, Solitons and Fractals.*

Gibbs, H. M., Hopf, F. A., Kaplan, D. L., & Schoemacker, R. L. (1981). Observation of chaos in optical bistability. *Physical Review Letters, 46*, 474-477.

Halle, K. S., Wu, C. W., Itoh, M., & Chua, L. O. (1993). Spread spectrum communication through modulation of chaos. *International Journal of Bifurcation Chaos, 3*(2), 469-478.

Hayes, S., Grebogi, C., & Ott. (1993). Communicating with chaos. *Physical Review Letters, 70*, 3031-3034.

He, R., & Vaidya, P. G. (1998). Implementation of chaotic cryptography with chaotic synchronization. *Physical Review E, 57*, 1532-1535.

Ikeda, K. (1979). Multiple-valued stationary state and its instability...transmitted light by a ring cavity system. *Optical Communications, 30*, 257.

Ikeda, K., Kondo, K., & Akimoto, O. (1982). Successive higher-harmonic bifurcations in systems with delayed feedback. *Physical Review Letter, 49*, 1467-1470.

Ikeda, K., & Matsumoto, K. (1987). High dimensional chaotic behavior in systems with time delayed feedback. *Physica D, 29*, 223-235.

Kennel, M. B., Brown, R., & Abarbanel, H. D. I. (1992). Determining embedding dimension for phase-space reconstruction using a geometrical construction. *Physical Review A, 45,* 3403-3411.

Kocarev, L., Halle, K. S., Eckert, K., Chua, L. O., & Parlitz, U. (1992). Experimental demonstration of secure communications via chaotic synchronization. *International Journal of Bifurcation Chaos, 2*(3), 709-714.

Lozi, R., & Chua, L. O. (1993). Secure communications via chaotic synchronization II: Noise reduction by cascading two identical receivers. *International Journal of Bifurcation and Chaos in Applied Sciences and Engineering, 3*(5), 1319-1325.

Mackey, M. C., & Glass, L. (1977). Oscillation and chaos in physiological control systems. *Science, 197*, 287-289.

Mackey, M. C., & Heiden, U. en der. (1984). The dynamics of recurrent inhibition. *Journal of Mathematical Biology, 19*, 211- 225.

Marcus, C. M., & Westervelt, R. M. (1989). Stability of analog neural networks with delay. *Physical Review A, 39*, 347-359.

Mensour, B., & Longtin, A. (1995). Controlling chaos to store information in delay-differential equations. *Physics Letter A, 205*, 18-24.

Milton, J. G., Heiden, U. en der, Longtin, A., & Hlackey, M. C. (1990). Complex dynamics and noise in simple neural networks with mixed feedback. *Biomedica Biochimica Acta, 49*, 697-707.

Parlitz, U., Chua, L. O., Kocarev, L., Halle, K. S., & Shang, A. (1992). Transmission of digital signals by chaotic synchronization. *International Journal of Bifurcation and Chaos in Applied Sciences and Engineering, 2*(4), 973-977.

Parlitz, U., & Ergezinger, S. (1994). Robust communication based on chaotic spreading sequences. *Physics Letter A, 188*, 146-150.

Pecora, L., & Carroll, T. (1990). Synchronization in chaotic systems. *Physical Review Letters, 64*, 821-824.

Plant, R. E. (1981). A Fitzhugh differential-difference equation modeling recurrent neural feedback. *SIAM Journal of Applied Mathematics, 40*(1), 150-162.

Wu, C. W., & Chua, L. O. (1993). A simple way to synchronize chaotic systems with applications to secure communication systems. *International Journal of Bifurcation Chaos, 3*(6), 1619-1628.

Chapter XIV
Portfolio Optimization Using Evolutionary Algorithms

Lean Yu
Chinese Academy of Sciences, China & City University of Hong Kong, Hong Kong

Shouyang Wang
Chinese Academy of Sciences, China

Kin Keung Lai
City University of Hong Kong, Hong Kong

ABSTRACT

In this study, a double-stage evolutionary algorithm is proposed for portfolio optimization. In the first stage, a genetic algorithm is used to identify good-quality assets in terms of asset ranking. In the second stage, investment allocation in the selected good-quality assets is optimized using another genetic algorithm based on Markowitz's theory. Through the two-stage genetic optimization process, an optimal portfolio can be determined. Experimental results obtained reveal that the proposed double-stage evolutionary algorithm for portfolio optimization provides a very useful tool to assist the investors in planning their investment strategy and constructing their portfolio.

INTRODUCTION

In modern portfolio theory, the mean-variance model originally introduced by Markowitz (1952) has been playing an important and critical role so far. Since Markowitz's pioneering work was published, the mean-variance model has revolutionized the way people think about portfolios of assets, and it has gained widespread acceptance as a practical tool for portfolio optimization (Yu, Wang, & Lai, 2008). However, Markowitz's portfolio theory only provides a solution to asset allocation among predetermined assets. In the investment markets, several hundred different assets, such as stocks, bonds, foreign exchanges, options, commodities, real estates, and future contracts, are available for trading. The qualities of these assets vary from very good to extremely poor. Usually, investors find it difficult to seek out those good-quality assets because of information asymmetry and asset price fluctuations. Therefore, it is not wise to use portfolio theory blindly for optimizing asset allocation among some low-quality assets. The suitable way of constructing a portfolio is first to select some good-quality assets and then to optimize asset allocation using portfolio theory.

An obvious challenge is how to select and optimize good assets. With focus on business computing, applying artificial intelligence to portfolio selection and optimization is one good way to meet the challenge. Some studies have been presented to solve the asset selection problem. Levin (1995) applied artificial neural networks (ANNs) to select valuable stocks. Chu, Tsao, and Shiue (1996) used fuzzy multiple attribute decision making (MADM) to select stocks for portfolio optimization. Similarly, Zargham and Sayeh (1999) used a fuzzy rule-based system to evaluate the listed stocks and realize stock selection. Recently, Fan and Palaniswami (2001) utilized support vector machines (SVMs) to train universal feed-forward neural networks (FNN) to perform stock selection. For portfolio optimization, Maranas, Androulakis, Floudas, Berger, and Mulvey (1997) applied tabu search to find the optimal asset allocation, while some researchers, such as Casas (2001) and Chapados and Bengio (2001), trained neural networks to predict asset behavior and used the neural network to make the asset allocation decisions. In addition, Mulvey, Rosenhaum, and Shetty (1997) applied dynamic programming to construct a multistage stochastic model for solving the asset allocation problem.

However, these approaches have some drawbacks in solving the portfolio selection problem.

For example, the fuzzy approach (Chu et al., 1996; Zargham & Sayeh, 1999) usually lacks learning ability, while the neural-network approach (Casas, 2001; Chapados & Bengio, 2001; Fan & Palaniswami, 2001; Levin, 1995) has an overfitting problem and it is often easy to get trapped into local minima. In order to overcome these shortcomings, we utilize evolutionary algorithms (EAs) to solve the portfolio selection and optimization problem. An EA is a generic population-based metaheuristic optimization algorithm. An EA uses some mechanisms inspired by biological evolution: reproduction, mutation, recombination, natural selection, and survival of the fittest. Candidate solutions to the optimization problem play the role of individuals in a population, and the cost function determines the environment within which the solutions "live." Typically, an EA includes four types: genetic algorithm (GA), genetic programming (GP), evolutionary programming (EP), and evolutionary strategy (ES). Of the four types, the GA is the popular one of EA. One seeks the solution of a problem in the form of strings of numbers (traditionally binary, although the best representations are usually those that reflect something about the problem being solved; these are not normally binary), virtually always applying recombination operators in addition to selection and mutation. This type of EA is often used in optimization problems. Compared to tabu search (Maranas et al., 1997), a GA is less problem dependent and provides a high chance of reaching the global optimum. In comparison with dynamic programming (Mulvey et al., 1997), GA allows the user to get the suboptimal solution while dynamic programming cannot, which is very important for some financial problems. Since time is limited in the financial world, investors often use a suboptimal but acceptable solution to allocate assets. Due to these advantages, we use a two-stage genetic algorithm to perform portfolio selection and solve the optimization problem.

The main motivation of this chapter is to employ a two-stage genetic algorithm for portfolio selection and optimization. In the first stage, a genetic algorithm is used to identify good-quality assets in terms of asset return ranking. In the second stage, investment allocation in the selected good-quality assets is optimized using a genetic algorithm based on Markowitz's theory. Through the two-stage genetic optimization process, an optimal portfolio can be determined. The rest of the chapter is organized as follows. The second section describes the basic selection and optimization process based on the two-stage genetic algorithm in detail. In order to test the efficiency of the proposed algorithm, a simulated experiment is performed in the third section. Finally the fourth section concludes the chapter.

PORTFOLIO OPTIMIZATION WITH A TWO-STAGE GENETIC ALGORITHM

As earlier noted, Markowitz's portfolio selection model only provides a solution to asset allocation among predetermined assets. However, in investment markets, several hundreds of assets are available for investment. Their qualities vary from very good to extremely poor. If these assets are not carefully chosen in advance, then it is difficult for us to obtain the most valuable portfolio via Markowitz's theory. Therefore, a prerequisite of obtaining a good portfolio is to select good-quality assets before applying Markowitz's model. In this study, genetic algorithms are used to perform this task. In addition, users can obtain a suboptimal but acceptable solution from Markowitz's model, which can avoid the difficulty of the quadratic programming (QP) solution. Thus, a two-stage genetic optimization algorithm can be generated to construct suitable portfolios.

Generally, GA imitates the natural selection process in biological evolution with selection, crossover, and mutation; the sequence of the different operations of a genetic algorithm is shown in the left part of Figure 1. That is, GA is a procedure modeled after genetics and evolution.

Genetics provides the chromosomal representation to encode the solution space of the problem while evolutionary procedures are designed to efficiently search for attractive solutions to large and complex problems. Usually, GA is based on the survival-of-the-fittest fashion by gradually manipulating the potential problem solutions to obtain more superior solutions in the population. Optimization is performed in the representation rather than in the problem space directly. To date, GA has become a popular optimization method as it often succeeds in finding the best optimum by global search in contrast to most common optimization algorithms. Interested readers are referred to Holland (1992), Goldberg (1999), and Yu, Wang, and Lai (2006) for more details.

Stage I: Selecting Good-Quality Assets Using GA

The aim of this stage is to identify the quality of each stock so that investors can choose some good ones for investment. Here a GA is used as a stock ranking tool. In this study, some financial indicators of the listed companies are employed to determine and identify the quality of each stock. That is, the financial indicators of the companies are used as input variables while a score is given to rank the stocks. The output variable is stock ranking. Throughout the study, four important financial indicators, return on capital employed (ROCE), price-earnings ratio (P/E ratio), earning per share (EPS), and the liquidity ratio, are utilized in this study.

ROCE is an indicator of a company's profitability related to the total financing, which is calculated as

ROCE = (Profit)/(Shareholder's equity)*100%.

(1)

The higher the indicator ROCE, the better the company's performance in terms of how efficient the company utilizes shareholder's capital to produce revenue.

The P/E ratio measures the multiple earnings per share at which the stock is traded on the stock exchange. The higher the ratio, the stronger the company's earning power. The calculation of this ratio is computed by

P/E ratio = (stock price)/(earnings per-share)*100%. (2)

EPS is a performance indicator that expresses a company's net income in relation to the number of ordinary shares issued. Generally, the higher the indicator, the better the company's investment value. The calculation of the indicator can be represented as

Earnings per share = (Net income)/(The number of ordinary shares). (3)

The liquidity ratio measures the extent to which a company can quickly liquidate assets to cover short-term liabilities. It is calculated as follows:

Liquidity Ratio = (Current Assets)/(Current Liabilities)*100%. (4)

If the liquidity ratio is too high, company performance is not good due to too much cash or stock on hand. When the ratio is too low, the company does not have sufficient cash to settle short-term debt.

When the input variables are determined, we can use the GA to distinguish and identify the quality of each stock, as illustrated in Figure 1. The detailed procedure is illustrated as follows.

First of all, a population that consists of a given number of chromosomes is initially created by randomly assigning 1 and 0 to all genes. In the case of stock ranking, a gene contains only a

Figure 1. Stock ranking with genetic algorithms

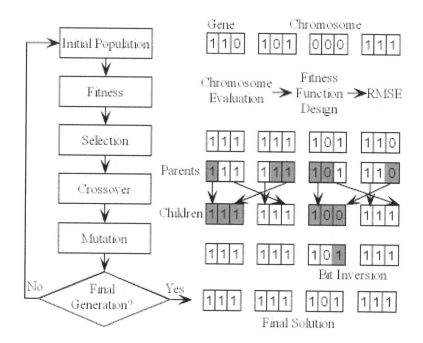

single bit string for the status of input variable. The top right part of Figure 1 shows a population with four chromosomes, and each chromosome includes different genes. In this study, the initial population of the GA is generated by encoding four input variables. For the testing case of ROCE, we design eight statuses representing different qualities in terms of different interval, varying from 0 (*extremely poor*) to 7 (*very good*). An example of encoding ROCE is shown in Table 1. Other input variables are encoded by the same principle. That is, the binary string of a gene consists of three single bits, as illustrated by Figure 1.

The subsequent work is to evaluate the chromosomes generated by previous operations by a so-called fitness function; the design of the fitness function is a crucial point in using GA, which determines what a GA should optimize. Since the output is some estimated stock ranking of designated testing companies, some actual stock ranking should be defined in advance for designing the fitness function. Here we use annual price return (APR) to rank the listed stock and the APR is represented as

$$APR_n = \frac{ASP_n - ASP_{n-1}}{ASP_{n-1}}, \tag{5}$$

where APR_n is the annual price return for year n, ASP_n is the annual stock price for year n. Usually,

the stocks with a high annual price return are regarded as good stocks. With the value of APR evaluated for each of the N trading stocks, they will be assigned for a ranking r ranging from 1 to N, where 1 is the highest value of the APR and N is the lowest. For convenience of comparison, the stock's rank r should be mapped linearly into stock ranking ranged from 0 to 7 according to the following equation:

$$R_{actual} = 7 \times \frac{N - r}{N - 1}. \tag{6}$$

Thus, the fitness function can be designed to minimize the root mean square error (RMSE) of the difference between the financial indicator derived ranking and next year's actual ranking of all the listed companies for a particular chromosome, represented by

$$RMSE = \sqrt{\frac{1}{m} \sum_{t=1}^{m} \left(R_{derived} - R_{actual} \right)^2}. \tag{7}$$

After evolving the fitness of the population, the best chromosomes with the highest fitness value are selected by means of the roulette wheel. Here, the chromosomes are allocated space on a roulette wheel proportional to their fitness and thus the fittest chromosomes are more likely selected. In the following crossover step, offspring chromosomes are created by some crossover

Table 1. An example of encoding ROCE

ROCE Value	Status	Encoding
(-∞, -30%]	0	000
(-30%, -20%]	1	001
(-20%,-10%]	2	010
(-10%,0%]	3	011
(0%, 10%]	4	100
(10%, 20%]	5	101
(20%, 30%]	6	110
(30%,+∞)	7	111

techniques. A so-called one-point crossover technique is employed, which randomly selects a crossover point within the chromosome. Then two parent chromosomes are interchanged at this point to produce two new offspring. After that, the chromosomes are mutated with a probability of 0.005 per gene by randomly changing genes from 0 to 1 and vice versa. The mutation prevents the GA from converging too quickly in a small area of the search space. Finally, the final generation will be judged. If they are satisfactory, then the optimized results are obtained. If not, then the evaluation and reproduction steps are repeated until a certain number of generations, a defined fitness, or a convergence criterion of the population is reached. In the ideal case, all chromosomes of the last generation have the same genes representing the optimal solution (Yu et al., 2006).

Stage II: Asset Allocation Optimization Using GA

In the previous stage, some good-quality stocks can be revealed in terms of stock return ranking. However, portfolio management does not only focus on the return but also on risk minimization. Therefore, good stock ranking is not enough for portfolio management; the risk factor must be taken into account by virtue of modern portfolio theory.

Modern portfolio theory originally discussed by Markowitz (1952) is based on a reasonable trade-off between expected return and risk. As earlier noted, the portfolio optimization model can be solved by QP. However, the QP model can also be solved by genetic algorithms. Since

it is a typical optimization model, GA is suitable for this task. The basic procedure of GA for this problem is similar to that discussed previously, but a suitable chromosome representation is needed to encode its solution space and an appropriate fitness function should be designed. In order to apply the model, the values of the expected return $E(R_i)$ and covariance σ_{ij} for all i and j should be determined, which are represented by

$$
\begin{cases}
\text{Expected Return} & E(R_i) = \sum_{t=1}^{n} R_t / n \\
& R_t = \dfrac{SCP_t - SCP_{i(t-1)}}{SCP_{i(t-1)}} \\
\text{Covariance} & s_{ij} = \dfrac{1}{n} \sum_{t=1}^{n} \left((R_t - E(R_i)) \times (R_t - E(R_j)) \right)
\end{cases}
\tag{8}
$$

where R_{it} is the return of stock i for time t, SCP_{it} is the stock closing price for stock i at time t, and n is the time period for available data.

The solution for asset allocation for stocks should be a composition of the stock quantity to be held so as to minimize the risk on a given level of expected return that will get the optimal solution. Thus, the chromosome can be designed as follows: Each stock's weight (w) is a composite of eight bits representing values 0 to 255; thus, the normalized weight (x) of each stock can be calculated with equation (9). The detailed chromosome representation is shown in Figure 2.

$$
x_i = \frac{w_i}{\sum_{i=1}^{n} w_i}
\tag{9}
$$

The fitness function is another important issue in genetic algorithms for solving the problem. In portfolio optimization, the fitness function must

Figure 2. The chromosome design of portfolio optimization

make a rational trade-off between minimizing risk and maximizing return. Thus, the fitness function can be designed as follows:

$$Fitness = \sum_{i=1}^{n} \sum_{j=1}^{n} \sigma_{ij} x_i x_j + \left(\sum_{i=1}^{n} E(R_i) x_i - R_p^* \right)^2 \quad (10)$$

From equation (10), we find that the fitness function can be broken up into two parts. The first one is required to minimize the risk while the second part also needs to be minimized so that the portfolio's overall return will stick to the expected return that we predefined. Therefore, the GA can be performed by minimizing this fitness function. The fitness function for each chromosome is the indicator for GA to perform the selection. After crossover and mutation, the new chromosome is generated for the next iterative evaluation procedure.

Through the optimization process of two-stage GA, the most valuable portfolio, that is, a good stock portfolio with optimal asset allocation, can be explored and discovered to support investors' decision making.

EXPERIMENT STUDY

For verification purposes, a simulated experiment with a real-world data set is performed in this study. First of all, the data description and experimental design are presented and then the experimental results are reported.

Data Description and Experiment Design

The daily data used in this study are stock closing prices obtained from the Shanghai Stock Exchange (SSE; http://www.sse.com.cn). The sample data span the period from January 2, 2001, to December 31, 2004. Monthly and yearly data in this study are obtained by daily data computation. For the simulation, 100 stocks are randomly selected. In this study, we select 100 stocks from Shanghai A's share, and their stock codes vary from 600000 to 600100.

In the first stage, the company financial information as the input variables is fed into the GA to obtain the derived company ranking. This output is compared with the actual stock ranking in terms of APR, as indicated by equations (7) and (8). In the process of GA optimization, the RMSE between the derived and the actual ranking of each stock is calculated and served as the evaluation function of the GA process. The best chromosome obtained is used to rank the stocks and the top n stocks are chosen for the portfolio optimization in the next stage. For practical operation purpose, the top 10, 20, and 30 stocks are chosen for testing according to the ranking of stock quality using GA.

In the second stage, the top 10, 20, and 30 stocks with the highest rank derived from the previous stage are selected. The portfolio optimization is then performed for asset allocation. Expected return of the previous 12 months and covariance of return are needed to calculate according to equation (8) for each stock. Consequently, the portfolio allocation and weight of stock in the portfolio will be obtained from the GA process by minimizing the fitness function (i.e., equation (10)). Therefore, the most valuable portfolio can be mined and discovered by the two-stage genetic optimization algorithm.

Experimental Results

In the first stage, four financial indicators of different stocks as input variables are fed into the GA process to derive the stock rank. The good-quality stock ranks are obtained by minimizing the discrepancies between the derived rank and the actual rank. Again, the RMSE is used to measure the quality of the solution. For simulation, the RMSE results of the top 10, 20, and 30 stocks are reported in Table 2. As can be seen from Table 2, the RMSE increases with the increase of the number of stocks selected.

Table 2. The RMSE results for stock ranking using GA optimization

Number of Stocks	Top 10	Top 20	Top 30
2001	0.8756	0.9231	0.9672
2002	0.8935	0.9056	0.9247
2003	0.8542	0.9098	0.9111
2004	0.9563	0.9352	0.9793

After ranking the stock, some good-quality stocks can be selected as the component of the portfolio. The selection of the good-quality stocks is depended on a threshold for the stock ranking that investor predefined. When the number of stocks is determined by investors in terms of stock ranking, the subsequent process is that these selected stocks will be sent to the second optimization stage for finding out the proportion of investment. For testing purposes, the best 10, 20, and 30 stocks are selected as the input values for the stock allocation process. Of course, the investor's expected return is also required as an input variable. It should be noted that for a month's basis evaluation process, the expected

monthly return should be the result of annual return divided by 12. Based upon the algorithm proposed by Section 2.2, the optimal asset allocation for the stocks can be obtained using GA. For interpretation, two important comparisons are performed. Assume that the expected return is set to 10% and the net accumulated return is used as performance evaluation criterion in the simulation.

Return Comparison between Optimal Portfolio and Equally Weighted Portfolio

In this comparison, an equally weighted portfolio means that assets are equally assigned to every

Figure 3. Return comparisons between optimal portfolio and equally weighted portfolio

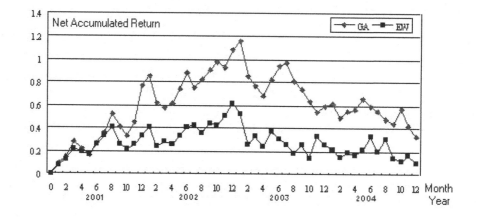

stock in the portfolio while the optimal portfolio is obtained by GA optimization. In addition, only the top 10 stocks are included in the portfolio in this comparison. Accordingly, the performance results are shown in Figure 3.

From Figure 3, the net accumulated return of the equally weighted portfolio is found to be the worse than that of the optimal portfolio. This implies that if one investor with no experience randomly chooses a portfolio of stock to invest, the expected return for the portfolio will be approximately the same as that value. It is not a surprising fact because there are so many bad-quality stocks in the stock market that they may lower the overall performance of the portfolio. Even if one gets no loss in the random investment, he or she has already had a loss due to the opportunity cost of capital. At the same time, this result also indicates that the selection of good-quality stock is a very important step in portfolio optimization, which is often neglected by Markowitz's theory.

The Return Comparison with Different Number of Stocks

In this study, three portfolios with 10, 20, and 30 stocks are compared. The optimal asset allocation

is performed by GA. Accordingly, the results are shown in Figure 4.

From Figure 4, we can find that the portfolio performance decreases with the increase of the number of stocks in the portfolio, and the portfolio performance of the 10 stocks is the best in the testing. As earlier noted, portfolio management does not only focus on the expected return but also on risk minimization. The larger the number of stocks in the portfolio, the more flexible the portfolio is to make the best composition to avoid risk. However, selecting good-quality stocks is the prerequisite for obtaining a good portfolio. That is, although the portfolio with the large number of stocks can lower the risk to some extent, some bad-quality stocks may be included in the portfolio, which influences the portfolio performance. This result also demonstrates that if the investors select good-quality stocks, the portfolio with the large number of stocks does not necessarily outperform the portfolio with the small number of stocks. Therefore it is wise for investors to select a limited number of good quality stocks for portfolio optimization.

In addition, Figure 4 also shows that the performance trend for different portfolios with different number of stocks is very similar except

Figure 4. Performance comparisons with different number of stocks

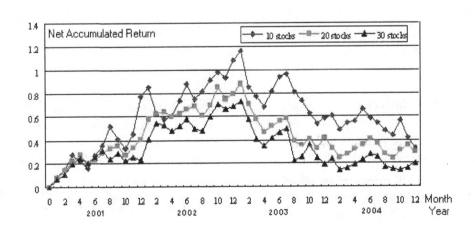

for the magnitude. Although a portfolio can reduce asymmetric risk, it can do little in the case where the overall market has poor performance. For example, the market condition was good for the first 2 years and all the portfolios performed well; however, for the last 2 years, especially for 2004, the market trend reversed and that caused all the portfolios to have reversal trends, too.

CONCLUSION

In this chapter, a two-stage genetic optimization algorithm is proposed to mine the most valuable portfolio. In the first stage, GA is used to rank the stock and select the good-quality stock for portfolio optimization. In the second stage, optimal asset allocation for portfolios can be realized by GA. Through the two-stage genetic optimization process, an optimal portfolio can be determined. For illustration purposes, a simulated experiment with a real-world data set is performed. Simulation results demonstrate that the proposed two-stage genetic optimization algorithm is an effective portfolio selection and optimization approach, which can mine the most valuable portfolio for investors.

In addition, experiment results also find that (a) selecting some good-quality stocks before portfolio asset allocation is very important, and (b) the quantity of stocks in the portfolio may not necessarily satisfy the principle of "the more, the better"; therefore, a limited number of stocks with high-quality assets in the portfolio can effectively improve the portfolio performance.

ACKNOWLEDGMENT

The authors would like to thank the editors and two anonymous referees for their valuable comments and suggestions. Their comments helped to improve the quality of the chapter immensely. This work is supported by grants from the National Natural Science Foundation of China (NSFC No. 70221001, 70601029), the Chinese Academy of Sciences (CAS No. 3547600), the Academy of Mathematics and Systems Science (AMSS No. 3543500) of CAS, and City University of Hong Kong (Strategic Research Grant No. 7001677, 7001806).

REFERENCES

Casas, C. A. (2001). Tactical asset allocation: An artificial neural network based model. *Proceedings of International Joint Conference on Neural Networks, 3*, 1811-1816.

Chapados, N., & Bengio, Y. (2001). Cost functions and model combination for VaR-based asset allocation using neural networks. *IEEE Transactions on Neural Networks, 12*, 890-906.

Chu, T. C., Tsao, C. T., & Shiue, Y. R. (1996). Application of fuzzy multiple attribute decision making on company analysis for stock selection. *Proceedings of the Soft Computing in Intelligent Systems and Information Processing* (pp. 509-514).

Fan, A., & Palaniswami, M. (2001). Stock selection using support vector machines. *Proceedings of International Joint Conference on Neural Networks, 3*, 1793-1798.

Goldberg, D. E. (1989). *Genetic algorithm in search, optimization, and machine learning.* Reading, MA: Addison-Wesley.

Holland, J. H. (1992). Genetic algorithms. *Scientific American, 267*, 66-72.

Levin, A. U. (1995). Stock selection via nonlinear multi-factor models. In *Advances in neural information processing systems* (pp. 966-972). San Francisco: Morgan Kaufmann Publishers.

Maranas, C. D., Androulakis, I. P., Floudas, C. A., Berger, A. J., & Mulvey, J. M. (1997). Solving long-term financial planning problems via global optimization. *Journal of Economic Dynamics and Control, 21*, 1405-1425.

Markowitz, H. M. (1952). Portfolio selection. *Journal of Finance, 7*, 77-91.

Mulvey, J. M., Rosenhaum, D. P., & Shetty, B. (1997). Strategic financial risk management and operations research. *European Journal of Operational Research, 97*, 1-16.

Yu, L., Wang, S. Y., & Lai, K. K. (2006). An integrated data preparation scheme for neural network data analysis. *IEEE Transactions on Knowledge and Data Engineering, 18*(2), 217-232.

Yu, L., Wang, S. Y., & Lai, K. K. (2008). Neural network-based mean-variance- skewness model for portfolio selection. *Computers & Operations Research, 35*(1), 34-46

Zargham, M. R., & Sayeh, M. R. (1999). A Web-based information system for stock selection and evaluation. *Proceedings of the First International Workshop on Advance Issues of E-Commerce and Web-Based Information Systems* (pp. 81-83).

Chapter XV
Financial Trading Systems:
Is Recurrent Reinforcement Learning the Way?

Francesco Bertoluzzo
University of Padua, Italy

Marco Corazza
University Ca'Foscari of Venice, Italy & School for Advanced Studies in Venice Foundation, Italy

ABSTRACT

In this chapter we propose a financial trading system whose trading strategy is developed by means of an artificial neural network approach based on a learning algorithm of the recurrent reinforcement type. In general terms, this kind of approach consists, first, of directly specifying a trading policy based on some predetermined investor's measure of profitability, and second, of directly setting the financial trading system while using it. In particular, with respect to the prominent literature, in this contribution we take into account as a measure of profitability the reciprocal of the returns weighted direction symmetry index instead of the widespread Sharpe ratio, and we obtain the differential version of the measure of profitability we consider and all the related learning relationships. Finally, we propose a simple procedure for the management of drawdown-like phenomena, and finally, we apply our financial trading approach to some of the most prominent assets of the Italian stock market.

INTRODUCTION

When an economic agent invests capital in financial markets, she or he has to make decisions under uncertainty. In such a context, the task consists of suitably dealing with financial risk in order to maximize some predetermined measure of profitability. A widespread class of tools that is used to support such risky decisions is the one of the financial trading system (FTS).

A standard approach that is usually followed to specify an FTS involves the following.

- Identifying one or more variables (asset prices, transaction volumes, etc.) related to the time behavior of one or more suitable quantities of interest (e.g., trading signals).
- Utilizing the current and past values of these variables to forecast (or, more in general, to extract information concerning them) the future values of the suitable quantities of interest.
- Using these predictions and information to implement a trading strategy by which to make effective trades.

The distinctly operative valence of FTSs has obviously made them popular for a long time among professional investors and practitioners. A lot of books have been devoted to the working utilization of these tools (see, among the various ones, Appel, 1979; Murphy, 1999; Nison, 1991; Wilder, 1978).

Nevertheless, although only in recent years, the academic world has also begun to (partially) recognize the soundness of some of the features related to FTSs (see, among the first ones, Lee & Swaminathan, 2000; Lo, Mamaysky, & Wang, 2000). Moreover, the really enormous, and continuously increasing, mass of collected financial data has led to the development of FTSs whose information extraction processes are based on data mining methodologies (see, for example, Corazza, Vanni, & Loschi, 2002; Plihon, Wu, & Gardarin, 2001).

Alternative approaches to the standard building of FTSs have been proposed both in the operative literature and in the academic ones. Among the approaches belonging to the latest category, in this chapter we consider the ones that exploit artificial neural network (ANN) methodologies

based on learning of the recurrent reinforcement type. In general terms, these approaches including the following.

- Directly specifying a trading policy based on some predetermined investor's measure of profitability (in such a manner one avoids to have to identify the quantities of interest, and avoids to have to perform the predictions and information extraction concerning such quantities).
- Directly setting the frame and the parameters of the FTS while using it (in such a way one can avoid to carry out the off-line setting of the trading system).

Among the first contributions in this research field, we recall Moody, Wu, Liao, and Saffell (1998), Moody and Saffell (2001), and Gold (2003). In general, they show that such strategies perform better than the ones based on supervised learning methodologies when market frictions are considered. In Moody et al., the authors develop and utilize a recurrent reinforcement learning (RRL) algorithm in order to set an FTS that, taking into account transaction costs, maximizes an appropriate investor's utility function based both on the well-known Sharpe ratio and on its differential version. Then, they show by controlled experiments that the proposed FTS performs better than standard FTSs. Finally, the authors use their FTS to make profitable trades with respect to assets of the U.S. financial markets. In Moody and Saffell, the authors mainly compare FTSs developed by using RRL methodologies with FTSs developed by using stochastic dynamic programming methodologies. In general, they show by extensive experiments that the former approach is better than the latter one. In Gold, the author considers an FTS similar to the one developed in Moody et al. and applies it to financial high-frequency data, obtaining profitable performances.

In this chapter, with respect to the cited contributions, we will do the following.

- Instead of considering as a measure of profitability the Sharpe ratio (which is the only one used in the quoted literature), we take into account the reciprocal of the returns weighted direction symmetry index reported in Abecasis, Lapenta, and Pedreira (1999).
- We obtain the differential version of the measure of profitability we consider and obtain all the new related learning relationships.
- We propose a simple procedure for the management of drawdown-like phenomena by which to integrate the considered FTS.
- We apply our financial trading approach (FTA) (i.e., FTS with drawdown-like phenomenon management) to some of the most prominent assets of the Italian stock market.

Finally, in the last section, we provide some concluding remarks.

RECURRENT REINFORCEMENT LEARNING: A SHORT RECALL

In this section, we give a short qualitative introduction of the learning of recurrent reinforcement type.

Generally speaking, this kind of learning concerns an agent (in our case, the FTS) dynamically interacting with an environment (in our case, a financial market). During this interaction, the agent perceives the state of the environment and undertakes a related action. In its turn, the environment, on the basis of this action, provides a positive or negative reward (in our case, the investor's gain or loss). Recurrent reinforcement learning consists of the online detection of a policy

(in our case, a trading strategy) that permits the maximization over the time of a predetermined cumulative reward (see, for technical details, Sutton & Barto, 1997).

It is good to notice that, given the well-known stochastic nature of financial markets, detecting such an optimal trading policy is equivalent to solving a suitable stochastic dynamic programming problem. Under this point of view, recurrent reinforcement learning provides approximate solutions to stochastic dynamic programming problems (see, for more details, Bertsekas, 1995; Bertsekas & Tsitsiklis, 1996).

THE FINANCIAL TRADING SYSTEM

In this section, at first we describe our discrete-time trading strategy, then we obtain all the new learning relationships related to the measure of profitability we consider.

The Trading Strategy

Let us start by considering a discrete time frame $t = 0,...,T$. Our trading strategy at time t, F_t, is simply based on the sign of the output, y_t, of a suitable ANN:[1]

- If $y_t < 0$, then $F_t = -1$ and one short sells the considered stock or portfolio.
- If $y_t = 0$, then $F_t = F_{t-1}$ and one does nothing.
- If $y_t > 0$, then $F_t = 1$ and one buys the considered stock or portfolio[2].

We reasonably assume that this trading strategy depends on the current and past values of one or more suitable variables related to the stock or portfolio to trade, and depends on the previous value of the trading strategy itself. In particular, in this chapter we consider only one variable, the logarithmic rate of return of the stock or portfolio to trade.

The ANN we consider is a simple no-hidden-layer perceptron model in which the squashing function is the tanh($\cdot$) one (both the architectural structure and the squashing function are the ones commonly used in the relevant literature):

$$y_t = \tanh\left(\sum_{i=0}^{M} w_{i,t}x_{t-i} + w_{M+1,t}F_{t-1} + w_{M+2,t}\right),$$

where

- $w_{0,\tau},..., w_{M+1,\tau}$ are the weights of the ANN at time τ,
- $x_\tau,...,x_{\tau-N}$ are the current and past values of the logarithmic rate of return of the stock or portfolio to trade at time τ, and
- $w_{M+2,\tau}$ is the threshold of the ANN at time τ.

As a reward at the generic time period $(t-1, t]$, we take into account the following quantity:

$$R_t = \mu[F_{t-1}r_t - \delta|F_t - F_{t-1}|],$$

where

- μ is the (prefixed) amount of capital to invest,
- r_τ is the geometric rate of return at time τ of the stock or portfolio to trade, and
- δ is the (prefixed) percent transaction cost related to the stock or portfolio quota to trade.

Notice the following.

- R_t is the net reward of the generic time period $(t-1, t]$.
- With respect to the cited contributions, in this chapter we consider a net reward formulated in terms of the rate of return instead of price.

Given the net reward of the period, it is easy to define as follows the (net) cumulative reward from time 1 to time t:

$$CR_t = CR_{t-1} + R_t = \sum_{i=1}^{t} R_i$$

where,

- CR_τ denotes the (net) capital gain at time τ.

The proposed expression for the net cumulative reward is a particularization of the following more general one:

$$CR_t = CR_{t-1} + R_t = \sum_{i=1}^{t} R_i(1+i_{fr})^{t-i},$$

where i_{fr} is the free-risk rate of return of the period.

Finally, we give the new investor's gain index at time t whose utilization permits the determination, via recurrent reinforcement learning, of the optimal values of the weights of the considered ANN:

$$I_t = \frac{\sum_{i=1}^{t} g_i|R_i|}{\sum_{i=1}^{t} b_i|R_i|}, \text{ with } \sum_{i=1}^{t} b_i|R_i| \neq 0, \qquad (1)$$

where

$$g_\tau = \begin{cases} 0 \text{ if } R_\tau \leq 0 \\ 1 \text{ if } R_\tau > 0 \end{cases}$$

and

$$b_\tau = \begin{cases} 1 \text{ if } R_\tau \leq 0 \\ 0 \text{ if } R_\tau > 0 \end{cases}.$$

This index, which is the reciprocal of the returns weighted directional symmetry measure reported in Abecasis et al. (1999), at each time t is given by the ratio between the cumulative "good" (i.e., positive) rewards and the cumulative "bad" (i.e., not positive) rewards.

A well-working trading strategy should guarantee that

$$\sum_{i=0}^{t} g_i |R_i| > \sum_{i=0}^{t} b_i |R_i|,$$

that is, after some arrangements, $I_t > 1$, with $t = 1,...,T$.

Recurrent Reinforcement Learning

The considered ANN is characterized by $M + 3$ parameters: $w_{0,t},...,w_{M+2,t}$. For determining their optimal values, we perform a well-founded economic approach consisting of the maximization of a suitable investor's utility function depending, at time t, on $R_1,...,R_t$. In particular, as a (nonstandard) utility function we take into account equation (1). At this point, we determine the optimal values of the considered parameters by using a usual weight updating method based on the following gradient ascent technique:

$$w_{i,t} = w_{i,t-1} + \rho_t \frac{dU_t}{dw_{i,t}}, \text{ with } i = 0,..., M+2,$$

$$(2)$$

where

- U_τ is the investor's utility function at time τ,
- and ρ_τ is a suitable learning rate at time τ.

It is important to notice that, in each generic time period $(t - 1, t]$, the investor is (obviously) interested in the marginal variation of the investor's utility function, that is, in $D_t = U_t - U_{t-1} = I_t - I_{t-1}$.

Now, in order to provide the expression for $dU_t/dw_{i,t} = dI_t/dw_{i,t}$, we should notice that computing I_t becomes harder as t increases. So, we resort to the following exponential moving formulation of equation (1):

$$\tilde{I}_t = \frac{A_t}{B_t},$$

$$(3)$$

where

$$A_\tau = \begin{cases} A_{\tau-1} & \text{if } R_\tau \leq 0 \\ \eta R_\tau + (1-\eta)A_{\tau-1} & \text{if } R_\tau > 0 \end{cases}$$

is the exponential moving estimates of the numerator of equation (1) at time τ,

$$B_\tau = \begin{cases} -\eta R_\tau + (1-\eta)B_{\tau-1} & \text{if } R_\tau \leq 0 \\ B_{\tau-1} & \text{if } R_\tau > 0 \end{cases}$$

is the exponential moving estimates of the denominator of equation (1) at time τ, and η is an adaptation coefficient. So, $U_t = \tilde{I}_t$.

Then, in order to provide an expression for D_t, we act in a way similar to the one used in Moody et al. (1998), Moody and Saffell (2001), and Gold (2003).

- First, we consider the expansion of equation (3) in Taylor's series about $\eta = 0$.
- Second, we utilize $d\tilde{I}_t / d\eta|_{\eta=0}$ as approximation of D_t, that is, after some arrangements,

$$D_t \cong \left. \frac{d\tilde{I}_t}{d\eta} \right|_{\eta=0} = \begin{cases} -\dfrac{A_{t-1}(R_t + B_{t-1})}{B_{t-1}^2} & \text{if } R_t \leq 0 \\ \dfrac{R_t - A_{t-1}}{B_{t-1}} & \text{if } R_t > 0 \end{cases}$$

At this point, it is possible to prove that (see, for more details, Moody et al., 1998; Moody & Saffell, 2001; and Gold, 2003),

$$\frac{dU_t}{dw_{i,t}} = \sum_{j=1}^{t} \frac{dU_j}{dR_j} \left(\frac{dR_j}{dF_j} \frac{dF_j}{dw_{i,t}} + \frac{dR_j}{dF_{j-1}} \frac{dF_{j-1}}{dw_{i,t-1}} \right),$$

where

$$\frac{dU_\tau}{dR_\tau} = \frac{d(U_\tau - U_{\tau-1})}{dR_\tau} = \frac{dD_\tau}{dR_\tau} = \begin{cases} \dfrac{A_{\tau-1}B_{\tau-1}}{B_{\tau-1}^3} & \text{if } R_\tau < 0 \\ \dfrac{1}{B_{\tau-1}} & \text{if } R_\tau > 0 \end{cases}$$

(notice that $\dfrac{dU_\tau}{dR_\tau} = \dfrac{d(U_\tau - U_{\tau-1})}{dR_\tau}$ as $U_{\tau-1}$ does not depend on R_τ),

$$\frac{dR_\tau}{dF_\tau} = -\mu\delta\,\text{sign}\left(F_\tau - F_{\tau-1}\right),$$

$$\frac{dR_\tau}{dF_{\tau-1}} = P_\tau - P_{\tau-1} - \mu\delta\,\text{sign}\left(F_\tau - F_{\tau-1}\right),$$

and $\dfrac{dF_\tau}{dw_{i,\tau}}$ which depends on the chosen squashing function and is easily obtainable (see, for instance, Bishop, 1995).

Finally, in order to implement equation (2), we approximate the previous exact relationship, which holds for batch learning, in the following one, which holds for online learning:

$$\frac{dU_t}{dw_{i,t}} \cong \frac{dU_t}{dR_t}\left(\frac{dR_t}{dF_t}\frac{dF_t}{dw_{i,t}} + \frac{dR_t}{dF_{t-1}}\frac{dF_{t-1}}{dw_{i,t-1}}\right)$$

APPLICATIONS

In this section, at first we present the experimental plan of our application, then we propose a simple procedure for the management of drawdown-like phenomena; finally, we give the results coming from the application of our FTA.

We apply the considered FTA to 13 assets of the most prominent of the Italian stock market, that is, to all the assets specifying the MIB30 on September 21, 2006, such that, on that date, were traded from more than 20 years: Alleanza Assicurazioni (AA), Banca Intesa (BI), Banca Popolare di Milano (BPM), Capitalia (C), Fiat (F), Finmeccanica (Fi), Fondiaria-Sai (FS), Generali Assicurazioni (GA), Mediobanca (M), Ras Fraz (RF), Saipem (S), Telecom Italia (TI), and Unicredito Italiano (UI). In detail, we consider close daily data from January 1, 1973, to September 21, 2006.

In order to make operative our FTA, we need to determine the optimal values and time evolution of the parameters M, δ, ρ_t, η, and the one related to the management of drawdown-like phenomena. For carrying out this optimal setting, we perform in a manner similar to the one utilized in Moody et al. (1998) and Gold (2003); that is, we articulate the whole trading time period (from 0 to T) in the following sequence of overlapping time subperiods:

$$[0, \Delta t_{off} + \Delta t_{on}], [\Delta t_{on} + \Delta t_{off} + 2\Delta t_{on}], \ldots, [i\Delta t_{on},$$
$$\Delta t_{off} + (i+1)2\Delta t_{on}], \ldots, [T - \Delta t_{off} - 2\Delta t_{on}, T$$
$$- \Delta t_{on}], [T - \Delta t_{off} - \Delta t_{on}, T],$$

where Δt_{off} is the length of the initial part of each time subperiod (from $i\Delta t_{on}$ to $\Delta t_{off} + i\Delta t_{on}$) during which the FTA works in an off-line modality for performing the optimal setting of the considered parameters, and Δt_{on} is the length of the final part of each time subperiod (from $\Delta t_{off} + i\Delta t_{on}$ to $\Delta t_{off} + (i+1)\Delta t_{on}$) during which the FTA works in an online modality for making the financial trading.[3]

By so acting, our FTA performs uninterruptedly from Δt_{off} to T, and in the meantime the parameters are periodically updated.

The Drawdown-Like Phenomenon Management

Any well-working FTS should be able to minimize large losses during its running since these losses could reduce so much the capital at an investor's disposal to make impossible the continuation of the trading itself.

So, our FTS should also be able to minimize large losses, and in case they occur, it should be able to guarantee the continuation of the trading.

In order to minimize large losses, the financial trading is not performed (and is definitively interrupted) at that first instant time $t \in \{1,\ldots,T\}$ in which the net capital gain, that is, CR_t, is negative. In such a case, the loss can be at most $-\mu$.

In order to (attempt to) guarantee the continuation of the financial trading in case a large loss occurs, we utilize an amount of capital to invest:

$\mu + \mu_0,$

where

$$\mu_0 = \left| \min\{ \min_{0<t\leq \Delta t_{off}} \{R_t : R_t < 0 \wedge CR_t < 0 \wedge F_{t-1}F_t = -1\}, 0\} \right|$$

that is, the absolute value of the largest loss (associated with the occurrence that the net capital gain is negative and the trading strategy is changed) happened during the initial part of the first time subperiod.

Of course, given such an amount of capital to invest, the loss can be at most $-(\mu + \mu_0)$.

The Results

In all 13 applications, we have used an amount of capital to invest μ, equal to 1. As far as the optimal setting of the parameters, we have determined that, in general, $M \in \{3, 4,..., 9, 10\}$, $\delta \in$

$\{0.005, 0.010,..., 0.070, 0.075\}$, $\rho_t = 0.01$, $\eta = 0.01$, $\Delta t_{off} = 500$, and $\Delta t_{on} = 50$; of course, μ_0 varies as the investigated stock asset varies. Moreover, in each application we initialize both the numerator and the denominator of equation (1) to a positive infinitesimally small quantity.

In Table 1 we present the main results of our applications. In particular, we report the following with respect to each investigated stock asset.

- In the first column we report the identifier.
- In the second column we report the CR_T, with $T =$ September 21, 2006, obtained from the application of our FTA.
- In the third column we report μ_0.
- In the fourth column we report the largest loss, that is, $\min_{\Delta t_{on} \leq t \leq T} \{R_t : R_t < 0 \wedge F_{t-1}F_t = -1\}$

•

Table 1. The main results of our applications

ID	FTA-Based CR_T	μ_0	Largest Loss	FTS-Based CR_T	No. of Trades	$\% R_t < 0$	$\% R_t = 0$	$\% R_t > 0$
AA	−0.559	0.143	−0.348	−0.683	201	0.468	0.034	0.498
BI	−1.161	0.161	−0.630	−1.785	187	0.503	0.069	0.428
BPM	0.311	0.179	−0.340	0.367	96	0.510	0.073	0.417
C	0.478	0.185	−0.778	0.567	189	0.444	0.112	0.444
F	1.609	0.083	−0.338	1.742	199	0.492	0.021	0.487
Fi	2.701	0.048	−0.415	2.841	147	0.463	0.088	0.449
FS	1.211	0.075	−0.250	1.303	145	0.448	0.049	0.503
GA	−0.076	0.228	−0.238	−0.093	152	0.520	0.033	0.447
M	1.472	0.146	−0.231	1.687	151	0.444	0.039	0.517
RF	0.988	0.197	−0.270	1.182	42	0.429	0.000	0.571
S	0.126	0.032	−0.488	0.130	344	0.485	0.088	0.427
TI	−0.807	0.497	−1.643	−1.208	236	0.483	0.059	0.458
UI	−1.112	0.207	−0.981	0.013	3	1.000	0.000	0.000

- In the fifth column we report as a benchmark the CR_T, with T = September 21, 2006, obtained from the application of our FTS (i.e., FTA without the drawdown-like phenomenon management). Notice that this CR_T has to be considered as an (sometimes unrealistic) upper bound for the CR_T reported in the second column because, lacking the management of the drawdown-like phenomena, the associated financial trading can unrealistically continue also when CR_T < 0, with t = 1,..., $T-1$.
- In the sixth column we report the number of performed trades.
- In the seventh, eighth, and ninth columns we report the percentages of the performed trades for which $R_t < 0 / R_t = 0 / R_t > 0$.

Concerning these results, the following has be noticed.

- Although 5 of the 13 investigated stock assets show a negative FTA-based CR_T, the summation of all these FTA-based CR_T is positive and equal to 5.181. That can be interpreted as the fact that, under a suitable diversification in the investments, our FTA is well working enough in the long run (see, for example, Figure 1).
- Of course, the magnitude of this summation is not satisfying. It certainly depends on the choice to utilize in the expressions for both the CR_T a free-risk rate of return equal to 0, and also depends on the need to effect

Figure 1. The case of Finmeccanica (the cumulative reward represented in the figure is the gross one, i.e., FTA-based $CR_T + \mu + \mu_0$)

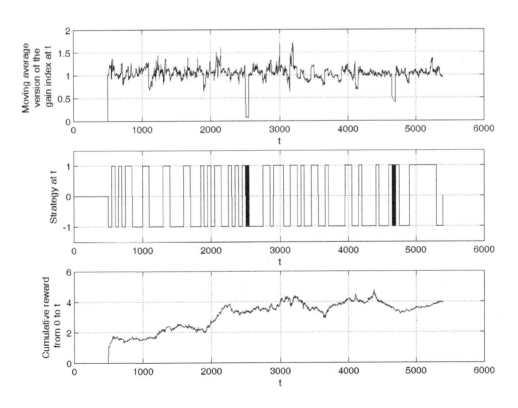

the setting of the parameters in some more refined way.

- Our drawdown-like phenomenon management is well performing enough. In fact, the utilization of an amount of capital to invest equal to $\mu + \mu_0$ appears able to reduce all the losses in T (and, as a counterpart, also all the gains in T); it also appears able to guarantee, among the three occurring critical cases (namely, Banca Intesa, Telecom Italia, and Unicredito Italiano), the continuation of the financial trading of the one Telecom Italia.

- In the critical case Banca Intesa, the behavior of our FTA before the large losses had been acceptable (see Figure 2 and Figure 3).

CONCLUSION

In this section, we provide some remarks for possible extensions of our contribution.

- In order to (attempt to) reduce the percentage of performed trades for which $R_t < 0$, we conjecture that it could be fruitful to utilize the following so-modified trading strategy:

if $y_t < -\varepsilon$, with $\varepsilon > 0$, then $F_t = -1$
if $-\varepsilon^- \leq y_t \leq \varepsilon^+$, with $\varepsilon^+ > 0$, then $F_t = F_{t-1}$
if $y_t > \varepsilon^+$, then $F_t = 1$

Of course, in such a case we should need to determine the optimal values of two other parameters, that is, ε^- and ε^+.

Figure 2. The critical case of Banca Intesa (the cumulative reward represented in the figure is the gross one, i.e., FTA-based $CR_T + \mu + \mu_0$)

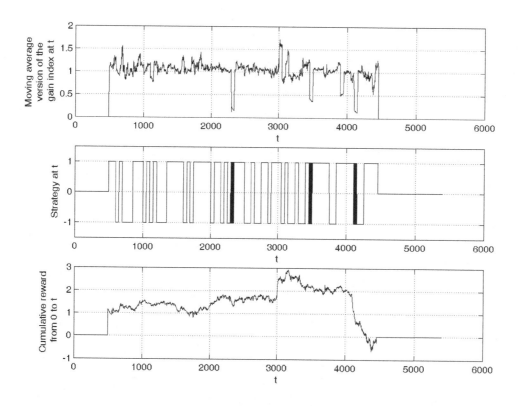

Figure 3. The critical case of Unicredito Italiano (the cumulative reward represented in the figure is the gross one, that is, FTA-based $CR_T + \mu + \mu_0$)

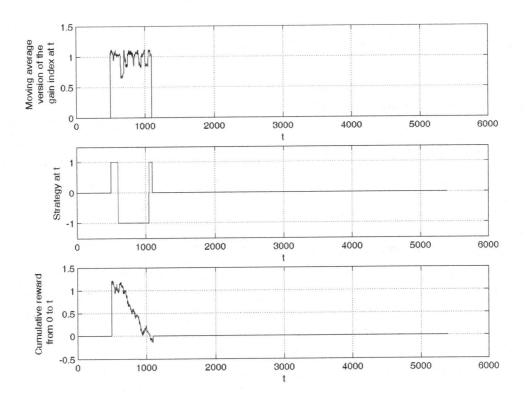

In order to (attempt to) improve the learning capabilities of the ANN, we conjecture that it could be profitable to use a multilayer perceptron model (to the best of our knowledge, such a check is carried out in Gold, 2003, but without meaningful results).

- In order to make more informative the set of the variables related to the time evolution of the quantities of interest, we conjecture that it could be fruitful to consider, beyond the logarithmic rate of return, at least the transaction volume.

- In order to (attempt to) explicitly take into account the risk in our FTA, we conjecture that it could be profitable to utilize some suit-

able risk-adjusted version of the investor's gain index (equation (1)).

- Finally, in order to (attempt to) make close our FTA, we conjecture that it could be fruitful to make the drawdown-like phenomenon management endogenous to the learning process.

REFERENCES

Abecasis, S. M., Lapenta, E. S., & Pedreira, C. E. (1999). Performance metrics for financial time series forecasting. *Journal of Computational Intelligence in Finance*, 5-23.

Appel, G. (1979). *The moving average convergence-divergence method.* Great Neck, NY: Signalert.

Bertsekas, D. P. (1995). *Dynamic programming and optimal control.* Belmont, MA: Athena Scientific.

Bertsekas, D. P., & Tsitsiklis, J. N. (1996). *Neurodynamic programming.* Belmont, MA: Athena Scientific.

Bishop, C. (1995). *Neural networks for pattern recognition.* Oxford, United Kingdom: Oxford University Press.

Corazza, M., Vanni, P., & Loschi, U. (2002). Hybrid automatic trading system: Technical analysis & group method of data handling. *Neural Nets: 13th Italian Workshop on Neural Nets, WIRN Vietri 2002* (pp. 47-55).

Gold, C. (2003). FX trading via recurrent reinforcement learning. *Proceedings of IEEE International Conference on Computational Intelligence in Financial Engineering* (pp. 363-370).

Lee, C. M. C., & Swaminathan, B. (2000). Price momentum and trading volume. *Journal of Finance, 55*, 2017-2069.

Lo, W. A., Mamaysky, H., & Wang, J. (2000). Foundations of technical analysis: Computational algorithms, statistical inference, and empirical implementation. *Journal of Finance, 55*, 1705-1769.

Moody, J., & Saffell, M. (2001). Learning to trade via direct reinforcement. *IEEE Transactions on Neural Networks, 12*, 875-889.

Moody, J., & Wu, L. (1997). Optimization of trading systems and portfolios. In Y. Abu-Mostafa, A. N. Refenes, & A. S. Weigend (Eds.), *Decision technologies for financial engineering* (pp. 23-35). London: World Scientific.

Moody, J., Wu, L., Liao, Y., & Saffell, M. (1998). Performance functions and reinforcement learning for trading systems and portfolios. *Journal of Forecasting, 17*, 441-470.

Murphy, J. J. (1999). *Study guide to technical analysis of the financial markets.* New York: Prentice Hall Press.

Nison, S. (1991). *Japanese candlesticks charting technique.* New York: Prentice Hall Press.

Plihon, V., Wu, F., & Gardarin, G. (2001). A financial data mining trading system. *Natural Language Processing and Information Systems: 5th International Conference on Applications of Natural Language to Information Systems, NLDB 2000* (p. 370).

Sutton, R. S., & Barto, A. G. (1997). *An introduction to reinforcement learning.* Cambridge, MA: MIT Press.

Wilder, J. W. (1978). *New concepts in technical trading.* Greensboro, NC: Trend Research.

Chapter XVI
About the Use of Computational Fluid Dynamics (CFD) in the Framework of Physical Limnological Studies on a Great Lake

Leonardo Castellano
Matec Modelli Matematici, Italy

Walter Ambrosetti
CNR – Istituto per lo Studio degli Ecosistemi, Italy

Nicoletta Sala
Università della Svizzera Italiana, Switzerland & Università dell'Insubria, Italy

ABSTRACT

The aim of this chapter is to discuss how far computational fluid dynamics (CFD) is currently able to simulate the limnological physics of a complex natural body of water. The experience reported by the authors is in progress at the CNR- ISE (Consiglio Nazionale delle Ricerche, Istituto per lo Studio degli Ecosistemi; National Research Council, Institute of Ecosystem Study) of Pallanza, Italy. The main features of the current state of the art in this field of application of mathematical modeling techniques are summarized and the characteristics of the computer code now in use for our studies on Lake Maggiore are described in detail. Examples of the kind of information that can be extracted from the outputs are given to show how knowledge collected by traditional analysis of the experimental data and in situ observations can be improved with this kind of support. Forecasts for future trends are also suggested.

INTRODUCTION

A large natural body of water with a free surface is a very complex system, and scientific observations on it, even restricted to its physical behavior (i.e., hydrodynamics, heat, and mass transfer mechanisms), require a considerable investment of human and material resources. Thus, any measurement campaign will usually be focused on a single process, and a fruitful exploitation of the collected results to assemble the puzzle of the overall phenomenology will depend on the experience and intelligence of the research team.

In the case of Lake Maggiore (Northern Italy and Switzerland), the CNR-ISE (Consiglio Nazionale delle Ricerche, Istituto per lo Studio degli Ecosistemi; National Research Council, Institute of Ecosystem Study) of Pallanza has for many years performed a quantitative analysis of the natural thermal stratification and destratification of the waters: the vertical mixing during the late winter, the recirculating flow induced by advective fluxes, and meteorological parameters (e.g., Ambrosetti & Barbanti, 1999; Ambrosetti, Barbanti, & Mosello, 1982; Ambrosetti, Barbanti, & Rolla, 1977; Ambrosetti, Barbanti, & Sala, 2002; Barbanti & Ambrosetti, 1990), all of which have aided our understanding of the main features governing the evolution of seasonal patterns in the hydrodynamic and thermal cycle of the water.

In the last decade, these studies have revealed signs of slow but progressive changes in the physical scenarios of the lake (i.e., increase in the stability of the bulk of the water body, reduction of the depth of the lake involved in the vertical mixing at the end of the limnological winter, deeper penetration of the heat coming from the atmosphere) similar to those observed in almost all the deep lakes of Southern Europe and the whole Temperate Zone, and which can be associated with global warming phenomena (in brief, an increase in air temperature and the infrared radiation remitted back to the Earth, changes in the composition and distribution of meteoric precipitations).

These changes are suspected of being the major causes of the observed decline in the aquatic ecosystem in that they increase the residence time in certain zones of the lake, reducing nutrient recycling and causing insufficient oxygenation of the deeper layers. Accordingly, a highly detailed picture of the dynamics of a lake is an essential prerequisite in devising worthwhile projects for its conservation and restoration.

As experience in other fields of applied research shows, a CFD (computational fluid dynamics) tool can play a decisive role by generating simulations that have the potential to provide distributions of all the variables of interest (velocity, temperature, density, mass fractions of species, and so on) at a number of spatial points up to several million for any desired time instant. The authors of this chapter are firmly convinced of the efficacy of this procedure, but their profound knowledge of the complexities of systems like large lakes also leads them to the conviction that the main problem is to avoid the application of a CFD model being reduced to a pure numerical exercise with an output consisting of attractive, plausible but indecipherable colored maps. The experience in progress at ISE-CNR is described below.

BACKGROUND

The design and implementation of multidimensional mathematical models and computer codes for hydrodynamics, heat, and mass transfer phenomena in large natural, free-surface water bodies has been one of the most pioneering applications of numerical fluid-dynamics methods in the fields of applied research and advanced engineering. It started many decades ago (Castellano & Dinelli, 1975; Cheng & Tung, 1970; Dailey & Harleman, 1972; Orlob, 1967), had a great boost from the publication of the famous report "Limits to Growth" (Meadows, Meadows, Randers, & Behrens, 1972), and reached its maximum point of creativity in the second half of the 1980s (Blumberg & Mellor, 1987; Hunter, 1987; Leendertse, 1989). The further progress made since then is mainly due to the enormous increase in the computational power of computers, which has allowed scientists to use a great number of computational cells to implement the numerical manipulation of sophisticated models of turbulence, such as large eddy simulation (LES; Rao & Agee, 1996; Yue, Lin, & Patel, 2004), and to take into account realistic interactions with meteorological events and more complex chemical and biochemical schemes (Leon, Lam, Schertzer, & Swayne, 2005; Pham Thi, Huisman, & Sommeijer, 2005; Wang, Song, Chao, & Zhang, 2005).

The above short review should suffice to demonstrate that today we have everything we need to perform reliable simulations of the physical, physical-chemical, and ecological behavior of lakes, seas, and rivers at almost any level of sophistication. This is actually true only in theory because from a practical point of view, it holds good only for academic research projects that have at their disposal great human and financial resources.

For routine studies in support of advanced engineering (e.g., as regards the potential physical impact of civil infrastructures and/or of sand and gravel extraction, the fate of warm water discharge, expected restoration by hypolimnetic oxygenation devices, and so on), it is too expensive, in the framework of a fully 3-D simulation, to provide an exact description of phenomena such as the influence of the optical properties of the water on the penetration of short-wave radiation, or local buoyancy effects at the inflow point of all the tributary rivers. The general strategy for this type of analysis is to choose the mathematical model that ensures the best description of the mechanisms of primary interest at the lowest cost and apply it to the smallest possible area of the water body for the minimum time interval necessary. A different approach is needed for limnological studies. The

two main missions here, to help in evaluating the spectrum of residence time at different depths and to clarify the mechanisms governing the seasonal cycle of stratification and destratification, require computations over the entire volume of the lake and for time intervals ranging from several months to years. The simulations have to consider the following.

- Mass flow rates and temperatures of all the tributary rivers
- Mass flow rates of all the effluents
- Mass flow rates and temperatures of meteoric precipitations
- Mass flow rate and temperature of runoff
- Velocity and direction of the wind
- All the meteorological parameters that affect the heat exchange across the free surface (i.e., temperature and vapor pressure of air, wind speed at standard reference height of 10 m, cloud cover, short-wave and long-wave radiation heat fluxes from the sun and atmosphere, emissivity of the water surface)

This is a comparison problem as can be deduced from the most thorough and in-depth studies published in the specialized technical literature (Laval, Imberger, Hodges, & Stocker, 2003; Leon et al., 2006). In any case, the level of goodness that can be expected for the output obviously depends on the goodness of the mathematical and numerical model, but also on the number, time scale, and correctness of the experimental values available for the above parameters.

A key question is just how to judge the actual goodness of the output. This is crucial if we are to be sure that the solutions are correct in all computational spatial and time points, and can be used to give reliable estimates of more global parameters like the vertical distribution of the renewal time, the position in time of the thermocline, the maximum extent of the epilimnion, and so on. This note looks at the availability and exploitation of experimental data on the physical behavior of a real system, in the absence of which any simulation is reduced merely to a numerical exercise. Our investigations followed these two questions.

- How much experimental data is required to build up a representative image of the lake?
- How many experimental and theoretical points have to be found in agreement in order to conclude that the numerical simulation is satisfactory?

In view of the complexity outlined above, we are convinced that in the field of limnological studies, the best use of sophisticated mathematical models is to open a dialog with the water body, that is, to proceed by analyzing step by step the response of the system to different hydrodynamic, thermal, and meteorological loads, and using the results of each single simulation to try to forecast the output of the next more complicated one and understand the discrepancies. Only after a careful study of this kind can an overall simulation give really useful results.

The CFD applications now in progress on Lake Maggiore follow this road map. A good reason for optimism is that we possess hydrometeorological, physical, chemical, and biological data acquired daily for almost 50 years, and more than 100 papers and reports interpreting them.

WORK IN PROGRESS ON LAKE MAGGIORE

The computer code adopted in the current phase of the study is based on a mathematical model that can be classified at a medium level of sophistication, within a range that encompasses all the developments briefly reviewed in the previous section. The major simplifications regarding the top solutions are of the description of the heat transfer across the free surface and the turbulence model.

The first release was implemented almost 30 years ago (Castellano, Colombo, & Tozzi, 1977) and has generated several specialized versions for lakes and rivers with an extensive history of comparison of experimental data. Its application to Lake Maggiore has required further improvements, and even more adjustments may have to be made as new insights arise.

The conceptual model is schematized in Figure 1 and shows the water body ideally subdivided into horizontal layers L for which the following equations are valid.

Figure 1. Diagram of the multilayer representation of the lake

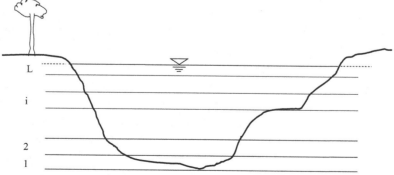

Equation 1.

$$\rho_0 h_i \frac{\partial u_i}{\partial t} + \rho_0 h_i \frac{\partial}{\partial x}(u_i u_i) + \rho_0 h_i \frac{\partial}{\partial y}(u_i v_i) + \rho_0 \left((uw)_{i+1} - (uw)_i\right) =$$

$$= -h_i \frac{\partial P_i}{\partial x} + h_i \frac{\partial}{\partial x}\left(\mu_{x,i} \frac{\partial u_i}{\partial x}\right) + h_i \frac{\partial}{\partial y}\left(\mu_{y,i} \frac{\partial u_i}{\partial y}\right) + \tau_{xz_{i+1}} - \tau_{xz_i} + S_{u_i}$$

$$i = 1, 2, \ldots, L-1$$

Equation 2.

$$\rho_0 h_i \frac{\partial v_i}{\partial t} + \rho_0 h_i \frac{\partial}{\partial x}(u_i v_i) + \rho_0 h_i \frac{\partial}{\partial y}(v_i v_i) + \rho_0 \left((vw)_{i+1} - (vw)_i\right) =$$

$$= -h_i \frac{\partial P_i}{\partial y} + h_i \frac{\partial}{\partial x}\left(\mu_{x,i} \frac{\partial v_i}{\partial x}\right) + h_i \frac{\partial}{\partial y}\left(\mu_{y,i} \frac{\partial v_i}{\partial y}\right) + \tau_{yz_{i+1}} - \tau_{yz_i} + S_{v_i}$$

$$i = 1, 2, \ldots, L-1$$

Equation 3.

$$h_i\left(\frac{\partial u_i}{\partial x} + \frac{\partial v_i}{\partial y}\right) + (w_{i+1} - w_i) = 0 \qquad i = 1, 2, \ldots, L-1$$

Equation 4.

$$P_i = g \sum_{j=0}^{L-1-i} h_{L-j} \rho_{L-j} + \frac{1}{2} g \rho_i h_i + P_a \qquad i = 1, 2, \ldots, L-1$$

Equation 5.

$$\rho = \frac{\rho_1(T)}{\rho_2(T) + 0.698\rho_1(T)}$$

Equation 6.

$$\rho_0 \frac{\partial(\phi_u)}{\partial t} + \rho_0 \frac{\partial}{\partial x}(\phi_u u_L) + \rho_0 \frac{\partial}{\partial y}(\phi_u v_L) - \rho_0 (uw)_L =$$

$$= -\frac{\partial(h_L P_L)}{\partial x} + \frac{\partial}{\partial x}\left(\mu_{x,L} \frac{\partial}{\partial x}\phi_u\right) + \frac{\partial}{\partial y}\left(\mu_{y,L} \frac{\partial}{\partial y}\phi_u\right) + \tau_{xz_a} - \tau_{xz_L} + S_{u_L}$$

Equation 7.

$$\rho_0 \frac{\partial(\phi_v)}{\partial t} + \rho_0 \frac{\partial}{\partial x}(\phi_v u_L) + \rho_0 \frac{\partial}{\partial y}(\phi_v v_L) - \rho_0 (vw)_L =$$

$$= -\frac{\partial(h_L P_L)}{\partial y} + \frac{\partial}{\partial x}\left(\mu_{x,L} \frac{\partial}{\partial x}\phi_v\right) + \frac{\partial}{\partial y}\left(\mu_{y,L} \frac{\partial}{\partial y}\phi_v\right) + \tau_{yz_a} - \tau_{yz_L} + S_{v_L}$$

Equation 8.

$$\frac{\partial}{\partial x}\phi_u + \frac{\partial}{\partial y}\phi_v - w_L + \frac{\partial h_L}{\partial t} = 0$$

Equation 9.

$$P_L = \frac{1}{2}g\rho_L h_L + P_a$$

Equation 10.

$$h_i \frac{\partial T_i}{\partial t} + h_i \frac{\partial}{\partial x}(u_i T_i) + h_i \frac{\partial}{\partial y}(v_i T_i) + \left((wT)_{i+1} - (wT)_i\right) =$$

$$i = 1, 2, ..., L-1$$

$$= h_i \frac{\partial}{\partial x}\left(\alpha_{x,i} \frac{\partial T_i}{\partial x}\right) + h_i \frac{\partial}{\partial y}\left(\alpha_{y,i} \frac{\partial u_i}{\partial y}\right) + q_{i+1} - q_i + S_{T_i}$$

Equation 11.

$$\frac{\partial(\phi_T)}{\partial t} + \frac{\partial}{\partial x}(\phi_T u_L) + \frac{\partial}{\partial y}(\phi_T v_L) - (wT)_L = \frac{\partial}{\partial x}\left(\alpha_{x,L}\frac{\partial}{\partial x}\phi_T\right) + \frac{\partial}{\partial y}\left(\alpha_{y,L}\frac{\partial}{\partial y}\phi_T\right) +$$

$$+q_a - q_L + S_{T_L}$$

$$\phi_u = h_L u_L \qquad (12)$$

$$\phi_v = h_L v_L \qquad (13)$$

$$\phi_T = h_L T_L \qquad (14)$$

$$\tau_{xz} = -\mu_z\left(\frac{\partial u}{\partial z} + \frac{\partial w}{\partial x}\right) \qquad (15)$$

$$\tau_{yz} = -\mu_z\left(\frac{\partial v}{\partial z} + \frac{\partial w}{\partial y}\right) \qquad (16)$$

$$q = -\alpha_z\frac{\partial T}{\partial z} \qquad (17)$$

The subscript *a* stands for the atmosphere, *i* for *i*th inner layer, L for the surface layer, g means

acceleration of gravity, h is thickness, P is pressure, q is the vertical component of heat fluxes, S_T are the internal heat sources, S_u are the internal sources of momentum in x-direction, S_v are the internal sources of momentum in y-direction, T is the temperature, u is the velocity in x-direction, v is the velocity in x-direction, w is the velocity in z-direction, (x, y) are the Cartesian coordinates on the horizontal planes, z is the Cartesian coordinate along the vertical direction, α is turbulent thermal diffusivity, η is the elevation of the free surface, μ is turbulent viscosity, ρ is mass density, $(\tau_{xz_i}, \tau_{yz_i})$ are the shear stresses between layers, and $(\tau_{xz_a}, \tau_{yz_a})$ are the shear stresses due to the wind.

The effect of the wind is modeled as follows.

Figure 2. Schematic of the vertical eddy viscosity model

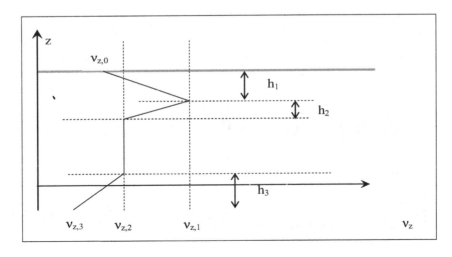

$$
\begin{cases}
\tau_{\sigma z_a} = \rho_a C_D U_{wind} U_{\sigma,wind} & , \quad \sigma = x, y \\[2mm]
C_D = a + b U_{wind}^c
\end{cases}
\tag{18}
$$

where U_{wind} is the strength of the wind, $U_{\sigma,wind}$ is the σ component, and C_D is a drag coefficient that depends on the empirical parameters (a,b,c) that depend on the U_{wind}.

The horizontal turbulent viscosities are defined as (e.g., Bird, Stewart, & Lightfoot, 1960),

$$
\mu_x = \rho (0.07 \delta x)^2 \sqrt{\left(\frac{\partial u}{\partial x}\right)^2 + \left(\frac{\partial v}{\partial x}\right)^2}
\tag{19}
$$

$$
\mu_y = \rho (0.07 \delta y)^2 \sqrt{\left(\frac{\partial u}{\partial y}\right)^2 + \left(\frac{\partial v}{\partial y}\right)^2}
\tag{20}
$$

where δx and δy are characteristic length scales of the computational grid.

The model for turbulence along the vertical direction is schematized in Figure 2, which shows a stratification defined by four values of viscosity for four different depth levels (Neumann & Pierson, 1966). On the free surface we have,

$$
\mu_L = \rho \nu_{z,0} = \rho \kappa U^* Z_0
\tag{21}
$$

where κ is the Von Karman universal constant ($\sim$0.4), Z_0 is the mean characteristic height of the surface waves, and U^* is the shear velocity given in terms of the wind shear stress (see equation (18)):

$$
U^* = (\tau_{wind} / \rho).
\tag{22}
$$

Equation 23.

$$
\begin{cases}
h_1 = 0.3\lambda \\[3mm]
\lambda = 0.2803 U_{wind}^2 \quad ; \quad \lambda \, (m), \; U_{wind} \, (m/s) \\[3mm]
\mu_1 = \rho \nu_1 = 0.3043 \cdot 10^{-4} \rho U_{wind}^3 \quad ; \quad \rho \left(kg/m^3\right), \; \nu_1 \left(m^2/s\right)
\end{cases}
$$

Equation 24.

$$
\begin{cases}
h_2 = 0.5 h_1 \\[3mm]
\mu_2 = \rho \nu_2 = \rho \left(a_{\nu_2} + b_{\nu_2} \left(K U_{water}^2 / \sigma\right)\right); \quad U_{water} \, (m/s), \; \nu_2 \left(m^2/s\right) \\[3mm]
\sigma = 10^{-4} \left(s^{-1}\right) \\[3mm]
K = 2.0 \cdot 10^{-5} \; (\text{dimensionless})
\end{cases}
$$

Equation 25.

$$\begin{cases} h_3 = a_{h_3} + b_{h_3} U_{water}^{c_{h_3}} \\[2ex] \mu_3 = \rho \nu_3 = \rho \left(a_{\nu_3} + b_{\nu_3} U_{water}^{c_{\nu_3}} \right) \end{cases}$$

The parameters of the first layer are given by, (see equation (23)).

Finally, for the underlying layers the equations are, (see equation (24) and (25)), where U_{water} is the local value of the velocity and a_{v2}, b_{v2}, a_{h3}, b_{h3}, c_{h3}, a_{v3}, b_{v3}, and c_{v3} are empirical constants.

The momentum source terms S_u and S_v can be used to take into account large structures that can cause localized pressure drops if present; their mathematical structure is,

$$\begin{cases} S_{u_i} = -h_i f_{u_i}\left(x, y; t\right) u_i \left| u_i \right| \\[2ex] S_{v_i} = -h_i f_{v_i}\left(x, y; t\right) v_i \left| v_i \right| \end{cases} \tag{26}$$

where f_{u_i} and f_{v_i} are friction factors.

The definition of the thermal source terms S_T belongs to the description of the heat exchange with the atmosphere. The main option implemented in the present version of our computer code is given by (Deas & Lowney, 2000; Jobson, 1997)

Figure 3. Grid mesh over the entire geometry of Lake Maggiore

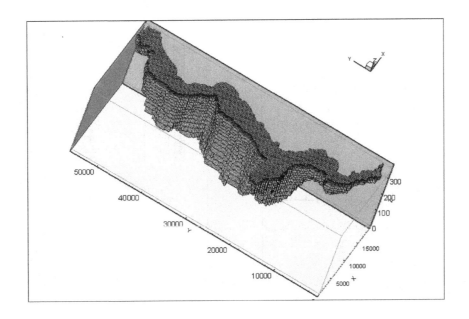

Figure 4. Flow pattern at the free surface

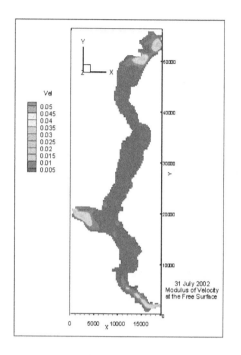

Figure 5. Modulus of velocity at the free surface

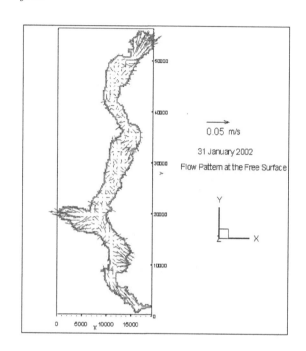

Figure 6. Temperature at the free surface

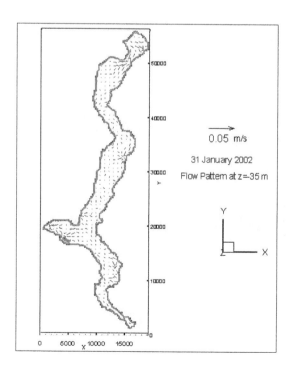

Figure 7. Flow pattern at z=-35 m

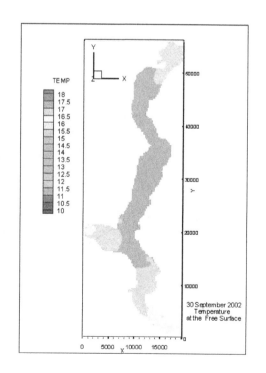

$$q_a = K_e (T_S - T_e), \qquad (27)$$

where T_S is the local value of the free surface temperature, T_e is the equilibrium temperature, and K_e is the kinetic surface exchange coefficient. These parameters can be **routinely** computed from the relations

$$K_e = 4\sigma(T_S + 273.)^3 + H_v\psi\rho(e_{o,p} - \gamma) \qquad (28)$$

$$T_e = T_a + 0.5\frac{K_a\left(T_h - T_l\right)}{m_a\left(t_s - t_f\right)}\cos(t + \theta) \qquad (29)$$

where σ is the Stefan-Boltzman constant, H_v is the latent heat of vaporization of water, ψ is an empirical coefficient or wind function dependent on wind speed, $e_{o,p}$ is the slope of the saturation vapor pressure curve with respect to temperature, γ is the psychrometric constant (reference value, 0.0598 kPa/°C), T_a is the air temperature, T_h and T_l are the high and low air temperature for the day, t_f and t_s are the time instants of the first and second temperature extremes, θ is the phase angle ($3\pi/2$ if the first extreme is the minimum temperature, and $\pi/2$ if the first extreme is the maximum temperature), and t is the current time. The ratio K_a/m_a between the heat exchange coefficient for the atmosphere and the mass of air per unit area can be determined using a rough discretization of equation (30),

$$\frac{\partial T_a}{\partial t} = K_a\left(T_a - T_e\right)/m_a \qquad (30)$$

and the mean lag between the time of the peak equilibrium temperature (solar noon) and the time of the peak air temperature.

Figure 8. Modulus of velocity at z=-35 m

Figure 9. Temperature at z=-35 m

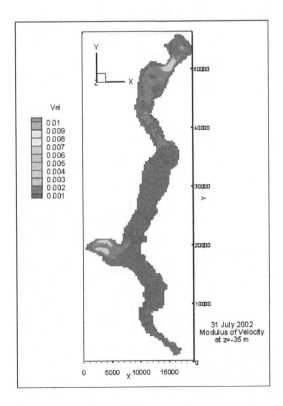

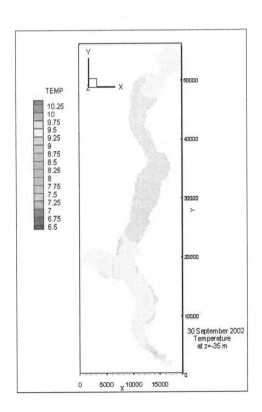

Figure 10. Velocity distribution in a vertical cross section

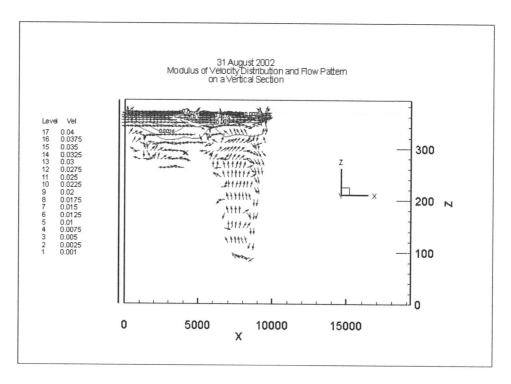

Figure 11. Temperature distribution and flow pattern in a vertical cross section

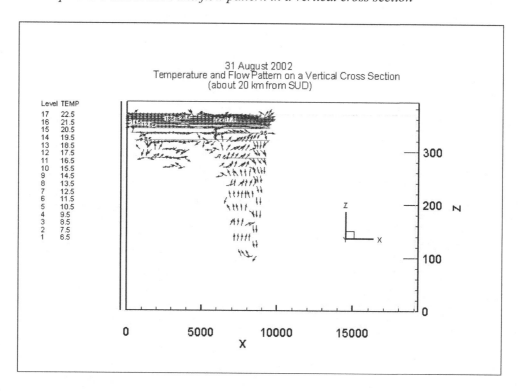

As a first approximation, the above computations can be performed out of line over a desired time scale and the results inserted in the code as input data. The source term S_T can be used to introduce a vertical distribution of a penalty factor that takes into account the extinction of the short-wave radiation as the depth increases.

Figure 12. Longitudinal movement of masses of water at various depth levels (positive sign means direction toward north)

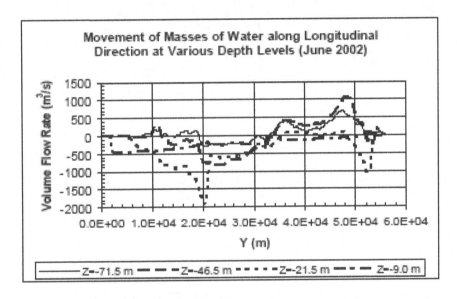

Figure 13. Transversal movement of masses of water at various depth levels (positive sign means direction toward east)

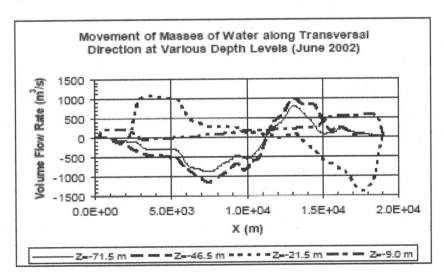

Figure 14. Vertical movement of masses of water at various depth levels (positive sign means direction toward free surface)

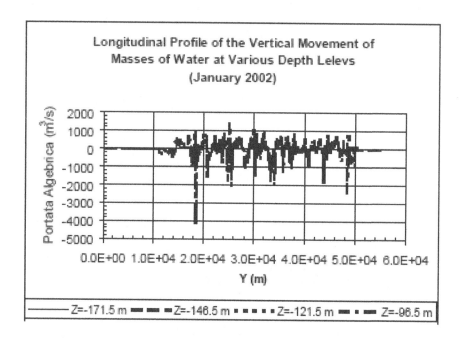

By inspection of equations (1) to (30), the following can be easily understood.

1. The main assumption is that the vertical distribution of pressure is hydrostatic.
2. The horizontal layers are coupled by this distribution of pressure, the shear stresses, and the vertical transfer of mass and energy.
3. The description of the turbulent regime is based on the eddy viscosity concept.
4. The description of the heat exchanges with the atmosphere is based on the heat transfer coefficient concept.

The first two statements are common to many other computer codes, even of much more recent date (e.g., Rueda & Schladow, 2003); in any **case**, they are acceptable in the absence of mechanisms of forced convection with a high value of vertical momentum component.

In the light of the details described above, the third statement appears equivalent to the vertical mixed-layer approach adopted by Hodges and Dallimore (2006) to improve the representativeness and performance of the computer code ELCOM (Estuary and Lake Computer Model). Finally, techniques and algorithms that can formulate more accurate models for heat transfer across the free surface are well known, but they are too time consuming to be used in simulations with a time scale of the order of years.

The numerical counterpart of the mathematical framework described above adopts a finite-volume method of discretization and uses structured meshes (e.g., Barth & Ohlberger, 2004). Assuming that all the variables are known at the time level n, the computational cycle to update the solution at the time level $n+1$ can be summarized as follows:

Figure 15. Vertical profile of temperature; comparison between experimental and numerical results at the end of May 2002

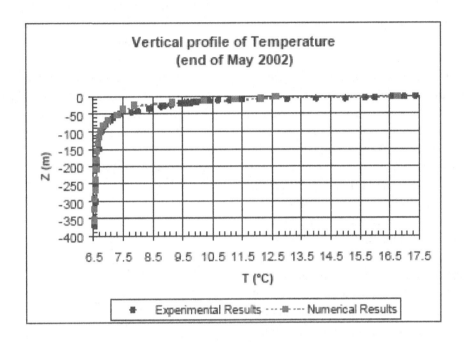

Figure 16. Vertical profile of temperature; comparison between experimental and numerical results at the end of September 2002

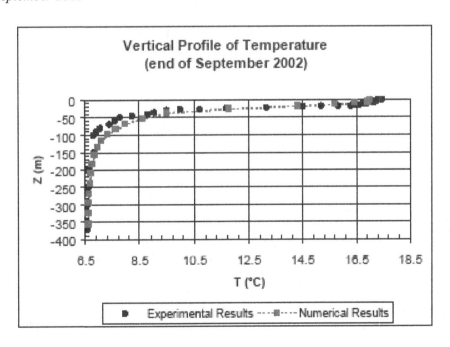

a. The initial distributions of the water temperature and the thickness of the surface layer, $\tilde{T}^{n+1}$ and $\tilde{h}_L^{\,n+1}$, are assumed to be equal to the values of the previous time (i.e., T^n and $h_L^{\,n}$).

b. These values are used in equations (4), (5), and (9) to give a first guess of the density and pressure distributions $\tilde{\rho}^{n+1}$, $\tilde{P}^{n+1}$.

c. $\tilde{\rho}^{n+1}$, $\tilde{P}^{n+1}$, $\tilde{h}_L^{\,n+1}$, T^n, u^n, v^n, w^n are used to compute a first guess $\tilde{u}_i^{n+1}$, $\tilde{v}_i^{n+1}$, $\tilde{T}_i^{n+1}$, $\tilde{\phi}_u^{n+1}$, $\tilde{\phi}_v^{n+1}$ $\tilde{\phi}_T^{n+1}$ of temperatures and horizontal velocities inside all layers. To do this, equations (1), (2), (6), (7), (10), and (11) are discretized to form linear algebraic systems of pentadiagonal structure, (see equation (31)), where the superscript γ counts the horizontal layers, the subscripts (i,j) indicate the spatial position, ψ are the nodal values of the unknowns, and AW, AE, AS, AN, AC, and S are coefficients and source terms that depend upon the metric properties of the computational mesh and the previous values of the thermal and hydrodynamic variables in that the nonlinear terms are linearized as:

$$u_i u_i \approx u_i^n \tilde{u}_i^{n+1} \tag{32a}$$

$$u_i v_i \approx v_i^n \tilde{u}_i^{n+1} \tag{32b}$$

$$v_i v_i \approx v_i^n \tilde{v}_i^{n+1} \tag{32c}$$

$$u_i T_i \approx u_i^n \tilde{T}_i^{n+1} \tag{32d}$$

$$v_i T_i \approx v_i^n \tilde{T}_i^{n+1} \tag{32e}$$

d. The results of the above step are used in equation (3) to compute $\tilde{w}_i^{n+1}$.

e. If the values guessed by Steps B to D satisfy equation (8), they are assumed to be the solutions at time level $n+1$ and the time cycle comes back to Step A; otherwise, the computation proceeds to the next step.

f. To find the increments η', φ'_u, φ'_v, u'_i, v'_i, which need to satisfy Constraint 8,

f1. one defines,

$$P' = \tilde{\rho}_L^{n+1} g \eta' \tag{33}$$

$$\phi'_u = -\frac{\tilde{\rho}_L^{n+1} g}{\rho_0 A C_{\phi_u}} \frac{\partial}{\partial x}(\tilde{h}_L^{n+1} \eta') \tag{34}$$

$$\phi'_v = -\frac{\tilde{\rho}_L^{n+1} g}{\rho_0 A C_{\phi_v}} \frac{\partial}{\partial y}(\tilde{h}_L^{n+1} \eta') \tag{35}$$

$$u'_i = -\frac{\tilde{\rho}_L^{n+1} g}{\rho_0 A C_u} \frac{\partial \eta'}{\partial x} \tag{36}$$

$$v'_i = -\frac{\tilde{\rho}_L^{n+1} g}{\rho_0 A C_v} \frac{\partial \eta'}{\partial y} \tag{37}$$

$$\tilde{\tilde{h}}_L = \tilde{h}_L^{n+1} + \eta' \tag{38}$$

$$\tilde{\tilde{\phi}}_u = \tilde{\phi}_u^{n+1} + \phi'_u \tag{39}$$

$$\tilde{\tilde{\phi}}_v = \tilde{\phi}_v^{n+1} + \phi'_v \tag{40}$$

$$\tilde{\tilde{u}}_i = \tilde{u}_i^{n+1} + u'_i \tag{41}$$

$$\tilde{\tilde{v}}_i = \tilde{v}_i^{n+1} + v'_i \tag{42}$$

Equation 31.

$$AW_{l,j}^{\gamma} \psi_{l-1,j}^{\gamma} + AE_{l,j}^{\gamma} \psi_{l+1,j}^{\gamma} + AS_{l,j-1}^{\gamma} \psi_{l,j-1}^{\gamma} + AN_{l,j}^{\gamma} \psi_{l,j+1}^{\gamma} + AC_{l,j}^{\gamma} \psi_{l,j}^{\gamma} =$$

$$= S_{\psi_{l,j}}^{\gamma}$$

f2. Solve the equation for η' that arises by summing the equations given by the substitution of equations (33) to (42) into equations (23) and (28).

f3. Update the values of h_L by equation (38) and comes back to Step B until $\eta' \approx 0$.

f4. Return to Step A.

g. The run stops when the final instant of the time simulation has been reached.

Figure 3 shows the grid mesh that was used to cover the geometric domain of Lake Maggiore for the first series of simulations we performed to evaluate the adequacy and/or points of weakness of the mathematical model compared to the real processes. It consists of about 400,000 computational cells distributed over 22 horizontal layers.

The outputs are real mines of information about the physical behavior of the lake. They consist of many millions of numbers for each time step, from which can be extracted graphical representations of velocity and temperature distributions in any desired section of the integration domain.

Figures 4 to 6 show some examples of flow pattern and the maps of velocity and temperature on the free surface as they were drawn from a 1-year simulation of the year 2002. The time step of the computation was 120 seconds, but the input parameters relevant to meteorology and to mass flow rates and temperature of tributary rivers were given as mean monthly values. Similar reconstructions can be done for all horizontal layers, for example, Figures 7 to 9, to get a complete overview of the entire scenario.

Much more useful for studying the physical limnology of the lake are plots like those shown in Figures 10 and 11, which report velocity and temperature on a vertical plane normal to the direction of the longer dimension of the lake.

The figures highlight the influence of the velocity field on the fate of the heat from the sun and the atmosphere. For instance, the figures show a weak (order of magnitude of millimeters per second, Figure 10) but well-defined upward motion that opposes the current by diffusion of heat from the warmer layers to the cooler ones below. The upward velocity components become zero at about 50 to 60 m deep as a consequence of the more effective and opposite momentum transfer in a horizontal direction produced by wind and tributary rivers to the more superficial layers. The vertical mixing in this zone is the result of turbulent diffusion and a weak recirculation flow due to entrainment and the boundaries of the water body.

Other useful information can also be obtained by managing the output data in such a way as to extract mean values and/or profiles of variables of interest on different spatial and/or time scales. Figures 12 and 13 show the longitudinal and transversal movement of masses of water at various depth levels, which are significant for a preliminary evaluation of the range of the vertical variation of the residence time. Similar profiles can be drawn for the natural exchange of water between the horizontal layers (Figure 14).

To complete the present discussion, it is worth giving some indications on the criteria for qualifying the results. The problem has been well summarized in the background section and on the practical ground the answer is straightforward: Apart from a good history of the mathematical model, the ability of the user, the correctness of constraints and boundary conditions, and the resolution power of the grid mesh and time step, all of which must be of a high standard, the reliability of a run is proportional to the number and variety of experimental observations that are in agreement with the theoretical results. In analyzing the simulations from which we extracted the figures, the comparison with the experimental vertical profiles of temperature proved to be the most significant. In fact, while the prediction of the values of the measured velocities is fairly satisfactory, the agreement between the thermal data is good only for the spring and summer months (Figure 15); at end of September, the computations begin to exhibit significant discrepancies (Figure 16). The difference in quality between hydrodynamic and thermal performance is justified by the fact that the measured velocities are of an inertial nature and then of an order of magnitude of centimeters per second, while the movement that opposes the penetration of the thermal energy into the lower layers of the lake is of a turbulent nature and then of an order of magnitude less than one millimeter per second, as shown in Figures 10 and 11. The conclusion is that improving the simulation of the physical behavior of the lake during autumn and winter requires a more thorough treatment of the turbulent regime and a finer grid mesh in the vertical direction.

FUTURE TRENDS

In confirmation of our remarks in the introduction section, we believe that for this kind of application, that is, CFD models that use a deterministic approach for large natural water bodies, the future is now. We would say once again that we have for many years possessed all the conceptual and theoretical tools to correctly describe the dynamics of such a system; and the most sophisticated of these tools are at the level of almost a full ab initio approach (e.g., full 3-D Navier-Stokes equations, Lambert-Beer-Bouguer law for heat exchange by radiation with the atmosphere, LES formulations of turbulence).

There is, therefore, a strong probability that the near future will be a continuation of the present, that is, resulting in even more fruitful applications of our current extensive knowledge but without any really significant improvements in basic know-how.

As regards our own experience, summarized in the previous section, there will be a natural evolution inside the framework of this road map, a step-by-step updating of the mathematical models now in use, fine-tuned according to the results of the dialog between the experimental and numerical data. In other words, the main aim of simulation campaigns will be to get to know the lake better instead of an academic wish to improve a priori the theoretical capabilities of the computer code. We do, however, believe that it is a matter of urgency to implement a subprogram to trace the fate of both Lagrangian massless and massive particles released at different depth levels for a more accurate evaluation of residence time.

As for the near future, generally speaking, a correct forecast would be that any net improvement in the simulations would be the consequence of (a) improvement in computer performance and rapid increase in computer memory capacity, in particular to enable the application of methods for direct simulations of turbulence, (b) the development of technologies for the low-cost collection of experimental data over time and spatial scales that match the time and spatial scales of the computations, at no more than an order of magnitude lower, and (c) the availability of tools for exploiting enormous numerical outputs.

From a practical point of view, the achievement and routine application of this kind of progress will demand a considerable investment of personnel with the highest scientific qualifications.

The above discussion does not take into account the futuristic possibilities that could be opened up by developments in quantum computing (e.g., Yepez, 2001), also in terms of theoretical aspects (i.e., suppression of Navier-Stokes equations and adoption of a lattice Boltzmann model). We are well aware of the progress being made in this field of scientific research and follow developments with great interest, but at present we cannot go beyond speculation as to what might be possible in the future.

CONCLUSION

This chapter offers a short but significant contribution to the discussion of the present capabilities of CFD in simulating the limnological physics of a complex natural water body such as a great subalpine lake. The discussion centers on the applications to a real system (Lake Maggiore) of a mathematical model that can be regarded as being at a medium level of sophistication compared to the entire gamma of the current state of the art. This tool was chosen intentionally to avoid the risk of emphasizing numerical efforts to the detriment of the research of insights into the system under discussion, at least in the first phase of this type of study. The development of the script has also made it possible to state the following about our present know-how. First, as far as a deterministic approach is concerned, the degree of development of the theoretical background can be considered at an almost full ab initio level. The possibility of describing some statistical peculiarities has been introduced by the application of LES for turbulence. Second, even today, the various products (i.e., computer codes) of the above knowledge are far from being fully exploited. The growth of computer technology can be a major support to limnological research; however, a decisive prerequisite for success is still the availability of enough experimental data. Third, no significant changes in the theoretical framework are envisaged in the near future, which will see only developments of the possibilities outlined above. The implementation of subprograms to simulate some random mechanisms (e.g., random-walk techniques) is straightforward, but is useful only when the main features of the lake are well known (on the other hand, LES models already cover a large part of the randomness of hydrodynamics). Fourth, in the near future, it should be possible to perform computations based on the direct simulation of turbulence. Finally, revolutionary innovations may arise from the theoretical approach to fluid dynamics suggested by conceptual developments in the field of quantum computing; but at the moment, this is mere speculation.

REFERENCES

Ambrosetti, W., & Barbanti, L. (1999). Deep water warming in lakes: An indicator of climatic change. *Journal of Limnology, 58*, 1-9.

Ambrosetti, W., Barbanti, L., & Mosello, R. (1982). Unusual deep mixing of Lago Maggiore during the winter 1980-1981. *Geografia Fisica e Dinamica Quaternaria, 5*, 183-191.

Ambrosetti, W., Barbanti, L., & Rolla, A. (1979). Mescolamento parziale o totale nel Lago Maggiore nell'ultimo trentennio. *Memorie dell'Istituto Italiano di Idrobiologia, 37*, 197-208.

Ambrosetti, W., Barbanti, L., & Sala, N. (2003). Residence time and physical processes in lakes. *Journal of Limnology, 62*(1), 1-15.

Barbanti, L., & Ambrosetti, W. (1990). The physical limnology on Lago Maggiore: A review. *Memorie dell'Itituto Italiano di Idrobiologia, 46*, 47-78.

Barth, T., & Ohlberger, M. (2004). Finite volume methods: Foundation and analysis. In E. Stein, R. de Borst, & T. J. R. Hughes (Eds.), *Encyclopedia of computational mechanics.* London: John Wiley & Sons, Ltd.

Bird, R. B., Stewart, W. E., & Lightfoot, E. N. (1960). *Transport phenomena.* New York: Wiley International Edition.

Blumberg, A. F., & Mellor, G. L. (1987). A description of a three-dimensional coastal ocean circulation model. In N. Heaps (Ed.), *Three-dimensional coastal ocean models* (pp. 1-16). Washington, DC: American Geophysical Union.

Castellano, L., Colombo, A., & Tozzi, A. (1977). *Numerical-differential model for the dispersion of heat and pollutants in sea environments* (Tech. Rep.). Milan: CALISMA/MATEC, ENEL-CRTN, Centro di Ricerca Termica e Nucleare.

Castellano, L., & Dinelli, G. (1975). Experimental and analytical evaluation of thermal alteration in the Mediterranean. *International Conference on Mathematical Models for Environmental Problems.*

Cheng, R. T., & Tung, C. (1970). Wind-driven lake circulation by finite element method. *Proceedings of the 13th Conference on Great Lakes Research* (pp. 891-903).

Dailey, J. E., & Harleman, D. R. F. (1972). *Numerical model for the prediction of transient water quality in estuary networks* (Rep. No. MITSG 72-15). Cambridge, MA: MIT, Department of Civil Engineering.

Deas, M. L., & Lowney, C. L. (2000). *Water temperature modeling review.* California Valley Modeling Forum, Central Valley, CA.

Hodges, B., & Dallimore, C. (2006). *Estuary, lake and coastal ocean model: ELCOM, v2.2 Science manual.* Australia: Centre for Water Research, University of Western Australia.

Hunter, J. R. (1987). The application of Lagrangian particle-tracking techniques to modelling of dispersion in the sea. In J. Noye (Ed.), *Numerical modelling: Applications to marine systems* (pp. 257-269). North-Holland: Elsevier Science Publishers.

Jobson, H. E. (1997). *Enhancements to the branched Lagrangian transport modeling system.* (Water-Resources Investigations Rep. No. 97-4050). U.S. Geological Survey.

Laval, B., Imberger, J., Hodges, B., & Stocker, R. (2003). Modeling circulation in lakes: Spatial and temporal variations. *Limnology and Oceanography, 48*(3), 983-994.

Leendertse, J. J. (1989). *A new approach to three-dimensional free-surface flow modeling* (Tech. Rep. No. R-3712-NETH/RC). Santa Monica, CA: Rand Corporation.

Leon, L. F., Lam, D., Schertzer, W. M., & Swayne, D. A. (2005). Lake and climate models linkage: A 3-D hydrodynamic contribution. *Advances in Geosciences, 4*, 57-62.

Leon, L. F., Lam, D. C. L., Schertzer, W. M., & Swayne, D. A. (2006). *A 3D hydrodynamic lake model: Simulation on Great Slave Lake.* Proceedings International Modelling and Software Society Biennial Conference, Burlington, VT.

Meadows, D. H., Meadows, D. L., Randers, J., & Behrens, W. W. (1972). *Limits to growth* (Report to the Club of Rome). New York: Universe Press.

Neumann, G., & Pierson, W. J., Jr. (1966). *Principles of physical oceanography.* Englewood Cliffs, NJ: Prentice-Hall Inc.

Orlob, G. T. (1967). *Prediction of thermal energy distribution in streams and reservoirs* (Tech. Rep.). Walnut Creek, CA: Water Resources Engineers, Inc.

Pham Thi, N. N., Huisman, J., & Sommeijer, B. P. (2005). Simulation of three-dimensional phytoplankton dynamics: Competition in light-limited environments. *Journal of Computational and Applied Mathematics, 174*(1), 57-77.

Rao, G.-S., & Agee, E. M. (1996). Large eddy simulation of turbulent flow in a marine convective boundary layer with snow. *Journal of Atmospheric Sciences, 53*(1), 86-100.

Rueda, F. J., & Schladow, S. G. (2003). Dynamics of large polymictic lake II: Numerical simulations. *Journal of Hydraulic Engineering, 129*(2), 92-101.

Wang, P., Song, Y. T., Chao, Y., & Zhang, H. (2005). Parallel computation of the regional ocean modeling system. *The International Journal of High Performance Computing Applications, 19*(4), 375-385.

Yepez, J. (2001). A quantum lattice-gas model for computational fluid dynamics. *Physical Review E, 63*, 1-37.

Yue, W., Lin, C.-L., & Patel, V. C. (2004). Large eddy simulation of turbulent open-channel flow with free surface simulated by level set method. *Physics of Fluids, 17*(2), 1-12.

Chapter XVII
Urban and Architectural 3–D Fast Processing

Renato Saleri Lunazzi

Laboratoire MAP aria UMR 694 CNRS: Ministère de la Culture et de la Communication, France

ABSTRACT

The main goal of this chapter is to present a research project that consists of applying automatic generative methods in design processes. The initial approach briefly explores early theoretical conjectures, starting with form and function balance within former conceptual investigations. The following experiments describe original techniques introducing integrated 2-D and 3-D generators for the enhancement of recent 3-D Earth browsers (Virtual Terrain©, MSN Virtual Earth©, or Google Earth©) and cellular-automata processes for architectural programmatic optimization.

INTRODUCTION

Present computer-aided design (CAD) tools should be able to assist the former exploration that leads the entire design process. However, present software often calls for an immediate actualization of geometrical intentions by forcing the user to use preset intentional clusters—geometric primitives, textural resources, design procedures—often uncompromising with poor intuitive feedback and generally restraining the imagination: "most of CAD software act like over-equipped hand-drafting assistants, assuming the maturity of the designer as much as the maturity of the project itself" (Chupin & Lequay, 2000).

We must quote Donald Shön, who remarks that research should concentrate on computer environments able to enhance the users ability to comprehend, store, manipulate, organize, and speculate over a project's matter. Many research projects explored this concept, introducing new operating methodologies able to schematize introductory project investigations long before any possible geometric formalization.

What we aim to achieve is a computer-assisted generation process of architectural and urban plausible geometries. These self-generated objects are intended to act like imagination enhancers serving the conceptual exploration of architectural design or providing credible 3-D environments in given historical context. In the next step, this pre-object could not only be the completion of a multidisciplinary integration process, but, in an autonomous-evolution Darwinian paradigm, the actualization of the most efficient genotype.

Some of the research tasks depicted hereby take advantage of recent generative methods developed within the MAP-ARIA research team. They are able to quickly produce architectural and urban geometric simulations, bringing to life wide 3-D databases connected to some of the most recent 3-D terrain browsers (Virtual Terrain©, MSN Virtual Earth©, or Google Earth©).

INTRODUCING GENERATIVE PARADIGM

Form vs. Function

In architecture, a modern acceptance of spatial interdependencies states that **form** should rise from **function**. Since the architectural thought of Frank Lloyd Wright (1869-1959), Robert Mallet-Stevens (1886-1945), and Ludwig Mies van Der Rohe (1886-1969), enlightened by their sublime work, we have believed in such a Manichean dogma, which could be, to be simple, the main contrast to centuries of academism, and a brand new unrestricted field of investigation.

Conversely, most examples of classical architecture appear to be in complete conceptual opposition to recurring high-geometric prevalence regarding function. The question is obviously not

Figure 1. Villa Almerigo (also known as La Rotonda, 1567-1569) designed by Andrea Palladio (1508-1580; image: Renato Saleri Lunazzi)

about how to overcome this conceptual dialog between **form** and **function,** but to consider further some hierarchical appraisal when it comes to selecting initial input data for our software.

In his *Entretien avec les Étudiants des Écoles D'architecture* (1958), even Le Corbusier (1887-1965) asserts how difficult it is to arrange a complex spatial distribution within simple shapes. According to this point of view, a profuse geometrical spread-out could rather facilitate the solving of programmatic intricacy.

According to German art historian Rudolf Wittkower (1901-1971), the most representative width-height ratios within Palladian architecture match the major chromatic musical scale (Wittkower, 1962, 1974). In this perspective, a C-G major chord could be quoted with a period ratio of 2:3 while a C-F major will be quoted as 3:4. In this perspective (and it is interesting to show how the music-interval notion rests on the Latin etymology of *intervallum*, which literally means *between the walls*). Deborah Howard and Malcolm Longhair underlined the recurrent use of musical ratios within Palladian architecture, emerging from a systematic frequency analysis of his major villas geometry and noticing that such reports are measurable horizontally and vertically.

George Stiny and William Mitchell (1978), among many others, pointed out some parametric grammars able to generate Palladian architectural patterns. This approach clearly refers to Professor Noam Chomsky's linguistics experiments. The amazing Palladio 1.0 Macintosh© Hypercard Stack (Freedman, 1990) is a noteworthy example of such a morphological synthesis. This concept is definitely not new, but its achievement could nowadays be handled by emerging technologies. The leading action of Vitruvius (70-23 BCE) in such a domain, a generative or algorithmic approach to automate the design process, massively influenced Renaissance's conceptual contents; philosophers and architects of this period, such as Leon Battista Alberti (1404-1472) or Antonio Rossellino (about 1427-1481), and moreover

contemporary theorists like Goethe (1749-1832), Monge (1746-1818), Froebel (1782-1852), Frege (1848-1925), and more recently Wittgenstein (1889-1951) and Le Corbusier through the research of Iannis Xenakis (1922-2001), certainly considered and applied theoretical aspects of this scheme in their very own work.

Morphologic studies of urban framework gave birth to various investigations; Philippe Panerai (1992), trying to define precisely *urban framework* (*tissu urbain* in French is closer to *fabric* or *cloth*) encloses its peculiar meaning within a combined structural and systemic approach, stating that "urban framework space closely follows roads, squares, boulevards and lanes spreadout as much as it can be the direct expression of the parcel's reverse influence" (Panerai, 1992).

Beyond the functionalist process that leads architectural and urban design through the correct response to constructive and programmatic needs, we can observe some peculiar design processes guided by specific interdisciplinary connections.

- physical analogies
- structural analogies
- geometric similarities
- multiscale patterns

In the domain of morphologic analysis, here intended as the backtrack of the conceptual pattern, we must mention the LAF research team within the Architecture School of Lyon (F). What Paulin and Duprat (1991) designate as a "morphological factorization of architecture" consists of splitting complex architectural arrangements in visible and pertinent subelements. Semantically speaking, this could be achieved in different manners, according to the specific knowledge we are willing to figure out: This is why a geometrical description of an architectural system does not necessary match the architectural or even its very deep constructive expression.

"We only could reason on models," stated Paul Valery (1871-1945) describing this very peculiar representation mode that supports artificial and symbolic mental depictions. The model, (emerging from the Latin *Modulus*, from *modus*, the measure) is resulting from a schematization process able to select certain discriminant properties of the real-life system, providing a plausible simulacre, a homotopic functional structure in a given abstraction level. This principle describes the model as a fully interactive set of elements with its own organization, information, and knowledge rules.

Noam Chomsky (born 1928) is the Institute Professor Emeritus of linguistics at the Massachusetts Institute of Technology. Chomsky is credited with the creation of the theory of generative grammar, considered to be one of the most significant contributions to the field of theoretical linguistics made in the 20th century.

Apophenic Approach: A Perceptive Disruption

Pareidolia is a type of illusion or misperception involving a vague or obscure stimulus being perceived as something clear and distinct.

Apophenia is the experience of seeing patterns or connections in random or meaningless data. The term was coined in 1958 by Klaus Conrad (1905-1961), who defined it as the "unmotivated seeing of connections" accompanied by a "specific experience of an abnormal meaningfulness."

According to Brugger (2001), it is "the propensity to see connections between seemingly unrelated objects or ideas most closely links psychosis to creativity...apophenia and creativity may even be seen as two sides of the same coin."

It seems that part of the cognitive (re)construction of depicted artifacts depends on a peculiar misperception of visual data; it is more the unconscious will to project some personal expectations that tend somehow to enhance the perceptual efficiency.

We can mark out the very famous painting *Ceci N'est pas une Pipe* (1929) by Magritte for stating how far the interpretation of an object from the object itself could be.

What we can call a look-alike effect, in some precise representative paradigm, acts as an imposter, a constructed distortions like something anamorphic: a distorted projection or representation that, when viewed from a certain point, appears regular and in proportion, a *trompe l'oeil* effect. The idea is that, in this case, the effect is not only

Figure 2. Ceci N'est pas une Pipe, René Magritte (1929)

Figure 3. Altered readability

Hello! **Hello!** **Hello!**

specifically geometric but more generically perceptive. Furthermore, we can observe that there is a very subjective perceptive limit to the legibility of a significant pattern: We can observe that this limit could have wide interpersonal variations that tend to enhance or weaken perceptual aptitudes. At which point do we perceive credible representations? Are what we perceive as doors, roofs, windows, and other single architectural details

making sense together, somehow matching some general discriminant criteria? Some interesting Malevitch tectonic assemblies are just geometrical clusters, solely made of boxes, prisms, and other cubic primitives. However, these primitives, even the significance of this word is proper to sustain the idea of an initiatory process, lead us to make artificial connections able to give sense to such a meaningless assemblage.

Figure 4. Plausible or meaningless? Random-generated rule-based 3-D objects

We can here depict a very interesting linguistics concept described as implicit and explicit typology. Culture is a manner of perceiving reality. Perception is, nevertheless, a subjective phenomenon and what we can perceive and describe is not reality but a possible, personal reality. One's experience tends to influence his or her very own perceptive methods. Each cultural content, in a very generic acceptance, has two components: what can be said (explicit) and what is not said or expressed because it is supposed to be obvious (implicit). Unspoken concepts are embedded in a bigger cultural context that imply their belonging in an implicit content.

It is clear that all artificial objects created are linked to a more generic implicit content, depending on personal, cultural, and subjective factors. The fact is that we can connect them immediately to specific know-how, related to a local tectonic and structural culture. The architectural and/or urban readability of depicted objects depends on a specific cognitive context, provided that all implicit dependencies are fulfilled. According to this point of view, we believe that any representation needs little apophenic projection to be understood, considering that it embeds in any case an implicit cultural content.

Even a map or a picture obviously implies some deep intrinsic contextual knowledge not to be misunderstood: The difficulty encountered in programming computer-based automatic 3-D extraction from 2-D images is still a bright proof of the unbeaten superiority of human thought; this peculiar ambiguity is somehow the cornerstone of the following research task.

EXPERIMENTING WITH GENERATIVE APPROACHES

Integrated Fast 3-D Urban Processing System

The proposal mainly of this approach consists of an integrated architectural and urban semiautomatic model-generation pipe, emerging from

Figure 5. Local database enhancing geo-related roof textures and generic facades

early research tasks about automatic generation of urban and architectural 2-D and 3-D patterns proposed by Saleri in 2004.

Our goal in this research task is to rapidly produce plausible urban environments, using existing data, such as digital maps, DEMs, and aerial photographs with a high level of detail, of 16 or 50 cm resolution.

Early stages of this project produced interesting results, combining complementary modeling techniques, according to the demanded LOD (level of detail): For instance, we prefer to use hybrid image-based modeling for relevant architectural objects, demanding high-level recognizability for close-up views and close-detail identification. If not specified, the model generation follows a generic approach.

The semiautomated process involved in rapid 3-D modeling for generic surrounding architecture (architectural sceneries) links two semiautomated generative processes considering separately 3-D elevation and facade generation: (a) the 3-D elevation step, and (b) the facade generation step.

- The **3-D elevation step** is a geometrical tool that mainly uses initial manual dot plotting on an aerial map and elevates the volume according to some simple contextual rules: the number of floors, entresol characteristics, and covering type. All we need first is to point out two vertices on the lower ledge of a roof face that will be kept horizontal in the next step of the computational process. Then we designate as cw or ccw all of the following coplanar vertices of the same roof face and validate them according to the initial position of the first two vertices. The program builds the geometric layout, adding the needed facade textures to side faces, as described in the facade generation step.

- The **facade generation step** consists of the prewrite of a specific texture look-up table, previously filled with contextualized facade-like tiles. In this system, the intrinsic coherence of the texture itself depends on the pertinence of single texture patches positioning and invoking. The consistence

Figure 6. Urban framework fast processing: Google Earth© browser 3-D upgrade using local database enhancing

of this approach is therefore limited by the local applicability of its generative process: On demand, we need to bring into conformity the initial set of generative rules in order to match to very local architectural components; we recently experimented such a rule-based generator over the Vieux Lyon urban framework to test the pertinence of the resulting representation. The visual discrimination at a certain distance is quite impressive and locally compares to classical virtual globe urban representations.

The scientific constriction of this artifact consists in its contextual urban and architectural possible transposition; the pertinence of generative rules should balance between a wide, low-level geometric descriptor's adaptability and a high-level of detail handling. If the low-level descriptors are too generic, we will not be able to build a satisfying architectural diversity, and resulting geometries will look too similar. On the other hand, it will be quite impossible to specify with such a generic approach the immense variety of architectural or urban expression; therefore we will have to handle carefully any prior semantic discrimination in order to avoid uncontrolled and meaningless geometric spread-outs.

Physical Cellular Automata

This research task involved some postgraduate students within the architecture school of Lyon; it emerges from a collective functional approach to generative processes as new project strategies. The scientific goal of this teamwork clearly aims to arbitrate very present questions about the pertinence of computer-aided design tools in conceptual, constructive processes, and more universally about representation processes in architecture and urban planning.

Early development stages of this project consider basic primitives within the Autodesk Maya©

3-D environment as structural guidelines for spatial-specific allocation. Using Autodesk Maya's© embedded physics engine, the idea consists of assigning specific attraction-repulsion attributes to scene objects according to their respective architectural programmatic connections. In this case, and within a specific generative process, we can generate a large number of plausible solutions responding to an initial set of connection rules. We can, for instance, force some elements to be attracted by specific allocation needs, like a panorama, or some attractive topological configuration, or, more trivial, the connection with existing power plants or road networks.

Declarative Modeling

Declarative modeling is quite a recent modeling technique, far from classical modeling techniques like geometric, parametric, or primitive-based modeling. First introduced in 1989 by Michel Lucas, its recent rise is due to novel project needs emerging from architecture design and furniture planning. Declarative modeling is able facilitate the design process through the implicit knowledge of former physical, geometric, or dimensional rules. In order to simplify what becomes an interactive settlement of a 3-D scene, we may introduce implicit relative-positioning sets of rules such as physical properties and nonoverlapping constraints.

As a matter of fact, we find, in the former structure of the research task introduced as a collaboration with Vincent Berger and other postgraduate students within the architecture school of Lyon, the main aspects of the declarative modeling inputs listed below as the **description**, **generative,** and **evaluation** phases (Berger & Saleri, 2005).

- **Description phase:** It is typically the foremost property formulation phase that takes place within a specific UI that is able to gather initial sets of input data. Its inner structure could match the natural language paradigm or other intuitive descriptive schemes.

- **Generation phase:** This step computes plausible solutions matching initial inputs. The user can formulate an initial query through a definite asset cluster that will be translated in some low-level computational constraints. The system should then be able to generate all the plausible solutions according to the initial model request. However, if the original description is inconsistent, the system can either return to an incongruous solution or give no response at all.

- **Evaluation phase:** This initiates the user-guided appraisal process, considering whether or not the suggested solutions consistently match initial needs. It should deliver

an appropriate feedback interface able to relaunch the generative phase with significant increase of computational constraint pertinence so as to recursively enhance the generative solutions.

The environment description is achieved through the description of a set of properties, as stated above. Properties are intended here as known descriptive elements, formerly defined by the user during the description phase. The system described below finds its solutions through the pseudo-random agglutination of physical active 3-D metaballs. Our experiment gives concrete expression to initial inputs with the use of appropriate 3-D geometry: Multipurpose spheres or metaballs within the Autodesk Maya© 3-D physical solver environment. *Appropriate* means

Figure 7. Initial metaball spread-out: major cluster plus natural light activators (Berger & Saleri, 2005)

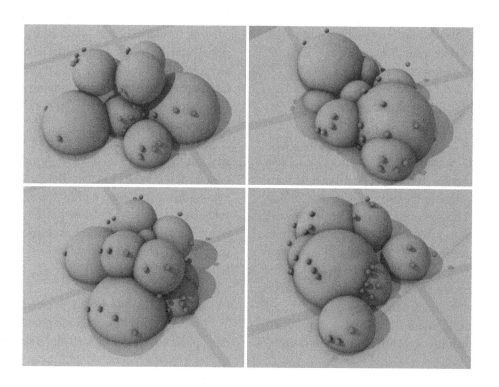

here the direct connection between size, mass, friction, and attraction-repulsion characteristics, embedded within the spheres' properties and the architectural programmatic initial set-up.

This means that we can model and handle immaterial connections and relationships between architectural indoor and outdoor spaces. For instance, the kitchen metaball will be most effectively connected to other servant spaces, such as carports; rooms such as the living room will be more likely attracted by lobbies and main entries. Eventually, servant metaball clusters may be also connected to specific outer spaces like backyards and secondary accesses as served clusters could be attracted by delightful points of views or major driveways.

These initial sprouts also embed natural-light activators: Clusters of 3-D points are generated at a distance in strategic positions toward a sun path or around a nice panorama or an attractive topographic configuration. They will stick to the main metaball cluster according to their initial position and create dimension-related openings through upcoming walls.

On the other hand, we could initially state about inner functional conflicts between listed

Figure 8. Geometric transform of former metaballs cluster. The light activators visible as small dots on Figure 7 generate rectangle-shaped openings.

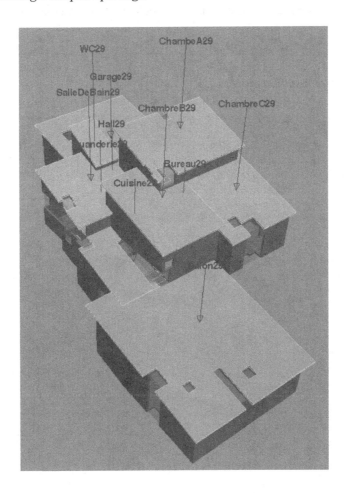

spaces; these conflicts can merge from acoustic or environmental pollutions or more generally from structural discord or incompatibilities. Such properties will indeed activate repulsive reactions between metaballs or heterogeneous subspaces when mismatching combinations are found out.

Through given input classes, we will generate, with such a pseudo-random process, lots of different geometric solutions, but all of them structurally isomorphic. This automated operation explores possible solutions within a conceptual pattern that works in a simulated real-life design process. Functions, properties, and connections are somehow modeled inside a former input graph that will structurally return many plausible solutions relatively to intentional programmatic needs.

This could be a very tectonic rebuild of the cellular automata concept. Former metaballs suit well to geometric self-investigation: The sphere shape brings an optimal surface-volume ratio and therefore the maximum combinational freedom. Computation time is normally less than a minute; it depends on the number of metaball clusters, the complexity of the initial constraint graph, and the number of recursive solving processes involved. At the end of the evaluation phase, the user can test-freeze the final solution, which consists in a geometric transformation of metaball clusters in respective size-related boxes. Successive Boolean operations will then subtract inner materials and hollow out openings with subsequent environmental connections as seen in Figure 9.

It is our belief that such a mechanism could shortly be implemented to help handle conceptual issues within product design and/or urban planning as soon as we are able to digitally master the homotopic nature of human genius.

Figure 9. External view of resultant process

CONCLUSION

We believe that the scientific goal of such a research task does not consist of trying to replace the architect's central responsibility within the design process. On the contrary, one should consider the interest of such innovative paradigm to offset increasing complexity of today's architect's activity. Its usefulness will balance between morphologic synthesis within geometric simulation tools on one hand and the secret hope of a possible instrumental operability in the field of urban and architectural management and design process on the other.

Fortunately, it seems that young professionals tend to easily endorse the mutability of emerging technologies and therefore they should be more prepared, in future, for embracing the increasing intricacy of the surrounding world in order to grant a sustainable balance between needs and resources.

REFERENCES

Berger, V., & Saleri, R. (2005). Instrumentation du hasard numérique dans la conception architecturale. In *Travail personnel de fin d'études*. Ecole d'architecture de Lyon.

Brugger, P. (2001). From haunted brain to haunted science: A cognitive neuroscience view of paranormal and pseudoscientific thought. In J. Houran & R. Lange (Eds.), *Hauntings and poltergeists: Multidisciplinary perspectives*. NC: McFarland & Company, Inc.

Chupin, J.-P., & Lequay, H. (2000). Escalade analogique et plongée numérique: Entre l'atelier tectonique et le studio virtuel dans l'enseignement du projet. In *Les cahiers de la recherche architecturale et urbaine* (pp. 21-28).

Le Corbusier. (1958). *Entretien avec les étudiants des écoles d'architecture*. Les Éditions de Minuit.

Freedman, R. (1990). *Palladio 1.0*. Apple Macintosh© Hypercard Stack.

Panerai, P. (1992). *L'étude pratique des plans de ville: Villes en parallèle n° 12-13*. Paris: Laboratoire de géographie urbaine, Université Paris X, Nanterre.

Paulin, M., & Duprat, B. (1991). *De la maison à l'école, élaboration d'une architecture scolaire à Lyon de 1875 à 1914*. Ministère de la Culture, Direction du Patrimoine, CRML.

Saleri, R. (2005). Pseudo-urban automatic pattern generation. *Chaos and Complexity Letters, 1*(3), 357-365.

Stiny, G., & Mitchell, W. J. (1978). The Palladian grammar. *Environment and Planning B, 5*, 5-8.

Wittkower, R. (1962). *Architectural principles in the age of humanism* (3rd ed.). London: The Warburg Institute, University of London.

Wittkower, R. (1974). *Palladio and Palladianism*. New York: George Braziller.

Chapter XVIII
Reflections of Spiral Complexity on Art

Ljubiša M. Kocić
University of Niš, Serbia

Liljana R. Stefanovska
Ss Cyril and Methodius University, R. of Macedonia

ABSTRACT

This chapter considers a relationship between spirals as proto-complex shapes and human intelligence organized in an information system (IS). We distinguish between old (precomputer ages) and new (computer ages) IS. It seems that actual intelligent machines, connected in an efficient network, inherit a much older structure: a collective consciousness being formed by an international group of artists who exchange their ideas of beauty with amazing speed and persistence. This "classical information system" was responsible for the recognition and propagation of the notion of the spiral shape as an archetypal form and its aesthetic implementation in many artifacts either consciously or not. Using modern technologies of IS, we proposed some methods for extracting spiral forms from pieces of visual arts. Sometimes, these forms are a consequence of a conscious and sometimes of an unconscious action of the artist. Both results support the thesis that there is a constant need of systematic recording of this important shape through history.

Where is the wisdom we have lost to knowledge? Where the knowledge we have lost in information? Where the information we have lost in Cyberspace?

INTRODUCTION

The age of IT has brought some new discoveries regarding complexity. One of the most important is a better understanding of the relationship between harmony and chaos. It seems now that the gap is not as wide as it was supposed to be before. In fact, it seems that chaos contains harmony and vice versa. Such harmonious behavior like oscillatory dynamics is a gate to complexity and chaos. The state of a steady oscillatory system is represented by a closed curve isomorphic to a circle *C* in a phase space (Figure 1a). The damped oscillation regime leads to an involving spiral trajectory, while the increase of amplitude results in an evolving spiral *S*.

The usual (folk) definition says that a spiral is a planar curve described by polar coordinates (θ, r) where $r = f(\theta)$, $\theta \in P$, and *f* is a monotone function. Then, if *f* is decreasing, the spiral winds in or is *involving*; if *f* is increasing, the spiral winds out or is *evolving*. In both cases, the pole is the center of the spiral. However, as Davis (1993) noticed, there is no satisfactory definition that will cover all our intuitive concepts of the spiral.

Sometimes, 3-D objects, known as helixes (the shape of a spiral staircase handrail), are mixed up with spirals. They are named after the old Greek word *helix* (snail) and are also called coils. The projection of a conic helix may be a spiral, and the conical lifting of a spiral is a conic helix, like Albrecht Dürer (1535) shows in his book (Figure 1b). The minimal surface having a helix as its boundary is called a *helicoid*. Leonardo Da Vinci came to the idea of using a conic helicoid as a flying device, an antecedent of the helicopter. The interest of these great renaissance artists in such unusual objects is a hint that spirals and helixes should be understood seriously.

The spiral's dynamics may be caused by an external force and is more complicated than a steady one. It usually leads to an increasing complexity of the system. Such oscillators, and their circle-spiral trajectories, appear everywhere in nature: in biology, chemistry, electrodynamics, psychology, sociology, and so forth. Figure

Figure 1. (a) Van der Pol's oscillator, (b) page from Dürer's book

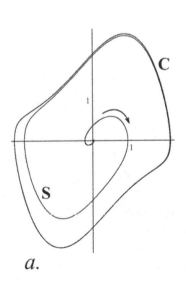

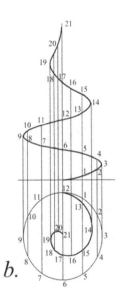

1a shows a phase diagram of the Van der Pol oscillator (Holden, 1992). In fact, many of the complex dynamics phenomena have their roots in spiral dynamics. They have been discovered by the science of the computer age, but it is also known that the spiral as a symbol was used in many forms by ancient people to express some contents of collective unconsciousness that may even be of an archetypal value (Jung, 1956, 1959, 1964). The collective unconsciousness is a kind of data bank. In fact, the international community of artists was always connected by fine strings of metalanguage that every one of them has spoken so well: the aesthetic. Artists of different kinds—musicians, masons, craftsman, poets, painters, sculptors, theater performers, and so forth—were members of this community. In the middle ages, when scholars were too isolated, the artist population was the only network for spreading progressive ideas. It was something like a Middle Age information system, a far ante-cedent of the Internet. The important part of this classical network was made by a group of people having extraordinary visual perception, that is, visual artists. If the spiral pattern was a part of our collective unconsciousness, it must have been noticed by this group of people. The purpose of this work is to explore this question.

TRIPLE SYMBOLISM OF THE SPIRAL

Aristotle, following his ingenious way, noticed that circular motion does not need extra space. Speaking in the Fourier language, Aristotle wanted to say that the circle's expansion in the Fourier series is a simple periodic function. A

Figure 2. On the left, (a) piston guide by symmetric Archimedes spiral segments, and (b) Archimedes snail. On the right, the triangle of human-nature relations through history

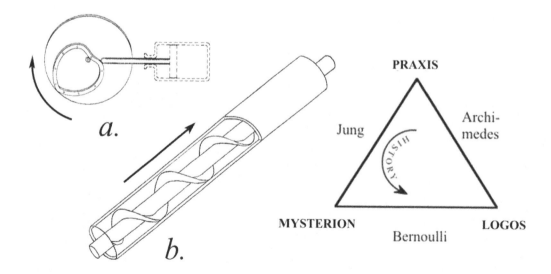

little mystery is that the spiral's expansion is much more complicated, but still the spiral motion does not need more space than the circle encompassing this spiral (like in Figure 1). The solution may be hidden in the fact that, in addition to the circle, the spiral motion also contains a linear component. In the case of spirals, this component acts as a radial from (or toward) its center (Figure 2a). If it is a helicoid, then the linear component acts vertically regarding the plane of the circular motion (Figure 2b).

So, probably the first application of the spiral or helicoid was its practical value since the praxis was historically the first of the three human relations with nature. The next one was the myth (*mysterion*), a spiritual activity that humankind tried to explain in a naïve way by different phenomena occurring in nature during the implementation of praxis. Since the myth was not enough, the new way of thinking, logic (from *logos*), prevailed. In this way, praxis, mysterion, and logos form a triangle that keeps repeating through time.

The earliest practical use of the spiral seems to go back to Archimedes, who combined the ratio and the praxis by inventing the mechanical application of the spiral (Figure 2a) and invented a device for pumping water to a higher level, the Archimedes snail (Figure 2b). In modern times, Carl Jung, the founder of analytic psychology, noticed that spiral forms appeared in dreams of his patients as an autochthonous symbol that came from collective unconsciousness (Jung, 1959). Jung combined practical purpose (help to psychotic patients) with myths (archetype) to discover this relationship. Somewhere between the Archimedes' and Jung's time, the professor of mechanics in Basel, Jacob Bernoulli, examined the nice mathematical properties of the logarithmic spiral $r = a \exp(b\theta)$ (*a* and *b* are constants), probably invented by Descartes in 1638. Bernoulli was captured by the metaphysical mystery of this spiral. By giving the name *spira mirabilis* (wonderful spiral), he expressed his deep impression that there was something irrational in this spiral. He even

made a testament asking his relatives to engrave a logarithmic spiral on his thumb encircled by the title *Eadem Mutata Resurgo* ("Though changed, I rise again the same"). Thus, Bernoulli represented those combining mystery with logic.

In this way, one may conclude that the spiral bears a very complex symbolism mixing the practical, logical, and mysterious up to nowadays, the IT epoch, always raising new questions and enigmas.

SPIRALS AND INFORMATICS

Information technologies are based on the simple physical phenomenon that a nonliving thing can have memory. A simple sawtooth signal generator is an unavoidable part of every intelligent electronic machine, like our personal computers, for example. This is a simple semiconductor-based electric circuit that turns constant electric voltage into a linearly increasing one (integrator) and then stops it when it reaches some maximal value and starts again, as in the diagram in Figure 3. The amount of memory that the circuit has comprises the capability of keeping this maximal value of voltage written down in part of its component. The mechanical analogy of such a sawtooth signal generator can be realized by using a segment of the Archimedes spiral having the simplest equation possible, $r = a\theta$, $\theta \in [0, 2\pi]$, where a is a positive real number (Figure 3). If such a segment rotates clockwise around the origin and pushes a mechanical piston toward the positive *x*-axis direction pressing a spring, the linear movement of the piston will be described by increasing of the affine function up to the moment (time is proportional to the angle θ) when a full circle is covered. Then, the piston is pushed back by a spring and the cycle starts again. In this way, a sawtooth diagram very similar to the electric one is obtained. Now, we are facing mechanical memory incorporated in the length of the spiral segment that will make the piston move to its maximal *x* position. The

Figure 3. On the top, an electric circuit generating a sawtooth signal, and on the bottom, a mechanical sawtooth generator that uses a segment of Archimedes' spiral

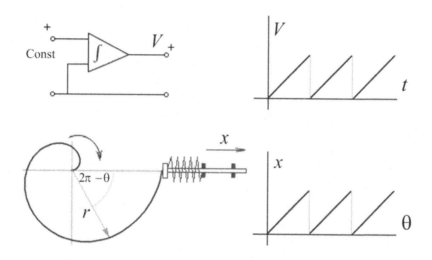

symmetric version (or cosine Fourier expansion) of the $[0, \pi]$ spiral segment is the piston-guiding device from Figure 2a. Its sawtooth diagram represents a symmetric function (triangle) over the $[0, 2\pi]$ interval. Also, the form of the triangles in both cases may be changed by various convex function segments, providing an adequate type of spiral. In this way, many electric circuits that our computers use in their work may be replaced by spiral dynamical elements. Therefore, the heart of the mechanical computer is available—if only we could make it work faster!

Getting back to Aristotle's objection on circular motion, it is evident that a mechanism analogous to the spiral sawtooth generator using a circle instead of a spiral will produce only a constant signal.

SPIRALS EVERYWHERE

IT ages brought new projects concerning the study of spirals, spiral patterns, and complexity based on them. Just compare the first steps in the chaos theory when Henri Poincare and Gaston Julia described fractal sets (now known as *Julia sets*), using only paper and intuition, and the pioneer work of Benoit Mandelbrot, who first saw such sets on the printer of one of the first IBM computers. Activities range from collecting and storing large amounts of data concerning celestial movements to the classification and description of ethnographic material around the world. Exploring, exchanging, and tracing down specific data are unthinkable without computer assistance and Internet connections.

Let us just scratch the surface by classifying some phenomena in Table 1 (see Appendix), where two typical dynamic patterns of involving and evolving spirals appear. Some of them are summarized concerning disciplines like the theory of dynamical systems, biology, psychology, sociology, and symbology.

Spiral forms were noted probably as early as the Paleolithic times, maybe from plant forms (Figure 4). Archeologists have found spiral patterns and decorative drawings in many localities all over the world: Newgrange (Ireland), Hadjilar (Anadoly), Russia, Scandinavia, the Mediterranean, Asia Minor, India, Oceania, China, the Americas, Africa, Australia, and so on. Jung (1956) referred to spiral shapes on the bronze figure of the god Frey (fertility) from Södermanland, Sweden, as well as in the form of a snake being carved in Assyrian boundary stone (Susa), where it represented the orbit of the moon. Spiral patterns are used to designate important places (like shrines, oracles, pilgrimage sites, etc.), to

help establish contact with the world of the dead, to make ordinary things sacred (by the magic value of the spiral decoration), and so on. In the old pre-Columbian civilization, Moche and Huari (South America) warriors decorated their bodies with double-spiral ornaments, motivated by the fact that the spiral may give them the power of a jaguar (*jahuar*). Namely, the jaguar's tail end made the form of a spiral before attacking. We will not review the huge amount of natural spiral forms that are excellently discussed in Blossfeldt (1985), Cook (1914), Ghyka (1927, 1977), Haeckel (1974), and so forth. The motif of circumambulation was found in dream symbols (Jung, 1959) in different transformed forms.

The authors of this text were told the story that depicts a very old belief among the people in the Morava valley (South Serbia) concerning the helicoid vortex of air, caused by wind in summer days. Not so long ago, during agricultural

Figure 4. Spiral plant forms (pencil drawings by Lj. Kocić after Blossfeldt, 1985) and similar configurations of magnified locations in Mandelbrot set

work, it was usual for country people and their families leave their homes and spend a day on farming estate land. So, mothers brought their babies along and put them into improvised swings made of wooden sticks and pieces of cloth. These primitive cradles were usually covered with a fine white fabric to protect the babies from the sun, dust, and insects. Sometimes, however, the wind made vortices that lifted dust funnels that moved quickly over the dusty roads. The local name for these vortices was *virishte*. A very old belief, which probably goes back to the pre-Christian times, is that virishte is a kind of evil spirit, and if it lifts the white cover from the baby's swing and tosses it away, the mother must not bring it back. If she does and covers the baby again, the baby will die within 3 days.

WORLD WIDE WEB THROUGH CENTURIES

Many of the phenomena described in the previous sections have been discovered by the science of the modern ages, but it has as well been discovered that the early civilizations also used the symbol of the spiral in many forms to express some contents of collective unconsciousness that may even be of an archetypal value. If the spiral patterns form some part of our collective unconsciousness, it must be deeply involved in old myths and artistic forms. In other words, it has to be recorded by the precomputer information system. This system was a society of people who praised beauty and art and had strong mutual connections and channels for exchanging their experiences. Even in war times, artists were active in transferring their knowledge and ideas all over the world. Just remember how the ancient Egyptian dome structure, based on a 3:4:5 triangle, found its way to the far Persian provinces, how the Buddhist *stupas* were spread in Japan, and how Mohenjo-Daro beads were brought down to the Mediterranean region. Every new and important art principle, canon, or procedure was quickly transferred and adopted by the most distanced parts of civilization. The same happened with the spiral patterns and ornaments (Figure 5).

The logic is simple: Artists learn from the living nature. They like the human body, vegetation, water, skies, and animals. The natural spiral laws of growth or movement imply spiral

Figure 5. Spiral ornaments

configurations of living organisms and these forms unintentionally become part of the artist's education and production. So, one may expect to see these configurations reproduced in a conscious or an unconscious way in art production through centuries.

Accordingly, the authors of this article were inspired to try the following. Using the IT technology, they examined over 2,000 pieces of art, from the Neolith to the post-modern: drawings, graphics, paintings, sculptures, installations, and so forth, looking for the formal presence of spiral patterns in compositions. The recognition and construction of these patterns were done by an interactive man-machine dialogue. The recognition was exclusively done by the authors while the construction of a geometrically precise spiral was left to the machine. The result was better than expected. About 15.5% of the artwork positively contained a spiral organization of forms. A refined study reveals that artists rarely use spirals as objects. The spiral patterns were rather hidden in the compositions of their works. Logarithmic spirals were usually found. This is not surprising since the human arm has the proportions of a decreasing "golden" sequence (looking from shoulder down to the fingers) so that a properly bent arm yields a good approximation of a logarithmic spiral. What is difficult to comprehend is whether artists make spiral compositions consciously or unconsciously. The authors believe that the great majority did it unconsciously, but have no proof for this claim. However, if this is true, it means that art is a real mirror of collective unconsciousness, a mirror that reflects the archetypal sense of the spiral pattern.

SPIRAL ANALYSIS

As we already mentioned, spirals were used by many artists. We may roughly split their works in two groups. The first group of artists uses the explicit form of the spiral. Some classical examples

are given in Figure 6a to 6e. Modern artists use spiral forms even more, such as Johannes Itten (*Tower of Fire*, 1920), Vladimir Tatlin (*Model of the Monument to the Third International*, 1920), Bruce Nauman (*Window of Wall Sign*, 1967), Robert Morris (*Ottawa Project*, 1970), Robert Smithson (*Spiral Jetty*, 1970), Zvonimir Kostić Palanski (Figure 6f), and so forth.

However, some artwork may contain an "invisible" spiral—a spiral that shows up after careful analysis of the composition of forms. Such analysis is similar to the classic geometric and proportional analysis that have been carried out by many authors like Ghyka (1927, 1977), Birkfoff (1931), Doczi (1981), Hambidge, Elam, Huntley, Lawlor, and so on. Some of them also use harmonic analysis based on rectangular subdivision, while others use circles or ellipses (Šejka, 1995).

With geometric analysis, an attempt is made to isolate some geometric forms (lines, squares, triangles, circles) from the art composition and establish some firm connections between them. The aim of proportional analysis is to find a relationship among different parts of a composition. The most popular proportion in art is the "golden section," $1:\phi$, where,

$$f = (1 + \sqrt{5})/2 \approx 1.618 .$$

If a rectangle has this proportion, it is called a golden rectangle. If one cuts a quadratic part of the golden rectangle, the rest is again a golden rectangle. This process may be continued to infinity, which is the reason why such a rectangle is said to have a dynamic symmetry.

If many proportions have the same ratio, we speak about harmonic analysis. In this scope, spiral analysis will be the fixing of spiral lines that naturally follow the visual dynamics of the composition masses. The most interesting spiral for applying spiral analysis is the logarithmic spiral, $r = a \exp(b\theta)$, where a and b are constants.

Searching for spiral patterns is a difficult task and needs the assistance of IT (hardware, software,

Figure 6. Some explicit spiral forms in art. (a) Inana's knot (summer), (b) Ionic capital, (c) Bishop's pastoral, (d) detail from Madonna and Child with Angels by Filippo Lippi, (e) detail from Annunciations by Leonardo Da Vinci, (f) Psalm 85:10, iron sculpture by Zvonimir Kostić Palanski

man-machine interaction, Web communications, etc.). Inspired by Davis' book (1993), with no pretensions to have any priority, the first author started systematic research on this topic in 2000. The first results were published in a paper (Kocić, 2001) and then in a book (Kocić, 2003).

Later in July 2006, when this paper was drafted, the authors found an interesting Web site of Ateş Gülcügil (2006) from Turkey, guided by his letter posted to the *WetCanvas!* forum on June 12, 2006. "I think that the rectangle of the whirling squares and the logarithmic spiral which are part of the Greek compositional system dynamic symmetry have been used in classic paintings," Gülcügil said. He also said that he had written a booklet on the subject. Gülcügil uses dynamic golden rectangles inscribed in each other that follow the dynamics of the masses in the classic

paintings. Although it is not quite clear what procedure Gülcügil's method exactly uses, it seems that it leans upon classic harmonic analysis that yields a series of inscribed golden rectangles with circular arcs that approximate a golden spiral. However, strictly speaking, a golden spiral does not uniquely exist, as Loeb and Varney (1992) show. Anyway, over 50 examples that Gülcügil provided are very nice.

SPIRAL FLOW, TWO METHODS

To follow such a sophisticated form as logarithmic spirals are, we need the assistance of IT. Then, let us agree to call an imagined spiral path over the analyzed picture a spiral flow. We will be interested in logarithmic spirals or spira mirabilis because of their beauty. According to Brand (2006), a logarithmic spiral is a curve of infinite dynamics since it cuts its radii with constant angle $a = \tan^{-1}(1/b)$, making its curvature invariant under differentiation. Infinite dynamics may imply infinite beauty of the logarithmic spiral flow. Anyway, the complex nature of the history of art is examined in Kocić and Stefanovska (2005).

Two main methods for determination of the spiral flow are used.

Gestalt flow

In some art work, the important characteristic of composition is asymmetry of some static mass. The masses themselves and their inclination or other kind of movement suggest a trace of line that helps the observer connect these masses into a whole. In fact, the observer uses the Gestalt effect to join what looks disjointed or separated. Sometimes, this line gives a spiral flow, as it is shown in the example of *Angelus*, and 18th century painting by Jean Francois Millet (Figure 7).

On the first site, we distinguish two oval regions. The inner region e_1 encompasses two peasants praying together during the Angelus time with a basket lying on the ground. The outer oval e_2 includes agricultural tools, a fork, and a wheelbarrow that surround the two people. But the mutual position of these two ovals indicates the dynamic flow as well. This flow is caused by the lack of equilibrium of the static masses contained in regions e_1 and e_2. The need for compensation of this nonequilibrium state causes the Gestalt effect: Our minds try to complete the uncompleted picture. This produces a virtual flow line, which is a spiral in our case. Its focus F should be placed in the center of the fork, basket, and wheelbarrow, that is, somewhere by the female's knees. The spiral flow then passes through Point 1 following the convex line of the apron's edge, then touches the basket (2), the female's feet (3), and the wheel (4). It cuts one sack (5) and goes up toward the woman's shoulders (6), passes over her Breton hat (7), bends down over her husband and passes over his chest (8), leaves his silhouette on his elbow (9), and then crosses the handle of the fork and ends on the ground.

This principle of forming the spiral flow will be called the Gestalt flow.

Figure 7. On the left, Millet's Angelus, and on the right, a grouping of masses into elliptic regions

Figure 8. Millet's Angelus: spiral flow of dynamic masses

Nystagmus Flow

Nystagmus is a medical term for rapid, involuntary rhythmic eye movement, with the eyes moving quickly in one direction, and then slowly in the other. A typical result of tracing the nystagmus of an art piece is a set of fixed viewpoints, scattered over the area of the art. Connecting these points yields a continuous polygonal line that approximates some curvilinear flow. In some cases, this polygonal line roughly follows a spiral flow. An example will be given using the Da Vinci's *Annunciation* dating back to 1475. By observing this picture, the majority of people first notice the silver apple (1) on the bottom of Madonna's distaff standing on a picturesque table. Then, the watching point skips over the details of the table's decorations over Points 2 to 5. After that, our seeing point jumps over the Madonna's figure (Points 6 to 9) and then hits the top of the cypress tree in the distanced background (10). The subsequent trajectory examines the Angel figure (12–20).

In this case, the polygonal line suggests a spiral flow line as it is shown in Figure 10. It can be seen that both spiral lines, the one from *Angelus* and the one from *Annunciation*, are similar in form: Both are logarithmic, with polar equation $r(\theta) = a \exp(b\theta)$, which reveals the similarity of these two compositions. More precisely, the *Angelus* spiral has parameters $a = -81.9573$ and $b = 0.2743$ and its focus is on point $F = (560, 220)$, provided that 860×710 pixels is the internal picture format. On

Figure 9. Da Vinci's Annunciation: Nystagmus analysis

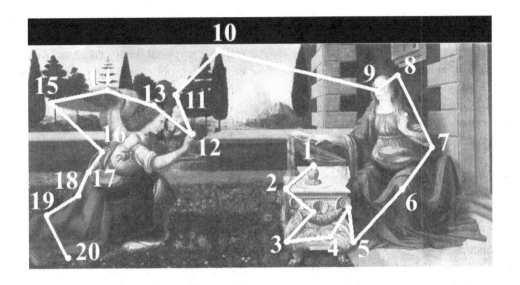

the other hand, if 770×360 pixels is the format of *Annunciation*, the focus is on F = (475,150) and the parameters are *a* = 137.873, *b* = 0.3339.

After having some experience, it is not difficult to recognize spiral compositions in pieces of art, no matter if they are 2-D (designs, graphics, pictures)

Figure 10. Da Vinci's Annunciation: Spiral interpolation of a subset of nystagmus points

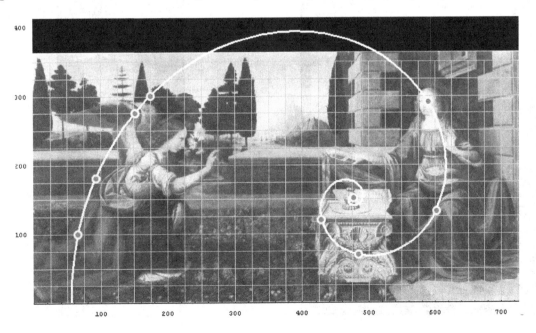

or 3-D (sculptures, architecture, plastic details). Some compositions may contain more than one spiral in their structure. So, all situations may be classified in five categories.

1. *Spiral flow.* This is a spiral line that interpolates distinguished points on some picture, like in the examples of *Angelus* (Figure 8) and *Annunciation* (Figure 10).
2. *Spiral proportion.* This is the occurrence of two spiral flows in the same composition, with different parameters *a* and *b*.
3. *Spiral similarity.* This involves two spiral flows in the same composition with proportional *a* parameters and identical *b* parameters.
4. *Spiral rhythm.* This is when there are two or more spiral flows with similar parameters in the same composition.
5. *Spiral harmony.* The existence of two or more spiral rhythms in the same composition.

SPIRAL PROPORTION

If one composition contains two or more different spiral flows, we say that this composition is spirally proportional. Let us consider two examples of spirally proportional compositions. One is the famous *Judith* by Sandro Botticelli, and the other is one of the nicest sculpture of all times, *Venus de Milo* (Figures 11 and 12).

The dimensions of *Judith* is 310×420 pixels; the elements of the first spiral are S_1: $F_1 = (165, 350)$, $a = -234.3078$, and $b = -0.3126$, and those of the second one are S_2: $F_2 = (100, 350)$, $a = 26.7719$, and $b = 0.3883$.

As far as *Venus de Milo* is concerned, its internal format is 425×1050 pixels. The elements of the spirals are S_1: $F_1 = (225, 950)$, $a = 37.9559$, and $b = 0.3497$, and S_2: $F_2 = (227, 640)$, $a = 96.5896$, and $b = 0.1935$.

In both cases, the spirals touch each other, forming interesting spiral diagrams that somehow

Figure 11. Sandro Botticelli: Judith

Figure 12. Venus de Milo

better explain the composition of the picture or the sculpture than either of the two spirals alone. Note that all the spirals are logarithmic.

SPIRAL SIMILARITY

We say that two spirals, S_1 and S_2, are similar if one can be transformed into the other by an affine transformation of the plane. More precisely, the spirals $r_1 = a_1 e^{b_1 q}$ and $r_2 = a_2 e^{b_2 q}$ are similar if and only if $b_1 = b_2$ and $a_1 = \lambda a_2$. The number λ is the similarity factor. If $\lambda = 1$, the spirals are identical.

If one piece of visual art is composed in such a manner that we may extract two parts dominated by spiral flows S_1 and S_2, and if S_1 and S_2 are similar, we speak about a composition with a spiral similarity.

The first example is the sculpture *Hercules and the Centaur* by Giovanni Bologna. The internal format of the picture is 260×360 pixels (Figure 13).

Hercules' body in swing contains the first spiral S_1 with elements $F_1 = (170, 270)$, $a_1 = -84.2597$, and $b_1 = -0.2232$; the second spiral S_2, which follows the twisted body of the centaur, has focus in $F_2 = (130, 158)$ and the parameters are $a_2 = -143.2415 = 1.7 \, a_1$ and $b_2 = b_1$. This means that these spirals are similar with similarity factor 1.7, which in turn means that S_2 is 1.7 times bigger than S_1.

In the second example, we will examine Da Vinci's painting *Saint Ana and Madonna with small Jesus* (Figure 14). The internal dimensions are 340×525 pixels; the focus of the bigger spiral S_1 is $F_1 = (181, 323)$, and the parameters are $a_1 = 38.4831$ and $b_1 = 0.2823$. The second spiral, S_2, is smaller and similar to S_1 since $a_2 = 0.45 \, a_1$.

SPIRAL RHYTHM

Spiral similarity introduces the next natural category, spiral rhythm. Indeed, the example of Figure 14 exhibits a serene rhythm made by two

Figure 13. Giovanni Bologna: Hercules and the Centaur

Figure 14. Da Vinci: St. Ana

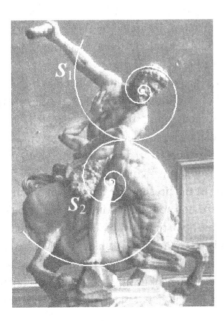

spirals, rhythm that resembles the rhythm of the sea waves. If there are more than two spiral similarities, such rhythmic feeling increases. The example of Da Vinci's unfinished *The Adoration*

Figure 15. Da Vinci: The Adoration of the Magi

Figure 16. (right) Claude Michel (Clodion): Amour and Psyche

of the Magi (Figure 15) is very rich in spiral flows, and we have selected a detail with three of them: S_1, S_2, and S_3, whose foci are situated in the vertices of an almost perfect equilateral triangle.

The parameters are the following: The internal format is 800×625 pixels, S_1: F_1 = (250, 300), a_1 = −52.0777, b_1 = 0.1528, S_2: F_2 = (425, 200), a_2 = −55.2738, b_2 = 0.2838, S_3: F_3 = (672, 225), a_3 = 50, and b_3 = 0.2421. Although these spirals are not similar, they are close to being similar, conveying the perfectionism of the old master.

The second example of spiral rhythm is the sculpture *Amour and Psyche* by the French sculptor Claude Michel called Clodion, with an internal format of 555×450 pixels (Figure 16). Here we also have three spirals: S_1: F_1 = (212, 412), a_1 = 43, b_1=0.5796, S_2: F_2 = (225, 470), a_2 = 31.6179, b_2 = 0.36, S_3: F_3 = (350, 425), a_3 = 72.9206, and b_3 = − 0.215691. These make a playful rhythm in the rich composition, characteristic of French neoclassicism and the times of Louis XVI.

SPIRAL HARMONY

If we can notice two or more spiral rhythms in the same picture, we speak about spiral harmony. As an example, we offer the famous Laocoön group, a group sculpture made by three sculptors from Rhodos: Agesander, Athenodorus, and Polydorus (Figure 17).

The group represents Laocoön, the Trojan priest of Poseidon, and his sons Antiphantes and Thymbraeus being strangled by sea serpents. The composition is crowded with helix movements and visual vortices so that the location of the spiral flows is not a difficult task.

All of the presented examples and many others were not possible without interactive action with highly sophisticated computer software. For all the examples we used the Mathematica 5.2 package. It has the ability to set the selected picture as a background and then to construct any mathematical object over it. The mighty

Figure 17. Rhodos school: Laocoön group

Parameters:
format 700×800 pixels

S_1: $F_1 = (260, 658)$
$a_1 = 23.8896$, $b_1 = 0.5084$

S_2: $F_2 = (130, 490)$
$a_2 = 19.1316$, $b_2 = 0.336$

S_3: $F_3 = (208, 340)$
$a_3 = 19.1316$, $b_3 = 0.3363$

S_4: $F_4 = (585, 438)$
$a_4 = -91.2617$, $b_4 = -0.2219$

S_5: $F_5 = (485, 338)$
$a_4 = -130.374$, $b_5 = -0.2219$

numerical performances of this package ensured the accurate construction of spirals and high precision in calculating the parameters of the spiral configurations.

CONCLUSION

As we already mentioned, about 15.5% of the examined artwork (more than 2,000 pictures) contained one of the above categories based on spirals: spiral flow, proportion, similarity, rhythm, or harmony incorporated in picture or sculpture compositions. What we could not comprehend is whether the authors used spiral geometry consciously or unconsciously. We are biased toward the *unconscious* hypothesis. The reason is simple:

The mathematical background for spiral construction is pretty advanced. It is hard to believe that these techniques were so widespread. Of course, there are exceptions like Da Vinci, Dürer, Luca Pacioli, and so forth, who were mathematically talented. But in many other works, the spiral form of the composition is so striking that it is difficult to drop the *conscious* hypothesis. The solution of this enigma may be the strong influence of the archetypal character of spiral forms on one hand and the special sensitivity related to the dictate of unconsciousness (the favorite surrealists' theme) during the creative process on the other hand. The same question may be raised for other pre-complex forms, like lines, circles, waves, and so on—the simpler ingredients of art complexity (Kocić & Stefanovska, 2005).

Anyway, further investigations are needed. Is it accidental that many logos for psychology or psychotherapy societies have the spiral as the main motif?

REFERENCES

Bidermann, H. (1998). *Knaurs lexikon der symbole*. München, Germany: Droemersche Verlagsanstalt Th. Knaur Nachf.

Birkfoff, G. D. (1931). A mathematical approach to aesthetics. *Scientia*, pp. 133-146.

Blossfeldt, K. (1985). *Art forms in the plant world*. New York: Dover Publications, Inc.

Brand, M. (2006). *Logarithmic spirals*. Retrieved July 10, 2006, from http://alumni.media.mit.edu/~brand/logspiral.html

Cook, T. A. (1914). *The curves of life*. London: Constable and Company Ltd.

Davis, P. J. (1993). *Spirals: From Theodorus to chaos*. Wellesley, MA: A. K. Peters.

Doczi, G. (1981). *The power of limits*. Boston: Shambhala Publications, Inc.

Dürer, A. (1535). *Unterweisung der messung*. Paris: Ex Officina Christiani Wecheli.

Ghyka, M. C. (1927). *Esthétique des proportions dans la nature et dans les arts*. Paris: Gallimard.

Ghyka, M. C. (1977). *The geometry of art and life*. New York: Dover Publications, Inc.

Gülcügil, A. (2006). *The rectangle of the whirling squares and the logarithmic spiral in classic art*. Retrieved July 16, 2006, from http://gulcugil.tripod.com

Haeckel, E. (1974). *Art forms in nature*. New York: Dover Publications, Inc.

Holden, A. V. (1992). Dynamical spirals. In I. Hargittai & C. Pickover (Eds.), *Spiral symmetry* (pp. 73-81). World Scientific Publishing Co.

Jung, C. G. (1956). *Symbols of transformation*. Princeton, NJ: Princeton University Press.

Jung, C. G. (1959). *The archetypes and the collective unconscious*. Princeton, NJ: Princeton University Press.

Jung, C. G. (Ed.). (1964). *Man and his symbols*. London: Aldus Book Ltd.

Kocić, Lj. (2001). Comments on "Peri Elikon." *Unus Mundus, 8*, 5-37.

Kocić, Lj. (2003). *Mathematics and aesthetics*. Niš, Serbia: Niš Cultural Center.

Kocić, Lj., & Stefanovska, L. (2005). Complex dynamics of visual arts. *Chaos and Complexity Letters, 1*(2), 207-235.

Loeb, A. L., & Varney, W. (1992). Does the golden spiral exist, and if not, where is its center? In I. Hargittai & C. Pickover (Eds.), *Spiral symmetry* (pp. 47-61). World Scientific Publishing Co.

Šejka, L. (1995). *Treatise on painting*. Sombor, Serbia: Zlatna Grana.

APPENDIX

Spiral Type	Dynamics	Biology	ψ	Sociology	Symbols
Involving spiral	f strictly increases	Involution	Calming down	Approaching stable society	Decreasing sun
	Dumping oscillations	Extinction of population	Success and pleasure	Settling down riots or citizen disobedience	Water eddy, dragon
	(Real) pendulum	Approaching stable population	Psycho-therapy	Extinction of settlements and civilizations	Star movement
			Mental concentration		Destructive powers
		Deterioration of an organism	Mandala	Approaching temples and spiritual places	
		Hunter approaches the prey	Oblivion		Death

	f strictly decreases	Evolution	Excitation	Riots, social disorder	Increasing sun
Evolving spiral	Increasing oscillations	Multiplying of population	Increasing of nervous tension	Citizen disobedience	Resurrection
	Inverse (real) pendulum	Approaching stable population	Complex development	Increasing social organization	Creative powers
		Growth of an organism	Learning	Forming settlements and new societies	Birth
			Unsuccessful trials		Orbit of the moon
		Prey escapes from hunter	Lack of concentration		Fertility

Chapter XIX
Fractal Geometry and Computer Science

Nicoletta Sala
Università della Svizzera Italiana, Switzerland & Università dell'Insubria, Italy

ABSTRACT

Fractal geometry can help us to describe the shapes in nature (e.g., ferns, trees, seashells, rivers, mountains) exceeding the limits imposed by Euclidean geometry. Fractal geometry is quite young: The first studies are the works by the French mathematicians Pierre Fatou (1878-1929) and Gaston Julia (1893-1978) at the beginning of the 20th century. However, only with the mathematical power of computers has it become possible to realize connections between fractal geometry and other disciplines. It is applied in various fields now, from biology to economy. Important applications also appear in computer science because fractal geometry permits us to compress images, and to reproduce, in virtual reality environments, the complex patterns and irregular forms present in nature using simple iterative algorithms executed by computers. Recent studies apply this geometry to controlling traffic in computer networks (LANs, MANs, WANs, and the Internet). The aim of this chapter is to present fractal geometry, its properties (e.g., self-similarity), and their applications in computer science.

INTRODUCTION

Fractal geometry is a recent discovery. It is also known as Mandelbrot's geometry in honor of its father, the Polish-born Franco-American mathematician Benoit Mandelbrot, who showed how fractals can occur in many different places in both mathematics and elsewhere in nature.

Fractal geometry is now recognized as the true geometry of nature. Before Mandelbrot, mathematicians believed that most of the patterns of nature were far too irregular, complex, and fragmented to be described mathematically. Mandelbrot's geometry replaces Euclidian geometry, which had dominated our mathematical thinking for thousands of years.

The *Britannica Concise Encyclopedia* ("Fractal Geometry," 2007) introduces fractal geometry as follows:

In mathematics, the study of complex shapes with the property of self-similarity, known as fractals. Rather like holograms that store the entire image in each part of the image, any part of a fractal can be repeatedly magnified, with each magnification resembling all or part of the original fractal. This phenomenon can be seen in objects like snowflakes and tree bark....This new system of geometry has had a significant impact on such diverse fields as physical chemistry, physiology, and fluid mechanics; fractals can describe irregularly shaped objects or spatially nonuniform phenomena that cannot be described by Euclidean geometry."

The multiplicity of the application fields had a central role in the diffusion of fractal geometry (Barnsley, Saupe, & Vrscay, 2002; Eglash, 1999; Mandelbrot, 1982; Nonnenmacher, Losa, Merlini, & Weibel, 1994; Sala, 2004, 2006; Vyzantiadou, Avdelas, & Zafiropoulos, 2007).

BACKGROUND: WHAT IS A FRACTAL?

A fractal could be defined as a rough or fragmented geometric shape that can be subdivided in parts, each of which is approximately a reduced-size copy of the whole (Mandelbrot, 1988). *Fractal* is a term coined by Benoit Mandelbrot (born 1924) to denote the geometry of nature, which traces inherent order in chaotic shapes and processes. The term derived from the Latin verb *frangere, to break*, and from the related adjective *fractus, fragmented and irregular*. This term was created to differentiate pure geometric figures from other types of figures that defy such simple classification. The acceptance of the word fractal was dated in 1975. When Mandelbrot presented the list of publications between 1951 and 1975, the date when

the French version of his book was published, people were surprised by the variety of the studied fields: linguistics, cosmology, economy, games theory, turbulence, and noise on telephone lines (Mandelbrot, 1975). Fractals are generally self-similar on multiple scales. So, all fractals have a built-in form of iteration or recursion. Sometimes the recursion is visible in how the fractal is constructed. For example, Koch's snowflake, Cantor's set, and Sierpinski's triangle are generated using simple recursive rules. Self-similarity, iterated function systems, and the Lindenmayer System are applied in different fields of computer science (e.g., in computer graphics, virtual reality, and traffic control for computer networks).

Self-Similarity

Self-similarity, or invariance against changes in scale or size, is a property by which an object contains smaller copies of itself at arbitrary scales. Mandelbrot (1982, p. 34) defined self-similarity as follows: "When each piece of a shape is geometrically similar to the whole, both the shape and the cascade that generate it are called self-similar."

A fractal object is self-similar if it has undergone a transformation whereby the dimensions of the structure were all modified by the same scaling factor. The new shape may be smaller, larger, translated, and/or rotated. Similar means that the relative proportions of the shapes' sides and internal angles remain the same. As described by Mandelbrot (1982), this property is ubiquitous in the natural world. Oppenheimer (1986) used the term fractal, exchanging it with self-similarity, and he affirmed that the geometric notion of self-similarity is evolving in a paradigm for modeling the natural world, in particular in the world of botany.

Self-similarity appears in objects as diverse as leaves, mountain ranges, clouds, and galaxies. Figure 1a shows a snowflake that is an example of self-similarity in nature. Figure 1b illustrates

Figure 1. (a) A snowflake is a natural fractal object, and (b) Koch's snowflake is a fractal generated using simple geometric rules.

(a)

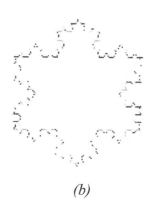

(b)

Koch's snowflake; it is built starting from an equilateral triangle, removing the inner third of each side, building another equilateral triangle at the location where the side was removed, and then repeating the process indefinitely. This fractal object represents an attempt to reproduce complex shapes present in nature using few simple geometric rules.

The Koch snowflake is an example of a shape with a finite area enclosed within an infinite boundary. This seems contrary to geometric intuition, but this is characteristic of many shapes in nature. For example, in the human body all the arteries, veins, capillaries, and bronchial structures occupy a relative small fraction of the body. Thus, inside the human body there is the presence of fractal geometry using two different points of view: spatial fractals and temporal fractals. Spatial fractals refer to the presence of self-similarity; for instance, the small intestine repeats its form, observed as various enlargements. Spatial fractals also refer to the branched patterns that are present inside the human body for enlarging the available surface for the absorption of substances (in the intestine) and the distribution and collection of solutes (in the blood vessels, and in the bronchial tree).

Temporal fractals are present in some dynamic processes, for example, in cardiac rhythm. The long-term variability of heart rate observed over a wide range of time scales with scale-invariant power-law characteristics has recently been associated with fractal scaling behavior and long-range correlation properties (Meyer, 2002).

The Iterated Function System

The iterated function system (IFS) is another fractal that can be applied in computer science. Barnsley (1993, p. 80) defined the IFS as follows:

*A (hyperbolic) iterated function system consists of a complete metric space (**X**, d) together with a finite set of contraction mappings w_n: **X**→ **X** with respective contractivity factor s_n, for n = 1, 2,.., N. The abbreviation "IFS" is used for "iterated function system." The notation for the IFS just announced is { **X**, w_n, n = 1, 2,.., N} and its contractivity factor is s = max {s_n : n = 1, 2, ..., N}.*

Barnsley put the word *hyperbolic* in parentheses because it is sometimes dropped in practice.

He also defined the following theorem (Barnsley, 1993, p. 81):

Let {$\mathbf{X}$, w_n, $n = 1, 2, ..., N$} be a hyperbolic iterated function system with contractivity factor s. Then the transformation W: H($\mathbf{X}$) → H($\mathbf{X}$) defined by:

$$W(B) = \cup_{n=1}^{n} w_n(B) \tag{1}$$

For all B∈ H($\mathbf{X}$), is a contraction mapping on the complete metric space (H($\mathbf{X}$), h(d)) with contractivity factor s. That is:

$$H(W(B), W(C)) \leq s \cdot h(B,C) \tag{2}$$

for all B, C ∈ H($\mathbf{X}$). Its unique fixed point, A ∈ H($\mathbf{X}$), obeys,

$$A = W(A) = \cup_{n=1}^{n} w_n(A) \tag{3}$$

and is given by A = $\lim_{n \to \infty}$ W^{on} (B) for any B ∈ H($\mathbf{X}$).

The fixed point A ∈ H($\mathbf{X}$), described in the theorem by Barnsley, is called the attractor of the IFS or invariant set.

Bogomolny (1998) affirms that two problems arise. One is to determine the fixed point of a given IFS, and it is solved by what is known as the *deterministic* algorithm.

The second problem is the inverse of the first: For a given set A∈H($\mathbf{X}$), find an iterated function system that has A as its fixed point (Bogomolny, 1998). This is solved approximately by the Collage Theorem (Barnsley, 1993).

The Collage Theorem (Barnsley, 1993, p. 94) states:

Let ($\mathbf{X}$, d), be a complete metric space. Let L∈H($\mathbf{X}$) be given, and let ε ≥ o be given. Choose an IFS (or IFS with condensation) {$\mathbf{X}$, (w_n), w_1, w_2, ..., w_n} with contractivity factor 0 ≤ s ≤ 1, so that,

$$h(L, \cup_{\substack{n=1 \\ (n=0)}}^{n} w_n(L)) \leq \varepsilon \tag{4}$$

Where h(d) is the Hausdorff metric. Then,

$$h(L, A) \leq \frac{\varepsilon}{1 - s} \tag{5}$$

Where A is the attractor of the IFS. Equivalently,

$$h(L, A) \leq (1 - s)^{-1} h(L, \cup_{\substack{n=1 \\ (n=0)}} w_n(L)) \tag{6}$$

for all L∈H($\mathbf{X}$).

The Collage Theorem describes how to find an IFS whose attractor is close to a given set; one must endeavor to find a set of transformations such that the union, or collage, of the images of the given set under transformations is near to the given set.

The Collage Theorem states that an iterated function system must represent an image.

Next Figure 2 shows a fern leaf created using the IFS. The IFS is produced by polygons: in this case, triangles that are put in one another. The final step of this iterative process shows a fern that has a high degree of similarity to a real one.

L-Systems

An L-system or Lindenmayer system is an algorithmic method for generating branched forms and structures such as plants. L-systems were invented in 1968 by Hungarian biologist Aristid Lindenmayer (1925-1989) for modeling biological growth. He worked with filamentous fungi and studied the growth patterns of various types of algae, for example, the blue-green bacteria Anabaena catenula. Originally, the L-systems were devised to provide a formal description of the development of such simple multicellular organisms, and to illustrate the neighborhood relationships between plant cells. Later on, this system was extended to describe higher plants and complex branching structures.

Figure 2. Fern leaf created using the IFS

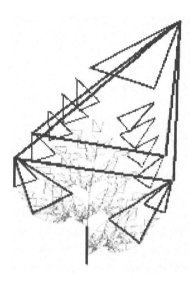

L-systems can also be used to generate self-similar fractals that are a particular type of symbolic dynamical system with the added feature of a geometrical interpretation of the evolution of the system. The components of an L-system are the following.

- An alphabet that is a finite set V of formal symbols containing elements that can be replaced (variables)
- The constants that are a set S of symbols containing elements that remain fixed
- The *axiom* (also called the *initiator*), which is a string ω of symbols from **V** defining the initial state of the system
- A *production* (or *rewriting rule*) P that is a set of rules or productions defining the way variables can be replaced with combinations of constants and other variables. A production consists of two strings: the predecessor and the successor.

The rules of the L-system grammar are applied iteratively starting from the initial state.

L-systems are also commonly known as parametric L-systems, and they are defined as a tuple **G** = {V, S, ω, P}.

Lindenmayer's original L-system for modeling the growth of algae and the blue-green bacteria (Anabaena catenula) is the following (Prusinkiewicz & Lindenmayer, 1990).

- variables: a, b
- constants: none
- start (axiom): b
- rules: (a $\rightarrow$ ab), (b $\rightarrow$ a)

The rule (a $\rightarrow$ ab) means that the letter a is to be replaced by the string ab, and the rule (b $\rightarrow$ a) means that the letter b is to be replaced by a. The symbols a and b represent cytological states of the cells (their size and readiness to divide). It produces the following.

n = 0: b
n = 1: a
n = 2: ab
n = 3: aba
n = 4: abaab
n = 5: abaababa

This is the simplest class of L-systems, those which are deterministic and context free, called DOL-systems. Using geometric interpretation of strings, it is possible to generate schematic images of Anabaena catenula.

An L-system can be also defined as a formal grammar (a set of rules and symbols) most famously used for modeling the growth processes of plant development, and it has been thought to be able to model the morphology of a variety of organisms.

The differences between L-systems and Chomsky grammars are well described by Prusinkiewicz and Lindenmayer (1990, pp. 2-3), who stated,

The essential difference between Chomsky grammars and L-systems lies in the method of applying

productions. In Chomsky grammars productions are applied sequentially, whereas in L-systems they are applied in parallel and simultaneously replace all letters in a given word. This difference highlights the biological motivation of L-systems. Productions are intended to capture cell divisions in multicellular organisms, where many divisions may occur at the same time. Parallel production application has an essential impact on the formal properties of rewriting systems.

Strings generated by L-systems may be interpreted geometrically in different ways. For example, L-system strings serve drawing commands for a LOGO-style turtle. The turtle interpretation of parametric L-systems was introduced by Szilard and Quinton (1979), and extended by Prusinkiewicz (1986, 1987) and Hanan (1988, 1992).

Prusinkiewicz and Lindenmayer defined a state of the turtle as a triplet (x, y, α), where the Cartesian coordinates (x, y) represent the turtle's position, and the angle α, called the heading, is interpreted as the direction in which the turtle is facing. Given the step size s and the angle increment δ, the turtle can respond to commands represented by the symbols in Table 1.

The Koch snowflake can be simply encoded as a Lindenmayer system with initial string F--F--F, string rewriting rule F $\rightarrow$ F+F--F+F, and angle 60°. Figure 3 shows an example of plant-like structures generated after four iterations by bracketed L-systems with the initial string F

Figure 3. Plant-like structures generated after four iterations by L-system

Table 1. Commands for LOGO-style turtle derived by L-systems

Symbols	Meaning
F	Move forward a step of length s. The state of the turtle changes; now it is (x', y', α), where $x' = x + s \cdot \cos \alpha$ and $y' = y + s \cdot \sin \alpha$. A segment between (x, y), the starting point, and the point (x', y') is drawn.
f	Move forward a step of length s without drawing a line.
+	Turn left by angle δ. The positive orientation of angles is counterclockwise, and the next state of the turtle is $(x, y, \alpha+\delta)$.
-	Turn right by angle δ. The next state of the turtle is $(x, y, \alpha - \delta)$.
[	Push the current state of the turtle onto a pushdown operations stack. The information saved on the stack contains the turtle's position and orientation, and possibly other attributes such as the color and width of lines being drawn.
]	Pop a state from the stack and make it the current state of the turtle. No line is drawn, although in general the position of the turtle changes.

(angle δ= 22.5°), and the replacement rule F → FF+[+F-F-F] -[-F+F+F].

APPLICATIONS OF FRACTAL GEOMETRY IN COMPUTER SCIENCE

Fractal geometry is one of the most exciting frontiers in the fusion between mathematics and computer science. Mandelbrot's geometry permits us to compress the images, and to reproduce in computer graphics and in virtual reality environments the textures and the irregular forms present in nature (e.g., mountains, clouds, and trees) using simple iterative or recursive algorithms. Recent studies also apply this geometry to the control of traffic in computer networks.

Fractal Geometry in Computer Graphics

Fractal geometry has been generalized by the computer graphics community and it includes objects outside Mandelbrot's original definition (Foley, van Dam, Feiner, & Hughes, 1997). It means anything that has a substantial measure of exact or statistical self-similarity. In the case of statistical fractals, it is the probability density that repeats itself on every scale. An application field of fractal geometry is in the compression of images (fractal compression). A fractal compressed image can be defined as follows: It is an encoding that describes (a) the grid partitioning (the range blocks), and (b) the affine transformations (one per range block) (Shulman, 2000). Research on fractal image compression derived from the mathematical ferment on chaos and fractals in the years 1978 to 1985. Barnsley was the principal researcher who worked on fractal compression. The basic idea was to represent by an IFS a fixed point that is close to the image (Barnsley, 1988; Barnsley, Jacquin, Malassenet, Reuter, & Sloane, 1988). This fixed point is also known as

a fractal (Fisher, 1995). Each IFS is coded as a contractive transformation with coefficients. The Banach fixed-point theorem (1922), also known as the contraction mapping theorem or contraction mapping principle, guarantees the existence and uniqueness of fixed points of certain self maps of metric spaces, and provides a constructive method to find those fixed points.

An image can be represented using a set of IFS codes rather than pixels. In this way, a good compression ratio can be achieved. This method was good for generating almost real images based on simple iterative algorithms. The inverse problem, going from a given image to an IFS that can generate the original (or at least closely resemble it), was solved by Jacquin according to Barnsley in March 1988. He introduced a modified scheme for representing images called partitioned iterated function systems (PIFSs). The main characteristics of this approach were that (a) it relied on the assumption that image redundancy can be efficiently exploited through self-transformability on a block-wise basis, and (b) it approximated an original image by a fractal image (Jacquin, 1992). In a PIFS, the transformations do not map from the whole image to the parts, but from larger parts to smaller parts. In Jacquin's method, the small areas are called range blocks, the big areas are called domain blocks, and the pattern of range blocks was called the partitioning of an image. Every pixel of the original image has to belong to one range block. This system of mappings is contractive; thus, when iterated, it quickly converges to its fixed-point image. Therefore, the key point for this algorithm is to find fractals that can best describe the original image and then represent them as affine transformations.

All methods are based on the fractal transform using iterated function systems that generate a close approximation of a scene using only a few transformations (Peitgen & Saupe, 1988; Wohlberg & de Jager, 1999; Zhao & Liu, 2005).

Fractal compression is a lossy compression method (compressing data and then decompress-

Figure 4. Fractal compression: Repeatedly compressing and decompressing the file will cause it to progressively lose quality

ing it retrieves data that may well be different from the original, but is close enough to be useful in some way), and most lossy compression formats suffer from generation loss: Repeatedly compressing and decompressing the file will cause it to progressively lose quality (as shown in Figure 4).

Mandelbrot's geometry and chaos theory can create beautiful images in 2-D and 3-D, as well as realistic, natural-looking structures and fractal textures used to add visual interest to relatively simple and boring geometric models (Ebert, Musgrave, Peachy, Perlin, & Worley, 2003). Fractal algorithms can also be used in computer graphics to generate complex objects using IFS.

Smith (1984) was the first to prove that L-systems were useful in computer graphics for describing the structure of certain plants in his paper "Plants, Fractals, and Formal Languages." He claimed that these objects should not be labeled as fractals for their similarity to fractals, introducing a new class of objects he called "graftals." This class captured great interest in the computer imagery field (Foley et al., 1997; Smith).

Fractal Geometry for Modeling Landscapes

Another interesting application of fractal geometry in computer science is for modeling landscapes. Fournier, Fussel, and Carpenter (1982) developed a mechanism for generating a kind of fractal mountain based on a recursive subdivision algorithm for a triangle. Here, the midpoints of each side of the triangle are connected, creating four new subtriangles. Figure 5a shows the subdivision of the triangle into four smaller triangles, and Figure 5b illustrates how the midpoints of the original triangle are perturbed in the y direction (Foley et al., 1997). To perturb these points, the properties of self-similarity can be used, and so can the conditional expectation properties of fractional Brownian motion (fBm). The fractional Brownian motion was originally introduced by Mandelbrot and Van Ness in 1968 as a generalization of the Brownian motion (Bm). Figure 6 shows a recursive subdivision of an initial polygon using triangles. Other polygons can be used to generate the grid (e.g., squares and hexagons).

This method evidences two problems that are classified as internal and external consistency

Figure 5. (a) The subdivision of a triangle into four smaller triangles, and (b) perturbation in the y direction of the midpoints of the original triangle

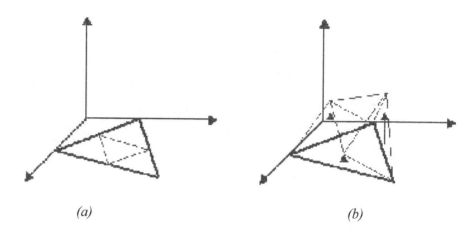

(a) *(b)*

Figure 6. Grid of triangles generated by a recursive subdivision and applying the fractional Brownian motion

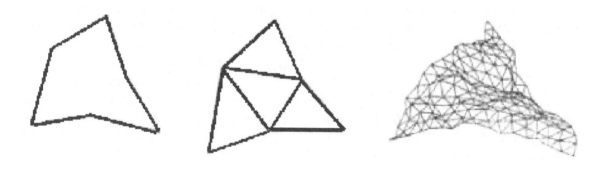

problems (Fournier et al., *1982*). Internal consistency is the reproducibility of the primitive at any position in an appropriate coordinate space and at any level of detail so that the final shape is independent of the orientation of the subdivided triangle. This is satisfied by a Gaussian random-number generator that depends on the point's position; thus, it generates the same numbers in the same order at a given subdivision level. External consistency concerns the midpoint displacement

at shared edges and their direction of displacement. This process, when iterated, produces a deformed grid that represents a surface; after the rendering phase (that includes a hidden line, colored and shaded) there can appear a realistic fractal mountain.

Using fractal algorithms, it is possible to create virtual mountains described in the virtual reality modeling language (VRML), as shown in Figure 7. VRML is a 3-D graphics language used on the

World Wide Web for producing virtual worlds that appear on the display screens using an appropriate VRML browser. This example shows that the connections between fractal geometry, virtual worlds, and the World Wide Web exist.

The last examples describe how to create fractal mountains, but not their erosion. Musgrave, Kolb, and Mace (1989) introduced techniques that are independent of the terrain creation. The algorithm can be applied to already generated data

Figure 7. Virtual mountains realized in VRML using fractal algorithms

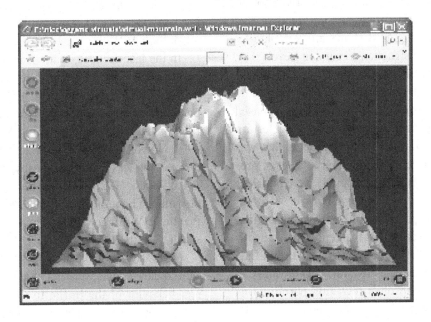

Figure 8. Squig-curve construction (recursion Levels 0-7)

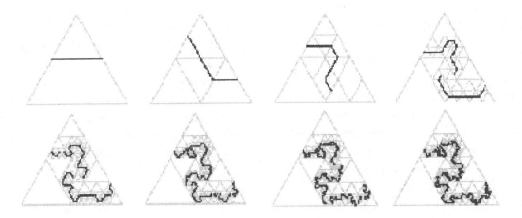

represented as regular height fields, which require separate processes to define the mountain and the river system. Prusinkiewicz and Hammel (1993) combined the midpoint-displacement method for mountain generation with the squig-curve model of a nonbranching river originated by Mandelbrot (1978, 1979). Their method created one nonbranching river as a result of a context-sensitive L-system operating on geometric objects (a set of triangles). Three key problems remained open: (a) The river flowed at a constant altitude, (b) the river flowed in an asymmetric valley, and (c) the river had no tributaries. Figure 8 shows an example of a squig-curve construction (recursion Levels 0–7; Prusinkiewicz & Hammel, 1993).

Marák, Benes, and Slavík (1997) reported a method for synthetic terrain erosion that is based on rewriting the matrices representing terrain parts. They found a rewriting process that was context sensitive. It was defined as a set of productions A → B, where A and B were matrices of numbers of type N ×N, where N>0.

The terrain parts were rewritten using certain user-defined sets of rules that represented an erosion process. The method consisted of three kinds of rewriting processes (Marák, 1997; Marák et al., 1997). The absolute rewriting permitted us to erode the objects in a predefined altitude. The rewriting with the reference point could erode an arbitrary object in any altitude. The third kind of rewriting process permitted us to erode some shapes in any scale. Its advantage was that the algorithm could be controlled by some external rules and could simulate different kinds of erosion (Marák et al.).

Guérin, Tosan, and Baskurt (2002) proposed an interesting model for fractal curves and surfaces. This method, called projected IFS, combined two classical models: a fractal model (IFS attractors) and a computer-aided geometric design model (CAGD). The model, based on IFS, generates a geometrical shape or an image with an iterative process. This method permitted us to reconstruct smooth surfaces and not only rough surfaces using

real data. The original surface generated has been extracted from a geological database (found at the United States Geological Survey home page, http://www.usgs.org).

Fractal Geometry for Controlling Network Traffic

Different models on the nature of network traffic have been proposed in the literature, but in contrast to traditional models, network traffic presents a kind of fractality (J. Liu, 2006; Norros, 1994, 1995; Park & Willinger, 2000).

In the last decades, many fractal traffic processes were described, but the fractality in the traffic was a complex concept, and different approaches were developed. Early models included fractional Brownian motion (Lévy Véhel & Riedi, 1997; Norros, 1994, 1995), the zero-rate renewal process model (Erramilli, Gosby, & Willinger, 1993; Veitch, 1992, 1993), and deterministic chaotic maps (Erramilli & Singh, 1992; Erramilli, Pruthi, & Willinger, 1994; Mondragon, Arrowsmith, & Pitts, 1999).

Many studies have shown that the classical Markovian models were not able to describe the real behavior of the traffic in networks. These models made unacceptable mistakes in the quantitative design in the allocation of the resources, in the connection and in admission control, in the scheduling, and in the traffic regulation. Markovian models supposed an autocorrelation that was decaying in an exponential way, but real examples showed a different behavior (Norros, 1995).

Other studies based on fractal geometry, in particular referring to the property of self-similarity, were realized. Self-similarity is an important notion for understanding the problems connected to the network traffic, including the modeling and analysis of network performances (Fowler & Leland, 1994; Lévy Véhel & Riedi, 1997; Norros, 1994, 1995; Park & Willinger, 2000).

Leland, Taqqu, Willinger, and Wilson (1993, 1994) reported that the Ethernet local area network

(LAN) traffic was statistically self-similar. In fact, the Ethernet LAN data were not only consistent with self-similarity at the level of aggregate packet traffic, but they were also in agreement with self-similarity in terms of the basic characteristics of the individual source-destination pair traffics that make up self-similar aggregate trace. None of the other traffic models were able to describe this fractal behavior, which has serious implications for the design, control, and analysis of high-speed networks. Aggregating streams of such traffic typically intensifies self-similarity ("burstiness") instead of smoothing it.

Figure 9 shows the Bellcore pOct traffic trace, a famous fractal trace, with a Hurst parameter of 0.78 (Norros, 1995).

Klivansky, Mukherjee, and Song (1994) presented an examination of packet traffic from geographically dispersed locations on the National Science Foundation Network (NSFNET) backbone. The analyses indicated that packet-level traffic over NSFNET core switches exhibited long-range dependence (LRD), and a subset of these showed the property of self-similarity (an asymptotic second-order self-similarity).

Willinger, Taqqu, Sherman, and Wilson (1995), using an approach suggested by Man-delbrot (1969), showed that the superposition of many on-off sources, each of which exhibited a phenomenon called the Noah effect, resulted in self-similar aggregate network traffic approaching fractional Brownian motion (the so-called Joseph effect).

Giordano, Pierazzini, and Russo (1995) reported some realistic traffic scenarios in the analysis of broadband telecommunication networks. They described the performance evaluation of a broadband network that provided a best-effort, asynchronous interconnection of several remote LANs, observing some relevant effects of the arrival processes on network performances considering a model of the distributed queue dual bus (DQDB) IEEE 802.6 network. The analysis of real traffic in LANs and in metropolitan area networks (MANs) and of its long-range dependence confirmed a self-similar nature of the traffic offered to a broadband network.

Paxson and Floyd (1994, 1995) reported the results of measurement and analysis on wide area network (WAN) traffic (transmission-control protocol [TCP] traffic) for applications like TELNET (teletype network) and FTP (file transfer protocol). Millions of connections and TCP packets from different sites, with traces ranging from 1 hour

Figure 9. Bellcore pOct traffic trace with Hurst parameter of 0.78 (Norros, 1995)

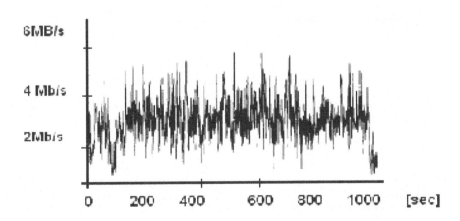

to 30 days, were collected. These studies showed the self-similar nature of WAN traffic.

Crovella and Bestavros (1995, 1996) reported that the World Wide Web's traffic is self-similar. They observed that (a) the traffic patterns generated by browsers have a self-similar nature, (b) every Web browser is modeled as an on-off source model and data fit well the Pareto distribution, and (c) the files available via the Web over the Internet seem to have a heavy-tailed size distribution (bimodal distribution).

Lévy Véhel and Riedi (1997) reported that the fractional Brownian motion, which has been used to model the long-range dependence of traffic traces, showed the property of self-similarity. They noticed that the multifractal approach to traffic was natural because it was a process of positive increments.

All these studies highlight that fractal traffic in LANs, MANs, WANs, and in the WWW has a correlation existing at multiple time scales, a kind of self-correlation that decays in a low-power way (as shown in Figure 10). This self-correlation has an important impact on network performance.

The Hurst parameter H is able to show a degree of self-similarity (for example, a degree of persistence of the statistical phenomenon under test). H has a value range of $0.5 \leq H \leq 1.0$. A value of $H = 0.5$ indicates the lack of self-similarity, a value for H close to 1.0 indicates a large degree of self-similarity or long-range dependence in the process.

Zhang, Shu, and Yang (1997) applied the Hurst parameter to capture the fractal behavior of the network traffic. They also made some interesting considerations of the multifractal behavior and the value of the Hurst parameter when the traffic is merged.

The fractal characterization of the Internet traffic has an exhaustive description by Park and Willinger in their book *Self-Similar Network Traffic and Performance Evaluation* (2000).

More recently, Salvador, Nogueira, Valadas, and Pacheco (2004) addressed the modeling of

Figure 10. Self-similarity in the traffic trace

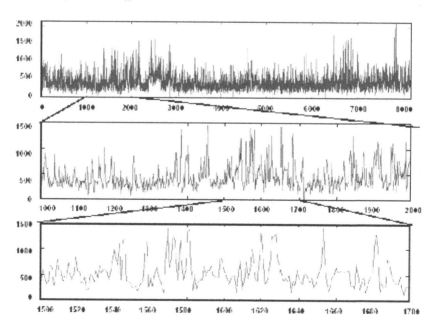

network traffic using a multi-time-scale framework. They evaluated the performance of two classes of traffic models: Markovian and Lindenmayer-systems-based traffic models. These traffic models included the notion of time scale using different approaches: indirectly in the model structure through a fitting of the second-order statistics in the case of the Markovian models, or directly in the model structure in the case of the Lindenmayer-systems-based models.

FUTURE TRENDS

In the field of the compression of images, novel methods are studied. For example, van Wijk and Saupe (2004) present a fast method to generate fractal imagery based on IFS. The high performance derives from three factors: (a) All steps are expressed in graphics operations that can be performed quickly by hardware, (b) frame-to-frame coherence is exploited, (c) only a few commands per image have to be passed from the CPU (central processing unit) to the graphics hardware, avoiding the classical CPU bottleneck.

Wang, Wu, He, and Hintz (2006) present an interactive progressive fractal decoding method, where the compressed file can be transmitted incrementally and reconstructed progressively at the users' side. The method requires no modification to encode or decode any fractal image compression algorithm, and it provides the user-controlled decoding procedure with the inherited fractal fast decoding feature. Their experimental results have shown that the method can be applied to various fractal compression techniques and in particular where the transmission bandwidth is relevant.

Other studies are based on the idea of integrating spiral architecture (SA) and fractal compression (He, Wang, Wu, Hintz, & Hur, 2006; D. Liu, 2006). SA is a recent approach to machine vision systems (Sheridan, 1996; Sheridan, Hintz, & Moore, 1991). It is inspired from anatomical consideration of the primate's vision system

(Schwartz, 1980). The natural data structure that emerges from geometric consideration of the distribution of photo receptors on the primate's retina has been called the spiral honeycomb mosaic (SHM; Sheridan & Hintz, 1999). Spiral architecture, inspired by the natural SHM, is an image structure on which images are displayed as a collection of hexagonal pixels placed in a hexagonal grid (as shown in Figure 11a). Each hexagonal pixel has six neighboring pixels that have the same distance to the center hexagon of unit of vision. In this way, SA has the possibility to save time for local and global processing. In the human eye, these hexagons would represent the relative position of the rods and cones on the retina. This arrangement is different from the traditional rectangular image architecture, a set of 3×3 rectangles used as a unit of vision, where each pixel has eight neighbor pixels (in Figure 11b).

This hexagonal representation has special computational features that are pertinent to the vision process, and it has features of higher degree of circular symmetry, uniform connectivity, greater angular resolution, and a reduced need of storage and computation in image processing operations.

Sheridan, Hintz, and Alexander (2000) introduced a one-dimensional addressing scheme for a hexagonal structure, together with the definitions of two operations, spiral addition and spiral multiplication, that correspond to image translation and rotation respectively. This hexagonal structure is called the spiral architecture. Each pixel on the spiral architecture is identified by a designated positive number, called a spiral address. Figure 12a shows a spiral architecture and the spiral addresses. The numbered hexagons form the cluster of size 7^n. In Figure 12a there is a collection of $7^2 = 49$ hexagons with labeled addresses. Every collection of seven hexagons is labeled starting from the center address as it was done for the first seven hexagons. The collection of hexagons in Figure 12a grows in powers of seven with uniquely assigned addresses. It is this pattern of growth of addresses

Figure 11. (a) Hexagonal grid, and (b) rectangular grid

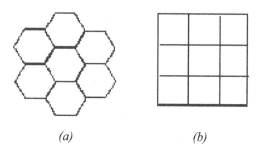

(a)   *(b)*

that generates the spiral; in fact, the hexagons tile the plane in a recursive modular manner along the spiral direction (Figure 12b).

Wu, He, and Hintz (2004) construct a virtual hexagonal structure that represents an important innovation in this field. Using a virtual spiral architecture, a rectangular structure can be smoothly converted to the spiral architecture. A virtual spiral architecture exists only during the procedure of image processing, which creates virtual hexagonal pixels in the computer memory. The data can be reorganized in a rectangular architecture for display. The term virtual refers

to the characteristic that the hexagonal pixels do not physically exist.

Figure 13 shows the phases of the image processing on a virtual spiral architecture (He, Hintz, Wu, Wang, & Jia, 2006). The accuracy and efficiency of image processing on SA have been demonstrated in many recently published papers (Bobe & Schaefer, 2006; He, Hintz, et al., 2006; He, Wang, et al., 2006; Wu et al., 2004). Spiral architecture applied into fractal image compression improves the compression performance in the compression ratio with little suffering in image quality. The methods present the following advantages: Little, if any, distortion is introduced and regular pixels are divided up into subpixels.

In the field of modeling landscapes, the future trends are oriented to use fractal geometry, in particular IFS, generating terrain from real data and extracting from geological databases. This is useful in the reconstruction of real terrain and landscapes (Guérin & Tosan, 2005; Guérin et al., 2002).

Fractal geometry also offers an alternative approach to conventional planetary terrain analysis. For example, Stepinski, Collier, McGovern, and Clifford (2004) describe Martian terrains, represented by topography based on the Mars

Figure 12. (a) Spiral architecture and (b) spiral addressing

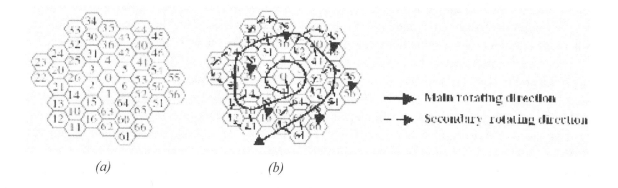

(a)   *(b)*

Figure 13. Image processing on virtual spiral architecture (He, Hintz, et al., 2006)

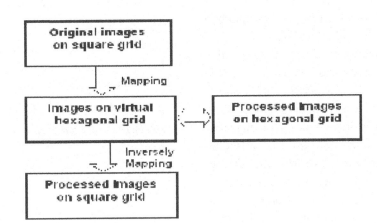

Orbiter Laser Altimetry (MOLA) data, as a series of drainage basins. Fractal analysis of each drainage network computationally extracts some network descriptors that are used for a quantitative characterization and classification of Martian surfaces.

In the field of network traffic control, recent studies intend to check the fractal behavior of network traffic supporting new applications and services (Chakraborty, Ashir, Suganuma, Mansfield, Roy, & Shiratori, 2004). Internet traffic being extremely variable and bursty in a wide range of time scales is usually characterized by self-similarity, which describes its statistics depending on the scales of resolution.

Marie, Bez, Blackledge, and Datta (2006) report a novel method to capture the fractal behavior of Internet traffic, adopting the random scaling fractal model (RSF) to simulate its self-affine characteristics. They realize the transmission of a digital file by splitting the file into a number of binary blocks (files) whose size and submission times are compatible with the bursty lengths of Internet traffic.

The fractal traffic analyses and their results will be useful to enhance the performance of real-time traffic, in particular in multimedia video applications (J. Liu, 2006). This is possible because video traffic is (a) self-similar and fractal, (b) time sensitive, and (c) bandwidth consuming.

CONCLUSION

This chapter has described some applications of fractal geometry in computer science. The fascination that surrounds fractal geometry seems to exist for two reasons. First, it is based on simple rules. The other reason is that fractal geometry is very suitable for simulating many phenomena. For example, fractal behavior and long-range dependence have been observed in the field of fluctuations in different systems, from black holes to quasars, rivers to fault lines, financial networks to computer networks, and brains to hearts; these and many other kinds of complex systems have all exhibited power law scaling relations in their behaviors.

Self-similarity, which characterizes fractal objects, is a unifying concept. In fact, it is an attribute of many laws of nature and innumerable phenomena in the world around us.

In computer science, fractals can be applied in different fields: to compress images using simple algorithms based on IFS, to model complex objects in computer graphics (e.g., mountains and rivers) using L-systems and the fractional Brownian motion, and to control network traffic. In particular, Internet traffic time series exhibit fractal characteristics with long-range dependence. This is due to the existence of several statistical properties that are invariant across a range of time scales, such as self-similarity and multifractality, which have an important impact on network performance. The traffic self-similarity existent in network and application traffic seems to be a ubiquitous phenomenon that is independent of technology, protocol, and environment. Therefore, traffic models must be able to include these properties in their mathematical structure and parameter inference procedures. This is one reason why fractal traffic analysis and modeling have been a popular research topic in network engineering for two decades.

Understanding the nature of traffic in computer networks is essential for engineering operation and their performance evaluation.

ACKNOWLEDGMENT

The author wishes to thank Professor Giovanni Degli Antoni (University of Milan) for his precious suggestions during the draft of the chapter.

REFERENCES

Barnsley, M. F. (1988). *Fractals everywhere*. Boston: Academic Press.

Barnsley, M. F. (1993). *Fractals everywhere* (2nd ed.). Boston: Academic Press.

Barnsley, M. F., Jacquin, A. E., Malassenet, F., Reuter, L., & Sloane, A. D. (1988). Harnessing chaos for image synthesis. *SIGGRAPH 1988* (pp. 131-140).

Barnsley, M. F., Saupe, D., & Vrscay, E. R. (Eds.). (2002). *Fractals in multimedia*. Berlin, Germany: Springer.

Bobe, S., & Schaefer, G. (2006). Image processing and image registration on spiral architecture with saLib. *International Journal of Simulation Systems, Science & Technology, 7*(3), 37-43.

Bogomolny, A. (1998). *The collage theorem.* Retrieved September 15, 2005, from http://www.cut-the-knot.org/ctk/ifs.shtml

Chakraborty, D., Ashir, A., Suganuma, G., Mansfield, K., Roy, T., & Shiratori, N. (2004). Self-similar and fractal nature of Internet traffic. *International Journal of Network Management, 14*(2), 119-129.

Crovella, M. E., & Bestavros, A. (1995). *Explaining World Wide Web traffic self-similarity* (Tech. Rep. No. TR-95-015). Boston: Boston University, Computer Science Department.

Crovella, M. E., & Bestavros, A. (1996). Self-similarity in World Wide Web traffic: Evidence and possible causes. *Proceedings of ACM SIGMETRICS'96*.

Ebert, D. S., Musgrave, F. K., Peachy, D., Perlin, K., & Worley, S. (2003). *Texturing and modeling: A procedural approach* (3rd ed.). Morgan Kaufmann Publishers Inc.

Eglash, R. (1999). *African fractals: Modern computing and indigenous design*. Piscataway, NJ: Rutgers University Press.

Erramilli, A., Gosby, D., & Willinger, W. (1993).

Engineering for realistic traffic: A fractal analysis of burstiness. Proceedings of ITC Special Congress, Bangalore, India.

Erramilli, A., Pruthi, P., & Willinger, W. (1994). *Modelling packet traffic with chaotic maps.* ISRN KTH/IT/R-94/18-SE, Stockholm-Kista, Sweden.

Erramilli, A., & Singh, R. P. (1992). *An application of deterministic chaotic maps to model packet traffic* (Bellcore Technical Memorandum). Bellcore.

Fisher, Y. (1995). *Fractal image compression: Theory and application.* New York: Springer-Verlag.

Foley, J. D., van Dam, A., Feiner, S. K., & Hughes, J. F. (1997). *Computer graphics: Principles and practice* (2nd ed.). New York: Addison Wesley.

Fournier, A., Fussel, D., & Carpenter, L. (1982). Computer rendering of stochastic models. *Communications of the ACM, 25*, 371-384.

Fowler, H., & Leland, W. (1994). Local area network traffic characteristics, with implications for broadband network congestion management. *IEEE Journal of Selected Areas in Communications, 9*(7), 1139-1149.

Fractal geometry. (2007). *Britannica concise encyclopedia.* Retrieved February 26, 2007, from http://concise.britannica.com/ebc/article-9364797/fractal-geometry

Giordano, S., Pierazzini, G., & Russo, F. (1995). *Multimedia experiments at the University of Pisa: From videoconference to random fractals.* Retrieved October 10, 2006, from http://www.isoc.org/HMP/PAPER/109/html/paper.html

Guérin, E., & Tosan, E. (2005). Fractal inverse problem: Approximation formulation and differential methods. In J. Lévy-Véhel & E. Lutton (Eds.), *Fractal in engineering: New trends in theory and applications* (pp. 271-285). London: Springer.

Guérin, E., Tosan, E., & Baskurt, A. (2002). Modeling and approximation of fractal surfaces with projected IFS attractors. In M. M. Novak (Ed.), *Emergent nature: Patterns, growth and scaling in the science* (pp. 293-303). NJ: World Scientific.

Hanan, J. S. (1988). *PLANTWORKS: A software system for realistic plant modelling.* Unpublished master's thesis, University of Regina.

Hanan, J. S. (1992). *Parametric L-systems and their application to the modelling and visualization of plants.* Unpublished doctoral dissertation, University of Regina.

He, X., Hintz, T., Wu, Q., Wang, H., & Jia, W. (2006). A new simulation of spiral architecture. *Proceedings of 2006 International Conference on Image Processing, Computer Vision, & Pattern Recognition (IPCV'06)* (pp. 570-575).

He, X., Wang, H., Wu, Q., Hintz, T., & Hur, N. (2006). Fractal image compression on spiral architecture. *International Conference on Computer Graphics, Imaging and Visualisation (CGIV'06)* (pp. 76-83).

Jacquin, A. E. (1992). Image coding based on a fractal theory of iterated contractive image transformations image processing. *IEEE Transactions, 1*(1), 18-30.

Klivansky, S. M., Mukherjee, A., & Song, C. (1994). On long-range dependence in NSFNET traffic (Tech. Rep. No. GIT-CC-94-61). Georgia Institute of Technology.

Leland, W. E., Taqqu, M. S., Willinger, W., & Wilson, D. V. (1993). On the self-similar nature of Ethernet traffic. *Proceedings of the ACM/SIGCOMM'93* (pp. 183-193).

Leland, W. E., Taqqu, M. S., Willinger, W., & Wilson, D. V. (1994). On the self-similar nature of Ethernet traffic (extended version). *IEEE/ACM Transactions on Networking, 2*(1), 1-15.

Lévy Véhel, J., & Riedi, R. (1997). Fractional Brownian motion and data traffic modeling: The other end of the spectrum. In J. Lévy Véhel, E. Lutton, & C. Tricot (Eds.), *Fractals in engineering* (pp. 185-202). London: Springer.

Liu, D. (2006). A parallel computing algorithm for improving the speed of fractal image compression based on spiral architecture. *Proceedings of 2006 International Conference on Image Processing, Computer Vision, & Pattern Recognition (IPCV'06)* (pp. 563-569).

Liu, J. (2006). *Fractal network traffic analysis with applications.* Retrieved January 10, 2007, from http://hdl.handle.net/1853/11477

Mandelbrot, B. B. (1969). Long-run linearity, locally Gaussian processes, H-spectra and infinite variances. *International Economic Review, 10*, 82-113.

Mandelbrot, B. (1975). *Les objects fractals: Forme, hasard et dimension.* Paris: Nouvelle Bibliothèque Scientifique Flammaron.

Mandelbrot, B. B. (1978). Les objets fractals. *La Recherche, 9*, 1-13.

Mandelbrot, B. B. (1979). Colliers all'eatoires et une alternative aux promenades aux hasard sans boucle: Les cordonnets discrets et fractals. *Comptes Rendus, 286A*, 933-936.

Mandelbrot, B. (1982). *The fractal geometry of nature.* W. H. Freeman & Company.

Marák, I. (1997). *On synthetic terrain erosion modeling: A survey.* Retrieved April 14, 2005, from http://www.cescg.org/CESCG97/marak/

Marák, I., Benes, B., & Slavík, P. (1997). Terrain erosion model based on rewriting of matrices. *Proceedings of WSCG-97, 2*, 341-351.

Marie, R. R., Bez, H. E., Blackledge, J. M., & Datta, S. (2006). *On the fractal characteristics of network traffic and its utilization in covert communications.* Retrieved January 2, 2007, from http://ima.org.uk/Conferences/mathssignalprocessing2006/Marie.pdf

Meyer, M. (2002). Fractal scaling of heartrate dynamics in health and disease. In G. A. Losa, D. Merlini, T. F. Nonnenmacher, & E. R. Weibel (Eds.), *Fractal in biology and medicine* (Vol. 3, pp. 181-193). Basel, Switzerland: Birkhauser.

Mondragon, R. J., Arrowsmith, D. K., & Pitts, J. M. (1999). Chaotic maps for traffic modelling and queueing performance analysis. *Performance Evaluation, 43*(4), 223-240.

Musgrave, F. K., Kolb, C. E., & Mace, R. S. (1989). The synthesis and rendering of eroded fractal terrain. *Computer Graphics, 23*(3), 41-50.

Nonnenmacher, T. F., Losa, G. A., Merlini, D., & Weibel, E. R. (Eds.). (1994). *Fractal in biology and medicine.* Basel, Switzerland: Birkhauser.

Norros, I. (1994). A storage model with self-similar input. *Queueing Systems Theory and Applications, 16*(3-4), 387-396.

Norros, I. (1995). On the use of fractional Brownian motion in the theory of connectionless networks. *IEEE Journal on Selected Areas in Communications, 13*(6), 953-962.

Oppenheimer, P. (1986). Real time design and animation of fractal plants and trees. *Computer Graphics, 20*(4), 55-64.

Park, K., & Willinger, W. (2000). *Self-similar network traffic and performance evaluation* (1st ed.). London: John Wiley & Sons.

Paxson, V., & Floyd, S. (1994). Wide area traffic: The failure of Poisson modeling. *Proceedings of ACM SIGCOMM'94* (pp. 257-268).

Paxson, V., & Floyd, S. (1995). Wide area traffic: The failure of Poisson modeling. *IEEE/ACM Transactions on Networking, 3*(3), 226-244.

Peitgen, H., & Saupe, D. (1988). *The science of fractal images.* New York: Springer-Verlag.

Prusinkiewicz, P. (1986). Graphical applications of L-systems. *Proceedings of Graphics Interface '86: Vision Interface* (pp. 247-253).

Prusinkiewicz, P. (1987). Applications of L-systems to computer imagery. In H. Ehrig, M. Nagl, G. Rozenberg, & A. Rosenfeld (Eds.), *Lecture notes in computer science: Vol. 291. Graph-Grammars and Their Application to Computer Science (3rd International Workshop)* (pp.534-548). Heidelberg, Germany: Springer-Verlag.

Prusinkiewicz, P., & Hammel, M. (1993). A fractal model of mountains with rivers. *Proceeding of Graphics Interface '93* (pp. 174-180).

Prusinkiewicz, P., & Lindenmayer, A. (1990). *The algorithmic beauty of plants.* New York: Springer-Verlag.

Sala, N. (2004). Fractal geometry in the arts: An overview across the different cultures. In M. M. Novak (Ed.), *Thinking in patterns: Fractals and related phenomena in nature* (pp. 177-188). Singapore: World Scientific.

Sala, N. (2006). Complexity, fractals, nature and industrial design: Some connections. In M. M. Novak (Ed.), *Complexus mundi: Emergent pattern in nature* (pp. 171-180). Singapore: World Scientific.

Salvador, P., Nogueira, A., Valadas, R., & Pacheco, A. (2004). Multi-time-scale traffic modeling using Markovian and L-systems models. In *Lecture notes in computer science: Vol. 3262. Proceedings of 3rd European Conference on Universal Multiservice Networks* (pp. 297-306). Heidelberg, Germany: Springer-Verlag.

Schwartz, E. (1980). Computation anatomy and functional architecture of striate cortex: A spatial mapping approach to perceptual coding. *Vision Research, 20*, 645-669.

Sheridan, P. (1996). *Spiral architecture for machine vision.* Unpublished doctoral dissertation, University of Technology, Sydney, Australia.

Sheridan, P., & Hintz, T. (1999). Primitive image transformations on hexagonal lattice (Tech. Rep.). Bathurst, Australia: Charles Sturt University.

Sheridan, P., Hintz, T., & Alexander, D. (2000). Pseudo-invariant image transformations on a hexagonal lattice. *Image and Vision Computing, 18*, 907-917.

Sheridan, P., Hintz, T., & Moore, W. (1991). Spiral architecture in machine vision. Proceedings of the Australian Occam and Transputer Conference, Australia.

Shulman, J. A. (2000). *Fractals and Benoit Mandelbrot: A computer science discovery often considered kind to prime numbers.* American Computer Science Association (ACSA). Retrieved December 28, 2006, from http://www.acsa2000.net/frac/

Smith, A. R. (1984). Plants, fractals, and formal languages. *International Conference on Computer Graphics and Interactive Techniques: Proceedings of the 11th Annual Conference on Computer Graphics and Interactive Techniques* (pp. 1–10).

Stepinski, T. F., Collier, M. L., McGovern, P. J., & Clifford, S. M. (2004). Martian geomorphology from fractal analysis of drainage networks. *Journal of Geophysical Research, 109*(nºE2), E02005.1-E02005.12.

Szilard, A. L., & Quinton, R. E. (1979). An interpretation for DOL systems by computer graphics. *The Science Terrapin, 4*, 8-13.

van Wijk, J. J., & Saupe, D. (2004). Image based rendering of iterated function systems. *Computers & Graphics, 28*(6), 937-943.

Veitch, D. (1992). *Novel models of broadband traffic.* Proceedings of the Seventh Australian Teletraffic Research Seminar, Murray River, Australia.

Veitch, D. (1993). Novel models of broadband traffic. *IEEE Global Telecommunications Conference, 1993, including a Communications Theory Mini-Conference: Technical Program Conference Record, IEEE in Houston. GLOBECOM '93, 2,* 1057-1061.

Vyzantiadou, M. A., Avdelas, A. V., & Zafiropoulos, S. (2007). The application of fractal geometry to the design of grid or reticulated shell structures. *Computer-Aided Design, 39*(1), 51-59.

Wang, H., Wu, Q., He, X., & Hintz, T. (2006). A novel interactive progressive decoding method for fractal image compression. *First International Conference on Innovative Computing, Information and Control (ICICIC'06), 3,* 613-617.

Willinger, W., Taqqu, M. S., Sherman, R., & Wilson, D. V. (1995). Self-similarity through high-variability: Statistical analysis of Ethernet LAN traffic at the source level. *ACM Sigcomm '95* (pp.100-113). Wohlberg, B., & de Jager, G. (1999). A review of the fractal image coding literature. *IEEE Transactions on Image Processing, 8*(12), 1716-1729.

Wu, Q., He, X., & Hintz, T. (2004). Virtual spiral architecture. *Proceedings of the International Conference on Parallel and Distributed Processing Techniques and Applications, 1,* 399-405.

Zhang, H. F., Shu, Y. T., & Yang, O. W. W. (1997). Estimation of Hurst parameter by variance time plots. *Proceedings IEEE Pacrim 97, 2,* 883-886.

Zhao, E., & Liu, D. (2005). Fractal image compression methods: A review. *ICITA 2005: Third International Conference on Information Technology and Applications, 1,* 756-759.

Glossary

A

Aconscious. It is mental content or activity that has always been placed outside of the consciousness domain and might never be brought to consciousness. It might include nondeclarative and procedural memory.

Action. In bios theory, it is the change of energy in time. Sabelli (2005) affirms that "action is the one and sole constituent of the universe."

ADHD (Attention Deficit/Hyperactivity Disorder). It is a neurobehavioral disorder characterized by pervasive inattention and/or hyperactivity-impulsivity and resulting in significant functional impairment, affecting 3 to 5% of the population. ADHD is most commonly diagnosed in children and, over the past decade, has been increasingly diagnosed in adults. It is hard for these people to control their behavior and/or pay attention. ADHD was first described by the German physician Heinrich Hoffman (1809-1894) in 1845; he wrote books on medicine and psychiatry. ADHD was first clinically observed by the English pediatrician George Still (1868-1941) in 1902.

ADMET Processes. It refers to the absorption, distribution, metabolism, excretion, and toxicity processes of a molecule within an organism. Optimizing these properties during early drug discovery is important for reducing ADMET problems later in the development process.

Agent. In computer science, an agent (or software agent) is a part of software that acts for a user or other program in a relationship of agency. Such action on behalf of another implies the authority to decide when (and if) action is appropriate. The idea is that agents are not strictly invoked for a task, but activate themselves.

Algorithm. In mathematics and in computing, it is an explicit step-by-step list of instructions for producing a solution to a problem given an initial state. The term is derived by the misspelling of the name of the Persian mathematician and astronomer Muhammad ibn Mūsā al-Khwārizmī (born around 780 in Khwārizm, now Khiva, Uzbekistan, and died around 850). He wrote a treatise in Arabic entitled *On Calculation with Hindu Numerals* in 850. It was translated in Latin in the 12th century with the title *Algoritmi de Numero Indorum*. During the translation, the term *algoritmi* was erroneously considered as a synonym of the term *calculation* and not the misspelling of the author's name.

Ant Colony Optimization Algorithm (ACO). It is a probabilistic technique inspired by the behavior of ants in searching for paths from the colony to food. This technique is used for solving computational problems that can be reduced to finding good paths through graphs, and it was introduced by the Italian engineer Marco Dorigo (born 1961) in his doctoral dissertation (1992). ACO is able to find approximate solutions to difficult optimization problems.

Apophenia. It is an unmotivated seeing of connections accompanied by a specific experience of an abnormal meaningfulness. Apophenia is the experience of making connections where none previously existed in random or meaningless data. Apophenia can be a normal phenomenon or an abnormal one, as in paranoid schizophrenia. The term was coined in 1958 by Klaus Conrad (1905-1961).

Arc. In graph theory, it is the line that connects different nodes in a graph.

Aristotelian Logic. It is a deductive method of logic introduced by the Greek philosopher Aristotle (384 B.C. to 322 B.C.). Logic is the study of the principles and criteria of valid demonstration and inference.

Artificial Intelligence (AI). It is a branch of computer science concerned with producing machines to automate tasks requiring intelligent

behavior. The term was coined in 1956 by John McCarthy (Massachusetts Institute of Technology) who considers it to mean "the science and engineering of making intelligent machines." AI is studied in overlapping fields of computer science, philosophy, psychology, neuroscience, and engineering. A possible classification is that between strong AI and weak AI. Strong AI affirms that computers can be made to think on a level (at least) equal to humans and possibly even be conscious of themselves. Weak AI makes no such claim and denies this possibility. Areas of artificial intelligence activity include (a) expert systems used in programming computers to make decisions in real-life situations (for example, helping doctors diagnose diseases based on symptoms), (b) neural networks, which are artificial systems that simulate intelligence by attempting to reproduce the types of physical connections that occur in the human brain, (c) robotics, in which scientists are programming computers to see and hear, and react to other sensory stimuli, and (d) in programming computers to play games (for example, chess).

Artificial Neural Network (ANN). ANN is a kind of computer model that finds inspiration from the neural network structure of the brain, consisting of interconnected processing units that send signals to one another and turn on or off depending on the sum of their incoming signals. Artificial neural networks may be composed of either computer software or hardware, or both. ANN is also called a simulated neural network (SNN) or just a neural network (NN), and it is an interconnected group of artificial neurons that uses a mathematical model or computational model for information processing based on a connectionist approach to computation.

Artificial Neuron. It is an abstraction of biological neurons. An artificial neuron is the basic unit in artificial neural networks. It is also called a McCulloch-Pitts neuron, binary neuron, or node. It receives different inputs and sums them, producing an output. Usually the sums of each node are weighted, and the sum is passed through a nonlinear function known as a transfer function. The canonical form of transfer functions is the sigmoid (a curve that has an S shape), but they also have the form of other linear functions, nonlinear functions, or step functions piecewise (a function whose definition is given differently on disjoint subsets of its domain).

Asymmetry. It is the absence of balanced proportions between parts of a thing, or to be without symmetry.

Attention. It is one of the cognitive processes associated with the human mind. It is the ability to concentrate mentally on one aspect of the environment while ignoring other things. Attention is one of the most intensely studied topics within cognitive neuroscience and psychology. Sometimes attention shifts to matters unrelated to the external environment; this phenomenon is referred to as "mind-wandering" or "spontaneous thought." Using an engineering point of view, attention is analyzed as the superior control system in the brain.

Attractor. In classical chaos theory, an attractor is an invariant set to which all nearby orbits converge. It represents a way to describe the long-term behavior of a system. Equilibrium and steady states correspond to fixed-point attractors, periodic states to limit-cycle attractors, and chaotic states to strange attractors. It can also be described as a fractal structure with noninteger dimensionality whose shape is shown in phase space and to which trajectories are attracted.

Augmented Reality (AR). It is a growing area in virtual reality research that deals with the combination of real-world and computer-generated data. Milgram and Kishino (1994) and Milgram, Takemura, Utsumi, and Kishino (1994) describe a taxonomy that identifies how augmented-reality and virtual-reality work are related, as shown in the figure.

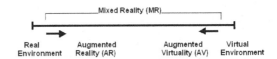

B

Bi-Causality. It is a neologism that shows the relation in which every action in the physical reality has an effect in the artificial reality, and vice versa. For example, a mouse click activates an object in a virtual world; this gesture can interact with a device that produces an effect on the physical reality. The term was coined by the Italian scientist Giovanni Degli Antoni (1989).

Bifurcation. It is a term used in chaos theory for a sensitive decision point of a complex system. At a bifurcation, a choice is made between two possible outcomes. Bifurcation occurs when a small, smooth change made to the parameter values (the bifurcation parameters) of a system causes a sudden qualitative or topological change in the system's long-term dynamical behavior.

Bioavailability. In pharmacology it is the degree to which a drug or other substance is absorbed or becomes available at the site of physiological activity after administration. Absolute bioavailability refers to the availability of the active drug in systemic circulation after nonintravenous administration.

Bionic. It is an application of biological principals to the study and design of engineering systems (especially electronic systems). The word bionic is formed from two terms: One is derived from the Greek word *βίον*, which means *unit of life*, and the other is the suffix *-ic*, which means *like* or *in the manner of*, hence, it means *like life*. Bionics is also known as biognosis, biomimicry, biomimetics, or bionical creativity engineering.

Bios Theory. It is a theory introduced by Hector Sabelli and colleagues who state,

BIOS is a causal and creative process that follows chaos in sequences of patterns of increasing complexity. Bios was first identified as the pattern of heartbeat intervals, and it has since then been found in a wide variety of processes ranging in size from Schrodinger's wave function to the temporal distribution of galaxies, and ranging in complexity from physics to economics to music.

Bios attempts to characterize the behavior of certain nonlinear dynamical systems that are sensitive to initial conditions and generate novelty. The term *bios*, adopted by Sabelli, derives from the Greek *bio*, meaning *life*, *course*, or *way of living*.

Biotic Logic. It integrates physics, logic, and dialectics by proposing that opposite processes display three different forms of interaction according to the size and complexity of the level of organization: quantum superposition, local macroscopic separation (logical, no contradiction), and global complementarity (dialectic contradiction; Sabelli, 2001).

Boolean. It is an item that can only have two states, like on or off, or yes or no, or true or false, often coded as 1 and 0, respectively. The term was coined in honor of the British mathematician George Boole (1815-1864) who introduced Boolean algebra, the basis of all modern computer arithmetic.

Bootstrapping. In computing, it is a process where a simple system activates another more complicated system that serves the same purpose. The

term is shortened to booting. This process is often applied to the process of starting up a computer, in which a mechanism is needed to execute the software program that is responsible for executing software programs (the operating system).

Broadband. It refers to telecommunication in which a wide band of frequencies is available to transmit information with high speed. Related terms are wideband (a synonym) and baseband (a one-channel band).

Broca's Area. It is the section of the human brain that is involved in language processing, speech production, and comprehension. It was discovered by the French physician, anatomist, and anthropologist Paul Broca (1824-1880).

Brownian Motion. It is a phenomenon that describes random movements. It was observed by the British botanist Robert Brown (1773-1858). In 1827, while examining pollen grains and the spores of mosses and equisetum suspended in water under a microscope, Brown saw some minute particles within vacuoles in the pollen grains executing a continuous jittery motion. He also observed the same motion in particles of dust. It is the random movement of particles suspended in a fluid. The mathematical model used to describe such random movements is often called the "Wiener process." Brownian motion has several real-world applications (e.g., in physics, economy, computer science, hydrodynamics).

Building Design. In architecture, it is the science of designing exterior and interior spaces, and constructing buildings and engineered elements.

C

CAD (Computer-Aided Design). It is a term used for indicating a wide range of computer-based tools that assist architects, engineers, and other design professionals in their design activities. There are 2-D and 3-D CADs.

Castration Anxiety (Castration Fears). In psychoanalysis, the word castration is associated with several others that define it and that it in turn defines. These include anxiety, fear, terror, disavowal, and above all, complex. Beyond the everyday connotations of the term, the specifically psychoanalytic definition of castration is rooted in the act feared by male children, namely, the removal of the penis.

Catastrophe Theory. It is a field of mathematics that studies how the behavior of dynamic systems can change drastically with small variations in specific parameters. This theory was introduced by the French mathematician René Thom (1923-2002) in the 1960s, and became very popular with the works of Christopher Zeeman (born 1925) in the 1970s.

Cellular Automaton or Automata (CA). Cellular automaton (cellular automata) is a simplified mathematical model that consists of an infinite, regular spatial lattice of cells, each of which can have any one of a finite number of states (the state represents a unique configuration of information in a program or machine). The lattice can be in any finite number of dimensions. The state of a cell at time t is a function of the states of a finite number of cells (called its neighborhood) at time t-1. CA are studied in mathematics, computer science, and theoretical biology. Cellular automata have their origin in systems described by John von Neumann (1903-1957) and Stanislaw Marcin Ulam (1909-1984) in the 1940s, followed by Arthur W. Burks (born 1915) and Edward F. Codd (1923-2003), to solve the problem of the nontrivial self-reproduction in a logical system.

Chaos. The term derives from the Greek *Χάος*, which in ancient Greece did not mean *disorder*, but meant *the primal emptiness space*. In physics and mathematics, the actual chaos theory presents the behavior of certain nonlinear dynamical systems that show dynamics, under particular initial conditions, that are sensitive to initial conditions (for example, the popular "butterfly effect" described by American mathematician and meteorologist Edward Lorenz, born 1917, in 1963). The chaotic systems have a behavior that appears to be random because it is generated by an exponential growth of errors in the initial conditions.

Chaos Theory. In physics, it is the qualitative study of unstable aperiodic behavior in deterministic nonlinear dynamical systems.

Characteristic Equation. In mathematics, it is any equation that has a solution, subject to specified boundary conditions, only when a parameter occurring in it has certain values. In linear algebra, the characteristic equation of a square matrix A is the equation in one variable λ: $det(A-\lambda I)=0$, where det is the determinant and I is the identity matrix. In physics, the characteristics equation is an equation relating a set of variables, such as pressure, volume, and temperature, whose values determine a substance's physical condition.

Chemostat. It is a device used in microbiology for growing and harvesting bacteria. It consists of two primary parts: a nutrient reservoir and a growth chamber or reactor, in which the bacteria reproduce. Via an inflow from the reservoir, fresh nutrition is added, and from an outflow bacteria are harvested.

Chinese Room (Argument). It is an experiment designed by John Searle in 1980 for supporting the studies in the artificial intelligence field. The heart of the experiment is an imagined human simulation of a computer, similar to Turing's paper machine. The human, a monolingual English speaker, is in the Chinese room and follows English instructions for manipulating Chinese characters, where a computer "follows" a program written in a computing language. The human produces the appearance of understanding Chinese by following the symbol-manipulating instructions, but does not thereby come to understand Chinese. The argument is intended to show that while suitably programmed computers may appear to converse in natural language, they are not capable of understanding language, even in principle. Searle argues that the thought experiment underscores the fact that computers merely use syntactic rules to manipulate symbol strings, but have no understanding of meaning or semantics.

Chromosome. It is a component in a cell that contains genetic information. Each chromosome contains numerous genes. In genetic algorithms, a chromosome is a set of parameters that represents a solution to the problem that the genetic algorithm is trying to solve. The chromosome is often represented as a simple string (sequence of characters), and the binary alphabet {0,1} is often used to represent these genes, but sometimes, depending on the application, integers or real numbers are used.

Ciphertext. It is a set of data that has been encrypted. It is unreadable until it has been converted into original text (decrypted) with a key.

CODAM (Corollary Discharge of Attention Movement). It is a generic model of consciousness that has been developed by John G. Taylor, where the prereflective self arises from experience of the attention copy signal at an early stage in the processing. This model considers the so-called "corollary discharge" or copy of the control signal causing the movement of the focus of attention to be the crucial element for consciousness creation.

Code. In communication, a code is the usage of a set of rules, characters, or words to represent words, sentences, or ideas. It is used for converting a piece of information (for example, a letter, or word) into another form or representation. Morse code is a common example, where the combinations of dashes and dots represent numbers and letters.

Coevolution. In biology, it is the mutual evolutionary influence between two species that become dependent on each other. In computer science, it is the evolutionary computation paradigm where both the measure of fitness and the solution evolve separately and affect each other.

Cognition. The term derives from the Latin *cognoscere* (that means *to know*). It is used in different ways by different disciplines. For example, in psychology and in artificial intelligence, it is used to refer to the mental processes involved in knowledge and comprehension including the knowing, remembering, thinking, learning, problem solving, and judging of intelligent entities (humans, human organizations, and autonomous robots).

Collage Theorem. The theorem describes how to find an iterated function system whose attractor is close to a given set. One must endeavor to find a set of transformations and contraction mappings on a suitable set, within which the given set lies, such that the union (or the collage) of the images of the given set under transformations is near the given set. The theorem has been enunciated and demonstrated by Michael Barnsley (1988).

Collective Unconsciousness. In analytical psychology, it is a part of the unconscious mind shared by a society, a people, or all humankind that is the product of ancestral experience and contains such concepts as morality, religion, and science. Thus, it refers to that part of a person's unconscious that is common to all human beings. The term was coined by Carl Jung (1875-1961).

Communication. It is a process of exchanging information and ideas. It is an active process that involves encoding, transmitting, and decoding intended messages. The term derives from the Latin *cum* (that means *with*) and *munire* (that means *bind* or *build*).

Complexity. It is the quality of being intricate and compounded. In physics, it is study of the behavior of macroscopic collections of simple units (e.g., atoms, molecules, bits, neurons) that are endowed with the potential to evolve in time. The term derives from Latin word *complexus* (that means *entwined, twisted together*).

Complex System. This is a system with a large number of interrelated parts.

Compression. It is a process that reduces the number of bytes required to define a digitized document in order to save disk space or transmission time. Compression is achieved by replacing commonly occurring sequences of pixels with shorter codes. It is possible to compress a movie or an image (see image compression).

Computational Fluid Dynamic (CFD). It is the branch of fluid mechanics that uses numerical methods and algorithms to solve and analyze problems that involve fluid flows. Computers are used to perform the millions of calculations required to simulate the interaction of fluids and gases with the complex surfaces used in engineering.

Computer Graphics. This is a branch of computer science that deals with the theory and techniques of computer image synthesis. Computer graphics uses methods and techniques for converting data to or from visual presentation using computers. It is concerned with generating and displaying three-dimensional objects in a two-dimensional space.

Computer Network. It is multiple computers connected together using a telecommunication system for the purpose of communicating and sharing resources.

Computer Networking. It is the engineering discipline concerned with communication between computer systems.

Computer Science. It is the study of the theoretical foundations of information and computation and their application in computer systems. It comprises many subfields. For example, some relate to the properties of computational problems (such as computational complexity theory), while others focus on the computation of specific results (such as computer graphics). Still others study the challenges in implementing computations. For example, programming language theory studies approaches to describing computations, while computer programming applies specific programming languages to solve specific computational problems with solutions.

Connectionism. It is an approach that models mental or behavioral phenomena as the emergent processes of interconnected networks of simple units. Connectionism is in the fields of artificial intelligence, cognitive psychology and cognitive science, neuroscience, and philosophy of the mind.

Connectivity. In computer science it is the ability to connect computer or communications systems to exchange data or share resources. It is a perception related to link to people and resources.

Consciousness. It is the quality of being aware of what is happening around us and responding in kind. It can also be defined as the process of a thinker focusing the thought on some aspect of existence. The term derives from Latin *conscientia* (that primarily meant *moral conscience*). There are many layers or levels of consciousness ranging from the ordinary, everyday consciousness of our body and mind to omniscient states of superconsciousness.

CPU (Central Processing Unit). It is the component in the computer that processes data and that interprets computer program instructions; sometimes it is called the processor. Today, the CPUs of almost all computers are contained on a single chip.

Crossover (Recombination). In genetic algorithms, it is a genetic operator that is used to modify the programming of a chromosome or chromosomes from one generation to the next. It is analogous to reproduction and biological crossover.

Cryptographic Encoding. In cryptography, it is the activity of converting a message from plain text into code.

Cryptography (Cryptology). It is the art of protecting information by transforming it (encrypting it) into an unreadable format, called ciphertext, for transmitting it over a public network. The original text, or plaintext, is converted into a coded equivalent called ciphertext via an encryption algorithm. The ciphertext is decoded (decrypted) at the receiving end and turned back into plaintext. The term derives from the Greek word κρυπτός (*kryptós* that means *hidden*), and from the verb γράφω (*gráfo* that means *write*).

Cryptosystem (Cryptographic System). It represents the entire process of using cryptography. This includes the actions of encrypting and decrypting a file or message, or authenticating the sender of an e-mail message.

Cybernetics. The science of communication and control processes as applied to the physiologic systems. The term derives from the Greek Κυβερνήτης (*kybernetes* meaning *governor* or *steersman*). Plato used it in *The Laws* to signify the governance of people. The French physicist André-Marie Ampère (1775-1836) used the word cybernetics to denote the sciences of government in his classification system of human knowledge. In 1948, the mathematician Norbert Wiener (1894-1964) used the word cybernetics to denote the science of communication and control in the animal and the machine. Cybernetics involves different disciplines such as electrical engineering, mathematics, biology, neurophysiology, anthropology, psychology, and computer science. First-order cybernetics studies a system as if it were a passive, objectively given thing that can be freely observed, manipulated, and taken apart. Second-order cybernetics studies how observers construct models of other cybernetic systems.

Cyberspace. It is a term coined by author William Gibson in his novel *Neuromancer* (1984) for indicating a futuristic computer network that people use by plugging their minds into it. Cyberspace refers to the electronic space created by computers connected together in networks like the Internet.

D

Darwinian Evolution. In biology, it is the Darwinian theory according to which higher forms of life have arisen out of lower forms with the passage of time.

Database (DB). It is a collection of information organized so that its contents can easily be accessed, managed, and updated. The most prevalent type of database is the relational database.

Decision Theory. It is a newly proposed extension to the theory of games that is based on the same logic as are causal processes in nature.

Decode. This means to convert coded data back into its original form.

Decoder. It is the device that executes a process of decoding.

Destratification. It is vertical mixing within a lake in which the water is mixed in order to eliminate stratified layers of temperature, plant, or animal life.

Deterministic Model. This is a mathematical model whose output is determined by the mathematical form of its equations and the selection of a single value for each input parameter. A mathematical model is deterministic if the relations between the variables involved take on values not allowing for any play of chance.

Dialectics. In philosophy, it represents an exchange of propositions (theses) and counter-propositions (antitheses) resulting in a qualitative transformation in the direction of the dialogue. The term derives from the Greek *διαλεκτική* (*dialektikē* that means *to converse, to discuss*).

Dynamic Systems. These are systems in motion. Most dynamic systems, and all living systems, are open. The human body, for example, is an open system. There are two main types of dynamic systems: discrete and continuous.

E

Ecosystem. An area that includes living organisms and nonliving substances interacting to produce an exchange of materials. It culminates in a stable, though not necessarily permanent, community of living organisms and nonliving components that have developed interrelationships with each other to form a distinct, self-sustaining system.

Ectoderm. It is the primary germ of a tissue that covers the body surfaces. Ectoderm gives rise to the nervous system and the epidermis of skin and its derivatives. The term derives from the Greek words *ecto (which means outside)* and *derma* (which means *skin*).

Electroencephalogram (EEG). It is a test that measures and records the electrical activity of the brain by using sensors (electrodes) attached to the head and connected by wires to a computer that records the brain's electrical activity (postsynaptic potentials) on the screen or on paper as wavy lines. EEG is a tool for monitoring and diagnosis in certain clinical situations, for example, for epilepsy, sleep disorders, coma, and brain death.

Emotion. It is a mental state that arises spontaneously rather than through conscious effort. It can evoke either a negative or positive psychological response. Many psychologists adopt a model based on three fundamental attributes for defining emotions: (a) physiological arousal, (b) behavioral expression (e.g., facial expressions), and (c) conscious experience, the subjective feeling of an emotion. The term emotion derives from the Latin *emovere* (that means *to set in motion*).

Encode. It means to convert from one format or signal to another, or to assign a code to represent data.

Epilepsy. The term sometimes is referred to as a seizure disorder. It is a chronic neurological condition that causes people to have recurring seizures. The seizures happen when clusters of nerve cells in the brain send out wrong signals. Epilepsy has many possible causes, including illness, brain injury, and abnormal brain development. In many cases, the cause is unknown.

Epilimnion. It is the upper layer of water in a thermally stratified lake or reservoir. This layer consists of the warmest water and has a fairly uniform (constant) temperature. The layer is readily mixed by wind action.

Erosion. The term is used in geology and it represents the carrying away of weathered soil, rock, and other materials on the Earth's surface by gravity, water, wind, or ice.

Ethernet. A physical and data link layer technology for local area networks (LANs). Ethernet was invented by engineer Robert Metcalfe.

Evolution. It is the changes in species as a consequence of processes such as mutation and natural selection. Evolution is a unifying principle of biology, but it extends beyond biology and can be used as an engineering principle that can be applied to computer science, where individuals in a population of candidate solutions to some particular problem undergo random variation (e.g., mutation and recombination) and face competition and selection based on their appropriateness for the final task.

Evolutionary Algorithms (EAs). They are computer programs that attempt to solve complex problems by mimicking the processes of Darwinian evolution: from natural selection and survival of the fittest in the biological world. An EA uses some mechanisms inspired by biological evolution, for example, reproduction, mutation, recombination, natural selection, and survival of the fittest. In an EA a number of artificial individuals (candidate solutions to the optimization problem) search over the space of the problem. The shared environment determines the fitness or performance of each individual in the population. The individuals compete continually with each other to discover optimal areas of the search space. It is hoped that over time the most successful of these creatures will evolve to discover the optimal solution. Each iteration of an EA involves a competitive selection that weeds out poor solutions. The fittest individuals are more likely to be selected for reproduction (retention or duplication), while recombination and mutation modify those individuals, yielding potentially superior ones. The solutions with high fitness are recombined with other solutions by swapping parts of a solution with another. The solutions can also be mutated by making a small change to a single element of the solution.

Evolutionary Computation. It is a general term used for several computational techniques that are based to some degree on the evolution of biological life in the natural world. A number of evolutionary computational models have been proposed, including evolutionary algorithms, genetic algorithms, the evolution strategy, evolutionary programming, and artificial life.

Evolutionary Systems. They are systems that undergo evolutionary processes.

Extinction. In biology, it is the elimination of a species (also applicable to levels other than species) due to natural processes or human activities.

F

False Nearest Neighbor. It is a method for determining the minimal sufficient embedding dimension. This method is important for the application of nonlinear methods in the reconstruction (embedding) of the time series in a phase space with appropriate dimension. The method determines when the points in dimension d are neighbors of one another by virtue of their projection onto too low a dimension. It was introduced by Kennel, Brown, and Abarbanel in a paper published in 1992.

Feedback. It is the mechanism whereby the consequences of an ongoing process become factors in modifying or changing that process. The original process is reinforced in positive feedback and suppressed in negative feedback.

Feed-Forward Networks. They are a particular kind of neural networks whose architectures are composed by neurons that can be divided into layers, with the neural activities in one layer only being able to influence the activity in later (not earlier) layers. They are also called multilayer perceptrons.

Financial Trading System (FTS). In economy, it is a widespread class of tools that are used to support risky financial decisions.

Fitness. In genetic algorithms and genetic programming, the term fitness is used to guide the search by deciding which individuals will be used as future points to look for better solutions. The fitness value is a comparative index for how close the corresponding value is to the ideal. This is in analogy with natural selection.

Fold Catastrophe. It is a catastrophe that can occur for one control parameter and one behavior axis.

Formal Grammar. In computer science, a formal grammar is the syntax of each programming language. The two main categories of formal grammar that exist are generative grammars and analytic grammars. Generative grammars are sets of rules for how strings in a language can be generated. A string is a sequence of symbols. Analytic grammars are sets of rules for how a string can be analyzed to determine whether it is a member of the language.

Fractal. It is an irregular or fragmented geometric shape that can be subdivided in parts, each of which is (at least approximately) a reduced-size copy of the whole. The term was coined by Benoit Mandelbrot in 1975. It derives from the Latin verb *frangere, to break,* and from the related adjective *fractus,* meaning *fragmented and irregular.*

Fractal Compression. In computer science, it is a method used to compress digitized images using fractal geometry for minimizing images' dimension. The fractal compression technique relies on the fact that in certain images, parts of the image resemble other parts of the same image. Fractal compression causes the loss of the quality of the images compressed.

Fractal Geometry. It is the geometry used to describe the irregular pattern and the irregular shapes present in nature. Fractals display the characteristic of self-similarity, an unending series of motifs within motifs repeated at all length scales.

Fractal Mountain. In computer graphics, it is a mountain generated using fractal algorithms based on iterative and recursive operations.

Fractality. It is the quality of an object that shows some typical properties of fractal geometry (e.g., self-similarity).

Fractional Brownian Motion (fBm). It is defined as W_t^H on $[0, T]$, $T \in R$. It is a continuous-time Gaussian process that starts at zero, with mean zero, and that has the following correlation function: $E[W_t^H W_s^H] = \frac{1}{2}(|t|^{2H} + |s|^{2H} + |s|^{2H} - |t-s|^{2H})$, where H is the Hurst parameter associated with the motion. H is a real number in the interval $[0, 1]$. Fractional Brownian motion has important properties: self-similarity, long-range dependence, regularity, and integration. The first two properties permit one to realize the connection between fBm and fractal geometry. The main difference between fBm and regular Brownian motion is that while the increments in Brownian Motion are independent they are dependent in fBm. This dependence means that if there is an increasing pattern in the previous steps, then it is likely that the current step will be increasing as well.

Frequency. It is the number of repetitions in a given interval of time. In mathematics it is the number of times that a specified periodic phenomenon occurs within a specified interval. In physics it is the number of complete cycles of a periodic process (or waveform) occurring per unit of time. It is usually measured in Hertz (Hz), where 1 Hz = 1 s^{-1}. In statistics the frequency is the ratio of the number of times an event occurs in a series of trials of a chance experiment to the number of trials of the experiment performed. The frequency also represents the number of measurements in an interval of a frequency distribution. The term derives from the Latin *frequentia* (that means *multitude*).

FTP (File Transfer Protocol). It is a communications protocol used to transmit files without loss of data over any network that supports the TCP/IP protocol (such as the Internet or an intranet). It is usually implemented as an application-level program, so it also uses the Telnet. A file transfer protocol can handle all types of files. The FTP transfer involves two computers: a server and a client.

G

Gene. It is a segment of nucleic acid that contains information necessary to produce a functional product, usually a protein. Genes correspond to units of inheritance.

Genetic Algorithm (GA). It is a technique used in computing to find true or approximate solutions to optimization and search problems. Genetic algorithms are categorized as global search heuristics. Genetic algorithms are a particular class of evolutionary algorithms that use techniques inspired by evolutionary biology such as inheritance, mutation, selection, and crossover (also called recombination).

Genetic Operator. In genetic algorithms, it is a process that is used to maintain genetic diversity. The genetic operators applied in this field are analogous to those that occur in the natural world that imply the survival of the fittest.

Genetic Programming (GP). Genetic programming is an automated method for creating a working computer program from a high-level problem statement of a problem. It uses some optimization techniques to evolve simple programs, mimicking the way humans construct programs by progressively rewriting them. It is a methodology inspired by biological evolution to find computer programs that perform a user-defined task. In nature, each species needs to adapt to a complicated and changing environment in order to maximize the likelihood of its survival. In GP, populations of programs are genetically bred to solve problems, for example, system identification, classification, control, robotics, optimization, game playing, and pattern recognition. The basis of GP began with the evolutionary algorithms first utilized by Nils Aall Barricelli in 1954 as applied to evolutionary simulations. Other works were developed by John Holland in the early 1970s. The first results on the GP methodology were reported by Stephen F. Smith (1980) and Nichael L. Cramer (1985). John R. Koza is a main proponent of GP and he was a pioneer in the application fields of genetic programming.

Gestalt. It is a German word typically translated as meaning *whole* or *form*.

Gradient Descent/Ascent Technique. It is a general framework for solving optimization problems to maximize or minimize functions of continuous (differentiable) parameters.

Grammar. It is the branch of linguistics that studies syntax and morphology with a set of rules (and sometimes also deals with semantics).

The set of those rules is also called the grammar of the language, and each language has its own distinct grammar. The term derives from the Greek γραμματική which is the feminine adjective of γράμμα (meaning *letter*), ultimately from γράφω (*write*).

Graph. In mathematics and in computer science, a graph is a set of objects called points, nodes, or vertices connected by links called lines or edges. The father of graph theory was the Swiss mathematician Leonhard Euler (1707-1783). In his paper entitled *Seven Bridges of Königsberg*, published in 1736, he presented a solution of the problem using a graph.

Group. In abstract algebra, it is a set (collection of elements) with a binary operation that satisfies certain axioms. A binary operation is an operation that involves two input elements.

H

Heat. A type of energy that is associated with atoms' and molecules' movement inside matter. It is capable of being transmitted through solid and fluid media by conduction, through fluid media by convection, and through empty space by radiation.

Homo Habilis. A species of the genus Homo that lived approximately 2.4 million to 1.5 million years ago in Tanzania, Kenya, Ethiopia, and South Africa. Homo habilis is an extinct species of humans considered to be an ancestor of modern humans and the earliest hominid to make tools. The terms derive from the Latin *Homō* (that means *man*) and *habilis* (meaning *skillful*).

Human-Computer Interaction. It is a discipline concerned with the design, evaluation, and implementation of interactive systems (both traditional and computerized systems) for human

use and with the study of major phenomena surrounding them.

Hydrodynamic. It is the study of fluids in motion, and it is based upon the physical conservation laws of mass, momentum, and energy. The mathematical models of these laws may be written in either integral or differential form. The integral form is useful for large-scale analyses particularly for engineering applications. The differential form of the equations is used for small-scale analyses.

Hypolimnion. It is the bottom and most dense layer of water in a thermally stratified lake. It is the layer that lies below the thermocline. Typically, it is noncirculatory and remains cold throughout the year.

I

Image (Picture). It is a representative reproduction of an object, especially an optical reproduction formed by a lens or mirror. Images may be classified as follows: two-dimensional images, such as a photograph, or three-dimensional images such as in a statue. In computer graphics, an image is an array of values, where a value is a collection of numbers describing the attributes of a pixel in the image. The dimensions of the array are called the width and height of the images, and the numbers of bits associated with each pixel in the array is called the depth.

Image Compression. In computer science, image compression is a technique that reduces the redundancy of the image data in order to be able to store or transmit data in an efficient form. Image compression can be **lossless** or **lossy**. Lossless compression is sometimes preferred for artificial images such as technical drawings. Lossless compression methods may also be preferred for high-value content, such as medical imagery or image scans made for archival purposes. This is because lossy compression methods, especially when used at low bit rates, introduce image quality loss. Lossy methods are especially suitable for natural images such as photos in applications where minor (sometimes imperceptible) loss of fidelity is acceptable to achieve a substantial reduction in bit rate.

Interaction. It is an action that involves two or more objects that have an effect upon one another. Interaction has different tailored meanings in various sciences. For example, in physics interaction represents one of four fundamental ways in which elementary particles and bodies can influence each other, classified as strong, weak, electromagnetic, and gravitational.

Interface. It is a surface that forms a common boundary between adjacent substances, bodies, phases, or regions. In computer science, an interface represents the point of interaction or communication between a computer and any other parts of software, hardware devices, or entities, such as printers or human operators.

Internet. It is the global network that connects millions of computers in the world via the TCP/IP protocol. The term derives from the phrase *interconnected network* and it was coined by the American computer scientist Vinton Cerf (born 1943) in 1974. The Internet evolved from the *ARPANET* of the late '60s and early '70s.

Isomorphism. It is a one-to-one mapping between two sets that preserves the relationship of elements under corresponding operations on each set.

Iterated Function System (IFS). It is a finite set of affine mappings in the plane that are combinations of translations, scalings, and rotations. Each mapping has a defined probability and should be contractive; that is, scalings are less than 1. Iterated function systems can be used for generating fractal objects and image compression. A finite

set of contraction $F_i: X \rightarrow X$ is defined on a metric space X.

Iterative Algorithm. It is a kind of algorithm that uses repetitive constructs like loops and sometimes additional data structures like stacks to solve given problems.

K

Key. In computer science, it is a set of bits, usually stored in a file, that is used to encrypt or decrypt a message.

L

Language. It is a set of finite arbitrary symbols combined according to rules of grammar for the purpose of communication. A language is a system of communicating based on sounds, symbols, and words in expressing a meaning, idea, or thought. A **natural language** is a language that is spoken, written, or signed by humans for general-purpose communication.

Large Eddy Simulation (LES). It is a numerical technique used to solve the partial differential equations governing turbulent fluid flow. Using this technique, only the large-scale motions of the flow are directly computed, while the effects of the smaller universal scales (called subgrid scales, SGS) are modeled using a subgrid scale model.

Lattice. In physics, it is a regular, periodic configuration of points, particles, or objects throughout an area or a space, especially the arrangement of ions or molecules in a crystalline solid.

Learning. Learning is the process of acquiring knowledge, attitudes, or skills from study, experience, or instruction.

Learning Environment. It is the physical or virtual setting in which learning takes place. It is also defined as the instructional, interpersonal, and physical characteristics of the classroom that may influence student performance.

Limnology. It is a branch of hydrology that concerns the study of fresh waters, specifically lakes, including their biological, physical, and chemical aspects. The term derives from the Greek *limne*, (that means *lake*) and λόγος (*logos* that means *knowledge*). The founder of limnology was the Swiss physician and scientist François-Alphonse Forel (1841-1912) with his studies concerning Lake Geneva. Limnology traditionally is closely related to hydrobiology, which is concerned with the application of the principles and methods of physics, chemistry, geology, and geography to ecological problems.

Local Area Network (LAN). A LAN is a computer network that is limited to a relatively small spatial area such as a room, a single building, a ship, or an aircraft. Local area networks are sometimes called a single-location network.

Logarithmic Spiral. It is a spiral whose polar equation is given by $r = \alpha e^{b\theta}$ where r is the distance from the origin, θ is the angle from the x-axis, and α and b are arbitrary constants. It is also known as an **equiangular spiral** or **growth spiral**. This curve was first described by the French mathematician René Descartes (1596-1650) and later extensively investigated by Jakob Bernoulli (1654-1705), who called it *spira mirabilis*, "the wonderful spiral." Bernoulli was charmed by this curve and he wanted its drawing on his tomb stone.

Logic. It is the study of principles and criteria that guide reasoning within a given field or situation. The term derives from the Greek λόγος (*logos* that means *word*, *account*, *reason*, or *principle*). Logic is studied as a branch of philosophy, one part of the classical trivium (that consisted of grammar, logic, and rhetoric).

L-System (Lindenmayer System). It is a formal grammar (a set of rules and symbols) commonly used to model the growth processes of plant development, but also able to model the morphology of a variety of organisms. L-systems were introduced and developed in 1968 by the Hungarian theoretical biologist and botanist Aristid Lindenmayer (1925-1989). L-systems can also be applied to generate self-similar fractals such as iterated function systems.

M

Machine Intelligence (see Artificial Intelligence).

Markovian Model. The most general Markovian model describes a set of random variables and is defined by a strong Markovian property.

Markovian Process. A process for generating a time series where the value at any new time depends only on the previous value plus some random component.

Markovian Property (Markov Property). In probability theory, it is a property that refers to a stochastic process that has its conditional probability distribution of future states depending only upon the present state and not on any past states. The system has the Markov property if only the present state predicts future states; that is, the process is memory-less.

Mars Orbiter Laser Altimetry (MOLA). An instrument currently in orbit around Mars on the Mars Global Surveyor (MGS) spacecraft. The instrument transmits infrared laser pulses toward Mars at a rate of 10 Hz and measures the time of flight to determine the range of the MGS spacecraft to the Martian surface.

Mathematical Model. It is a representation of a system, process, or relationship in mathematical form, for example, using equations for simulating the behavior of the system or process under study. This model consists of two parts: the mathematical structure and some particular constants, or parameters associated with it.

MEA (Microelectrode Arrays). It is an implementation of passive metal electrodes, typically 60, allowing the targeting of several sites for stimulation and extracellular recording of electrically active cells (single cells, neuronal, muscle, or cardiac tissue) at once. MEA offers the unique possibility for noninvasive extracellular recording. MEA represents an ideal system to monitor both acute and chronic effects of drugs and toxins and to perform functional studies under physiological or induced pathophysiological conditions that mimic in vivo damages.

Meme. The term was coined in 1976 by the biologist Richard Dawkins in his book *The Selfish Gene*. It refers to a "unit of cultural information" that can propagate from one mind to another in a manner analogous to genes (the units of genetic information). Dawkins derived the term from a shortening of the Greek *mimeme*, making it sound similar to *gene*.

Memetics. This is the study of memes and their social and cultural effects. The term was introduced in 1904 by the German evolutionary biologist Richard Semon (1859-1918) in his work entitled *Die Mnemische Empfindungen in ihren Beziehungen zu den Originalenempfindungen*. The work was translated into English in 1921 as *The Mneme*. The term is made of two parts: *meme* and *tics* (derived from *aesthetics*).

Memory. It is the function of the brain for storing, retaining, and subsequently recalling information about past events or knowledge. Different ways are used to classify memories based on the duration, the nature, and the retrieval of information. A general classification of memory is based on the duration of memory retention, and identifies three distinct types of memory: (a) **sensory memory**, which is the ability to retain impressions of sensory information after the original stimulus has ceased, (b) **short-term memory** (or **working memory**), which recovers memories of recent events, and (c) **long-term memory**, which is concerned with recalling the more distant past. In computer science, memory (also called **computer memory**) is the device where information is stored while being actively processed.

Message. A primary element of the communication process, a message consists of the information passed from the sender (communicator) to the receiver. Thus, the message is an object of communication. In computer science, a message is any set of transmitted data.

Metabolism. It is the sum of chemical and physiological processes by which the living organism builds and maintains itself and by which it breaks down food and nutrients to produce energy. These processes include both synthesis (anabolism) and breakdown (catabolism) of body constituents.

Metaheuristic. It is a heuristic method for solving a general class of computational problems by combining user-given black-box procedures in a hopefully efficient way. The name combines the Greek prefix *meta* (*beyond*, here in the sense of *higher level*) and *heuristic* (from ευρισκειν, *heuriskein, to find*).

Metaphor. It is a rhetorical device of saying something as if it were something else. The term derives from the Greek *metapherin* (that means *rhetorical trope*). It is also defined as an indirect comparison between two or more seemingly unrelated subjects that typically uses *is-a* to join the first subjects, for example, "Time is money."

Metaphorical Thinking. It is the linking of a topic and a vehicle through a common ground. The topic is what the metaphor is about. The vehicle is the means by which the speaker refers to the topic. The ground is the sum of possible attributes shared by the topic and vehicle. Thus, metaphors can create strong images that can be used to great effect in everyday communications and thinking.

Metropolitan Area Network (MAN). It is a network that connects two or more local area networks or controller area networks together, but does not extend beyond the boundaries of the immediate town, city, or metropolitan area. Multiple routers, switches, and hubs are connected to create a MAN.

Microtubules. They are protein structures found within cells, composed chiefly of tubulin. They have a diameter of about 24 nanometers and have varying length from several micrometers to possible millimeters in axons of nerve cells.

Mind-Body Problem. It is a famous problem that tries to find an explanation for the relationships between minds, or mental processes, and bodily states or processes. The philosophers who work in this area tried to explain how a supposedly nonmaterial mind can influence a material body and vice versa. The modern mind-body problem stems from the thought of the French philosopher René Descartes (1596-1650), who was responsible for the classical formulation of dualism (which is a set of views about the relationship between mind and matter).

Mirror Neuron. It activates itself when an animal performs an action and when the animal observes the same action performed by another animal (possibly of the same species). This neuron mirrors the behavior of another animal as though the observer were itself performing the action. Mirror neurons have been argued to support simulation theories of action understanding and mind reading (Gallese & Goldman, 1998).

Mirror System Hypothesis. It states that the matching of neural code for execution and the observation of hand movements in the monkey is present in the common ancestor of monkey and human.

Mobile Network. It is the set of facilities operated by a carrier for the purposes of providing public mobile telecommunications services. Mobile network is the synonym of cellular network, which is a radio network constituted by a number of radio cells (or cells) each served by a fixed transmitter that is known as a cell site or base station.

Model. It is a description, illustration, small reproduction, or other representation that is used to explain an object, a system, or a concept.

Modulation. It is the process of imposing an information signal on a carrier. The process modifies some characteristic of a wave (the carrier or channel signal) so that it varies in step with the instantaneous value of another wave (the modulating wave) in order to transmit a message. This can be done by changing the frequency (frequency modulation, FM), the amplitude (amplitude modulation, AM), or the phase (phase modulation, PM), or any combination of these.

Möbius Strip (Möbius Band). It is a one-sided surface that can be created by taking a strip of paper and taping the two ends together with a half-turn in the middle. German mathematicians

August Ferdinand Möbius (1790-1868) and Johann Benedict Listing (1808-1882) independently discovered this surface in 1858.

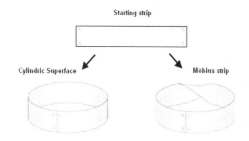

Monte Carlo (Method). It is an analytical technique in which a large number of simulations are run using random quantities for uncertain variables and looking at the distribution of results to infer which values are most likely. The name of this method comes from the city of Monte Carlo, which is known in the world for its casinos.

Mutability. Mutability is the quality of being capable of mutation.

Mutation. It is a permanent change, a structural alteration, in the DNA or RNA. In genetic algorithms, the term mutation refers to a genetic operator used to maintain genetic diversity from one generation of a population of chromosomes to the next. It is analogous to biological mutation.

Mythology. This is a collection of stories belonging to a people and addressing their origin, history, and heroes. It typically involves supernatural beings or forces, and embodies and provides an explanation or justification for something such as the early history of a society, a religious belief or ritual, or a natural phenomenon.

N

Neighborhood (Neighbourhood). The term is used for indicating a vicinity: a surrounding or nearby region. In mathematics, it is a small set of points surrounding and including a particular point. More rigorously, a subset N of a topological space is called a neighborhood of a subset K if every point of K belongs to the interior of N.

Network. It is a set of connections among a multiplicity of separate entities sharing a common characteristic. In computer science, a network, also called net, is a system of computers interconnected by telephone wires or other means in order to share information.

Networking. It is the linking of a number of devices, such as computers, workstations, and printers into a network (system) for the purpose of sharing resources.

Network Topology (Physical Topology). It refers to the configuration of cables, computers, and other peripherals. Physical topology should not be confused with logical topology, which is the method used to pass information between workstations.

Neural Darwinism. It is a theory of brain development presented by the American neurobiologist Gerald Edelman (born 1929) in his book *Neural Darwinism: The Theory of Neural Group Selection* (1989). Natural Darwinism is the process of selection that is the basis of evolution and operates not only on the individual and species levels, but also on the cellular level, in the various major systems of an organism. Two different contexts of application can be identified. One refers to the theory that human intelligence can be explained using the Darwinian selection and evolution of neural states. The other context presents a physical process in neurodevelopment where the used neural connections (synapses) are strengthened, while unused connections weaken and are eventually pruned for establishing some efficient neural pathways.

Neural Network (NN). It is an interconnected group of artificial neurons that uses a computational model for information processing based on a connectionist approach to computation. In most cases an NN is an adaptive system that changes its structure based on external or internal information that flows through the network.

Neurobiology. This is the branch of biological sciences that studies the cells of the nervous system and the organization of these cells into functional circuits that process information and mediate behavior.

Neurofeedback (NFB). It is a noninvasive treatment approach that allows us to gain information about the brainwave activity as measured by electrodes on the scalp, and uses the information to produce changes in brainwave activity. The brainwave activity is presented as feedback in the form of a video display, sound, or vibration.

Neuron. It is also known as *neurone* and nerve cell. It is an electrically excitable cell in the nervous system that transmits and processes information. Neurons are composed of a soma, or cell body, a dendritic tree, and an axon. In vertebrate animals, neurons are the core components of the brain, spinal cord, and peripheral nerves.

Neuroscience. It is the branch of biological sciences that is devoted to the scientific study of the anatomy, physiology, and pathology of the nervous system. The scope of neuroscience includes any systematic scientific experimental and theoretical investigation of the central and peripheral nervous system of biological organisms.

Niche. In ecology, it is a term that describes the relational position of a population (or species) in an ecosystem. The term was coined by the American naturalist Joseph Grinnell (1877-1939) in 1917, but it was the British ecologist Charles

Sutherland Elton (1900-1991) that gave the first working definition of the niche concept in 1927.

Niche Construction. It refers to the activities, choices, and metabolic processes of organisms, through which they define, choose, modify, and partly create their own niches.

Node. An object (gene, molecule, or computer) connected in a network.

Nystagmus. An involuntary rhythmic shaking or wobbling of the eyes of a sleepy or inebriated individual. Nystagmus may be inherited, be idiopathic (no known cause), or be associated with a sensory problem. The term derives from the Greek word *nýstagma* (that means *drowse*). Nystagmus has also been described as "dancing eyes" or "jerking eyes."

O

Object Relations Theory. It is a branch of psychoanalytic theory that emphasizes interpersonal relations, primarily in the family and especially between mother and child. The object is that to which a subject relates (e.g., persons, parts of persons, or symbols of one of these). The fundamental idea is that the ego-self exists only in relation to other objects that can be classified as external objects and internal objects. An external object is an actual person, place, or thing that a person has invested in with emotional energy. An internal object is one person's representation of another, such as a reflection of the child's way of relating to the mother. The theory was developed in the 1940's and 1950's by British psychologists Ronald Fairbairn (1889-1964), Donald Winnicott (1896-1971), Harry Guntrip (1901-1975), and others.

Oedipus Myth. Oedipus (*Οἰδίπους, Oidípous,* that means *swollen-footed*) was the mythical son of the king of Thebes Laius and Jocasta. In ancient Greece, Thebes was the richest city in the world. The myth begins with Laius and Jocasta received a warning from the Delphic oracle that their soon-to-be-born son will kill his father and marry his mother. To avoid the prophecy, after his birth Oedipus' feet were pierced and bound, and he was given to a shepherd who was instructed to abandon the child on Mount Cithaeron. Oedipus was instead brought to Polybus and Merope, king and queen of Corinth, who adopted him as their son. When he reached adulthood, Oedipus learned from an oracle that he was destined to kill his father and marry his mother. To evade his fate, he left Corinth and during the journey, his chariot met another at a point where three roads cross. Neither occupant was willing to cede the other's right of way. During the violent discussion, Oedipus killed the other man who was King Laius, his biological father. Sometime later, Oedipus reached Thebes and was confronted at the city's gate by the Sphinx, a mythological creature with the head of a woman and the body of a lion. She terrorized the city by asking all travelers who attempted to pass through the gate a riddle, and killing them when they could not answer it. The Sphinx asked Oedipus the same riddle: "Which creature in the morning goes on four feet, at noon on two, and in the evening upon three?" He answered "Man," solving the riddle (man crawls on all fours as a baby, then walks on two feet as an adult, and walks with a cane in old age). The Sphinx threw herself from her high rock and died. Oedipus came into Thebes as the victor. He married Jocasta, his biological mother. Four children were born from this marriage: two sons, Eteokles and Polynices, and two daughters, Antigone and Ismene. During a long time, Oedipus reigned over Thebes. Then, suddenly, a plague broke out. Oedipus sent Kreon to the oracle of Delphi to ask the cause of the divine punishment. He brought back the answer that the wrath of the gods was upon the people because the murderer of Laius

had not been punished and exiled. Upon discovery of the truth, Jocasta hangs herself, while Oedipus blinded himself, going away from Thebes with his daughter Antigone.

OOP (Object-Oriented Programming). It is a programming paradigm that uses the concept of objects to design applications and computer programs. An object is a collection of private data and a set of operations that can be performed on that data. This paradigm originated in the 1960s, but OOP was not commonly used in mainstream software application development until the 1990s. OOP uses several techniques different from previously established paradigms, including inheritance, modularity, polymorphism, and encapsulation. Encapsulation means that a user sees only the services that are available from an object, but not how those services are implemented. Today, many popular programming languages support OOP.

P

Paradigm. It is a thought pattern in any scientific discipline or other epistemological context. The term derives from the Greek word παράδειγμα (*paradeigma*, which means *pattern*) and from the word παραδεικνύναι (*paradeiknunai*, that means *demonstrate*).

Paradox. It is a statement formulated in clear contradiction to the common experience or its elementary beginnings of logic, but when submitted to a strict criticism proves to be valid. The sentence "Less is more" is an example of paradox. The term derives from the Greek *paràdoxos*, which is composed of *parà* and *doxa* (meaning *against the opinion*).

Pareidolia. It is a type of illusion or misperception involving a vague or obscure stimulus being perceived as something clear and distinct. The term derives from the Greek *para* (that means *amiss*, *faulty*, *wrong*) and *eidolon* (that means *image*). Pareidolia is a type of apophenia.

Pattern. It is a repeated sequence of natural occurrences, or a configuration of shapes or other objects arranged in such a way as to demonstrate a specific repeat in design.

Perceptron. It is a simple computational model of a biological neuron that comprises some input channels, a processing element, and a single output. Each input value is multiplied by a channel weight, summed by the processor, passed through a nonlinear filter, and put into the output channel. The perceptron was invented by the American scientist Frank Rosenblatt (1928-1969) in 1957.

Phase Space. Phage space is the state space of a system, a mathematical abstract space used to visualize the evolution of a dynamic system. Phase space for the ego is defined here as a two-dimensional chart showing relationships between consciousness, the personal unconscious, and the collective unconscious over time.

Pixel. It is the smallest part of a digitized or digital image. It is the smallest individual dot that can be displayed on a computer screen, and it can be also used in measuring image size and resolution. The term is an abbreviation for *picture element*.

Plaintext. It is information used as input to an encryption algorithm or the output of a decryption algorithm (decryption transforms ciphertext into plaintext).

Portfolio. In finance, it is a collection of the financial assets held by an individual or a bank or other financial institution. In marketing and strategic management, a portfolio is a set of products, projects, services, or brands that are offered for sale by a company. The term derives from the Italian word *portafoglio*, composed of *porta* (meaning *to carry*) and *foglio* (meaning *sheet*).

Portfolio Theory. It is a theory that proposes to the investors a diversification for optimizing their portfolios, and how a risky asset should be priced.

Principle of Least Action. It describes action as an integral quantity used to determine the evolution of a physical system between two defined states, that is, a change of energy in time; influenced by the economic spirit, the principle requires the action to be least.

Psychoanalysis. The theory of personality developed by the Austrian neurologist Sigmund Freud (1856-1939) in which free association, dream interpretation, and analysis of resistance and transference are used to explore repressed or unconscious impulses, internal conflicts, and anxieties. Psychoanalysis was devised in Vienna in the 1890s.

Psychology. It is the science that studies human behavior, mental processes, and how they are affected and/or affect an individual's or group's physical state, mental state, and external environment.

Psychoneurobiology. It is the field of scientific research into the relationship between psyche (spirit, emotions), neurones (nervous system, mind), and biology. Psychoneurology represents a scientific reframing of the ancient mind, body, and spirit concept of traditional Chinese medicine.

Q

Quantum Computer. It is a device for computation that directly uses the quantum mechanics phenomena (e.g., entanglement and superposition) to perform operations on data. The amount of data is measured by qubits (quantum bits). Quantum computer encodes information as a set of quantum-mechanical states such as the spin directions of electrons or the polarization orientations of a photon that might represent a 1 or a 0, might represent a combination of the two, or might represent a number expressing that the state of the qubit is somewhere between 1 and 0, or a superposition of many different numbers at once.

Quantum Computing. It is the area of study focused on the development of computer technology based on the laws of quantum mechanics, and the way that atoms can be in more than one state at once to do computational tasks. The physicist Paul Benioff, working at Argonne National Labs, is credited with first applying quantum theory to computers in 1981. Benioff theorized about creating a quantum Turing machine.

Quantum Entanglement. It is a phenomenon that happens in quantum mechanics where the quantum states of two or more particles have to be described with reference to each other, even though the individual particle may be spatially separated.

Quantum Gate. It is a basic quantum circuit operating on a small number of qubits. The quantum gate is also known as the quantum logic gate, and it is the analogue for quantum computers as the classical logic gate is for conventional digital computers.

Quantum Mind (Theory). It is a set of theories that propose that classical mechanics cannot explain consciousness. It suggests that quantum mechanics phenomena (for example, superposition and quantum entanglement) may play an important role in the brain's function and could form the basis of an explanation of consciousness.

Quantum Mechanics. A branch of physics that studies the light, the elementary particles, and the atoms replacing classical mechanics and classical electromagnetism at the atomic and subatomic scales. The foundations of quantum mechanics were established during the first half of the 20th century by Werner Heisenberg (1901-1976), Max Planck (1858-1947), Louis de Broglie (1892-1987), Niels Bohr (1885-1962), Erwin Schrödinger (1887-1961), Max Born (1882-1970), John von Neumann (1903-1957), Paul Dirac (1902-1984), Wolfgang Pauli (1900-1958), and others. It was developed between 1900 and 1930 and it was combined with the general and special theory of relativity, revolutionizing the field of physics. Quantum mechanics introduced new concepts, for example, the particle properties of radiation, the wave properties of matter, and the quantization of physical properties. The Latin term *quantum* (*how much*, *quantity*) in quantum mechanics refers to a discrete unit that quantum theory assigns to certain physical quantities, such as the energy of an atom at rest.

Quantum Superposition. It is a principle of quantum theory that describes a challenging concept about the nature and behavior of matter and forces at the atomic level. The principle of superposition states that any given particle that is unobserved and has more than one possible state is simultaneously in all possible states until it is observed.

Qubit. It is a short term for *quantum digit*, the basic unit of a quantum computer; it can be in state 0, 1, or a quantum superposition of the two.

R

Radiation. The term generally means the transmission of waves, objects, or information from a source into a surrounding medium or destination.

In physics, the radiation is the energy that travels through empty space or through a transparent material without heating the empty space or transparent material.

Receiver. In information theory, it is the receiving end of a communication channel. It receives decoded messages and decoded information from the sender, who first encoded them.

Recursive Algorithm. It is a kind of algorithm that invokes (makes reference to) itself repeatedly until a certain condition matches.

Reflexivity. In mathematics and in logic it is a relation such that it holds between an element and itself. In sociology, the reflexivity refers to circular relationships between cause and effect.

Rendering. In computer graphics, it is the process of adding realism to a graphics object by adding three-dimensional qualities such as shadows, variations in color, and variations in light source.

Residence Time. It is usually defined as "the time taken by a water/tracer parcel to leave the domain of interest." This time scale is one of the most widely used concepts to quantify the renewal of water in semi-enclosed water bodies. In environmental studies, it provides, for instance, a quantitative measure of the time of exposure to pollution stresses.

Recombination (see Crossover).

Robot. It is an electromechanical system that responds to sensory inputs. It sometimes resembles a human and is capable of performing a variety of complex human tasks on command or by being programmed in advance. The term derives from the Czech noun *robota* (meaning *servitude, forced labour*). The word robot was introduced by Czech writer Karel Čapek (1890-1938) in his science fiction work *R.U.R.* (*Rossum's Universal Robots*) written in 1920. Robotics is the science and technology of robots and their design, manufacture, and application.

Routing. It is the techniques for selecting paths in a computer network along which to send data. Routing directs forwarding, the passing of logically addressed packets from their source network toward their ultimate destination through intermediary nodes; typically hardware devices called routers.

S

Schrödinger Equation. It is the fundamental equation of physics for describing quantum mechanical behavior (the space- and time-dependence of quantum mechanical systems). It has been proposed by the Austrian physicist Erwin Schrödinger (1887-1961) in 1925. It is also called the Schrödinger wave equation, and is a partial differential equation that describes how the wave function of a physical system evolves over time.

Second-Order Cybernetics (also known as Cybernetics of Cybernetics). It is a branch of cybernetics that studies how observers construct models of other cybernetic systems.

Security. It is the condition of being protected from danger or risk. In computer science, the term is used in a variety of contexts. For example, information security is the process of protecting data from unauthorized accesses. Network security consists of the provisions in the computer network infrastructures for defining the policies adopted by the network administrator to protect the network and the network-accessible resources from unauthorized accesses.

Selection. In a genetic algorithm, it is the stage of a in which individual genomes are chosen from a population for later breeding (recombination or crossover).

Self-Reference. In natural or formal languages, it is a phenomenon consisting of a sentence or formula referring to itself directly.

Self-Similar. It is an object that is exactly or approximately similar to a part of itself, for example, the whole has the same shape as one or more of the parts. There are many self-similar shapes in nature, for example, ferns, and in the human body.

Self-Similarity. It is the property of fractal objects whereby a shape is repeated on different scales. The object need not exhibit exactly the same structure at all scales, but the same type of structure must appear on all scales. Many objects in the real world, for example, coastlines, are statistically self-similar. Parts of them show the same statistical properties at many scales.

Self-Organization. It represents the spontaneous emergence of nonequilibrium structural organization on a macroscopic level due to collective interactions between a large number of simple, usually microscopic, objects.

Sender (Source). In information and communication processing, it is an object that encodes message data and transmits the information, via a channel, to one or more receivers.

Simulation. It is the practice to mime some or all the behaviors of one system. Generally, it refers to the use of a mathematical model to recreate a situation, often repeatedly, so that the likelihood of various outcomes can be more accurately estimated.

Skill. It is a natural or acquired facility by training in a specific activity. This term also means an ability to produce solutions in some problem domain.

Social Learning. It means learning something from other people. It is a kind of learning that involves observing, retaining, and replicating behavior observed in others. Social learning includes true imitation, but there are other kinds of social learning as well.

Spiral. It is a curve that emanates from a central point, getting progressively farther away as it revolves around the point.

Spiral Architecture (SA). In computer graphics, it is an image structure on which images are displayed as a collection of hexagonal pixels. SA is an approach to create a machine vision system. It is inspired from anatomical consideration of the primate's vision system. The natural data structure that emerges from geometric consideration of the distribution of photo receptors on the primate's retina has been called the spiral honeycomb mosaic (SHM).

Spiral Honeycomb Mosaic (SHM). It is a structure that emerges observing the distribution of photo receptors on the primate's retina. SHM is made up of hexagonal lattices that consist of groups of 7^n hexagons ($n > 0$). It has very useful geometric properties. Two operations are defined on spiral honeycomb mosaic: spiral addition and spiral multiplication.

Spiral Similarity. It is a combination of central similarity and rotation with the same center.

Stratification (Water). It is the phenomenon that occurs when cold water and warm water (thermocline) form some layers that act as barriers to water mixing.

String. In computer science, it is a sequence of symbols, where these symbols are chosen from a predetermined set.

Structured Mesh. It is a mesh that has a regular arrangement of its cells, and that can be defined by specifying the parameters of the arrangement. Each cell is not defined separately. The topology of the cells in an structured mesh is specified for the mesh as a whole, and is not deduced from the nodes. Using this application module, the number of instances is independent of the number of cells in the mesh.

Stochastic Model. It is a model of a system that includes some sort of random forcing. Its inputs are expressed as random variables, and its output is a distribution of possible results.

Stochastic Process. It is a set of random variables dependent upon a parameter that usually denotes time.

Stochastic Universal Sampling (SUS). In genetic algorithms, it is a genetic operator used for selecting useful solutions for recombination.

Symmetry. It is a property of a mathematical object that causes it to remain invariant under certain classes of transformations (for example, rotation, reflection, inversion, or more abstract operations). The mathematical study of symmetry is systematized and formalized in the area of mathematics called group theory. The term symmetry derives from the Greek word συμμετρία (*summetria*, that means *same measurement*), and is composed of σύν (*sun*, that means *with*, *together*) and of μέτρον (metron, that means measures). The concept of symmetry can be generalized, thus the objects can be symmetric (a) over time (if they do not change over time), (b) over space (if they look the same even from different points of view), and (c) over size (if it looks the same even if we zoom in or out).

Synchronization. It is the process that involves events occurring at the same time. For example, a hearing system uses information from each ear arriving at a common (synchronized) set of signal processing parameters.

System. A set of objects or parts connected in some way so as to form a whole. Modern thermodynamics classifies three basic kinds of systems: isolated, closed, and open. **Isolated systems** are those that are totally independent of their environment. **Closed systems** are closed to matter (no matter may pass through the boundaries of the system) but are open to energy and information. **Open systems** are dependent on environment. Matter, energy, and information may pass through the boundaries of open systems.

Systems Biology. It is an emergent field that seeks to integrate high-throughput biological studies to understand how biological systems function.

T

TCP (Transfer Control Protocol). It is a set of rules (protocol) used along with the Internet protocol (IP) to send data in the form of message units between computers over the Internet. TCP takes care of keeping track of the individual units of data (called packets) that a message is divided into for efficient routing through the Internet. TCP/IP is the suite of protocols that defines the Internet.

TELNET (Teletype Network). It is a network protocol that enables a computer to function as a terminal working from a remote computer. It is used on the Internet, on TCP/IP-based networks, on a local area network, or on connections. In origin, it was developed for ARPAnet in 1969. Telnet is a common utility in the TCP/IP protocol suite now. It has limitations that are considered to be security risks; in fact, it is not secure and transfers commands in the clear. The term telnet also refers to software that implements the client part of the protocol.

Temperature. It is the measure of the average energy of motion of the particles of a substance. The temperature is a physical property of a system.

Texture. In computer graphics, it is the digital representation of the surface of an object.

Thermocline. It is the middle layer in a thermally stratified lake or reservoir. In this layer there is a rapid decrease in temperature with depth. Thermocline is also called the metalimnion.

TNGS (Theory of Neural Groups Segregation). It is also referred to as the Darwinian brain, and is an application of this principle. This theory is based on three principles: ontogenetical selection, secondary synaptic reinforcements or decay, and interactions among cerebral repertoires by a bidirectional reentry.

Topology. It is a branch of mathematics that studies the properties of geometric figures or solids that are not changed by homeomorphisms, such as stretching or bending. The term derives from the Greek words τοπος and λογος (*topos* and *logos* that mean *place* and *study*).

Traffic Control. In computer science, it is the control of the flow of traffic in the computer networks (local area networks, metropolitan area networks, wireless area networks, and the Internet).

Triadicity. It is a fundamental form that repeats in many processes at multiple levels of organization.

Turing Test. A hypothetical test for computer intelligence, proposed by the English mathematician Alan Turing (1912-1954) in 1950. In his paper *Computing Machinery and Intelligence*, Turing described a dialogue in which a person tries to guess which of two conversations is being conducted with a person and which with a computer. This test has become a standard model used to judge the intelligence of many AI applications.

U

Unconscious. This is all psychic contents or processes that are not conscious. It represents the lacking of the awareness and the capacity for sensory perception. It is usually divided into **repressed** or **dynamic unconscious** (which has been conscious and can be recalled to consciousness) and **primary unconscious**, which has never been conscious and might never be brought to consciousness.

Universal Grammar. It is a system of grammatical rules and constraints shared by all languages. It does not describe specific languages but attempts to explain language acquisition in general.

Universal Turing Machine. It is a general-purpose programmable computer that can perform any computable sequence of operations.

Utility Function. It is a function that measures the utility of an investment for an economic agent.

V

Virtual Reality. This is a form of human-computer interaction in which a real or imaginary environment is simulated and users interact with and manipulate that world. It is a modern technology that gives to its users the illusion of being immersed in a computer-generated virtual world with the ability to interact with it. The origin of the term is uncertain. It has been credited to *The Judas Mandala*, a 1982 novel by Damien Broderick where the context of use was somewhat different from that defined now.

VRML (Virtual Reality Modeling Language, originally known as the Virtual Reality Markup Language). VRML is a language that specifies the parameters to create virtual worlds networked together via the Internet and accessed via World Wide Web hyperlinks. The aim of VRML is to bring to the Internet the advantages of 3-D spaces, known in VRML as worlds whether they compromise environments or single objects. It was conceived in the spring of 1994 and it has been presented to the first annual WWW conference in Geneva, Switzerland. Mark Pesce (born 1962) was one of the inventors of this language, and he is recognized as the man who brought virtual reality into the World Wide Web.

Virtual Spiral Architecture. In computer graphics, it is a geometrical arrangement of pixels on a hexagonal structure described in terms of a hexagonal grid. This method is used to smoothly convert images to and from rectangular and hexagonal representations. The methods present the following advantages: Little, if any, distortion is introduced, and regular pixels are divided up into subpixels. The term virtual refers to the characteristic that the hexagonal pixels do not physically exist.

Virtual World. It is an artificial world maintained by a computer that a user may interact with or view.

W

Wide Area Networks (WAN). A WAN is a data communications network that covers a relatively broad geographic area and that often uses transmission facilities provided by common carriers, such as telephone companies. WAN technologies generally function at the lower three layers of the OSI reference model: the physical layer, the data link layer, and the network layer.

Working Memory (Short-Term Memory). In cognitive psychology, it is the collection of structures and processes within the brain used for temporarily storing and manipulating information. Working memory is a mental work space consisting of a small set of data items representing the current state of knowledge of a system at any stage in the performance of a task, and that is transformed into a new set, in humans by the application of a discrete mental operation (operator), and in production systems on the firing of a new production rule.

World Wide Web (WWW or Web). A system of Internet servers that support particular formatted documents. The documents are written using a markup language called HTML (hypertext markup language) that supports links to other documents, as well as graphics, audio, and video files. The World Wide Web uses the HTTP (hypertext transfer protocol) protocol to transmit data over the Internet. The Web was invented around 1990 by the Englishman Timothy (Tim) Berners-Lee (born 1955) and the Belgian Robert Cailliau (born 1947) while working at CERN (European Center for Nuclear Research) in Geneva, Switzerland. The World Wide Web is not the same thing as the Internet. The Internet is a massive network of networks, a networking infrastructure. WWW is a way of accessing information over the medium of the Internet.

REFERENCES

Gallese, V., & Goldman, A. (1998). Mirror neurons and the simulation theory of mind reading. *Trends in Cognitive Sciences, 12*, 493-501.

Kennel, M. B., Brown, R., & Abarbanel, H. D. (1992). Determining embedding dimension for phase-space reconstruction using a geometrical construction. *Physics Reviews A, 45*, 3403-3411.

Milgram, P., & Kishino, F. (1994). A taxonomy of mixed reality visual displays. *IEICE Transactions on Information Systems, E77-D*(12), 1321-1329.

Milgram, P., Takemura, H., Utsumi, A., & Kishino, F. (1994). Augmented reality: A class of displays on the reality-virtuality continuum. *SPIE Proceedings: Telemanipulator and Telepresence Technologies, 2351*, 282-292.

Sabelli, H. (2005). *Bios: A study of creation.* Singapore: World Scientific.

Sala, N., & Sala, M. (2005). *Geometrie del design: Forme e materiali per il progetto.* Milan: Franco Angeli.

Scholarpedia, the free peer reviewed encyclopedia. (2007). Retrieved March 10, 2007, from http://www.scholarpedia.org

Taylor, J. G. (2003). *The CODAM model and deficits of consciousness.* Proceedings of the Conference of Knowledge-Based Expert Systems, Oxford, United Kingdom.

Wikipedia, the free encyclopedia. (2007). Retrieved February 20, 2007, from http://en.wikipedia.org

Compilation of References

Abarbanel, H. D. I., & Kennel, M. B. (1993). Local false nearest neighbors and dynamical dimensions from observed chaotic data. *Physics Review E, 47*, 3057-3068.

Abecasis, S. M., Lapenta, E. S., & Pedreira, C. E. (1999). Performance metrics for financial time series forecasting. *Journal of Computational Intelligence in Finance*, 5-23.

Aida, T., & Davis, P. (1992). Oscillation modes of laser diode pumped hybrid bistable system with large delay and application to dynamical memory. *IEEE Journal of Quantum Electronics, 28*(3), 686-699.

Aiello, L. C., & Wheeler, P. (1995). The expensive-tissue hypothesis. *Current Anthropology, 36*, 199-221.

Akaike, H. (1973). Information theory and an extension of maximum likelihood principle. *2nd International Symposium on Information Theory* (pp. 267-281).

Akin, T., Najafi, K., Smoke, R. H., & Bradley, R. M. (1994). A micromachined silicon electrode for nerve regeneration applications. *IEEE Transactions of Biomedical Engineering, 41*, 305-313.

Albert, R., Jeong, H., & Barabasi, A. L. (2000). Error and attack tolerance of complex networks. *Nature, 406*, 378-382.

Altenberg, L. (1998). B2.7.2. NK fitness landscapes. In T. Baeck, D. F. Fogel, & Z. Michalewicz (Eds.), *Handbook of evolutionary computation*. New York: Oxford University Press.

Ambrose, S. H. (2001). Paleolithic technology and human evolution. *Science, 291*, 1748-1753.

Ambrosetti, W., & Barbanti, L. (1999). Deep water warming in lakes: An indicator of climatic change. *Journal of Limnology, 58*, 1-9.

Ambrosetti, W., Barbanti, L., & Mosello, R. (1982). Unusual deep mixing of Lago Maggiore during the winter 1980-1981. *Geografia Fisica e Dinamica Quaternaria, 5*, 183-191.

Ambrosetti, W., Barbanti, L., & Sala, N. (2003). Residence time and physical processes in lakes. *Journal of Limnology, 62*(1), 1-15.

Ambrosetti, W., Barbanti, L., & Rolla, A. (1979). Mescolamento parziale o totale nel Lago Maggiore nell'ultimo trentennio. *Memorie dell'Istituto Italiano di Idrobiologia, 37*, 197-208.

Andreassi, J. L. (2000). *Psychophysiology: Human behaviour and physiological response* (4th ed.). Mahwah, NJ: LEA.

Andrews, D. L., & Bradshaw, D. S. (2005). Laser-induced forces between carbon nanotubes. *Optics Letters, 30*(7), 783-785.

Aoki, K., & Feldman, M. V. (1987). Toward a theory for the evolution of cultural. *Proceedings of the National Academy of Sciences, 84*, 7164-7168.

Appel, G. (1979). *The moving average convergence-divergence method*. Great Neck, NY: Signalert.

Arbib, M. A. (2002). The mirror system, imitation, and the evolution of language. In C. Nehaniv & K. Dautenhahn (Eds.), *Imitation in animals and artifacts*. The MIT Press.

Arbib, M. A. (2005). From monkey-like action recognition to human language: An evolutionary framework for neurolinguistics. *Behavioral and Brain Sciences, 28*, 105-167.

Archetti, F., Lanzeni, S., Messina, E., & Vanneschi, L. (2006). Genetic programming for human oral bio-availability of drugs. *Proceedings of the Genetic and Evolutionary Computation Conference* (GECCO'06, pp. 255-262).

Arecchi, F., Gadomski, W., & Meucci, R. (1986). Generation of chaotic dynamics by feedback on a laser. *Physical Review A, 34*, 1617-1620.

Aristotle. (1982). *Poetics* (Vol. 23, Loeb Classical Library). Cambridge, MA: Harvard University Press.

Asimov, I. (1950). *I, robot.* Boston: Gnome Press.

Atwood, G., & Stolorow, R. (1993). *Faces in a cloud: Intersubjectivity in personality theory.* Northvale, NJ: Jason Aronson. (Original work published 1979)

Aunger, R. (Ed.). (2001). *Darwinizing culture: The status of memetics as a science.* New York: Oxford University Press.

Awh, E. & Jonides, J. (2001). Overlapping mechanisms of attention and spatial working memory. *Trends in Cognitive Sciences, 5*, 119-126.

Awh, E., Jonides, J., & Reuter-Lorenz, P. A. (1998). Rehearsal in spatial working memory. *Journal of Exp. Psychol. Hum. Percept. Perform., 24*, 780-790.

Babaoglu, O., Canright, G., Deutsch, A., Di Caro, G. A., Ducatelle, F., Gambardella, L. M., et al. (2006). Design patterns from biology for distributed computing. *ACM Transactions on Autonomous and Adaptive Systems (TAAS), 1*(1).

Baddeley, A. D. (1986). *Working memory.* Oxford, United Kingdom: Oxford University Press.

Baldwin, J. M. (1896). A new factor in evolution. *American Naturalist, 30*, 441-451.

Banzhaf, W., Nordin, P., Keller, R. E., & Francone, F. D. (1998). *Genetic programming: An introduction.* San Francisco: Morgan Kaufmann.

Barabasi, A. L., & Albert, R. (1999). Emergence of scaling in random networks. *Science, 286*, 509-512.

Baran, B., & Sosa, R. (2000). *A new approach for AntNet routing.* Proceedings of the Ninth International Conference on Computer Communications Networks, Las Vegas, NV.

Baras, J., & Mehta, H. (2003). A probabilistic emergent routing algorithm for mobile ad hoc networks. *WiOpt03: Modeling and Optimization in Mobile, Ad Hoc and Wireless Networks.*

Barbanti, L., & Ambrosetti, W. (1990). The physical limnology on Lago Maggiore: A review. *Memorie dell'Itituto Italiano di Idrobiologia, 46*, 47-78.

Barnsley, M. F. (1988). *Fractals everywhere.* Boston: Academic Press.

Barnsley, M. F. (1993). *Fractals everywhere* (2nd ed.). Boston: Academic Press.

Barnsley, M. F., Jacquin, A. E., Malassenet, F., Reuter, L., & Sloane, A. D. (1988). Harnessing chaos for image synthesis. *SIGGRAPH 1988* (pp. 131-140).

Barnsley, M. F., Saupe, D., & Vrscay, E. R. (Eds.). (2002). *Fractals in multimedia.* Berlin, Germany: Springer.

Barth, T., & Ohlberger, M. (2004). Finite volume methods: Foundation and analysis. In E. Stein, R. de Borst, & T. J. R. Hughes (Eds.), *Encyclopedia of computational mechanics.* London: John Wiley & Sons, Ltd.

Basch-Kahre, E. (1985). Patterns of thinking. *International Journal of Psychoanalysis, 66*(4), 455-470.

Bates, E., & MacWhinney, B. (1987). Competition, variation and language learning. In B. MacWhinney (Ed.), *Mechanisms of language acquisition* (pp. 157-193). Hillsdale, NJ: Erlbaum.

Bateson, G. (1979). *Mind and nature: A necessary unity.* Toronto, Canada: Bantam.

Bauer, R. H. (1976). Short-term memory: EEG alpha correlates and the effect of increased alpha. *Behavioural Biology, 17*, 425-433.

Belew, R. K., & Mitchel, M. (Eds.). (1996). *Adaptive individuals in evolving populations: Models and algorithms*. Reading, MA: Addison-Wesley.

Berger, V., & Saleri, R. (2005). Instrumentation du hasard numérique dans la conception architecturale. In *Travail personnel de fin d'études*. Ecole d'architecture de Lyon.

Bertsekas, D. P. (1995). *Dynamic programming and optimal control*. Belmont, MA: Athena Scientific.

Bertsekas, D. P., & Tsitsiklis, J. N. (1996). *Neuro-dynamic programming*. Belmont, MA: Athena Scientific.

Bertsekas, D., & Gallager, R. (1992). *Data networks*. Prentice-Hall.

Bidermann, H. (1998). *Knaurs lexikon der symbole*. München, Germany: Droemersche Verlagsanstalt Th. Knaur Nachf.

Bilotta, E., & Pantano, P. (2005). Emergent patterning phenomena in 2D cellular automata. *Artificial life, 11*(3), 339-362.

Bilotta, E., & Pantano, P. (2006). Structural and functional growth in self-reproducing cellular automata. *Complexity, 11*(6), 12-29.

Bilotta, E., Lafusa, A., & Pantano, P. (2002). Is self replication an embedded characteristic of artificial/living matter? In R. K. Standish, M. A. Bedau, & H. A. Abbass (Eds.), *Artificial life VIII* (pp. 38-48). Cambridge, MA: The MIT Press.

Bilotta, E., Lafusa, A., & Pantano, P. (2003). Life-like self-reproducers. *Complexity, 9*(1), 38-55.

Binkofski, F., Fink, G. R., Geyer, S., Buccino, O., Grfuber, O., Shah, N. J., et al. (2002). Neural activity in human motor cortex areas 4a and 4p is modulated differentially by attention to action. *Journal of Neurophysiology*.

Bion, W. (1983). *Elements of psycho-analysis*. Northvale, NJ: Jason Aronson.

Bird, R. B., Stewart, W. E., & Lightfoot, E. N. (1960). *Transport phenomena*. New York: Wiley International Edition.

Birkfoff, G. D. (1931). A mathematical approach to aesthetics. *Scientia*, pp. 133-146.

Bishop, C. (1995). *Neural networks for pattern recognition*. Oxford, United Kingdom: Oxford University Press.

Blackmore, S. (1999). *The meme machine*. New York: Oxford University Press.

Blossfeldt, K. (1985). *Art forms in the plant world*. New York: Dover Publications, Inc.

Blumberg, A. F., & Mellor, G. L. (1987). A description of a three-dimensional coastal ocean circulation model. In N. Heaps (Ed.), *Three-dimensional coastal ocean models* (pp. 1-16). Washington, DC: American Geophysical Union.

Bobe, S., & Schaefer, G. (2006). Image processing and image registration on spiral architecture with saLib. *International Journal of Simulation Systems, Science & Technology, 7*(3), 37-43.

Bodmer, W. F., & Cavalli-Sforza, L. L. (1976). *Genetics, evolution and man*. San Francisco: Freeman.

Bogomolny, A. (1998). *The collage theorem*. Retrieved September 15, 2005, from http://www.cut-the-knot.org/ctk/ifs.shtml

Bonabeau, E., Dorigo, M., & Theraulaz, G. (1999). *Swarm intelligence: From natural to artificial systems*. Oxford University Press.

Bonabeau, E., Henaux, F., Guérin, S., Snyers, D., Kuntz, P., & Theraulaz, G. (1998). Routing in telecommunication networks with "smart" ant-like agents. *Proceedings of IATA'98, Second International Workshop on Intelligent Agents for Telecommunication Applications*.

Bork, P., Jensen, L. J., Von Mering, C., Ramani, A. K., Lee, I., & Marcotte, E. M. (2004). Protein interaction networks from yeast to human. *Current Opinion on Structural Biology, 7*, 292-299.

Bourbaki, N. (1962). L'architecture des mathématiques. In F. Le Lionnais (Ed.), *Les grands courants de la pensée mathématique*. Blanchard. (Reprinted from *Cahiers du Sud*, 1948)

Boyd, R., & Richerson, P. J. (1985). *Culture and the evolutionary process*. Chicago: University of Chicago Press.

Brand, M. (2006). *Logarithmic spirals*. Retrieved July 10, 2006, from http://alumni.media.mit.edu/~ brand/logspiral.html

Branigan, H. P., Pickering, M. J., & Cleland, A. A. (2000). Syntactic co-ordination in dialogue. *Cognition, 75*, B13-B25.

Broch, J., Maltz, D. A., Johnson, D. B., Hu, Y.-C., & Jetcheva, J. (1998). A performance comparison of multi-hop wireless ad hoc network routing protocols. *Proceedings of the Fourth Annual ACM/IEEE International Conference on Mobile Computing and Networking (MobiCom98)*.

Bruer, J., & Freud, S. (1895). *Studies on hysteria*. SE 2.

Brugger, P. (2001). From haunted brain to haunted science: A cognitive neuroscience view of paranormal and pseudoscientific thought. In J. Houran & R. Lange (Eds.), *Hauntings and poltergeists: Multidisciplinary perspectives*. NC: McFarland & Company, Inc.

Bucci, W. (1997). *Psychoanalysis and cognitive science*. New York: Guilford Press.

Bull, L., Holland, O., & Blackmore, S. (2000). On meme-gene coevolution. *Artificial Life, 6*, 227-235.

Burgess, N., & Hitch, G. (2005). Computational models of working memory: Putting long-term memory into context. *Trends in Cognitive Sciences, 9*(11), 535-541.

Câmara, D., & Loureiro, A. (2000). A novel routing algorithm for ad hoc networks. *Proceedings of the 33rd Hawaii International Conference on System Sciences*.

Campbell, J. (1973). *The hero with a thousand faces*. Princeton, NJ: Bollingen Series, Princeton University. (Original work published 1949)

Canepari, M., Bove, M., Mueda, E., Cappello, M., & Kawana, A. (1997). Experimental analysis of neural dynamics in cultured cortical networks and transitions between different patterns of activity. *Biological Cybernetics, 7*, 153-162.

Capra, F. (1975). *The Tao of physics*. Boulder, CO: Shambala.

Carbonara, D. (Ed.). (2005). *Technology literacy applications in learning environments*. Hershey, PA: Idea Group.

Carlson-Sabelli, L., & Sabelli, H. C. (1992). Phase plane of opposites: A method to study change in complex processes, and its application to sociodynamics and psychotherapy. *The Social Dynamicist, 3*, 1-6.

Carlson-Sabelli, L., Sabelli, H. C., Zbilut, J., Patel, M., Messer, J., Walthall, K., et al. (1994). How the heart informs about the brain: A process analysis of the electrocardiogram. *Cybernetics and Systems, 94*(2), 1031-1038.

Carlson-Sabelli, L., Sabelli, H., Patel, M., & Holm, K. (1992). The union of opposites in sociometry: An empirical application of process theory. *The Journal of Group Psychotherapy, Psychodrama and Sociometry, 44*, 147-171.

Carmena, J. M., Lebedev, M. A., Crist, R. E., O'Doherty, J. E., Santucci, D. M., Dimitrov, D. F., et al. (2003). Learning to control a brain-machine interface for reaching and grasping by primates. *M.A.L. PLoS Biology, 1*, 193-208.

Carrillo, L., Marzo, J., Fμabrega, L., Vila, P., & Guadall, C. (2004). Ant colony behaviour as routing mechanism to provide quality of service. *Ants Algorithms: Proceedings of ANTS 2004, Fourth International Workshop on Ant Algorithms*.

Casas, C. A. (2001). Tactical asset allocation: An artificial neural network based model. *Proceedings of International Joint Conference on Neural Networks, 3*, 1811-1816.

Castellano, L., & Dinelli, G. (1975). Experimental and analytical evaluation of thermal alteration in the Mediterranean. *International Conference on Mathematical Models for Environmental Problems.*

Castellano, L., Colombo, A., & Tozzi, A. (1977). *Numerical-differential model for the dispersion of heat and pollutants in sea environments* (Tech. Rep.). Milan: CALISMA/MATEC, ENEL-CRTN, Centro di Ricerca Termica e Nucleare.

Cavalli-Sforza, L. L., & Feldman, M. W. (1981). *Cultural transmission and evolution: A quantitative approach.* Princeton: Princeton University Press.

Chabot, R. J., di Michele, F., Prichep, L., & John, E. R. (2001). The clinical role of computerized EEG in the evaluation and treatment of learning and attention disorders in children and adolescents. *Journal of Neuropsychiatry and Clinical Neuroscience, 13*(2), 171-186.

Chakraborty, D., Ashir, A., Suganuma, G., Mansfield, K., Roy, T., & Shiratori, N. (2004). Self-similar and fractal nature of Internet traffic. *International Journal of Network Management, 14*(2), 119-129.

Chalmers, D. (1995). Facing up the problem of consciousness. *Journal of Consciousness Studies, 2*(3), 200-219.

Chalmers, D. (1997). *The conscious mind: In search of a fundamental theory.* Oxford University Press.

Chan, P. A., & Rabinowitz, T. (2006). A cross-sectional analysis of video games and attention deficit hyperactivity disorder symptoms in adolescents. *Ann Gen Psychiatry, 5*, 16.

Chapados, N., & Bengio, Y. (2001). Cost functions and model combination for VaR-based asset allocation using neural networks. *IEEE Transactions on Neural Networks, 12*, 890-906.

Chemical Information Systems Inc. (2006). *The company that introduced SMILES molecule representation.*

Retrieved January 10, 2007, from http://www.daylight.com/dayhtml/smiles

Cheng, R. T., & Tung, C. (1970). Wind-driven lake circulation by finite element method. *Proceedings of the 13th Conference on Great Lakes Research* (pp. 891-903).

Chomsky, N. (1975). *Reflections on language.* New York: Pantheon.

Chou, H. H., & Reggia, J. A. (1997). Emergence of self-replicating structures in a cellular automata space. *Physica D, 110*(3-4), 252-276.

Chu, T. C., Tsao, C. T., & Shiue, Y. R. (1996). Application of fuzzy multiple attribute decision making on company analysis for stock selection. *Proceedings of the Soft Computing in Intelligent Systems and Information Processing* (pp. 509-514).

Chupin, J.-P., & Lequay, H. (2000). Escalade analogique et plongée numérique: Entre l'atelier tectonique et le studio virtuel dans l'enseignement du projet. In *Les cahiers de la recherche architecturale et urbaine* (pp. 21-28).

Clarke, A. R., Barry, R. J., McCarthy, R., & Selikowitz, M. (1998). EEG analysis in attention-deficit/hyperactivity disorder: A comparative study of two subtypes. *Psychiatry Research, 81*(1), 19-29.

Clarke, A. R., Barry, R. J., McCarthy, R., Selikowitz, M., & Brown, C. R. (2002). EEG evidence for a new conceptualisation of attention deficit hyperactivity disorder. *Clinical Neurophysiology, 113*(7), 1036-1044.

Clausen, T., Jacquet, P., Laouiti, A., Muhlethaler, P., Qayyum, A., & Viennot, L. (2001). Optimized link state routing protocol. *Proceedings of the IEEE International Multi Topic Conference (INMIC).*

Conte, R., Hegselmann, R., & Terna, P. (Eds.). (1997). *Simulating social phenomena.* Berlin, Germany: Springer Verlag.

Cook, T. A. (1914). *The curves of life.* London: Constable and Company Ltd.

Corazza, M., Vanni, P., & Loschi, U. (2002). Hybrid automatic trading system: Technical analysis & group method of data handling. *Neural Nets: 13ᵗʰ Italian Workshop on Neural Nets, WIRN Vietri 2002* (pp. 47-55).

Corbetta, M., & Shulman, G. L. (2002). Control of goal-directed and stimulus-driven attention in the brain. *Nature Reviews, Neuroscience, 3*, 201-215.

Corbetta, M., Tansy, A. P., Stanley, C. M., Astafiev, S. V., Snyder, A. Z., & Shulman, G. L. (2005). A functional MRI study of preparatory signals for spatial location and objects. *Neuropsychologia, 43*, 2041-2056.

Crovella, M. E., & Bestavros, A. (1995). *Explaining World Wide Web traffic self-similarity* (Tech. Rep. No. TR-95-015). Boston: Boston University, Computer Science Department.

Crovella, M. E., & Bestavros, A. (1996). Self-similarity in World Wide Web traffic: Evidence and possible causes. *Proceedings of ACM SIGMETRICS'96*.

Crucitti, P., Latora, V., Marchiori, M., & Rapisarda, A. (2004). Error and attack tolerance of complex networks. *Physica A, 340*, 388-394.

Cuomo, K. M., & Oppenheim, A. V. (1993). Circuit implementation of synchronized chaos with applications to communications. *Physical Review Letters, 71*, 65-68.

Cuomo, K. M., Oppenheim, A. V., & Strogatz, S. H. (1993). Robustness and signal recovery in a synchronized chaotic system. *International Journal of Bifurcation and Chaos in Applied Sciences and Engineering, 3*(6), 1629-1638.

D'Esposito, M., Postle, B. R., & Rypma, B. (2000). Prefrontal cortical contributions to working memory: Evidence from event-related fMRI studies. *Exp. Brain Res., 133*, 3-11.

Dailey, J. E., & Harleman, D. R. F. (1972). *Numerical model for the prediction of transient water quality in estuary networks* (Rep. No. MITSG 72-15). Cambridge, MA: MIT, Department of Civil Engineering.

Dale, R., & Spivey, M. J. (2006). Unravelling the dyad: Using recurrence analysis to explore patterns of syntactic coordination between children and caregivers in conversation. *Language Learning, 56*, 391-430.

Davis, P. J. (1993). *Spirals: From Theodorus to chaos.* Wellesley, MA: A. K. Peters.

Dawkins, R. (1976). *The selfish gene.* Oxford: Oxford University Press.

Dawkins, R. (1982). *The extended phenotype.* San Francisco: Freeman.

De Jong, H. (2002). Modeling and simulation of genetic regulatory systems: A literature review. *Journal of Computational Biology, 9*, 67-103.

De Marse, T. B., Wagenaar, D. A., & Potter, S. M. (2002). *The neurally controlled artificial animal: A neural computer interface between cultured neural networks and a robotic body.* Proceedings of SFN 2002, Orlando, FL.

Deas, M. L., & Lowney, C. L. (2000). *Water temperature modeling review.* California Valley Modeling Forum, Central Valley, CA.

Deco, G., & Rolls, E. T. (2005). Attention, short-term memory, and action selection: A unifying theory. *Prog. Neurobiol., 76*, 236-256.

Deneubourg, J.-L., Aron, S., Goss, S., & Pasteels, J.-M. (1990). The self-organizing exploratory pattern of the Argentine ant. *Journal of Insect Behavior, 3*, 159-168.

Dennett, D. (1995). *Darwin's dangerous idea.* Hammondsworth, United Kingdom: The Penguin Press.

Dennett, D. C. (1978). *Brainstorms.* Cambridge, MA: MIT Press/Bradford Books.

Dennett, D. C. (1991). *Consciousness explained.* Boston: Little, Brown & Co.

Desimone, R., & Duncan, J. (1995). Neural mechanics of selective visual attention. *Annual Reviews of Neuroscience, 18*, 193-222.

Desmurget, M., & Grafton, S. (2000). Forward modeling allows feedback control for fast reaching movements. *Trends in Cognitive Neurosciences, 4*, 423-431.

Desmurget, M., Epstein, C. M., Turner, R. S., Prablanc, C., Alexander, G. E., & Grafton, S. T. (1999). Role of the posterior parietal cortex in updating reaching movements to a visual target. *Nature Neuroscience, 2*, 563-567.

Di Caro, G. A. (2004). *Ant colony optimization and its application to adaptive routing in telecommunication networks*. Unpublished doctoral dissertation, Faculté des Sciences Appliquées, Université Libre de Bruxelles, Brussels, Belgium.

Di Caro, G. A., & Dorigo, M. (1997). Adaptive learning of routing tables in communication networks. *Proceedings of the Italian Workshop on Machine Learning*.

Di Caro, G. A., & Dorigo, M. (1998b). Extending Ant-Net for best-effort quality-of-service routing. *ANTS'98: From Ant Colonies to Artificial Ants. First International Workshop on Ant Colony Optimization*.

Di Caro, G. A., & Vasilakos, T. (2000). Ant-SELA: Ant-agents and stochastic automata learn adaptive routing tables for QoS routing in ATM networks. *ANTS2000: From Ant Colonies to Artificial Ants. Second International Workshop on Ant Colony Optimization*.

Di Caro, G. A., & Dorigo, M. (1998a). AntNet: Distributed stigmergetic control for communications networks. *Journal of Artificial Intelligence Research (JAIR), 9*, 317-365.

Di Caro, G. A., Ducatelle, F., & Gambardella, L. M. (2004). AntHocNet: An ant-based hybrid routing algorithm for mobile ad hoc networks. In *Lecture notes in computer science: Vol. 3242. Proceedings of Parallel Problem Solving from Nature (PPSN) VIII* (pp. 461-470). Springer-Verlag.

Di Caro, G. A., Ducatelle, F., & Gambardella, L. M. (2005a). AntHocNet: An adaptive nature-inspired algorithm for routing in mobile ad hoc networks. *European Transactions on Telecommunications, 16*(5), 443-455.

Di Caro, G. A., Ducatelle, F., & Gambardella, L. M. (2005b). Swarm intelligence for routing in mobile ad hoc networks. *Proceedings of the IEEE Swarm Intelligence Symposium*.

Di Caro, G. A., Ducatelle, F., & Gambardella, L. M. (2006). *Studies of routing performance in a city-like testbed for mobile ad hoc networks* (Tech. Rep. No. 07-06). Lugano, Switzerland: Istituto Dalle Molle di Studi sull'Intelligenza Artificiale.

Dittrich, P., Ziegler, J., & Banzhaf, W. (2001). Artificial chemistries: A review. *Artificial Life, 7*, 225-275.

Doczi, G. (1981). *The power of limits*. Boston: Shambhala Publications, Inc.

Doi, S., & Yamamura, M. (2000). BntNetL: Evaluation of its performance under congestion. *Journal of IEICE B*.

Donald, M. (1997). Origins of the modern mind: Three stages in the evolution of culture and cognition. *Behavioral and Brain Sciences, 16*(4), 737-791.

Donchin, E., & Coles, M. G. H. (1988). Is the P300 component a manifestation of context updating. *The Behavioral and Brain Sciences, 11*, 406-425.

Dorigo, M., & Di Caro, G. A. (1999). The ant colony optimization meta-heuristic. In D. Corne, M. Dorigo, & F. Glover (Eds.), *New ideas in optimization* (pp. 11-32). McGraw-Hill.

Dorigo, M., & Gambardella, L. M. (1997). Ant colony system: A cooperative learning approach to the traveling salesman problem. *IEEE Transactions on Evolutionary Computation, 1*(1), 53-66.

Dorigo, M., & Stützle, T. (2004). *Ant colony optimization*. Cambridge, MA: MIT Press.

Dorigo, M., Di Caro, G. A., & Gambardella, L. M. (1999). Ant algorithms for discrete optimization. *Artificial Life, 5*(2), 137-172.

Dorizzi, B., Grammaticos, B., Berre, M. L., Pomeau, Y., Ressayres, E., & Tallet, A. (1987). Statistics and dimension of chaos in differential delay systems. *Physical Review A, 35*, 328-339.

Dovrolis, C., Ramanathan, P., & Moore, D. (2004). Packet-dispersion techniques and a capacity-estimation methodology. *IEEE/ACM Transactions on Networking, 12*(6), 963-977.

Drug Bank, a recently developed database of FDA approved and experimental drugs. (2006). Retrieved January 10, 2007, from http://redpoll.pharmacy.ualberta.ca/drugbank/

Ducatelle, F., Di Caro, G. A., & Gambardella, L. M. (2005a). Ant agents for hybrid multipath routing in mobile ad hoc networks. *Proceedings of the Second Annual Conference on Wireless on Demand Network Systems and Services (WONS).*

Ducatelle, F., Di Caro, G. A., & Gambardella, L. M. (2005b). Using ant agents to combine reactive and proactive strategies for routing in mobile ad hoc networks. *International Journal of Computational Intelligence and Applications, 5*(2), 169-184.

Ducatelle, F., Di Caro, G. A., & Gambardella, L. M. (2006). An analysis of the different components of the AntHocNet routing algorithm. In *Lecture notes in computer science: Vol. 4150. Proceedings of ANTS 2006, Fifth International Workshop on Ant Algorithms and Swarm Intelligence* (pp. 37-48). Springer-Verlag.

Ducatelle, F., Di Caro, G. A., & Gambardella, L. M. (2007). *A study on the use of MANETs in an urban environment* (Tech. Rep. No. 01-07). Lugano, Switzerland: Istituto Dalle Molle di Studi sull'Intelligenza Artificiale.

Dürer, A. (1535). *Unterweisung der messung.* Paris: Ex Officina Christiani Wecheli.

Durham, W. H. (1991). *Coevolution: Genes, culture and human diversity.* Stanford, CA: Stanford University Press.

Ebert, D. S., Musgrave, F. K., Peachy, D., Perlin, K., & Worley, S. (2003). *Texturing and modeling: A procedural approach* (3rd ed.). Morgan Kaufmann Publishers Inc.

Eckmann, J.-P., Kamphorst, S. O., & Ruelle, D. (1987). Recurrence plots of dynamical systems. *Europhysics Letters, 5*, 973-977.

Edelman, G. M. (1992). *Bright air, brilliant fire: On the matter of the mind.* London: Penguin Group.

Egert, U., Schlosshauer, B., Fennrich, S., Nisch, W., Fejtl, M., Knott, T., et al. (2002). A novel organotypic long-term culture of the rat hippocampus on substrate-integrated microelectrode arrays. *Brain Resource Protocol, 2*, 229-242.

Eglash, R. (1999). *African fractals: Modern computing and indigenous design.* Piscataway, NJ: Rutgers University Press.

Egner, T., & Gruzelier, J. (2003). Ecological validity of neurofeedback: Modulation of slow wave EEG enhances musical performance. *NeuroReport, 14*(9), 1221-1224.

Egner, T., & Gruzelier, J. (2004). EEG biofeedback of low beta band components: Frequency-specific effects on variables of attention and event-related brain potentials. *Clinical Neurophysiology, 115*, 131-139.

Egner, T., & Gruzelier, J. H. (2001). Learned self-regulation of EEG frequency components affects attention and event-related brain potentials in humans. *NeuroReport, 12*(18), 4155-4159.

Eiben, A. E., & Smith, J. E. (2003). *Introduction to evolutionary computing.* Berlin, Germany: Springer.

Eigen, M. (1971). Self organization of matter and the evolution of biological macro molecules. *Naturwissenschaften, 58*, 465-523.

Eigen, M., & Schuster, P. (1977). The hypercycles: A principle of natural evolution. *Naturwissenschaften, 64*, 541; *65*, 7; *65*, 341.

Ellenberger, H. (1981). *The discovery of the unconscious.* New York: Basic Books.

Erdelyi, M. H. (1985). *Psychoanalysis: Freud's cognitive psychology.* New York: W. H. Freeman & Company.

Erdos, P., & Renyi, A. (1960). On the evolution of random graphs. *Publ. Math. Inst. Hung. Acad. Sci., 2*, 17-61.

Erramilli, A., & Singh, R. P. (1992). *An application of deterministic chaotic maps to model packet traffic* (Bellcore Technical Memorandum). Bellcore.

Erramilli, A., Gosby, D., & Willinger, W. (1993). *Engineering for realistic traffic: A fractal analysis of burstiness.* Proceedings of ITC Special Congress, Bangalore, India.

Erramilli, A., Pruthi, P., & Willinger, W. (1994). *Modelling packet traffic with chaotic maps.* ISRN KTH/IT/R-94/18-SE, Stockholm-Kista, Sweden.

Fan, A., & Palaniswami, M. (2001). Stock selection using support vector machines. *Proceedings of International Joint Conference on Neural Networks, 3*, 1793-1798.

Farmer, J. D. (1982). Chaotic attractors of an infinite-dimensional dynamical system. *Physica D, 4*, 366-393.

Feder, L. (1988). Adoption trauma: Oedipus myth/clinical reality. In G. Pollock & J. Ross (Eds.), *The Oedipus papers.* Madison, CT: International Universities Press. (Original work published 1974)

Feinberg, I. (1978). Efference copy and corollary discharge: Implications for thinking and its disorders. *Schizophrenia Bulletin, 4*, 636-640.

Feldman, M. W., & Laland, K. N. (1996). Gene-culture coevolutionary theory. *Trends in Ecology and Evolution, 11*, 453-457.

Feynman, R. P. (1974). Statistical mechanics: A set of lectures. *American Journal of Physics.*

Feynman, R. P., Leighton, R. B., & Sands, M. (1963). *The Feynman lectures on physics, v1-3.* Reading, MA: Addison-Wesley.

Fisher, Y. (1995). *Fractal image compression: Theory and application.* New York: Springer-Verlag.

Flavell, J. H. (1963). *The developmental psychology of Jean Piaget.* New York: Van Nostrand.

Fodor, J. A. (1983). *The modularity of mind.* Cambridge, MA: *MIT Press.*

Fogel, D. B. (1995). *Evolutionary computation.* IEEE Press.

Fogel, L. J., Owens, A. J., & Walsh, M. J. (1966). *Artificial intelligence through simulated evolution.* New York: John Wiley.

Foley, J. D., van Dam, A., Feiner, S. K., & Hughes, J. F. (1997). *Computer graphics: Principles and practice* (2nd ed.). New York: Addison Wesley.

Fonagy, P., & Target, M. (1997). Attachment and reflective function: Their role in self-organization. *Development and Psychopathology, 9*, 679-700.

Fournier, A., Fussel, D., & Carpenter, L. (1982). Computer rendering of stochastic models. *Communications of the ACM, 25*, 371-384.

Fowler, H., & Leland, W. (1994). Local area network traffic characteristics, with implications for broadband network congestion management. *IEEE Journal of Selected Areas in Communications, 9*(7), 1139-1149.

Fractal geometry. (2007). *Britannica concise encyclopedia.* Retrieved February 26, 2007, from http://concise.britannica.com/ebc/article-9364797/fractal-geometry

Fragopanagos, N., Kockelkoren, S., & Taylor, J. G. (2003). A neurodynamic model of the attentional blink. *Cognitive Brain Research, 24*, 568-586.

Freedman, R. (1990). *Palladio 1.0.* Apple Macintosh© Hypercard Stack.

Freeman, L. C. (2004). *The development of social networks analysis: A study in the sociology of science.* Vancouver, Canada: Booksurge Publishing.

Freeman, R. L. (2004). *Telecommunication system engineering.* Wiley-IEEE Press.

Freeman, W. J. (1975). *Mass action in the nervous system.* New York: Academic Press.

Freud, S. (n.d.). Beyond the pleasure principle. In J. Strachey (Ed. & Trans.), *The standard edition of the complete psychological works of Sigmund Freud* (Vol. 18, pp. 1-64). London: Hogarth Press. (Original work published 1920)

Freud, S. (n.d.). *The interpretation of dreams* (J. Strachey, Trans.). New York: Basic Books. (Original work published 1900)

Freud, S. (n.d.-a). Studies on hysteria. In J. Strachey (Ed. & Trans.), *The standard edition of the complete psychological works of Sigmund Freud* (Vol. 2). London: Hogarth Press. (Original work published 1893-1895)

Freud, S. (n.d.-b). Project for a scientific psychology. In J. Strachey (Ed. & Trans.), *The standard edition of the complete psychological works of Sigmund Freud* (Vol. 1, pp. 295-391). London: Hogarth Press. (Original work published 1895)

Freud, S. (n.d.-c). The "uncanny." In J. Strachey (Ed. & Trans.), *The standard edition of the complete psychological works of Sigmund Freud* (Vol. 17, pp. 217-256). London: Hogarth Press. (Original work published 1919)

Frith, C. (1992). *The cognitive neuropsychology of schizophrenia*. Hillsdale, NJ: Erlbaum.

Fromherz, P. (2002). Electrical interfacing of nerve cells and semiconductor chips. *Chemphyschem, 3*, 276-284.

Fromherz, P., & Schaden, H. (1994). Defined neuronal arborisations by guided outgrowth of leech neurons in culture. *European Journal of Neuroscience, 6*.

Fromherz, P., Muller, C. O., & Weis, R. (1993). Neuron-transistor: Electrical transfer function measured by the patch-clamp technique. *Physical Review Letters, 71*.

Fromherz, P., Offenhäusser, A., Vetter, T., & Weis, J. (1991). A neuron-silicon-junction: A Retzius-cell of the leech on an insulated-gate field-effect transistor. *Science, 252, 1290-1293*.

Fuster, J. M., & Alexander, G. E. (1971). Neuron activity related to short-term memory. *Science, 173*, 652-654.

Gaddini, E. (1969). On imitation. *International Journal of Psycho-Analysis, 50*, 475-484.

Gaddini, E. (1989). Fenomeni PSI e processo creativo. In *Scritti*. Milan: Cortina. (Original work published 1969)

Gaddini, E. (1992). On imitation. In Limentani (Ed.), *A psychoanalytic theory of infantile experience*. London: Routledge. (Original work published 1969)

Galatzer-Levy, R. (1988). On working through: A model from artificial intelligence. *Journal of the American Psychoanalytic Association, 38*(1), 125-151.

Gallager, R. (1977). A minimum delay routing algorithm using distributed computation. *IEEE Transactions on Communications, 25*, 73-84.

Gallagher, S. (2000). Philosophical conceptions of the self. *Trends in Cognitive Sciences, 4*(1), 14-21.

Gallego-Schmid, M. (1999). Modified AntNet: Software application in the evaluation and management of a telecommunication network. *Genetic and Evolutionary Computation Conference (GECCO-99)*.

Gao, G., Cagin, T., & Goddard, W. A., III. (1998). Energetics, structure, mechanical and vibrational properties of single walled carbon nanotubes (SWNT). *Nanotechnology, 9*, 184-191.

Garcia, P. S., Calabrese, R. L., DeWeerth, S. P., & Ditto, W. (2003). Simple arithmetic with firing rate encoding in leech neurons: Simulation and experiment. *Proceedings of the XXVI Australasian Computer Science Conference, 16*, 55-60.

Gardner, T. S., & Faith, J. J. (2005). Reverse-engineering transcriptional control networks. *Physics of Life Review, 2*, 65-88.

Garey, M. R., & Johnson, D. S. (1979). *Computers and intractability*. W. H. Freeman & Company.

Gauthier, Y. (1984). Hegel's logic from a logical point of view. In R. S. Cohen & M. W. Wartofsky (Eds.), *Hegel and the sciences* (pp. 303-310). New York: D. Reidel Publishing Co.

Gazzaniga, M. S. (2005). *The ethical brain*. New York: The Dana Press.

Ghosh, D., Saha, P., & Chowdhury, A. R. (in press). Multiple delay Rössler system-bifurcation and chaos control. *Chaos, Solitons and Fractals*.

Ghyka, M. C. (1927). *Esthétique des proportions dans la nature et dans les arts.* Paris: Gallimard.

Ghyka, M. C. (1977). *The geometry of art and life.* New York: Dover Publications, Inc.

Gibbs, H. M., Hopf, F. A., Kaplan, D. L., & Schoemacker, R. L. (1981). Observation of chaos in optical bistability. *Physical Review Letters, 46,* 474-477.

Gibson, J. J. (1979). *The ecological approach to visual perception.* NJ: Lawrence Erlbaum Associates.

Gillespie, D. T. (1977). Exact stochastic simulation of coupled chemical reactions. *Journal of Phys. Chem., 81,* 2340- 2361.

Giordano, S., Pierazzini, G., & Russo, F. (1995). *Multimedia experiments at the University of Pisa: From videoconference to random fractals.* Retrieved October 10, 2006, from http://www.isoc.org/HMP/PAPER/109/html/paper.html

Giray, M., & Ulrich, R. (1993). Motor coactivation revealed by response force in divided and focused attention. *Journal of Experimental Psychology, Human Perception and Performance, 19*(6), 1278-1291.

GNOSYS. (2006). Retrieved from http://www.ics.forth.gr/gnosys

Gold, C. (2003). FX trading via recurrent reinforcement learning. *Proceedings of IEEE International Conference on Computational Intelligence in Financial Engineering* (pp. 363-370).

Goldberg, D. E. (1989). *Genetic algorithm in search, optimization, and machine learning.* Reading, MA: Addison-Wesley.

Goss, S., Aron, S., Deneubourg, J.-L., & Pasteels, J. M. (1989). Self-organized shortcuts in the Argentine ant. *Naturwissenschaften, 76,* 579-581.

Gould, S. J., & Eldredge, N. (1977). Punctuated equilibria: The tempo and mode of evolution reconsidered. *Paleobiology, 3,* 115-151.

Grassé, P. P. (1959). La reconstruction du nid et les coordinations interindividuelles chez bellicositermes natalensis et cubitermes sp: La théorie de la stigmergie. Essai d'interprétation du comportement des termites constructeurs. *Insectes Sociaux, 6,* 41-81.

Green, C. S., & Bavelier, D. (2003). Action video game modifies visual selective attention. *Nature, 423,* 534-537.

Greenberg, J. R., & Mitchell, S. A. (1983). *Object relations in psychoanalytic theory.* Cambridge, MA: Harvard University Press.

Greenberg, L. (1987). An objective measure of methylphenidate response: Clinical use of the MCA. *Psychopharmacology Bulletin, 23*(2), 279-282.

Griffin, I. C., & Nobre, A. C. (2003). Orienting attention to locations in internal representations. *Journal of Cognitive Neuroscience, 15,* 1176-1194.

Griffiths, M. (2000). Does Internet and computer "addiction" exist? Some case study evidence. *CyberPsychology & Behavior, 3*(2), 211-218.

Groves, C., Wilson, D. E., & Reeder, D. M. (Eds.). (2005). *Mammal species of the world (3rd ed.).* Johns Hopkins University Press.

Guérin, E., & Tosan, E. (2005). Fractal inverse problem: Approximation formulation and differential methods. In J. Lévy-Véhel & E. Lutton (Eds.), *Fractal in engineering: New trends in theory and applications* (pp. 271-285). London: Springer.

Guérin, E., Tosan, E., & Baskurt, A. (2002). Modeling and approximation of fractal surfaces with projected IFS attractors. In M. M. Novak (Ed.), *Emergent nature: Patterns, growth and scaling in the science* (pp. 293-303). NJ: World Scientific.

Gülcügil, A. (2006). *The rectangle of the whirling squares and the logarithmic spiral in classic art.* Retrieved July 16, 2006, from http://gulcugil.tripod.com

Günes, M., Sorges, U., & Bouazizi, I. (2002). ARA: The ant-colony based routing algorithm for MANETS. *Proceedings of the 2002 ICPP International Workshop on Ad Hoc Networks (IWAHN).*

Haeckel, E. (1974). *Art forms in nature*. New York: Dover Publications, Inc.

Hagan, S., Hameroff, S., & Tuszynski, J. (2002). Quantum computation in brain microtubules? Decoherence and biological feasibility. *Physical Reviews E, 65*.

Halle, K. S., Wu, C. W., Itoh, M., & Chua, L. O. (1993). Spread spectrum communication through modulation of chaos. *International Journal of Bifurcation Chaos, 3*(2), 469-478.

Hameroff, S. R., & Penrose, R. (1996). Orchestrated reduction of quantum coherence in brain microtubules: A model for consciousness? In S. R. Hameroff, A. W. Kaszniak, & A. C. Scott (Eds.), *Toward a science of consciousness: The first Tucson discussions and debates* (pp. 507-540). Cambridge, MA: MIT Press.

Hanan, J. S. (1988). *PLANTWORKS: A software system for realistic plant modelling*. Unpublished master's thesis, University of Regina.

Hanan, J. S. (1992). *Parametric L-systems and their application to the modelling and visualization of plants*. Unpublished doctoral dissertation, University of Regina.

Harlow, H. V. (1991). Asset allocation in a downside-risk framework. *Financial Analysts Journal*, pp. 30-40.

Hayes, S., Grebogi, C., & Ott. (1993). Communicating with chaos. *Physical Review Letters, 70*, 3031-3034.

Haykin, S. (1999). *Neural networks: A comprehensive foundation*. London: Prentice Hall.

Hayman, D. (1999). *The life of Jung*. New York: W. W. Norton.

He, R., & Vaidya, P. G. (1998). Implementation of chaotic cryptography with chaotic synchronization. *Physical Review E, 57*, 1532-1535.

He, X., Hintz, T., Wu, Q., Wang, H., & Jia, W. (2006). A new simulation of spiral architecture. *Proceedings of 2006 International Conference on Image Processing, Computer Vision, & Pattern Recognition (IPCV'06)* (pp. 570-575).

He, X., Wang, H., Wu, Q., Hintz, T., & Hur, N. (2006). Fractal image compression on spiral architecture. *International Conference on Computer Graphics, Imaging and Visualisation (CGIV'06)* (pp. 76-83).

Heims, S. (1991). *The cybernetics group*. Cambridge, MA: The MIT Press.

Heissenbüttel, M., & Braun, T. (2003). Ants-based routing in large scale mobile ad-hoc networks. *Kommunikation in Verteilten Systemen (KiVS03)*.

Heusse, M., Snyers, D., Guérin, S., & Kuntz, P. (1998). Adaptive agent-driven routing and load balancing in communication networks. *Advances in Complex Systems, 1*(2).

Hey, A. J. G., & Allen, R. W. (Eds.). (1996). *Feynman lectures on computation*. Reading, MA: Addison-Wesley Publishing Company.

Hodges, B., & Dallimore, C. (2006). *Estuary, lake and coastal ocean model: ELCOM, v2.2 Science manual*. Australia: Centre for Water Research, University of Western Australia.

Hofbauer, J., & Sigmund, K. (1988). *The theory of evolution and dynamical systems*. Cambridge: Cambridge University Press.

Hofstadter, D. R. (1979). *Gödel, Escher, Bach: An eternal golden braid*. New York: Basic Books.

Hofstadter, D. R., & Dennett, D. C. (1981). *The mind's I: Fantasies and reflections on self and soul*. New York: Basic Books.

Holden, A. V. (1992). Dynamical spirals. In I. Hargittai & C. Pickover (Eds.), *Spiral symmetry* (pp. 73-81). World Scientific Publishing Co.

Holland, J. (1975). *Adaptation in natural and artificial systems*. Ann Arbor, MI: The University of Michigan Press.

Holland, J. H. (1992). Genetic algorithms. *Scientific American, 267*, 66-72.

Hölldobler, B., & Wilson, E. O. (1990). *The ants*. Berlin, Germany: Springer-Verlag.

Hopf, J.-M., et al. (2000). Neural sources of focused attention in visual search. *Cerebral Cortex, 10*, 1231-1241.

Hopfield, J. J. (1984). Neural networks and physical systems with emergent collective computational abilities. *Proceedings National Academy of Sciences US, 81*.

Hopfield, J., & Tank, D. W. (1985). Neural computation of decisions in optimization problems. *Biological Cybernetics, 52*.

Houde, O., & Tzourio-Mazayer, N. (2003). Neural foundations of logical and mathematical cognition. *Nature Review, Neuroscience, 4*, 507-514.

Hunter, J. R. (1987). The application of Lagrangian particle-tracking techniques to modelling of dispersion in the sea. In J. Noye (Ed.), *Numerical modelling: Applications to marine systems* (pp. 257-269). North-Holland: Elsevier Science Publishers.

Husserl, E. (1980). *Collected works*. Boston: The Hague.

Ikeda, K. (1979). Multiple-valued stationary state and its instability...transmitted light by a ring cavity system. *Optical Communications, 30*, 257.

Ikeda, K., & Matsumoto, K. (1987). High dimensional chaotic behavior in systems with time delayed feedback. *Physica D, 29*, 223-235.

Ikeda, K., Kondo, K., & Akimoto, O. (1982). Successive higher-harmonic bifurcations in systems with delayed feedback. *Physical Review Letter, 49*, 1467-1470.

Ioannides, A. A., & Taylor, J. G. (2003). Testing models of attention with MEG. *Proceedings of IJCNN'03*.

Jacquin, A. E. (1992). Image coding based on a fractal theory of iterated contractive image transformations image processing. *IEEE Transactions, 1*(1), 18-30.

Jain, P. (2002). *Validation of AntNet as a superior single path, single constrained routing protocol*. Unpublished master's thesis, Department of Computer Science and Engineering, University of Minnesota, MN.

Jasper, H. H. (1958). Report of the committee on methods of clinical examination in electroencephalography. *Electroencephalography and Clinical Neurophysiology, 10*, 370-375.

Jaynes, J. (1976). *The origin of consciousness in the breakdown of bicameral mind*. New York: Houghton Mifflin.

Jaynes, J. (1995). The diachronicity of consciousness. In G. Trautteur (Ed.), *Consciousness: Distinction and reflection*. Napoli, Italy: Bibliopolis.

Jobson, H. E. (1997). *Enhancements to the branched Lagrangian transport modeling system*. (Water-Resources Investigations Rep. No. 97-4050). U.S. Geological Survey.

John, A., Wheeler, J. A., & Zurek, W. H. (1983). *Quantum theory and measurement*. Princeton University Press.

Johnson, D. B., & Maltz, D. A. (1996). Dynamic source routing in ad hoc wireless networks. In *Mobile computing* (pp. 153-181). Kluwer.

Joja, A. (1969). *La lógica dialéctica y las ciencias* [M. Serrano Pérez, Trans.]. Buenos Aires, Argentina: Juárez.

Jolliffe, I. T. (1986). *Principal component analysis* (2nd ed.). Berlin, Germany: Springer

Jones, B. L., Enns, R. H., & Rangnekar, S. S. (1976). On the theory of selection of coupled macromolecular systems. *Bulletin of Mathematical Biology, 38*, 15-23.

Josephson, B. D., & Pallikari-Viras, F. (1991). Biological utilisation of quantum nonlocality. *Foundations of Physics, 21*, 197-207.

Jung, C. (1956). Symbols of transformation. In *Collected works*. London: Routledge & Kegan Paul.

Jung, C. (1961). *Memories, dreams, reflections*. New York: Random House.

Jung, C. G. (1956). *Symbols of transformation.* Princeton, NJ: Princeton University Press.

Jung, C. G. (1959). *The archetypes and the collective unconscious.* Princeton, NJ: Princeton University Press.

Jung, C. G. (Ed.). (1964). *Man and his symbols.* London: Aldus Book Ltd.

Kamiya, J. (1968). Conscious control of brain waves. *Psychology Today, 1,* 57-60.

Kanwisher, N., & Wojciulik, E. (2000). Visual attention: Insights from brain imaging. *Nature Review, Neuroscience, 1,* 91-100.

Kasderidis, S., & Taylor, J. G. (2004). Attentional agents and robot control. *International Journal of Knowledge-Based & Intelligent Systems 8,* 69-89.

Kasderidis, S., & Taylor, J. G. (2005). *Rewarded attentional agents.* Proceedings of ICANN2005, Warsaw, Poland.

Kassabalidis, I., Das, A., El-Sharkawi, M., Marks, R., II, Arabshahi, P., & Gray, A. (2002). Intelligent routing and bandwidth allocation in wireless networks. *Proceedings of the NASA Earth Science Technology Conference.*

Kassabalidis, I., El-Sharkawi, M., Marks, R., II, Arabshahi, P., & Gray, A. (2002). Swarm intelligence for routing in communication networks. *Proceedings of the IEEE World Congress on Computational Intelligence.*

Kastner, S., & Ungerleider, L. G. (2000). Mechanisms of visual attention. *Annual Reviews of Neuroscience, 23,* 315-341.

Kastner, S., & Ungerleider, L. G. (2001). The neural basis of biased competition in human visual cortex. *39,* 1263-1276.

Katura, H. (1999). Optical properties of single-wall carbon nanotubes. *Synthetic Metals, 103,* 2555-2558.

Katznelson, R. D. (1981). Normal modes of the brain: Neuroanatomical basis and a physiological theoretical model. In P. L. Nunez (Ed.), *Electric fields of the brain:* *The neurophysics of EEG* (pp. 401-442). New York: Oxford University Press.

Kauffman, L. H. (2002). Biologic II. In N. Tongring & R. C. Penner (Eds.), *Woods hole mathematics: World Scientific series on knots and everything 34* (pp. 94-132). Singapore: World Scientific.

Kauffman, L. H. (2004). Biologic. *AMS Contemporary Mathematics Series, 304,* 313 - 340.

Kauffman, L., & Sabelli, H. (1998). The process equation. *Cybernetics and Systems, 29,* 345-362.

Kauffman, S. (1993). *The origins of order: Self-organization and selection in evolution.* Oxford, United Kingdom: Oxford University Press.

Keijzer, M. (2003). Improving symbolic regression with interval arithmetic and linear scaling. In C. Ryan et al. (Eds.), *Lecture notes in computer science: Vol. 2610. Genetic Programming: Proceedings of the 6th European Conference* (pp. 71-83). Berlin, Germany: Springer.

Kennedy, T. (1997). Managing the drug discovery development interface. *Drug Discovery Today, 2,* 436–444.

Kennel, M. B., Brown, R., & Abarbanel, H. D. I. (1992). Determining embedding dimension for phase-space reconstruction using a geometrical construction. *Physical Review A, 45,* 3403-3411.

Kephart, J., & Chess, D. (2003). The vision of autonomic computing. *IEEE Computer, 36*(1), 41-50.

Kernberg, P. F. (2007). *Beyond the reflection: The role of the mirror paradigm in clinical practice.* New York: Other Press.

Kerr, J. (1995). *A most dangerous method.* New York: Vintage Books/Random House.

Klein, M. (1932). *The psycho-analysis of children.* London: Hogarth.

Klimesch, W., Schimke, H., & Pfurtscheller, G. (1993). Alpha frequency, cognitive load and memory performance. *Brain Topography, 5*(3), 241-251.

Klimesch, W., Schimke, H., Ladurner, G., & Pfurtscheller, G. (1990). Alpha frequency and memory performance. *Psychophysiology, 4*, 381-390.

Klipp, E., Herwig, R., Kowald, A., Wierling, C., & Lehrach, H. (2005). *Systems biology in practice*. Weinheim, Germany: Wiley-VCH.

Klivansky, S. M., Mukherjee, A., & Song, C. (1994). On long-range dependence in NSFNET traffic (Tech. Rep. No. GIT-CC-94-61). Georgia Institute of Technology.

Kocarev, L., Halle, K. S., Eckert, K., Chua, L. O., & Parlitz, U. (1992). Experimental demonstration of secure communications via chaotic synchronization. *International Journal of Bifurcation Chaos, 2*(3), 709-714.

Kocić, Lj. (2001). Comments on "Peri Elikon." *Unus Mundus, 8*, 5-37.

Kocić, Lj. (2003). *Mathematics and aesthetics*. Niš, Serbia: Niš Cultural Center.

Kocić, Lj., & Stefanovska, L. (2005). Complex dynamics of visual arts. *Chaos and Complexity Letters, 1*(2), 207-235.

Kohut, H. (1971). *The analysis of the self*. New York: International Universities Press.

Kohut, H. (1977). *The restoration of the self*. New York: International Universities Press.

Koppens, F. H. L., Buizert, C., Tielrooij, K. J., Vink, L. T., Nowack, K. C., Meunier, T., et al. (2006). Driven coherent oscillations of a single electron spin in a quantum dot. *Nature, 442*, 766-771.

Kornhuber, H. H., & Deecke, L. (1965). Hirnpotentialänderungen bei willkürbewegungen und passiven bewegungen des menschen: Bereitschaftspotential und reafferente potentiale. *Pflügers Arch. Ges. Physiol., 284*, 1-17.

Kosok, M. (1984). The dynamics of Hegelian dialectics, and nonlinearity in the sciences. In R. S. Cohen & M. W. Wartofsky (Eds.), *Hegel and the Sciences* (pp. 311-348). New York: D. Reidel Publishing Co.

Koza, J. R. (1992). *Genetic programming*. Cambridge, MA: MIT Press.

Kuhn, T. (1962). *The structure of scientific revolutions*. Chicago: University of Chicago Press.

Kvasnicka, V., & Pospichal, J. (1999a). Evolutionary study of interethnic cooperation. *Advances in Complex Systems, 2*, 395-421.

Kvasnicka, V., & Pospichal, J. (1999b). Simulation of Baldwin effect and Dawkins memes by genetic algorithm. In R. Roy, T. Furuhashi, & P. K. Chawdhry (Eds.), *Advances in soft computing* (pp. 481-496). London: Springer-Verlag.

Kvasnicka, V., & Pospichal, J. (1999c). Simulation of evolution of Dawkins memes. *Evolution and cognition, 5*, 75-86.

Kvasnicka, V., & Pospichal, J. (2000). An emergence of coordinated communication in populations of agents. *Artificial Life, 5*, 319-342.

Kvasnicka, V., & Pospichal, J. (2003). Artificial chemistry and molecular Darwinian evolution in silico. *Collection of Czechoslovak Chemical Communications, 68*(1), 139-177.

Lacan, J. (2005). The mirror stage. In *Ecrits*. W. W. Norton. (Original work published 1937)

Lakoff, G., & Johnson, M. (1980). *Metaphors we live by*. Chicago: University of Chicago Press.

Lakoff, G., & Johnson, M. (1999). *Philosophy in the flesh: The embodied mind and its challenge to Western thought*. New York: Basic Books.

Laland, K. N., Odling-Smee, J., & Feldman, M. W. (1999). Niche construction, biological evolution and cultural change. *Behavioral and Brain Sciences, 23*, 131-175.

Laland, K. N., Odling-Smee, J., & Feldman, M. W. (2000). Niche construction, biological evolution, and cultural change. *Behavioral and brain sciences, 23*, 131-175.

Landauer, R. (1961). Irreversibility and heat generation in the computing process. *IBM Journal of Research and Development*, 183-191.

Landers, D. M., Petruzzello, S. J., Salazar, W., Crews, D. J., Kubitz, K. A., Gannon, T. L., et al. (1991). The influence of electrocortical biofeedback on performance in pre-elite archers. *Medicine and Science in Sports and Exercise, 23*(1), 123-129.

Langdon, W. B., & Barrett, S. J. (2004). Genetic programming in data mining for drug discovery. In *Evolutionary computing in data mining* (pp. 211-235). Berlin, Germany: Springer.

Langton, C. G. (1984). Self-reproduction in cellular automata. *Physica D, 10*, 135-144.

Lassig, M., Bastolla, U., Manrubia, S. C., & Valleriani, A. (2001). Shape of ecological networks. *Physical Review Letters, 86*, 4418-4421.

Laval, B., Imberger, J., Hodges, B., & Stocker, R. (2003). Modeling circulation in lakes: Spatial and temporal variations. *Limnology and Oceanography, 48*(3), 983-994.

Le Corbusier. (1958). *Entretien avec les étudiants des écoles d'architecture.* Les Éditions de Minuit.

Lee, C. M. C., & Swaminathan, B. (2000). Price momentum and trading volume. *Journal of Finance, 55*, 2017-2069.

Leendertse, J. J. (1989). *A new approach to three-dimensional free-surface flow modeling* (Tech. Rep. No. R-3712-NETH/RC). Santa Monica, CA: Rand Corporation.

Lefebvre, H. (1947). *Logique formelle, logique dialectique.* Paris: Editions Sociales.

Leland, W. E., Taqqu, M. S., Willinger, W., & Wilson, D. V. (1993). On the self-similar nature of Ethernet traffic. *Proceedings of the ACM/SIGCOMM'93* (pp. 183-193).

Leland, W. E., Taqqu, M. S., Willinger, W., & Wilson, D. V. (1994). On the self-similar nature of Ethernet traffic (extended version). *IEEE/ACM Transactions on Networking, 2*(1), 1-15.

Leon, L. F., Lam, D. C. L., Schertzer, W. M., & Swayne, D. A. (2006). *A 3D hydrodynamic lake model: Simulation on Great Slave Lake.* Proceedings International Modelling and Software Society Biennial Conference, Burlington, VT.

Leon, L. F., Lam, D., Schertzer, W. M., & Swayne, D. A. (2005). Lake and climate models linkage: A 3-D hydrodynamic contribution. *Advances in Geosciences, 4*, 57-62.

Levin, A. U. (1995). Stock selection via nonlinear multifactor models. In *Advances in neural information processing systems* (pp. 966-972). San Francisco: Morgan Kaufmann Publishers.

Lévi-Strauss, C. (1977). *Structural anthropology 1* (C. Jacobson & B. G. Schoepf, Trans.). Harmondsworth, United Kingdom: Penguin.

Lévy Véhel, J., & Riedi, R. (1997). Fractional Brownian motion and data traffic modeling: The other end of the spectrum. In J. Lévy Véhel, E. Lutton, & C. Tricot (Eds.), *Fractals in engineering* (pp. 185-202). London: Springer.

Levy, A., Alden, D., & Levy, C. (2006, August). *Biotic patterns in music.* Paper presented at the Society for Chaos Theory in Psychology & Life Sciences 16th Annual International Conference, Baltimore.

Levy-Carciente, S., Sabelli, H., & Jaffe, K. (2004). Complex patterns in the oil market. *Intersciencia, 29*, 320-323.

Lewontin, R. C. (1983). Gene, organism, and environment. In D. S. Bendall (Ed.), *Evolution from molecules to men.* Cambridge University Press.

Libet, B. (1993). *Neurophysiology of consciousness: Selected papers and new essays.* Boston: Birkhauser.

Libet, B., Freeman, A., & Sutherland, K. (1999). *The volitional brain, towards a neuroscience of free will.* Thorverton, United Kingdom: Imprint Academic.

Lieberman, P. (1991). *Uniquely human: The evolution of speech, thought, and selfless behavior.* Cambridge, MA: Harvard University Press.

Linden, M., Habib, T., & Radojevic, V. (1996). A controlled study of the effects of EEG biofeedback on cognition and behaviour of children with ADD and LD. *Biofeedback and Self Regulation, 21*(1), 35-49.

Lindner, J. F., & Ditto, W. (1996). Exploring the nonlinear dynamics of a physiologically viable model neuron. *AIP Conference Proceedings, 1*, 375-385.

Liu, D. (2006). A parallel computing algorithm for improving the speed of fractal image compression based on spiral architecture. *Proceedings of 2006 International Conference on Image Processing, Computer Vision, & Pattern Recognition (IPCV'06)* (pp. 563-569).

Liu, J. (2006). *Fractal network traffic analysis with applications.* Retrieved January 10, 2007, from http://hdl.handle.net/1853/11477

Liu, L., & Feng, G. (2005). A novel ant colony based QoS-aware routing algorithm for MANETs. *Proceedings of the First International Conference on advances in Natural Computation (ICNC).*

Liu, Z., Kwiatkowska, M., & Constantinou, C. (2005). A self-organised emergent routing mechanism for mobile ad hoc networks. *European Transactions on Telecommunications (ETT), 16*(5).

Lo, W. A., Mamaysky, H., & Wang, J. (2000). Foundations of technical analysis: Computational algorithms, statistical inference, and empirical implementation. *Journal of Finance, 55*, 1705-1769.

Loeb, A. L., & Varney, W. (1992). Does the golden spiral exist, and if not, where is its center? In I. Hargittai & C. Pickover (Eds.), *Spiral symmetry* (pp. 47-61). World Scientific Publishing Co.

Lohn, J. D., & Reggia, J. A. (1995). Discovery of self-replicating structures using a genetic algorithm. In *Proceedings of 1995 IEEE International Conference on Evolutionary Computation* (ICEC'95, pp. 678-683).

Lovett, B. W., Reina, J. H., Nazir, A., Kothari, B., & Briggs, G. A. D. (2003). Resonant transfer of excitons and quantum computation. *Physics Letters A, 315*, 136-142.

Lozi, R., & Chua, L. O. (1993). Secure communications via chaotic synchronization II: Noise reduction by cascading two identical receivers. *International Journal of Bifurcation and Chaos in Applied Sciences and Engineering, 3*(5), 1319-1325.

Lubar, J. F. (1995). Neurofeedback for the management of attention-deficit/hyperactivity disorders. In M. S. Schwartz (Ed.), *Biofeedback: A practitioner's guide* (2nd ed., pp. 493-522). New York: Guildford Press.

Lubar, J. F., & Shouse, M. N. (1976). EEG and behavioral changes in a hyperkinetic child concurrent with training of the sensorimotor rhythm (SMR): A preliminary report. *Biofeedback and Self Regulation, 1*(3), 293-306.

Lubar, J. F., Swartwood, M. O., Swartwood, J. N., & O'Donnell, P. H. (1995). Evaluation of the effectiveness of EEG neurofeedback training for ADHD in a clinical setting as measured by changes in T.O.V.A. scores, behavioural ratings, and WISC-R performance. *Biofeedback and Self Regulation, 20*(1), 83-99.

Lukovits, I. (2000). A compact form of adjacency matrix. *Journal of Chemical Information and Computer Sciences, 40*, 1147-1150.

Ma, H. W., & Zeng, A. P. (2003). The connectivity structure, giant strong component and centrality of metabolic networks. *Bioinformatics, 19*, 1423-1430.

Mackey, M. C., & Glass, L. (1977). Oscillation and chaos in physiological control systems. *Science, 197*, 287-289.

Mackey, M. C., & Heiden, U. en der. (1984). The dynamics of recurrent inhibition. *Journal of Mathematical Biology, 19*, 211-225.

Maher, M. P., Pine, J., Wright, J., & Tai, Y. C. (1999). The neurochip: A new multielectrode device for stimulating and recording from cultured neurons. *Neuroscience Methods, 87*, 45-56.

Malkin, G. S. (1999). *RIP: An intra-domain routing protocol.* Addison-Wesley.

Mandelbrot, B. (1975). *Les objects fractals: Forme, hasard et dimension.* Paris: Nouvelle Bibliothèque Scientifique Flammaron.

Mandelbrot, B. (1982). *The fractal geometry of nature.* W. H. Freeman & Company.

Mandelbrot, B. B. (1969). Long-run linearity, locally Gaussian processes, H-spectra and infinite variances. *International Economic Review, 10,* 82-113.

Mandelbrot, B. B. (1978). Les objets fractals. *La Recherche, 9,* 1-13.

Mandelbrot, B. B. (1979). Colliers all´eatoires et une alternative aux promenades aux hasard sans boucle: Les cordonnets discrets et fractals. *Comptes Rendus, 286A,* 933-936.

Mann, C. A., Lubar, J. F., Zimmerman, A. W., Miller, C. A., & Muenchen, R. A. (1992). Quantitative analysis of EEG in boys with attention-deficit-hyperactivity disorder: Controlled study with clinical implications. *Pediatric Neurology, 8*(1), 30-36.

Marák, I. (1997). *On synthetic terrain erosion modeling: A survey.* Retrieved April 14, 2005, from http://www.cescg.org/CESCG97/marak/

Marák, I., Benes, B., & Slavík, P. (1997). Terrain erosion model based on rewriting of matrices. *Proceedings of WSCG-97, 2,* 341-351.

Maranas, C. D., Androulakis, I. P., Floudas, C. A., Berger, A. J., & Mulvey, J. M. (1997). Solving long-term financial planning problems via global optimization. *Journal of Economic Dynamics and Control, 21,* 1405-1425.

Marcus, C. M., & Westervelt, R. M. (1989). Stability of analog neural networks with delay. *Physical Review A, 39,* 347-359.

Marie, R. R., Bez, H. E., Blackledge, J. M., & Datta, S. (2006). *On the fractal characteristics of network traffic and its utilization in covert communications.* Retrieved January 2, 2007, from http://ima.org.uk/Conferences/mathssignalprocessing2006/Marie.pdf

Markowitz, H. M. (1952). Portfolio selection. *Journal of Finance, 7,* 77-91.

Markowitz, H. M. (1959). *Portfolio selection.* New York: John Wiley.

Marwaha, S., Tham, C. K., & Srinivasan, D. (2002). Mobile agents based routing protocol for mobile ad hoc networks. *Proceedings of IEEE Globecom.*

Marwan, N. (2003). *Encounters with neighbours.* Unpublished doctoral dissertation, University of Potsdam.

Marx, A., & Mandelkow, E. M. (1994). A model of microtubule oscillations. *European Biophysics Journal, 22*(6), 405-421.

Masson, J. (1984). *The assault on truth: Freud's suppression of the seduction theory.* Horizon Book Promotions.

Masson, J. M. (Ed.). (1985). *The complete letters of Sigmund Freud to Wilhelm Fliess 1887-1904.* Cambridge, MA: Belknap.

Mathiak, K., & Weber, R. (2006). Toward brain correlates of natural behavior: fMRI during violent video games. *Human Brain Mapping, 27*(12), 948-956.

Matsuno, K. (1999). Cell motility as an entangled quantum coherence. *BioSystems, 51,* 15-19.

Matsuo, H., & Mori, K. (2001). Accelerated ants routing in dynamic networks. *2nd International Conference on Software Engineering, Artificial Intelligence, Networking and Parallel/Distributed Computing.*

Maturana, H. (2002). Autopoiesis, structural coupling and cognition: A history of these and other notions in the biology of cognition. *Cybernetics & Human Knowing, 9*(3-4), 5-34.

Maturana, H. R., & Varela, F. J. (1980). *Autopoiesis and cognition: The realization of the living.* Dordrecht, the Netherlands: D. Reidel Publishing Co.

McAdams, C. J., & Maunsell, J. H. R. (1999). Effects of attention on orientation tuning functions of single neurons in macaque cortical area V4. *Journal of Neuroscience, 19*(1), 431-441.

McDermott, J. J. (Ed.). (1967). *The writings of William James.* New York: Random House.

McMahon, S. M., Miller, K. H., & Drake, J. (2001). Networking tips for social scientists and ecologists. *Science, 293*, 1604-1605.

Meadows, D. H., Meadows, D. L., Randers, J., & Behrens, W. W. (1972). *Limits to growth* (Report to the Club of Rome). New York: Universe Press.

Mehta, A. D., Ulbert, I., & Schroeder, C. E. (2000). Intermodal selective attention in monkeys II: Physiological mechanisms of modulation cerebral cortex. *10*, 359-370.

Mensour, B., & Longtin, A. (1995). Controlling chaos to store information in delay-differential equations. *Physics Letter A, 205*, 18-24.

Meyer, M. (2002). Fractal scaling of heartrate dynamics in health and disease. In G. A. Losa, D. Merlini, T. F. Nonnenmacher, & E. R. Weibel (Eds.), *Fractal in biology and medicine* (Vol. 3, pp. 181-193). Basel, Switzerland: Birkhauser.

Miall, R. C., & Wolpert, D. M. (1996). Forward models for physiological motor control. *Neural Networks, 9*(8), 1265-1279.

Michalareas, T., & Sacks, L. (2001a). Link-state and ant-like algorithm behaviour for single-constrained routing. *IEEE Workshop on High Performance Switching and Routing (HPSR).*

Michalareas, T., & Sacks, L. (2001b). Stigmergic techniques for solving multi-constraint routing for packet networks. *Proceedings of the First International Conference on Networking (ICN), Part II.*

Michalewicz, Z. (1996). *Genetic algorithms + data structures = evolution programs* (3rd ed.). Berlin, Germany: Springer.

Milton, J. G., Heiden, U. en der, Longtin, A., & Hlackey, M. C. (1990). Complex dynamics and noise in simple neural networks with mixed feedback. *Biomedica Biochimica Acta, 49*, 697-707.

Minsky, M. (1985). *The society of mind.* New York: Simon & Schuster.

Minsky, M. (2006). *The emotion machine: Commonsense thinking, artificial intelligence, and the future of the human mind.* Simon & Schuster.

Mitchell, M. (1996). *An introduction to genetic algorithms.* Cambridge, MA: The MIT Press.

Monastra, V. J., Monastra, D. M., & George, S. (2002). The effects of stimulant therapy, EEG biofeedback and parenting style on the primary symptoms of attention deficit/hyperactivity disorder. *Applied Psychophysiology and Biofeedback, 27*(4), 231-249.

Mondragon, R. J., Arrowsmith, D. K., & Pitts, J. M. (1999). Chaotic maps for traffic modelling and queueing performance analysis. *Performance Evaluation, 43*(4), 223-240.

Monte, C., & Sollod, R. (2003). *Beneath the mask: An introduction to theories of personality.* New York: John Wiley & Sons.

Moody, J., & Saffell, M. (2001). Learning to trade via direct reinforcement. *IEEE Transactions on Neural Networks, 12*, 875-889.

Moody, J., & Wu, L. (1997). Optimization of trading systems and portfolios. In Y. Abu-Mostafa, A. N. Refenes, & A. S. Weigend (Eds.), *Decision technologies for financial engineering* (pp. 23-35). London: World Scientific.

Moody, J., Wu, L., Liao, Y., & Saffell, M. (1998). Performance functions and reinforcement learning for trading systems and portfolios. *Journal of Forecasting, 17*, 441-470.

Morita, K., & Imai, K. (1996). Self-reproduction in a reversible cellular space. *Theoretical Computer Science, 168*, 337-366.

Moy, J. (1998). *OSPF anatomy of an Internet routing protocol.* Addison-Wesley.

Mozer, M. C., & Sitton, M. (1998). Computational modeling of spatial attention. In H. Pashler (Ed.), *Attention* (pp. 341-393). New York: Taylor & Francis.

Mulvey, J. M., Rosenhaum, D. P., & Shetty, B. (1997). Strategic financial risk management and operations research. *European Journal of Operational Research, 97*, 1-16.

Murphy, J. J. (1999). *Study guide to technical analysis of the financial markets.* New York: Prentice Hall Press.

Musgrave, F. K., Kolb, C. E., & Mace, R. S. (1989). The synthesis and rendering of eroded fractal terrain. *Computer Graphics, 23*(3), 41-50.

Nehaniv, C. L. (2002). Evolution in asynchronous cellular automata. In R. K. Standish, M. A. Bedau, & H. A. Abbass (Eds.), *Artificial life VIII* (pp 65-73). Cambridge, MA: The MIT Press.

Nelakuditi, S., & Zhang, Z.-L. (2001). On selection of paths for multipath routing. In *Lecture notes in computer science: Vol. 2092. Proceedings of the International Workshop on QoS (IWQoS)* (pp. 170-182).

Neumann, E. (1993). *The origins and history of consciousness.* Princeton, NJ: Princeton. (Original work published 1954)

Neumann, G., & Pierson, W. J., Jr. (1966). *Principles of physical oceanography.* Englewood Cliffs, NJ: Prentice-Hall Inc.

Nielsen, J. (1998). Metabolic engineering: Techniques of analysis of targets for genetic manipulations. *Biotechnology & Bioengineering, 58*, 125-132.

Nielsen, M. A., & Chuang, I. L. (2000). *Quantum computation and quantum information.* Cambridge, United Kingdom: Cambridge University Press.

Nietzsche, F. (1999). *The birth of tragedy and other writings* (Cambridge texts in the history of philosophy). Cambridge, United Kingdom: Cambridge University Press. (Original work published 1871)

Nison, S. (1991). *Japanese candlesticks charting technique.* New York: Prentice Hall Press.

Nobre, A. C. (2001). The attentive homunculus: Now you see it, now you don't. *Neuroscience and Biobehavioral Reviews, 25*, 477-496.

Nonnenmacher, T. F., Losa, G. A., Merlini, D., & Weibel, E. R. (Eds.). (1994). *Fractal in biology and medicine.* Basel, Switzerland: Birkhauser.

Norman, D. A. (1988). *The design of everyday things.* New York: Doubleday.

Norman, D. A. (1999). Affordances, conventions, and design. *Interactions, 6*(3), 38-41.

Norros, I. (1994). A storage model with self-similar input. *Queueing Systems Theory and Applications, 16*(3-4), 387-396.

Norros, I. (1995). On the use of fractional Brownian motion in the theory of connectionless networks. *IEEE Journal on Selected Areas in Communications, 13*(6), 953-962.

Nunez, P. L. (1981). *Electric fields of the brain: The neurophysics of EEG.* New York: Oxford University Press.

Ogden, C. K. (1967). *Opposition.* London: Indiana State University. (Original work published 1932)

Oida, K., & Kataoka, A. (1999). Lock-free AntNet and its evaluation for adaptiveness. *Journal of IEICE B.*

Oida, K., & Sekido, M. (2000). ARS: An efficient agent-based routing system for QoS guarantees. *Computer Communications.*

Oppenheimer, P. (1986). Real time design and animation of fractal plants and trees. *Computer Graphics, 20*(4), 55-64.

Orlob, G. T. (1967). *Prediction of thermal energy distribution in streams and reservoirs* (Tech. Rep.). Walnut Creek, CA: Water Resources Engineers, Inc.

Ornstein, R. (Ed.). (1973). *The nature of human consciousness.* San Francisco: W. H. Freeman.

Orsucci, F. (2006). The paradigm of complexity in clinical neuro-cognitive science. *The Neuroscientist, 12*(4), 1-10.

Orsucci, F. (Ed.). (1998). *The complex matters of the mind.* Singapore: World Scientific.

Orsucci, F., & Sala, N. (2005). Virtual reality, telemedicine and beyond. In D. Carbonara (Ed.), *Technology literacy applications in learning environments* (pp. 349-357). Hershey, PA: Idea Group.

Orsucci, F., Giuliani, A., & Zbilut, J. (2004). Structure & coupling of semiotic sets. *Experimental Chaos: AIP Proceedings, 742,* 83-93.

Orsucci, F., Giuliani, A., Webber, C., Zbilut, J., Fonagy, P., & Mazza, M. (2006). Combinatorics & synchronization in natural semiotics. *Physica A: Statistical Mechanics and its Applications, 361,* 665-676.

Orsucci, F., Walters, K., Giuliani, A., Webber, C., Jr., & Zbilut, J. (1999). Orthographic structuring of human speech and texts. *International Journal of Chaos Theory and Applications, 4*(2), 80-88.

Ott, E., Grebogi, C., & Yorke, J. A. (1990). *Phys. Rev. Lett., 64*(11), 1196.

Palumbo, M. C., Colosimo, A., Giuliani, A., & Farina, L. (2005). Functional essentiality from topology features in metabolic networks: A case study in yeast. *FEBS Letters, 579,* 4642-4646.

Palumbo, M. C., Farina, L., Colosimo, A., Tun, K., Dhar, P., & Giuliani, A. (2006). Networks everywhere? Some general implications of an emergent metaphor. *Current Bioinformatics, 1*(2), 219-234.

Panerai, P. (1992). *L'étude pratique des plans de ville: Villes en parallèle n° 12-13.* Paris: Laboratoire de géographie urbaine, Université Paris X, Nanterre.

Papadimitriou, C. H., & Steiglitz, K. (1982). *Combinatorial optimization.* NJ: Prentice-Hall.

Park, K., & Willinger, W. (2000). *Self-similar network traffic and performance evaluation* (1st ed.). London: John Wiley & Sons.

Parlitz, U., & Ergezinger, S. (1994). Robust communication based on chaotic spreading sequences. *Physics Letter A, 188,* 146-150.

Parlitz, U., Chua, L. O., Kocarev, L., Halle, K. S., & Shang, A. (1992). Transmission of digital signals by chaotic synchronization. *International Journal of Bifurcation and Chaos in Applied Sciences and Engineering, 2*(4), 973-977.

Passingham, D., & Sakai, K. (2004). The prefrontal cortex and working memory: Physiology and brain imaging. *Current Opinion in Neurobiology, 14,* 163-168.

Patel, M., & Sabelli, H. (2003). Autocorrelation and frequency analysis differentiate cardiac and economic bios from 1/F noise. *Kybernetes, 32,* 692-702.

Paulin, M., & Duprat, B. (1991). *De la maison à l'école, élaboration d'une architecture scolaire à Lyon de 1875 à 1914.* Ministère de la Culture, Direction du Patrimoine, CRML.

Paxson, V., & Floyd, S. (1994). Wide area traffic: The failure of Poisson modeling. *Proceedings of ACM SIGCOMM'94* (pp. 257-268).

Paxson, V., & Floyd, S. (1995). Wide area traffic: The failure of Poisson modeling. *IEEE/ACM Transactions on Networking, 3*(3), 226-244.

Pecora, L. M., & Carroll, T. L. (1990). *Phys. Rev. Lett., 64,* 821.

Pecora, L., & Carroll, T. (1990). Synchronization in chaotic systems. *Physical Review Letters, 64,* 821-824.

Peitgen, H., & Saupe, D. (1988). *The science of fractal images.* New York: Springer-Verlag.

Peitgen, H., Jürgens, H., & Saupe, D. (1992). *Chaos and fractals.* New York: Springer.

Penrose, R. (1994). *Shadows of the mind.* Oxford University Press.

Perkins, C. E., & Royer, E. M. (1999). Ad-hoc on-demand distance vector routing. *Proceedings of the Second IEEE Workshop on Mobile Computing Systems and Applications.*

Perline, R. (1996). Zipf's law, the central limit theorem, and the random division of the unit interval. *Physical Review E, 54,* 220-223.

Perrier, J. Y., Sipper, M., & Zahnd, J. (1996). Toward a viable, self-reproducing universal computer. *Physica D, 97*, 335-352.

Petitot, J. (1999). *Naturalizing phenomenology: Issues in contemporary phenomenology and cognitive science.* Stanford, CA: Stanford University Press.

Petrides, M. (2000). Dissociable roles of mid-dorsolateral prefrontal and anterior inferotemporal cortex in visual working memory. *Journal of Neuroscience, 20*, 7496-7503.

Pham Thi, N. N., Huisman, J., & Sommeijer, B. P. (2005). Simulation of three-dimensional phytoplankton dynamics: Competition in light-limited environments. *Journal of Computational and Applied Mathematics, 174*(1), 57-77.

Phillips, C., & Harbour, R. (2000). *Feedback control systems.* NJ: Prentice Hall.

Piaget, J. (1950). *Introduction à l'épistémologie génétique* (3 Vols.). Paris: Presses Universitaires de France.

Pisella, L., Grea, H., Tillikete, C., Vighetto, A., Desmurget, M., Rode, G., et al. (2000). An "automatic pilot" for the hand in human posterior parietal cortex: Toward reinterpreting optic ataxia. *Nature Neuroscience, 3*, 729-736.

Pizzi, R., de Curtis, M., & Dickson, C. (2002). Evidence of chaotic attractors in cortical fast oscillations tested by an artificial neural network. In J. Kacprzyk (Ed.), *Advances in soft computing.* Physica Verlag.

Pizzi, R., Fantasia, A., Gelain, F., Rossetti, D., & Vescovi, A. (2004). *Behavior of living human neural networks on microelectrode array support.* Proceedings of the Nanotechnology Conference and Trade Show 2004, Boston.

Pizzi, R., Fantasia, A., Gelain, F., Rossetti, D., & Vescovi, A. (2004). *Non-local correlations between separated neural networks.* Proceedings of the SPIE Conference on Quantum Information and Computation, Orlando, FL.

Pizzi, R., Rossetti, D., Cino, G., Gelain, F., & Vescovi, A. (in press). Learning in human neural networks on microelectrode arrays. *BioSystems.*

Plant, R. E. (1981). A Fitzhugh differential-difference equation modeling recurrent neural feedback. *SIAM Journal of Applied Mathematics, 40*(1), 150-162.

Planty-Bonjour, G. (1965). *Le catégories du matérialisme dialectique.* Paris: Presses Universitaires de France.

Plihon, V., Wu, F., & Gardarin, G. (2001). A financial data mining trading system. *Natural Language Processing and Information Systems: 5th International Conference on Applications of Natural Language to Information Systems, NLDB 2000* (p. 370).

Pollock, G., & Ross, J. (1988). *The Oedipus papers.* Madison, CT: International Universities Press.

Potter, S. M. (2001). Distributed processing in cultured neuronal networks. In M. A. L. Nicolelis (Ed.), *Progress in brain research.* Elsevier Science B.V.

Praamstra, P., & Oostenveld, R. (2003). Attention and movement-related motor cortex activation: A high density EEG study of spatial stimulus-response compatibility. *Cognitive Brain Research, 16*, 309-323.

Prusinkiewicz, P. (1986). Graphical applications of L-systems. *Proceedings of Graphics Interface '86: Vision Interface* (pp. 247-253).

Prusinkiewicz, P. (1987). Applications of L-systems to computer imagery. In H. Ehrig, M. Nagl, G. Rozenberg, & A. Rosenfeld (Eds.), *Lecture notes in computer science: Vol. 291. Graph-Grammars and Their Application to Computer Science (3rd International Workshop)* (pp. 534-548). Heidelberg, Germany: Springer-Verlag.

Prusinkiewicz, P., & Hammel, M. (1993). A fractal model of mountains with rivers. *Proceeding of Graphics Interface '93* (pp. 174-180).

Prusinkiewicz, P., & Lindenmayer, A. (1990). *The algorithmic beauty of plants.* New York: Springer-Verlag.

Putman, J. A. (2001). Technical issues involving bipolar EEG training protocols. *Journal of Neurotherapy, 5*(3), 51-58.

Qualls, P. J., & Sheehan, P. W. (1981). Role of the feedback signal in electromyograph biofeedback: The relevance of attention. *Journal of Experimental Psychology, General, 110*(2), 204-216.

Rajagopalan, S., & Shen, C. (2005). ANSI: A unicast routing protocol for mobile ad hoc networks using swarm intelligence. *Proceedings of the International Conference on Artificial Intelligence.*

Ramachandran, V. S., & Hirstein, W. (1998). The perception of phantom limbs. The DO Hebb lecture. *Brain, 121*, 1603-1630.

Rao, F., & Caflisch, A. (2004). The protein folding network. *Journal of Molecular Biology, 342*, 299-306.

Rao, G.-S., & Agee, E. M. (1996). Large eddy simulation of turbulent flow in a marine convective boundary layer with snow. *Journal of Atmospheric Sciences, 53*(1), 86-100.

Rasey, H. W., Lubar, J. F., McIntyre, A., Zoffuto, A. C., & Abbott, P. L. (1996). EEG biofeedback for the enhancement of attentional processing in normal college students. *Journal of Neurotherapy, 1*(3), 15-21.

Rechenberg, I. (1973). *Evolutionsstrategie: Optimierung technischer systeme nach prinzipien der biologischen evolution.* Stuttgart, Germany: Fromman-Holzboog Verlag.

Reger, B., Fleming, K. M., Sanguineti, V., Alford, S., & Mussa-Ivaldi, F. A. (2000). Connecting brains to robots: An artificial body for studying the computational properties of neural tissues. *Artificial Life, 6*, 307-324.

Richardson, D. C., & Dale, R. (2005). Looking to understand: The coupling between speakers' and listeners' eye movements and its relationship to discourse comprehension. *Cognitive Science, 29*, 39-54.

Ricoeur, P. (1970). *Freud and philosophy.* Cambridge, MA: Yale University Press.

Rizzolatti, G., & Arbib, M. A. (1998). Language within our grasp. *Trends in Neuroscience, 21*, 188-194.

Robertson, R. (1995). *Jungian archetypes.* York Beach, ME: Nicholas-Hay.

Rothkrantz, L., & van der Put, R. (1998). Routing in packet switched networks using agents. *First International Workshop on Ant Colony Optimization (ANTS).*

Rothschild, B. (2000). *The body remembers: The psychophysiology of trauma and trauma treatment.* New York: W. W. Norton.

Rousseeuw, P. J., & Leroy, A. M. (1987). *Robust regression and outlier detection.* New York: Wiley.

Royer, E. M., & Toh, C.-K. (1999). A review of current routing protocols for ad hoc mobile wireless networks. *IEEE Personal Communications, 6*(2), 46-55.

Ruaro, M. E., Bonifazi, P., & Torre, V. (2005). Toward the neurocomputer: Image processing and pattern recognition with neuronal cultures. *IEEE Transactions on Biomedical Engineering, 3.*

Rueda, F. J., & Schladow, S. G. (2003). Dynamics of large polymictic lake II: Numerical simulations. *Journal of Hydraulic Engineering, 129*(2), 92-101.

Rushworth, M. F. S., Ellison, A., & Walsh, V. (2001). Complementary localization and lateralization of orienting and motor attention. *Nature Neuroscience, 4*(6), 656-661.

Rushworth, M. F. S., Krams, M., & Passingham, R. E. (2001). *Journal of Cognitive Neuroscience, 13*, 698-710.

Rushworth, M. F. S., Nixon, P. D., Renowden, S., Wade, D. T., & Passingham, R. E. (1997). The left parietal cortex and motor attention. *Neuropsychologia, 35*(9), 1261-1273.

Sabelli, H. (1971). An attempt to formalize some aspects of dialectic logic. In W. R. Beyer (Ed.), *Hegel-Jahrbuch 1970* (pp. 211-213). Meisenheim am Glan, Germany: Verlag Anton Hain.

Sabelli, H. (1989). *Union of opposites: A comprehensive theory of natural and human processes.* Lawrenceville, VA: Brunswick.

Sabelli, H. (1995). Non-linear dynamics as a dialectic logic. *Proceedings of International Systems Society* (pp. 101-112).

Sabelli, H. (1998). The union of opposites: From Taoism to process theory. *Systems Research, 15*, 429-441.

Sabelli, H. (2001). The co-creation hypothesis. In G. Ragsdell & J. Wilby (Eds.), *Understanding complexity.* London: Kluwer Academics/Plenum Publishers.

Sabelli, H. (2005). *Bios: A study of creation.* Singapore: World Scientific.

Sabelli, H. C. (1972). A pharmacological approach for modeling neuronal nets. In H. Drischeland & P. Dattmar (Eds.), *Biocybernetics* (Vol. 4, pp. 1-9). Jena, Germany: Veb Gustav Fischer Verlag.

Sabelli, H. C. (1984). Mathematical dialectics, scientific logic and the psychoanalysis of thinking. In R. S. Cohen & M. W. Wartofsky (Eds.), *Hegel and the sciences* (pp. 349-359). New York: D. Reidel Publishing Co.

Sabelli, H., & Carlson-Sabelli, L. (1989). Biological priority and psychological supremacy: A new integrative paradigm derived from process theory. *American Journal of Psychiatry, 146*, 1541-1551.

Sabelli, H., & Carlson-Sabelli, L. (1996). As simple as one, two, three. Arithmetic: A simple, powerful, natural and dynamic logic. *Proceedings of International Systems Society* (pp. 543-554).

Sabelli, H., & Carlson-Sabelli, L. (2005). Bios: A process approach to living system theory. In honor to James and Jessie Miller. *Systems Research and Behavioral Science, 23*, 323-336.

Sabelli, H., & Kovacevic, L. (2006). Biotic population dynamics and the theory of evolution. *International Journal* 2006. Retrieved from http://www.interjournal.org/manuscript_abstract.php?82762892

Sabelli, H., & Kovacevic, L. (2006). Quantum bios and biotic complexity in the distribution of galaxies. *Complexity, 11*, 14-25.

Sabelli, H., Carlson-Sabelli, L., Patel, M., Zbilut, J., Messer, J., & Walthall, K. (1995). Psychocardiological portraits: A clinical application of process theory. In F. D. Abraham & A. R. Gilgen (Eds.), *Chaos theory in psychology* (pp. 107-125). Westport, CT: Greenwood Publishing.

Sabes, M. (2000). The planning and control of reaching movements. *Current Opinion in Neurobiology, 10*, 740-746.

Saha, D., & Mukherjee, A. (2003). Pervasive computing: A paradigm for the 21st century. *IEEE Computer, 36*(3).

Sala, N. (2004). Fractal geometry in the arts: An overview across the different cultures. In M. M. Novak (Ed.), *Thinking in patterns: Fractals and related phenomena in nature* (pp. 177-188). Singapore: World Scientific.

Sala, N. (2006). Complexity, fractals, nature and industrial design: Some connections. In M. M. Novak (Ed.), *Complexus mundi: Emergent pattern in nature* (pp. 171-180). Singapore: World Scientific.

Saleri, R. (2005). Pseudo-urban automatic pattern generation. *Chaos and Complexity Letters, 1*(3), 357-365.

Salvador, P., Nogueira, A., Valadas, R., & Pacheco, A. (2004). Multi-time-scale traffic modeling using Markovian and L-systems models. In *Lecture notes in computer science: Vol. 3262. Proceedings of 3rd European Conference on Universal Multiservice Networks* (pp. 297-306). Heidelberg, Germany: Springer-Verlag.

Sandalidis, H., Mavromoustakis, K., & Stavroulakis, P. (2001). Performance measures of an ant based decentralized routing scheme for circuit switching communication networks. *Soft Computing, 5*(4).

Saunders, P. T. (1980). *An introduction to catastrophe theory.* Cambridge, United Kingdom: Cambridge University Press.

Sayama, H. (1998). Introduction of structural dissolution into Langton's self-reproducing loop. In C. Adami, R.

K. Belew, H. Kitano, & C. E. Taylor (Eds.), *Artificial life VI* (pp.114-122). Los Angeles: MIT Press.

Sayama, H. (2000). Self-replicating worms that increase structural complexity through gene transmission. In M. A. Bedau, J. S. McCaskill, N. H. Packard, & S. Rasmussen (Eds.), *Artificial life VII* (pp. 467-476). MIT Press.

Scalable Network Technologies, Inc. (2006). *Qualnet simulator, Version 3.9*. Retrieved from http://www.scalable-networks.com

Schluter, N. D., Krams, M., Rushworth, M. F. S., & Passingham, R. E. (2001). Cerebral dominance for action in the human brain: The selection of actions. *Neuropsychologia, 39*, 105-113.

Schoonderwoerd, R., Holland, O., Bruten, J., & Rothkrantz, L. (1996). Ant-based load balancing in telecommunications networks. *Adaptive Behavior, 5*(2), 169-207.

Schore, A. (2001). Minds in the making: Attachment, the self-organizing brain, and developmentally-oriented psychoanalytic psychotherapy. *British Journal of Psychotherapy, 17*(3), 299-328.

Schore, A. (2007). Dissociation chapter Schore on implicit memory

Schrödinger, E. (1956). *Science and humanism*. Cambridge University Press.

Schwartz, E. (1980). Computation anatomy and functional architecture of striate cortex: A spatial mapping approach to perceptual coding. *Vision Research, 20*, 645-669.

Schwoebel, J., Boronat, C. B., & Coslett, H. B. (2002). The man who executed "imagined" movements: Evidence for dissociable components of the body schema. *Brain and Cognition, 50*, 1-16.

Searle, J. R. (1980). Minds, brains, and programs. *Behavioural and Brain Sciences, 3*, 417-424.

Searle, J. R. (1980). Minds, brains, and programs. In *The behavioral and brain sciences* (3). Cambridge University Press.

Šejka, L. (1995). *Treatise on painting*. Sombor, Serbia: Zlatna Grana.

Sept, D., Limbach, H.-J., Bolterauer, H., & Tuszynski, J. A. (1999). A chemical kinetics model for microtubule oscillations. *Journal of Theoretical Biology, 197*, 77-88.

Sergent, C., & Dehaene, S. (in press). Is consciousness a gradual phenomenon? Evidence for an all-or-none bifurcation during the attentional blink. *Nature Neuroscience*.

Sergent, C., Baillet, S., & Dehaene, S. (2005). Timing of the brain events underlying access to consciousness during the attentional blink. *Nature Neuroscience, 8*, 1391-1400.

Shannon, C. E. (1938). A symbolic analysis of relay and switching circuits. *Trans. Am. Inst. Elec. Eng., 57*, 713-723.

Shannon, C. E. (1948). *A mathematical theory of communication. Bell System Technical Journal, 27*, 379-423, 623-656.

Shapiro, K. L., Arnell, K. M,. & Raymond, J. E. (1997). The attentional blink. *Trends in Cognitive Science, 1*, 291-295.

Shapiro, K. L., Hillstrom, A. P., & Husain, M. (2002). Control of visuotemporal attention by inferior parietal and superior temporal cortex. *Current Biology, 12*, 1320-1325.

Sheridan, P. (1996). *Spiral architecture for machine vision*. Unpublished doctoral dissertation, University of Technology, Sydney, Australia.

Sheridan, P., & Hintz, T. (1999). Primitive image transformations on hexagonal lattice (Tech. Rep.). Bathurst, Australia: Charles Sturt University.

Sheridan, P., Hintz, T., & Alexander, D. (2000). Pseudo-invariant image transformations on a hexagonal lattice. *Image and Vision Computing, 18*, 907-917.

Sheridan, P., Hintz, T., & Moore, W. (1991). Spiral architecture in machine vision. Proceedings of the Australian Occam and Transputer Conference, Australia.

Shinba, T. (1999). Neuronal firing activity in the dorsal hippocampus during the auditory discrimination oddball task in awake rats. *Cognitive Brain Research, 8*, 241-350.

Shockley, K., Santana, M.-V., & Fowler, C. A. (2003). Mutual interpersonal postural constraints are involved in cooperative conversation. *Journal of Experimental Psychology: Human Perception and Performance, 29*, 326-332.

Shoemaker, S. (1968). Self-reference and self-awareness. *Journal of Philosophy, 65*, 556-570.

Shulman, J. A. (2000). *Fractals and Benoit Mandelbrot: A computer science discovery often considered kind to prime numbers.* American Computer Science Association (ACSA). Retrieved December 28, 2006, from http://www.acsa2000.net/frac/ Smith, A. R. (1984). Plants, fractals, and formal languages. *International Conference on Computer Graphics and Interactive Techniques: Proceedings of the 11th Annual Conference on Computer Graphics and Interactive Techniques* (pp. 1–10).

Siegel, D. (2001). Memory: An overview, with emphasis on developmental, interpersonal, and neurobiological aspects. *Journal of the Academy of Child & Adolescent Psychiatry, 40*(9), 997-1011.

Siegel, D. J. (2007). *The mindful brain.* New York: Norton.

Sigel, E., Denby, B., & Heárat-Mascle, S. L. (2002). Application of ant colony optimization to adaptive routing in a LEO telecommunications satellite network. *Annals of Telecommunications, 57*(5-6).

Sim, K., & Sun, W. (2003). Ant colony optimization for routing and load-balancing: Survey and new directions. *IEEE Transactions on Systems, Man, and Cybernetics: Part A, 33*(5).

Smola, A. J., & Scholkopf, B. (1998). A tutorial on support vector regression (Tech. Rep. No. NC2-TR-1998-030). NeuroCOLT2.

Solms, M. (2004). Freud returns. *Scientific American,* pp. 83-89.

Solms, M., & Turnbull, O. (2002). *The brain and the inner world: An introduction to the neuroscience of subjective experience.* New York: Other Press/Karnac Books.

Spencer-Brown, G. (1979). *Laws of form.* New York: E. P. Dutton. (Original work published 1969)

Stapp, H. (1993). *Mind, matter, and quantum mechanics.* Springer-Verlag.

Steenstrup, M. E. (Ed.). (1995). *Routing in communications networks.* Prentice-Hall.

Stepinski, T. F., Collier, M. L., McGovern, P. J., & Clifford, S. M. (2004). Martian geomorphology from fractal analysis of drainage networks. *Journal of Geophysical Research, 109*(nE2), E02005.1-E02005.12.

Sterman, M. B. (1973). Neurophysiologic and clinical studies of sensorimotor EEG biofeedback training: Some effects on epilepsy. *Seminal Psychiatry, 5*(4), 507-525.

Sterman, M. B. (2000). Basic concepts and clinical findings in the treatment of seizure disorders with EEG operant conditioning. *Clinical Electroencephalography, 31*(1), 45-55.

Sterman, M. B., & Friar, L. (1972). Suppression of seizures in an epileptic following sensorimotor EEG feedback training. *Electroencephalography and Clinical Neurophysiology, 33*(1), 89-95.

Sterman, M. B., & Macdonald, L. R. (1978). Effects of central cortical EEG feedback training on incidence of poorly controlled seizures. *Epilepsia, 19*(3), 207-222.

Sterman, M. B., Macdonald, L. R., & Stone, R. K. (1974). Biofeedback training of the sensorimotor electroencephalogram rhythm in man: Effects on epilepsy. *Epilepsia, 15*(3), 395-416.

Stern, D. (1985). *The interpersonal world of the infant.* New York: Basic Books.

Sternberg, R. (1990). *Metaphors of mind: Conceptions of the nature of intelligence.* New York: Cambridge University Press.

Stiny, G., & Mitchell, W. J. (1978). The Palladian grammar. *Environment and Planning B, 5,* 5-8.

Stojmenovic, I. (Ed.). (2002). *Mobile ad-hoc networks.* John Wiley & Sons.

Stolorow, R., Brandchaft, B., & Atwood, G. (1987). *Psychoanalytic treatment: An intersubjective approach.* Hillsdale, NJ: The Analytic Press.

Straker, L. M., Pollock, C. M., Zubrick, S. R., & Kurinczuk, J. J. (2006). The association between information and communication technology exposure and physical activity, musculoskeletal and visual symptoms and socio-economic status in 5-year-olds. *Child Care Health Development, 32*(3), 343-351.

Subing, Z., & Zemin, L. (2001). A QoS routing algorithm based on ant algorithm. *Proceedings of the IEEE International Conference on Communications (ICC).*

Subramanian, D., Druschel, P., & Chen, J. (1997). Ants and reinforcement learning: A case study in routing in dynamic networks. *Proceedings of IJCAI-97, International Joint Conference on Artificial Intelligence.*

Sugerman, A., & Sabelli, H. (2003). Novelty, diversification and nonrandom complexity define creative processes. *Kybernetes, 32,* 829-836.

Sutton, R. S., & Barto, A. G. (1997). *An introduction to reinforcement learning.* Cambridge, MA: MIT Press.

Sutton, R. S., & Barto, A. G. (1998). *Reinforcement learning: An introduction.* Cambridge, MA: MIT Press.

Szilard, A. L., & Quinton, R. E. (1979). An interpretation for DOL systems by computer graphics. *The Science Terrapin, 4,* 8-13.

Tadrus, S., & Bai, L. (2003). A QoS network routing algorithm using multiple pheromone tables. *Proceedings of the IEEE/WIC International Conference on Web Intelligence.*

Tanenbaum, A. (2002). *Computer networks.* Prentice-Hall.

Tansey, M. A. (1993). Ten-year stability of EEG biofeedback results for hyperactive boy who failed fourth grade perceptually impaired class. *Biofeedback and Self Regulation, 18*(1), 33-44.

Tansey, M. A., & Bruner, R. L. (1983). EMG and EEG biofeedback training in the treatment of a 10-year-old hyperactive boy with a developmental reading disorder. *Biofeedback and Self Regulation, 8*(1), 25-37.

Tatomir, B., & Rothkrantz, L. (2004). Dynamic routing in mobile wireless networks using abc-adhoc. *Proceedings of the Fourth International Workshop on Ant Colony Optimization and Swarm Intelligence (ANTS).*

Tausk, V. (1933). On the origin of the "influencing machine" in schizophrenia. *Psychoanalytic Quarterly, 2,* 519-556. (Original work published 1919)

Taylor, J. G. (1996). Breakthrough to awareness. *Biological Cybernetics.*

Taylor, J. G. (2000). Attentional movement: The control basis for consciousness. *Society for Neuroscience Abstracts, 26,* 2231.

Taylor, J .G. (2002). Paying attention to consciousness. *Trends in Cognitive Sciences, 6*(5), 206-210.

Taylor, J. G. (2002). From matter to mind. *Journal of Consciousness Studies, 6,* 3-22.

Taylor, J. G. (2003). Neural models of Consciousness. In M. A. Arbib (Ed.), *The handbook of brain theory and neural networks* (pp. 263-267). Cambridge, MA: MIT Press.

Taylor, J. G. (2003). *The CODAM model and deficits of consciousness.* Proceedings of the Conference of Knowledge-Based Expert Systems, Oxford, United Kingdom.

Taylor, J. G. (2003). Paying attention to consciousness. *Progress in Neurobiology 71*, 305-335.

Taylor, J. G. (2004). A review of brain-based cognitive models. *Cognitive Processing, 5*(4), 190-217.

Taylor, J. G. (2005). From matter to consciousness: Towards a final solution? *Physics of Life Reviews, 2*, 1-44.

Taylor, J. G. (2006). *The mind: A user's manual.* Wiley & Son.

Taylor, J. G., & Fragopanagos, N. (2003). Simulation of attention control models of sensory and motor paradigms. *Proceedings of IJCNN'03.*

Taylor, J. G., & Fragopanagos, N. (2005). The interaction of attention and emotion. *Neural Networks, 18*(4), 353-369.

Taylor, J. G., & Rogers, M. (2002). A control model of the movement of attention. *Neural Networks, 15*, 309-326.

Taylor, J. G., Fragopanagos, N., & Korsten, N. (2006). *Modelling working memory through attentional mechanisms.* Proceedings of the International Conference on Artificial Neural Networks (ICANN06), Athens, Greece.

Taylor, J. G., Nobre, C. A., & Shapiro, K. (Eds.). (2006). Special issue on brain and attention. *Neural Networks, 19*(7).

Taylor, N., Hartley, M., & Taylor, J. G. (2006). *Value learning for goal decisions* (KCL preprint).

Tempesti, G. (1995). A new self-reproducing cellular automaton capable of construction and computation. In F. Morán, A. Moreno, J. J. Merelo, & P. Chacón (Eds.), *Lecture notes in computer science: Vol. 929. ECAL'95: Third European Conference on Artificial Life* (pp. 555-563). Heidelberg, Germany: Springer-Verlag.

Tettamanzi, A., & Tomassini, M. (2001). *Soft computing: Integrating evolutionary, neural, and fuzzy systems.* Berlin, Germany: Springer.

Theraulaz, G., & Bonabeau, E. (1999). A brief history of stigmergy. *Artificial Life, 5*, 97-116.

Thom, R. (1983). *Mathematical models of morphogenesis.* Chichester, United Kingdom: Ellis Horwood.

Thomas, G. H. (2006). *Geometry, language and strategy.* Singapore: World Scientific.

Thomas, G. H., Sabelli, H., Kauffman, L. H., & Kovacevic, L. (2006). Biotic patterns in Schrödinger's equation and the evolution of the universe. *International Journal.* Retrieved from http://www.interjournal.org/manuscript_abstract.php?1161328888

Thompson, L., & Thompson, M. (1998). Neurofeedback combined with training in metacognitive strategies: Effectiveness in students with ADD. *Applied Psychophysiology and Biofeedback, 23*(4), 243-263.

Thompson, W. I. (1996). *Coming into being: Artefacts and texts in the evolution of consciousness.* New York: St. Martin's Press.

Tomasello, M. (2003). *A usage-based theory of language.* Cambridge, MA: Harvard University Press.

Trautteur, G. (1987, February). *Intelligenza umana e intelligenza artificiale.* Paper presented at Centro Culturale San Carlo of Milan.

Trautteur, G. (1997-1998). Distinzione e riflessione. *ATQUE, 16*, 127-141.

Turing, A. M. (1964). *Minds and machines.* Englewood Cliffs, NJ: Prentice Hall. (Original work published 1950)

Turkle, S. (1988). Artificial intelligence and psychoanalysis: A new alliance. *Daedalus, 117*(1), 241-268.

Tuszynski, J. A., Trpisova, B., Sept, D., & Sataric, M. V. (1997). The enigma of microtubules and their self-organizing behavior in the cytoskeleton. *BioSystems, 42*, 153-175.

van der Maas & van Geert (Eds.). (1999). *Non-linear analysis of developmental processes.* Amsterdam: Elsevier.

van Wijk, J. J., & Saupe, D. (2004). Image based rendering of iterated function systems. *Computers & Graphics, 28*(6), 937-943.

Vandervert, L. R. (1988). Systems thinking and a proposal for a neurological positivism. *Systems Research, 5,* 313-321.

Varela, F. J., Thompson, E., & Rosch, E. (1991). *The embodied mind, cognitive science and human experience.* Cambridge, MA: MIT Press.

Vazirani, V. V. (2001). *Approximation algorithms.* Berlin, Germany: Springer-Verlag.

Veitch, D. (1992). *Novel models of broadband traffic.* Proceedings of the Seventh Australian Teletraffic Research Seminar, Murray River, Australia.

Veitch, D. (1993). Novel models of broadband traffic. *IEEE Global Telecommunications Conference, 1993, including a Communications Theory Mini-Conference: Technical Program Conference Record, IEEE in Houston. GLOBECOM '93, 2,* 1057-1061.

Vernon, D. (2005). Can neurofeedback training enhance performance? An evaluation of the evidence with implications for future research. *Applied Psychophysiology and Biofeedback, 30*(4), 347-364.

Vernon, D., & Withycombe, E. (2006). *The use of alpha neurofeedback training to enhance mental rotation performance.* Paper presented to the Society of Applied Neuroscience, Swansea, United Kingdom.

Vernon, D., Egner, T., Cooper, N., Compton, T., Neilands, C., Sheri, A., et al. (2003). The effect of training distinct neurofeedback protocols on aspects of cognitive performance. *International Journal of Psychophysiology, 47*(1), 75-85.

Vernon, D., Egner, T., Cooper, N., Compton, T., Neilands, C., Sheri, A., et al. (2004). The effect of distinct neurofeedback training protocols on working memory, mental rotation and attention performance. *Journal of Neurotherapy, 8*(1), 100-101.

Vernon, D., Frick, A., & Gruzelier, J. (2004). Neurofeedback as a treatment for ADHD: A methodological review with implications for future research. *Journal of Neurotherapy, 8*(2), 53-82.

von Neumann, J. (1958). *The computer and the brain.* London: Yale University Press.

von Neumann, J. (1966). *Theory of self-reproducing automata* (Edited and completed by A. W. Burks). IL: University of Illinois Press.

Vyzantiadou, M. A., Avdelas, A. V., & Zafiropoulos, S. (2007). The application of fractal geometry to the design of grid or reticulated shell structures. *Computer-Aided Design, 39*(1), 51-59.

Walrand, J., & Varaiya, P. (1996). *High-performance communication networks.* Morgan Kaufmann.

Wang, H., Wu, Q., He, X., & Hintz, T. (2006). A novel interactive progressive decoding method for fractal image compression. *First International Conference on Innovative Computing, Information and Control (ICICIC'06), 3,* 613-617.

Wang, P., Song, Y. T., Chao, Y., & Zhang, H. (2005). Parallel computation of the regional ocean modeling system. *The International Journal of High Performance Computing Applications, 19*(4), 375-385.

Wang, Y., Kempa, K., Kimball, B., Carlson, J. B., Benham, G., Li, W. Z., et al. (2004). Receiving and transmitting light-like radio waves: Antenna effect in arrays of aligned carbon nanotubes. *Applied Physics Letters, 85,* 2607-2609.

Watts, D. J., & Strogatz, S. H. (1998). Collective dynamics of "small world" networks. *Nature, 393,* 440-442.

Webber, C. L., Jr., & Zbilut, J. P. (1994). Dynamical assessment of physiological systems and states using recurrence plot strategies. *Journal of Applied Physiology, 76,* 965-973.

Wheeler, J. A. (1957). Assessment of Everett's "relative state" formulation of quantum theory. *Reviews of Modern Physics.*

White, T., Pagurek, B., & Oppacher, F. (1998). ASGA: Improving the ant system by integration with genetic algorithms. *Proceedings of the Third Genetic Programming Conference.*

Wigner, E. (1961). Remarks on the mind-body question. In I. J. Good (Ed.), *The scientist speculates.* London: W. Heinemann.

Wigner, E. (1972). The place of consciousness in modern physics. In C. Muses & A. M. Young (Eds.), *Consciousness and reality.* New York: Outerbridge & Lazard.

Wilder, J. W. (1978). *New concepts in technical trading.* Greensboro, NC: Trend Research.

Willinger, W., Taqqu, M. S., Sherman, R., & Wilson, D. V. (1995). Self-similarity through high-variability: Statistical analysis of Ethernet LAN traffic at the source level. *ACM Sigcomm '95* (pp.100-113). Wohlberg, B., & de Jager, G. (1999). A review of the fractal image coding literature. *IEEE Transactions on Image Processing, 8*(12), 1716-1729.

Winnicott, D. W. (1987). *The child, the family, and the outside world.* Reading, MA: Addison-Wesley Publishing Co.

Wisdom, J. O. (1961). A methodological approach to the problem of hysteria. *International Journal of Psychoanalysis, 42,* 224-237.

Wittkower, R. (1962). *Architectural principles in the age of humanism* (3rd ed.). London: The Warburg Institute, University of London.

Wittkower, R. (1974). *Palladio and Palladianism.* New York: George Braziller.

Wolfram, S. (2002). *A new kind of science.* Champaign, IL: Wolfram Media.

Wolpert, D. M., & Ghahramani, Z. (2000). Computational principles of movement neuroscience. *Nature Neuroscience, 3,* 1212-1217.

Worrall, J., & Zahar, E. (Eds.). (1976). *Proofs and refutations.* Cambridge, United Kingdom: Cambridge University Press.

Wright, S. (1932). The roles of mutation, inbreeding, crossbreeding, and selection in evolution. *Proceedings of the Sixth International Congress of Genetics, 1,* 356-366. Retrieved from http://www.blackwellpublishing.com/ridley/classictexts/wright.pdf

Wu, C. W., & Chua, L. O. (1993). A simple way to synchronize chaotic systems with applications to secure communication systems. *International Journal of Bifurcation Chaos, 3*(6), 1619-1628.

Wu, Q., He, X., & Hintz, T. (2004). Virtual spiral architecture. *Proceedings of the International Conference on Parallel and Distributed Processing Techniques and Applications, 1,* 399-405.

Wuensche, A. (1999). Classifying cellular automata automatically: Finding gliders, filtering and relating space-time patterns, attractors basins and the Z parameter. *Complexity, 4*(3), 47-66.

Xu, L. D., & Li, L. X. (1989). Complementary opposition as a systems concept. *Systems Research, 6,* 91-101.

Yepez, J. (2001). A quantum lattice-gas model for computational fluid dynamics. *Physical Review E, 63,* 1-37.

Yoo, H. J., Cho, S. C., Ha, J., Yune, S. K., Kim, S. J., Hwang, J., et al. (2004). Attention deficit hyperactivity symptoms and Internet addiction. *Psychiatry Clinical Neuroscience, 58*(5), 487-494.

Yoshida, F., & Topliss, J. G. (2000). QSAR model for drug human oral bioavailability. *Journal of Medicinal Chemistry, 43,* 2575-2585.

Yu, L., Wang, S. Y., & Lai, K. K. (2006). An integrated data preparation scheme for neural network data analysis. *IEEE Transactions on Knowledge and Data Engineering, 18*(2), 1-13.

Yu, L., Wang, S. Y., & Lai, K. K. (in press). Neural network-based mean-variance-skewness model for portfolio selection. *Computers & Operations Research.*

Yue, W., Lin, C.-L., & Patel, V. C. (2004). Large eddy simulation of turbulent open-channel flow with free surface simulated by level set method. *Physics of Fluids, 17*(2), 1-12.

Zahavi, D. (1999). *Self-awareness and alterity.* Evanston, IL: North-Western University Press.

Zargham, M. R., & Sayeh, M. R. (1999). A Web-based information system for stock selection and evaluation. *Proceedings of the First International Workshop on Advance Issues of E-Commerce and Web-Based Information Systems* (pp. 81-83).

Zeilinger, A., Weihs, G., Jennewein, T., & Aspelmeyer, M. (2005). Happy centenary, photon. *Nature, 433,* 230-238.

Zhang, H. F., Shu, Y. T., & Yang, O. W. W. (1997). Estimation of Hurst parameter by variance time plots. *Proceedings IEEE Pacrim 97, 2,* 883-886.

Zhang, Y., Kuhn, L. D., & Fromherz, M. P. J. (2004). Improvements on ant routing for sensor networks. *Proceedings of the Fourth International Workshop on Ant Colony Optimization and Swarm Intelligence (ANTS).*

Zhao, E., & Liu, D. (2005). Fractal image compression methods: A review. *ICITA 2005: Third International Conference on Information Technology and Applications, 1,* 756-759.

Zheng, X., Guo, W., & Liu, R. (2004). An ant-based distributed routing algorithm for ad-hoc networks. *Proceedings of the International Conference on Communications, Circuits and Systems (ICCCAS).*

About the Contributors

Franco Orsucci received his first degree in medicine and second degree in psychiatry at La Sapienza University in Rome (Italy). He has been a researcher at the Italian National Research Council. Now he is professor of clinical psychology and psychiatry at the Catholic University and Gemelli University Hospital in Rome. He is also a research fellow at the London University College, and founder and editor in chief of *Chaos and Complexity Letters: International Journal of Dynamical System Research* (Nova Science, New York). His last published books are *Changing Mind: Transitions in Natural and Artificial Environments* (World Scientific, Singapore, 2002) and *Bioethics in Complexity* (Imperial College Press, London, 2004). He has also published more than 80 scientific articles on neuroscience and cognitive science.

Nicoletta Sala received a laurea in physics and applied cybernetics at the University of Milan (Italy); a PhD in communication science at Università della Svizzera Italiana of Lugano (USI, Lugano, Switzerland); and postgraduate degrees (2 years for each) in didactics of the communication and multimedia technologies, and journalism and mass media. She is professor of information technology and electronics and teaches at the University of Lugano (Mendrisio, Switzerland) and the University of Insubria (Varese, Italy). She is founder and coeditor of *Chaos and Complexity Letters: International Journal of Dynamical System Research* (Nova Science, New York). Her research interests concern various scientific topics from an interdisciplinary point of view and comprise the following areas: fractal geometry and complexity; mathematics in arts, architecture, and industrial design; new media and IT in the learning environments; and virtual reality in education. She has authored 20 mathematics and information technology books, and edited four others. She has written 280 scientific papers.

*   *   *

Walter Ambrosetti is first researcher at the Istituto per lo Studio degli Ecosistemi (ISE, Institute for Ecosystem's Study) of the Research National Council in Pallanza, carrying out this function in several areas (physical limnology, hydrology, and meteorology). He was responsible for research in physical limnology in the unit of biology, engaged in a national Italian research program in Antartide. He also participated as ISE's representative in the Interreg II-Italia-Svizzera project from 1994 to 1999 approved by the European Union. He did the same in many other similar projects in CEE. He was the secretary of the Italian Oceanology and Limnologic Association and afterward was elected as a member of the president's council. He is author and coauthor of 150 scientific dissertations published in national and international reviews.

Santo Banerjee has been working in the field of nonlinear systems and chaos since 1998. He wrote several research papers published in international journals such as *Physics Letters A, Chaos, Physica Scripta, International Journal of Nonlinear Mechanics*, and *Chaos, Solitons & Fractals*. He submitted his thesis for a PhD degree in 2006 at Jadavpur University (Kolkata, India) and is presently working as a lecturer in an engineering college in the Department of Mathematics (West Bengal, India). His current field of research interest is synchronization and chaotic cryptography, and he is also interested in movies, especially film making and music.

Francesco Bertoluzzo is a PhD student at the Department of Statistics of the University of Padua (Italy). His main research interests are in techniques for stochastic dynamic modelization, financial time-series modeling and forecasting, and financial trading systems' design and development. He participated in a research project on environmental questions financially supported by the Italian Ministry of Education, University and Research. He collaborated as external counselor with the Venice Research Consortium (Italy).

Eleonora Bilotta is full professor of general psychology at the Department of Linguistics of the University of Calabria (Italy), and is the coordinator of the PhD course Psychology of Programming and Artificial Intelligence. Her research interests concern various scientific topics from an interdisciplinary point of view and comprise the following areas: cognitive psychology and intelligent systems in education, animal and human behavior, human-computer interaction, the psychology of music, and artificial life. She published more than 150 scientific papers and is coauthor of various books. Some covers of issues of scientific journals such as *Complexity* and the *International Journal of Bifurcation and Chaos* are dedicated to research papers published by Eleonora Bilotta.

Leonardo Castellano graduated with a degree in physics at the University of Milan (Italy) with a thesis entitled *A Quasi-Three Dimensional Model for the Thermal Pollution of the Po River*. Encouraged by international success of the model in his thesis, he initiated a long career as consultant of the most important Italian and European research centers in the field of mathematical modeling for any sort of environmental and industrial processes and systems. He has published over 100 scientific papers. For many years he served as an invited professor at the Department of General Physics of the University of Milan, and from 1998 he has been an invited professor at the Department of Computer Science.

Roy Chowdhury graduated with degrees in physics and mathematics from Presidency College, Calcutta University. He received his PhD in high-energy physics in 1972. After that, he worked on projects regarding integrable systems, solitons, plasma physics, nonlinear optics, and chaos. He has guided 32 scholars in their PhD work and has completed 11 projects. At present, he is professor of physics at Jadavpur University. He has authored *Lie Algebraic Methods in Integrable Systems, Painleve Analysis and its Application*, and *Quantam Integrable Systems*, all published by CRC press (Chapman & Hall, USA). He is a member of the Indian Physical Society.

Marco Corazza is associate professor at the Department of Applied Mathematics of the University Ca' Foscari of Venice (Italy). His main research interests are in quantitative finance (with particular attention to modern portfolio theory, nonstandard stochastic processes for the modeling of financial return dynamics, and credit risk), soft-computing methodologies (with particular attention to artificial neural networks and GMDH-based approaches), multicriteria decision analysis, mixed-integer nonlinear programming, and operational research models for productive process optimization. He participates and has participated in several national and international research projects. His contributions have appeared as papers in refereed international journals (for instance, *Economics & Complexity*, *European Journal of Operational Research*, *Multinational Finance Journal*, and *The Journal of Futures Markets*) and as chapters in refereed international books.

Gianni Andrea Di Caro received his laurea degree in physics with full honors from the Università di Bologna (Italy) in 1992 and his PhD in applied sciences from the Université Libre de Bruxelles (Belgium) in 2004. He has worked in several leading scientific laboratories worldwide. His general interests are in adaptive network routing, ant colony optimization and other metaheuristics for combinatorial optimization, reinforcement learning, the immune system, autonomous robotics, and parallel computing. He is currently at IDSIA (Dalle Molle Institute for Artificial Intelligence) in Lugano (Switzerland) where he works on adaptive algorithms for network routing and on swarm robotics.

Frederick Ducatelle obtained an MS in commercial engineering in management informatics from the Katholieke Universiteit Leuven in Belgium in 2000 and an MS in artificial intelligence from the University of Edinburgh in Scotland in 2001. He is currently a PhD student at IDSIA in Lugano (Switzerland) where his work is mainly focused on swarm intelligence and its application to problems in networking and robotics.

Walter J. Freeman studied physics and mathematics at the Massachusetts Institute of Technology (MIT), electronics in the Navy during World War II, philosophy at the University of Chicago, medicine at Yale University, internal medicine at Johns Hopkins, and neuropsychiatry at the University of California, Los Angeles (UCLA). He has taught brain science in the University of California at Berkeley since 1959, where he is professor at the graduate school. Dr. Freeman received his MD cum laude in 1954, and he has more than 20 awards, among which are the Bennett Award from the Society of Biological Psychiatry in 1964, a Guggenheim in 1965, the MERIT Award from NIMH (National Institute of Mental Health) in 1990, and the Pioneer Award from the Neural Networks Council of the IEEE (Institute of Electrical and Electronics Engineers) in 1992. He was president of the International Neural Network Society in 1994, is life fellow of the IEEE, and was chair of the IEEE Oakland-East Bay Section, EMBS, in 2006. He has authored over 450 articles and four books: *Mass Action in the Nervous System* (1975), *Societies of Brains* (1995), *Neurodynamics* (2000), and *How Brains Make up Their Minds* (2001).

Luca Maria Gambardella is a research director of IDSIA. His major research interests are in the areas of optimization, simulation, robotics learning, and adaptation applied to both academic and real-world problems. In particular, he has studied and developed several ant colony optimization algorithms to solve scheduling and routing problems. In these domains, the best known solutions for many benchmark instances have been computed. He is responsible for IDSIA metaheuristic and robotic projects. He has led several research and industrial projects, both at the Swiss national and European levels.

Alessandro Giuliani is senior scientist at the Department of Environment and Health, Computational and Experimental Carcinogenesis Unit, at the Istituto Superiore di Sanita (Italian NIH). He is mainly involved in the generation and testing of soft physical and statistical models for life sciences, with a special emphasis on the elucidation of mesoscopic complex systems like protein sequence and structure prediction, quantitative structure and activity relations in medicinal chemistry, the analysis of physiological time series, and the analysis of ecological systems. He is on the editorial boards of *Current Bioinformatics*, *Systems and Synthetic Biology*, and *BMC Applied Informatics*. He acts as a reviewer for the journals *American Journal of Physiology*, *Journal of Medicinal Chemistry*, *Chemical Toxicology*, *Medical and Biological Engineering and Computing*, *Physics Letters A*, *Journal of Chemical Information and Computer Science*, *Chemical Research in Toxicology*, *Biophysical Journal*, *Neuroscience Letters*, *Bioinformatics*, *Biopolymers*, *FEBS Journal*, and *Genome Biology*.

Ljubiša M. Kocić is full professor with the Faculty of Electronic Engineering, University of Niš (Serbia). He was born 1952, and received a PhD in 1985 from the University if Niš in applied mathematics. His fields of interest include chaos theory, fractal geometry, computer-aided design, and approximation theory. He is a member of AMS and different national scientific forums, and is an editorial board member of *Chaos and Complexity Letters*.

Vladimir Kvasnicka received a degree in nuclear chemistry from Czech Technical University in Prague in 1964, and a PhD degree in chemistry from Heyrovsky Institute of Czech Academy of Sciences in Prague in 1968. From 1973 to 2003 he held the positions of assistant professor, associate professor, professor, and head of the Department of Mathematics with the Faculty of Chemical and Food Technologies, Slovak University of Technology (Bratislava). Since 2004 he has been a deputy head of the Institute of Applied Informatics with the Faculty of Informatics and Information Technology at the same university. His fields of research are artificial intelligence, cognitive science, neural networks, evolutionary algorithms, and theoretical and mathematical chemistry.

Kin Keung Lai is the chair professor of management science at City University of Hong Kong, and he is also the associate dean of the Faculty of Business. Currently, he is also acting as the dean of the College of Business Administration at Hunan University (China). Prior to his current post, he was a senior operational research analyst at Cathay Pacific Airways and the area manager of marketing information systems at Union Carbide Eastern. Professor Lai received his PhD at Michigan State University (USA). Professor Lai's main research interests include logistics and operations management, computational intelligence, and business decision modeling.

Renato Saleri Lunazzi was born in 1964. He lived in Belgium, Switzerland, and Italy, and is currently in France. He is an architect and postgraduate in industrial design and informatics productive processes. He joined the MAP (Modèles et Simulations pour L'Architecture, L'Urbanisme et le Paysage) ARIA research team in 1995. He was recently involved in research tasks on automatic generative design processes.

Terry Marks-Tarlow, PhD, is a clinical psychologist in private practice in Santa Monica, California (http://www.markstarlow.com). Dr. Marks-Tarlow teaches advanced sequencing yoga workshops while adopting a strong mind-body focus clinically. During long-term psychotherapy with patients, she specializes in productive blocks and highlights creative expression. As a visual artist, she specializes in figure drawing (http://www.contemporary-art-gallery.de). Her first book, *Creativity Inside Out: Learning* *through Multiple Intelligences* (Addison-Wesley, 1996), is a creativity curriculum for educators. Her book in progress, *Psyche's Fractal Veil: Complexity and Psychotherapy*, combines nonlinear science with the art of psychotherapy.

Pietro Pantano is full professor of mathematical physics with the Faculty of Engineering of the University of Calabria. His research interests concern various scientific themes that are studied by an interdisciplinary point of view. His most relevant research fields are the theory of complexity and self-organizing systems, discrete and continuous dynamical systems, Chua's oscillator, biological models based on cellular automata, artificial life, and generative and evolutionary music. He has published more than 200 scientific papers on these subjects and has coauthored various books. The journals *Complexity* and *International Journal of Bifurcation and Chaos* have dedicated the covers of some issues to papers that Pantano coauthored.

Rita Pizzi received a degree in physics at the University of Milan and a PhD in electronic and information engineering at the University of Pavia. Currently she is aggregate professor at the Department of Information Technologies of the University of Milan, where she teaches the courses Artificial Intelligence and Medical Informatics. Her research interests are artificial intelligence and the study of the biological processes implied in natural intelligence. She presently coordinates the Living Networks Labgroup, which is concerned with the study of the computational aspects of natural neural networks adhering to microelectrode arrays.

Jiri Pospichal received a degree in physical chemistry from the University of Jan Evangelista Purkyne in Brno (Czech Republic) in 1984, and a PhD degree in chemistry from the Faculty of Chemical and Food Technologies at Slovak University of Technology (Bratislava) in 1990. From 1990 to 2003, he held the positions of assistant professor and associate professor of applied informatics in the Department of Mathematics, Faculty of Chemical and Food Technologies, Slovak University of Technology (Bratislava). Since 2006, he has held the position of professor at the Institute of Applied Informatics at the same university. His research interests are evolutionary algorithms, artificial intelligence, cognitive science, neural networks, mathematical chemistry, and graph theory.

Hector Sabelli, MD, PhD, an Argentine-born American scientist and psychiatrist, is the former director of the Institute of Pharmacology, University of Litoral (Argentina). He is also a professor and chairman of pharmacology at the Health Sciences University (Chicago), and a pharmacology professor and associate professor of psychiatry at Rush University (Chicago). He studies creative processes from mathematical, empirical, and clinical perspectives. Earlier work includes the discovery of phenylethylamine, a stimulant neurohormone reduced in depression. He has published six books and scientific articles in leading journals (*Nature, Science, American Journal of Psychiatry*). Among other scientific awards, he received a doctorate honoris causa (University of Rosario, Argentina).

Franco Scalzone was born in Napoli where he graduated with a degree in medicine and surgery. He specialized in psychiatry in Roma and worked in public psychiatric centers. He is a member of the Italian Psychoanalytical Society (SPI) and currently practices as a private psychoanalyst. His main fields of interest are the hysteria syndrome and the interchange between psychoanalysis and neuroscience.

He is the author of several scientific papers such as "Notes for a Dialogue between Psychoanalysis and Neuroscience" (*International Journal of Psychoanalysis*, Volume 86, Issue 5, pp. 1405-1423; 2005), and the editor, together with Dr. G. Zontini, of the anthology *Perché L'Isteria?* (Liguori, Napoli, 1999).

Liljana R. Stefanovska is full professor with the Faculty of Technology and Metallurgy, University S. S. Cyril and Methodius, Skopje (Republic of Macedonia). She was born in 1951, and received her PhD in 1994 from the University S. S. Cyril and Methodius in mathematics. Her fields of interest include differential equations, theory of dynamical systems, mathematics, and art. She is a member of AMS, the Harmony Society, the Society of Mathematicians of Macedonia, the Society of Informatics of Macedonia, and the Society of Physicists of Macedonia.

John G. Taylor is the European editor in chief of *Neural Networks*, and was president of the International Neural Network Society (1995) and European Neural Network Society (1993-1994); emeritus professor of mathematics at King's College, London; and member of the EC projects MATHESIS, GNOSYS (building cognitive robot), and NoE HUMAINE, plus U.K. projects on attention. He published over 500 scientific papers (in theoretical and particle physics, neural networks, higher cognitive processes, brain imaging, consciousness), authored 12 books, and edited 13 others, including *Artificial Neural Networks* (North-Holland, 1992), *The Promise of Neural Networks* (Springer,1993), *Mathematical Approaches to Neural Networks* (Elsevier,1994), *Neural Networks* (A. Waller,1995), *The Race for Consciousness* (MIT Press, 1999), and *The Mind: A User's Manual* (Wiley, 2006).

Gerald H. Thomas holds a PhD in theoretical physics, and has practiced at CERN in Geneva and at Argonne National Laboratory (USA). He has extensive experience as a senior manager for Fortune 500 companies as well as small venture companies, building a wealth of knowledge about real-world decisions and strategies. He currently teaches computer engineering at Milwaukee School of Engineering. He has published numerous research articles on high-energy physics in international journals, and more recently a book on decision theory.

Marco Tomassini is a professor of computer science at the Information Systems Department of the University of Lausanne (Switzerland). He graduated in physical and chemical sciences in Mendoza (Argentina) and received a doctorate in theoretical chemistry from the University of Perugia (Italy) working on computer simulations of condensed-matter systems. His current research interests are centered on the application of biological ideas to artificial systems. He is active in evolutionary computation, especially spatially structured systems, genetic programming, and the structure of program search spaces. He is also interested in machine learning, evolutionary games, and the dynamical properties of networked complex systems. He has been program chairman of several international events and has published many scientific papers and several authored and edited books in these fields.

Leonardo Vanneschi received a master's degree (laurea) in computer science at the University of Pisa (Italy) in 1996 (summa cum Laude), and a PhD in computer science at the University of Lausanne in 2004 (for which his thesis was honored with the excellence award of the science faculty). He has been an assistant professor in the Department of Informatics, Communication, and Systems of the University of Milano-Bicocca (Milan, Italy) since September 2004. His main research interests include machine learning, the study of complex systems, data mining, evolutionary computation and genetic programming, techniques of classification and clustering, and using paradigms of parallel and distributed computing. Vanneschi has participated in various collaborations, both national and internationals, and is a member of the steering committees and program committees of various international conferences. He is a teacher of the course Algoritmi e Strutture Dati (Soft Computing) and assistant in various other computer science courses. He has produced 42 publications, among which 9 have been honored with international awards.

David Vernon is a senior lecturer in psychology at Canterbury Christ Church University. His research interests include the use of electroencephalographic (EEG) biofeedback as a potential mechanism to enhance human performance, as well as its use within clinical settings. Dr. Vernon was part of the team that originally showed that specific aspects of human memory could be enhanced via the use of EEG biofeedback. He also has research interests in human memory, in particular the use and flexibility of implicit memory. He is an active council member of the Society of Applied Neuroscience, which is an international organization that focuses on advancing neuroscientific knowledge, as well as a member of the B27 European Union working group examining electrical neuronal oscillations and cognition (COST-B27).

Shouyang Wang received a PhD degree in operations research from the Institute of Systems Science, Chinese Academy of Sciences (CAS; Beijing) in 1986. He is currently a Bairen distinguished professor of management science at the Academy of Mathematics and Systems Sciences of CAS and a Lotus chair professor of Hunan University (Changsha). He is the editor in chief or coeditor of 12 journals. He has published 18 books and over 150 journal papers. His current research interests include financial engineering, e-auctions, knowledge management, and decision analysis.

Lean Yu received a PhD degree in management sciences and engineering from the Institute of Systems Science, Academy of Mathematics and Systems Sciences, Chinese Academy of Sciences in 2005. He is currently a research fellow in the Department of Management Sciences of City University of Hong Kong. He has published about 20 papers in journals including *IEEE Transactions on Knowledge and Data Engineering*, *Expert Systems with Applications*, *European Journal of Operational Research*, *International Journal of Intelligent Systems*, and *Computers & Operations Research*. His research interests include artificial neural networks, evolutionary computation, decision support systems, and financial forecasting.

Gemma Zontini was born in Napoli where she graduated with a degree in medicine and surgery, specializing in psychiatry. She is a full member of the SPI and director of a center for diagnosis and treatment. Her interests are hysteria and the relation between psychoanalysis and neuroscience. She published several scientific papers such as "The Dream's Navel between Chaos and Thought" with Franco Scalzone (*International Journal of Psychoanalysis,* Volume 82, Issue 2, pp. 263-282; 2001), and papers on the psychiatry-medicine relation. She also edited with Scalzone the anthology *Tra Psiche e Cervello* (Liguori, Napoli, Italy, 2004), an introduction to a dialogue between psychoanalysis and neuroscience.

Index

C

CAD (computer-aided design), definition 332

CAD software 278

calculator-machine 56

canonic GP 133

castration anxiety, definition 333

castration fears, definition 333

catastrophe theory, definition 333

cell assemblies (CAs) 14

cellular-automata processes 278

cellular automata (CA) 109, 110

cellular automata (CA), definition 333

cellular automata (CA), self-replacating 109

cellular automaton, definition 333

CFD (computational fluid dynamics) 258

CFD applications 260

CFD model 258

CFD models 274

Chalmers, David 85

chaos, definition 333

chaos theory 87

chaos theory, definition 333

chaotic communication 219

chaotic communication system, diagram 218

chaotic dynamical systems 217

chaotic Lorenz system 230

chaotic signal 230

characteristic equation, definition 333

chemostat, definition 333

Chinese room (argument), definition 333

Chomsky, Noam 7

Chomsky's hierarchy 29

Chomsky grammars 312

chromodynamics 143

chromosome, definition 334

ciphertext 221

ciphertext, definition 334

ciphertext message 221

classical information system 290

closed systems, definition 353

clustering algorithms 177

CNR- ISE 257

cocreation paradigm 158

CODAM (corollary discharge of attention movement), definition 334

CODAM model 68

CODAM model of attention 69

code, definition 334

codetermination 158

coevolution, definition 334

coevolution of genes and memes 33

coevolution of genes and memes, chemostat simulation 40

cognition 146

cognition, definition 334

cognitive abilities 98

cognitive development 28

cognitive functions 2

cognitive neuroscience of the reflexive function 1

cognitive psychology 47

cognitive tasks 65

coherence 95

coils 291

Collage Theorem 311

Collage Theorem, definition 334

collective unconsciousness, definition 334

combinatorial chemistry techniques 131

communication 224

communication, definition 334

communicational cyberspaces 56

complex chaotic behavior 218

complexity 111

complexity, definition 335

complex networks 65

complex system, definition 335

compression, definition 335

computational fluid dynamic (CFD), definition 335

computational fluid dynamics (CFD) 257

computational logic 143

computer-aided design (CAD) tools 278

computer-aided geometric design model (CAGD) 318

computer graphics, definition 335

computer logic 138

computer memory, definition 344

computer network, definition 335

computer networking, definition 335

computerphilia 56

computerphobia 56

computer science 308